MW00813907

New Testament
GREEK
INTERMEDIATE

New Testament
GREEK
INTERMEDIATE

From Morphology to Translation

GERALD L. STEVENS

CASCADE *Books* · Eugene, Oregon

NEW TESTAMENT GREEK INTERMEDIATE
From Morphology to Translation

Cascade Books
A Division of Wipf and Stock Publishers
199 W. 8th Ave., Suite 3
Eugene, OR 97401

www.wipfandstock.com

ISBN 13: 978-1-55635-580-6

Cataloging-in-Publication data:

Stevens, Gerald L.

   New Testament Greek intermediate : from morphology to translation / Gerald L. Stevens.

   xxvi + 612 p. ; 23 cm. — Includes index.

   ISBN 13: 978-1-55635-580-6

   1. Bible. N.T.—Language, style. 2. Greek language, Biblical—Grammar. I. Title

PA817 .S73 2008

Manufactured in the U.S.A.

dedicated to my students

past, present, and future

CONTENTS

LIST OF FIGURES, CHARTS

▧▧▧▧▧▧▧▧▧ FIGURES ▧▧▧▧▧▧▧▧▧

▧▧▧▧▧▧▧▧▧ CHARTS ▧▧▧▧▧▧▧▧▧

LIST OF TABLES

LIST OF TABLES

ᕰᕰᕰᕰᕰᕰᕰ MANUSCRIPTS 1 ᕰᕰᕰᕰᕰᕰᕰ

Latin New Testament manuscripts developed rich traditions of beautiful ornamentation and full illustrations of biblical texts and themes, especially during the medieval period. A fine example is Ms. 180, the Douce Apocalypse, c. 1270, held in the Bodleian Library in Oxford. Along with the text in smaller script are selections from Berengaudus's Revelation commentary, a common medieval practice. Most illuminations include John the Seer as he auditions each vision; he is the figure to the right in the image below. This lavish illumination depicts Rev 12. John's dramatic and vivid imagery describes a great sign in heaven: a woman clothed with the sun with the moon at her feet, opposed by a great, seven-headed red dragon crowned with diadems, whose tail sweeps a third of the stars of heaven down to earth. The dragon awaits to devour the child whom the woman bears. The child, however, miraculously is caught up to God in heaven.

Fig. 1. Ms. 180 Douce Apocalypse at Rev 12.

PREFACE
TEXTBOOK STRATEGY

This textbook was born of the need to bridge the gap between an initial foray into New Testament Greek by the beginning student and the full-blown analysis of advanced courses that focus primarily or exclusively on syntax. In our system, students must assimilate all of Greek grammar in one semester. Such a task is considerable, and their grasp on Greek can be a struggle. In addition, we have students coming to us from our colleges who have had Greek grammar in their religion majors, so they cannot take our introductory grammar for credit. Yet, their initial study sometimes is several years in the past, and they can be pretty cold on the subject. Or, we have students who have had some exposure to New Testament Greek in an online course or some other delivery system and instantly sense inadequacies in their training the first day of class. As a result, students with varied backgrounds of education and experience struggle to get on to the same page with our students who only recently have finished grammar at the seminary level and are hot on the subject. Thus, one purpose for our intermediate grammar course is as a leveler to get all these students in the mix and on the same page.

A second purpose for our intermediate Greek grammar is to review all of Greek grammar. This review, however, reorganizes the material topically for a fresh approach to the subject and adds more depth to the discussion. Also, an attempt is made to build a bridge to syntactical questions to prepare the student for our advanced Greek grammar, which is our syntax course.

A third purpose for our intermediate Greek grammar is to expose the student to more Greek from different New Testament authors and with more surrounding context. Thus, translations move from snippets that illustrate specific grammar to example paragraphs that reoccur from chapter to chapter in the exercises, but with different grammatical focus each time. Eventually, the student will be translating the entire text of 1 John and part of the nativity story from Luke's Gospel.

A fourth purpose for our intermediate Greek grammar is to expand Greek vocabulary. Our introductory course brings the student to mastering words that occur fifty or more times in the New Testament. This level, of course, is not enough for continuous reading of paragraphs of Greek without constant consultation of a lexicon. Therefore, this textbook expands Greek vocabulary by including seven vocabulary lists that can comprise seven vocabulary exams easily distributed during the course as the instructor desires. These lists will bring the student's vocabulary acquisition to words that occur fifteen or more times in the New Testament.

In sum, this text is meant to:

(1) level differing backgrounds of introductory Greek
(2) review Greek grammar and raise syntactical issues
(3) explore the varieties of New Testament Greek in context
(4) expand Greek vocabulary to fifteen or more times

Perhaps this text, then, can serve your purposes in the study of New Testament Greek.

Each chapter is organized topically in a total review of Greek grammar and includes exercises taken from the Greek New Testament to illustrate the grammar discussed. "Manuscripts" sections include illustrations that introduce the student to handwritten copies of the New Testament and issues of textual criticism. Five appendixes include a glossary, paradigms, principal parts, lexical middle, and an answer key. These appendixes are followed by seven evenly divided vocabulary lists of decreasing frequency to be used for vocabulary exams, concluding with a total vocabulary list of Greek to English and a list of English derivatives. Finally, a comprehensive and detailed subject index adds to the usability of the text.

ACKNOWLEDGMENTS

Any writer has to recognize how much of any book is the result of many contributions, known and unknown, large or small, of many individuals over a lifetime. A heartfelt sense of gratitude is felt to all who have enriched my understanding of the Bible in general and the Greek New Testament in particular. I thank my colleagues, students, teachers, friends, and family. Especially do I thank my wife, Jean, who has seen all the action, endured all the isolation, and faithfully and tirelessly supported every project, including this one.

Akademische Druck-u. Verlagsanstalt, Austria (ADEVA), Uersperggasse 12, A-8010 Graz, for the image of Ms. 180 Douce Apokalypse on p. xviii. Used by permission. All rights reserved.

Öffentliche Bibliothek der Universität Basel, Schöbeinstrasse 18-20, 4056 Basel, Switzerland, for the image of Greek Gospel MS. 2 on p. 202 from Mscr. A N IV 1, f. 138r. Used by permission. All rights reserved.

The Chester Beatty Library, Dublin Castle, Dublin 2, Ireland, for the image of $\mathfrak{P}^{46}$ on p. 314 from Frederic G. Kenyon, *The Chester Beatty Biblical Papyri: Descriptions and Texts of Twelve Manuscripts on Papyrus of the Greek Bible; Fasciculus III Supplement: Pauline Epistles* (Oxford, 1937), © The Trustees of the Chester Beatty Library, Dublin. By permission of the Trustees of the Chester Beatty Library. All rights reserved.

Bibliotheca Apostolica Vaticana, 00120 Città del Vaticano, for the images of MS. Vat. gr. 1209 (Codex Vaticanus) on pp. 94, 170, and 520, from Bibliothecae Apostolicae Vaticanae, *Codex Vaticanus Graecus 1209, Bibliorum Sacrorum Graecorum, Codex Vaticanus B,* "Millennium Edition," Istituto Poligrafico E Zecca Dello Stato. Used by permission. All rights reserved.

Martin Bodmer Foundation, Bibliotheca Bodmeriana, 19-21, Route Du Guignard, CH-1223, Cologny-Genève, Switzerland for the image of $\mathfrak{P}^{66}$

on pp. 72 and the lines from $\mathfrak{P}^{66}$ and $\mathfrak{P}^{75}$ used on p. 454, from *Papyrus Bodmer II, Supplement, Evangile de Jean, chap. 14-21*; Nouvelle édition augmentée et corrigée: avec reproduction photographique complète du manuscrit, chap. 1-21 (Cologny-Genève, Switzerland: Bibliothèque Bodmer, 1962) and from *Papyrus Bodmer XIV-XV: Evangiles de Luc et Jean, Tome II, XV: Jean, chap. 1-15* (Cologny-Genève, Switzerland: Bibliothèque Bodmer, 1961). Used by permission. All rights reserved.

Cambridge University Library, West Road, Cambridge, England CB3 9DR, for the image of Codex Bezae, p. 232, from *Codex Bezae Cantabrigiensis, Quattuor Euangelia et Actus Apostolorum, Complectens Graece et Latine, Sumptibus Academiae Phototypice Repraesentatus; Tomus Posterior*. (London: Cantabrigiae, 1899). Reproduced by kind permission of the Syndics of Cambridge University Library. All rights reserved.

Deutsche Bibelgesellschaft/German Bible Society, Kirchliche Stiftung des öffentlichen Rechts/Foundation Balinger Straße 31 70567 Stuttgart, for use in examples and exercises of selections from *The Greek New Testament, Fourth Revised Edition, edited by Barbara Aland, Kurt Aland, Johannes Karavidopoulos, Carlo M. Martini, and Bruce M. Metzger, in cooperation with the Institute for New Testament Textual Research, Münster/ Westphalia*, © 1993 Deutsche Bibelgesellschaft, Stuttgart. Used by permission. All rights reserved.

Harvard University Press, 79 Garden Street, Cambridge, Mass. 02138, for the image of Lectionary 59 on p. 6, Synod Collection, Moscow State Historical Museum, COD. 41, from William Henry Paine Hatch, *Facsimiles and Descriptions of Minuscule Manuscripts of the New Testament* (Cambridge, Mass.: Harvard University Press, 1951). Used by permission. All rights reserved.

OakTree Software, Inc., 498 Palm Springs Drive, Suite 100, Altamonte, Fla., for the map on p. 1, and the chart on pp. 141 derived from *Accord-ance*, ver. 7.4.1. Used by permission. All rights reserved.

Oxford University Press, Walton Street, Oxford, England OX2 6DP, for the images of Codex Sinaiticus on pp. xxiv and 11 from Helen and Kirsopp

ACKNOWLEDGMENTS

Lake, *Codex Sinaiticus Petropolitanus: The New Testament, The Epistle of Barnabas and the Shepherd of Hermas, Preserved in the Imperial Library of St. Petersburg, Now Reproduced in Facsimile From Photographs by Helen and Kirsopp Lake, with a Description and Introduction to the History of the Codex by Kirsopp Lake* (The Clarendon Press, 1911); Codex Alexandrinus on p. 72 from Frederick G. Kenyon, *The Codex Alexandrinus (Royal MS. 1 D v-viii) in Reduced Photographic Facsimile; New Testament and Clementine Epistles* (1909). By permission of Oxford University Press. All rights reserved.

The John Rylands University Library, University of Manchester, Oxford Road, Manchester M13 9PP, England, for the image of $\mathfrak{P}^{52}$ on p. 208. Reproduced by courtesy of the University Librarian and Director, The John Rylands University Library. The University of Manchester. Used by permission. All rights reserved.

Gerald L. Stevens, 3777 Mimosa Ct., New Orleans, La. 70131, for images: the Ionic Greek capital, Athens Academy, as used in the front cover artwork; images and artwork of the Athena Statue, Athens Academy (p. v, passim); Athenian Hoplite Warrior on Wine Crater, c. 6th cent. B.C., Thessalonikki Museum (p. 1, passim); Aphrodite Inscription from Rhodes (p. 2); Bust of Alexander the Great, from Cyrene, c. 3rd cent. B.C., Istanbul Museum (p. 3); Pediment of Zeus and the Gods, Athens Academy (p. 28, passim); Terracotta Bowl Gymnasium Scenes from Lydos's Workshop, c. 550 B.C., Athens Museum (p. 477, passim); Proconsul Inscription of Gaius Laecanius Bassus, Archeological Museum of Ephesus (p. 408); Politarch Inscription, Berea Archeological Museum (p. 536); Proconsul Inscription of Lucius Junius Gallio, Archeological Museum of Delphi (p. 548). © Gerald L. Stevens. All rights reserved.

MANUSCRIPTS 2

Sinaiticus is one of our best New Testament manuscripts, and the only one with a complete New Testament. For more information on this valuable manuscript, see p. 94.

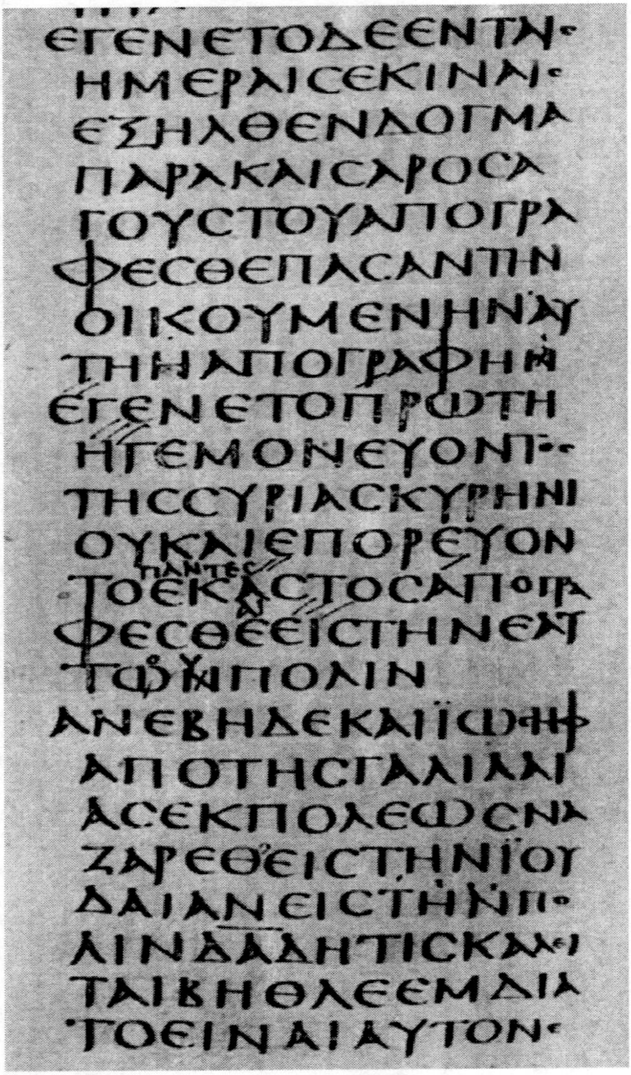
ΕΓΕΝΕΤΟΔΕΕΝΤΑΙ
ΗΜΕΡΑΙCΕΚΙΝΑΙ
ΕΞΗΛΘΕΝΔΟΓΜΑ
ΠΑΡΑΚΑΙCΑΡΟCΑ
ΓΟΥCΤΟΥΑΠΟΓΡΑ
ΦΕCΘΕΠΑCΑΝΤΗΝ
ΟΙΚΟΥΜΕΝΗΝΑΥ
ΤΗΗΑΠΟΓΡΑΦΗΗ
ΕΓΕΝΕΤΟΠΡΩΤΗ
ΗΓΕΜΟΝΕΥΟΝΤ
ΤΗCCΥΡΙΑCΚΥΡΗΝΙ
ΟΥΚΑΙΕΠΟΡΕΥΟΝ
ΠΑΝΤΕC
ΤΟΕΚΑCΤΟCΑΠΟΓΡΑ
ΦΕCΘΕΕΙCΤΗΝΕΑΥ
ΤΩΝΠΟΛΙΝ
ΑΝΕΒΗΔΕΚΑΙΙΩCΗΦ
ΑΠΟΤΗCΓΑΛΙΛΑΙ
ΑCΕΚΠΟΛΕΩCΝΑ
ΖΑΡΕΘΕΙCΤΗΝΙΟΥ
ΔΑΙΑΝΕΙCΤΗΝΠΟ
ΛΙΝΔΑΔΗΤΙCΚΑΛΕΙ
ΤΑΙΒΗΘΛΕΕΜΔΙΑ
ΤΟΕΙΝΑΙΑΥΤΟΝ

Fig. 2. Codex Sinaiticus at Lk 2:1-4. *Codex Sinaiticus* (Lake, 1911) © Oxford University Press. By permission of Oxford University Press.

CHAPTER 1
HISTORY AND LANGUAGE

This chapter briefly reviews the history of the Greek language, the Greek alphabet, and Greek accents. Understanding history puts New Testament Greek into its proper historical context. Understanding the alphabet puts our New Testament manuscripts into their proper canonical context. Finally, understanding Greek accents puts the edited Greek text into its proper literary context.

The Greek Language

Hellenic Dialects

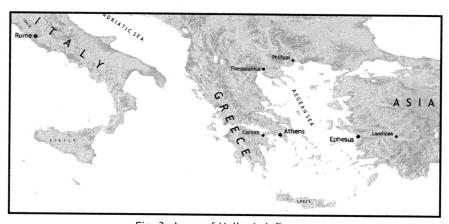

Fig. 3. Areas of Hellenic Influence

Dorian

Ancient Greeks had several dialects, among them the Dorian, Ionic, and Attic. The Dorian Hellenes invaded Greece about 1100 B.C. and maintained their cultural and linguistic traits. Dorian city-states such as Sparta and Corinth transmitted Dorian influence to the Greek world. The Doric dialect was heard in the Peloponnesus, Crete, and various Aegean islands, as well as Sicily and southern Italy.

Ionic

Many of the Greek isles were colonized by another group of Hellenes, the Ionians, who also populated western Asian coastal cities such as Miletus and Ephesus. The Ionians provided the basic Greek alphabet later adopted at Athens.

Fig. 4. Inscription, Temple of Aphrodite, Rhodes

Attic

Hellenes of Attica (Athens) had the greatest influence upon the Greek language. This Attic dialect developed a remarkable beauty and style and became the premier literary dialect. Precision and elegance marked Attic Greek, which impacted Greek language for centuries.

Hellenistic Greek

Literary Hellenistic Greek

Greek rhetoricians were big advocates of the Attic style. They considered this Classical period the golden age of Greece. They had tremendous influence on concepts of proper style and literary production, even to the point of using obsolete terms. One might compare praying today with "Thee's" and "Thou's," even though these old seventeenth-century English terms are obsolete. Some New Testament documents show an "Attic influence," especially Luke when he is not following his source material closely.

Non-Literary Hellenistic Greek

Alexander the Great (336-323 B.C.) expanded the Macedonian power base his father had welded together from unwilling Greek city-states into a world empire. Alexander tutored under the famous Aristotle, loved all things Greek, and promoted the already expanding influence of the Greek language in his cosmopolitan vision for his empire. Thus, Greek became a second tongue for the world.

Fig. 5. Alexander the Great

Over time, non-native speakers altered spoken Greek. A continual metamorphosis transformed the ancient native dialects within the new world order of Alexander. Fine nuances in the sophisticated Attic Greek began to blur. Grammatical principles were "broken." This second-language Greek became the universal tongue used in commerce and conversation. We call this universal tongue *Koine*. Koine Greek developed spontaneously, amorphously, and without imposed standards. This Greek, unlike a dialect, was not regional. Thus, while Paul could address the populace of Lystra in Greek, they speculated among themselves in their own regional tongue (Lycaonian, Acts 14:11).

Koine Style

Koine style has numerous distinctive characteristics. One major example is over-striving for emphasis, appearing in various forms:

- *Historical Present*. Narration in aorist tense unexpectedly will shift to present tense, called the historical present (e.g., ἐκβάλλει, Mk 1:12).
- *Vivid Future*. The future tense is rendered more vivid with the present (e.g., ἔρχομαι, Rev 22:20).
- *Vivid Perfect*. Perfect tense stands in for present tense (e.g., most occurrences of οἶδα).
- *Comparative for Superlative*. The comparative adjective stands in for the superlative, so must be translated with superlative meaning (e.g., μικρότερον, Mt 13:32).
- *Direct Discourse*. Direct discourse is preferred over indirect (e.g., καὶ λέγων ὅτι πεπλήρωται ὁ καιρὸς, Mk 1:15).

Another dominant habit in the Koine style is pleonasm (over-fullness). Examples would include:

- *Pronoun Subjects*. Pronoun subjects are used even though the verb is inflected. Determining when a pronoun actually is meant as emphatic is ambiguous (e.g., προσκαλεῖται οὓς ἤθελεν αὐτός, Mk 3:13).
- *Pronoun Abundance*. Use of pronouns is abundant (e.g., Hebrews, about 8/100 words vs. John's 13/100 words).
- *Parenthetical Remarks*. Remarks can be inserted to explain something in the text or provide a gloss (e.g., Γολγοθᾶ, ὅ ἐστιν Κρανίου Τόπος λεγόμενος, Mt 27:33).
- *Adverbial Abundance*. Modifying the verb with adverbs and adverbial prepositional phrases is a favorite pastime (e.g., Καὶ πρωῒ ἔννυχα λίαν ἀναστὰς, Mk 1:35).
- *Compound Verbs*. Use of compound verbs is common, and even followed by the same preposition (e.g., ἐκβάλλει ἐκ τοῦ θησαυροῦ αὐτοῦ, Mt 13:52).
- *Prepositional Phrases*. One often finds prepositions when the inflected noun would do (e.g., ἀπὸ τῆς Γαλιλαίας ἐπὶ τὸν Ἰορδάνην πρὸς τὸν Ἰωάννην, Mt 3:13).
- *Periphrasis*. The periphrastic participle, εἰμί followed by a complementary participle, takes the place of an indicative

verb (e.g., ἦν γὰρ διδάσκων αὐτούς, taking the place of ἐδίδασκεν, Mk 1:22; cf. Jn 7:14; 8:2).

In addition to overemphasis and overfullness, Koine Greek has other stylistic elements. Examples would include:

- *Absence of Conjunctions.* A preference for καί seems to displace other conjunctions. Mark, as one good example, is notorious for his overuse of καί—1,100 times!
- *Coordinate Clauses.* Literary style would use subordinate clauses, but Koine seems to lean heavily toward coordinate conjunctions (e.g., the stringing of καί in Jn 1:1-5).
- *Infinitive Loss.* The infinitive is a sophisticated element of Greek. Koine style shows a notable loss of infinitive use (cf. John's 0.8/100 words vs. Acts's 2.3/100 words).

Adolf Deissmann (1866-1937)

Knowledge of the true nature of New Testament Greek as Koine is a modern discovery of the twentieth century. New Testament Greek always had befuddled scholars. The rules of grammar and syntax were mysteriously different from the Classical style of Homer. The unexplained phenomena of New Testament Greek generated abundant, sometimes fantastic, theories. Two of the most favorite explanations included "Hebraisms" and "Holy Ghost Greek." Some thought the unusual Greek of the New Testament was the result of disciples who spoke Aramaic and tried to write in Greek, creating a mutant or "Hebrew" Greek. Others—substituting piety for history—wildly speculated that the Greek of the New Testament represented the "perturbations of inspiration." That is, the New Testament must have been the natural result of almost uncontrollable Spirit ecstasy which threw all grammar and rules of grammar to the four winds. After all, God was not subject to the rules of humans! Some more moderately suggested that New Testament Greek simply was tailor-made, a sort of "God's Greek" created uniquely for the New Testament revelation!

However, at the turn of the twentieth century, a German New Testament scholar by the name of Adolf Deissmann revolutionized our understanding of New Testament Greek. While he knew well the Greek of the New Testament, he could not explain the grammar and syntax according to Classical Greek standards. Now, papyri documents recently had been discovered in the hot sands of Egypt, written in Greek, with which Deissmann became acquainted by pure serendipity. These Egyptian papyri represented a typical ancient Egyptian "trash basket" of incantations, receipts, wills, old letters, and the like. Deissmann was surprised to discover he could translate these documents almost effortlessly. He began to realize that his "training" had been his study of New Testament Greek. Suddenly, New Testament Greek was discovered to be not some specially commissioned "Holy Ghost Greek" but the commonly spoken, vernacular Greek. The grammar and syntax was that of a *non-literary* Hellenistic Greek, *spoken* Greek, the Greek of the marketplace, such as in these Egyptian materials. New Testament Greek was the everyday Greek spoken by any commoner in the Hellenistic world, from slave to free. With Deissmann's discovery, the study of New Testament Greek took a quantum leap in under-standing. Deissmann catalyzed the production of the great, magis-terial Greek lexicons of last century, thus revolutionizing our study of the New Testament.[1]

The Greek Alphabet

Our term "alphabet" comes from the first two Greek letter names, "alpha" and "beta." The table gives the Koine Greek alphabet. Ancient Greek included other letters, such as the letter digamma (Ϝ), which was no longer used in the first century.

---

[1]Cf. Gustav Adolf Deissmann, *Light from the Ancient East: The New Testament Illustrated by Recently Discovered Texts of the Graeco-Roman World* (original, 1908; trans. Lionel R. M. Strachan: 1927; repr., Eugene, Ore.: Wipf and Stock, 2004).

Table 1.1 The Greek Alphabet

Letter		Name	English	Pronunciation
A	α	alpha	a	*a*lms, *a*lley (short)
B	β	beta	b	*b*etter
Γ	γ	gamma	g, n	*g*ambit
Δ	δ	delta	d	*d*elta
E	ε	epsilon	e	*e*pic
Z	ζ	zeta	z	*z*oo, a*dz*e (internal)
H	η	eta	e	pr*e*y
Θ	θ	theta	th	*th*in
I	ι	iota	i, y	id*i*om, *i*diom (short)
K	κ	kappa	k, c	*k*ayak
Λ	λ	lamba	l	*l*amb
M	μ	mu	m	*m*usic
N	ν	nu	n	*n*uclear
Ξ	ξ	xi	x	he*x*
O	ο	omicron	o	*o*melet
Π	π	pi	p	*p*ie
P	ρ	rho	r	*r*oad
Σ	σ, ς	sigma	s	*s*ignal
T	τ	tau	t	*t*aunt
Υ	υ	upsilon	u, y	*u*se, *u*sher (short)
Φ	φ	phi	ph	*ph*ilosophy
X	χ	chi	ch	*ch*iropractic
Ψ	ψ	psi	ps	li*ps*
Ω	ω	omega	o	*o*mit

Pronunciation

Vowels and Diphthongs

Vowels are short, long, or variable. The short vowels are ε and o. The long vowels are the corresponding η and ω. Variable vowels are α, ι, and υ and are deduced by observation (see table above). Beginning vowels have a breathing mark. *Rough breathing* aspirates the vowel (ἅγιος); *smooth breathing* does not (ἀγρός).

Diphthongs are two-vowel combinations pronounced together as one (see table below). Diphthongs are built on the closure provided by the two closed vowels ι and υ (see the *Glossary*). Iota diphthongs are αι, ει, οι, and υι. Upsilon diphthongs are: αυ, ευ, ου, and the rare ηυ, ωυ. *Diaeresis* is a mark to separate two vowels for pronunciation (Μωϋσῆς). *Improper diphthongs* are the three vowels with *iota subscript*: ᾳ, ῃ, ῳ. This iota when subscripted goes unpronounced, hence, creating what is called an "improper" diphthong (no diphthong pronunciation).

Table 1.2 Diphthong Pronunciation

αι = *aisle*	ου = group
αυ =*out*	υι = s*ui*te
ει = *eight*	ηυ = a-oo
ευ = eh-oo	ωυ = s*ou*l

♦ *Syllable quantity is the vowel quantity in the syllable.*

Consonants

Consonants are distinguished from vowels by airflow. Airflow through the nose or mouth creates three consonant categories.

Sibilants are consonants that have an "s," or hissing, sound due to constant airflow over the teeth. The *simple sibilant* is σ. The *complex sibilants* represent certain consonants combined with a sigma: (1) ψ = πσ, βσ, φσ; (2) ξ = κσ, γσ, χσ; (3) ζ = δσ and σδ.

Liquids are consonants with airflow directed through the nasal cavity, which creates *liquid* (λ, ρ) and *nasal* (μ, ν) consonants. Usually liquids and nasals are grouped together as simply "liquids."

Stops are consonants with airflow directed through the mouth cavity. Stop consonants can be analyzed by the square of stops as voiced, controlled, and restricted. Airflow voiced by including the larynx creates voiced stops, without the larynx, voiceless stops. Airflow controlled or obstructed by the lips creates labial stops, by the palate, palatal stops, and by the teeth, dental stops. Airflow restricted completely before expiration creates smooth stops, restricted moderately, flat (or middle) stops, and restricted slightly, rough (or aspirated) stops. The crux of the matter in terms of word formation will be the voiceless stops, or, in terms of aspiration, the smooth and rough stops.

Table 1.3 The Square of Stops

		Physiology of Production (Voicing)		
		Voiceless	Voiced	Voiceless
Place of	Labial—	π	β	φ
Obstruction	Palatal—	κ	γ	χ	(Square of Stops)
(Classes)	Dental—	τ	δ	θ
		Smooth	Middle	Rough
			(Orders)	
		Degree of Expiration		

Modern Debate

The exact pronunciation of Koine Greek is debated, so we are not sure exactly how Aristotle or even Paul spoke. The Renaissance scholar Erasmus is credited with devising a system based on Latin for standardizing pronunciation, now known as the "academic" system because of its use in colleges and seminaries. Some argue that Biblical Greek actually is pronounced closer to modern Greek.

Argued letters, in fact, are a small subset. Of consonants, only the voiced stops β, γ, and δ are disputed with any significant consequence. The β is given as in "**ve**ry," the γ as in "**ye**ar," and the δ as in "**th**is." Of the vowels, those in dispute are η, ι, and υ, which are all given like "sk*i*." The short ο is undistinguished from the long ω. All diphthongs except ου are disputed, based on the close vowel (either ι or υ). Thus, αι is said to be like ε. Both ει and οι are given as in "sk*i*." Both αυ and ευ are given as their corresponding short vowel sounds closing with "v." (Observe in these disputed vowel and diphthong patterns that "ee" and "v" type vocalizations dominate.)

Observations

We give some additional observations about the Greek alphabet related to pronunciation and transliteration:

- *Combinations:* Some consonant sounds require two English consonants. Thus, θ = th, φ = ph, χ = ch, and ψ = ps.
- *Gamma:* Before palatal stops (κ, γ, χ) and ξ, gamma has an "n" sound, or *gamma nasal*. The γκ in ἐγκαίνια is pronounced like "i<u>nk</u>"; the γγ in ἄγγελος like "si<u>ng</u>"; the γχ in σπλάγχνα like "I<u>nc</u>a"; and γχ in λάρυγξ like "lary<u>nx</u>."
- *Zeta:* Within a word the ζ is voiced as "dz." For example, one can contrast ζάω and σῴζω.
- *Iota:* First, the iota subscript can be written *after* a capital vowel, a feature in some of our Greek manuscripts that is called *iota adscript*. Second, Hebrew terms beginning with *yod* (׳) come into Greek as iota, transliterated in two different ways, depending on whether a vowel follows. When a vowel follows, the *yod* is transliterated as "Y," and the equivalent English sound is "J." Thus, יַעֲקֹב comes into Greek as Ἰακώβ and is given in English as "Jacob." In contrast, when no vowel follows, *yod* is transliterated as "I," and the equivalent English sound is as in "sk*i*." Thus, יִשְׂרָאֵל comes into Greek as Ἰσραήλ, which is "Israel" in English.

- *Kappa:* Greek words with κ coming into English through Latin use a hard "c" for the κ. Thus, "canon" is from the Latin *canon*, which is itself from the Greek κανών.
- *Upsilon:* The υ is transliterated as "y," but "u" is used for diphthongs. For example, ὑπό = *hypo*, but αὐτός = *autos*.
- *Diphthong ευ:* The tradition of giving the diphthong ευ as the English "feud," ubiquitous in Greek grammars, should stop. English "feud" is f(y)üd, pronounced "fee-üd," which is *not* the pronunciation of this Greek diphthong ευ.

Formation

Majuscules

Majuscules are capital letters. *Uncial* is a special style in our ancient Greek manuscripts in formal literary works using all capital letters. This style had virtually no word divisions, or accents, or punctuation! This running of letters and words together is called *scripto continua* for "continuous script." Many ancient copies of the New Testament are uncials written in this *scripto continua*, the best coming from the third to sixth centuries. One example is Codex Vaticanus in the Vatican Library, a fourth-century uncial written in *scripto continua*, but having a few accent marks added by a second hand at a later time (pp. 94, 520). Another example is Codex Sinaiticus, a fourth-century uncial and our only complete Greek uncial copy of the New Testament (pp. xxvi, 11, 94). Capital letters in an edited Greek text are used: (1) as the first letter of proper names, (2) at the beginning of a direct quotation, (3) at the beginning of a paragraph, or (4) at the beginning of a sentence understood to be a new thought.

Minuscules

Minuscules are small letters. Since the uncial style eventually deteriorated over time, literary handwriting went through reform about the ninth century in a transition to a cursive minuscule hand.

Copying of Greek manuscripts took place mostly in Byzantium, capital of the eastern Roman Empire until the city fell to the Turks in 1493. The majority of New Testament manuscripts are this later "Byzantine" type. New Testament manuscripts fall fairly well into two major camps: the earlier uncials and the later minuscules. The point is that our great uncial manuscripts were unknown when the English translators worked on the King James Version. All they had with which to work were a few, late Byzantine minuscules.[2]

Table 1.4 Greek Manuscript Styles

Codex Sinaiticus. Section image of Sinaiticus, 4th cent., one of our best uncials, the only one with the entire New Testament. Each of four columns is just over 2 inches wide. The image shows a column at Lk 2:1-2. *Codex Sinaiticus* (Lake, 1911) © Oxford University Press. By permission of Oxford University Press.

Lectionary 59. Section image of the Greek lectionary 59 (Fol. 81, verso), about the 10th cent. This manuscript has two columns, each about 2.7 inches wide. One easily can see that a minuscule cursive hand is quite different than the stylized uncial script of Sinaiticus. The large capital alpha (A) begins at Rom 12:1.

---

[2]For the material in the text above, see Bruce Manning Metzger, *The Text of the New Testament: Its Transmission, Corruption and Restoration*, 3d ed. (New York and Oxford: Oxford University Press, 1992).

Punctuation

Commas and periods are the same as in English. Partial stops (colon, semicolon) are a raised dot, and questions are like our semicolon: ἐάν τις ὑμῖν εἴπῃ· τί ποιεῖτε τοῦτο; (Mk 11:3). For the most part, our oldest Greek manuscripts are not punctuated. An exception is 𝔓⁶⁶, about A.D. 200. Punctuation, then, in our edited Greek text has to be decided by a committee of scholars. Likewise, all punctuation in all translations represents editorial decisions of the translators. Thus, one must be alert to possible punctuation issues that could affect the sense of a given text. Note the options with the period in Jn 1:3-4: (1) "what was created in him was life." or (2) "what was created. In him was life . . ."

Greek manuscripts do not use quotation marks. Direct quotes are indicated two ways in the edited text: (1) by a capital letter following a comma, or (2) by ὅτι recitative ("*hoti* recitative"), when ὅτι is understood as introducing a quote. The ὅτι as "*hoti* recitative" is not translated. The word after ὅτι that begins the direct quote will be capitalized. Thus, for example, one will have καὶ λέγει, Οὐκ εἰμί (Jn 1:21), or ὡμολόγησεν ὅτι Ἐγὼ οὐκ εἰμι ὁ Χριστός (Jn 1:20). The job of assessing what is a direct quote can be difficult. Study carefully Jn 3:16, for example. Is this most famous verse of the Bible to be read as a direct discourse of Jesus, or as the writer's own commentary about Jesus?

Elision is the dropping of a letter. *Crasis* is the merging of two words into one for pronunciation, with the elision of one or more letters. A mark like an apostrophe indicating crasis is called a *coronis*. Crasis does not affect meaning. The resultant word still is translated as the two originally separate words. The phenomenon of crasis usually involves the conjunction καί, in the following forms: κἀγώ (καὶ ἐγώ), κἀμέ (καὶ ἐμέ), κἀμοί (καὶ ἐμοί), κἀκεί (καὶ ἐκεί), κἀκεῖθεν (καὶ ἐκεῖθεν), κἀκεῖνος, -η, -ο (καὶ ἐκεῖνος, -η, -ο), κἄν (καὶ ἐν or καὶ ἐάν or καὶ ἄν). The neuter article τό adds two other forms: τοὔνομα (τὸ ὄνομα) and τοὐναντίον (τὸ ἐναντίον).

Accents

History

Greek accents began to be used about the fourth century B.C., but not systematically until about 200 B.C. Even so, the oldest copies of the Greek New Testament usually do not have accent marks. One of the earliest accented New Testament manuscripts is 𝔓⁷⁵ (ca. 2nd cent.), which seems to have breathing marks and diaeresis. As New Testament documents continued being copied over the centuries, accents were added, but not fully until the 9th to 11th centuries. Later copyists added the Greek accents to aid in the pronunciation of a Greek language no longer spoken. Originally, accents reflected inflection. Now, accents simply mark stress. The acute is strong, the grave weak, circumflex a modest rise and fall.

Some Greek words have exactly the same letters, but different accents. English is similar. Notice how different accents can change a word from a noun to a verb. "Prógress" is a noun but "progréss" is a verb. With Greek, πότε is the interrogative adverb "when?" but ποτέ is a particle meaning "at the same time."

Syllables

Modern edited Greek texts of the New Testament are accented. We choose to remove their mystery. So, how do accents work? To answer this question we first must learn to divide a Greek word into syllables, the names of the last three syllables, and syllable quantity. We then present key principles, such as possible accent positions, the limitations of syllable quantity, accent sustain, and general rules of accent. We will discuss each of these in turn.

Syllable Divisions

The table below illustrates syllable divisions. A brief discussion will explain the principles involved.

The fundamental principle is simple:

♦ *A Greek word has as many syllables as vowels and/or diphthongs.*

Starting from the left, syllable divisions occur after each vowel or diphthong, except the last vowel or diphthong. A final consonant goes with the last vowel or diphthong. A single vowel can be a syllable. Divide a syllable: (1) after each vowel unit, and (2) after the first consonant in a group. These consonant groups have two exceptions: (2a) non-divisible consonants, and (2b) nasal units.

Table 1.5 Syllable Divisions

Principle	Example	Division
simple, single vowel	λόγος	λό-γος
simple, double vowel	θέος	θέ-ος
simple, diphthong	αὐτοῦ	αὐ-τοῦ
two consonants	εὐαγγέλιον	εὐ-αγ-γέ-λι-ον
three consonants	ἄνθρωπος	ἄν-θρω-πος
consonant unit (first)	σχίσμα	σχί-σμα
consonant unit (int.)	πάσχα	πά-σχα
nasal -μ unit (first)	σμύρνα	σμύρ-να
nasal -μ unit (int.)	ἀριθμός	ἀ-ρι-θμός
nasal -ν unit (first)	πνεῦμα	πνεῦ-μα
nasal -ν unit (int.)	ἔγνωσαν	ἔ-γνω-σαν
compound	ἐκβάλλω	ἐκ-βάλ-λω

Multiple Consonants. Two consonants together (including doubled consonants) are split. The first consonant closes the syllable before; the second consonant opens the syllable following. Of three consonants together, the first closes the syllable before; the last two open the syllable following.

Consonant Units. Certain consonant combinations *never* divide, and are called "consonant units" (or "clusters" or "groups"). These units are learned by observation with vocabulary. One tip is:

- ◆ *Any consonant unit that may begin a word will not divide within a word.*

An indivisible unit will go with the following vowel/diphthong. For example, with liquids, observe βλ, κλ, θλ, πλ, μν, πν, γρ, θρ, κρ, πρ, τρ, and χρ. For others, note πτ, σκ, σπ, στ, σμ, and σχ.

Nasal Units. The two nasal consonants are μ and ν. Nasals do not divide when *second* in a consonant pair. So, units such as σμ, θμ, πν, and γν would not divide.

Compound Words. Greek words can be compounded to form new words, as with verbs. Compounds are divided where the words are joined together.

Syllable Positions

Table 1.6 Final Three Syllable Positions

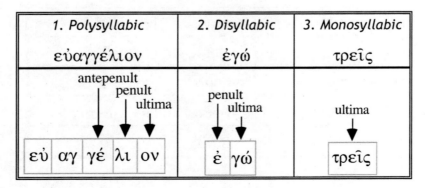

A Greek word with three or more syllables is *polysyllabic*. A *disyllabic* word has two syllables. *Monosyllabic* is a one syllable word. Syllable "position" relates only to the final three syllables of a Greek word, regardless of the total number of syllables. The *last three* syllables of a Greek word are called the *antepenult*, the *penult*, and the *ultima*. Whether a word is polysyllabic, disyllabic, or monosyllabic, the last syllable is the ultima.

Syllable Quantity

Syllable quantity is the vowel or diphthong quantity in that syllable. A long vowel (η, ω, diphthong) creates a long syllable. A short vowel (ε, ο, and αι, οι when final) creates a short syllable. Syllables with α, ι, or υ may be long or short, given by observation.

Preliminary Principles

Once the basic idea of Greek syllables is grasped, we can apply accenting principles. Preliminary principles include possible accent positions, how syllable quantity limits the circumflex, and the idea of accent sustain.

Possible Accent Positions

Table 1.7 Possible Accent Positions

	Antepenult	*Penult*	*Ultima*
acute	╱	╱	╱
circumflex		⌒	⌒
grave			╲

Possible accent positions involve the last three syllables of any word. An acute accent can occur on any of the last *three* syllables.

The circumflex can occur only on the last *two* syllables. The grave can occur only on the *last* syllable. The table above provides a visual summary of these possibilities.

Circumflex Restriction

Syllable quantity—as long or short—affects accents. Both acute and grave accents can stand over either long or short syllables; these two accents are unrestricted by a syllable's quantity. In contrast:

♦ *The circumflex accent can stand over long syllables only.*

This restriction of the circumflex to long syllables is important and has numerous implications for accent.

Accent Sustain

Sustain is the ability of a particular accent to carry the sylla-bles that follow. The acute can sustain *three* syllables, but *only two adjacent can be long*. The circumflex can sustain *two* sylla-bles, but *the second must be short*. The grave can sustain only *one* syllable (not really stressed at all).

Table 1.8 Maximum Accent Sustain

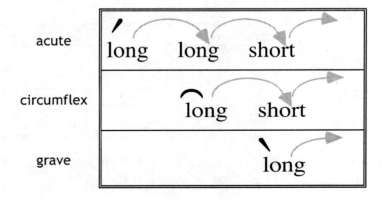

Accenting Rules

Word Class Rules

Accent behavior depends on word class. Word class is whether the word is a noun or verb. Word class generates two rules. One is:

♦ *Noun accents are persistent.*

Table 1.9 Noun Accent: Persistent

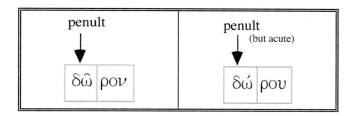

Noun accent tries to stay in the syllable of the lexical form. The circumflex penult changes to acute penult in δῶρον to δώρου. Note how λόγος show a penult persistence (λόγος, λόγου, λόγῳ, λόγον, λόγοι, λόγων, λόγοις, λόγους), but ἄνθρωπος antepenult persistence (ἄνθρωπος, ἀνθρώπου, ἀνθρώπῳ, ἄνθρωπον, ἄνθρωποι, ἀνθρώπων, ἀνθρώποις, ἀνθρώπους); here, though, long ultimas forces the *antepenult* acute back to the *penult*.

Table 1.10 Noun Accent: Antepenult Acute

The other word class rule applies to verbs:

♦ *Verb accents are recessive.*

Table 1.11 Verb Accent: Recessive

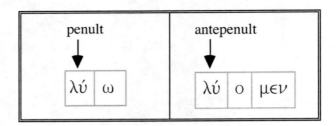

Verb accent tries to recede from the ultima as far as possible, if rules allow. Note the shift from penult back to the antepenult: λύω, λύεις, λύει, λύομεν, λύετε, λύουσι. The forms λύομεν, λύετε, and λύουσι show the acute *penult* of the disyllabic form (λύω) receding back to the *antepenult* in the polysyllabic forms of the plurals, because the ultima is short and allows this shift.

Special Rules

Special rules apply to two accents, circumflex and grave. We already have presented the circumflex rule:

    ◆ *The circumflex accent can stand over long syllables only.*

So, we have forms such as the long vowel δῶρον or the diphthong αὐτοῦ. For a variable vowel, note ἡμῖν. The circumflex accent reveals that the iota, which is a variable vowel that can be long or short, is declared *long* by the presence of the circumflex accent.

    The other special rule applies to grave accents. The rule for a grave accent is simple:

    ◆ *An acute ultima becomes grave in composition.*

"In composition" simply means when composed with other words in an actual sentence. Thus, the grave accent shows up when no punctuation breaks the flow to the next word (πρὸς τὸν θεόν).

Ultima Quantity Rules

Greek accents can be conquered by the following dictum:

♦ *The deciding factor for accents is the quantity of the ultima.*

The above dictum has one exception:

♦ *The diphthongs -οι and -αι are considered short when final.*

The word "final" means the last two letters of the word. Six rules follow this dictum of the ultima quantity:

Table 1.12 Six Ultima Quantity Rules

	If the ultima is short:
1.	The accented antepenult must be acute (κύριος).
2.	The accented, *long* penult *must* be circumflex, but acute if short (δῶρον; λόγος).
3.	The accented ultima is acute (θεός).
	If the ultima is long:
4.	The antepenult *cannot* be accented (κυρίου).
5.	The accented penult is acute (δώρου).
6.	The accented ultima can be any accent (γραφή; in composition: γραφὴ λέγει; γραφῆς).

These six rules can be summarized visually, as given below:

Table 1.13 If Syllable Accented and Short Ultima

Antepenult	Penult		Ultima	
✓	⌢	✓	✓	╲
	Long	Short	Short	Short

Table 1.14 If Syllable Accented and Long Ultima

Antepenult	Penult	Ultima		
-----	/	/	⌢	\
(cannot be accented)		Long	Long	Long

So, how does one proceed to determine the correct accent of an inflected form of a Greek word? The following table summarizes questions to ask to determine accent.

Table 1.15 Accent Determination Procedure

1. **What is the word class?**
   a. If a *noun*, apply the *persistent* rule of accent.
   b. If a *verb*, apply the *recessive* rule of accent.
2. **What is the lexical form?**
   Both *accent* and *position* in the lexical form first must be known in advance in order to apply the rules of accent.
3. **What is the ultima quantity?**
   Keeping in mind both preliminary principles and special rules for circumflex and grave accents, then:
   a. If *short*, apply ultima rules one through three.
   b. If *long*, apply ultima rules four through six.

Additional Accent Rules

Oxytone Rule

An *oxytone* is a noun with acute accent in the ultima of the nominative singular. (Oxytone means "sharp-toned.") Examples are: the masculine nouns θεός, ἀδελφός, οὐρανός, υἱός, and Χριστός, and the neuter noun ἱερόν. Oxytones have a distinct accent pattern: *interior cases (genitive, dative) have a circumflex ultima*. (For the concept of "interior cases," see Table 2.6.)

Neuter oxytone nouns of the second declension actually are rare in the New Testament. These include: ἑρπετόν ("reptile"), ἱερόν ("temple"), Ἰλλυρικόν ("Illyricum"), λουτρόν ("bath"), πετεινόν ("bird"), σφυδρόν ("ankle"),[3] and ᾠόν ("egg"). Yet, though the noun is rare, the neuter oxytone noun paradigm helps because many neuter *adjectives* are oxytone and follow the second declension neuter noun paradigm of ἱερόν.

Table 1.16 Oxytone Paradigms: Masculine and Neuter

	ὁ υἱός			τὸ ἱερόν	
Case	Singular	Plural	Case	Singular	Plural
N	υἱός	υἱοί	N	ἱερόν	ἱερά
G	υἱοῦ	υἱῶν	G	ἱεροῦ	ἱερῶν
D	υἱῷ	υἱοῖς	D	ἱερῷ	ἱεροῖς
A	υἱέ	υἱοί	A	ἱερόν	ἱερά

Enclitic Rules

Table 1.17 Enclitic Accent Rules

> ***Acute enclitic rules:***
> 1. The acute antepenult adds an acute to the ultima (κύριός ἐστιν).
> 2. The acute penult:
>   a. causes any monosyllabic enclitic to loose accent (λόγος μου).
>   b. allows any disyllabic enclitic to retain accent (λόγος ἐστίν).
> 3. The acute ultima does not revert to grave (υἱός ἐστιν).

---

[3]The variant σφυρόν occurs in ℵ² B² D E Ψ 𝔐 at Acts 3:7.

Circumflex enclitic rules:

4. The circumflex penult adds an acute to the ultima (δοῦλοί εἰσιν).
5. The circumflex ultima causes enclitics to loose accent (φωνῆς μού αὐτῶν ἐστιν).

Double enclitic rule:

6. A preceding word itself an enclitic retains accent (μού ἐστιν).

Emphatic enclitic rule:

7. Enclitics may retain accent for emphasis or when beginning a clause or sentence (Ἔστιν δὲ ἐν τοῖς Ἱεροσολύμοις).

Compound enclitic rule:

8. A word compounded by an enclitic treats the enclitic as a separate word (ὥστε = ὡς + τέ).

An *enclitic* is a word that looses accent by "leaning on" the *previous* word for accent. The enclitic has no accent of its own. Such words, one might suspect, would generate exceptions to our general accent rules. The accenting that results from the presence of an enclitic is understandable if one remembers that an enclitic is just an extra syllable being considered for accent. Thus, a word might receive *two* accents, or a grave accent fails to show.

Proclitic Rule

A *proclitic* is a word that looses accent by "leaning on" the *following* word for accent. The proclitic has no accent of its own. Proclitics have oxytone accent ("interiors go circumflex").

Contract Rules

Contract verbs create a distinct set of accents distinguished by whether the contract or thematic vowel is accented prior to the contraction process. If one knows which vowel is accented prior to contraction, then one can apply the following rules.

Epsilon Contracts. All of the epsilon contracts accent the stem vowel in the lexical form (penult). Thus, according to the stem vowel rule, *all epsilon contract verbs have circumflex accents throughout the present active indicative.* Resultant contract forms are spelled just as their thematic verb counterparts in all but first and second persons plural (φιλοῦμεν, φιλεῖτε). Otherwise, the circumflex accent alone distinguishes what is a regular verb and what is a contract verb.

Two-syllable suffixes push an accent back to the antepenult (as far back as the accent can recede). This antepenult comprised of the thematic vowel becomes long in the process of contraction. A long antepenult *must* be acute. An example suffix is -ομεθα. This accented antepenult o in the first person plural that contracts to the long diphthong ου *must* be acute (φιλεόμεθα = φιλούμεθα).

Table 1.18 Contract Accent Rules

> *Stem vowel rule:*
> 1. Accented stem vowels create circumflex contract accents (φιλέεις→φιλεῖς).
>
> *Thematic vowel rule:*
> 2. Accented thematic vowels create acute contract accents (φιλεόμεθα→φιλούμεθα).
>
> *Diphthong rule:*
> 3. Final -οι and -αι, normally considered short for accenting, are considered *long* in contracts (δηλόει→δηλοῖ).
>
> *Accented alpha rule:*
> 4. Accented α always is considered long (τιμάετε→τιμᾶτε).

Omicron Contracts. Recall that the diphthongs αι and οι when final are considered short for accenting purposes. This general rule is *not* observed in contracts. A final -οι, if accented, is considered *long* in contracts. Thus, a circumflex accent occurs over the final οι in δηλοῖ, the third person singular contraction (δηλο + ει = δηλόει = δηλοῖ).

Alpha Contracts. The vowel α is variable—either long or short. However, in accented contract syllables, an α always is considered long. Thus, a circumflex occurs over the α in τιμᾶτε (τιμά + ετε = τιμάετε = τιμᾶτε).

Subjunctive Mood Contraction

Aorist Passive. Aorist passive subjunctive has a -θε voice suffix. The subjunctive mood has the long thematic vowel. Thus, aorist passive subjunctive looks like an epsilon contract, with the typical circumflex accent result (λυθῶ, λυθῇς, λυθῇ, λυθῶμεν, λυθῆτε, λυθῶσι).

MI Verbs. Similarly, -μι verbs can have short vowel stems. Such stems will contract with the long thematic vowel of the subjunctive, yielding all circumflex accents (διδῶ, διδῷς, διδῷ, διδῶμεν, διδῶτε, διδῶσι).

Substantive Contraction

First Declension Nouns. Three first declension nouns are "α pure" in inflectional endings, but their stem vowels contract in a pattern similar to contraction in verbs. The contraction leaves a tell-tale sign in the circumflex accent. These three nouns are γῆ (γέ + α), συκῆ (συκέ + α), and μνᾶ (μνά + α). These nouns are found in the New Testament in singular forms only.

Adjectives. Various adjectives have stem vowels ending with ε or ο and can contract. Typical inflection is affected. In a few *second* declension adjectives, one will have nominative in -οῦς, not -ος; accusative in -οῦν, not -ον. One example is χρυσοῦς, -ῆ, -οῦν ("gold"). Another is χαλκοῦς, -ῆ, -οῦν ("made of copper").

Two other adjectives end in a variation with rho (-ρε) and show a pattern similar to χρυσοῦς, only with -ᾶ, -ᾶς, -ᾷ, -ᾶν in the singular. These are σιδηροῦς, -ᾶ, -οῦν ("made of iron"), and ἀργυροῦς, -ᾶ, -οῦν ("made of silver").

The *singular* forms of *third* declension adjective contraction can be confused with cases of other inflections, as in ἀληθῆς, "true" (cf. -ῆς, -οῦς, -εῖ, -ῆ). The plural forms of this adjective are like the third declension noun πίστις (e.g., ἀληθεῖς).

Liquid Future Accents

Liquid future verbs use the alternate future tense suffix -εσ instead of the simple -σ. However, these verbs drop the sigma, which creates contraction of the thematic vowel and the remaining suffix vowel -ε. The result looks just like an epsilon contract verb (μενῶ, μενεῖς, μενεῖ, μενοῦμεν, μενεῖτε, μενοῦσι).

Third Declension Noun Accents

Third declension noun accents follow a different drummer. For example, these nouns do not follow the rule of persistence (e.g., dative singular, λιβί, but plural, λίψι). The genitive plural does not always have circumflex, even if feminine (e.g., χαρίτων). Again, the accent, regardless of its syllable position in other forms, sometimes may recede to the antepenult (e.g., ἔθνεσι). Thus, third declension accents simply have to be observed and noted.

Optative Accent

The optative uses an iota mood sign. Two endings of the third singular create the forms λύοι and λύσαι (present and aorist). The final οι and αι in these forms are considered *long*, which is an exception to the standard rule; hence, acute accents are used in the penult.

Infinitive Accents

Infinitive accents look "irregular." However, accent rules for finite verbs do not apply to infinitives. The accent is learned by observation for each form.

Participle Accents

Active Participles. Participle accent is not "irregular," since, like infinitives, rules for finite verbs do not apply. Accent follows that of nouns and adjectives. Once the accent of the nominative masculine singular in a tense and voice is known, one can observe that: (1) general rules of accent are followed, (2) accent is persistent, (3) the genitive feminine plural of active voice (and aorist passive) has the typical circumflex on the ultima, as in first declension nouns. The present and future have penult acute (λύων, λύσων), which generally become antepenult acute in the paradigms (λύοντος, λύσοντος).

The aorist active participle generally is penult acute (λύσας), but the neuter nominative and accusative singular (λῦσαν) and genitive feminine plural (λυσασῶν) are circumflex. The second aorist is like present, but ultima acute (λιπών). The aorist passive also is ultima acute (λυθείς), which generally becomes penult acute in the paradigm (λυθέντος), but dative plural has circumflex (λυθεῖσιν). Some feminine forms have circumflex accent (e.g., λυθεῖσα, λυθεισῶν).

The perfect participle is ultima acute (λελυκώς). This accent generally becomes penult acute in the paradigms (λελυκότος).

Middle Participles. Nominative masculine singular accent is antepenult acute. Then observe that: (1) general rules of accent are followed, (2) accent is persistent, (3) the genitive feminine plural does *not* have the typical circumflex on the ultima, as in first declension nouns.

EXERCISE 1

1. Answer the following on Hellenic dialects and Hellenistic Greek.

   1.1 _____ Which dialect provided the basic Greek alphabet?

   1.2 Convert each line of the majuscule letters of the Aphrodite inscription (Fig. 4, p. 2) into minuscule letters.

   Line 1: _____

   Line 2: _____

   Line 3: _____

   1.3 _____ Which dialect spoken at Athens became the premier language of literary expression?

   1.4 _____ and _____ are the two major forms of Hellenistic Greek.

   1.5 _____ Who especially promoted the Greek of the Classical period and greatly influenced Greek style?

   1.6 _____ Whose cosmopolitan program of world empire over time revolutionized the Greek language?

1.7 a. _____ The theory that the Greek of the New Testament was the result of Aramaic speaking disciples who did not know Greek trying to write in Greek.

b. _____ The theory that the Greek of the New Testament was the result of uncontrollable Spirit ecstasy.

c. _____ The theory that the Greek of the New Testament was a divine dialect created uniquely for the New Testament revelation.

d. _____ The scholar whose work on Egyptian papyri blew all these theories out of the water.

1.8 Identify elements of Koine style in the following narrative taken from Mk 1:21-26, 29-30. You do not have to translate the passage to spot Koine style. Be able to classify as over-emphasis, overfullness, or other.

Καὶ εἰσπορεύονται εἰς Καφαρναούμ· καὶ εὐθὺς τοῖς σάββασιν εἰσελθὼν εἰς τὴν συναγωγὴν ἐδίδασκεν. καὶ ἐξεπλήσσοντο ἐπὶ τῇ διδαχῇ αὐτοῦ· ἦν γὰρ διδάσκων αὐτοὺς ὡς ἐξουσίαν ἔχων καὶ οὐχ ὡς οἱ γραμματεῖς.

Καὶ εὐθὺς ἦν ἐν τῇ συναγωγῇ αὐτῶν ἄνθρωπος ἐν πνεύματι ἀκαθάρτῳ καὶ ἀνέκραξεν λέγων· τί ἡμῖν καὶ σοί, Ἰησοῦ Ναζαρηνέ; ἦλθες ἀπολέσαι ἡμᾶς; οἶδά σε τίς εἶ, ὁ ἅγιος τοῦ θεοῦ. καὶ ἐπετίμησεν αὐτῷ ὁ Ἰησοῦς λέγων· φιμώθητι καὶ ἔξελθε ἐξ αὐτοῦ. καὶ σπαράξαν αὐτὸν τὸ πνεῦμα τὸ ἀκάθαρτον καὶ φωνῆσαν φωνῇ μεγάλῃ ἐξῆλθεν ἐξ αὐτοῦ. . . .

Καὶ εὐθὺς ἐκ τῆς συναγωγῆς ἐξελθόντες ἦλθον εἰς τὴν οἰκίαν Σίμωνος καὶ Ἀνδρέου μετὰ Ἰακώβου καὶ Ἰωάννου. ἡ δὲ πενθερὰ Σίμωνος κατέκειτο πυρέσσουσα, καὶ εὐθὺς λέγουσιν αὐτῷ περὶ αὐτῆς.

2. Answer the following on the Greek alphabet.

2.1 _____ Identify the three smooth stops.

2.2 _____ Are the three smooth stops voiced or voiceless?

2.3 _____ Identify the three rough stops.

2.4 _____ Are the three rough stops voiced or voiceless?

2.5 Convert the first 11 lines of the uncial letters of Codex Sinaiticus (Table 1.4, p. 12) into minuscule letters in order to illustrate the _scripto continua_ style. Use your UBS text as a guide. The uncial sigma is C. The alpha λ, delta Δ, and lambda λ are easily confused, according to a given scribe's particular hand.

Line 1: _____

Line 2: _____

Line 3: _____

Line 4: _____

Line 5: _____

Line 6: _____

Line 7: _____

Line 8: _____

Line 9: _____

Line 10: _____

Line 11: _____

3. Answer the following on Greek accents.

3.1 Divide the following lines into syllables:

Line 1: Καὶ εἰσπορεύονται εἰς Καφαρναούμ· καὶ εὐθὺς

Line 2: ἐξεπλήσσοντο ἐπὶ τῇ διδαχῇ αὐτοῦ· ἦν γὰρ

Line 3: Καὶ εὐθὺς ἦν ἐν τῇ συναγωγῇ αὐτῶν ἄνθρωπος ἐν

3.2 Answer true or false:

_____ a. The circumflex can stand in the antepenult.

_____ b. The grave can stand in the penult.

_____ c. The circumflex can stand over long syllables only.

_____ d. The acute is the only accent that can sustain two adjacent long syllables.

_____ e. The circumflex can sustain two syllables, but only if the second is short.

_____ f. Verb accents are persistent.

_____ g. The diphthongs αι and οι are considered short when final.

_____ h. If the ultima is short and the penult long, the accented penult must be acute.

_____ i. If the ultima is long, the accented penult must be acute.

3.3 Using Table 1.12, accent the following verb forms; participle forms have their own patterns according to voice:

a. ἀκουωσιν[4]   ἀκουετε   ἀκουετω

b. βλεπομεν   βλεπει   βλεπομενη

c. λεγωμεν   λεγομενοι   λεγομενοις

3.4 Using Table 1.12, accent the following noun forms:

a. ανθρωποι   ανθρωπου   ανθρωπον

b. λογοι   λογοις   λογω

c. κυριοι   κυριου   κυριον

---

[4]Consider the iota short.

CHAPTER 2
NOUNS: 1ST AND 2ND DECLENSION

Greek has three declensions. Any particular word belongs to only one declension. Gender varies within a declension, yet the first declension is mostly feminine, the second declension is mostly masculine and neuter, but the third declension mixes all three. This chapter covers first and second declensions.

First Declension

Vowel Stems

First declension and second declension are comprised of vowel stem nouns. First declension is called the "-α declension," for most of the noun stems end in the vowel -α. Second declension is called the "-ο declension," because all the nouns stems end in -ο. The two vowels α and ο actually function as "theme vowels" (as verbs have), for these vowels help join case suffixes to the noun stem. For simplicity, the second declension endings normally are learned in their volatilized forms, in which the stem vowel -ο is obscured.

Feminine Inflection

Feminine nouns of the first declension have three basic stem types: (1) -ε, -ι, -ρ, (2) nominatives in -η, and (3) sibilants. The noun endings are either -α or -η. Inflection patterns can be arranged according to these stem types, but only singular forms are affected. Regardless of singular stem type:

♦ *In first declension, all the plurals are all the same.*

The student should focus on the three simple singular patterns: one builds on the vowel α, another on the vowel η; the third mixes the two. Genitive singular (-ας, -ης) and accusative plural (-ας) *always* are long. The genitive plural *always* is circumflex. The -ε, -ι, -ρ stems are called "α pure." The nominatives in -η stems are called "η pure." The sibilant stems are called "α/η mixed." Note that dative singular always has iota subscript.

Table 2.1 First Declension Inflection Patterns By Stem Type

Case	Singulars by Stem Type			Plurals
	-ε, -ι, -ρ	Nom. in -η	Sibilant	
N	-α	-η	-α	-αι
G	-ας	-ης	-ης	-ων
D	-ᾳ	-ῃ	-ῃ	-αις
A	-αν	-ην	-αν	-ας

Type 1: Alpha Pure (-ε, -ι, -ρ stems)

Notice the -α vowel throughout the singular inflection. This alpha can be long or short; two paradigms are given to represent either case. When long (καρδία), this long alpha generates acute accents, *except in the genitive plural, which always is circumflex in first declension regardless of accent rules* (καρδιῶν). Final -αι always is short, so the nominative plural is acute. A short alpha allows an acute accent on the antepenult (ἀλήθεια). If the nominative singular α is long (καρδία), the accusative singular will be long (καρδίαν). Likewise, if the nominative singular α is short (ἀλήθεια), the accusative singular will be short (ἀλήθειαν). The oxytone paradigm (χαρά) provides both an alternate example using a -ρ stem and an illustration of the oxytone accent pattern, summarized by the phrase "interiors go circumflex." (For an explanation of the concept of "interior cases," see Table 2.6)

Type 2: Eta Pure (Nominatives in -η)

This class represents stems other than Type 1 or Type 3. Notice the -η throughout the singular inflection. Any first declension noun whose lexical form ends in -η will retain that η throughout the singular (= "η pure"). The γραφή paradigm represents oxytone accent for this η pure inflection ("interiors go circumflex").

Type 3: Alpha/Eta Mixed (Sibilant stems)

Type 3 stems end with three sibilants (-σ, -ξ, -ζ). *Notice how the interior singular slips to -η.* The singular starts with -α in the nominative, as if a Type 1, but the genitive and dative take the -η vowel of Type 2, then returns to the -α of Type 1 in the accusative. The plural is the same as *all* plurals. No oxytone first declension sibilant *noun* occurs in the New Testament. Other forms are discussed later (-ης, -ας masculines). Contracted feminines γῆ, συκῆ, and μνᾶ were given in chapter one in discussing accents.

Masculine Inflection

All first declension nouns whose nominative forms end in -ης or -ας are *masculine* in gender but first declension in their inflection (similar to "η pure" and "α pure"). First declension inflection is regular, with two exceptions: the -ου of the genitive singular and the -α of the vocative singular. In terms of concord, notice that the article will have second declension inflection, but the noun will have first declension inflection; e.g., τῷ μαθητῇ or τοὺς μαθητάς These -ης nouns sometimes are categorized as "occupation" or "agent" nouns. Like the English suffix "-er" in "learn*er*," they can indicate an occupation or agent.

Which words comprise this list? One can use a sentence, "John the prophet's disciples await Messiah," to sum up first declension masculines Ἰωάννης, προφήτης, μαθητής, and μεσσίας. One can use another phrase, "a way in the wilderness," to catch the second declension feminines ὁδός and ἔρημος. This leaves only παρθένος from typical vocabulary lists.

Additional patterns for first declension masculine nouns focus on variations in nominative and genitive singular: (1) -ας/-ου, as in Ἠσαΐας, Ἠσαΐου, (2) -ας/-α, as in σατανᾶς, σατανᾶ, (3) -ης/ -η, as in Μανασσῆς, Μανασσῆ. These forms are uncommon, the last quite rare.

The following paradigms are given to summarize the discussion of first declension inflection patterns. Some paradigms, however, are given not for inflection but to illustrate an accent pattern, such as long or short alpha or the oxytone pattern.

Table 2.2 First Declension: -ε, -ι, -ρ ("α pure") Stems

ἡ καρδία (long α in N, Ac)		ἡ ἀλήθεια (short α in N, Ac)	
Singular	Plural	Singular	Plural
καρδία	καρδίαι	ἀλήθεια	ἀλήθειαι
καρδίας	καρδιῶν	ἀληθείας	ἀληθειῶν
καρδίᾳ	καρδίαις	ἀληθείᾳ	ἀληθείαις
καρδίαν	καρδίας	ἀλήθειαν	ἀληθείας

Table 2.3 First Declension: Nom. in -η ("η pure") and Sibilant

ἡ ἀγάπη (nom. in -η)		ἡ δόξα (sibilant)	
Singular	Plural	Singular	Plural
ἀγάπη	ἀγάπαι	δόξα	δόξαι
ἀγάπης	ἀγαπῶν	δόξης	δοξῶν
ἀγάπῃ	ἀγάπαις	δόξῃ	δόξαις
ἀγάπην	ἀγάπας	δόξαν	δόξας

Table 2.4 First Declension: Oxytone Accent

ἡ χαρά		ἡ γραφή	
(oxytone)		(oxytone)	
Singular	*Plural*	*Singular*	*Plural*
χαρά	χαραί	γραφή	γραφαί
χαρᾶς	χαρῶν	γραφῆς	γραφῶν
χαρᾷ	χαραῖς	γραφῇ	γραφαῖς
χαράν	χαράς	γραφήν	γραφάς

Table 2.5 First Declension: *Mas.*—Ὁ Μαθητής, Ὁ Μεσσίας

ὁ μαθητής		ὁ μεσσίας	
(masculine)		(masculine)	
Singular	*Plural*	*Singular*	*Plural*
μαθητής	μαθηταί	μεσσίας	μεσσίαι
μαθητοῦ	μαθητῶν	μεσσίου	μεσσιῶν
μαθητῇ	μαθηταῖς	μεσσίᾳ	μεσσίαις
μαθητήν	μαθητάς	μεσσίαν	μεσσίας
μαθητά	μαθηταί	μεσσία/ας	μεσσίαι

The Second Declension

Vowel Stems

The second declension has an omicron theme vowel; that is, the noun stems end in -o. Words such as λόγος or δῶρον have the stems λογο- and δωρο-. This stem vowel, however, gets lost in the shuffle to inflectional endings. Thus, second declension endings usually are learned in their *resultant* forms, *after* contraction has taken place. Notice that the dative singular always has an iota subscript.

Table 2.6 Second Declension Inflections

		Mas./Fem.		Neuter	
		Sing.	Plu.	Sing.	Plu.
	N	-ος	-οι	-ον	-α
	G	-ου	-ων	-ου	-ων
	D	-ῳ	-οις	-ῳ	-οις
	A	-ον	-ους	-ον	-α
	V	-ε	-οι	-ον	-α

Mas./neu. interiors the same

Neuter acc. exactly like nominative

In the format of the table, we can refer to the genitive and dative cases as the "interior" cases. Notice the interior cases. Masculine and neuter forms are identical. This neuter replication of the masculine is true across the board in all paradigms of the various substantives (i.e., nouns, pronouns, adjectives). So, learn the masculine paradigm, and you already have learned half of any neuter paradigm! Further still, the other two cases of the neuter, nominative and accusative, duplicate each other. These two observations are important inflection patterns to pick up quickly in order to reduce memorization work:[1]

♦ *Neuter forms replicate masculine forms in the interior cases.*

♦ *Neuter accusative replicates the neuter nominative.*

---

[1]For this reason, we swap the traditional masculine, feminine, neuter order in the tables to illustrate by juxtaposition how similar neuter is to masculine.

Paradigms

Table 2.7 Second Declension: Masculine, Neuter

ὁ λόγος (masculine)	
Singular	Plural
λόγος	λόγοι
λόγου	λόγων
λόγῳ	λόγοις
λόγον	λόγους
λόγε	λόγοι

τὸ δῶρον (neuter)	
Singular	Plural
δῶρον	δῶρα
δώρου	δώρων
δώρῳ	δώροις
δῶρον	δῶρα
δῶρον	δῶρα

Observe that the omicron theme vowel is obscured in some forms by contraction processes. Also, note the distinct vocative form in the masculine singular. (Most of the time, the vocative is the same as the nominative.) Then, observe the neuter pattern:

- Neuter interior cases replicate the masculine interior.
- Neuter accusative replicates neuter nominative.

Lastly, paradigms for the masculine and neuter oxytone pattern already have been given in chapter 1 using ὁ υἱός and τὸ δῶρον (Table 1.16). The interior cases take circumflex accent.

Table 2.8 Second Declension: Feminine

	ἡ ὁδός	
	Singular	Plural
N	ἡ ὁδός	αἱ ὁδοί
G	τῆς ὁδοῦ	τῶν ὁδῶν
D	τῇ ὁδῷ	ταῖς ὁδοῖς
A	τὴν ὁδόν	τὰς ὁδούς
V	ὁδέ	ὁδοί

By way of reminder:

♦ *Declension is not gender.*

Declension is simply an inflection pattern. Thus, first declension, though mostly feminine, can have masculine nouns (ὁ προφήτης), and, similarly, second declension, though mostly masculine, can have feminine nouns (ἡ ὁδός).

Proper Names

Proper names are mixed in declension and are unpredictable. Words of Semitic origin usually are indeclinable. In contrast, Greek and Latin names generally are declined. Thus, while Ἰωάννης is masculine first declension, Ἰησοῦς might be analyzed as a contracted second declension. Even if that were so, the dative and vocative forms using -ου are still irregular and unexpected.

Table 2.9 Proper Names

John	Jesus
Ἰωάννης	Ἰησοῦς
Ἰωάννου	Ἰησοῦ
Ἰωάννῃ	Ἰησοῦ
Ἰωάννην	Ἰησοῦν
Ἰωάννης	Ἰησοῦ

Number

As all the paradigms in this chapter show, Greek substantives are either singular or plural in number. Classical Greek had three inflections for number: singular, dual, and plural. Dual was used for pairs, such as the two eyes, two hands, etc. Dual had just two inflections. One inflection was for nominative, accusative, and vocative cases (none or -ε); the other inflection was for genitive and dative (-ιν or -οιν). This dual inflection of Classical Greek, however, disappeared in spoken Greek centuries before Christ.

EXERCISE 2

1. Answer true or false:

    _____ a. All first declension nouns are feminine gender.

    _____ b. All first declension plural forms are the same.

    _____ c. First and second declension are "vowel" declensions because the noun stem has a theme vowel.

    _____ d. The nominative in -η stem will have a mixed pattern in singular forms.

    _____ e. Second declension is learned as resultant endings because the -ο is lost in the shuffle in some forms.

2. Answer the following.

    2.1 _____ What is the name of the type of accent with an acute in the ultima?

    2.2 _____ What accent is over all interior forms for the above accent type?

2.3 Describe the two inflection patterns that are true across the board for all neuter paradigms:

Pattern 1: _____

Pattern 2: _____

2.4 _____ To what declension does the proper name "John" (Ἰωάννης) belong?

2.5 _____ What is the dative inflectional ending for the proper name "Jesus" (Ἰησοῦς)?

3. Answer the following questions related to the passage below:

> Καὶ εἰσπορεύονται εἰς Καφαρναούμ· καὶ εὐθὺς τοῖς σάββασιν εἰσελθὼν εἰς τὴν συναγωγὴν ἐδίδασκεν. καὶ ἐξεπλήσσοντο ἐπὶ τῇ διδαχῇ αὐτοῦ· ἦν γὰρ διδάσκων αὐτοὺς ὡς ἐξουσίαν ἔχων καὶ οὐχ ὡς οἱ γραμματεῖς.
> Καὶ εὐθὺς ἦν ἐν τῇ συναγωγῇ αὐτῶν ἄνθρωπος ἐν πνεύματι ἀκαθάρτῳ καὶ ἀνέκραξεν λέγων· τί ἡμῖν καὶ σοί, Ἰησοῦ Ναζαρηνέ; ἦλθες ἀπολέσαι ἡμᾶς; οἶδά σε τίς εἶ, ὁ ἅγιος τοῦ θεοῦ. καὶ ἐπετίμησεν αὐτῷ ὁ Ἰησοῦς λέγων· φιμώθητι καὶ ἔξελθε ἐξ αὐτοῦ. καὶ σπαράξαν αὐτὸν τὸ πνεῦμα τὸ ἀκάθαρτον καὶ φωνῆσαν φωνῇ μεγάλῃ ἐξῆλθεν ἐξ αὐτοῦ. . . .
> Καὶ εὐθὺς ἐκ τῆς συναγωγῆς ἐξελθόντες ἦλθον εἰς τὴν οἰκίαν Σίμωνος καὶ Ἀνδρέου μετὰ Ἰακώβου καὶ Ἰωάννου. ἡ δὲ πενθερὰ Σίμωνος κατέκειτο πυρέσσουσα, καὶ εὐθὺς λέγουσιν αὐτῷ περὶ αὐτῆς.

3.1a _____ How many different first declension nouns are present? Identify them:

1st Declen.: _____

   b. Can you identify what stem type is represented in each one?

   c. Be ready to locate ("parse") these forms.

3.2a _____ How many different second declension nouns are present? Identify them:

2nd Declen.: _____

    b. Can you identify what stem type is represented in each one?

    c. Be ready to locate ("parse") these forms.

3.3a _____ How many different proper names are present? Identify them:

Names: _____

_____

    b. Can you identify any declension patterns for these names?

    c. Which proper noun(s) has/have vocative inflection?

Vocative: _____

4. Translate:

Καὶ εἰσπορεύονται εἰς Καφαρναούμ· καὶ εὐθὺς τοῖς

_____

σάββασιν εἰσελθὼν εἰς τὴν συναγωγὴν ἐδίδασκεν. καὶ

_____

ἐξεπλήσσοντο ἐπὶ τῇ διδαχῇ αὐτοῦ· ἦν γὰρ διδάσκων

_____

αὐτοὺς ὡς ἐξουσίαν ἔχων καὶ οὐχ ὡς οἱ γραμματεῖς.

_____

🔲🔲🔲🔲🔲🔲🔲 MANUSCRIPTS 3 🔲🔲🔲🔲🔲🔲🔲

Ancient manuscripts have two forms, the scroll and the codex. The codex is used today, with leaves folded and sewn together to make pages. Two types of material were used in these codexes, papyrus and parchment. Papyrus was paper made from a reed plant grown along the Nile River. As fragile paper, papyrus was easily destroyed. Parchment was leather made from animal skin, so more durable, but also much more expensive. The Bodmer Library in Cologny, Switzerland, near Geneva, holds one of our oldest, extensive copies of John's Gospel, papyrus $\mathfrak{P}^{66}$, dated A.D. 200 or earlier.

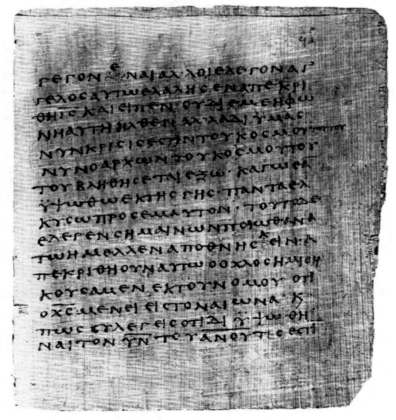

Fig. 6. Papyrus $\mathfrak{P}^{66}$ at Jn 12:29-34.

CHAPTER 3
CASE AND SENTENCE ROLES

Greek makes sentence sense by inflection. Simply put, the spelling of the word tells what the word does in a sentence. Since English makes sentence sense by word order more than inflection, then we have to learn to part our hair on the other side of our grammatical heads.

Inflection

Sentence Sense

English puts words in linear order for sentence sense. "John hit the ball" can be changed completely in sense just by swapping order: "The ball hit John." English, that is, is as simple as one, two, three: subject, verb, object. Greek, instead, uses inflection. A word's inflection, not position, indicates word relationships such as subject, direct object, indirect object, and so forth.

Table 3.1 Inflection as Word Relationships

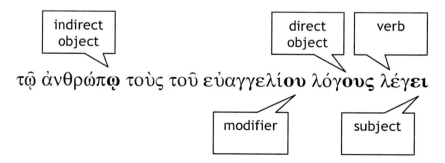

The example shows one of many possible configurations in Greek of the sentence, "He is saying the words of the gospel to the man." Notice linear English: one, two, three, "He is saying words,"

subject, verb, object. Other items are objects and modifiers. Since Greek does not rely on word order, English students heavily conditioned to expect word order to generate sense out of a sentence are caught off guard. One must think word *endings*, not word *order* for sentence sense in Greek (and that is Greek to you). What are these endings, and what is their meaning in a sentence?

Sentence Roles

♦ *Case is specific word relationship expressed through inflection.*

Word relationships are roles that words play in sentences. Case is a specific grammatical function that takes on a distinct role in a sentence. The table summarizes these grammatical functions and corresponding sentence roles for each case.

Notice in the table below the use of various prepositions, such as "of," "from," "to," "for," "in," "by." These prepositions are meant to indicate that these case functions in a sentence often require prepositional phrases in translation. Thus, we have this generalization:

♦ *Genitive and dative cases often express prepositional phrases.*

Table 3.2 Case, Function, and Sentence Role

Case/Func.	Grammatical Function	Sentence Role
Nominative	designation, naming	**subject**
Genitive	description, possession	*of*
Ablative	separa., origin, source	*of, from, by*
Dative	personal interest	*to, for,* **indirect object**
Locative	location	*in, on, at, by, among*
Instrum.	means, agency	*by, with*
Accusative	extension	**direct object**
Vocative	direct address	[not connected]

Greek has five cases with three additional case functions. The student needs to be alerted to the variation of terminology among older grammars. Grammarians debated the descriptive accuracy of labeling Greek as a "five" or an "eight" case system. A few grammars still refer to Greek as an "eight case" system, under the influence of A. T. Robertson. Modern grammars refer to Greek as a "five case" system. The genitive case form also has an "ablative" function. The dative case form also has both "locative" and "instrumental" functions. That is, not only does the Greek student need to learn five case *forms* in paradigms, the student also needs to recognize three additional case *functions* in translation.[1] In the discussion to follow, a brief description of each case is given, along with illustrations of various sentence roles.

Nominative Case

The nominative is the case of *designation* or naming. The sentence role usually is naming the subject: ὁ κόσμος παράγεται (1 Jn 2:17). The nominative case, however, can play other roles in a sentence as well.

Nominative Absolute. This nominative is independent; that is, the word has no grammatical relationship in the sentence. Several scenarios generate this possibility:
  • *Book Titles.* This is a publishing form in the first century. The book title is the first word and is nominative. For example, the header to the book of Revelation in our Greek manuscripts is: Ἀποκάλυψις Ἰωαννοῦ (Rev 1:1).
  • *Exclamations.* An interjection or exclamation will use a nominative. Observe: ἴδε ποταποὶ λίθοι καὶ ποταπαὶ

---

[1]Neuter nouns illustrate a problem of attempting to use forms to distinguish "cases." For any neuter noun, the nominative, vocative, and accusative endings always are the same *form*—yet we have three distinct *functions*. The question of form versus function in context is a question of syntax. Cf. Gerald L. Stevens and William F. Warren, Jr., *New Testament Greek Syntax: From Translation to Exegesis* (Eugene, Ore.: Cascade Books, 2009).

οἰκοδομαί = "Behold, what manner of *stones* and what wonderful *buildings!*" (Mk 13:1).

- *Broken Construction.* A second nominative follows closely after another nominative. This second nominative is in apposition to the subject or to some other word or phrase. The second nominative breaks the thought, "renaming" the first before the statement moves on. For example: ἐγώ εἰμι, ὁ λαλῶν σοι = "I, *the one speaking* to you, am (he)" (Jn 4:26).

- *Letter Openings.* In a letter, the sender's name is inscribed in the nominative case. Further self-description might be added, using another nominative (or phrase) in apposition to the sender's name. Thus: Παῦλος δοῦλος Χριστοῦ Ἰησοῦ = "*Paul, a servant* of Jesus Christ" (Rom 1:1).

Nominative of Appellation. A proper noun may be written as nominative, regardless of its grammatical function. Thus, we have ὑμεῖς φωνεῖτέ με· ὁ διδάσκαλος, καί· ὁ κύριος = "you call me *Teacher* and *Lord*" (Jn 13:13). One might have expected the accusative case for "Teacher" and "Lord."

Predicate Nominative. A nominative will follow a form of the verb εἰμί. For example: ἐγώ εἰμι ὁ ἄρτος τῆς ζωῆς (Jn 6:35).

Genitive Case

Descriptive Genitive. All genitives *describe*. Essentially, the genitive answers the question, "what kind?" Genitive descriptions particularly indicate possession or ownership, specification or kind. In English, for example, we use an "apostrophe s" to show ownership, as in "the student's book." Here are some examples of this case function:

1. τέκνα θεοῦ γενέσθαι (Jn 1:12; possession)
2. τὸ σῶμα τῆς ἁμαρτίας (Rom 6:6; description)
3. Σίμων Ἰωάννου, ἀγαπᾷς με (Jn 21:15; relationship)

The third example, "genitive of relationship," is an interesting extension of the genitive idea of possession. A proper name in the genitive expresses some familial or other relationship (son or daughter, wife, sister, or other relationship, decided by context). Literally, the Greek has "James, *of Zebedee*," but one supplies "son of" for meaning. Even when such a genitive is used, the relationship still might be spelled out, as in Jn 6:8. Observe:

1. Ἰάκωβον τὸν <u>τοῦ Ζεβαδαίου</u> = "James, *the son of* Zebedee" (Mt 4:21)
2. Μαρία ἡ <u>Ἰωσῆτος</u> = "Mary, the *mother of* Joses" (Mk 15:47)
3. Μαρία ἡ <u>Ἰακώβου</u> = "Mary, the *mother of* James" (Lk 24:10)
4. Μαρία ἡ <u>τοῦ κλωπᾶ</u> = "Mary, *the wife of* Cleopas" (Jn 19:25)
5. τὸν Ἰούδαν <u>Σίμονος Ἰσκαριώτου</u> = "Judas, the *son of* Simon Iscariot" (Jn 6:71)
6. οἱ <u>τοῦ Χριστοῦ</u> = "*the (followers) of* Christ" (Gal 5:24)

In fact, the genitive case was growing in significance, eventually swallowing up other functions. By Byzantine times, the dative case was almost defunct, all its functions having been absorbed by the genitive case.

Subjective Genitive. Two important uses of the genitive in the New Testament are the *subjective* and the *objective* genitive. The ambiguity of the preposition "of" is the issue. When one says, "the love of God," what is meant? Does this phrase mean the love God has for an individual (subjective genitive), or the love an individual has for God (objective genitive)?

The key to spotting a subjective or objective genitive problem is a *noun of action*, a noun that inherently carries a verbal idea. Certain nouns of action are easy to spot, because a cognate verb has the same root. Thus, the verb ἀγαπάω has the cognate noun ἀγάπη, the verb φοβέομαι the cognate noun φόβος, and so forth. In distinction, other nouns suggest no verbal idea at all, as in ἰχθύς or θάλασσα. Other noun of action words tip themselves off by the two endings -μος or -σις (e.g., ἔρημος, κρίσις), for which an associated verb is lurking nearby (ἐρημόομαι, κρίνω)—though this is not an infallible indication. This subjective or objective co-nundrum *requires* that the noun modified be a noun of action.

The subjective genitive *generates* the quality of the noun of action modified. Thus, for example, when Paul wrote, τίς ἡμᾶς χωρίσει ἀπὸ τῆς ἀγάπης τοῦ <u>Χριστοῦ</u>; (Rom 8:35), he meant Christ's love for believers. This is the subjective genitive use. That is, the genitive Χριστοῦ is a *subjective* genitive, understood as generating the quality of the modified noun of action, ἀγάπης.

Table 3.3 Genitive Use

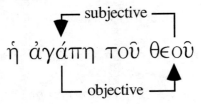

To test for a subjective genitive, make the modified noun of action a verb and make the genitive noun subject of that verb (the idea of "subjective" genitive). So, in Rom 8:35, make the modified noun of action (ἀγάπης) into the corresponding verb (ἀγαπᾷ) and make the genitive Χριστοῦ subject, i.e., Χριστός ἀγαπᾷ ἡμᾶς. This likely is Paul's meaning. The love in τῆς ἀγάπης τοῦ Χριστοῦ is Christ's love for believers.

Objective Genitive. The objective genitive *receives* the verbal idea of the noun of action modified. Thus, for example, in the ex-pression διὰ τὸν φόβον τῶν Ἰουδαίων ("because of fear *of the Jews*," Jn 7:13), the Ἰουδαίων is an *objective* genitive, here understood as *receiving* (being the object of) the verbal idea of the modified noun of action, φόβον.

The choice between subjective or objective genitive is not always clear. Each instance has to be decided on the basis of context. One example of ambiguity would be 1 Jn 2:5, ἀληθῶς ἐν τούτῳ ἡ ἀγάπη τοῦ <u>θεοῦ</u> τετελείωται = "truly in this one the love *of God* has been perfected." Is this a subjective or objective genitive?

Ablative Function. The *ablative* function is a subcategory of the genitive case. The form is genitive, but the function is ablative. Ablative function is to show *origin, source, separation, departure.* With passive voice the ablative shows *personal* agency. A common preposition to use for ablative function is "from." Examples are:

1. ἀπ᾽ <u>αὐτοῦ</u> ἐν τῇ παρουσίᾳ αὐτοῦ = *from him* at his appearing (1 Jn 2:28; separation)
2. καὶ ἰδοὺ φωνὴ ἐκ τῶν <u>οὐρανῶν</u> = and, behold, a voice *from heaven* (Mt 3:17; source)
3. ἐγὼ χρείαν ἔχω ὑπὸ <u>σοῦ</u> βαπτισθῆναι = I have need to be baptized *by you* (Mt 3:14; personal agency)

Direct Object. Some verbs take their direct object in the genitive, such as ἄρχω (ἄρχειν ἐθνῶν, Rom 15:12). Other verbs can take either accusative or genitive, such as ἀκούω (ἀκούουσι τὴν φωνήν, Acts 22:9; ἀκούουσι τῆς φωνῆς, Acts 9:7). Basic case ideas may be involved. For example, the genitive direct object may emphasize the *kind* of sound heard, and the accusative may emphasize hearing with *comprehension.* Distinctions, however, should be drawn carefully, calculating other factors, such as an author's style, which, for example, would argue against a distinction between Luke's accusative direct object in Acts 9:4 and his genitive direct object with the same verb in Acts 22:7.

Dative Case

The dative indicates *personal interest.* One common use is as the *indirect object* ("to whom" or "for whom" something is done). Another type of personal interest is personal advantage. Common dative prepositions are "to" and "for." Examples are:

1. προσέφερον <u>αὐτῷ</u> παιδία = they were bringing little children *to him* (Mk 10:13; indirect object)
2. Ἔκρινα γὰρ <u>ἐμαυτῷ</u> τοῦτο = For I determined this *for myself* (2 Cor 2:1; personal advantage)
3. ὄνομα <u>αὐτῷ</u> Ἰωάννης = *his* name is John (Jn 1:6; the idea is possession, but including personal interest)

Locative Function. The *locative* function is the first of two sub-categories of the dative case. The form is dative, but the function is locative. As the name implies, the locative indicates *location* or *position* (the "in" case). Common locative prepositions to use are "in," "at," "on." Examples:

1. εἴ τις ἐν Χριστῷ = if anyone is *in Christ* (2 Cor 5:17; locative of sphere)
2. ἐπέθηκαν αὐτοῦ τῇ κεφαλῇ = they placed it *on* his *head* (Jn 19:2; locative of place)
3. Τῇ δὲ μιᾷ τῶν σαββάτων = but *on the first* day of the week (Lk 24:11; locative of time)

Instrumental Function. The *instrumental* function is a second subcategory of the dative case. The form is dative, but the function is instrumental. As the name implies, the instrumental function is *means* or *agency*. The instrumental shows *impersonal* agency when used with the passive voice. Common prepositions to use are "by" and "with."

1. ἀποκτεῖναι ἐν ῥομφαίᾳ = to kill *with the sword* (Rev 6:8; instrumental of means)
2. ἐγὼ δὲ λιμῷ ὧδε ἀπόλλυμαι = but I am perishing here *because of famine* (Lk 15:17; instrumental of cause)
3. ἐπιθυμίᾳ ἐπεθύμησα τοῦτο τὸ πάσχα φαγεῖν = I have longed *with great desire* to eat this Passover (Lk 22:15; manner, i.e., circumstances accompanying an action)
4. συνεσθίει αὐτοῖς = he eats *with them* (Lk 15:2; instrumental of association)
5. ἐξέβαλεν τὰ πνεύματα λόγῳ = he casts out the spirits *with a word* (Mt 8:16; impersonal agency)

Direct Object. Some verbs take their direct object in the dative, such as ἀκολουθέω (ἠκολούθει αὐτῷ, Mt 26:58), ἀπειθέω (ἀπειθοῦσι τῇ ἀληθείᾳ, Rom 2:8), ἀποκρίνομαι (ἀπεκρίθη αὐτοῖς, Jn 1:26), ἀρέσκω (πᾶσιν ἀρέσκω, 1 Cor 10:33), βοηθέω (βοήθει μοι, Mt 15:25), and δουλεύω (δουλεύω σοι, Lk 15:29). Other verbs can take either accusative or dative, as is the case for ὁμολογέω (ὁμολογῶ δὲ τοῦτο σοι, Acts 24:14; ὁμολογήσει ἐν αὐτῷ, Lk 12:8) and πιστεύω (πεπιστεύκαμεν τὴν ἀγάπην, 1 Jn 4:16; πιστεύω γὰρ τῷ θεῷ, Acts 27:25).

Accusative Case

Accusative is the case of *extension*. Accusative extends the action of the verb, or in some way enriches the verb. Direct object is one way to extend the action of the verb—a major one—but not the only one. The accusative is used to indicate measure, manner, reference, intensity, or other *adverbial* quality. This extension of the verb inherently limits the verbal action. A verb can have *two* accusatives, variously called the *double accusative* or the *object complement*; practically, this effect is like a double direct object. After a few examples, we then detail two particular categories:

1. ἐδίδασκεν τοὺς <u>ὄχλους</u> = he was teaching the *crowds* (Lk 5:3; direct object)
2. θέλω δὲ ὑμᾶς σοφοὺς εἶναι εἰς τὸ <u>ἀγαθόν</u> = I want you to be wise *with reference to the good* (Rom 16:19; accusative of reference)
3. Δαυὶδ οὖν <u>κύριον</u> <u>αὐτὸν</u> καλεῖ = Therefore, David calls him *Lord* (Lk 20:44, double accusative; complement)

Adverbial of Measure. The accusative adds *extent in time* or *extent in space* to refine the precision of the expressed verbal action. This accusative inherently answers such questions as "how far?" (in distance) or "how long?" (in time). Use of ὡς or a prepositional phrase can set up this grammar, frequently with εἰς, but others as well. The two phrases εἰς τὸν αἰῶνα = "forever" or εἰς τοὺς αἰῶνας τῶν αἰώνων = "forever and ever" occur often, and illustrate this adverbial of measure role. Other examples are:

1. ἐληλακότες οὖν ὡς <u>σταδίους</u> εἴκοσι πέντε ἢ τριάκοντα = "When they had rowed, therefore, about twenty-five or thirty *stadia*" (Jn 6:19; about three or four miles, if a stadion was about two hundred yards, as given by Josephus)
2. ὃ μὲν ἔπεσεν παρὰ τὴν <u>ὁδόν</u> = which fell alongside the *road* (Mk 4:4)

3. ὅς ἐστιν ἐν δεξιᾷ [τοῦ] θεοῦ, πορευθεὶς εἰς <u>οὐρανόν</u> = "who is at the right hand of God, having gone *unto heaven*" (1 Pet 3:22)

4. Ἔνεκεν σοῦ θανατούμεθα ὅλην τὴν <u>ἡμέραν</u> = "For your sake we are being killed *all day long*" (Rom 8:36)

5. <u>τριετίαν νύκτα</u> καὶ <u>ἡμέραν</u> οὐκ ἐπαυσάμην μετὰ δακρύων νουθετῶν ἕνα ἕκαστον = "*night and day for three years* I did not cease to admonish each one with tears" (Acts 20:31)

Adverbial of Manner. This accusative adds *how* the action takes place. The preposition would be εἰς. Observe:

1. ὅτι οὐκ εἰς <u>κενὸν</u> ἔδραμον = "that I had not run *in vain*" (Phil 2:16)

2. ἔφθασεν δὲ ἐπ᾽ αὐτοὺς ἡ ὀργὴ εἰς <u>τέλος</u> = "but the wrath has fallen upon them *completely*" (1 Thess 2:16)

Purpose, Result, Cause. This accusative adds *purpose, result,* or *cause* to the action of the verb. If prepositions are used, purpose can have πρός, result will have εἰς (always), and cause can have εἰς or διά. Observe:

1. πρὸς <u>κατάκρισιν</u> οὐ λέγω = "I am not speaking **for the purpose of condemnation**" (2 Cor 7:3, purpose; necessary, because in an earlier letter he *had* spoken to shame: πρὸς <u>ἐντροπὴν</u> ὑμῖν λέγω, 1 Cor 6:5; cf. 15:34)

2. οὐ γὰρ ἐλάβετε πνεῦμα δουλείας πάλιν εἰς <u>φόβον</u> = "for we have not received a spirit of slavery *unto fear* again" (Rom 8:15, result)

3. τὸ μὲν σῶμα νεκρὸν διὰ <u>ἁμαρτίαν</u>, τὸ δὲ πνεῦμα ζωὴ διὰ <u>δικαιοσύνην</u> = "the body is dead *because of sin*, but the spirit is alive *because of righteousness*" (Rom 8:10, cause)

Predicate Accusative. An εἰς with accusative following εἰμί is the *predicate accusative*. (Normally, a nominative is used with the εἰμί verb.) The verb εἰμί is not always explicit.

1. ὥστε αἱ γλῶσσαι εἰς <u>σημεῖον</u> εἰσιν = "so then tongues are *a sign*" (1 Cor 14:22)

2. καὶ ἔσομαι αὐτοῖς εἰς <u>θεὸν</u> καὶ αὐτοὶ ἔσονταί μοι εἰς <u>λαόν</u> = "and I will be *their God,* and they will be *my people*" (Heb 8:10)

Vocative Case

Vocative is the case of direct address. Technically, the vocative is not a case, because the vocative has no grammatical relationship to the rest of the sentence. The vocative: (1) is infrequent in the New Testament, (2) regularly has the same form as the nominative, and (3) is set off by commas in the edited Greek text. In other words, one hardly can miss a vocative. The end result is that in noun paradigms, a fifth row for the vocative rarely is included, since its form often is the same as the nominative. Examples:

1. <u>κύριε</u>, ἔρχου καὶ ἴδε = *Lord,* come and see (Jn 11:34)
2. <u>υἱὲ</u> διαβόλου = *you son* of the devil (Acts 13:10)
3. <u>ἄνδρες Ἰουδαῖοι</u> καὶ οἱ κατοικοῦντες Ἰερουσαλὴμ πάντες = *Men of Judea,* and all inhabitants of Jerusalem (Acts 2:14)

Case Frequency

Finally, a few remarks on frequency of the cases can orient the student to New Testament usage. Across the board (i.e., nouns, adjectives, articles, pronouns, participles), the cases show an emphasis on subject and direct object type uses, with genitive a not too distant third. The dative, in contrast, already is showing lower percentages in the New Testament, indicating this case eventually will be on its way out by modern times. Vocative use is almost negligible, since nominative stands in just as well for this function. Noun (and pronoun) usage shows a slight shift to accusative and genitive cases; the pattern with dative and vocative, however, is the same. All other usage (adjective, article, participle) reflects the general pattern.

Chart 1: Case Usage

General Usage:

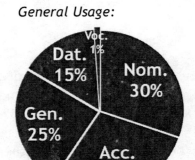

Noun Usage:

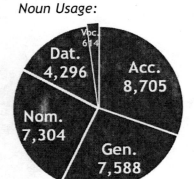

EXERCISE 3

1. Answer questions of case, case function, and sentence role in the following narrative taken from Mk 1:21-26, 29-30. (Note: an asterisk indicates the word is third declension.)

Καὶ εἰσπορεύονται εἰς Καφαρναούμ· καὶ εὐθὺς τοῖς σάββασιν εἰσελθὼν εἰς τὴν συναγωγὴν ἐδίδασκεν. καὶ ἐξεπλήσσοντο ἐπὶ τῇ διδαχῇ αὐτοῦ· ἦν γὰρ διδάσκων αὐτοὺς ὡς ἐξουσίαν ἔχων καὶ οὐχ ὡς οἱ γραμματεῖς.

Καὶ εὐθὺς ἦν ἐν τῇ συναγωγῇ αὐτῶν ἄνθρωπος ἐν πνεύματι ἀκαθάρτῳ καὶ ἀνέκραξεν λέγων· τί ἡμῖν καὶ σοί, Ἰησοῦ Ναζαρηνέ; ἦλθες ἀπολέσαι ἡμᾶς; οἶδά σε τίς εἶ, ὁ ἅγιος τοῦ θεοῦ. καὶ ἐπετίμησεν αὐτῷ ὁ Ἰησοῦς

λέγων· φιμώθητι καὶ ἔξελθε ἐξ αὐτοῦ. καὶ σπαράξαν
αὐτὸν τὸ πνεῦμα τὸ ἀκάθαρτον καὶ φωνῆσαν φωνῇ
μεγάλῃ ἐξῆλθεν ἐξ αὐτοῦ. . . .
   Καὶ εὐθὺς ἐκ τῆς συναγωγῆς ἐξελθόντες ἦλθον εἰς
τὴν οἰκίαν Σίμωνος καὶ Ἀνδρέου μετὰ Ἰακώβου καὶ
Ἰωάννου. ἡ δὲ πενθερὰ Σίμωνος κατέκειτο πυρέσσουσα,
καὶ εὐθὺς λέγουσιν αὐτῷ περὶ αὐτῆς.

1.1 _____ What case is σάββασιν[2] in line 2?

_____ What is its function in this context?

1.2 _____ What case is συναγωγήν in line 2?

_____ What is its function in this context?

1.3 _____ What case is αὐτούς in line 4?

_____ What is its sentence role?

1.4 _____ What case is ἐξουσίαν in line 4?

_____ What is its sentence role?

1.5 _____ What case is συναγωγῇ in line 5?

_____ What is its function in this context?

1.6 _____ What case is αὐτῶν in line 5?

_____ What is its function in this context?

1.7 _____ What case is ἄνθρωπος in line 5?

_____ What is its sentence role?

1.8 _____ What case is πνεύματι* in line 6?

_____ What is its function in this context?

1.9 _____ What case is τίς* in line 7?

_____ What is its sentence role?

1.10 _____ What case is Ναζαρηνέ in line 7?

_____ What is its sentence role?

1.11 _____ What case is θεοῦ in line 8?

---

[2]Second declension neuter, but this particular case form curiously imitates the *third* declension pattern of neuter nouns whose stems end in the dental -τ.

_____	What is its function in this context?
1.12 _____	What case is αὐτοῦ in line 9?
_____	What is its function in this context?
1.13 _____	What case is φωνῇ in line 10?
_____	What is its function in this context?
1.14 _____	What case is Σίμωνος* in line 13?
_____	What is its function in this context?
1.15 _____	What case is Σίμωνος* in line 14?
_____	What is its function in this context?
1.16 _____	What case is αὐτῷ in line 15?
_____	What is its function in this context?

2. Translate:

2.1 ἡ πίστις ὑμῶν καταγγέλλεται ἐν ὅλῳ τῷ κόσμῳ. (Rom 1:8)

_____

_____ Is ὑμῶν subjective or objective genitive?

2.2 δι᾽ ἀποκαλύψεως Ἰησοῦ Χριστοῦ (Gal 1:12)

_____

_____ Is Ἰησοῦ Χριστοῦ subjective or objective?

3. Translate:

Καὶ εὐθὺς ἦν ἐν τῇ συναγωγῇ αὐτῶν ἄνθρωπος ἐν

_____

πνεύματι ἀκαθάρτῳ καὶ ἀνέκραξεν λέγων· τί ἡμῖν καὶ

_____

σοί, Ἰησοῦ Ναζαρηνέ; ἦλθες ἀπολέσαι ἡμᾶς; οἶδά σε τίς

_____

εἶ, ὁ ἅγιος τοῦ θεοῦ.

_____

CHAPTER 4
THE GREEK ARTICLE

English has both a *definite* article ("the") and an *indefinite* article ("a"/"an"). Greek, however, has no indefinite article. Greek is more efficient than English in this regard, for the English indefinite article is, in fact, superfluous. Thus, properly, one would not say, "the Greek definite article," simply because Greek does not have the corresponding grammatical category of "indefinite article." One would just say, "the Greek article." This is one key feature distinguishing Greek:

♦ *Greek has no indefinite article.*

Construction

Articular and Anarthrous

Articular (or *arthrous*) construction means "with the article," as in ὁ λόγος. *Anarthrous* construction means "without the article," as in λόγος. An anarthrous Greek noun is understood naturally to be indefinite. Our terms "arthrous" and "anarthrous" actually derive from the Greek word ἄρθρον, "article."

Postpositives are Greek words that never occur first in their clause, that is, in "positive" (or "primary") position. English has no equivalent. Two common postpositives are the conjunctions γάρ and δέ. In English, these conjunctions always are first in their clause, but never in Greek. Thus, an articular noun can be separated from its article by a postpositive conjunction that cannot be first in the clause, but must be second or later. As examples, note the position in ὁ δὲ Ἰησοῦς λέγει αὐτῷ (Mt 8:22), or in ἡ γὰρ καρδία σου οὐκ ἔστιν εὐθεῖα (Acts 8:21).

Inherently Articular

Inherently articular refers to nouns that are considered as articular even if the actual Greek article is not explicitly present. These nouns have a distinctive character, or uniqueness in a class; they are considered articular inherently, so expressing the article is redundant. Thus, an anarthrous noun still can be so definitely conceived as to be considered articular even without the article. For example, ἥλιος without the article still can be translated "the sun," since only one sun in the Greek sky existed. Notice how "sun," "moon," and "stars" all are anarthrous in Lk 21:25, but are translated variously with or without English definite articles (cf. RSV and NRSV). Other words one might find without the article yet articular in idea are: θεός, πνεῦμα, κόσμος, and νόμος. Thus, translating Jn 1:1 as "the Word was a god" (θεὸς ἦν ὁ λόγος) does not reflect actual Greek grammar in that context.

Inflection

Basic Function

Table 4.1 Articular Function

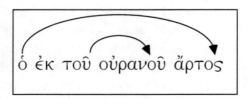

The Greek article began its grammatical life as a demonstrative pronoun. The basic function of a demonstrative pronoun is to point out some other element. This function is retained by the article:

◆ *The basic function of the Greek article is to point.*

The article often points to a noun, but the article can point to an entire group of words or verbal units, such as participles or infinitives. The article can be separated by other words from the noun to which the article points, such as in a prepositional phrase (e.g., ὁ ἐκ τοῦ οὐρανοῦ ἄρτος). To find to what the article points, one must note concord. *Concord* is grammatical agreement in case, gender, and number. Thus, an article expresses the same case, gender, and number of the noun to which the article points. The principle of concord also gives this little gender gem:

♦ *The gender of the article declares the gender of the noun.*

This gender gem from the concord principle helps spot those pesky first declension masculines, second declension feminines, and any third declension noun.

Paradigms

♦ *The article does not belong to any one declension.*

Table 4.2 Greek Article Inflection

Proclitic, rough breathing	ὁ		τό		ἡ		Proclitic, rough breathing
	Sing.	*Plur.*	*Sing.*	*Plur.*	*Sing.*	*Plur.*	
	ὁ	οἱ	τό	τά	ἡ	αἱ	
	τοῦ	τῶν	τοῦ	τῶν	τῆς	τῶν	
	τῷ	τοῖς	τῷ	τοῖς	τῇ	ταῖς	
	τόν	τούς	τό	τά	τήν	τάς	

Observe that nominative forms of the article have no accent for masculine and feminine. These unaccented forms are *proclitics.* For accenting, they are treated as another syllable prefixed to the following word. Nominative forms have *rough* breathing for masculine and feminine. The first letter is τ for most forms, similar to the English definite article with its beginning "t."

As for inflection, the endings are first and second declension. Second declension exceptions are nominative masculine singular (ὁ, not ὅς), and nominative and accusative neuter singular (τό, not τόν).[1] Observe the consistent neuter paradigm principles: neuter interior cases replicate the masculine, and neuter accusative replicates neuter nominative. The feminine article follows the γραφή paradigm of first declension (nominative in -η). Finally, in all genders, accent follows the *oxytone* pattern ("interiors go circumflex"). Remember that the principle of concord helps to locate any noun constructed with these article forms.

Translation

The Greek article functions in ways that go well beyond its use in English. Such idiomatic usage provides translation issues, since an English speaker would not anticipate translating "the" should be much trouble at all! Here we deal with three problematic areas: (1) basic grammatical features, (2) substitution idioms, and (3) a principle often referred to as Sharp's Rule.

Basic Features

Various grammatical features offer English translation issues for the Greek article. The following are common:

- *Multiple Occurrences.* The article can occur more times in Greek than needs translating into English. For example, one has Μακάριοι οἱ πτωχοὶ τῷ πνεύματι. Literally, this is "blessed are *the* poor in *the* spirit," but proper translation into English is "the poor in spirit."

---

[1]These neuter forms are following the neuter *pronoun* pattern, in which neuter pronouns drop the -v in nominative and accusative singular.

- *Proper Names.* Proper names usually take an article, but translating this pointer is not imperative. So, one can have ὁ Ἰησοῦς, which is translated "Jesus," not "the Jesus." Again, note that τοῦ θεοῦ is translated "of God," not "of the God."
- *Abstract Nouns.* Abstract nouns take the article in Greek, but not in English. Hence, ἡ ἀγάπη is rendered "love," not "the love," as in 1 Cor 13:13.
- *Inherently Articular.* This idea has been discussed already. The noun ἥλιος can be translated "the sun" even without the article.

Substitution Idioms

Greek articles can substitute for various substantives, often pronouns. English has no equivalent. Gender helps determine how to construe this substantive idea. Study the following idioms.

Article as Personal Pronoun

A *nominative* article can refer to a person(s) previously mentioned substituting in the role of a third personal *pronoun subject* of the related verb. In such cases, "he," "she," or "they" can be used. Examples:

1. A sequence in which Rhoda and the disciples are arguing Peter's miraculous release from prison: οἱ δὲ πρὸς αὐτὴν εἶπαν, Μαίνῃ. ἡ δὲ διϊσχυρίζετο οὕτως ἔχειν. οἱ δὲ ἔλεγον . . . = "But *they* said to her, 'You are crazy.' But *she* kept on asserting the fact. So *they* began saying . . ." (Acts 12:15)

2. Jesus as he appears to the women at the tomb: αἱ δὲ προσελθοῦσαι ἐκράτησαν αὐτοῦ τοὺς πόδας = "and *they* came up and seized his feet" (Mt 28:9)

Article as Demonstrative Pronoun

The article's original function surfaces here. A translation can use either "this," "that," if singular, or "these," those," if plural. Examples:

1. εἰ δέ τις οὐχ ὑπακούει τῷ λόγῳ ἡμῶν διὰ <u>τῆς</u> ἐπιστολῆς = "But if anyone is not obedient to our instruction through *this* letter" (2 Thess 3:14)

2. ὁ δὲ Πέτρος καὶ <u>οἱ</u> σὺν αὐτῷ = "Now Peter and *those* with him" (Lk 9:32)

3. <u>αἱ</u> δὲ οὖσαι ὑπὸ θεοῦ τεταγμέναι εἰσίν = "and *those* [authorities] which exist are established by God" (Rom 13:1)

4. καὶ λάμπει πᾶσιν <u>τοῖς</u> ἐν τῇ οἰκίᾳ = "and it gives light to all *those* in the house" (Mt 5:15)

Article as Alternative Pronoun

One has a literary device using the μέν . . . δέ construction and definite articles before each element as alternative pronouns. Singular articles are translated as "one . . . another," or, if plural, "some . . . others." Examples:

1. The equivocal Roman Jews' response to Paul: καὶ <u>οἱ</u> μὲν ἐπείθοντο τοῖς λεγομένοις, <u>οἱ</u> δὲ ἠπίστουν = "and while *some* were persuaded by the things being spoken, *others* were unbelieving" (Acts 28:24)

2. καὶ αὐτὸς ἔδωκεν <u>τοὺς</u> μὲν ἀποστόλους, <u>τοὺς</u> δὲ προφήτας, <u>τοὺς</u> δὲ εὐαγγελιστάς, <u>τοὺς</u> δὲ ποιμένας καὶ διδασκάλους = "and he himself gave *some* apostles, *others* prophets, *others* evangelists, *others* pastors and teachers (Eph 4:11)

Article as Possessive Pronoun

Possession is so obvious as to obviate the need for the possessive pronoun. The article alone is sufficient. Examples:

1. Οἱ ἄνδρες, ἀγαπᾶτε <u>τὰς</u> γυναῖκας = "Husbands, love *your* wives." (Eph 5:25)
2. Κύριε, μὴ τοὺς πόδας μου μόνον ἀλλὰ καὶ <u>τὰς</u> χεῖρας καὶ <u>τὴν</u> κεφαλήν = "Lord, not my feet only but also *my* hands and *my* head" (Jn 7:44)

Article as Relative Pronoun

An article or second repeating article in a modifying phrase functions as a relative pronoun. This use is common. Examples:
1. ὅτι οὐκ ἐστὲ ἐκ τῶν προβάτων <u>τῶν</u> ἐμῶν = "because you are not from the sheep *which* are mine" (Jn 10:26)
2. ταῖς ἐκκλησίαις τῆς Ἰουδαίας <u>ταῖς</u> ἐν Χριστῷ = "to the churches of Judea *which* are in Christ" (Gal 1:22)
3. ἐν πίστει <u>τῇ</u> ἐν Χριστῷ Ἰησοῦ = "in the faith *which* is in Christ Jesus" (1 Tim 3:13)

Article as Noun

The article replaces some noun idea within the context of the verbal expression. The *neuter plural article* frequently is used this way. Examples:
1. <u>τὰ</u> ἄνω φρονεῖτε, μὴ <u>τὰ</u> ἐπὶ τῆς γῆς = "Concentrate on the *things* above, not the *things* on earth" (Col 3:2)
2. Ἐν δὲ <u>τοῖς</u> περὶ τὸν τόπον ἐκεῖνον = "Now in the *neighborhood* of that place" (Acts 28:7, context crucial for making sense of the article)

Sharp's Rule

The Problem: One or Two?

English handbooks used to make a distinction about the use of the definite article with the coordinate conjunction. If one said, "the black and white cat," one meant the same two-colored cat. Notice that the article is *not repeated* with the second adjective after the conjunction. On the other hand, if one said, "the black and the white cat," in which the article *is repeated* with the second adjective following the conjunction, then one meant two different cats, one being black, the other being white.

A somewhat similar issue arises with the Greek article, but tied specifically to nouns of personal description (referring to persons or human entities). In the use of the Greek conjunction καί, how does one know whether one person or entity is meant, or two distinct persons are meant?

The Solution: The Article

The solution, called "Sharp's Rule," first was enunciated in 1798.[2] Sharp observed that article position clarifies the relationship of nouns of personal description of the same case joined by καί. The nouns are correlated, but their relationships have two possibilities: (1) each noun is a separate person or distinctive aspect, or (2) all nouns are descriptive of, or related to, aspects of the same person. A simple grammatical principle helps spell out the relationship indicated by καί.

Repeated Articles (distinctive aspects). If all nouns before and after the καί are articular, then each noun functions as a separate entity or distinctive aspect (similarly, by symmetry, if *all* nouns constructed with καί are anarthrous). Examples are:

1. ἀπὸ <u>τῆς</u> ἐκκλησίας <u>καὶ τῶν</u> ἀποστόλων <u>καὶ τῶν</u> πρεσβυτέρων = "by *the* church *and the* apostles *and the* elders" (Acts 15:4, three separate groups presented, each with a distinct involvement)

---

[2]Granville Sharp, *Remarks on the Uses of the Definitive Article in the Greek Text of the New Testament*, Durham: L. Pennington, 1798, 1802, pp. xxxv-xxxvi). Sharp actually formulated six rules; but in only one configuration with καί do the nouns apply to the same person, and that only if the first noun alone is articular. For all six rules, refer to the Glossary.

2. οὗτος καὶ <u>τὸν</u> πατέρα <u>καὶ</u> <u>τὸν</u> υἱὸν ἔχει = "this one has both *the* Father *and the* Son" (2 Jn 9, in which one has mutual yet distinct operations of Father and Son)

3. ὑμεῖς γάρ ἐστε <u>ἡ</u> δόξα ἡμῶν <u>καὶ ἡ</u> χαρά. = "For you are our glory *and* joy" (1 Thess 2:20, glory as a distinct eschatological reality, but joy in its present reality)

Single Article (common aspect). The article used with only the first personal noun in a καί construction means that all nouns function corporately; together they describe the same person or personal entity. Examples are:

1. ἀπὸ <u>τῶν</u> πρεσβυτέρων <u>καὶ</u> ἀρχιερέων <u>καὶ</u> γραμματέων = "by *the* elders *and* chief priests *and* scribes" (Lk 9:22, various elements of Jewish leadership here conceived together in a common bond of opposition, and all acting in concert seeking Jesus' death)

2. <u>τοῦ</u> θεοῦ ἡμῶν <u>καὶ</u> σωτῆρος Ἰησοῦ Χριστοῦ = "of our God *and* Savior, Jesus Christ" (2 Pet 1:1, an often used example, grammar leaving no doubt Jesus is regarded here in the same category as God; other examples include 2 Pet 2:20 and Tit 2:13)

Καί Absent. What about constructions in which καί is absent? *Any* construction minus καί implies the same person or aspect in Sharp's Rules (see the Glossary).

EXERCISE 4

1. Answer the following general questions related to the Greek article.

   1.1 Answer true or false:

   _____ a. Greek has an indefinite article, but rarely uses the form.

   _____ b. The basic function of the Greek article is to point.

   _____ c. The article is not always a reliable indicator of the gender of the noun.

   _____ d. The article does not belong to any one declension.

   1.2 Define a "postpositive":

   _____

2. Answer questions on Greek article construction related to the following passage:

   Καὶ εἰσπορεύονται εἰς Καφαρναούμ· καὶ εὐθὺς τοῖς σάββασιν εἰσελθὼν εἰς τὴν συναγωγὴν ἐδίδασκεν. καὶ ἐξεπλήσσοντο ἐπὶ τῇ διδαχῇ αὐτοῦ· ἦν γὰρ διδάσκων αὐτοὺς ὡς ἐξουσίαν ἔχων καὶ οὐχ ὡς οἱ γραμματεῖς.
   Καὶ εὐθὺς ἦν ἐν τῇ συναγωγῇ αὐτῶν ἄνθρωπος ἐν πνεύματι ἀκαθάρτῳ καὶ ἀνέκραξεν λέγων· τί ἡμῖν καὶ σοί, Ἰησοῦ Ναζαρηνέ; ἦλθες ἀπολέσαι ἡμᾶς; οἶδά σε τίς

εἰ, ὁ ἅγιος τοῦ θεοῦ. καὶ ἐπετίμησεν αὐτῷ ὁ Ἰησοῦς
λέγων· φιμώθητι καὶ ἔξελθε ἐξ αὐτοῦ. καὶ σπαράξαν
αὐτὸν τὸ πνεῦμα τὸ ἀκάθαρτον καὶ φωνῆσαν φωνῇ
μεγάλῃ ἐξῆλθεν ἐξ αὐτοῦ. . . .

Καὶ εὐθὺς ἐκ τῆς συναγωγῆς ἐξελθόντες ἦλθον εἰς
τὴν οἰκίαν Σίμωνος καὶ Ἀνδρέου μετὰ Ἰακώβου καὶ
Ἰωάννου. ἡ δὲ πενθερὰ Σίμωνος κατέκειτο πυρέσσουσα,
καὶ εὐθὺς λέγουσιν αὐτῷ περὶ αὐτῆς.

2.1 _____ Is the noun συναγωγήν (line 2) articular or anarthrous?

2.2 _____ Is the noun ἐξουσίαν (line 4) articular or anarthrous?

2.3 _____ How many anarthrous nouns does the passage contain?

2.4 _____ Is the article in ὁ Ἰησοῦς (line 8) translated or not translated? Why?

2.5 _____ Does the passage contain a noun that is inherently articular? If so, which?

2.6 _____ Does the passage contain an example of a postpositive? If so, which word(s), in what line(s)?

3. Match the following categories of substitution idioms with the Greek articles that are underlined:

_____ 1. personal pronoun   _____ 4. possessive pronoun

_____ 2. demonstrative pronoun   _____ 5. relative pronoun

_____ 3. alternative pronoun   _____ 6. noun

a. τίς ἡ πρόσλημψις εἰ μὴ ζωὴ ἐκ νεκρῶν; (Rom 11:15)

b. ὑμᾶς ἀναμνήσει τὰς ὁδούς μου <u>τὰς</u> ἐν Χριστῷ (1 Cor 4:17)

c. <u>οἱ</u> γὰρ κατὰ σάρκα ὄντες (Rom 8:5)

d. <u>ὁ</u> μὲν οὕτως, <u>ὁ</u> δὲ οὕτως (1 Cor 7:7)

e. <u>τὰ</u> τῆς σαρκὸς φρονοῦσιν (Rom 8:5)

f. <u>οἱ</u> δὲ πρὸς αὐτὸν εἶπαν (Acts 28:21)

4. Translate the following and be prepared to analyze the καί constructions according to Sharp's Rule:

4.1   ἐποικοδομηθέντες ἐπὶ τῷ θεμελίῳ τῶν ἀποστόλων

_____

καὶ προφητῶν (Eph 2:20)

_____

4.2   ἀμεταμέλητα γὰρ τὰ χαρίσματα καὶ ἡ κλῆσις τοῦ θεοῦ. (Rom 11:29)

_____

4.3   Ἡ χάρις τοῦ κυρίου Ἰησοῦ Χριστοῦ καὶ ἡ ἀγάπη

_____

τοῦ θεοῦ καὶ ἡ κοινωνία τοῦ ἁγίου πνεύματος

_____

μετὰ πάντων ὑμῶν. (2 Cor 13:13)

_____

4.4   ἵνα . . . δοξάζητε τὸν θεὸν καὶ πατέρα τοῦ κυρίου

_____

ἡμῶν Ἰησοῦ Χριστοῦ. (Rom 15:6)

_____

5. Translate:

καὶ ἐπετίμησεν αὐτῷ ὁ Ἰησοῦς λέγων· φιμώθητι καὶ

ἔξελθε ἐξ αὐτοῦ. καὶ σπαράξαν αὐτὸν τὸ πνεῦμα τὸ

ἀκάθαρτον καὶ φωνῆσαν φωνῇ μεγάλῃ ἐξῆλθεν ἐξ αὐτοῦ.

⧉⧉⧉⧉⧉⧉⧉ MANUSCRIPTS 4 ⧉⧉⧉⧉⧉⧉⧉

Alexandrinus (A), a fifth-century parchment of the Bible, was given by Cyril Lucar, Patriarch of Constantinople, to James I, reaching Britain in 1627. The Catholic Epistles are before the letters of Paul. Books not in our canon include 3 and 4 Maccabees (Old Testament) and 1 and 2 Clement (New Testament). A "text type" is a common pattern of readings among some manuscripts that reveals the historical stream from which those manuscripts flowed. Alexandrinus's text type is not uniform: in the Gospels, the inferior "Byzantine"; in Acts and Pauline letters, "Alexandrian"; yet, in Revelation, Alexandrinus is probably our best text.

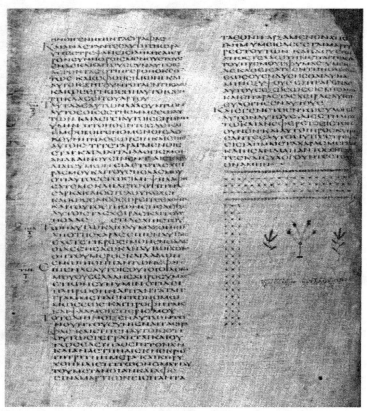

Fig. 7. Codex Alexandrinus at Lk 24:32-53. *Codex Alexandrinus* (Kenyon, 1909)
© Oxford University Press. By permission of Oxford University Press.

CHAPTER 5
NOUNS: 3RD DECLENSION

Greek has three declensions. Any particular word belongs to only one declension. First and second declensions are vowel stems; that is, their stems end in a vowel. Third declension contains consonant stems; that is, these stems end in consonants. These consonant stems will volatilize when joined to inflections that themselves begin with a consonant, such as a sigma, for example. For analysis, they can be divided into two major categories: (1) stop and sibilant stems, and (2) liquid and semivowel stems. Before we discuss these two stem categories, we will introduce the inflection pattern.

Inflection

Basic Pattern

Third declension can be daunting to the novice. The plethora of paradigms is intimidating. One key observation, however, can help the student focus on the fundamentals:

♦ *Third declension endings never change.*

Their forms simply volatilize in certain reactions. The following table summarizes the basic inflection pattern. A dash line indicates no ending, meaning the inflection ends with the stem consonant. Note that the basic neuter pattern holds (interiors = masculine, accusative = nominative). In addition, one has this maxum:

♦ *Third declension interiors are the same for all genders.*

Table 5.1 Third Declension Inflections

	Mas./Fem.		Neuter	
	Sing.	Plu.	Sing.	Plu.
N	-ς, ---	-ες	---	-α
G	-ος	-ων	-ος	-ων
D	-ι	-σι	-ι	-σι
A	-α, -ν	-ας	---	-α

Overview

General Observations

First, we will offer some general observations about the basic inflection pattern. Then, we will give four key points based on these observations that boil down recognizing what is happening with these endings on actual third declension stems.

1. Third declension mixes all three genders. Form does not give gender. Gender must be memorized with vocabulary.
2. Masculine and feminine inflections are the same.
3. The iota does *not* subscript in dative forms as in the vowel declensions.
4. A "no ending" option—indicated by the dash line in the table (nom./acc. forms)—means the word ends in the stem consonant. However, this stem consonant ending creates a problem. Of consonants, only ν, ρ, or ς may end a Greek word![1] If a no ending option is taken, this can leave a consonant not allowed at the end of a Greek word. The Greek solution is simply to drop the final stem consonant if that consonant is not a ν, ρ, or ς.

---

[1]One also can have ψ and ξ, but these are just complex sibilant variations of the simple sibilant ς. An exception is the negative οὐ, which can alter to οὐκ or οὐχ for pronunciation purposes if the next letter is a vowel or rough breathing.

5. The masculine/feminine *accusative* singular has either of two options, -α or -ν. However, regularly the -α is used.
6. The *genitive* singular -ος easily is confused with second declension *nominative* singular. So, with an -ος inflection, does one have the subject of the verb or a prepositional phrase using "of" or "from"? One has to know declensions to which nouns belong or depend on hints in context.
7. *Nominative singular* and *dative plural* forms will show the most changes, due to their sigma forms (-ς, -σι). These forms generate sigma volatilization with stop consonants, yielding a resultant sibilant. The sigma volatilization table below must be memorized to master these changes.
8. Volatilization in their nominative forms means these *third declension noun stems are hidden by the vocabulary form*. Instead, the *genitive singular* form must be known to produce the inflectional stem of a third declension noun.

Table 5.2 Sigma Volatilization: Stops

Formation	Volatilization Pattern		
	stop consonant	simple sibilant	resultant sibilant
labials	π, β, φ	+ σ	= ψ
palatals	κ, γ, χ	+ σ	= ξ
dentals	τ, δ, θ	+ σ	= σ

Key Points

Here are some key points, or "tricks of the trade," that will help you negotiate your way through third declension paradigms. Among these, we also include an observation about -ντ pairs.

1. *Final Letters.* Of consonants, only ν, ρ, or ς may end a Greek word. Thus, a final stem consonant may drop.

2. *Lengthening.* Stem vowels may lengthen when letters drop, a process called *compensatory lengthening.* Thus, an -o lengthens to its diphthong form, -ου, or on other occasions to its corresponding long vowel form, -ω.
3. *Sigma Volatilization.* Stop consonants will volatilize with sigma inflections. Know the sigma volatilization table.
4. *Any -ντ Pair.* Any -ντ pair will drop before a sigma.

Keeping these key points in mind, we will describe specific examples of formation changes to illustrate that third declension endings do not change. Their forms simply volatilize according to predictable patterns. Notice how these key points apply below.

Stop and Sibilant Stems

The first major category of third declension nouns are the stop and sibilant stems. These noun stems end in either a stop or sibilant, which basically is the bulk of consonants.

Formation Examples

Sigma is the most reactive consonant in Greek. Third declension volatilization is found in the nominative singular and dative plural forms, because these inflections involve a sigma (-ς, -σι). Our examples, therefore, will focus on these two inflections.

The Noun ὁ ἄρχων

Nominative Singular. Unlike first and second declension, in which the noun stem is derived from the nominative form, the third declension noun stem is derived from the *genitive* singular form, ἄρχοντος, minus the -ος inflectional ending. So, the stem of ἄρχων is not ἀρχ-, but ἀρχοντ-. The nominative form opts for no ending. This leaves just the stem ἀρχοντ. However, a Greek word cannot end in a -τ, so the -τ drops, leaving the form ἀρχον. The stem vowel -o is lengthened to compensate for the dropped -τ. The nominative form, then, finally winds up as ἄρχων.

Dative Plural. The dative plural inflection is -σι. Added to the ἀρχοντ- stem yields ἀρχοντσι. However, a -ντ pair drops before a sigma, which yields ἀρχοσι. Compensatory lengthening kicks in, but this time, instead of the long vowel form, the diphthong form is used (often with moveable nu): ἄρχουσι(ν).

The Noun ἡ σάρξ

Nominative Singular. The stem is derived from the genitive singular form, σαρκός, minus the -ος inflectional ending: σαρκ-. The nominative form opts for the sigma ending, yielding σαρκς. However, the palatal stop -κ volatilizes with the -ς, according to the standard sigma volatilization table, resulting in the form σάρξ.

Dative Plural. The dative plural inflection is -σι. Added to the σαρκ- stem, this form yields σαρκσι. However, the palatal stop -κ volatilizes with the -σ, resulting in the form σάρξι(ν).

Stem Patterns

We now briefly describe some basic stem patterns one will find in third declension nouns. Notice that most changes to inflectional endings simply are following predictable patterns as in the illustrations using ἄρχων and σάρξ based on the four key points.

Stop Stems

Basic Examples. Stop stems react with sigma volatilization. For example, the masculine labial stem λιβ- produces the nominative λίψ. The feminine palatal stem σαρκ- produces the nominative σάρξ. The feminine dental stem χαριτ- produces the nominative χάρις, whose accusative opts for the -ν form (χάριν).[2] The

---

[2] The accusative singular drops the dental τ before the -ν ending (no fixed rule). Twice in the New Testament one finds the alternate form, χάριτα (Acts 24:27; Jude 4).

feminine dental stem ἐλπιδ- produces the nominative ἐλπίς, whose accusative opts for the -α (ἐλπίδα). The only dental stem in θ is the feminine ὄρνιθ-, producing the nominative ὄρνις.³

One common palatal stem is γυνή. The stem is γυναικ-, so one might expect either γύναιξ or γύναι in the nominative singular; however the form is γύνη—simply called "irregular." The vocative singular, γύναι, is more regular, as the γυναικ- stem takes the no ending option of the nominative singular to become γύναικ, but the κ must drop at the end of the word; hence, we have the resultant form γύναι.

Dental Subgroups. Of the stop stems, the dental group can be subdivided into -ητος, -ματ, -ντ, and -κτ stems. We briefly overview these dental subgroups.

Dental stems ending in -ητος follow a dental pattern, so the feminine dental stem πραΰτητ- produces the nominative πραΰτης, whose declension is normal.

♦ *All dental stems in -ματ are neuter.*

All dental stems in -ματ are neuter gender. Third declension neuter has no ending for the nominative singular. In a -ματ noun, no ending exposes the final -τ, which must be dropped, producing a -μα noun. So, the stem σωματ- produces the nominative σῶμα.

♦ *All dental stems in -ντ are masculine.*

All dental stems in -ντ are masculine gender. Some -ντ stems opt for no ending in the nominative singular, exposing the final -τ, which must be dropped, calling for compensatory lengthening of the stem vowel. So, the masculine dental stem αρχοντ- produces the nominative ἄρχων (with stem vowel lengthening). Other -ντ stems opt for the -ς ending of the nominative singular, calling for the expulsion of the ντ pair before this -ς, which generates stem

---

³Only twice in the New Testament (Mt 23:37; Lk 13:34).

vowel lengthening. Thus, the dental stem ὀδοντ- will result in the nominative form ὀδούς.

Dental stems in -κτ are mixed gender. A two-stage reaction is involved. First, the final dental τ drops before the sibilant ending of -ς. Secondarily, the now-exposed palatal stop, κ, itself also volatilizes with the -ς ending. So, the feminine dental stem νυκτ- produces the nominative form νύξ.[4]

Sibilant Stems

Sibilant stems here refers to stems ending in the simple sibilant (σ). These include genitive stems in -εσ, and the rare forms -οσ and -ασ. The only sibilant stem of real consequence is the -εσ stem.[5] All sibilant stems in -εσ with nominatives in -ος are neuter.

For this stem type, we have additional reaction patterns. These reactions involve either an intervocalic sigma or coalescence. An *intervocalic sigma* is a sigma between two vowels. An intervocalic sigma often drops, leaving two vowels to contract in standard contraction patterns. *Coalescence* is the merging of the same two letters into one. Two sigmas together will coalesce into one sigma.

The neuter sibilant stem γενεσ-, then, in the genitive singular transforms: γενεσ + ος = γενεσος → γενεος → γένους. Again, the dative plural is γενεσ + σι = γενεσσι → γένεσι(ν); dative singular creates a diphthong: ε + ι = ει; nominative plural contracts: ε + α = η; genitive plural contracts: ε + ω = ω. However, the nominative singular is in -ος. Thus, the nominative form is γένος, which is also the accusative singular form. With this stem, all nominative and accusative forms are the same. The bottom line is, these forms for the sibilant -εσ stem *can be easily confused with first and second declension endings in both case and number.*

---

[4]The only New Testament -κτ stem—but occurring sixty-one times. Other dental stems in -τ are irregular; e.g., the masculine type ending of φῶς; the noun ὕδωρ adding a -ρ; the noun οὖς with some type of vowel gradation. No paradigm can summarize them.

[5]The only -οσ stem example in the New Testament is αἰδῶς ("modesty"). The only two -ασ stem examples are κρέας ("meat") and γέρας ("old man").

Table 5.3 Third Declension Stops: Labial and Palatal Stems

ὁ λίψ Labial (-π, -β, -φ)		ἡ σάρξ Palatal (-κ, -γ, -χ)	
Singular	Plural	Singular	Plural
λίψ	λίβες	σάρξ	σάρκες
λιβός	λίβων	σαρκός	σαρκῶν
λιβί	λίψι(ν)	σαρκί	σαρξί(ν)
λίβα	λίβας	σάρκα	σάρκας

Table 5.4 Third Declension Stops: Dental Stems

ἡ χάρις Dental (-τ, -δ, -θ; -ν acc.)		ἡ ἐλπίς Dental (-τ, -δ, -θ; -α acc.)	
Singular	Plural	Singular	Plural
χάρις	χάριτες	ἐλπίς	ἐλπίδες
χάριτος	χαρίτων	ἐλπίδος	ἐλπίδων
χάριτι	χάρισι(ν)	ἐλπίδι	ἐλπίσι(ν)
χάριν	χάριτας	ἐλπίδα	ἐλπίδας

Table 5.5 Third Declension Stops: Dental Subgroup Stems 1

ἡ πραΰτης Dental (-ητος stem)		τό σῶμα Dental (neuter -ματ stem)	
Singular	Plural	Singular	Plural
πραΰτης	πραΰτητες	σῶμα	σώματα
πραΰτητος	πραυτήτων	σώματος	σωμάτων
πραΰτητι	πραΰτησι(ν)	σώματι	σώμασι(ν)
πραΰτητα	πραΰτητας	σῶμα	σώματα

Table 5.6 Third Declension Stops: Dental Subgroup Stems 2

ὁ ἄρχων	
Dental (-ντ stem; no ending)	
Singular	*Plural*
ἄρχων	ἄρχοντες
ἄρχοντος	ἀρχόντων
ἄρχοντι	ἄρχουσι(ν)
ἄρχοντα	ἄρχοντας

ὁ ὀδούς	
Dental (-ντ stem; -ς ending)	
Singular	*Plural*
ὀδούς	ὀδόντες
ὀδόντος	ὀδόντων
ὀδόντι	ὀδοῦσι(ν)
ὀδόντα	ὀδόντας

Table 5.7 Third Declension: Dental Subgroup and Sibilant Stems

ἡ νύξ	
Dental (-κτ stem)	
Singular	*Plural*
νύξ	νύκτες
νυκτός	νυκτῶν
νυκτί	νύξι(ν)
νύκτα	νύκτας

τό ἔθνος	
Sibilant (-εσ stem; -ος nom.)	
Singular	*Plural*
ἔθνος	ἔθνη (ε + α)
ἔθνους	ἐθνῶν (ε + ω)
ἔθνει (ε + ι)	ἔθνεσι(ν)
ἔθνος	ἔθνη (ε + α)

Articular Concord

In the final analysis, concord always gives away any information hidden in an unusual third declension form. If a third declension noun is articular, locate the article, and you *already* have located any unrecognized inflection. When dealing with third declension, do not forget that the Greek article is your best friend!

The following table gives an idea of some Greek vocabulary that fall under these paradigm patterns. Changes from standard inflectional forms will be in nominative singular and dative plural forms. Thus, the form of the word as a vocabulary entry in the dictionary hides the stem you will see in the rest of the paradigm.

Table 5.8 Third Declension Stop/Sibilant Vocabulary

Labial stops (-π, -β, -φ stem)
λίψ, λίβος, ὁ, *southwest wind*
Palatal stops (-κ, -γ, -χ stem)
γυνή, γυναικός, ἡ, *woman*
θρίξ, τριχός, ἡ, *hair*
σάλπιγξ, -πιγγος, ἡ, *trumpet*
σάρξ, σαρκός, ἡ, *flesh*
Dental stops (-τ, -δ, -θ stem)
ἐλπίς, ἐλπίδος, ἡ, *hope*
πούς, ποδός, ὁ, *foot*
χάρις, χάριτος, ἡ, *grace*
Dental stops (-ητος stem)
πραΰτης, -ητος, ἡ, *humility*
Dental stops (neu. -ματ stem)
αἷμα, -ατος, τό, *blood*
βάπτισμα, -ατος, τό, *baptism*
γράμμα, -ατος, τό, *letter*
θέλημα, -ατος, τό, *will*
ὄνομα, -ατος, τό, *name*
πνεῦμα, -ατος, τό, *spirit*
ῥῆμα, -ατος, τό, *word*
σπέρμα, -ατος, τό, *seed*

στόμα, -ατος, τό, *mouth*
σῶμα, -ατος, τό, *body*
Dental stops (-ντ stem)
ἄρχων, -οντος, ὁ, *ruler*
λέων, -οντος, ὁ, *lion*
ὀδούς, -οντος, ὁ, *tooth*
Dental stops (-κτ stem)
νύξ, νυκτός, ἡ, *night*
Dental stops (neuter -τ stem)
οὖς, ὠτός, τό, *ear*
ὕδωρ, ὕδατος, τό, *water*
φῶς, φωτός, τό, *light*
Sibilant (neuter -εσ stem)
γένος, γένους, τό, *race*
ἔθνος, ἔθνους, τό, *nation*
ἔτος, ἔτους, τό, *year*
μέλος, μέλους, τό, *member*
μέρος, μέρους, τό, *part*
ὄρος, ὄρους, τό, mountain
πλῆθος, -ους, τό, crowd
σκότος, -ους, τό, darkness
τέλος, τέλους, τό, end

Liquid and Semivowel Stems

The second major category of third declension nouns is the liquid and semivowel stems. These noun stems end in a liquid (λ, μ, ν, ρ) or one of the two semivowels, -ι or -υ.

Liquid Stems (-ρ, -ν)

Technically, liquid stems are those ending in -λ or -ρ, and nasal stems are those ending in -μ or -ν. Liquids and nasals can be treated together, as their reactions are similar. So, by "liquids" we practically include the nasals too. In fact, the small liquid category quickly reduces to just noun stems ending in -ρ, for only one noun stem in the New Testament ends in -λ. This word is the Attic noun "salt," ἅλς, ἁλός, τό.[6] Similarly, the nasals are μ and ν, but, in fact, no noun stem ends in -μ in the New Testament. So this nasal category, like the liquid, also quickly reduces to just noun stems ending in -ν.

♦ *Liquid stems show stem vowel variations.*

The characteristic feature of liquids (-ρ stems and nasal -ν stems) is that they show vowel variations in the stem. These vowel variations are patterned. The patterns are: (1) all forms using a long vowel in the stem, (2) forms shifting from a long vowel to a short vowel in the stem, or (3) vowels dropping out of the stem altogether. These stem vowel variations are used to classify liquid and nasal stem nouns into paradigm subgroups.

Long Vowel

In this pattern, the long vowel in the nominative form holds throughout the entire inflection. Thus, the vowel you see in the memorized vocabulary word is the vowel you see in the entire paradigm. These nouns opt for no ending in the nominative.

Rho Stems. The long vowel -ρ stem paradigm is the masculine σωτήρ, σωτῆρος. A neuter example is πῦρ, πυρός. One minor exception is the feminine χείρ, χειρός, whose dative plural

---

[6]Actually in a variant reading in the textual apparatus at Mk 9:49 (as ἁλί). The form in the next verse, ἅλας (9:50), seems derived from a dental stem variation, ἅλας, -ατος, τό.

inexplicably degrades the long ει seen in all other inflections to a short ε (χερσίν). Another exception is the masculine μάρτυς, μάρτυρος. The stem is μαρτυρ-, but inexplicably the final ρ drops before the nominative singular and dative plural endings (μάρτυς, μάρτυσιν).

♦ *Nasal ν will drop before a sibilant σ.*

Nu Stems. Since a nasal ν will drop before a sibilant σ, the dative plural -σι ending causes the ν to drop. Usually when the nasal ν does this, compensatory lengthening occurs; however, in this instance the stem vowel does not change. Our long vowel -ν stem paradigm is αἰών, αἰῶνος.

Short Vowel

These stems show a long vowel in the nominative form, but the vowel degrades to a short vowel in all other forms. These nouns opt for no ending in the nominative.

Rho Stems. Short vowel -ρ stems are all masculine. The short vowel -ρ stem paradigm is ἀστήρ, ἀστέρος. This short vowel -ρ stem has two subgroups based on a feature called syncopation.

Syncopation is the dropping of a vowel between two consonants for the express purpose of bringing the two consonants together for pronunciation. In this instance the purpose is to allow the ρ to be "trilled," as in most Mediterranean languages. Syncopation has two forms:

(1) *Weak syncopation* is syncopation in only three inflections: genitive and dative singular and dative plural. The short stem vowel drops out. However, a syncopated dative plural throws *three* consonants together (e.g., πατρσι), which actually renders the ρ unpronounceable. To preserve the pronunciation, Greeks added the vowel α, creating the dative plural form πατράσιν. The paradigm illustrating weak syncopation is πατήρ, πατρός.

(2) *Strong syncopation* is syncopation in all forms besides the nominative. The short vowel drops out in every inflection but nominative singular. The paradigm illustrating strong syncopation is ἀνήρ, ἀνδρός.

Nu Stems. The long vowel of the nominative is short elsewhere. Nasal ν will drop before a sibilant σ. Thus, in the sigma form of the dative plural (σι), ν before the sibilant drops. The short vowel -ν stem paradigm is εἰκών, εἰκόνος.[7]

Semivowel Stems (-ι, -υ)

Semivowels are the vowels ι and υ that can have consonantal effect in their pronunciation, because these semivowels replaced the old digamma consonant, Ϝ, that used to be used. In such cases, the ι used for the Ϝ is sounded like a "y"; the υ used for the Ϝ is sounded like a "w." This semivowel function also includes the use of the υ in certain diphthongs, such as ευ and ου.[8]

Iota Stems

Most -ι stems are feminine. This type actually is an -ε stem that becomes -ι only in the nominative and accusative singular. All other forms show -ε or -ει.[9] The genitive singular is the distinctive Attic form -εως. The accusative singular opts for -ν. A striking feature for these feminine nouns is the accusative plural using the same ending as the nominative plural (like the neuter pattern). The paradigm is πίστις, πίστεως, ἡ.

---

[7]Two short vowel -ν stem nouns in the New Testament also show strong syncopation, expelling the short vowel altogether in most forms. These two nouns are the masculine ἀρήν, ἀρνός ("lamb," once, Lk 10:3), and the masculine κύων, κυνός ("dog," semivowel υ), occurring five times (Mt 7:6; Lk 16:21; Phil 3:2; 2 Pet 2:22; Rev 22:15).

[8]Extremely rare stems include the diphthong -αυ (ναῦς, νεώς) and the -υ stem with -ε before vowels (πῆχυς, πήχεως). Only one iota diphthong pattern occurs (-οι stem) in a variant reading in 1 Cor 2:4, that is, πειθώ, πειθοῦς, ἡ.

[9]Diphthongizing in dative singular (ε + ι = ει), contracting in nominative plural (ε + ε = ει).

Upsilon Stems

The -υ stem retains the υ throughout. The old stem had the equivalent of a "w" sound from the archaic letter digamma, Ϝ, later vocalized as a semivowel υ. This semivowel did not undergo any further changes. The accusative opts for -ν. The paradigm is ἰχθύς, ἰχθύος, ὁ.

Several *diphthong stems* represent old stems originally ending with a "w" sound, later vocalized with the semivowel υ. The diphthong stem -ευ shows -ευ only before consonants (i.e., the sigmas of nominative singular, dative plural). Otherwise, the stem falls to -ε before vowels. The genitive inflection is Attic. All -ευ nouns are masculine. The paradigm is ἱερεύς, ἱερέως, ὁ.

The diphthong stem -ου shows -ου only before consonants. Otherwise, the stem falls to -ο before vowels. The accusative singular opts for -ν. Most are masculine. The most important New Testament example is the paradigm itself, νοῦς, νοός, ὁ.

Paradigms

Paradigm Summary

Perusing the paradigms, one can see that the basic third declension inflection is evidenced everywhere. Basic inflectional patterns are very similar overall. The multiplicity of paradigms simply represents variations on the theme. In short, after learning the nominative singular form as vocabulary, the differences mostly focus on minor variations in the stems. Note that the majority of accusative singular forms opt for the -α.

The only truly unusual forms are in the semivowels, particularly the -ι and -ευ stems. Here one has the distinctive Attic -εως of the genitive singular, as well as the -εις nominative and accusative plural (the point of the πίστις and ἱερεύς paradigms). This -εις plural inflection will show up again in personal pronouns.

Table 5.9 Third Declension Liquids: Long Vowel Stems

ὁ σωτήρ			ὁ αἰών		
Liquid (-ρ stem, long vowel)			Liquid (-ν stem, long vowel)		
Singular	Plural		Singular	Plural	
σωτήρ	σωτῆρες		αἰών	αἰῶνες	
σωτῆρος	σωτήρων		αἰῶνος	αἰώνων	
σωτῆρι	σωτῆρσι(ν)		αἰῶνι	αἰῶσι(ν)	
σωτῆρα	σωτῆρας		αἰῶνα	αἰῶνας	

Table 5.10 Third Declension Liquids: Short Vowel Stems

ὁ ἀστήρ			ἡ εἰκών		
Liquid (-ρ stem, short vowel)			Liquid (-ν stem, short vowel)		
Singular	Plural		Singular	Plural	
ἀστήρ	ἀστέρες		εἰκών	εἰκόνες	
ἀστέρος	ἀστέρων		εἰκόνος	εἰκόνων	
ἀστέρι	ἀστέρσι(ν)		εἰκόνι	εἰκόσι(ν)	
ἀστέρα	ἀστέρας		εἰκόνα	εἰκόνας	

Table 5.11 Third Declension Liquids: Rho Stem Syncopation

ὁ πατήρ			ὁ ἀνήρ		
Liquid (-ρ stem, weak sync.)			Liquid (-ρ stem, strong sync.)		
Singular	Plural		Singular	Plural	
πατήρ	πατέρες		ἀνήρ	ἄνδρες	
πατρός	πατέρων		ἀνδρός	ἀνδρῶν	
πατρί	πατράσι(ν)		ἀνδρί	ἀνδράσι(ν)	
πατέρα	πατέρας		ἄνδρα	ἄνδρας	

Table 5.12 Third Declension Semivowels: Iota, Upsilon Stems

ἡ πίστις		ὁ ἰχθύς	
Vowel (-ι stem, -ε vowel)		Liquid (-υ stem, pure υ)	
Singular	Plural	Singular	Plural
πίστις	πίστεις	ἰχθύς	ἰχθύες
πίστεως	πίστεων	ἰχθύος	ἰχθύων
πίστει	πίστεσι(ν)	ἰχθύι	ἰχθύσι(ν)
πίστιν	πίστεις	ἰχθύν	ἰχθύας

Table 5.13 Third Declension Semivowels: Diphthongs

ὁ ἱερεύς		ὁ νοῦς	
Vowel (-ευ diphthong)		Vowel (-ου diphthong)	
Singular	Plural	Singular	Plural
ἱερεύς[10]	ἱερεῖς	νοῦς	νόες
ἱερέως	ἱερέων	νοός	νοῶν
ἱερεῖ	ἱερεῦσι(ν)	νοΐ	νουσί(ν)
ἱερέα	ἱερεῖς	νοῦν	νόας

Articular Concord

Remember that the Greek article is your best friend! That is, if a third declension noun is articular, locate the article and you have located the noun.

The following table gives an idea of some Greek vocabulary that fall under these paradigm patterns. Study the vocabulary to anticipate how words would appear in inflected forms in the New Testament.

---

[10]The vocative is ἱερεῦ (cf. Acts 25:24; but see Rev 15:3).

Table 5.14 Third Declension Liquid/Semivowel Vocabulary

Liquids (long stem vowel)
αἰών, αἰῶνος, ὁ, age
ἀμπελών, -ῶνος, ὁ, vineyard
Ἕλλην, -ηνος, ὁ, Greek
μάρτυς, -τυρος, ὁ, witness
πῦρ, πυρός, τό, fire
Σίμων, Σίμωνος, ὁ, Simon
σωτήρ, σωτῆρος, ὁ, savior
χείρ, χειρός, ἡ, hand
Liquids (short stem vowel)
ἀήρ, ἀέρος, ὁ, air
ἀλέκτωρ, -τορος, ὁ, rooster
ἀστήρ, ἀστέρος, ὁ, star
εἰκών, εἰκόνος, ἡ, image
ἡγεμών, -μόνος, ὁ, ruler
ποιμήν, -μένος, ὁ, shepherd
Liquids (syncopated -ρ stem)
ἀνήρ, ἀνδρός, ὁ, man
θυγάτηρ, -τρός, ἡ, daughter
μήτηρ, μητρός, ἡ, mother

πατήρ, πατρός, ὁ, father
Vowels (-ι stem = feminine)
ἀνάστασις, -εως, ἡ, resurrect.
γνῶσις, -εως, ἡ, knowledge
δύναμις, -εως, ἡ, power
θλῖψις, θλίψεως, ἡ, trouble
κρίσις, κρίσεως, ἡ, judgment
πίστις, πίστεως, ἡ, faith
πόλις, πόλεως, ἡ, city
Vowels (-υ stem)
ἰσχύς, ἰσχύος, ἡ, strength
ἰχθύς, ἰχθύος, ὁ, fish
ὀσφῦς, ὀσφύος, ἡ, waist
Vowels (-ευ stem = masculine)
ἀρχιερεύς, -έως, ὁ, chief prt.
βασιλεύς, -έως, ὁ, king
γραμματεύς, -έως, ὁ, scribe
ἱερεύς, -έως, ὁ, priest
Vowels (-ου stem = mas.)
νοῦς, νοός, ὁ, mind, thought

EXERCISE 5

1. Answer true or false:

   _____ a. Third declension has different endings for different words.

   _____ b. Third declension gender must be memorized as a part of vocabulary.

   _____ c. Third declension has only one set of interior endings regardless of gender.

   _____ d. All dental stems in -ματ are masculine gender.

   _____ e. All dental stems in -ντ are feminine gender.

   _____ f. Liquid and nasal stems consistently show the same stem vowel throughout their inflections.

   _____ g. A nasal ν will drop before a sibilant σ.

2. Answer the following on endings and inflection patterns.

   2.1 _____ Of consonants, only what letters may end a Greek word?

   2.2 _____ What are the two options for masculine and feminine *accusative singular* endings?

   2.3 _____ Which third declension case easily can be confused with the second declension *nominative* singular?

2.4 _____ Which case forms show the most changes due to their sigma inflections?

2.5 _____ What is the name for the lengthening process that can follow the dropping of a consonant?

2.6 _____ What letter pair characteristically will drop before a sigma?

2.7 _____ What is the name for a sigma between two vowels that drops, causing the two vowels to contract?

2.8 _____ What is the name for the merging of the same two letters into one?

2.9 _____ Which stem forms easily can be confused with first and second declensions in both case and number, and what paradigm word reflects this formation?

2.10 Match the following items:

_____ 1. Liquids	a.	syncopation in gen./dat. singular and dat. plural
_____ 2. -ειϛ	b.	syncopation in all forms except nom. singular
_____ 3. -εωϛ	c.	show variations in stem vowel between long and short forms
_____ 4. strong	d.	the sound of the iota as a semivowel
_____ 5. weak	e.	the sound of the upsilon as a semivowel
_____ 6. "w"	f.	the distinctive Attic genitive of certain semivowel stems
_____ 7. "y"	g.	the distinctive nom./acc. plu. of certain semivowel stems

3. Provide inflections according to stem categories and be ready to answer questions about stem types (see vocabulary lists).

3.1 Provide the inflection of φῶς, φωτός, τό:[11]

_____   _____

_____   _____

_____   _____

_____   _____

3.2 Provide the inflection of ποιμήν, -μένος, ὁ:

_____   _____

_____   _____

_____   _____

_____   _____

3.3 Provide the inflection of πόλις, πόλεως, ἡ:

_____   _____

_____   _____

_____   _____

_____   _____

3.4 Provide the inflection of βασιλεύς, βασιλέως, ὁ:

_____   _____

_____   _____

_____   _____

_____   _____

---

[11]This *neuter* noun strangely opts for the -ς ending in the nom. sing. form.

4. Identify the *third* declension words in the passage below. Be ready to locate and describe the stem type, if applicable:

Καὶ εἰσπορεύονται εἰς Καφαρναούμ· καὶ εὐθὺς τοῖς σάββασιν εἰσελθὼν εἰς τὴν συναγωγὴν ἐδίδασκεν. καὶ ἐξεπλήσσοντο ἐπὶ τῇ διδαχῇ αὐτοῦ· ἦν γὰρ διδάσκων αὐτοὺς ὡς ἐξουσίαν ἔχων καὶ οὐχ ὡς οἱ γραμματεῖς.

Καὶ εὐθὺς ἦν ἐν τῇ συναγωγῇ αὐτῶν ἄνθρωπος ἐν πνεύματι ἀκαθάρτῳ καὶ ἀνέκραξεν λέγων· τί ἡμῖν καὶ σοί, Ἰησοῦ Ναζαρηνέ; ἦλθες ἀπολέσαι ἡμᾶς; οἶδά σε τίς εἶ, ὁ ἅγιος τοῦ θεοῦ. καὶ ἐπετίμησεν αὐτῷ ὁ Ἰησοῦς λέγων· φιμώθητι καὶ ἔξελθε ἐξ αὐτοῦ. καὶ σπαράξαν αὐτὸν τὸ πνεῦμα τὸ ἀκάθαρτον καὶ φωνῆσαν φωνῇ μεγάλῃ ἐξῆλθεν ἐξ αὐτοῦ. . . .

Καὶ εὐθὺς ἐκ τῆς συναγωγῆς ἐξελθόντες ἦλθον εἰς τὴν οἰκίαν Σίμωνος καὶ Ἀνδρέου μετὰ Ἰακώβου καὶ Ἰωάννου. ἡ δὲ πενθερὰ Σίμωνος κατέκειτο πυρέσσουσα, καὶ εὐθὺς λέγουσιν αὐτῷ περὶ αὐτῆς.

3rd Declen.: _____

5. Translate:

Καὶ εὐθὺς ἐκ τῆς συναγωγῆς ἐξελθόντες ἦλθον εἰς

_____

τὴν οἰκίαν Σίμωνος καὶ Ἀνδρέου μετὰ Ἰακώβου καὶ

_____

Ἰωάννου. ἡ δὲ πενθερὰ Σίμωνος κατέκειτο πυρέσσουσα,

_____

καὶ εὐθὺς λέγουσιν αὐτῷ περὶ αὐτῆς.

_____

𝕲𝕲𝕲𝕲𝕲𝕲𝕲 MANUSCRIPTS 5 𝕲𝕲𝕲𝕲𝕲𝕲𝕲

Vaticanus (B) and Sinaiticus (ℵ) are fine uncial manuscripts. Constantin von Tischendorf discovered Sinaiticus at St. Catherine's monastery on Mount Sinai, going to the Czar of Russia in 1859, and the British Museum in 1933. Sinaiticus, our only complete uncial New Testament, includes the Epistle of Barnabas and the Shepherd of Hermes beyond our canon. Vaticanus is held in the Vatican Library, first mentioned in library records in 1475. Vaticanus has the entire Bible, but parts are missing, including part of Hebrews, the Pastorals, Philemon, and Revelation. Vaticanus is the best example of the "Alexandrian" text type in the Gospels and Acts. The image below shows the ending of the Gospel of Mark.

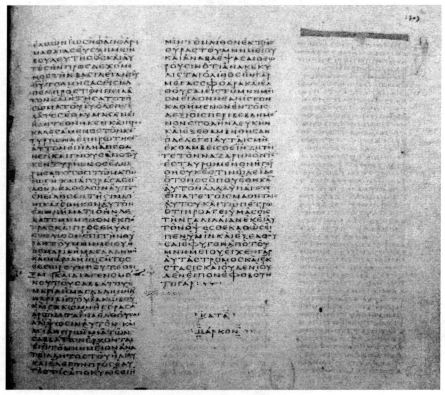

Fig. 8. Codex Vaticanus at Mk 15:43–16:8.

CHAPTER 6
ADJECTIVES AND ADVERBS

Adjectives and adverbs are two other important parts of speech. English grammar orders these to make sentence sense: adjectives normally come *before* what they modify ("*good* book"), whereas adverbs normally come *after* what they modify ("spoke *well*")—even though these positions can vary, especially with adverbs. Greek inflects the adjective, providing grammatical concord to show modifying relationships.

Adjectives

Inflection Patterns

First and Second Declension

Most adjectives (80-85%) follow first and second declension inflection. The remainder follows third declension, which can be subdivided by stem types. Some adjectives show hybrid inflections, mixing declension patterns by gender. Masculine and neuter adjectives follow second or third declension. Feminine often follows first declension, either "α pure" (-ε, -ι, -ρ stems) or "η pure."

Third Declension

One third declension category is the liquid (nasal) -ν, whose long stem vowel in the nominative singular is short elsewhere (cf. εἰκών, εἰκόνος). For example, an -ην stem goes to -εν outside the nominative singular. Another shows an -ων stem going to -ον. What happens is that the nominative singular opts for no ending. The remaining -εν or -ον stem then undergoes compensatory lengthening to -ην and -ων, respectively. In the dative plural, the typical nasal rule is invoked: *nasal ν drops before the sibilant σ.*

Mixed Declensions

In mixed declensions, masculine and neuter will vary between second and third declension, but the feminine always is first. One set uses only third for masculine and neuter ($3^{rd}/1^{st}$). Another set mixes third and second for masculine and neuter ($3^{rd}/2^{nd}/1^{st}$).

$3^{rd}/1^{st}$ Mixed. In this type pattern, both masculine and neuter adjectives are third declension. Feminine is first declension. Three variations are observed, based on third declension stems.

The -υ/ε stem shows -ε everywhere except the nominative and accusative singular for masculine and neuter, which show -υ. This is a third declension noun pattern that follows a stem type that was not covered for these nouns.

The -ντ stem opting for -ς in the nominative shows similarity to the noun ὁδούς. The feminine is like the first declension sibilant δόξα. The major example in the New Testament is the very common πᾶς, πᾶσα, πᾶν (1,243 times!), so this paradigm should be learned well.

The -ν stem yields only one New Testament example, μέλας. Again, as one might expect, the dative plural form shows the nasal ν dropping before the sibilant σ.

$3^{rd}/2^{nd}/1^{st}$ Mixed. Here, masculine and neuter forms are *mostly* second declension. One distinction to note is that singular forms of the nominative and accusative reveal an *altered* stem with third declension endings. The feminine is -η pure first declension. Two variations are observed, specifically the two paradigms provided and their cognates. Notice minor stem alterations (nom./acc. sing.): μεγαλ- to μεγα- in the first paradigm (μέγας), and πολλ- to πολυ- in the second.

Two Termination

A "two termination" adjective simply uses the same inflection for both masculine and feminine forms, leaving only two patterns for all three genders. Most third declension adjectives are "two termination" by default, since masculine and feminine inflections are the same in third declension. In addition, a small subset of adjectives is two termination in the *second* declension.

Vowel Contraction

Second Declension. Some adjectives show vowel contraction of stem vowels and endings, producing a resultant circumflex accent. Contractions can be irregular, such as absorbing a vowel. Two adjectives with stems in ε and ο show various forms of contraction in inflected forms. Besides the paradigm χρυσοῦς ("golden"), only one other New Testament adjective fits this category, which is χαλκοῦς, -ῆ, -οῦν ("made of copper"). Two adjectives end in a variation with rho (-ρε) and show a pattern similar to χρυσοῦς, only having -ᾶ, -ᾶς, -ᾷ, -ᾶν in the singular. These two are the adjectives σιδηροῦς, -ᾶ, -οῦν ("made of iron"), and the related term, ἀργυροῦς, -ᾶ, -οῦν ("made of silver"). Note how these contracted forms *disguise* or *confuse* second declension endings in certain forms: nominative -οῦς, not -ος; accusative -οῦν, not -ον.

Third Declension. The neuter -εσ stem with an -ος nominative (cf. ἔθνος, τό) is an example. The endings are the typical third declension masculine-feminine patterns. The nominative opts for no ending, and the remaining -ες stem undergoes compensatory lengthening to -ης. In other case forms, an intervocalic sigma drops and the remaining vowels contract. Notice typical third declension phenomena (all interiors are all the same, neuter singular and plurals are the same for nominative and accusative, etc.) Singular forms of third declension contraction can be confused with cases of other inflections (-ῆς, -οῦς, -εῖ, -ῆ). The plurals are like third declension πίστις (e.g., ἀληθεῖς).

Table 6.1 Adjectives: First and Second Declension

| Masculine | | Neuter | | Feminine | |
Singular	Plural	Singular	Plural	Singular	Plural
ἀγαθός	ἀγαθοί	ἀγαθόν	ἀγαθά	ἀγαθή	ἀγαθαί
ἀγαθοῦ	ἀγαθῶν	ἀγαθοῦ	ἀγαθῶν	ἀγαθῆς	ἀγαθῶν
ἀγαθῷ	ἀγαθοῖς	ἀγαθῷ	ἀγαθοῖς	ἀγαθῇ	ἀγαθαῖς
ἀγαθόν	ἀγαθούς	ἀγαθόν	ἀγαθά	ἀγαθήν	ἀγαθάς
δίκαιος	δίκαιοι	δίκαιον	δίκαια	δικαία	δίκαιαι
δικαίου	δικαίων	δικαίου	δικαίων	δικαίας	δικαίων
δικαίῳ	δικαίοις	δικαίῳ	δικαίοις	δικαίᾳ	δικαίαις
δίκαιον	δικαίους	δίκαιον	δίκαια	δικαίαν	δικαίας
μικρός	μικροί	μικρόν	μικρά	μικρά	μικραί
μικροῦ	μικρῶν	μικροῦ	μικρῶν	μικρᾶς	μικρῶν
μικρῷ	μικροῖς	μικρῷ	μικροῖς	μικρᾷ	μικραῖς
μικρόν	μικρούς	μικρόν	μικρά	μικράν	μικράς

Table 6.2 Adjectives: Liquid, Short Vowel (Third Declension)

| Mas./Fem. | | Neuter | |
Singular	Plural	Singular	Plural
ἄφρων	ἄφρονες	ἄφρον	ἄφρονα
ἄφρονος	ἀφρόνων	ἄφρονος	ἀφρόνων
ἄφρονι	ἄφροσιν	ἄφρονι	ἄφροσιν
ἄφρονα	ἄφρονας	ἄφρον	ἄφρονα

Table 6.3 Adjectives: 3ʳᵈ/1ˢᵗ Mixed (-υ/ε stem)

Masculine		Neuter		Feminine	
Singular	Plural	Singular	Plural	Singular	Plural
ταχύς	ταχεῖς	ταχύ	ταχέα	ταχεῖα	ταχεῖαι
ταχέως	ταχέων	ταχέως	ταχέων	ταχείας	ταχειῶν
ταχεῖ	ταχέσιν	ταχεῖ	ταχέσιν	ταχείᾳ	ταχείαις
ταχύν	ταχεῖς	ταχύ	ταχέα	ταχεῖαν	ταχείας

Table 6.4 Adjectives: 3ʳᵈ/1ˢᵗ Mixed (-ντ stem)

Masculine		Neuter		Feminine	
Singular	Plural	Singular	Plural	Singular	Plural
πᾶς	πάντες	πᾶν	πάντα	πᾶσα	πᾶσαι
παντός	πάντων	παντός	πάντων	πάσης	πασῶν
παντί	πᾶσιν	παντί	πᾶσιν	πάσῃ	πάσαις
πάντα	πάντας	πᾶν	πάντα	πᾶσαν	πάσας

Table 6.5 Adjectives: 3ʳᵈ/1ˢᵗ Mixed (-ν stem)

Masculine		Neuter		Feminine	
Singular	Plural	Singular	Plural	Singular	Plural
μέλας	μέλανες	μέλαν	μέλανα	μέλαινα	μέλαιναι
μέλανος	μελάνων	μέλανος	μελάνων	μελαίνης	μελαινῶν
μέλανι	μέλασιν	μέλανι	μέλασιν	μελαίνῃ	μελαίναι
μέλανα	μέλανας	μέλαν	μέλανα	μέλαιναν	μελαίνας

Table 6.6 Adjectives: $3^{rd}/2^{nd}/1^{st}$ Mixed (altered stem)

Masculine		Neuter		Feminine	
Singular	*Plural*	*Singular*	*Plural*	*Singular*	*Plural*
μέγας	μεγάλοι	μέγα	μεγάλα	μεγάλη	μεγάλαι
μεγάλου	μεγάλων	μεγάλου	μεγάλων	μεγάλης	μεγάλων
μεγάλῳ	μεγάλοις	μεγάλῳ	μεγάλοις	μεγάλη	μεγάλαις
μέγαν	μεγάλους	μέγα	μεγάλα	μεγάλην	μεγάλας

Table 6.7 Adjectives: $3^{rd}/2^{nd}/1^{st}$ Mixed (altered stem)

Masculine		Neuter		Feminine	
Singular	*Plural*	*Singular*	*Plural*	*Singular*	*Plural*
πολύς	πολλοί	πολύ	πολλά	πολλή	πολλαί
πολλοῦ	πολλῶν	πολλοῦ	πολλῶν	πολλῆς	πολλῶν
πολλῷ	πολλοῖς	πολλῷ	πολλοῖς	πολλῇ	πολλαῖς
πολύν	πολλούς	πολύ	πολλά	πολλήν	πολλάς

Table 6.8 Adjectives: Two-Termination (Second Declension)

Mas./Fem.		Neuter	
Singular	*Plural*	*Singular*	*Plural*
ἔρημος	ἔρημοι	ἔρημον	ἔρημα
ἐρήμου	ἐρήμων	ἐρήμου	ἐρήμων
ἐρήμῳ	ἐρήμοις	ἐρήμῳ	ἐρήμοις
ἔρημον	ἐρήμους	ἔρημον	ἔρημα

Table 6.9 Adjectives: Contraction (Second Declension)

| Masculine | | Neuter | | Feminine | |
Singular	Plural	Singular	Plural	Singular	Plural
χρυσοῦς	χρυσοῖ	χρυσοῦν	χρυσᾶ	χρυσῆ	χρυσαῖ
χρυσοῦ	χρυσῶν	χρυσοῦ	χρυσῶν	χρυσῆς	χρυσῶν
χρυσῷ	χρυσοῖς	χρυσῷ	χρυσοῖς	χρυσῇ	χρυσαῖς
χρυσοῦν	χρυσοῦς	χρυσοῦν	χρυσᾶ	χρυσῆν	χρυσᾶς

Table 6.10 Adjectives: Contraction (Third Declension)

| Mas./Fem. | | Neuter | |
Singular	Plural	Singular	Plural
ἀληθής	ἀληθεῖς	ἀληθές	ἀληθῆ
ἀληθοῦς	ἀληθῶν	ἀληθοῦς	ἀληθῶν
ἀληθεῖ	ἀληθέσιν	ἀληθεῖ	ἀληθέσιν
ἀληθῆ	ἀληθεῖς	ἀληθές	ἀληθῆ

Adjective Function

Adjectives either modify nouns or are used as nouns. When adjectives modify nouns they are *attributive*. When adjectives are used as nouns they are *substantival*. With transitive verbs, substantival roles include subject and direct object. With intransitive (i.e., copulative) verbs, substantival roles include subject and predicate. This predicate use also is called the verb *complement*, because the predicate structure completes the verbal expression. When adjectives are used as the predicate complement they are *predicative*. Finally, adjectives can have other noun roles that are independent of the verb, such as, for example, the object of a preposition in a prepositional phrase.

Attributive Use

Adjectives modify nouns. When attributive, they show concord in case, gender, and number. They can be articular or anarthrous, and they can be positioned before or after the noun modified:

- τὰ καλὰ ἔργα (Mt 5:16)
- τὴν γῆν τὴν καλὴν (Mt 13:8)
- πολλοὶ προφῆται (Mt 13:17)
- καρποὺς καλοὺς (Mt 7:17)

Restrictive attributive position is an *articular* adjective that follows an *articular* noun, implying emphasis (Mt 13:8 above; cf. Jn 10:11, ὁ ποιμὴν ὁ καλός, "the *good* shepherd"). Otherwise, adjectives are in simple attributive position, called *ascriptive attributive*. Note that the adjective ὅλος *always* is attributive.

Substantival Use

♦ *Adjectives standing alone are substantival.*

Transitive Verbs. A *transitive verb* has a direct object; an *intransitive verb* does not have a direct object. A *copulative* is an intransitive verb that can take a nominative complement in the predicate. Adjectives used substantivally stand alone; whether articular or anarthrous, the key is, they stand alone. With transitive verbs, substantival use is often as subject or direct object:

- ὁ ἕτερος ἦλθεν (Lk 19:20)
- πολλοὶ ἐροῦσίν μοι (Mt 7:22)
- τοὺς πτωχοὺς ἔχετε μεθ᾽ ἑαυτῶν (Mt 26:11)
- νεκροὺς ἐγείρετε (Mt 10:8)

The substantival adjective also can be object of a preposition:

- ἀπὸ μικροῦ ἕως μεγάλου αὐτῶν (Heb 8:11)
- νίκα ἐν τῷ ἀγαθῷ τὸ κακόν (Rom 12:21)

Intransitive Verbs. With intransitive verbs, substantival use is as subject or predicate. The intransitive verb is copulative, that is, a form of "I am," "I become." Greek has three copulatives: εἰμί, γίνομαι, and ὑπάρχω. Copulative constructions will have two nominatives: one is the subject; the other is the predicate. Thus:

- ἄνθρωπός τις ἦν πλούσιος (Lk 16:1)
- πολλοὶ γάρ εἰσιν κλητοί, ὀλίγοι δὲ ἐκλεκτοί (Mt 22:14)

In the second example, both adjectives κλητοί and ἐκλεκτοί are predicative. Since the copulative verb is expressed in the first part of the parallel construction, the verb is assumed in the second.

Note carefully that of the three adjective functions, *attributive* and *substantival* adjectives can be any construction (articular or anarthrous). However, in contrast, for the predicative function:

♦ *The predicate adjective always is anarthrous.*

Verbless Predicative. Greek idiom can drop an explicit form of the copulative verb and still assume a copulative construction. We can label this idiom the "verbless predicative." Greek signals this verbless idiom with the articular noun. The adjective, of course, is anarthrous. Thus, we have the "verbless predicative" dictum:

♦ *Articular nouns with anarthrous adjectives are predicative if both are nominative.*

In these cases, you supply the correct form of the "to be" verb in English translation:

- πιστὸς ὁ θεός = "God *is* faithful" (1 Cor 1:9)
- ὁ ἄνθρωπος οὗτος δίκαιος = "this man *was* righteous" (Lk 2:25)

Colwell's Rule

The Problem: Subject or Predicate?

The predicate nominative is a noun or adjective in nominative case that renames or describes the subject following a copulative verb. In Greek one has two nominatives: one is subject, the other predicate. For example: ἐγώ εἰμι ὁ ἄρτος τῆς ζωῆς (Jn 6:35). The question is, which nominative is subject, and which nominative is predicate? The answer is different for English and for Greek.

How does English establish subject and predicate nominative? English depends on word order for sentence sense, not inflection. English is as simple as one, two, three—subject, verb, object. The subject is first, the verb second, the object third. Thus, in English, the subject will be *first*, positioned *before* the copulative verb, and the predicate noun or adjective will be *third*, positioned *after* the verb. For example, as a predicate noun: "The student is president"; as a predicate adjective: "The baby is hungry."

Greek, on the other hand, is inflected. Thus, word order does not determine which nominative is subject and which is predicate. So, how does one decide which nominative in Greek is subject and which is predicate, that is, which Greek nominative to put *before* the verb in English translation and which nominative to put *after* the verb? Before one prematurely concludes the matter is insignificant, think through the following two statements, which are worlds apart in meaning, simply by swapping English subject and predicate positions one and three:

(1) God is love.
(2) Love is god.

Whereas the issue is not always crucial to accurate translation because the grammar can be a logical redundancy, on occasion the issues can be divided sharply, with theological implications.

The Solution: Levels of Precedence

Principles for deciding the question of the predicate nominative are associated with the name of Ernest Colwell, and so are called "Colwell's Rule."[1] The key is establishing "levels of precedence" among three grammatical constructions:

---

[1]Actually, in particular, Colwell's discussion focused on the definitive nature of an anarthrous predicate nominative when positioned prior to the verb. See

(1) The *articular noun* is subject over an anarthrous noun.

(2) The *proper name* is subject over an articular noun.

(3) The *pronoun* is subject over anything.

Using these principles, notice that, in the Jn 6:35 example above (ἐγώ εἰμι ὁ ἄρτος τῆς ζωῆς), the ἐγώ as a pronoun would trump anything, so functions as the subject nominative, and the noun, even though articular, is the predicate nominative.

Such rules have idiomatic and contextual exceptions. One example is the idiom for giving an individual's name. The name itself usually will take predicate position in English translation: Ἰωάννης ἐστὶν ὄνομα αὐτοῦ, "His name is John" (Lk 1:63).

The following provide more examples illustrating this simple hierarchy. In the examples, the subject nominative is underlined.

1. *Articular Noun Precedence* (two nouns)

   καὶ θεὸς ἦν ὁ λόγος = "The Word was God" (Jn 1:1)

2. *Proper Name Precedence*

   Ἰησοῦς ἐστιν ὁ χριστός = "Jesus is the Christ"(Jn 20:31)

3. *Pronoun Precedence*

   a. *Over nouns:*

   Οὗτός ἐστιν ὁ υἱός μου = "'This is my son'" (Mt 3:17)

   b. *Over proper names:*

   Οὗτός ἐστιν Ἰησοῦς = "'This is Jesus'" (Mt 27:37)

4. *Symmetry* = decision by context

   a. *Both articular:*

   ὁ δὲ ἀγρός ἐστιν ὁ κόσμος = "and the field is the world" (Mt 13:38; subject implied by pre-positioning)

   b. *Both anarthrous:*

   πολλοὶ γάρ εἰσιν κλητοί = "For many are called" (Mt 22:14)

Ernest C. Colwell, "A Definite Rule For the Use of the Article in the Greek New Testament," *Journal of Biblical Literature* 52 (1933): 12-21. The importance of these observations is demonstrated in the fallacy of a well-known mistranslation of Jn 1:1, καὶ θεὸς ἦν ὁ λόγος.

Uses of Πᾶς

The πᾶς, πᾶσα, πᾶν adjective is used frequently in the New Testament. The two common uses are the meanings "all" or "the whole," grammatical construction often distinguishing the two. The following summary statements do not represent hard and fast rules. Context always is your guide, but these guidelines may be useful in deciphering all the ways "all" is used.

Articular Constructions

These uses correspond to English. The English definite article's position makes a difference in meaning. The article used with the *noun* and the adjective is given as "all," as in "all *the city*." The article used with the *adjective* and the adjective is understood as "whole," as in "*the whole* city."

Similarly, in Greek observe article construction with πᾶς. The article used with the *noun* and πᾶς means "all." The article used with the *adjective* itself and the meaning is "the whole." Note:

1. πᾶσα ἡ πόλις = "*all* the city" (Acts 13:44)
2. τὸν πάντα χρόνον = "*the whole* time" (Acts 20:18)

Table 6.11 Articular Construction: Πᾶς

πᾶς + [article + noun] = "all the ____"

[article + πᾶς] + noun = "the whole ____"

Anarthrous Constructions

Here, the problem is lack of understanding of English grammar. We fail to make the proper distinction between "every" as *singular* in meaning and "all" as *plural* in meaning. "*Every* bowling pin" is singular in meaning, a reference to each individual bowling pin, the one, the two, the three, and so forth. "*All* bowling pins" is plural in meaning, a reference to all the pins together as a group.

This English confusion between singular and plural distinctions for "every" and "all" bleeds over into translation of πᾶς. When both adjective and noun are anarthrous and *singular*, one properly should translate πᾶς as "every." When both adjective and noun are anarthrous and *plural*, one properly should translate πᾶς as "all."

1. πᾶσα γλῶσσα = "*every* tongue" (Phil 2:11)
2. ὑπὲρ πάντων ἀνθρώπων = "for *all* men" (1 Tim 2:1)

Table 6.12 Anarthrous Constructions: Πᾶς

$$\text{πᾶς}_{sg} + \text{noun}_{sg} = \text{"every \_\_\_\_\_"}$$

$$\text{πάντες}_{pl} + \text{noun}_{pl} = \text{"all \_\_\_\_\_"}$$

Substantival Constructions

Finally, do not forget that gender can figure into translation of the adjective πᾶς. Used substantivally (alone, without a noun) a masculine πᾶς or feminine πᾶσα can include the idea of person in the translation, such as "everyone" or "every person" in the singular or "all people," "all men," or "all women" in the plural. Similarly, the neuter πᾶν could be "everything" in the singular or "all things" in the plural.

1. Πᾶς οὖν ὅστις ἀκούει = "Therefore *everyone* who hears" (Mt 7:24)
2. πάντες γὰρ ἥμαρτον "for *all* have sinned" (Rom 3:23)
3. καθὼς κἀγὼ πάντα πᾶσιν ἀρέσκω = "just as I also please all things *to all men*" (1 Cor 10:33)
4. πᾶν κοινὸν καὶ ἀκάθαρτον = "*anything* common or unclean" (Acts 10:14)
5. πάντα συνεργεῖ εἰς ἀγαθόν = "(God) works together *all things* for the good" (Rom 8:28)

6. καθὼς κἀγὼ <u>πάντα</u> πᾶσιν ἀρέσκω = "just as I also please *all things* to all men" (1 Cor 10:33)

Table 6.13 Substantival Constructions: Πᾶς

$$\boxed{\pi \hat{α} \varsigma_{sg} = \text{"everyone"}}$$

$$\boxed{\pi άντε \varsigma_{pl} = \text{"all men"}}$$

Guidelines for translating πᾶς must be weighed by context and usage. For example, nouns thought of as a unit will have singular number, so the πᾶς adjective will be singular, but translated "all." Note πᾶσαν τὴν οἰκουμένην, "all the inhabitants" (Lk 2:1); ἥτις ἔσται παντὶ τῷ λαῷ "which shall be to all the people" (Lk 2:10).

Adverbs

Formation

One often forms the English adverb by adding the suffix "-ly" to an adjective, as in "quick" to "quickly." Similarly, many adverbs in Greek are generated from the genitive plural adjective ending by substituting -ως for the -ων. Thus, the adjective καλῶν ("good") becomes the adverb καλῶς ("well"); κακῶν ("bad") becomes κακῶς ("badly"); δικαίων ("just") becomes δικαίως ("justly").

Other adverbs are created from other cases. For example, ποῦ ("where?") is genitive, παλίν ("again") is accusative, and κύκλῳ ("around") is locative. Some adverbs may preserve artifacts of old endings now lost, as the -δον in ὁμοθυμαδόν ("of one accord").[2] Another process is the blending of words, such as in κατέναντι ("opposite").[3] In any case, from the standpoint of morphology,

---

[2]Almost exclusive to Acts (10 times), except for one occurrence in Paul in Rom 15:6.

[3]Eight occurrences, mostly in Mark and Paul; cf. Mk 13:3, Rom 4:17.

once an adverb is memorized as vocabulary, recognition is easy—
the adverb is not declined.

Analysis

"Adverbs add to the verb." Of course, this statement, while
partially true, is an oversimplification. Adverbs have several other
functions that we will outline briefly below.

Functions

Verbal Qualifiers. The main triad of adverbial use is to add
manner, *time*, and *place* qualifiers to verbal action. So, adverbs
characteristically answer
questions such as "when,"
"where," "how," or "how
much," etc. For example,
"I am coming" is a simple
verbal idea. "I am coming
quickly" is a verbal idea
enhanced by an adverb of
manner ("hurriedly," or, if
adverb of time, "soon");
e.g., ἔρχομαι ταχύ, "I am
coming *soon*" (Rev 22:20).

Table 6.14 Adverbs: Qualifiers

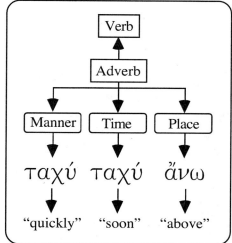

Modifiers. Adverbs do
more than modify verbs.
They also can modify sub-
stantives. For example,
"The Jerusalem *above* is
free" (Gal 4:26). Further, adverbs even can modify other adverbs.

Substantives. As with adjectives, adverbs also can be used substantivally. For example, Paul wrote, "Behold, *now* is the day of
salvation" (2 Cor 6:2). In addition, adverbs themselves even can be
the substantival object of a prepositional phrase. An article in this

construction will be neuter singular. Thus, the prepositional phrase ἀπὸ τοῦ <u>νῦν</u> literally is "from the *now*"; however, the idea better would be translated "from the *present*."

Case Clarifiers ("adverbial prepositions"). Case usage can be ambiguous. One can perceive this ambiguity especially in the interior cases in which one form can have several translations depending on the context. Some adverbs over time were used more and more with nouns. Such use was to clarify case (function) connected to the verbal action. These adverbs less and less were constructed with verbs only and moved into a more prepositional function (more with nominal structures than verbal). Such adverbs are called "adverbial prepositions."[4] One example of an adverbial preposition is ἔξω, "outside." Notice Heb 11:13, Ἰησοῦς . . . <u>ἔξω</u> τῆς πύλης ἔπαθεν, "Jesus . . . suffered *outside* the gate." The adverb ἔξω relates πύλης ("gate") in a directional manner back to the verb ἔπαθεν ("he suffered").

History

This adverb evolution from the original old adverbs to adverbial prepositions actually defines the history of prepositions. In reality, *prepositions are adverbs*—adverbs so fixed in usage with noun-type structures for clarifying case as to have lost any vestige of the original verbal composition. That is, a proper preposition simply is an old adverb used exclusively with nouns. Prepositions and their use will be discussed in the next chapter. One category will be the proper preposition, which creates prepositional phrases with nouns as their object. The other category will be the adverbial pre-position, which can be used either to modify a verb or to set up a prepositional phrase.

---

[4]To be rejected is labeling these adverbs "improper prepositions."

EXERCISE 6

1. Answer true or false:

_____ a. The attributive adjective always will be articular in construction.

_____ b. The substantival adjective always will be articular in construction.

_____ c. The predicate adjective always will be anarthrous in construction.

_____ d. In the "verbless predicative" idiom, the noun will be articular in construction.

2. Answer questions on Greek article construction related to the following passage:

Καὶ εὐθὺς ἦν ἐν τῇ συναγωγῇ αὐτῶν ἄνθρωπος ἐν πνεύματι ἀκαθάρτῳ καὶ ἀνέκραξεν λέγων· τί ἡμῖν καὶ σοί, Ἰησοῦ Ναζαρηνέ; ἦλθες ἀπολέσαι ἡμᾶς; οἶδά σε τίς εἶ, ὁ ἅγιος τοῦ θεοῦ. καὶ ἐπετίμησεν αὐτῷ ὁ Ἰησοῦς λέγων· φιμώθητι καὶ ἔξελθε ἐξ αὐτοῦ. καὶ σπαράξαν αὐτὸν τὸ πνεῦμα τὸ ἀκάθαρτον καὶ φωνῆσαν φωνῇ μεγάλῃ ἐξῆλθεν ἐξ αὐτοῦ. . . .

2.1 _____ How many adverbs are in this passage? Identify them by circling them.

2.2a _____ Which paradigm table summarizes the inflection pattern for the adjective ἀκαθάρτῳ (line 2)?

b. _____ What is the construction of the adjective ἀκαθάρτῳ (line 2, articular or anarthrous)?

c. _____ What is the function of the adjective ἀκαθάρτῳ (line 2, attributive, substantival, or predicative)?

2.3a _____ Which paradigm table summarizes the inflection pattern for the adjective ἅγιος (line 4)?

b. _____ What is the construction of the adjective ἅγιος (line 4, articular or anarthrous)?

c. _____ What is the function of the adjective ἅγιος (line 4, attributive, substantival, or predicative)?

2.4a _____ Which paradigm table summarizes the inflection pattern for the adjective μεγάλη (line 7)?

b. _____ What is the construction of the adjective μεγάλη (line 7, articular or anarthrous)?

c. _____ What is the function of the adjective μεγάλη (line 7, attrib., substan., or pred.)?

3. Using Colwell's Rule identify the subject and predicate in the following constructions. Circle the subject and underline the predicate, and translate:

3.1 ὁ πατὴρ ἡμῶν Ἀβραάμ ἐστιν (Jn 8:39)

_____

3.2 Ἰησοῦς ἐστιν ὁ υἱὸς τοῦ θεοῦ (1 Jn 4:15)

_____

3.3 φονεύς ἐστιν ὁ ἄνθρωπος οὗτος (Acts 28:4)

3.4 Σαμαρίτης εἶ σὺ καὶ δαιμόνιον ἔχεις (Jn 8:48)

3.5 Τῶν δὲ δώδεκα ἀποστόλων τὰ ὀνόματά ἐστιν ταῦτα (Mt 10:2)

3.6 Ἔστιν δὲ αὕτη ἡ παραβολή· ὁ σπόρος ἐστὶν ὁ λόγος τοῦ θεοῦ. (Lk 8:11)

4. Translate and be ready to explain the usage of πᾶς:

4.1 ὁ γὰρ πᾶς νόμος ἐν ἑνὶ λόγῳ πεπλήρωται (Gal 5:14)

4.2 καθὼς πανταχοῦ ἐν πάσῃ ἐκκλησίᾳ διδάσκω (1 Cor 4:17)

4.3 ἰδοὺ γὰρ ἀπὸ τοῦ νῦν μακαριοῦσίν με πᾶσαι αἱ γενεαί, (Lk 1:48)

5. Translate the following:

5.1 μεγάλη ἡ Ἄρτεμις Ἐφεσίων (Acts 19:28)

5.2 ὁ δὲ μὴ πιστεύων ἤδη κέκριται (Jn 3:18)

5.3 καὶ ἡ ἐλπὶς ἡμῶν βεβαία ὑπὲρ ὑμῶν (2 Cor 1:7)

5.4 ἡ δὲ ἄνωθεν σοφία πρῶτον μὲν ἁγνή ἐστιν (Jas 3:17)

5.5 ἐκέλευσεν ἔξω βραχὺ τοὺς ἀνθρώπους ποιῆσαι (Acts 5:34)

5.6 μηδὲν πράξῃς σεαυτῷ κακόν, ἅπαντες γάρ ἐσμεν ἐνθάδε (Acts 16:28)

5.7 κραταιωθῆναι διὰ τοῦ πνεύματος αὐτοῦ εἰς τὸν ἔσω ἄνθρωπον (Eph 3:16)

5.8 καὶ ἔλεγεν αὐτοῖς· ὑμεῖς ἐκ τῶν κάτω ἐστέ, ἐγὼ ἐκ τῶν ἄνω εἰμί· (Jn 3:28)

5.9 γάλα ὑμᾶς ἐπότισα, οὐ βρῶμα· οὔπω γὰρ ἐδύνασθε. ἀλλ᾽ οὐδὲ ἔτι νῦν δύνασθε (1 Cor 3:2)

CHAPTER 7
PREPOSITIONS AND CONJUNCTIONS

Prepositions are petrified adverbs. They developed to clarify case usage connected to verbs, brought in to help the overloaded case system. They are divided into two types: proper prepositions and adverbial prepositions. Conjunctions join words, phrases, clauses, and sentences.

Prepositions

Proper Prepositions

Preposition History

Table 7.1 Preposition History

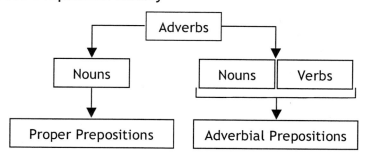

Certain adverbs began to be used so regularly with noun structures that they lost their use with verbs. Adverbial heritage of English prepositions is seen in English infinitives—always with "to," as in "to say" or "to know." *Proper prepositions* are old adverbs frozen in use *exclusively with nouns*. *Adverbial prepositions* display a dual nature: as old adverbs they show their original function by modifying verbs; yet sometimes, like proper prepositions, they can be composed with noun structures. As a result, then, note that adverbial prepositions can be found by themselves, modifying a verb; proper prepositions never are by themselves—they always are part of a "prepositional phrase," that is, part of a noun phrase.

Table 7.2 Prepositions: Case Usage

	Gen	Abl	Dat	Loc	Ins	Acc
ἀνά						✓
ἀντί		✓				
ἀπό		✓				
διά	✓	✓				✓
εἰς						✓
ἐκ		✓				
ἐν			✓	✓	✓	
ἐπί	✓		✓	✓	✓	✓
κατά	✓	✓				✓
μετά	✓					✓
παρά		✓		✓	✓	✓
περί	✓	✓				✓
πρό		✓				
πρός	✓			✓		✓
σύν					✓	
ὑπέρ	✓					✓
ὑπό		✓				✓

Prepositions were brought into play to clarify case. Conventions of such usage changed over time. Some prepositions became fixed in usage with one case only. Other prepositions developed uses with several cases. Even in just one case, a Greek preposition can have several meanings. As a result, one simply cannot give one "meaning" for a preposition. One has to observe case and context. Note that seven of the proper prepositions are used in just one case/function (bold in table), including any preposition starting with alpha: ἀνά, ἀντί, ἀπό, εἰς, ἐκ, πρό, σύν. These we can dub the "magnificent seven," for they help in locating nouns.

Table 7.3 Prepositions: The Magnificent Seven

Case/Function	Preposition
Ablative	ἀντί, ἀπό, ἐκ, πρό
Instrumental	σύν
Accusative	ἀνά, εἰς

These one-hit wonders help you locate any grammatical structure with which they are associated. For example, whenever you see εἰς in the text, you *know* the noun following has to be accusative. Note: εἰς τὰ μέρη τῆς Γαλιλαίας, *"unto the regions* of Galilee" (Mt 2:22). Regardless the confusion that might be generated by the inflection of the third declension noun μέρη, you *know* that that noun is *accusative*, because the noun here is the object of the preposition εἰς, and εἰς is used only with the accusative. Thus:

♦ *Know the seven prepositions used in one case/function only.*

Preposition Use

Prepositional phrases work two ways: (1) *adjectivally*, either modifying a noun ("the people *on the grass*"), or standing in for a noun ("*on the grass* was better"), and (2) *adverbially*, modifying a verb ("they walked *on the grass*"). Such phrases add direction, position, time, cause, agency, means, relation, association, or purpose to the context. The following table illustrates preposition use. Note: prepositions do not "have meaning." They have usage in context. Part of that context is the case of the noun that follows. In fact, the case of the noun is a crucial element for translation:

♦ *Always note noun case to establish preposition use.*

Table 7.4 Prepositions and Case Usage

	Usage	Example
ἀνά	**up**	ἀναβαίνομεν = "we are going *up*" (Mt 20:18)
acc.	*through, in*	ἀνὰ μέσον τοῦ σίτου = "*in* the midst of the wheat" (position, Mt 13:25)
acc.	*each one; the measure of*	ἀνὰ μετρητὰς δύο ἢ τρεῖς = "twenty or thirty gallons *each*" (distributive, Jn 2:6)
ἀντί	**against**	ἀντιλέγει = "he speaks *against*" (Jn 19:12)
abl.	*because of*	ἀντὶ τούτου = "*because of* this" (cause, Eph 5:31)
abl.	*for, instead of*	ἀντὶ τοῦ πατρὸς αὐτοῦ = "*instead of* his father" (relation, Mt 2:22)
ἀπό	**away from, off**	ἀποχωρεῖτε = "you depart (*from* me)" (Mt 7:23)
abl.	*away from*	ἀπὸ σοῦ = "*away* **from** you" (separation, Mt 5:29)
abl.	*from*	ἀπὸ Ἰησοῦ Χριστοῦ = "*from* Jesus Christ" (source, Rev 1:5)
abl.	*by*	ἀπὸ τῆς σαρκὸς = "*by* the flesh" (agency, Jude 23)
abl.	*because of*	ἀπὸ τῆς εὐλαβείας = "*because of* his reverence" (cause, Heb 5:7)
διά	**through**	διαγινώσκειν = "to investigate" (Acts 23:15)
gen.	*through*	διὰ τῆς Γαλιλαίας = "*through* Galilee" (adverbial of place, Mk 9:30)
abl.	*through*	διὰ τοῦ εὐαγγελίου = "*through* the gospel" (agency, 2 Tim 1:10)
abl.	*through*	διὰ πίστεως = "*through* faith" (means, Eph 2:8)
acc.	*because of*	διὰ τὸ ἔργον αὐτῶν = "*because of* their work" (cause, 1 Thess 5:13)

εἰς	*into*	εἰσέρχεται = "he enters *into*" (Heb 9:25)
acc.	*to, unto*	εἰς οὐρανὸν = "*unto* heaven" (adverbial of measure, 1 Pet 3:22)
acc.	*in*	οὐκ εἰς κενὸν = "not *in* vain" (adverbial of manner, Phil 2:16)
acc.	*with respect to*	εἰς τὸ ἴδιον σῶμα = "*with respect to* his own body" (adverbial of reference, 1 Cor 6:18)
acc.	*resulting in*	εἰς δικαίωσιν ζωῆς = "*resulting in* the righteousness of life" (result, Rom 5:18)
ἐκ	*out of*	ἐκβάλλει = "he is casting *out*" (Mt 12:24)
abl.	*out of*	ἐκ γῆς Αἰγύπτου = "*out of* the land of Egypt" (separation, Jude 9)
abl.	*from*	ἐκ τῶν ἡδονῶν ὑμῶν = "*from* your desires" (source, Jas 4:1)
abl.	*by*	ἐκ θεοῦ = "*by* God" (personal agency, Jn 1:18)
abl.	*by*	ἐκ τῶν ἔργων μου = "*by* my works" (means, Jas 2:18)
abl.	*because of*	Ἐκ τούτου = "*because of* this" (cause, Jn 6:66)
abl.	*on (rare)*	εἷς ἐκ δεξιῶν = "one *on* the right" (position, Mt 20:21)
ἐν	*in*	ἐνετύλιξεν = "he wrapped [him] *in*" (Lk 23:53)
dat.	*to*	ἐν τοῖς ἀπολλυμένοις = "*to* those who are perishing" (indir. ob., 2 Cor 4:3)
dat.	*with respect to*	ἐν ἀνθρώποις = "*with respect to* men" (adverbial of reference, 1 Cor 3:21)
loc.	*among*	ἐν τῷ λαῷ = "*among* the people" (place, Acts 6:8)
loc.	*in*	ἐν ἀγρῷ = "*in* the field" (place, Lk 15:25)
loc.	*in, at, on*	ἐν τῇ παρουσίᾳ = "*at* the appearing" (time, 1 Thess 3:13)

loc.	in	ἐν Χριστῷ = "in Christ" (sphere, 2 Cor 5:17)
ins.	by, with	ἐν πυρὶ = "with fire" (means, 1 Cor 3:13)
ins.	because of	ἐν ἐμοὶ = "because of me" (cause, Mt 26:31)
ins.	in, with	ἐν δυνάμει = "in power" (manner, 1 Thess 1:5)
ins.	by	ἐν τῷ Βεελζεβούλ = "by Beelzebul" (personal agency, Mt 12:24)
ἐπί	on, upon	ἐπιβάλλουσιν = "they put on" (Mk 11:7)
gen.	during	ἐπ᾽ ἐσχάτου τοῦ χρόνου = "during the last time" (adverbial of time, Jude 18)
gen.	on, upon	ἐπὶ τῆς θαλάσσης = "upon the sea" (adverbial of place, Mk 6:48)
dat.	to, for	ἐπὶ τοῖς ἀνθρώποις τούτοις = "to these men" (indirect object, Acts 5:35)
dat.	with respect to	ἐπὶ Στεφάνῳ = "concerning Stephen" (reference, Acts 11:19)
loc.	on, at	ἐπὶ τῷ ποταμῷ = "at the river" (place, Rev 9:14)
loc.	during	ἐπὶ παροργισμῷ ὑμῶν = "during your wrath" (time, Eph 4:26)
loc.	in	ἐπ᾽ ἐλπίδι = "in hope" (sphere, Acts 2:26)
ins.	because of	ἐπὶ τῷ λόγῳ = "because of the word" (cause, Acts 20:38)
acc.	on, upon	ἐπὶ τοὺς πόδας αὐτῶν = "upon their feet" (adverbial of measure, Rev 11:11)
κατά	down	καταβαίνει = "came down" (Rev 16:21)
gen.	by	κατὰ τοῦ θεοῦ = "by God" (oath, Mt 26:63)
abl.	against	κατὰ σοῦ = "against you" (opposition, Mt 5:23)
acc.	(distributive)	κατὰ τοὺς οἴκους = "house by house" (adverbial of measure, Acts 8:3)
acc.	as	κατὰ ἄνθρωπον = "as a man" (adverbial of reference, Rom 3:5)

acc.	according to	κατὰ τὸν νόμον = "*according to* the law" (adverbial of reference, Jn 19:7)
μετά	*with*	μεταβεβήκαμεν = "we have crossed *over*" (1 Jn 3:14)
gen.	with	μετὰ Μαρίας = "*with* Mary" (association, Mt 2:11)
gen.	with	μετὰ τῶν νεφελῶν = "*with* the clouds" (attendant circumstances, Rev 1:7)
acc.	after	μετὰ τὴν θλῖψιν ἐκείνην = "*after* that tribulation" (adv. of meas., Mk 13:24)
παρά	*beside*	παράγει = "was passing *by*" (Mt 20:30)
abl.	from	παρὰ ἀνθρώπων = "*from* men" (source, Jn 5:41)
abl.	by	παρὰ Κυρίου = "*by* the Lord" (agency, Lk 1:45)
loc.	with	παρὰ σοί = "*with* you" (place, Mt 18:19)
loc.	beside	παρὰ τῷ σταυρῷ = "*beside* the cross" (place, Jn 19:25)
loc.	with	μωρία παρὰ τῷ θεῷ = "foolishness *with* God" (sphere, 1 Cor 3:19)
ins.	with	παρὰ τινι Σίμωνι = "*with* a certain Simon" (association, Acts 9:43)
acc.	beside	παρὰ τὴν θάλασσαν = "*beside* the sea" (adverbial of measure, Mt 13:1)
acc.	than	παρὰ Κάϊν = "*than* Cain" (comparison, Heb 11:4)
περί	*around*	περιάγετε = "you travel *around*" (Mt 23:15)
gen.	for, concerning	περὶ τῆς βασιλείας = "*concerning* the kingdom" (adverb. of refer., Acts 1:3)
gen.	for	περὶ ὑμῶν = "*for* you" (advan., 1 Pet 5:7)
acc.	around	περὶ τὴν ὀσφὺν αὐτοῦ = "*around* his waist" (adverbial of measure, Mt 3:4)
acc.	in regard to	περὶ τὴν πίστιν = "*in regard to* the faith" (adverbial of reference, 1 Tim 1:19)

πρό	before	προάγουσιν = "they go *before*" (Mt 21:31)
abl.	before,	πρὸ καταβολῆς κόσμου = "*before* the
	from	foundation of the world" (sep., Eph 1:4)
abl.	above	πρὸ πάντων = "*above* all" (rank, Jas 5:12)
πρός	near, to-ward	προσάγειν = "(they) drew *near to*" (Acts 27:27)
loc.	at, on	πρὸς τῇ θύρᾳ = "*at* the door" (place, Jn 18:16)
acc.	beside	πρὸς τὸν ἄνδρα = "*beside* her husband" (place, Acts 5:10)
acc.	with, to	πρὸς ἐμαυτὸν = "*with* me" (adverbial of measure, Phlm 13)
acc.	with re-spect to	πρὸς ζωὴν καὶ εὐσέβειαν = "*with respect to* life and godliness" (adverbial of reference, 2 Pet 1:3)
acc.	for (pur-pose)	πρὸς εὐσέβειαν = "*for* (the purpose of) godliness" (purpose, 1 Tim 4:7)
σύν	with, to-gether	συνεσθίει = "he eats *with*" (Lk 15:2) συνεργεῖ = "work *together*" (Rom 8:28)
ins.	with	σὺν τοῖς μαθηταῖς αὐτοῦ = "*with* his disciples" (association, Mk 8:34)
ὑπέρ	over, above	ὑπερνικῶμεν = "we *overwhelmingly* conquer" (Rom 8:37)
gen.	for	ὑπὲρ δικαίου = "*for* a righteous man" (advantage, Rom 5:7)
gen.	in behalf of	ὑπὲρ σοῦ = "*in* your *behalf*" (adverbial of reference, Phlm 13)
gen.	concerning	ὑπὲρ τῆς ὑπομονῆς ὑμῶν καὶ πίστεως = "*concerning* your perseverance and faith" (adv. of reference, 2 Thess 1:4)
acc.	than	τομώτερος ὑπὲρ πᾶσαν μάχαιραν δίστομον = "sharper *than* any two-edged sword" (comparison, Heb 4:12)

ὑπό	under	ὑπομένω = "I endure (abide *under*)" (2 Tim 2:10)
abl.	*by*	ὑπὸ τοῦ ἀγγέλου = "*by* the angel" (personal agency, Lk 2:21)
abl.	*by*	ὑπὸ τοῦ νόμου = "*by* the law" (impersonal agency = means, Rom 3:21)
acc.	*under*	ὑπὸ νόμον = "*under* law" (adverbial of measure, Rom 6:14)

The uses in the table above involve analysis of syntax and context that informs translating Greek prepositions. Over time, the student will learn prepositions inductively through translation.[1]

Table 7.5 Prepositions and Directional Use

---

[1]The advanced student should consult Stevens and Warren, *New Testament Greek Syntax*; also, cf. Stanley E. Porter, *Idioms of the Greek New Testament*, Biblical Languages: Greek, 2 (Sheffield: JSOT Press, 1992), p. 142; Daniel B. Wallace, *Greek Grammar Beyond The Basics: An Exegetical Syntax of the New Testament* (Grand Rapids: Zondervan Publishing House, 1996), p. 363.

One specific function of proper prepositions is to indicate direction. *Directional usage is case specific.* The diagram above might be helpful in summarizing directional use of prepositions.

Articular Phrases

Table 7.6 Articular Prepositional Phrases

Remember that the basic function of the Greek article is to point. The article can point to a prepositional phrase. This phrase then functions as a substantive in the attributive position. For example, notice ὁ ἄρτος ὁ ἐκ τοῦ οὐρανοῦ (Jn 6:50). Here, the second ὁ, in concord with the articular noun ὁ ἄρτος, points to the prepositional phrase ἐκ τοῦ οὐρανοῦ as an adjective modifier of ἄρτος; hence, "the bread *from heaven*" or "the *heavenly* bread." Compare ὁ ναὸς τοῦ θεοῦ ὁ ἐν τῷ οὐρανῷ = "the temple of God *which is in heaven*" (Rev 11:19). Further, since an adjective can be used substantivally, then articular prepositional phrases also can be used substantivally.

Elision and Aspiration

Minor spelling changes occur with prepositions in composition (and in compounds). *Elision* is the dropping of a letter. A preposition's final vowel elides before a following vowel. A few exceptions are inconsequential because such forms appear "normal"; that is, the final vowel does not elide: πρὸ ἐμοῦ. Exceptions include περί and πρό, occasionally ὑπό, rarely ἀντί, and ἀνά once (Rev 21:21). Also, the sharp stop consonants π and τ alter into their corresponding aspirate forms, φ and θ, before rough breathing (for euphony). The table below summarizes alternate spellings for prepositions.

Table 7.7 Prepositions: Elision and Aspiration

	Smooth	Elision Example
ἀνά	ἀν᾽	-------
ἀντί	ἀντ᾽	-------
ἀπό	ἀπ᾽	ἀπ᾽ ἐμοῦ (Mt 7:23)
διά	δι᾽	δι᾽ ἄλλης (Mt 2:12)
ἐπί	ἐπ᾽	ἐπ᾽ αὐτόν (Mt 3:16)
κατά	κατ᾽	κατ᾽ ὄναρ (Mt 1:20)
μετά	μετ᾽	μετ᾽ αὐτοῦ (Mt 2:3)
παρά	παρ᾽	παρ᾽ αὐτῶν (Mt 2:4)
ὑπό	ὑπ᾽	ὑπ᾽ αὐτοῦ (Mt 3:6)

	Rough	Aspiration Example
ἀνά	ἀν᾽	-------
ἀντί	ἀνθ᾽	ἀνθ᾽ ὧν (Lk 1:20)
ἀπό	ἀφ᾽	ἀφ᾽ ὑμῶν (Mt 21:43)
διά	δι᾽	δι᾽ ὑμᾶς (Rom 2:24)
ἐπί	ἐφ᾽	ἐφ᾽ ὅσον (Mt 9:15)
κατά	καθ᾽	καθ᾽ ὑμῶν (Mt 5:11)
μετά	μεθ᾽	Μεθ᾽ ἡμῶν (Mt 1:23)
παρά	παρ᾽	παρ᾽ ἡμέραν (Rom 14:5)
ὑπό	ὑφ᾽	ὑφ᾽ ὑμῶν (Acts 4:11)

Adverbial Prepositions

Basic Function

Adverbial prepositions modify verbs and, on occasion, are used with noun structures like proper prepositions. Almost all of these noun structures are genitive (20) or ablative (21). Two are locative (ἐγγύς, which also can be genitive, and παραπλήσιον), and one is instrumental (ἅμα). The table below illustrates the use of these adverbial prepositions; an asterisk indicates that that preposition has only one occurrence in the New Testament.

Table 7.8　Adverbial Prepositions

Preposition	Usage	Example
ἅμα inst.	together	ἅμα καὶ ἐλπίζων = "at the same time he was hoping" (Acts 24:26)
ἄνευ abl.	apart from	ἄνευ τοῦ πατρὸς ὑμῶν = "apart from your Father" (Mt 10:29)
ἄντικρυς* gen.	straight; opposite	κατηντήσαμεν ἄντικρυς Χίου = "we arrived opposite Chios" (Acts 20:15)
ἀντιπέρα* gen.	opposite	ἀντιπέρα τῆς Γαλιλαίας = "opposite Galilee" (Lk 8:26)
ἀπέναντι abl.	opposite; before	ἀπέναντι πάντων ὑμῶν = "before all of you" (Acts 3:16)
ἄτερ gen.	without	ἄτερ βαλλαντίου = "without a coin bag" (Lk 22:35)
ἄχρι gen.	until	ἄχρι ἡμερῶν πέντε = "until five days" (Acts 20:6)
ἄχρι gen. loc.	near near	τὴν χώραν ἐγγὺς τῆς ἐρήμου = "the region near the desert" (Jn 11:54) καὶ εἰρήνην τοῖς ἐγγύς = "and peace to those who are near" (Eph 2:17)
ἐκτός abl.	outside	ἐκτὸς τοῦ σώματός ἐστιν = "is outside the body" (1 Cor 6:18)

ἔμπροσθεν abl.	before	γέμοντα ὀφθαλμῶν ἔμπροσθεν καὶ ὄπισθεν = "full of eyes before and behind" (Rev 4:6)
ἔναντι gen.	before, presence	ἐν τῷ ἱερατεύειν αὐτὸν . . . ἔναντι τοῦ θεοῦ = "while he was serving as priest . . . before God" (Lk 1:8)
ἐναντίον gen.	before, presence	ἦσαν δὲ δίκαιοι ἀμφότεροι ἐναντίον τοῦ θεοῦ = "both were righteous before God" (Lk 1:6)
ἕνεκεν abl.	for the sake of	ἕνεκεν ἐμοῦ = "for my sake" (Mk 10:29)
ἐντός gen.	inside, within	τὸ ἐντὸς τοῦ ποτηρίου = "the inside of the cup" (Mt 23:26)
ἐνώπιον gen.	before, presence	ἐνώπιον παντὸς τοῦ λαοῦ = "before all the people" (Lk 8:47)
ἔξω abl.	outside	ἔξω τῆς οἰκίας = "outside the house" (Mt 10:14)
ἔξωθεν abl.	outside	τὸ ἔξωθεν τοῦ ποτηρίου = "the outside of the cup" (Lk 11:39)
ἐπάνω gen.	above, over	ἐπάνω πάντων ἐστίν = "he is above all" (Jn 3:31)
ἐπέκεινα* abl.	beyond	ἐπέκεινα Βαβυλῶνος = "beyond Babylon" (Acts 7:43)
ἔσω gen.	inside	ἔσω τῆς αὐλῆς = "inside the gate" (Mk 15:16)
ἕως gen.	until, as far as	ἕως ἔξω τῆς πόλεως = "until outside the city" (Acts 21:5)
κατέναντι gen.	opposite	κατέναντι τοῦ ἱεροῦ = "opposite the temple" (Mk 13:3)
κατενώπι-ον (gen.)	before, presence	κατενώπιον τῆς δόξης αὐτοῦ = "in the presence of his glory" (Jude 24)
κυκλόθεν gen.	around	κυκλόθεν τοῦ θρόνου = "around the throne" (Rev 4:4)

κύκλῳ gen.	around	εἰς τοὺς κύκλῳ ἀγροὺς = "into the *surrounding* countryside" (Mk 6:36)
μέσον gen.	midst, middle	ἔστη εἰς τὸ μέσον = "he stood in their *midst*" (Jn 20:19)
μεταξύ abl.	between	μεταξὺ δύο στρατιωτῶν = "*between* two soldiers" (Acts 12:6)
μέχρι(ς) gen.	until, up to	ἀπὸ Ἀδὰμ μέχρι Μωϋσέως = "from Adam *until* Moses" (Rom 5:14)
ὄπισθεν abl.	behind	γέμοντα ὀφθαλμῶν ἔμπροσθεν καὶ ὄπισθεν = "full of eyes before and *behind*" (Rev 4:6)
ὀπίσω abl.	after	ὀπίσω μου ἀκολουθεῖν = "to follow *after* me" (Mk 8:34)
ὀψέ gen. abl.	evening after	ὅταν ὀψὲ ἐγένετο = "when *evening* came" (Mk 11:19) Ὀψὲ δὲ σαββάτων = "*after* the sabbath" (Mt 28:1)
παραπλή- σιον* (loc.)	near	παραπλήσιον θανάτῳ· = "[he was] *near* death" (Phil 2:27)
παρεκτός abl.	except	παρεκτὸς λόγου πορνείας = "*except* on ground of unchastity" (Mt 5:32)
πέραν abl.	after	πέραν τοῦ Ἰορδάνου = "*beyond* the Jordan" (Mt 19:1)
πλήν abl.	except	πλὴν τῶν ἀποστόλων = "*except* the apostles" (Acts 8:1)
πλησίον gen.	near	πλησίον τοῦ χωρίου = "*near* the field" (Jn 4:7)
ὑπεράνω abl.	far above	ὑπεράνω πάντων τῶν οὐρανῶν = "*far above* all the heavens" (Eph 4:10)
ὑπερέκει- να* (abl.)	beyond	εἰς τὰ ὑπερέκεινα ὑμῶν = "unto the regions *beyond* you" (2 Cor 10:16)
ὑπερεκπε- ρισσοῦ (abl.)	very high- ly, above	ὑπερεκπερισσοῦ ἐν ἀγάπῃ = "*very highly* in love" (1 Thess 5:13)

ὑποκάτω abl.	under, beneath	ὑποκάτω τῆς γῆς = "under the earth" (Rev 5:13)
χάριν abl.	for the sake of	Τούτου χάριν κάμπτω = "For this reason I bow" (Eph 3:14)
χωρίς abl.	apart fr., without	Νυνὶ δὲ χωρὶς νόμου = "But now, apart from the Law" (Rom 3:21)

Directional Use

Adverbial prepositions can be directional too. They occasionally can be guessed from the proper prepositions from which they sometimes have been derived. One can notice, for example, the πρός in ἔμπροσθεν, the ἐπί and ἀνά in ἐπάνω, or the ὑπό and κατά in ὑποκάτω.

Compound Verbs

Function

A *compound verb* is a verb with a prefixed preposition. The phenomenon can be observed in English verbs, as in "downsize," "uplift," or "outrun." The function of the compound is to enhance the verb's meaning. The result is that the verb might be:

1. *strengthened:* as in γινώσκω, "I know" to ἐπιγινώσκω, "I know fully"
2. *changed:* as in γινώσκω, "I know" to ἀναγινώσκω, "I read"
3. *directed:* as in βάλλω, "I throw" to ἐκβάλλω, "I throw out"
4. *unaffected:* that is, the original compound force was trivialized into insignificance by overuse, as with the verb ἐπιγινώσκω, sometimes meaning no more than "I know"

Koine Greek sometimes shows a redundancy with compound verbs. The preposition compounded onto the verb could be uselessly repeated after the verb. Note, for example, ἐκ τῆς ἐκκλησίας ἐκβάλλει = "he is throwing *out of* the church" (3 Jn 10). Prepositions commonly repeated in this way are ἀπό, ἐκ, εἰς, ἐν, and ἐπί. In translation, the redundant preposition is ignored.

Formation

Prepositions are prefixed to verbs in Greek just as in English. The typical form does not alter the spelling of

Table 7.9 Compound Verbs

$$\dot{\alpha}\pi\acute{o} + \ddot{\alpha}\gamma\omega \longrightarrow \dot{\alpha}\pi\acute{\alpha}\gamma\omega$$

the verb, as in ἐκβάλλω. However, verbs with a beginning vowel cause elision of the preposition's final vowel. So, ἀπό plus ἄγω generates the compounded form ἀπάγω. Also, be sure to note that the preposition ἐκ changes to ἐξ before vowels, as in ἐξ αὐτῶν; thus, in compounds, observe the form ἐξέρχομαι, for example.

Principal Parts

The compounded preposition is not reckoned part of the tense stem in the formation of principal parts for verbs. Therefore:

♦ *Compounds are disregarded in verb formation.*

If a prefix is to be added to a tense stem, such as a past time augment, and the verb is compounded, the prefix will go *between* the compound preposition and the tense stem. That is, the prefix is attached directly to the tense stem, not the preposition. Thus, the verb περιβάλλω, "I put on," as aorist tense has the past time prefix ε not before the π of the preposition περί but before the verb stem -βαλ-, as in περιέβαλον.

Conjunctions

A *phrase* is a word group that does not have a subject, such as "on the grass" or "knowing this." A *clause* is a word group that has a subject: "since she knows." *Conjunctions* join words, phrases, clauses, and sentences. The joined elements make a compound. So, a *compound subject* is two or more subjects joined by a conjunction: "Bill *and* Jane"; a *compound verb* is two or more verbs joined by a conjunction: "study *and* learn"; a *compound phrase* joins two or more phrases: "in the air *and* on the ground"; a *compound clause* joins two or more clauses: "while she sang *and* as he played." Finally, a *compound sentence* is two or more sentences joined by a conjunction: "she sang *and* he played."

We now focus our attention on the use of conjunctions in clauses. Conjunctions have two forms: coordinate and subordinate.

Coordinating Conjunctions

Coordinate conjunctions join coordinate clauses. A *coordinate clause* has equal status with a related clause. Such clauses are joined in four ways, outlined in the table below.

Table 7.10 Coordinate Conjunctions

Type	Greek	English
1. Copulative	καί	and
2. Adversative	δέ, ἀλλά	and, but
3. Inferential	οὖν, δίο, ἄρα	therefore, then
4. Causal	γάρ	for

Copulative (καί)

A *copulative* coordinating conjunction expresses equality or similarity of clauses. The workhorse conjunction is the copulative καί, used 9161 times! Καί can join sentence strings, perhaps showing continuity of thought (cf. the Gospel of Mark). The Greek adjective ἀμφότεροι means "both," but is used only fourteen times in the New Testament. An alternate form for "both" is a series using καί . . . καί, which can be translated "both . . . and."

Note Jn 15:24: <u>καὶ</u> ἐμὲ <u>καὶ</u> τὸν πατέρα μου = "*both* me *and* my Father."

The conjunction καί has numerous nuances.[2] Observe:

1. *Adjunctive* ("also," "likewise"): ὡς <u>καὶ</u> ἡμεῖς ἀφήκαμεν τοῖς ὀφειλέταις ἡμῶν = "as we *also* have forgiven our debtors" (Mt 6:12); <u>καὶ</u> τὴν ἄλλην, "*likewise* the other one" (Mt 5:39)

2. *Adversative* ("and yet," "but"): <u>καὶ</u> ἡδέως αὐτοῦ ἤκουεν = "*and yet* he liked to listen to him" (Mk 6:20); <u>καὶ</u> ἐφοβήθησαν τὸν λαόν = "*but* they feared the people" (Lk 20:19)

3. *Ascensive* ("even"): <u>καὶ</u> γὰρ τὰ κυνάρια ἐσθίει ἀπὸ τῶν ψιχίων = "For *even* the dogs eat from the crumbs" (Mt 15:27); ὥστε ἐξαπορηθῆναι ἡμᾶς <u>καὶ</u> τοῦ ζῆν, "so that we despaired *even* of life" (2 Cor 1:8)

4. *Explanatory* ("namely," "indeed"): ἔρχεται ὥρα <u>καὶ</u> νῦν ἐστιν = "an hour is coming, *indeed*, now is" (Jn 5:25)

Adversative (δέ, ἀλλά)

An *adversative* coordinating conjunction expresses contrast, antitheses, or opposition. The coordinating conjunctions δέ and ἀλλά are adversatives. The relative degree of contrast is distinguished between the two: δέ communicates *slight contrast*, while ἀλλά communicates *strong contrast*. Thus, δέ can serve as a simple connecting particle or can mark new development in the narrative or argument, translated as "and" or "now." A stylistic variant of δέ is τέ. Of the 215 uses of τέ in the New Testament, the lion's share goes to Acts alone (151 times). This stylistic pen-

---

[2]Cf. Frederick William Danker, ed., *A Greek-English Lexicon of the New Testament and Other Early Christian Literature, Third Edition (BDAG)*, revised and edited by Frederick William Danker, based on Walter Bauer's *Griechisch-deutsches Wörterbuch zu den Schriften des Neuen Testaments und der frühchristlichen Literatur*, sixth edition, ed. Kurt Aland and Barbara Aland, with Viktor Reichmann and on previous English editions by W. F. Arndt, F. W. Gingrich, and F. W. Danker (Chicago/London: University of Chicago Press, 2000).

chant is reminiscent of the Greek historian Polybius (ca. 203-120 B.C.). In contrast, the ἀλλά is a stronger conjunction, translated "but," "yet," or "rather." This conjunction sets a following clause in strong contrast, sometimes suggesting antithesis or opposition. How does one know these different uses of δέ and ἀλλά? *Context* is key. The point here is that the student learn flexibility in translating the adversatives δέ and ἀλλά by carefully noting the context. Note that the conjunction δέ always is postpositive, that is, never first in its clause. Study the following examples:

1. Ἐγένετο δὲ ἐν ταῖς ἡμέραις ἐκείναις = "*Now* it happened in those days" (Lk 2:1; weak connective)
2. Ἀνέβη δὲ καὶ Ἰωσὴφ ἀπὸ τῆς Γαλιλαίας = "*And* Joseph went up also from Galilee" (Lk 2:4; weak connective)
3. ἡ δὲ Μαριὰμ πάντα συνετήρει τὰ ῥήματα ταῦτα συμβάλλουσα ἐν τῇ καρδίᾳ αὐτῆς. = "*But* Mary treasured up all these words in her heart." (Lk 2:19; contrast)
4. ἀνδρῶν τε καὶ γυναικῶν = "*both* men and women" (Acts 5:14; weak connective)
5. καὶ ἀποκριθεῖσα ἡ μήτηρ αὐτοῦ εἶπεν, Οὐχί, ἀλλὰ κληθήσεται Ἰωάννης. = "And his mother answering said, 'Absolutely not; *rather* he will be called John!'" (Lk 1:60; strong contrast)
6. ὁ Ἰησοῦς εἶπεν πρὸς αὐτούς, Οὐ χρείαν ἔχουσιν οἱ ὑγιαίνοντες ἰατροῦ ἀλλὰ οἱ κακῶς ἔχοντες = "Jesus said to them, 'It is not those are healthy who need a physician, *but* those who are sick.'" (Lk 5:31; antithesis)
7. ἀλλ' οὐχὶ ἐρεῖ αὐτῷ = "*yet* will he not say to him?" (Lk 17:8; opposition)

Inferential (οὖν, διό, ἄρα)

The *inferential* coordinating conjunction occurs as οὖν, διό, and ἄρα, translated as "therefore," "so," "consequently," and "then" (ἄρα). An inferential conjunction is used in the process of reasoning, argument, and drawing logical conclusions. The clause following the conjunction is a logical conclusion of the previous statement or argument, the inference made by the writer or speaker. Note that the conjunction οὖν always is postpositive. Observe: Γίνεσθε οὖν μιμηταὶ τοῦ θεοῦ, *"Therefore,* be imitators of God" (Eph 5:1). Another inferential example is: Διὸ παρέδωκεν αὐτοὺς ὁ θεὸς ἐν ταῖς ἐπιθυμίαις τῶν καρδιῶν αὐτῶν = *"Therefore,* God delivered them over to the lusts of their hearts" (Rom 1:24). Finally, note Mt 19:25: τίς ἄρα δύναται σωθῆναι; = *"Then* who is able to be saved?"

Causal (γάρ)

The *causal* coordinating conjunction is γάρ, "for." A causal conjunction is used in the process of reasoning and provides the explanation or basis or the previous statement or argument. The conjunction γάρ always is postpositive in its clause. Note: Αὐτὸς γάρ ἐστιν ἡ εἰρήνη ἡμῶν, *"For* he is our peace" (Eph 2:14), explaining the reason why the dividing wall has been abolished and Jew and gentile believers have been brought together in Christ.

Subordinating Conjunctions

A *dependent clause* is a clause that fulfills a noun, adjective, or adverb role related to its associated independent clause. Thus, a dependent clause has no life of its own and cannot stand by itself. Three types of conjunctions introduce dependent clauses. These are subordinate conjunctions, relative pronouns, and conjunctive adverbs. (The conjunctive adverb simply is an adverb that is used as a conjunction.) Thus, the presence of a subordinate conjunction, a relative pronoun, or a conjunctive adverb indicates a dependent clause and a complex sentence. An adjective clause can be introduced by any of the three conjunctions. An adverb clause can be introduced by the subordinate conjunction and the conjunctive adverb. A noun clause can be introduced only by a relative pronoun. The table below illustrates these relationships.

Table 7.11 Dependent Clauses

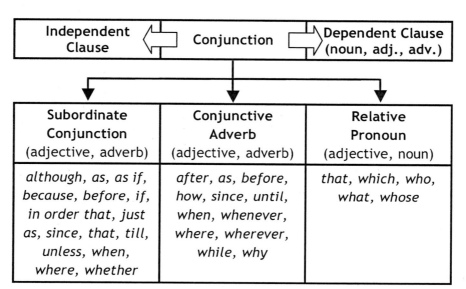

Subordinate Conjunction (adjective, adverb)	Conjunctive Adverb (adjective, adverb)	Relative Pronoun (adjective, noun)
although, as, as if, because, before, if, in order that, just as, since, that, till, unless, when, where, whether	after, as, before, how, since, until, when, whenever, where, wherever, while, why	that, which, who, what, whose

A *complex sentence* combines an independent clause with at least one dependent clause. Therefore, subordinating conjunctions indicate complex sentences. Our focus here is on subordinate conjunctions. Subordinate conjunctions have seven major types in Greek. These seven types are summarized in the table below.

Table 7.12 Subordinate Conjunctions

Type	Greek	English
1. Consecutive	ὅτι	that
2. Causal	ὅτι, διότι	because
3. Final	ἵνα	in order that
4. Temporal	ὅτε	when
5. Conditional	εἰ, ἐάν	if
6. Comparative	ὡς, καθώς	as, just as
7. Concessive	ἐάν	although

Consecutive (ὅτι)

The conjunction ὅτι can function two ways. One is to introduce consecutive clauses. The other is to introduce causal clauses. Context is the key to distinguishing ὅτι as consecutive or ὅτι as causal. We start with ὅτι as consecutive, which has two types, explanatory and substantival. Note that the second type, substantival, includes a special function indicating discourse.

Explanatory ὅτι. First, consecutive ὅτι can be explanatory, or "epexegetic." The ὅτι clause elaborates on the preceding word or clause. (Grammatically, the two clauses are in apposition.) An example is Mt 16:8: Τί διαλογίζεσθε ἐν ἑαυτοῖς . . . <u>ὅτι</u> ἄρτους οὐκ ἔχετε; = "Why are you discussing among yourselves . . . *that* you have no bread?" Another is Jn 3:19: αὕτη δέ ἐστιν ἡ κρίσις <u>ὅτι</u> τὸ φῶς ἐλήλυθεν = "and this is the judgment, *that* light has come."

Substantival ὅτι. Second, consecutive ὅτι can be substantival, introducing a clause that functions as a substantive, commonly as the subject or direct object of the main verb. An example of a ὅτι clause functioning as the subject is Heb 7:14: πρόδηλον γὰρ <u>ὅτι</u> ἐξ Ἰούδα ἀνατέταλκεν ὁ κύριος ἡμῶν = "For *that* our Lord has arisen out of Judah is clearly obvious." A frequent direct object use of a ὅτι clause is after verbs of perception (see, hear, think, know, read). An example is Mt 5:21: Ἠκούσατε <u>ὅτι</u> ἐρρέθη = "You have heard *that* it has been said." Another is 1 Jn 2:5: γινώσκομεν <u>ὅτι</u> ἐν αὐτῷ ἐσμεν = "we know *that* we are in Him."

Discourse ὅτι. Both direct and indirect discourse (speech and reported speech) are introduced with ὅτι. We briefly discuss each in turn, with special attention to the problem of English idiom regarding use of tenses in indirect discourse.

Direct discourse is introduced with ὅτι, called "ὅτι recitative." This ὅτι is left untranslated, and the material following is put within quotation marks. In the edited Greek text, the direct quote is set off by using ὅτι followed by a capital letter. (Without the ὅτι one will have just a comma followed by a capital letter.)

Indirect discourse is introduced with ὅτι (translated as "that"). This entire ὅτι clause functions as direct object of the verb of saying (i.e., another example of substantival ὅτι). Numerous verbs can introduce indirect discourse, including verbs of saying, reporting, proclaiming, thinking, showing, hoping, marveling, etc. In reporting indirect discourse, English idiom converts the tense of the original verb in the direct discourse one step back in time in the indirect report. Present tense direct statements convert to preterit; preterit tense direct statements convert to pluperfect.

Table 7.13 English Indirect Discourse: Tense Conversion

Statement	English Conversion	Indirect Discourse
"I go."	Present → Past	He said that he *went*.
"I went."	Past → Pluperfect	He said that he *had gone*.

Greek has a problem with this English idiom, because:

♦ *Greek always preserves the tense of direct discourse.*

Greek tense, then, in indirect discourse often must be adjusted for English translation. Two basic structures for Greek indirect discourse are given below with suggestions on how to translate them. Do not treat these as hard and fast "rules." Be flexible to allow for context to help you decide how to translate:

1. *Tenses preserved.* Greek indirect discourse, for example, preserves the present tense of the original statement. If the context involves a supposition generally held, or something considered generally known, etc., English translation also can use this present tense. For example, οἴδαμεν ὅτι ἁμαρτωλῶν ὁ θεὸς οὐκ ἀκούει = "we know that God does not *hear* sinners" (Jn 9:31).

2. *Tenses converted.* English idiom regularly converts tenses moving from direct to indirect discourse. Thus, often when

translating tenses of Greek verbs within indirect discourse, the English translator must supply the correct past tense for proper English idiom. Study the table.

Table 7.14 Greek Indirect Discourse: Tense Conversion

Indirect Discourse	Greek to English	Translation
ἐκεῖνοι δὲ ἔδοξαν ὅτι περὶ τῆς κοιμήσεως τοῦ ὕπνου λέγει	Present → Past	"but they supposed that he *was speaking* about actual sleep" (Jn 11:13)
ἔγνωσαν γὰρ ὅτι πρὸς αὐτοὺς τὴν παραβολὴν εἶπεν	Past → Pluperfect	"for they began to understand that he *had spoken* the parable against them" (Mk 12:12)

- First, one might move from *present to past tense.* The Greek indirect discourse preserves the present tense of the original statement; however, the translator should supply the past tense for proper English translation. For example, ἐκεῖνοι δὲ ἔδοξαν ὅτι περὶ τῆς κοιμήσεως τοῦ ὕπνου λέγει = "but they supposed that he *was speaking* about actual sleep" (Jn 11:13). Observe carefully how the Greek idiom preserves the present tense of the original state- ment. ("He *is speaking* about actual sleep.") However, English idiom requires tense conversion.
- Second, one might move from *past to pluperfect* tense. The Greek indirect discourse preserves the past tense of the original statement; however, the translator should sup- ply the pluperfect tense for proper English translation. For example, ἔγνωσαν γὰρ ὅτι πρὸς αὐτοὺς τὴν παραβολὴν εἶπεν = "for they began to understand that he *had spoken*

the parable against them" (Mk 12:12, ἔγνωσαν taken as
ingressive). Observe carefully how the Greek idiom preserves the past tense of the original statement. ("He *spoke*
the parable against them.") However, the English idiom
requires tense conversion.

Other conjunctions are used occasionally for indirect discourse.
Indirect commands or requests take a ἵνα or ὅπως clause, which
also calls for the subjunctive mood. For example, οὐκ ἐρωτῶ ἵνα
ἄρῃς αὐτοὺς ἐκ τοῦ κόσμου, "I am not asking *that* you take
them out of the world" (Jn 17:15). Another is τί used to ask a
question, as in τάραχος οὐκ ὀλίγος ἐν τοῖς στρατιώταις τί ἄρα
ὁ Πέτρος ἐγένετο, "no small commotion among the soldiers *what*
had happened with Peter" (Acts 12:18).

Causal (ὅτι, διότι)

Besides consecutive, the other major use of ὅτι is causal. That
is, the ὅτι clause provides the cause or basis for the preceding
clause, translated "because" or "for." Note Mt 5:3: Μακάριοι οἱ
πτωχοὶ τῷ πνεύματι, ὅτι αὐτῶν ἐστιν ἡ βασιλεία τῶν οὐρανῶν
= "Blessed are the poor in spirit, *for* theirs is the kingdom of heav-
en." Again, observe Jn 7:29: ἐγὼ οἶδα αὐτόν, ὅτι παρ᾽ αὐτοῦ
εἰμι, "I know him, *because* I am from him."

An alternate causal subordinate conjunction is διότι. Note:
διότι οὐ παραδέξονταί σου μαρτυρίαν περὶ ἐμοῦ = "*because*
they will not receive your testimony concerning me" (Acts 22:18),
explaining why God never wanted Paul testifying in Jerusalem.

Final (ἵνα)

The final subordinate conjunction is ἵνα, "in order that." The
mood will be subjunctive. An example is Mt 7:1: Μὴ κρίνετε, ἵνα
μὴ κριθῆτε· = "Do not judge *in order that* you not be judged."

Temporal (ὅτε)

The temporal subordinate conjunction is ὅτε, "when." As an example, note 1 Thess 3:4: καὶ γὰρ <u>ὅτε</u> πρὸς ὑμᾶς ἦμεν = "For, indeed, *when* we were with you."

Conditional (εἰ, ἐάν)

The conditional subordinate conjunction is εἰ, "if." Some of these conditional constructions call for the alternate form, ἐάν. An example is 1 Pet 3:14: ἀλλ᾽ <u>εἰ</u> καὶ πάσχοιτε διὰ δικαιοσύνην, μακάριοι = "but *if* indeed you should suffer for the sake of righteousness, you are blessed."

Comparative (ὡς, καθώς)

The comparative subordinate conjunction occurs as ὡς and καθώς, "as," "just as." An example is Rom 12:3: ἑκάστῳ <u>ὡς</u> ὁ θεὸς ἐμέρισεν μέτρον πίστεως = "to each one *as* God has distributed a measure of faith." As another example one has Rom 15:7: Διὸ προσλαμβάνεσθε ἀλλήλους, <u>καθὼς</u> καὶ ὁ Χριστὸς προσελάβετο ὑμᾶς εἰς δόξαν τοῦ θεοῦ. = "Therefore receive one another, *just as* also Christ received you unto the glory of God."

Concessive (ἐάν)

The concessive subordinate conjunction is ἐάν, "although." This use of ἐάν is rare, as the dominant use by far is conditional. Other rare birds are καίτοιγε and καίπερ. (The concessive participle is the normal grammar for this type subordinate clause.) One example is Mk 14:31: <u>ἐὰν</u> δέῃ με συναποθανεῖν σοι, οὐ μή σε ἀπαρνήσομαι = "*even though* I might die with you, I never will deny you."

Finally, note how conjunctions can pile up. Rom 5:18 has three conjunctions front-loaded: Ἄρα οὖν ὡς δι᾽ ἑνὸς παραπτώματος = "*Therefore, then, just as* through one person's transgression."

Preposition Frequency

Finally, a few remarks on frequency of the prepositions can orient the student to New Testament usage. Notice how "e is high frequency." That is, the prepositions that begin with epsilon are the most frequent. In terms of preposition usage with case, the accusative, genitive, and dative are fairly evenly divided by thirds (acc.: 38%, gen.: 32%, dat.: 30%). This even division demonstrates prepositions in their role as case clarifiers.

Chart 2: Preposition Frequency

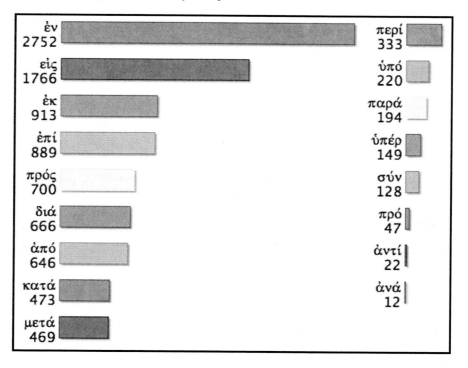

ἐν 2752	περί 333
εἰς 1766	ὑπό 220
ἐκ 913	παρά 194
ἐπί 889	ὑπέρ 149
πρός 700	σύν 128
διά 666	πρό 47
ἀπό 646	ἀντί 22
κατά 473	ἀνά 12
μετά 469	

𝔢𝔢𝔢𝔢𝔢𝔢𝔢𝔢𝔢 EXERCISE 7 𝔢𝔢𝔢𝔢𝔢𝔢𝔢𝔢𝔢

1. Answer the following on Greek prepositions.

   1.1 _____ Greek prepositions originally derive from what part of speech?

   1.2 _____ What prepositions are used only with noun structures?

   1.3 _____ What prepositions can be used both with noun structures and to modify verbs?

   1.4 Identify the single case or case function of the following prepositions:

   a. _____ ἀνά   e. _____ ἐκ

   b. _____ ἀντί   f. _____ πρό

   c. _____ ἀπό   g. _____ σύν

   d. _____ εἰς

   1.5 Fill in the following chart on the directional use of prepositions:

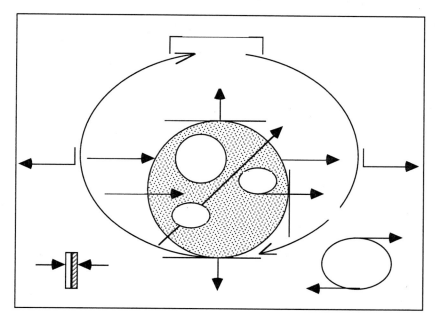

1.6 Explain the process involved in the alteration of the spelling in the following forms of prepositions:

a. κατ᾽ ὄναρ = _____

b. καθ᾽ ὑμῶν = _____

1.7 Circle all compound verbs in the following passage. Be ready to describe spelling changes for these compound verbs. Also, be ready to identify any past time augments.

    Καὶ εἰσπορεύονται εἰς Καφαρναούμ· καὶ εὐθὺς τοῖς σάββασιν εἰσελθὼν εἰς τὴν συναγωγὴν ἐδίδασκεν. καὶ ἐξεπλήσσοντο ἐπὶ τῇ διδαχῇ αὐτοῦ· ἦν γὰρ διδάσκων αὐτοὺς ὡς ἐξουσίαν ἔχων καὶ οὐχ ὡς οἱ γραμματεῖς.
    Καὶ εὐθὺς ἦν ἐν τῇ συναγωγῇ αὐτῶν ἄνθρωπος ἐν πνεύματι ἀκαθάρτῳ καὶ ἀνέκραξεν λέγων· τί ἡμῖν καὶ σοί, Ἰησοῦ Ναζαρηνέ; ἦλθες ἀπολέσαι ἡμᾶς; οἶδά σε τίς εἶ, ὁ ἅγιος τοῦ θεοῦ. καὶ ἐπετίμησεν αὐτῷ ὁ Ἰησοῦς

λέγων· φιμώθητι καὶ ἔξελθε ἐξ αὐτοῦ. καὶ σπαράξαν αὐτὸν τὸ πνεῦμα τὸ ἀκάθαρτον καὶ φωνῆσαν φωνῇ μεγάλῃ ἐξῆλθεν ἐξ αὐτοῦ. . . .

Καὶ εὐθὺς ἐκ τῆς συναγωγῆς ἐξελθόντες ἦλθον εἰς τὴν οἰκίαν Σίμωνος καὶ Ἀνδρέου μετὰ Ἰακώβου καὶ Ἰωάννου. ἡ δὲ πενθερὰ Σίμωνος κατέκειτο πυρέσσουσα, καὶ εὐθὺς λέγουσιν αὐτῷ περὶ αὐτῆς.

2. Answer the following on Greek conjunctions.

2.1 _____ What is the term used for a word group that does *not* have a subject?

2.2 _____ What is the term used for a word group that *does* have a subject?

2.3 _____ Two or more grammatical elements joined by a conjunction is called what?

2.4 Define a complex sentence: _____

_____

2.5 What are the three dependent clause connectors?

    a. _____

    b. _____

    c. _____

2.6 What are the three roles that a dependent clause will fulfill related to the independent clause?

    a. _____

    b. _____

    c. _____

2.7 Identify the following conjunctions as coordinate (c) or subordinate (s). Specify the category type each conjunction represents (copulative, adversative, etc.). Then, give a gloss. Finally, circle the conjunctions that always are postpositive.

		Clause:	Type:	Gloss:
a.	ἀλλά	_____	_____	_____
b.	ἄρα	_____	_____	_____
c.	γάρ	_____	_____	_____
d.	δέ	_____	_____	_____
e.	διο	_____	_____	_____
f.	διότι	_____	_____	_____
g.	εἰ	_____	_____	_____
h.	ἐάν	_____	_____	_____
i.	ἐάν	_____	_____	_____
j.	ἵνα	_____	_____	_____
k.	καί	_____	_____	_____
l.	καθώς	_____	_____	_____
m.	οὖν	_____	_____	_____
n.	ὅτι	_____	_____	_____
o.	ὅτι	_____	_____	_____
p.	ὅτε	_____	_____	_____
q.	ὡς	_____	_____	_____

2.8 _____ How many times does καί occur in Mk 4:30-41? What does this potentially illustrate about the passage?

3. Translate the following and be prepared to describe the grammar of prepositions and conjunctions. Identify all conjunctions as either coordinate (c) or subordinate (s). For the dependent clauses, note whether they function as nouns, adjectives, or adverbs related to the independent clause.

3.1 εἶπεν γὰρ ὅτι θεοῦ εἰμι υἱός (Mt 27:43)

_____

3.2 σὺ οὖν ἐὰν προσκυνήσῃς ἐνώπιον ἐμοῦ, ἔσται σοῦ

πᾶσα. (Lk 4:7)

_____

3.3 πῶς λέγουσιν ἐν ὑμῖν τινες ὅτι ἀνάστασις νεκρῶν

οὐκ ἔστιν; 1 Cor 15:12)

_____

3.4 ἄρα καὶ τοῖς ἔθνεσιν ὁ θεὸς τὴν μετάνοιαν εἰς

ζωὴν ἔδωκεν. (Acts 11:18)

_____

3.5 Ὅτε οὖν ἤκουσεν ὁ Πιλᾶτος τοῦτον τὸν λόγον,

μᾶλλον ἐφοβήθη. (Jn 19:8)

_____

3.6 Αὕτη ἐστὶν ἡ ἐντολὴ ἡ ἐμή, ἵνα ἀγαπᾶτε ἀλλήλους

καθὼς ἠγάπησα ὑμᾶς. (Jn 15:12)

_____

3.7 Οἴδατε ὅτι ὅτε ἔθνη ἦτε πρὸς τὰ εἴδωλα τὰ ἄφωνα

ὡς ἂν ἤγεσθε ἀπαγόμενοι. (1 Cor 12:2)

3.8 τῇ γὰρ ἐλπίδι ἐσώθημεν· ἐλπὶς δὲ βλεπομένη οὐκ

ἔστιν ἐλπίς· ὃ γὰρ βλέπει τίς ἐλπίζει; (Rom 8:24)

3.9 μακάριος εἶ, Σίμων Βαριωνᾶ, ὅτι σὰρξ καὶ αἷμα

οὐκ ἀπεκάλυψέν σοι ἀλλ᾽ ὁ πατήρ μου ὁ ἐν τοῖς

οὐρανοῖς. (Mt 16:17)

3.10 Ἄρα οὖν ὡς καιρὸν ἔχομεν, ἐργαζώμεθα τὸ

ἀγαθὸν πρὸς πάντας, μάλιστα δὲ πρὸς τοὺς

οἰκείους τῆς πίστεως. (Gal 6:10)

3.11 Διὸ οὐκ ἐγκακοῦμεν, ἀλλ᾽ εἰ καὶ ὁ ἔξω ἡμῶν

ἄνθρωπος διαφθείρεται, ἀλλ᾽ ὁ ἔσω ἡμῶν

ἀνακαινοῦται ἡμέρᾳ καὶ ἡμέρᾳ. (2 Cor 4:16)

3.12 Εἶπεν δὲ ὁ κύριος ἐν νυκτὶ δι᾽ ὁράματος τῷ

Παύλῳ· μὴ φοβοῦ, ἀλλὰ λάλει καὶ μὴ σιωπήσῃς,

διότι ἐγώ εἰμι μετὰ σοῦ καὶ οὐδεὶς ἐπιθήσεταί

σοι τοῦ κακῶσαί σε, διότι λαός ἐστί μοι πολὺς ἐν

τῇ πόλει ταύτῃ. (Acts 18:9-10)

CHAPTER 8
COMPARISONS AND NUMERALS

Comparisons use adjectives and adverbs as their base or standard of comparison. Degrees of comparison are analyzed. Numerals are used as adjectives and adverbs. Numerals are divided logically into three basic categories: cardinal, ordinal, and adverbial. Cardinals are "counting" numbers ("one," "two," "three," etc.). Ordinals are "ordering" numbers ("first," "second," "third," etc.). Adverbials are verbal modifiers ("once," "twice").

Comparisons

Adjective Comparisons

English Usage

Overview. Comparison is a figure of speech offering two levels of distinction from a given adjective or adverb. The given adjective or adverb is the positive degree, or base of comparison. The next level of comparison is the *comparative* degree. The last level of comparison is the *superlative* degree. Thus, adjectives and adverbs can be constructed in three degrees of comparison: positive, comparative, and superlative.

Table 8.1 Comparisons: Formation of Three Degrees

Formation	Positive	Comparative	Superlative
Regular	Adjective	Suffix: "-er"	Suffix: "-est"
Regular	Adjective	Word: "more"	Word: "most"
Irregular	Adjective	(Vocabulary)	(Vocabulary)

Formation. Forms of comparison may be regular or irregular. *Regular* forms have two patterns in English:

(1) *Suffixes.* The first regular pattern uses the suffixes "-er" and "-est." For example, the positive form would be the adjective itself, such as "new," the comparative "new*er*," and the superlative "new*est.*"

(2) *Supplementary words.* The second regular pattern uses supplementary words, such as "more" and "most." For example, the positive form would be the adjective itself, such as "beautiful," the comparative "*more* beautiful," and the superlative "*most* beautiful."

Other forms of comparison are *irregular*. Irregular simply means the comparative and superlative forms actually are completely different words altogether, as in "good," "better," "best."

Greek Usage

Overview. Greek comparison is much like English. That is, Greek has three degrees of comparison. Further, these degrees are formed regularly or irregularly. The basic difference is inflection. As usual, Greek shows inflection for case, gender, and number. Regular Greek formation uses the suffix -τερ- for comparative (very similar in sound to the English suffix "-er") and -τατ- for superlative (with a similar final "t" sound like the English "-est").

Formation. Inflection for adjective comparisons is like that of first and second declension adjectives. Masculine comparisons show -τερος and -τατος endings; feminine comparisons show -τερα and -τατη endings; and neuter show -τερον and -τατον endings.

A much smaller subset of comparisons shows third declension patterns. These forms will have masculine/feminine suffixes -ιων and -ιστος (and -ιστη), and neuter suffixes -ιον and -ιστον. Comparative third declension inflexion follows the liquid short vowel stem ἄφρων. Superlative third declension inflexion actually is rare in the New Testament. An -ιστ suffix is distinctive; the endings are -ος, -η, -ον. Just eight words are involved in this category in the New Testament: ἐλάχιστος (13), ὕψιστος (13), κράτιστος (4), πλεῖστος (4), μέγιστος (1), as well as the rare suffix -τατ, on ἁγιώτατος, ἀκριβέστατος, and τιμώτατος (2).

Table 8.2 Comparisons: Adjectives (First, Second Declension)

	Comparative "newer"		Superlative "newest"	
	Singular	Plural	Singular	Plural
masculine	νεώτερος	νεώτεροι	νεώτατος	νεώτατοι
	νεωτέρου	νεωτέρων	νεωτάτου	νεωτάτων
	νεωτέρῳ	νεωτέροις	νεωτάτῳ	νεωτάτοις
	νεώτερον	νεωτέρους	νεώτατον	νεωτάτους
neuter	νεώτερον	νεώτερα	νεώτατον	νεώτατα
	νεωτέρου	νεωτέρων	νεωτάτου	νεωτάτων
	νεωτέρῳ	νεωτέροις	νεωτάτῳ	νεωτάτοις
	νεώτερον	νεώτερα	νεώτατον	νεώτατα
feminine	νεωτέρα	νεώτεραι	νεωτάτη	νεώταται
	νεωτέρας	νεωτέρων	νεωτάτης	νεωτάτων
	νεωτέρα	νεωτέραις	νεωτάτῃ	νεωτάταις
	νεωτέραν	νεωτέρας	νεωτάτην	νεωτάτας

Irregular adjective comparisons show third declension forms. Because these words are "irregular" in form, their related positive degree adjectives simply must be memorized to connect the dots. For example:

- ἀγαθός ("good") and κρείττων ("better")
- κακός ("bad") and χείρων ("worse")
- μέγας ("great") and μείζων ("greater")
- πολύς ("much") and πλείων ("more")

Note that the superlative forms given in the table below are *not* for πλείων. Rather, they are given as an example only.

Table 8.3 Comparisons: Adjectives (Third Declension)

	Comparative "more than"		Superlative "least, smallest"	
	Sing.	Plur.	Sing.	Plur.
mas.	πλείων	πλείονες	ἐλάχιστος	ἐλάχιστοι
	πλείονος	πλειόνων	ἐλαχίστου	ἐλαχίστων
	πλείονι	πλείοσιν	ἐλαχίστῳ	ἐλαχίστοις
	πλείονα	πλείονας	ἐλάχιστον	ἐλαχίστους
fem.	πλείων	πλείονες	ἐλαχίστη	ἐλάχισται
	πλείονος	πλειόνων	ἐλαχίστης	ἐλαχίστων
	πλείονι	πλείοσιν	ἐλαχίστῃ	ἐλαχίσταις
	πλείονα	πλείονας	ἐλαχίστην	ἐλαχίστας
neu.	πλεῖον	πλείονα	ἐλάχιστον	ἐλάχιστα
	πλείονος	πλειόνων	ἐλαχίστου	ἐλαχίστων
	πλείονι	πλείοσιν	ἐλαχίστῳ	ἐλαχίστοις
	πλεῖον	πλείονα	ἐλάχιστον	ἐλάχιστα

Koine Idiom. Use of the superlative form was dying out in New Testament times. The comparative form simply was conscripted for double duty. Thus, sometimes in the New Testament a comparative form is used with superlative meaning. Context usually makes this idiomatic usage clear. An example is: μικρότερον ὂν πάντων τῶν σπερμάτων = "*least* of all the seeds" (Mk 4:31). Context is clear that a superlative sense is meant by the comparative form. Also, the basic adjective itself can be superlative in sense: ὅτι πάντες εἰδήσουσίν με ἀπὸ μικροῦ ἕως μεγάλου αὐτῶν, "because all will know me from *the least* to *the greatest*" (Heb 8:11).

Adverb Comparisons

Overview

Comparison of adverbs is easier, since the comparative degree uses the neuter accusative *singular* of the comparative adjective and the superlative degree uses the neuter accusative *plural* of the superlative adjective. This superlative adverb form usually is *third* declension. For example, the comparative of ἐγγύς is the second declension form ἐγγύτερον, but the superlative form is ἔγγιστα, a third declension neuter ending. Twelve of fifteen occurrences of superlative adverb forms in the New Testament are the one word μάλιστα ("especially").

Table 8.4 Comparisons: Adjectives vs. Adverbs

Adjective Comparisons				
Comparative	2nd D	-τερος	-τερα	-τερον
	3rd D	-ιων	-ιων	-ιον
Superlative	2nd D	-τατος	-τατη	-τατον
	3rd D	-ιστος	-ιστη	-ιστον
Adverb Comparisons				
Comparative		-----	-----	-τερον
Superlative	2nd D	-----	-----	-τατα
	3rd D	-----	-----	-ιστα

Methods of Comparison

Greek has three methods for comparisons. The one most similar to English uses the conjunction ἤ ("than"). The other two use distinct case forms, the ablative and the accusative. Before engaging a discussion of these Greek constructions, however, we need to clarify the matter of the logical omission of words.

Clarification of Ellipsis

Ellipsis is any process of the omission of words, grammatically necessary but logically unnecessary. Ellipsis is common in adverbial clauses, such as participial constructions: "while taking notes" actually is "while [*I was*] taking notes." Ellipsis also occurs in many comparisons, which often leave words unexpressed but understood. The following comparison illustrates: "Jesus was making and baptizing more disciples *than John*" (Jn 4:1). Grammatically, this comparison when expanded into a complete thought becomes: "Jesus was making and baptizing more disciples *than John [was making and baptizing disciples]*."

Table 8.5 Methods of Comparison

Structure	Construction
Conjunction	ἤ
Ablative	-ου, -ης, -ας, -ων, etc.
Accusative	παρά or ὑπέρ

Method 1: Conjunction ἤ

The first method of setting up a comparison in Greek is familiar to the English student due to English idiom for making comparisons: explicit use of the comparative conjunction "than" (ἤ). In Greek the cases of the items compared are the same. In Jn 4:1, the compared elements are constructed in the same case (nominative):

Ἰησοῦς <u>πλείονας</u> μαθητὰς ποιεῖ καὶ βαπτίζει <u>ἤ</u> Ἰωάννης

The comparative adjective is πλείονας. The compared elements are Ἰησοῦς and Ἰωάννης, which both are nominative. Hence: "Jesus was making and baptizing <u>more</u> disciples *than* John." Notice the logical ellipsis of most of the second element. Another example is Lk 10:14, but here using the dative case for both elements:

πλὴν Τύρῳ καὶ Σιδῶνι <u>ἀνεκτότερον</u> ἔσται ἐν τῇ κρίσει ἢ ὑμῖν.

Here, the comparative adjective is ἀνεκτότερον. The compared elements are Τύρῳ καὶ Σιδῶνι and ὑμῖν, which are both dative. Hence: "'However, it will be <u>more tolerable</u> for Tyre and Sidon in the judgment *than* for you.'" Again notice the ellipsis of words: "than [it will be tolerable] for you."

Compared elements even can be entire clauses. This type can occur in logical argument. One example is Rom 13:11:

νῦν γὰρ <u>ἐγγύτερον</u> ἡμῶν ἡ σωτηρία ἢ ὅτε ἐπιστεύσαμεν.

"For now our salvation is <u>nearer</u> *than* when we (first) believed." Notice even here the logical omission of words: "than [our salvation was near] when we (first) believed."

The comparative conjunction "than" always is present to express comparisons in English. Greek, on the other hand, actually has two other methods for comparison in which the comparative conjunction ἤ is not used. These two methods are idiomatic uses of cases. One uses the genitive case with ablative function. The other incorporates the accusative case with certain prepositions.

Method 2: The Ablative of Comparison

Comparison implies separation. Separation is ablative function. A substantive in the genitive (with ablative function) provides the standard of the comparison. The word "than" necessarily must be supplied in English translation of this Greek idiom. An example is Jn 13:16:

<u>μείζων</u> τοῦ κυρίου αὐτοῦ

Observe the genitive case following the comparative adjective μείζων. This genitive case is idiomatic and is called the *ablative of comparison*. The ablative function is what calls for the "than" to be inserted into the English translation: "greater *than* his master." Notice again 1 Cor 1:25:

$$\text{σοφώτερον τῶν ἀνθρώπων}$$

Once again, observe the genitive case following the comparative adjective σοφώτερον: "wiser *than* men." In each example, the ablative function declares the comparison idea that generates the need to supply the "than" conjunction in English translation.

Method 3: The Accusative of Comparison

The accusative of comparison uses the prepositions παρά and ὑπέρ, translated as "than," followed by the accusative case (and can occur without the comparative adjective). Note Heb 11:4:

$$\text{Πίστει πλείονα θυσίαν Ἄβελ παρὰ Κάϊν προσήνεγκεν}$$

The comparative adjective is πλείονα. The preposition παρά gives the "than." Note that the case following παρά is accusative. Thus: "By faith Abel offered a more acceptable sacrifice *than* Cain." As another example, observe the construction in Heb 4:12:

$$\text{Ζῶν γὰρ ὁ λόγος τοῦ θεοῦ καὶ ἐνεργὴς καὶ τομώτερος ὑπὲρ}$$
$$\text{πᾶσαν μάχαιραν δίστομον}$$

The comparative adjective is τομώτερος. The preposition ὑπέρ gives the "than." Note that the case following ὑπέρ is accusative. Thus: "For the Word of God is living, energetic, and sharper *than* any two-edged sword." (Cf. Lk 3:13; Heb 3:3; 9:23; 11:4; 12:24.)

Note that a comparative adjective does not *have* to be explicit. For example: Ὃς μὲν [γὰρ] κρίνει ἡμέραν παρ᾽ ἡμέραν, "Who judges one day *more than* another day" (Rom 14:5).

Finally, Rom 8:18 is our only example of an accusative of comparison using πρός. Paul wrote: οὐκ ἄξια τὰ παθήματα τοῦ νῦν καιροῦ πρὸς τὴν μέλλουσαν δόξαν, "the present sufferings are not worthy *compared with* the coming glory."

Adjective Functions

We give one final word about comparative adjectives. These forms can have normal adjective functions. When articularized (constructed with an article), the comparative adjective becomes a simple adjective, or, if alone, a substantive. Note this adjective:

$$\text{ἐκβληθήσονται εἰς τὸ σκότος } \underline{\text{τὸ ἐξώτερον}}$$

"They will be cast into the *outer* darkness" (Mt 8:12). Or, note this substantival function as subject of this copulative sentence:

$$\underline{\text{ὁ}} \text{ δὲ } \underline{\text{μικρότερος}} \text{ ἐν τῇ βασιλείᾳ τῶν οὐρανῶν μείζων αὐτοῦ}$$
$$\text{ἐστιν}$$

"But *the least* in the kingdom of heaven is greater than he" (Mt 11:11). As a mirror image, note this substantival function as predicate adjective in this copulative construction:

$$\text{τί γάρ ἐστιν } \underline{\text{εὐκοπώτερον}}$$

"For which is *easier*?" Jesus asked, in reference to pronouncing healing or pronouncing forgiveness (Mt 9:5).

Numerals

Numbers are used as adjectives and adverbs. Numbers can be broken down into cardinal, ordinal, and adverbial categories.

Cardinal Numbers

Cardinal numbers are the counting numbers. The formulation patterns are logical. These patterns can be subdivided into singles (1–10), teen units (11, 12, 13, etc.), ten units (20, 30, 40, etc.), hundred units (100, 200, 300, etc.), and thousand units (1000, 2000, 3000, etc.). Units use vocabulary words and suffixes.

Table 8.6 Cardinals: Unit Divisions

Singles	Teen Units	Ten Units	Hundred Units	Thousand Units	Ten Thousand	Above
(Vocab.)	δέκα	εἴκοσι	ἑκατόν	χίλιοι	μύριοι	μυριάδες
---	δέκα +	-κοντα	-κοσιοι	-χιλιοι	---	---

Singles (vocabulary)

Only the first four cardinals are declined. (Those above two hundred are declined too.) The other single units (5, 6, 7, etc.) are simply vocabulary words to learn.

The number one is only singular. The numbers two, three, and four are only plural. The number one is third declension singular in masculine and neuter, first declension singular in feminine. The number two winds up in only two case forms, and these two are used for all genders. The number three is similar to ἱερεύς in the masculine/feminine plural and to σῶμα in the neuter plural. The number four is similar to σωτήρ in the masculine/feminine plural and to σῶμα in the neuter plural.

Teen Units (δέκα, δέκα +)

The base unit is δέκα. Formulations add to the base. The numeral added can be as a prefix, as in ἕνδεκα, or as a suffix, as in δεκατρεῖς. A more pedantic method simply combines units with καί, as in ἑπτά καὶ δέκα. Formulations are not fixed. One might encounter δεκαοκτώ or δέκα καὶ ὀκτώ; compare these two variations in Lk 13:4, 11 and 13:16.

Ten Units (εἴκοσι, -κοντα)

The number twenty is its own word (εἴκοσι). Since the twenty unit is its own word, one can form other numbers in the twenties

by: (1) placing the smaller numeral first joined to εἴκοσι with
καί, as in δύο καὶ εἴκοσι; (2) placing the εἴκοσι first and
joining the smaller number with καί, as in εἴκοσι καὶ δύο; or
(3) placing the εἴκοσι first and the smaller number second without καί, as in εἴκοσι δύο.

All other ten units above twenty use a -κοντα suffix. Thus, we
have τριάκοντα, τεσσεράκοντα, etc. Other numbers are given by
addition. That is, to these ten units are added the basic numbers,
for example, τριάκοντα εἷς.

One Hundred Units (ἑκατόν, -κοσιοι)

The number one hundred is its own word (ἑκατόν). All other
hundred units above one hundred use a -κοσιοι suffix. Thus, we
have διακόσιοι, τριακόσιοι, etc. These hundred intervals are
declined on the δίκαιος, -α, -ον adjective pattern. The declension, naturally, is plural only. Other numbers above each unit are
played out in Greek exactly as spoken out in English. Thus, "one
hundred twenty three" is ἑκατὸν εἴκοσι τρεῖς.

One Thousand Units (χίλιοι, -χιλιοι)

The number one thousand is its own word (χίλιοι). All other
thousand units above one thousand use a -χιλιοι suffix. Thus, we
have δισχίλιοι, τρισκίλιοι, etc. The declension, naturally, is
plural only. Other numbers above each unit are played out in Greek
exactly as spoken out in English. Thus, "two thousand thirty three"
is δισχίλιοι τριάκοντα τρεῖς.

An alternate form for one thousand is the word χιλιάδες,
which occurs twenty-three times in the New Testament, but almost
exclusively in Revelation.[1] This word can be found in context with
a number or a series of numbers for which χιλιάδες is the maximum unit. Note the following: ἔπεσαν μιᾷ ἡμέρᾳ εἴκοσι τρεῖς
χιλιάδες, "*twenty-three thousand* fell in one day" (1 Cor 10:8).

---

[1]With the exception of Lk 14:31 (2x); Acts 4:4; and 1 Cor 10:8.

Ten Thousand (μύριοι)

The number ten thousand is its own word (μύριοι). Greeks did not have interval units above ten thousand. In the New Testament, this particular form occurs only once, at Mt 18:24.

Above Ten Thousand (μυριάδες)

Greeks did not have a cardinal unit above ten thousand. The force of a number in the thousands, however, also was carried by another term, μυριάς, μυριάδες, from which English derives the term "myriads." This term was not a specific unit but a generic term used quite flexibly. Its translation has to be by context on a case-by-case basis. Sometimes the idea is "thousands." Sometimes a number is included to be multiplied to the μυριάδες, as if the μυριάδες is to be taken as a stand-in number for the ten thousand number (μύριοι). The following are illustrative examples:

- ἐπισυναχθεισῶν <u>τῶν μυριάδων</u> τοῦ ὄχλου = "the crowd was gathered *by the thousands*" (Lk 12:1)
- πόσαι <u>μυριάδες</u> εἰσὶν = "how many *thousands* there are" (Acts 21:20)
- εὗρον ἀργυρίου <u>μυριάδας πέντε</u> = "it was found to be *fifty thousand* silver pieces" (Acts 19:19)
- ἀλλὰ προσεληλύθατε . . . <u>μυριάσιν</u> ἀγγέλων = "but you have come . . . *to innumerable* angels" (Heb 12:22)
- ἰδοὺ ἦλθεν κύριος ἐν ἁγίαις <u>μυριάσιν</u> αὐτοῦ = "Behold, the Lord comes with *ten thousands* of his holy ones" (Jude 14)
- καὶ ἦν ὁ ἀριθμὸς αὐτῶν <u>μυριάδες μυριάδων</u> καὶ χιλιάδες χιλιάδων = "and their number was *myriads of myriads* and thousands of thousands"; or, another translation might be "*ten thousand times ten thousand*" (Rev 5:11)
- καὶ ὁ ἀριθμὸς τῶν στρατευμάτων τοῦ ἱππικοῦ <u>δισμυριάδες μυριάδων</u> = "and the number of cavalry troops was *two hundred million*" (Rev 9:16)

Study the following New Testament examples of the formation of cardinal numbers. Inflection patterns represent the function of the number in each context.

1. ἑκατὸν εἴκοσι = "one hundred twenty" (Acts 1:15)
2. διακόσιαι ἑβδομήκοντα ἕξ = "two hundred seventy-six" (Acts 27:37)
3. τετρακοσίος καὶ πεντήκοντα = "four hundred and fifty" (Acts 13:20)
4. ἑξακόσιοι ἑξήκοντα ἕξ = "six hundred sixty-six" (Rev 13:18)
5. χιλίας διακοσίας ἑξήκοντα = "one thousand two hundred sixty (Rev 11:3)
6. χιλιάδες ἑπτὰ = "seven thousand" (Rev 11:13)
7. δώδεκα χιλιάδες = "twelve thousand" (Rev 7:5)
8. ἑκατὸν τεσσεράκοντα τέσσαρες χιλιάδες = "one hundred forty-four thousand" (Rev 7:4)

Paradigms for the numbers one to four are given below. Notice that, with the exception of the feminine form of the number one, all paradigms follow third declension patterns. The inflection of two hundred and above is first and second declension.

Table 8.7 Numerals: One (3rd/3rd/1st Declension)

εἷς (mas.)		ἕν (neu.)		μία (fem.)	
Singular	Plural	Singular	Plural	Singular	Plural
εἷς	-------	ἕν	-------	μία	-------
ἑνός	-------	ἑνός	-------	μιᾶς	-------
ἑνί	-------	ἑνί	-------	μιᾷ	-------
ἕνα	-------	ἕν	-------	μίαν	-------

Table 8.8 Numerals: Two (3rd Declension)

δύο (mas.)		δύο (fem.)		δύο (neu.)	
Singular	*Plural*	*Singular*	*Plural*	*Singular*	*Plural*
-------	δύο	-------	δύο	-------	δύο
-------	δύο	-------	δύο	-------	δύο
-------	δυσί	-------	δυσί	-------	δυσί
-------	δύο	-------	δύο	-------	δύο

Table 8.9 Numerals: Three (3rd Declension)

τρεῖς (mas.)		τρεῖς (fem.)		τρία (neu.)	
Singular	*Plural*	*Singular*	*Plural*	*Singular*	*Plural*
-------	τρεῖς	-------	τρεῖς	-------	τρία
-------	τριῶν	-------	τριῶν	-------	τριῶν
-------	τρισί	-------	τρισί	-------	τρισί
-------	τρεῖς	-------	τρεῖς	-------	τρία

Table 8.10 Numerals: Four (3rd Declension)

τέσσαρες (mas.)		τέσσαρες (fem.)		τέσσαρες (neu.)	
Singular	*Plural*	*Singular*	*Plural*	*Singular*	*Plural*
-------	τέσσαρες	-------	τέσσαρες	-------	τέσσαρα
-------	τεσσάρων	-------	τεσσάρων	-------	τεσσάρων
-------	τέσσαρσι	-------	τέσσαρσι	-------	τέσσαρσι
-------	τέσσαρας	-------	τέσσαρας	-------	τέσσαρα

Table 8.11 Numerals: Two Hundred and Units (like δίκαιος)

200 (mas.)		200 (neu.)		200 (fem.)	
Singular	*Plural*	*Singular*	*Plural*	*Singular*	*Plural*
------	διακόσιοι	------	διακόσια	------	διακόσιαι
------	διακοσίων	------	διακοσίων	------	διακοσίων
------	διακοσίοις	------	διακοσίοις	------	διακοσίαις
------	διακοσίους	------	διακόσια	------	διακοσίας

Ordinal Numbers

Adjective Inflection

Ordinal numbers are the ordering numbers. Ordinals follow the pattern of the adjective ἀγαθός, -ή, -όν, except for δεύτερος. This stem ends in -ρ, so follows that of the adjective δίκαιος, -α, -ον (feminine in -α). Both alternate forms are illustrated in:

κἂν ἐν τῇ <u>δευτέρᾳ</u> κἂν ἐν τῇ <u>τρίτῃ</u> φυλακῇ ἔλθῃ

The translation is: "and whether he should come in the *second* or even in the *third* watch" (Lk 12:38). An articular ordinal grammatically functions as an adjectival substantive. This means the ordinal stands in the place of a noun, such as the subject, direct object, etc. An example is:

ἐγώ εἰμι <u>ὁ πρῶτος</u> καὶ ὁ ἔσχατος

Notice in this example, "I am *the first* and the last" (Rev 1:17), that the articular ordinal (ὁ πρῶτος) has the same substantival function as the following articular adjective (ὁ ἔσχατος) found standing alone (i.e., used substantivally).

Table 8.12 Numerals: Ordinals (like ἀγαθός, δίκαιος)

| πρῶτος (mas.) | | πρῶτον (neu.) | | πρώτη (fem.) | |
Singular	Plural	Singular	Plural	Singular	Plural
πρῶτος	πρῶτοι	πρῶτον	πρῶτα	πρώτη	πρῶται
πρώτου	πρώτων	πρώτου	πρώτων	πρώτης	πρώτων
πρώτῳ	πρώτοις	πρώτῳ	πρώτοις	πρώτῃ	πρώταις
πρῶτον	πρώτους	πρῶτον	πρῶτα	πρώτην	πρώτας

Idiomatic Usage

In English the ordinal "first" is used with many nuances, including priority, rank, status, and so forth. Greek is similar, so context is a key for translation of πρῶτος. The term πρῶτον is used as an adverb (hence, not declined) with the varied meanings "first," "in the first place," "above all else," "earlier," "to begin with" and so on. Note the following:

ζητεῖτε δὲ <u>πρῶτον</u> τὴν βασιλείαν [τοῦ θεοῦ] καὶ τὴν δικαιοσύνην αὐτοῦ

Here, the idea is more than simple ordering—first, second, and so forth. The idea is life priority, more like: "But *above all else*, seek the kingdom and His righteousness" (Mt 6:33). Another illustrative use is: <u>πρῶτον</u> λέγετε, Εἰρήνη τῷ οἴκῳ τούτῳ, "*first* say, 'Peace to this house!'" (Lk 10:5).

An adverb form of πρῶτος is πρώτως, meaning, "for the first time." This adverb form is found only at Acts 11:26: χρηματίσαι τε <u>πρώτως</u> ἐν Ἀντιοχείᾳ τοὺς μαθητὰς Χριστιανούς, "the disciples *first* were called Christians in Antioch."

Adverbials

Adverbials quantify the frequency of verbal action with the terms "once" and "twice." Archaic English used to have another term, "thrice," but this word has dropped out of spoken English today. After "twice," English idiom reverts to a cardinal number and the word "times," such as "three times," "four times," etc. As adverbs, adverbials are not declined. Thus:

πρὶν ἢ <u>δὶς</u> ἀλέκτορα φωνῆσαι <u>τρίς</u> με ἀπαρνήσῃ

The meaning is, "before the rooster crows *twice*, you will deny me *three times*" (Mk 14:30).

One should distinguish the grammatical roles of adverbials and ordinals. Adverbials such as "once" are adverbs. They would diagram under the verb. Ordinals such as "first" are adjectives. They would diagram under the noun modified, if attributive, or in the place of a noun if substantival.

EXERCISE 8

1. Answer the following on Greek cardinal numbers.

    1.1 Matching (list continues on next page)

    ___ 1. Single units   a. ἑκατόν, -κοσιοι

    ___ 2. Teen units   b. μύριοι

    ___ 3. Ten units   c. χιλιάδες

    ___ 4. Hundred units   d. μυριάδες

    ___ 5. Thousand units   e. vocabulary

_____ 6. Alternate 1000   f. εἴκοσι, -κοντα

_____ 7. Ten thousand   g. χίλιοι, -χιλιοι

_____ 8. Above   h. δέκα, δέκα +

1.2 _____ With the lone exception of feminine gender for the numeral one, the cardinal numbers one to four are all inflected according to what declension?

1.3 _____ What Greek numeral actually has only two inflected forms?

2. Answer the following on Greek ordinal numbers.

   2.1 _____ Ordinals follow the inflection pattern of what adjective?

   2.2 _____ An articular ordinal functions in what adjectival role?

   2.3 _____ Which ordinal number is quite flexible in meaning and has to be handled idiomatically in context?

3. Answer the following on Greek adverbial numbers.

   3.1 _____ What do adverbials do to the frequency of verbal action?

   3.2 _____ What are the only two adverbial numbers remaining in the English language?

   3.3 _____ What does English do to express verbal frequency beyond these two adverbials?

4. Answer the following on adjective comparisons.

   4.1 _____ What are the two suffixes for adjective comparisons following first and second declension inflection?

4.2 _____ What are the two suffixes for adjective comparisons following third declension inflection?

4.3 Matching (irregular comparisons):

_____ 1. ἀγαθός   a. μείζων

_____ 2. κακός   b. πλείων

_____ 3. μέγας   c. χείρων

_____ 4. πολύς   d. κρείττων

5. Answer the following on adverb comparisons.

    5.1 _____ What is the suffix for the comparative adverb?

    5.2 _____ What are two possible suffixes for the superlative adverb?

    5.3 _____ Which word actually represents 12 of the 15 occurrences of the superlative adverb in the NT?

6. Answer the following on methods of comparisons.

    6.1 Define ellipsis:

    _____

    6.2 What does ellipsis have to do with comparisons?

    _____

    6.3 _____ What Greek conjunction means "than" when used in comparisons?

    6.4 _____ What two cases are used when the Greek conjunction is not used for comparison?

6.5 _____ Which two prepositions are used in one of these cases to express comparison?

7. Translate the following and be prepared to analyze the grammar of comparisons and numbers:

7.1   νηστεύω δὶς τοῦ σαββάτου (Lk 18:12)

_____

7.2   καὶ αὐτὴ χήρα ἕως ἐτῶν ὀγδοήκοντα τεσσάρων (Lk 2:37)

_____

7.3   καὶ καθελὼν ἔθνη ἑπτὰ ἐν γῇ Χανάαν

κατεκληρονόμησεν τὴν γῆν αὐτῶν ὡς ἔτεσιν

τετρακοσίοις καὶ πεντήκοντα. (Acts 13:20)

7.4   καὶ ὁ Κορνήλιος ἔφη· ἀπὸ τετάρτης ἡμέρας μέχρι

ταύτης τῆς ὥρας ἤμην τὴν ἐνάτην προσευχόμενος

ἐν τῷ οἴκῳ μου (Acts 10:30)

7.5   καὶ τοὺς πλείονας τῶν ἀδελφῶν ἐν κυρίῳ

πεποιθόταςτοῖς δεσμοῖς μου περισσοτέρως τολμᾶν

ἀφόβως τὸν λόγον λαλεῖν. (Phil 1:14)

_____

7.6 ὃς ἐὰν οὖν λύσῃ μίαν τῶν ἐντολῶν τούτων τῶν

ἐλαχίστων καὶ διδάξῃ οὕτως τοὺς ἀνθρώπους,

ἐλάχιστος κληθήσεται ἐν τῇ βασιλείᾳ τῶν

οὐρανῶν· (Mt 5:19)

𒀭𒀭𒀭𒀭𒀭𒀭 MANUSCRIPTS 6 𒀭𒀭𒀭𒀭𒀭𒀭

The ending of Mark's Gospel varies in our Greek manuscripts. In several of our ancient uncial manuscripts Mark ends at 16:8 with the word ΓΑΡ (γάρ), as with both Codex Sinaiticus and Codex Vaticanus. Note in Vaticanus below how the typical text decoration showing the end of a book is drawn. The usual closing notation is seen in ΚΑΤΑ ΜΑΡΚΟΝ (κατὰ Μᾶρκον) = "According to Mark." Finally, as is the normal procedure at the end of a book, the rest of that column is left blank (and the entire last column of that page in the case of Mark; see Fig. 8, p. 94). On the next page the Gospel of Luke begins. These decorative markings and empty columns show how the scribe concluded Mark's Gospel. Notice that no notations of any kind are given to indicate that the scribe thought any verses were missing after Mk 16:8.

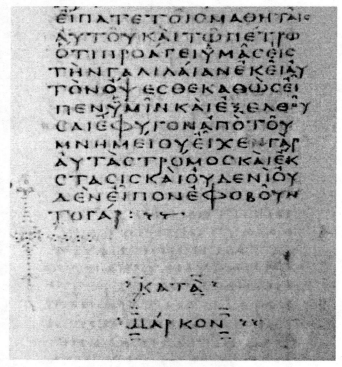

Fig. 9. Codex Vaticaus at Mk 16:7-8.

CHAPTER 9
PRONOUNS

The twelve Greek pronoun categories can be grouped into four systems: personal, demonstrative, relative, and interrogative. The personal system refers. The demonstrative points. The relative relates. The interrogative asks.

Pronouns can take the place of nouns to avoid monotony. The substituted noun is called the *antecedent*. The pronoun will agree with the antecedent in gender and number. On the other hand:

♦ *Pronoun case is determined by its grammatical function.*

Some pronouns can be used as adjectives. Such use includes all three of the adjective functions: attributive, substantival, and predicative. In regards to the standard adjective function:

♦ *Attributive adjectival pronouns show full concord.*

Personal System

The personal system refers to person in some manner. These pronouns break down into seven basic categories: personal ("I"), intensive ("myself"), possessive ("my"), reflexive ("myself"), reciprocal ("ourselves"), indefinite ("someone"), and negative ("no one") pronouns. The following table provides a synopsis of this personal system. Use of italics for the type of pronoun indicates that we have no distinct English pronouns as counterparts. English uses some other device to communicate the idea. After the table, a brief discussion of each personal system category is given. The basic usage of the category is outlined, as well as any pertinent idiomatic constructions.

Table 9.1 Pronouns: Personal System

Type	English	Greek
Personal	I	ἐγώ
	we	ἡμεῖς
	you (s)	σύ
	you (p)	ὑμεῖς
	he, she, it	αὐτός, -ή, -ό
	they	αὐτοί, -αί, -ά
• Intensive	-self	αὐτός, -ή, -ό
	the same	ὁ (αὐτός, -ή, -ό)
• Possessive	my	ἐμός, ἐμή, ἐμόν
	our	ἡμέτερος, -α, -ον
	your (s)	σός, σή, σόν
	your (p)	ὑμέτερος, -α, -ον
	his, her, its	[ἴδιος, -α, -ον]
	their	[ἴδιοι, -αι, -α]
• Reflexive	myself	ἐμαυτοῦ, -ῆς, --
	ourselves	ἑαυτῶν, -ῶν, --
	yourself	σεαυτοῦ, -ῆς, --
	yourselves	ἑαυτῶν, -ῶν, --
	himself (etc.)	ἑαυτοῦ, -ῆς, -οῦ
	themselves	ἑαυτῶν, -ῶν, --
• Reciprocal	one another	ἀλλήλων, -οις, -ους
• Indefinite	someone (s)	τις, τις, τι
	someone (p)	τινές, τινές, τινά
• Negative	no one	οὐδείς, οὐδεμία, οὐδέν

Personal Pronouns ("I")

Table 9.2 Personal Pronouns: First and Second

First Person		Second Person	
Singular	*Plural*	*Singular*	*Plural*
(I, me)	*(we, us)*	*(you)*	*(you)*
ἐγώ	ἡμεῖς	σύ	ὑμεῖς
ἐμοῦ (μου)	ἡμῶν	σοῦ (σου)	ὑμῶν
ἐμοί (μοι)	ἡμῖν	σοί (σοι)	ὑμῖν
ἐμέ (με)	ἡμᾶς	σέ (σε)	ὑμᾶς

Table 9.3 Personal Pronouns: Third

Third: Masculine		Third: Neuter		Third: Feminine	
Singular	*Plural*	*Singular*	*Plural*	*Singular*	*Plural*
(he, him)	*(they, them)*	*(it)*	*(they, them)*	*(she, her)*	*(they, them)*
αὐτός	αὐτοί	αὐτό	αὐτά	αὐτή	αὐταί
αὐτοῦ	αὐτῶν	αὐτοῦ	αὐτῶν	αὐτῆς	αὐτῶν
αὐτῷ	αὐτοῖς	αὐτῷ	αὐτοῖς	αὐτῇ	αὐταῖς
αὐτόν	αὐτούς	αὐτό	αὐτά	αὐτήν	αὐτάς

Basic Usage

Personal pronouns often stand for the subject of the verb. First person is the person speaking. Second person is the person spoken to. Third person is the person spoken about. English personal pronouns distinguish in form between the nominative and objective, or *oblique*, cases (genitive, dative, accusative). For example, the nominative is "I," but the objective is "me"; nominative is "we," but the objective is "us"; etc. English *second* person does *not* make this distinction (both nominative and objective is "you").

Greek first and second personal pronouns do not show gender, just like English ("I," "you"). English third person *singular* shows gender ("he," "she," "it"), but not the plural ("they"). *All* Greek third person forms, in contrast, show gender. Inflection is close to the adjective ἀγαθός. First and second person have enclitic forms (μου, σου, etc.), but these forms do not affect translation. The third person *neuter* shows a "pronoun pattern"—the dropping of the final -ν in neuter nominative and accusative singular forms.

♦ *The "pronoun pattern" is the dropping of the neuter -ν.*

Subject Emphasis

The verb has the subject built in by inflection. Restating the subject with a personal pronoun of the same person and number as the verb is often for emphasis. By default, this *emphatic* pronoun will be *nominative* and *anarthrous*. Koine Greek was beginning to overuse personal pronouns with the verb, especially third person. So, evaluating true subject emphasis is contextually driven. Note:

Ὑμεῖς ἐστε τὸ ἅλας τῆς γῆς

"*You* are the salt of the earth" (Mt 5:13).

Intensive Pronouns ("-self," "the same")

The *intensive* pronoun really is just the *third* personal pronoun (αὐτός) kidnapped to play two other roles besides its normal "he, she, it" role. One role is intensifying a substantive, the equivalent of a using reflexive pronoun ("-self"). The other role intensifies a substantive with the equivalent of the adjective "the same." These uses are idiomatic for which English has no comparison. Therefore, the English student will have to work hard to assimilate these uses and spot them in the Greek text. One tip off is that the presence of the third person pronoun simply does not translate easily in the context, and a literal wording becomes almost nonsensical.

Reflexive Intensification ("-self")

The effect is like a reflexive pronoun in English ("-self"). The third person pronoun is put in concord with a substantive nearby to intensify the substantive. This third person pronoun is *anarthrous* and shows only case and number concord. (Obviously, since the third person pronoun is used, the person always is third person.) If nominative, the third person pronoun could be intensifying the subject of the verb—that is, going one step beyond emphasizing the subject (i.e., repetition with the personal pronoun *in the same person and number*, as described above). Thus, the subject of the verb can be expressed in four grammatical levels in Greek:

Table 9.4 Verb Subject: Four Grammatical Levels

Type	Greek	English
1. Inflected:	γινώσκω	"I know"
2. Emphatic:	ἐγὼ γινώσκω	"*I* know"
3. Intensive:	αὐτὸς γινώσκω	"I *myself* know"
4. Doubled:	<u>αὐτὸς</u> <u>ἐγὼ</u> γινώσκω	"*I* <u>*myself*</u> know"

Notice the resulting effect like a double-barrel shotgun approach in the doubled, emphatic + intensive construction in the following:

<u>αὐτοὶ</u> <u>ὑμεῖς</u> μοι μαρτυρεῖτε

"<u>*You*</u> <u>*yourselves*</u> are my witnesses!" (Jn 3:28). One can detect the intense rhetoric conveyed by the Greek grammar.

For other examples of reflexive intensification of a substantive using the third personal pronoun, study the following:

1. <u>αὐτὸν</u> οἶμαι τὸν κόσμον = "I suppose the world *itself*" (Jn 21:25)
2. καθὼς <u>αὐτοὶ</u> οἴδατε = "just as you *yourselves* know" (Acts 2:22)

3. αὐτοὶ γὰρ οἴδατε ὅτι εἰς τοῦτο κείμεθα = "for you *yourselves* know we were destined for this" (1 Thess 3:3)
4. αὐτὸς ἤμην ἐφεστὼς = "I *myself* was standing by" (Acts 22:20)
5. αὐτὴ ἡ κτίσις ἐλευθερωθήσεται = "creation *itself* will be freed" (Rom 8:21)
6. αὐτό τε τὸ βιβλίον = "both the book *itself*" (Heb 9:19)

Adjectival Intensification ("the same")

Notice how the English adjective "same" regularly is used with the article: "I bought *the same* book." In a similar way, put the article with the third person pronoun in concord with a substantive nearby and you have the equivalent of the English adjective "the same." The third personal pronoun is conscripted to intensify the substantive adjectivally. The key is that the third personal pronoun is articular. Hence:

♦ *Adjectival intensification always is articular.*

The following phrase from Heb 10:1 illustrates the idea:

ταῖς αὐταῖς θυσίαις

This phrase would be translated, "by *the same* sacrifices." You can suspect you might be dealing with this idiom of adjectival intensification when the literal translation makes no sense: "by *the them* sacrifices"?

Possessive Pronouns ("my")

Possessive pronouns are uncommon in the New Testament, the third person being absent altogether. Most frequent are inflected forms of the first person singular ἐμός.[1] The preferred method was a genitive *personal* pronoun (e.g., μου, σου, ἡμῶν, ὑμῶν, αὐτοῦ, αὐτῆς, αὐτῶν). Possessive pronouns, however, unlike personal, express possession inherently, not only by the genitive case. Such pronouns really are adjectives: (1) they maintain *full concord* and (2) always are *attributive*. Four observations on form follow:

1. First, *even singular forms of possessive pronouns have plural inflection in order to show plural concord*. English is not so (cf. "my book," "my books"). So, *singular* possessive pronouns can have *plural* inflection—if the noun modified is plural. However, these plural inflections will not have plural translation into English. For example, the singular form τὸν ἐμὸν οἶκον translates as "*my* house," but the plural form τοὺς ἐμοὺς οἴκους also still translates as "*my*," as in "*my* houses."

2. Second, plural pronoun inflections are almost exact copies of each other, except for the first letter. Compare the forms ἡμέτερος and ὑμέτερος. This similarity is like first and second person plural pronouns (cf. ἡμεῖς and ὑμεῖς).

3. Third, *Greek possessive pronouns have no third person forms*. Instead, the *personal* pronoun is used, thrown into genitive case. In addition, an alternate method uses the *adjective*, ἴδιος, with possessive force: "his own," "her own," "its own" (for forms, see "Paradigms," p. 496). This alternate method makes the possession emphatic. Observe these examples: ἀγαπήσας τοὺς ἰδίους, "having loved *his own*" (Jn 13:1); ἐν τῷ ἰδίῳ ὀφθαλμῷ, "in *his own* eye" (Lk 6:41); ὑπὸ τῆς ἰδίας ἐπιθυμία, "by *his own* lust" (Jas 1:14).

4. Fourth, English distinguishes possessive pronouns employed as nouns rather than as adjectives. The suffix "s" is added,

---

[1]Seventy-six times in the New Testament, over half in John's Gospel (forty-one). Forms of σός twenty-six times; ἡμέτερος seven times; ὑμέτερος eleven times.

creating "yours," "ours," "hers," and "theirs." (However, contrast the first person singular, "mine." The neuter "its" is an adjective, not a pronoun.) For example: "The choice is *yours*." "The decision was *mine*." "*Ours* were the only votes." Greek does not make this inflectional distinction between noun and adjective roles for possessive pronouns. Still, possessive constructions can be translated with these alternate English forms as appropriate to the context. Notice 1 Cor 1:2, αὐτῶν καὶ ἡμῶν, "*theirs* and *ours*." Again, Mt 5:3, αὐτῶν ἐστιν ἡ βασιλεία τῶν οὐρανῶν = "*theirs* is the kingdom of heaven."

Table 9.5 Possessive Pronouns: First Singular ("my")

Masculine		Neuter		Feminine	
Singular	*Plural*	*Singular*	*Plural*	*Singular*	*Plural*
ἐμός	ἐμοί	ἐμόν	ἐμά	ἐμή	ἐμαί
ἐμοῦ	ἐμῶν	ἐμοῦ	ἐμῶν	ἐμῆς	ἐμῶν
ἐμῷ	ἐμοῖς	ἐμῷ	ἐμοῖς	ἐμῇ	ἐμαῖς
ἐμόν	ἐμούς	ἐμόν	ἐμά	ἐμήν	ἐμάς

Table 9.6 Possessive Pronouns: First Plural ("our")

Masculine		Neuter		Feminine	
Singular	*Plural*	*Singular*	*Plural*	*Singular*	*Plural*
ἡμέτερος	ἡμέτεροι	ἡμέτερον	ἡμέτερα	ἡμετέρα	ἡμέτεραι
ἡμετέρου	ἡμετέρων	ἡμετέρου	ἡμετέρων	ἡμετέρας	ἡμετέρων
ἡμετέρῳ	ἡμετέροις	ἡμετέρῳ	ἡμετέροις	ἡμετέρα	ἡμετέραις
ἡμέτερον	ἡμετέρους	ἡμέτερον	ἡμέτερα	ἡμετέραν	ἡμετέρας

Table 9.7 Possessive Pronouns: Second Singular ("your")

Masculine		Neuter		Feminine	
Singular	*Plural*	*Singular*	*Plural*	*Singular*	*Plural*
σός	σοί	σόν	σά	σή	σαί
σοῦ	σῶν	σοῦ	σῶν	σῆς	σῶν
σῷ	σοῖς	σῷ	σοῖς	σῇ	σαῖς
σόν	σούς	σόν	σά	σήν	σάς

Table 9.8 Possessive Pronouns: Second Plural ("your")

Masculine		Neuter		Feminine	
Singular	*Plural*	*Singular*	*Plural*	*Singular*	*Plural*
ὑμέτερος	ὑμέτεροι	ὑμέτερον	ὑμέτερα	ὑμετέρα	ὑμέτεραι
ὑμετέρου	ὑμετέρων	ὑμετέρου	ὑμετέρων	ὑμετέρας	ὑμετέρων
ὑμετέρῳ	ὑμετέροις	ὑμετέρῳ	ὑμετέροις	ὑμετέρα	ὑμετέραις
ὑμέτερον	ὑμετέρους	ὑμέτερον	ὑμέτερα	ὑμετέραν	ὑμετέρας

Reflexive Pronouns ("myself")

This pronoun intensifies a substantive, often the subject. (This role also can be achieved by the *intensive* pronoun.) One can see in the formation a combination of ἐμέ and σέ with the objective cases of αὐτός. Only third person includes neuter forms. Within a gender, *plural forms are the same for any person*. Examples are:

1. ἀφ᾽ ἑαυτῶν γινώσκετε = "you can know for *yourselves*" (Lk 21:30)
2. ἐβουλόμην πρὸς ἐμαυτὸν κατέχειν = "I wished to retain for *myself*" (Phlm 13)
3. Σὺ περὶ σεαυτοῦ μαρτυρεῖς = "You are bearing witness about *yourself*" (Jn 8:13)

4. θησαυρίζεις <u>σεαυτῷ</u> ὀργὴν = "you are storing up wrath for *yourself*" (Rom 2:5)

5. ἁγνίζει <u>ἑαυτὸν</u> καθὼς ἐκεῖνος ἁγνός ἐστιν = "he purifies *himself* just as that one is pure" (1 Jn 3:3)

Table 9.9 Reflexive Pronouns: 1st ("myself," "ourselves")

| Masculine | | Neuter | | Feminine | |
Singular	Plural	Singular	Plural	Singular	Plural
---------	---------	---------	---------	---------	---------
ἐμαυτοῦ	ἑαυτῶν	---------	---------	ἐμαυτῆς	ἑαυτῶν
ἐμαυτῷ	ἑαυτοῖς	---------	---------	ἐμαυτῇ	ἑαυταῖς
ἐμαυτόν	ἑαυτούς	---------	---------	ἐμαυτήν	ἑαυτάς

Table 9.10 Reflexive Pronouns: 2nd ("yourself," "yourselves")

| Masculine | | Neuter | | Feminine | |
Singular	Plural	Singular	Plural	Singular	Plural
---------	---------	---------	---------	---------	---------
σεαυτοῦ	ἑαυτῶν	---------	---------	σεαυτῆς	ἑαυτῶν
σεαυτῷ	ἑαυτοῖς	---------	---------	σεαυτῇ	ἑαυταῖς
σεαυτόν	ἑαυτούς	---------	---------	σεαυτήν	ἑαυτάς

Table 9.11 Reflexive Pronouns: 3rd ("himself," "themselves")

| Masculine | | Neuter | | Feminine | |
Singular	Plural	Singular	Plural	Singular	Plural
---------	---------	---------	---------	---------	---------
ἑαυτοῦ	ἑαυτῶν	ἑαυτοῦ	ἑαυτῶν	ἑαυτῆς	ἑαυτῶν
ἑαυτῷ	ἑαυτοῖς	ἑαυτῷ	ἑαυτοῖς	ἑαυτῇ	ἑαυταῖς
ἑαυτόν	ἑαυτούς	ἑαυτό	ἑαυτά	ἑαυτήν	ἑαυτάς

Reciprocal Pronouns ("one another")

Only masculine and only plural, the reciprocal pronoun has only three inflected forms in the New Testament: ἀλλήλων, ἀλλήλοις, and ἀλλήλους. The repetitive opening part of each inflection gives a hint of their origin, which is the doubling of the stem of the adjective ἄλλος, "other." Thus:

1. ἐσμὲν ἀλλήλων μέλη = "we are members *of one another*" (Eph 4:25)
2. ἀλλήλους προκαλούμενοι, ἀλλήλοις φθονοῦντες = "irritating *one another*, envying *one another*" (Gal 5:26)

Indefinite Pronouns ("someone")

Table 9.12 Indefinite Pronouns ("someone")

Mas./Fem.		Neuter	
Singular	*Plural*	*Singular*	*Plural*
τις	τινές	τι	τινά
τινός	τινῶν	τινός	τινῶν
τινί	τισί(ν)	τινί	τισί(ν)
τινά	τινάς	τι	τινά

These pronouns clone the interrogative, but are enclitic (no accent in composition; only table forms have accent). Inflection is third declension: masculine and feminine are the same, and *all* interiors are the same. Substantive use translates as "someone" (ἔρχεταί τις = "*someone* comes"). Adjective use translates as "a certain . . ." (ἄνθρωπός τις = "*a certain* man"). As examples:

1. ἄνθρωπός τις εἶχεν δύο υἱούς = "*a certain* man had two sons" (Lk 15:11)
2. ἐν τῷ εἶναι αὐτὸν ἐν τόπῳ τινὶ προσευχόμενον = "while he was praying in *a certain* place" (Lk 11:1)

3. λέγειν <u>τι</u> ἢ ἀκούειν <u>τι</u> καινότερον = "telling *anything* or hearing *anything* new" (Acts 17:21)

4. Εἰ δέ <u>τινες</u> τῶν κλάδων = "But if *some* of the branches" (Rom 11:17)

5. <u>τινας</u> περιπατοῦντας ἐν ὑμῖν ἀτάκτως = "*some* among you are acting lazy" (2 Thess 3:11)

Negative Pronouns ("no one")

Table 9.13 Negative Pronouns ("no one")

Masculine		Neuter		Feminine	
Singular	*Plural*	*Singular*	*Plural*	*Singular*	*Plural*
οὐδείς	-------	οὐδέν	-------	οὐδεμία	-------
οὐδενός	-------	οὐδενός	-------	οὐδεμιᾶς	-------
οὐδενί	-------	οὐδενί	-------	οὐδεμιᾷ	-------
οὐδένα	-------	οὐδέν	-------	οὐδεμίαν	-------

These pronouns are only singular ("no *one*"). Their morphology combines "one" in declined forms (εἷς, ἕν, μία) with the indicative mood negative particle οὐδέ ("not even"), or its subjunctive counterpart, μηδέ. Often, a negative pronoun can be constructed in any case to function as a substantive. Inflection mixes third and first declension:

1. <u>Μηδεὶς</u> πειραζόμενος λεγέτω = "Let *no one* say when he is tempted" (Jas 1:13a)

2. πειράζει δὲ αὐτὸς <u>οὐδένα</u> = "and he himself tempts *no one*" (Jas 1:13b)

3. <u>μηδεμίαν</u> ἐν <u>μηδενὶ</u> διδόντες προσκοπήν = "giving <u>*not even one*</u> cause for offense in <u>*anything*</u>" (2 Cor 6:3)

4. παρ᾽ <u>οὐδενὶ</u> τοσαύτην πίστιν ἐν τῷ Ἰσραὴλ εὗρον. = "Such great faith I have not found with *anyone* in Israel!" (Mt 8:10)

Table 9.14 Pronouns: The Other Three Systems

Type	English	Greek
Demonstrative	*this/these* (prox.)	οὗτος, αὕτη, τοῦτο
• Remote	*that/those*	ἐκεῖνος, -η, -ο
Relative	who	ὅς, ἥ, ὅ
• *Indefinite Rel.*	who/whoever	ὅστις, ἥτις, ὅτι
• *Correlative*	such so much as as much as	τοιοῦτος, -αύτη, -ο τοσοῦτος, -αύτη, -ο οἷος, οἷα, οἷον ὅσος, ὅσα, ὅσον
Interrogative	who?	τίς, τίς, τί (τίνες, τίνα)
• Qualitative	what type?	ποῖος, ποία, ποῖον
• Quantitative	how much?	πόσος, πόσα, πόσον

Besides the large group of pronouns in the personal system, the three other smaller systems are the demonstrative, relative, and interrogative. These systems are summarized in the table above. Italics means we have no distinct English pronouns as counterparts. A brief discussion of each system is given. The basic usage is outlined, as well as any pertinent idiomatic constructions.

Demonstrative System

The demonstrative system points out a grammatical element. This system has two categories: proximate and remote. These categories are abstractions, based on relative distance. Proximate is (relatively) near the speaker ("this"). Remote is (relatively) far from the speaker ("that"). Forms are similar to the third personal pronoun. Observe the neuter "pronoun pattern" in inflection (dropping of the -ν ending in nominative, accusative singular).

Proximate Demonstratives ("this")

Singular translates as "this," plural "these." *Masculine* and *feminine nominative* do not have the initial τ-. Inflection is second and first declension, but note the "pronoun pattern."

Table 9.15 Demonstrative Pronouns: Prox. ("this," "these")

Masculine		Neuter		Feminine	
Singular	*Plural*	*Singular*	*Plural*	*Singular*	*Plural*
οὗτος	οὗτοι	τοῦτο	ταῦτα	αὕτη	αὗται
τούτου	τούτων	τούτου	τούτων	ταύτης	τούτων
τούτῳ	τούτοις	τούτῳ	τούτοις	ταύτῃ	ταύταις
τοῦτον	τούτους	τοῦτο	ταῦτα	ταύτην	ταύτας

Examples of the proximate demonstrative are:
1. <u>οὗτος</u> καὶ τὸν πατέρα καὶ τὸν υἱὸν ἔχει = "*this one* has both the Father and the Son" (2 Jn 9)
2. τὸ πλοῦτος τῆς δόξης τοῦ μυστηρίου <u>τούτου</u> = "the riches of the glory of *this* mystery" (Col 1:27)
3. <u>Ταῦτα</u> λάλει καὶ παρακάλει καὶ ἔλεγχε = "*These things* speak and exhort and reprove" (Tit 2:15)

Remote Demonstratives ("that")

Table 9.16 Demonstative Pronouns: Remote ("that," "those")

Masculine		Neuter		Feminine	
Singular	*Plural*	*Singular*	*Plural*	*Singular*	*Plural*
ἐκεῖνος	ἐκεῖνοι	ἐκεῖνο	ἐκεῖνα	ἐκείνη	ἐκεῖναι
ἐκείνου	ἐκείνων	ἐκείνου	ἐκείνων	ἐκείνης	ἐκείνων
ἐκείνῳ	ἐκείνοις	ἐκείνῳ	ἐκείνοις	ἐκείνη	ἐκείναις
ἐκεῖνον	ἐκείνους	ἐκεῖνο	ἐκεῖνα	ἐκείνην	ἐκείνας

The remote demonstrative is a different word, unrelated in form to the proximate pronoun. Singular translates as "that," plural "those." Inflection is second and first declension, but note the "pronoun pattern" in the neuter forms.

Whether proximate or remote, the demonstrative pronoun can function adjectivally in predicate position (and is anarthrous). The following are examples of remote demonstrative pronouns:

1. τί ποιήσει τοῖς γεωργοῖς ἐκείνοις; = "What will he do to *those* vinegrowers?" (Mt 21:40)

2. μετὰ τὰς ἡμέρας ἐκείνας, λέγει κύριος = "after *those* days, says the Lord" (Heb 8:10)

3. ἀγοράζει τὸν ἀγρὸν ἐκεῖνον = "he buys *that* field" (Mt 13:44)

4. καὶ ἀπ᾽ ἐκείνης τῆς ὥρας ἔλαβεν ὁ μαθητὴς αὐτὴν = "and from *that* very hour the disciple took her" (Jn 19:27)

Relative System

The relative system has three categories: relative ("who"), indefinite relative ("whoever"), and correlative ("such"). Relative pronouns relate to a grammatical element as the antecedent. Observe the neuter "pronoun pattern" in all inflections.

Relative Pronouns ("who")

Table 9.17 Relative Pronouns ("who," "whom," "which")

Masculine		Neuter		Feminine	
Singular	*Plural*	*Singular*	*Plural*	*Singular*	*Plural*
ὅς	οἵ	ὅ	ἅ	ἥ	αἵ
οὗ	ὧν	οὗ	ὧν	ἧς	ὧν
ᾧ	οἷς	ᾧ	οἷς	ᾗ	αἷς
ὅν	οὕς	ὅ	ἅ	ἥν	ἅς

Relative pronoun inflection is similar to the article minus the τ but is *accented* with *rough breathing*. One should remember the phrase, "relatives are rough (and accented)." This observation will help you distinguish forms of the relative pronoun from other short words that have the same two or three letters—but either are not rough breathing, or if rough breathing, do not have accent. Notice the difference in the relative pronoun αἵ with its rough breathing and acute accent and the article αἱ with its rough breathing but no accent. Thus, <u>αἵ</u> εἰσιν <u>αἱ</u> προσευχαὶ τῶν ἁγίων, "<u>which</u> are <u>the</u> prayers of the saints" (Rev 5:8). So, remember:

♦ *Relatives are rough (and accented).*

The Greek relative pronoun distinguishes number as singular or plural to show concord with its antecedent. This distinction is lost in translation, however, since English does not ("the <u>man</u> *who*" versus "the <u>men</u> *who*").

Table 9.18 Relative Pronouns: Concord Versus Function

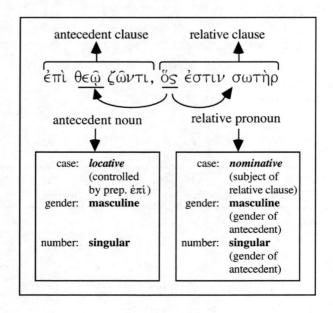

The relative pronoun introduces a dependent relative clause. A key issue with the relative pronoun is its case. Relative pronoun case is governed by the pronoun's *function within the relative clause*. Thus, if the relative pronoun is subject in its own clause, the relative pronoun will be nominative case, regardless the case of its antecedent, which could be dative, for example. So, one could have ἐπὶ θεῷ ζῶντι, ὅς ἐστιν σωτήρ, "in the living God, *who* is savior" (1 Tim 4:10). The relative pronoun, ὅς, is nominative because the pronoun is subject in its own clause, even though its antecedent, θεῷ, is dative.

One exception to relative pronoun case is "attraction." A word close to the relative pronoun seems to exert more influence on case than the pronoun's actual grammatical function in its own clause. The pronoun takes on the case of the grammatical element close by, sort of like a chameleon changing colors by proximity.

◆ *Relative pronouns always occur first in their clause.*

Relative pronouns always occur first in their clause, regardless of their grammatical function. Thus, a relative pronoun could be direct object in its clause, which in normal English order would be slot three (1-2-3, subject-verb-object). However, the pronoun even as direct object still will be positioned at the head of the clause. For example, in the expression, "the man *whom* you saw," the dependent clause, "*whom* you saw," is fronted by the relative pronoun, "whom." The pronoun here takes *objective* inflection ("whom," not "who") because the pronoun is *direct object* in its own clause. In English order, the direct object normally would be positioned in slot three: "you saw *whom*." This positive positioning of the relative pronoun is true both for English and for Greek.

Uncommon relative pronoun forms appearing in the New Testament are the following. The relative ὁποῖος ("as," "such as," "of what kind") occurs five times, as ὁποῖος (Acts 26:29; Jas 1:24), ὁποῖον (1 Cor 3:13), ὁποῖοι (Gal 2:6), and ὁποίαν (1 Thess

1:9). The relative ἡλίκος ("how great") occurs three times, as ἡλίκον (Col 2:1; Jas 3:5) and ἡλίκην (Jas 3:5). Finally, the relative πηλίκος ("how large") occurs just twice, as πηλίκοις (Gal 6:11) and πηλίκος (Heb 7:4).

Study the following examples. Identify illustrations of the relative pronoun positioned first regardless of its clause function:

1. εἷς θεὸς ὁ πατήρ ἐξ <u>οὗ</u> τὰ πάντα . . . καὶ εἷς κύριος Ἰησοῦς Χριστός δι' <u>οὗ</u> τὰ πάντα = "one God, the Father, *from whom* are all things . . . and one Lord, Jesus Christ, *through whom* are all things" (1 Cor 8:6)

2. Γνωρίζω δὲ ὑμῖν, ἀδελφοί, τὸ εὐαγγέλιον <u>ὃ</u> εὐηγγελισάμην ὑμῖν, <u>ὃ</u> καὶ παρελάβετε, ἐν <u>ᾧ</u> καὶ ἐστήκατε, δι' <u>οὗ</u> καὶ σῴζεσθε = "Now I make known to you, brothers, the gospel *which* I proclaimed to you, *which* also you received, *in which* also you stand, *through which* also you are being saved" (1 Cor 15:1-2)

3. <u>ἅ</u> ἐστιν σκιὰ = "*which* are a shadow" (Col 2:17; the antecedent occurs in previous elements of 2:16; note that the neuter plural subject takes a singular verb)

4. τὸ μυστήριον τῶν ἑπτὰ ἀστέρων <u>οὓς</u> εἶδες = "the mystery of the seven stars *which* you saw" (Rev 1:20)

5. φιάλας χρυσᾶς . . . <u>αἵ</u> εἰσιν αἱ προσευχαὶ τῶν ἁγίων = "golden bowls . . . *which* are the prayers of the saints" (Rev 5:8)

Indefinite Relative Pronouns ("whoever")

Table 9.19 Indefinite Relative Pronouns ("whoever")

| Masculine | | Neuter | | Feminine | |
Singular	Plural	Singular	Plural	Singular	Plural
ὅστις	οἵτινες	ὅτι	ἅτινα	ἥτις	αἵτινες

The indefinite relative pronoun, as its name suggests, combines inflected forms of the relative (ὅς) and indefinite pronoun (τις). Inflection is third declension. Such pronouns often occur as *subject* of a relative clause, so are encountered *mostly as nominative*. The genitive form ὅτου occurs five times; the accusative ὅτι only once.

1. δέκα παρθένοις, <u>αἵτινες</u> λαβοῦσαι τὰς λαμπάδας ἑαυτῶν = "to ten virgins, *who* took their lamps" (Mt 25:1)
2. <u>ἅτινα</u> ἦν μοι κέρδη = "*whichever things* were gain to me" (Phil 3:7)
3. <u>ὅστις</u> γὰρ ὅλον τὸν νόμον τηρήσῃ = "For *whoever* keeps the whole law" (Jas 2:10)

Correlative Pronouns ("such")

The terms "relative" and "correlative" are not as distinct as one might desire. Classification among grammars and lexicons is inconsistent. Some terms classified as "correlative" just as easily could be placed under the relative pronoun category. Types can be distinguished by noting initial patterns: τοι-, τοσ-, οἱ-, ὁσ.

Table 9.20 Correlative Pronouns: Initial Patterns

Initial Patterns		
Greek	*Gloss*	*NT Freq.*
τοι-	such	57 times
τοσ-	so much	20 times
οἱ-	as	14 times
ὁσ-	as much	110 times

Four main varieties of correlative pronoun occur in the New Testament. One is τοιοῦτος "such," occurring fifty-seven times. The pronoun τοσοῦτος ("so much," "so great," "so many") occurs some twenty times; οἷος, -α, -ον ("as") is used fourteen times; finally, ὅσος, -η, -ον ("as much as") is most frequent—110 times.

Other forms also appear in the New Testament. First, the pronoun ὅδε ("this," "thus") is found only in three forms τῇδε (Lk 10:39), τήνδε (Jas 4:13), and τάδε (Acts 21:11; Rev 2:1, 8, 12, 18; 3:1, 7, 14). Second, the pronoun τηλικοῦτος ("so great") is found in the four forms τηλικούτου (2 Cor 1:10), τηλικαύτης (Heb 2:3), τηλικαῦτα (Jas 3:4), and τηλικοῦτος (Rev 16:18). Third, the pronoun τοιόσδε ("such as this") is found only at 2 Pet 1:17.

Table 9.21 Correlative Pronouns ("such")

Masculine		Neuter		Feminine	
Singular	*Plural*	*Singular*	*Plural*	*Singular*	*Plural*
τοιοῦτος	τοιοῦτοι	τοιοῦτο	τοιαῦτα	τοιαύτη	τοιαῦται
τοιούτου	τοιούτων	τοιούτου	τοιούτων	τοιαύτης	τοιαύτων
τοιούτῳ	τοιούτοις	τοιούτῳ	τοιούτοις	τοιαύτῃ	τοιαύταις
τοιοῦτον	τοιούτους	τοιοῦτο	τοιαῦτα	τοιαύτην	τοιαύτας

Correlative τοιοῦτος ("such")

Sometimes considered as a special class of the demonstrative pronoun, these forms prefix a τοι- to forms of the demonstrative οὗτος (minus the opening τ- in objective forms). Observe:

1. Καὶ <u>τοιαύταις</u> παραβολαῖς πολλαῖς ἐλάλει αὐτοῖς τὸν λόγον = "And with many *such* parables he was speaking the word to them" (Mk 4:33)

2. <u>τῶν</u> γὰρ <u>τοιούτων</u> ἐστὶν ἡ βασιλεία τοῦ θεοῦ = "for *of such ones* is the kingdom of God" (Lk 18:16, substantive construction)

3. καὶ οἶδα <u>τὸν τοιοῦτον</u> ἄνθρωπον = "and I know *such* a man" (2 Cor 12:3)

4. ἡμεῖς οὖν ὀφείλομεν ὑπολαμβάνειν <u>τοὺς τοιούτους</u> = "Therefore, we ought to support *such men*" (3 Jn 8, substantive construction)

Correlative τοσοῦτος ("so much")

Similar in form to τοιοῦτος, this pronoun prefixes τοσ- to the inflectional endings -ουτος, -αυτη, and -ουτον. Observe:

1. παρ᾽ οὐδενὶ <u>τοσαύτην</u> πίστιν ἐν τῷ Ἰσραὴλ εὗρον = *"Such great* faith I have not found with anyone in Israel!" (Mt 8:10)
2. <u>Τοσούτῳ</u> χρόνῳ μεθ᾽ ὑμῶν εἰμι καὶ οὐκ ἔγνωκάς με, Φίλιππε; = "I have been with you for *so* long yet you do not know me, Philip?" (Jn 14:9)
3. καὶ <u>τοσούτῳ</u> μᾶλλον ὅσῳ βλέπετε ἐγγίζουσαν τὴν ἡμέραν = "and *so much* more as you see the day drawing near" (Heb 10:25)

Correlative οἷος ("as")

These forms prefix a οἱ- to the relative pronoun. They occur in the New Testament only as masculine οἷος, οἷοι, οἷον, οἷους, neuter οἷον, οἷα, and feminine οἵα (note accent). Observe:

1. <u>οἷος</u> ὁ χοϊκός, τοιοῦτοι καὶ οἱ χοϊκοί = "*As* is the earthly, such also are those who are earthly" (1 Cor 15:48)
2. οὐχ <u>οἵους</u> θέλω εὕρω ὑμᾶς = "not *as* I wish will I find you" (2 Cor 12:20)
3. καὶ σεισμὸς ἐγένετο μέγας, <u>οἷος</u> οὐκ ἐγένετο = "and a great earthquake took place, *such as* had not happened" (Rev 16:18)

Correlative ὅσος ("as much as")

These forms prefix a ὁσ- to the relative pronoun. Actually, the translation is by context. Several alternatives may be appropriate. Compare the following:

1. πωλεῖ πάντα <u>ὅσα</u> ἔχει = "he sells all *as much as* he has" or "he sells all *that* he has" (Mt 13:44)
2. δώσει αὐτῷ <u>ὅσων</u> χρῄζει = "he will give him *as much as* he needs" (Lk 11:8)

3. ὅσα ἐστὶν ἀληθῆ = "*whatever* is true" (Phil 4:8)

Interrogative System

The interrogative system has three main types. These types are divided by function. The first *asks* ("who?"), the second *qualifies* ("of what type?"), and the third *quantifies* ("how much?").

Know that two other forms also appear in the New Testament. These other forms are rare. The first is the interrogative ποταπός ("what sort of?" "what kind?"), occurring seven times, as ποταπός (Mt 8:27; Lk 1:29), ποταποί (Mk 13:1), ποταπαί (Mk 13:1), ποταπή (Lk 7:39), ποταπούς (2 Pet 3:11), and ποταπήν (1 Jn 3:1). The second, πότερος ("which?"), occurs only once (Jn 7:17).

Basic Interrogatives ("who?")

Table 9.22 Interrogative Pronouns ("who?")

Mas./Fem.		Neuter	
Singular	*Plural*	*Singular*	*Plural*
τίς	τίνες	τί	τίνα
τίνος	τίνων	τίνος	τίνων
τίνι	τίσι(ν)	τίνι	τίσι(ν)
τίνα	τίνας	τί	τίνα

Substantival ("who?", "what?")

The basic interrogative (τίς, τίς, τί) *asks* "who?" or "what?" and is used to initiate a direct question or to report a question indirectly. Pattern is third declension (i.e., feminine = masculine) and clones the indefinite pronoun—*except acute accent*. Observe:

1. οἱ βασιλεῖς τῆς γῆς ἀπὸ τίνων λαμβάνουσιν = "from *whom* do the kings of the earth receive?" (Mt 17:25)

2. τί ἐστιν εὐκοπώτερον = "*which* is easier?" (Mk 2:9)
3. πρὸς <u>τίνα</u> ἀπελευσόμεθα = "to *whom* shall we go?" (Jn 6:68)
4. ἐκεῖνοι δὲ οὐκ ἔγνωσαν <u>τίνα</u> ἦν = "but they did not understand *what* those things were" (Jn 10:6)
5. <u>τί</u> ποιοῦμεν = "*what* are we doing?" (Jn 11:47)
6. οὗτοι . . . <u>τίνες</u> εἰσὶν = "*who* are these?" (Rev 7:13)

Adverbial ("why?")

The neuter interrogative τί (asking "what?") can be used at the front of a clause. On occasion, though, the interrogative form τί at the front of a clause can be used adverbially to ask the question, "why?" For example:

1. <u>τί</u> με περάζετε; = "*why* are you testing me?" (Mt 22:18)
2. <u>τί</u> ταῦτα διαλογίζεσθε; = "*why* do you discuss these things?" (Mk 2:8)

Qualitative Interrogatives ("of what type?")

The *qualitative* interrogative *qualifies*, asking, "of what type?" Translation as "what?" or "which?" is the typical usage for this pronoun. The form is ποῖος, ποία, ποῖον. Occurring thirty-three times, this pronoun is mostly singular in the New Testament. Observe:

1. <u>ποία</u> ἐντολὴ μεγάλη ἐν τῷ νόμῳ; = "*which* commandment is greatest in the law?" (Mt 22:36)
2. <u>ποῖον</u> οἶκον οἰκοδομήσετέ ´μοι; = "*What kind of* house will you build for me?" (Acts 7:49)
3. διὰ <u>ποίου</u> νόμου; = "Through *what type* of law?" (Rom 3:27)
4. <u>ποίῳ</u> δὲ σώματι ἔρχονται; = "And *with what kind of* body do they come?" (1 Cor 15:35)
5. <u>ποία</u> ἡ ζωὴ ὑμῶν = "*what* your life (will be like)" (Jas 4:14)

Quantitative Interrogatives ("how much?")

The *quantitative* interrogative *quantifies* by asking, "how much?" The form is πόσος, -η, -ο and occurs twenty-seven times. One use is in a dramatic context, in which the pronoun itself is exclamatory. Another use is to report indirectly a statement that could be framed as a question. Often, this pronoun works in concert with the adverb μᾶλλον. Observe:

1. εἰ οὖν τὸ φῶς τὸ ἐν σοὶ σκότος ἐστίν, τὸ σκότος πόσον. = "If the light in you is darkness, *how great* is that darkness!" (Mt 22:18)

2. πόσων σπυρίδων πληρώματα κλασμάτων ἤρατε; = "*how many* large baskets full of left-over pieces did you pick up?" (Mk 8:20)

3. Πόσον ὀφείλεις τῷ κυρίῳ μου; = "*How much* do you owe my master?" (Lk 16:5)

4. πόσῳ μᾶλλον τὸ πλήρωμα αὐτῶν = "*how much* more their fullness!" (Rom 11:12)

Pronoun Summary

Twelve pronouns are organized into four systems. The personal refers; demonstrative points; relative relates; interrogative asks.

Table 9.23 Pronoun Systems

Personal	Demonstrative	Relative	Interrogative
• personal	• proximate	• relative	• interrogative
• intensive	• remote	• indef. rel.	• qualitative
• possessive		• correlative	• quantitative
• reflexive			
• reciprocal			
• indefinite			
• negative			

Pronoun Frequency

Finally, a few remarks on frequency of the pronouns can orient the student to New Testament usage. The overwhelming majority of pronouns in the New Testament are the personal, used 69% of the time compared to the other major classes, almost three out of four pronouns encountered. After the personal pronouns, relative and demonstrative pronouns are encountered the most.

Chart 3: Pronoun Frequency

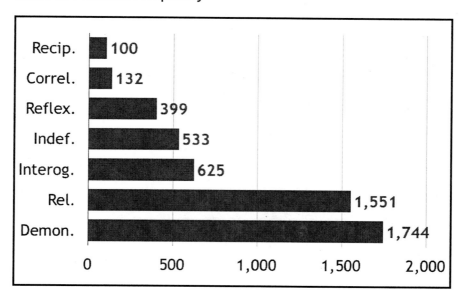

EXERCISE 9

1. Answer the following on Greek pronoun categories in general and the personal pronoun system in particular.

   1.1 Fill in the following table on the four pronoun systems and their basic function:

Pronoun System:	*Basic Function:*
1. _____	_____
2. _____	_____
3. _____	_____
4. _____	_____

   1.2 Answer true or false:

   _____ a. A pronoun's case is determined by its grammatical function.

   _____ b. Pronouns that function as attributive adjectives show only partial concord with the noun modified.

   _____ c. The "pronoun pattern" is the dropping of the final -ν in neuter nominative and accusative singular.

   _____ d. The idiom of adjectival intensification using the third person personal pronoun always is anarthrous.

   _____ e. Relative pronouns have smooth breathing and most frequently are enclitic.

1.3 Matching

____	1. Personal	a.	ἐμαυτοῦ
____	2. Intensive	b.	αὐτός
____	3. Possessive	c.	οὗτος
____	4. Reflexive	d.	ὅστις
____	5. Reciprocal	e.	τις
____	6. Indefinite	f.	ἐμός
____	7. Negative	g.	τοιοῦτος
____	8. Demonstrative (prox.)	h.	ἐκεῖνος
____	9. Demonstrative (rem.)	i.	τοσοῦτος
____	10. Relative	j.	τίς
____	11. Indefinite Relative	k.	πόσος
____	12. Correlative ("such")	l.	ὅσος
____	13. Correlative ("so much")	m.	οὐδείς
____	14. Correlative ("as")	n.	ὅς
____	15. Correlative ("as much as")	o.	ἐγώ
____	16. Interrogative ("who?")	p.	ποῖος
____	17. Interrogative ("what?")	q.	οἷος
____	18. Interrogative ("how much?")	r.	ἀλλήλων

1.4 Fill in the following table on the four grammatical levels for expressing the verbal subject in Greek using the *first person plural* of the verb ἀκούω:

Type:	Greek:	English:
1. _____	_____	_____

Type:	Greek:	English:
2. _____	_____	_____
3. _____	_____	_____
4. _____	_____	_____

1.5 _____ A third personal pronoun used for adjectival intensification is equivalent to what English adjective?

1.6 _____ Possessive pronouns, even though they are pronouns, always have what role in a sentence?

1.7a _____ Possessive pronouns are missing in what person?
    b. Possessive pronouns substitute for this person in what two ways?

        1. _____

        2. _____

1.8 _____ What pronoun category clones the form of the interrogative, but is enclitic in composition?

2. Answer the following on the three other pronoun systems.

2.1 _____ What determines the case of the relative pronoun?

2.2 _____ Relative pronouns always have what position in their clause?

2.3 _____ What term is used for the one exception to relative pronoun case?

2.4 What is the correct form of the relative pronoun in the following clauses and why (what is the sentence function)?

a. _____ "the man (*who/whom?*) you saw"

b. _____ "the player (*who/whom?*) scored"

c. _____ "the lady (*who/whom?*) is president"

2.5 What is the sentence function of the following relative pronouns in their own clause?

a. _____ καὶ οὐ ποιεῖτε ἃ λέγω

b. _____ ἡ μαρτυρία ἣν μαρτυρεῖ περὶ ἐμοῦ

c. _____ εἰσὶν τινες οἳ οὐ πιστεύουσιν

2.6 _____ The formation of the indefinite relative pronoun combines the relative pronoun with what pronoun?

2.7 _____ The indefinite relative pronoun is almost always what case? Why? _____

2.8 Match the following correlative pronoun patterns of the opening Greek letters to the English gloss for that category:

____ 1. "such"   a. ὁσ-

____ 2. "so much"   b. τοσ-

____ 3. "as"   c. τοι-

____ 4. "as much"   d. οἱ-

2.9 Identify the three categories of the interrogative pronoun by giving the category type, the Greek form, and English gloss:

	Category	Greek	Gloss
1.	_____	_____	_____
2.	_____	_____	_____
3.	_____	_____	_____

3. Translate the following and be prepared to analyze the grammar of pronouns:

3.1 ποία ἐστὶν ἐντολὴ πρώτη πάντων; (Mk 12:28)

3.2 ἀλλὰ ταῦτα τί ἐστιν εἰς τοσούτους; (Jn 6:9)

3.3 ὁ δὲ λέγει αὐτοῖς· πόσους ἄρτους ἔχετε; (Mk 6:38)

3.4 ἡμεῖς καὶ αὐτοὶ ἐν ἑαυτοῖς στενάζομεν (Rom 8:23)

3.5 οἵτινές εἰσιν Ἰσραηλῖται, ὧν ἡ υἱοθεσία καὶ ἡ δόξα (Rom 9:4)

3.6 Περὶ δὲ τῆς ἡμέρας ἐκείνης καὶ ὥρας οὐδεὶς οἶδεν (Mt 24:36)

3.7 δεῦτε ἴδετε ἄνθρωπον ὃς εἶπέν μοι πάντα ὅσα ἐποίησα (Jn 4:29)

3.8 ἔλεγον οὖν οἱ μαθηταὶ πρὸς ἀλλήλους· μή τις

ἤνεγκεν αὐτῷ φαγεῖν; (Jn 4:33)

3.9 ἔσονται γὰρ αἱ ἡμέραι ἐκεῖναι θλῖψις οἵα οὐ

γέγονεν τοιαύτη ἀπ᾽ ἀρχῆς κτίσεως (Mk 13:19)

3.10 πάντα ὅσα ἔχει ὁ πατὴρ ἐμά ἐστιν· διὰ τοῦτο

εἶπον ὅτι ἐκ τοῦ ἐμοῦ λαμβάνει καὶ ἀναγγελεῖ

ὑμῖν. (Jn 16:15)

4. Refer to the manuscript reproduced on the following page, one of the few that were available to Erasmus when he was producing an edited Greek New Testament for publication in Basel, Switzerland. (For help, use the Internet; also consult Metzger, *The Text of the New Testament*, pp. 99-100.)

    4.1 Erasmus used what few manuscripts he could find in Basel. He had just one for the Gospels and just one for Acts and the Epistles. None were earlier than the twelfth century. Among other notations on the page, notice corrections for the printer to incorporate hurriedly scribbled in Erasmus's own hand at the bottom of the page. How many manuscripts and fragments do we have available today for this work? How early are they compared to the twelfth century?

    4.2 Erasmus's one Revelation manuscript was missing the last verses. Erasmus translated *backwards* from the Latin Vulgate to produce these verses in Greek. What would be the result of such a faulty process?

    4.3 Erasmus was competing with Cardinal Ximenes of Spain to be the first to publish an edited Greek text. Did he win?

    4.4 Finally, the edited Greek text produced and published by Erasmus was the basis of what later would be known as the Beza text. Which famous English translation was based on this Beza text?

🏛 MANUSCRIPTS 7 🏛

The Greek New Testament first was published by the Dutch scholar Erasmus on the Gutenberg printing press in 1516. Erasmus had only *six* Greek manuscripts. His rushed project had numerous errors, yet his text became the basis of many others.

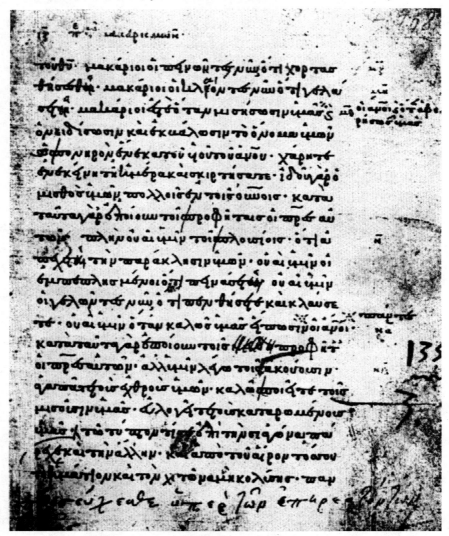

Fig. 10. Greek Gospel MS. 2 at Lk 6:20-30.

CHAPTER 10
THE GREEK VERB: AN OVERVIEW

Finite verbs are limited by a subject. The finite Greek verb has two conjugations, three kinds of action, four moods, five components, and six principal parts. The student who masters these key elements will master the finite Greek verb.

Two Conjugations

The Greek verb system has two major conjugations, thematic and non-thematic. The second is much less frequent and on its way out in the New Testament period.

Thematic Verbs

The first conjugation of Greek verbs is called the *thematic verb,* because in its

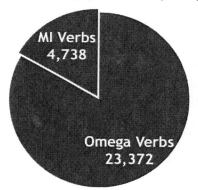

Chart 4: Conjugation Frequency

MI Verbs
4,738

Omega Verbs
23,372

formation a theme vowel (ε/ο) is used to join endings to tense stems. Thematic verbs also are called "-ω verbs," because the dictionary form of these verbs ends in -ω. In fact, the -ω ending actually is a *resultant* interaction of the first person singular ending with the thematic vowel. The majority of New Testament verbs are of this class. Note that thematic verbs that are so-called "deponent" are given in a lexicon with the middle ending -ομαι. (The issue of so-called "deponents" will be discussed under the topic of voice later in this chapter.)

Non-thematic Verbs

The second conjugation of Greek verbs is called the *non-thematic* verb, because a theme vowel typically is not used. The ending is joined directly to the tense stem. Non-thematic verbs also are called "-μι verbs," because the dictionary form of these verbs ends in -μι. The most frequent -μι verb is εἰμί, usually introduced early in grammars. Historically, -μι verbs are older than -ω verbs. As a result, some -μι verb endings show more primitive forms (such as the first person singular, -μι). This earlier conjugation eventually began losing out to the growing dominance of -ω verbs. Depending on who is counting, some thirty distinct -μι verb stems appear in the New Testament. With compounds, the total is about 116-119. Besides εἰμί, other frequent New Testament -μι verbs are δίδωμι, δύναμαι, ἵστημι, and τίθημι, for example.

The -μι verb conjugation in the main actually follows that of the -ω verb. The main difference in formation patterns resides in the first principle part of present and imperfect tenses. A few verbs in the New Testament show up in *both* an old -μι verb form (ἀπόλλυται, Mk 2:22), as well as an -ω verb form (ἀπολλύει, Jn 12:25). These hybrid forms illustrate the -ω verb system in the actual process of taking over the older -μι verb conjugation.

Three Kinds of Action

Verbs have tense. Our word "tense" has a Latin root, *tempus*, which means time. Latin, unfortunately, does not describe Greek. Greek tense is *not* time. *Tense* in Greek boils down to kind of action. That is, Greek verbs use tense not to express time but to express kind of action. Greek has three kinds of action. Time in Greek actually is a function of mood and context. Note carefully:

♦ *Greek tense is kind of action, not time of action.*

Durative Action

Many descriptive words could be used here for this kind of action. Take your pick: durative, continuous, progressive, linear, or incomplete. Action is ongoing. The durative tenses are present and imperfect, and, on rare occasions, future. Translation infers simple, iterative, or continuous action: "I say," "am saying." Imperfect is durative past: "I was saying."

Perfective Action

Many descriptive words could be used here for this kind of action. Take your pick: perfective, completed, or existing. Action is completed, but the emphasis in Greek, in contrast to English, is on-going result. A permanent state arises from the completed action. Action is completed; result is on-going. The perfective tenses are pluperfect, perfect, and future perfect. Pluperfect is distinctive: Not only is the action completed, but the results are completed as well (results no longer continue into the present). Translation uses auxiliary verbs: "had" for pluperfect; "have," "has" for perfect; "will have" for future perfect. On-going result is not clear in English translation, only the completed action. Hence, the Greek perfect meaning must be brought out in exposition.

Table 10.1 Perfective Action: On-going Results

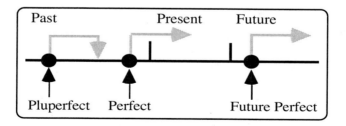

Undefined Action

Many descriptive words could be used here for this kind of action. Take your pick: undefined, simple, indefinite, unlimited, momentary, instantaneous, or punctiliar. This category is a default slot, a way of saying neither of the other two (not durative, not perfective). Action is undefined. The undefined tenses are aorist and future, and, on rare occasions, present. Translation for the aorist is preterit tense, as in "I went." Future uses the auxiliary "will," as in "I will go."

Four Moods

Verbs have mood. This component is the relative degree of contingency in the verbal action in the speaker's mind. Indicative has no contingency. The other moods show increasing contingency. While the indicative mood occurs far more frequently than the other moods, the other moods have their own

Chart 5: Verb Mood Frequency

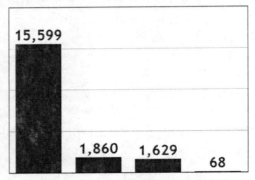

exegetical significance that rewards the translator and interpreter of the New Testament in passages in which they occur.

Indicative Mood (Reality)

Indicative mood indicates reality and time. These two elements are overviewed briefly. As will be seen, "reality" in this context is used in only a relative way, not as indicating objective fact or as phenomenological essence.

Indicative as Reality (No Contingency)

Indicative mood presents no contingency in the action. Thus, reality here means no contingency. The speaker affirms or asserts the action's reality, that is, that the action took place, is taking place, or will take place without any contingency. One could affirm as reality, "I did my homework." Or, one could assert a falsehood, such as, "I did my homework." Either way, affirmed or asserted, the statement is *presented* as reality, i.e., with no contingency.

The three main types of indicative mood sentences are: (1) declarative fact statements or assertions, (2) interrogatives, and (3) first class conditional sentences, in which the condition is assumed true. For example:

- *affirmation:* "now we *are* children of God" (1 Jn 3:2)
- *assertion:* "he *has* Beelzebul" (Mk 3:22)
- *interrogative:* "Why do you *speak* to them in parables?" (Mt 13:10)
- *first class conditional sentence:* "if they *persecuted* me" (Jn 15:20, condition assumed true)

Indicative as Time

Indicative mood indicates time. Time is a factor for the Greek verb only in the indicative mood.[1] The Greek verb system has two sets of endings based on time. Primary endings are used for present (5534x), perfect (835x), and future (1610x) tenses. (The future perfect occurs only once in the New Testament.) Secondary

---

[1]The matter continues to be debated, especially in publications by Fanning and Porter. Cf. Bruce M. Fanning, *Verbal Aspect in New Testament Greek* (Oxford: Clarendon Press, 1990) and Stanley E. Porter, *Verbal Aspect in the Greek of the New Testament, with Reference to Tense and Mood* (New York: Peter Lang, 1989). A more accessible form of Porter's views is found in Porter, *Idioms of the Greek New Testament*. The debate is summarized concisely in Stanley E. Porter and D. A. Carson, eds., *Biblical Greek Language and Linguistics: Open Questions in Current Research*, Journal for the Study of the New Testament Supplement Series 80 (Sheffield: JSOT Press, 1993).

endings are used for imperfect (1680x), aorist (5875x), and pluperfect (86x), which are past time.

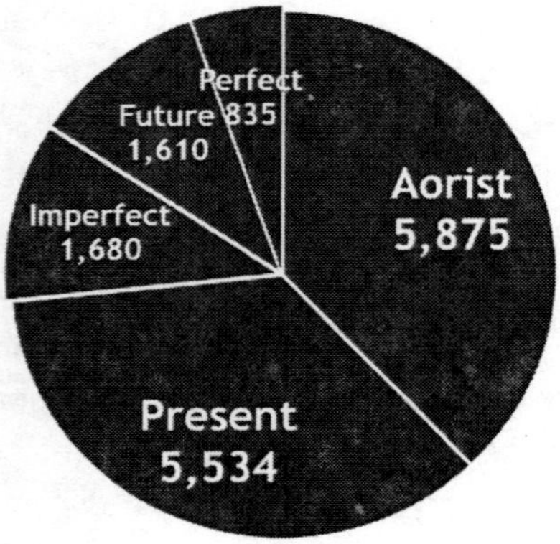

Notice the tense triads for primary and secondary endings. Each tense triad represents the three kinds of action (durative, perfective, undefined) within that time frame. For example, any of *three* of the Greek tenses can indicate past time. Any distinctions made are based on the three *kinds* of action in past time. Thus, past *durative* action would call for the imperfect tense, past *perfective* action the pluperfect tense, and past *undefined* action the aorist tense.

Chart 6: Indicative Tenses

Table 10.2 Primary and Secondary Tenses

Kind of Action	Time of Action		
	Secondary	Primary	
	Past	Present	Future
Durative	Imperfect	Present	(Future)
Perfective	Pluperfect	Perfect	Fut. Perf.
Undefined	Aorist	(Present)	Future

With exceptions, we may derive two important generalizations:

◆ *Primary tenses take primary endings.*

◆ *Secondary tenses take secondary endings.*

To these primary and secondary tenses the indicative mood endings, or *pronominal suffixes*, are added. See the table below.

Table 10.3 Indicative Mood Endings (Pronominal Suffixes)

Subject		Indicative Mood Endings			
		Primary Tenses		*Secondary Tenses*	
Num.	Per.	Active	Mid/Pass	Active	Mid/Pass
Sing.	1st	-ω	-μαι	-ν	-μην
	2nd	-εις	-σαι (η)	-ς	-σο (ου)
	3rd	-ει	-ται	(-εν)	-το
Plu.	1st	-ομεν	-μεθα	-μεν	-μεθα
	2nd	-ετε	-σθε	-τε	-σθε
	3rd	-ουσι(ν)	-νται	-ν, -σαν	-ντο

A few observations relate to these endings:

1. *Thematic vowel.* The thematic vowel is included only in the primary active set. The vowel is not given in the other patterns. The thematic vowel in the primary active is lost to sight due to interactions. (The vowel is clearly visible only on the first and second persons plural.) So the primary active endings are learned *with* the thematic vowel.

2. *"Movable nu."* Primary active, third plural can end with -ν, called "movable nu." This -ν does not affect meaning but smoothes pronunciation for a following word beginning with a vowel, or when the verb comes at the end of a clause or sentence. (Compare the use of the alternate forms of the English indefinite article: "a," "an.") Again, the secondary active, third person singular has no ending. No ending exposes the thematic vowel -ε, to which a "movable nu" can be added. The result is an -εν ending.

3. *Intervocalic sigma.* The *intervocalic sigma* is a sigma between two vowels that elides. In the primary middle, second person singular the σ between the two vowels drops out, exposing a theme vowel (ε) to a diphthong (αι).

These vowels combine into an improper diphthong, ῃ. This phenomenon also occurs in the secondary middle, second person singular. A remaining ε and ο contract into -ου.

4. *Third plural.* The secondary active, third person plural exists in *two* forms. Most verbs take the -ν option. A few take the -σαν.

5. *Non-thematic.* The -μι verb conjugation takes the same indicative endings. The only exceptions are the three primary active singulars -μι, -ς, -σι, and third plural -ασι.

Subjunctive Mood (Probability)

The subjunctive mood in-dicates *some contingency* bearing upon the statement made. The two main types are *probable reality* state-ments and third class condi-tional sentences (in which the main condition is assumed *probably* true). In translation, contingency can be conveyed by the use of auxiliary verbs,

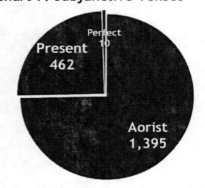

Chart 7: Subjunctive Tenses

Perfect 10
Present 462
Aorist 1,395

such as "could," "should," or "would." Or, contingency could be inherent in the context, such as the use of a temporal conjunction ("*when* he comes") or a prohibition ("*Do not think* that I came to destroy the law," Mt 5:17). A conditional example would be, "If anyone *loves* the world" (1 Jn 2:15).

Optative Mood (Possibility)

The optative mood indicates even *greater contingency* about the statement made, basically a weaker form of the subjunctive. The statement is considered *possible reality*, but remote. Use of optative mood was fading in New Testament times, so the optative is uncommon in the New Testament (68 total: aorist 45x, present 23x). The main uses are in fourth class conditional sentences (main condition only remotely possible) and in wishes, benedictions, and prayers. The use in benedictions and prayers is a *literary* convention, not actual doubt on the part of the author. Auxiliary verbs would include "may" or "might," and, on occasion, "could" or "should." Optative examples would include, "For *how am I able* unless someone guides me?" (Acts 8:31); "what *would he wish* to say?" (Acts 17:18). As a benediction, "*May* mercy, peace, and love *be multiplied*" (Jude 2).

Imperative Mood (Command)

The imperative mood in-
dicates *greatest contingency*
bearing upon the statement
made. Imperative, then, is
the conventional mood for
commands or entreaties. This
mood is the most straightforward mood in application. As
examples, "*Let* your kingdom
come" (Mt 6:10); "*Do not be
conformed*" (Rom 12:2).

Chart 8: Imperative Tenses

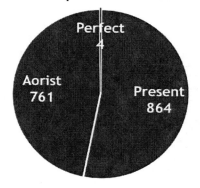

In sum, the four moods depict reality, probability, possibility, and command. Non-indicative moods relate decreasing reality and increasing contingency from the speaker's perspective. Remember, in the moods of contingency, tense is kind of action only. Thus, a present subjunctive and an aorist subjunctive can translate the same into English, because time is not a factor, and kind of action is obscured in the translation. Note the present subjunctive, ὁ δὲ χριστὸς ὅταν ἔρχηται, "but when the Messiah *comes*," (Jn 7:27), compared to aorist subjunctive, ὅταν οὖν ἔλθῃ ὁ κύριος, "there-fore, when the master *comes*" (Mt 21:40).

Table 10.4 Mood and Contingency

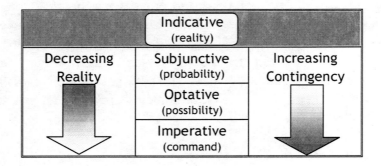

Five Components

Verbs have five components: tense, voice, mood, person, and number. Tense (as kind of action) and mood already have been discussed under their own separate headings. We now overview the remaining components of voice, person, and number.

Table 10.5 Verb Components

Tense	Voice	Mood	Person	Number
Present	Active	Indicative	First	Singular
Imperfect	Middle	Subjunct.	Second	Plural
Future	Passive	Optative	Third	
Aorist		Imperative		
Perfect				
Pluperfect				
Future Per.				

Voice

Voice and Subject

Voice of a verb indicates the relationship of the verb's subject to the verb's action. This relationship takes one of three forms: active, middle, and passive. English has only *two* voices, the active and the passive. English has no equivalent to the Greek middle voice. Translating middle voice, therefore, is a prob-

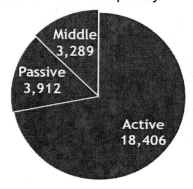

Chart 9: Voice Frequency

Middle 3,289

Passive 3,912

Active 18,406

lem, since English has no counterpart. Use of the active voice outnumbers middle and passive combined almost three to one.

Table 10.6 Voice as Subject and Action

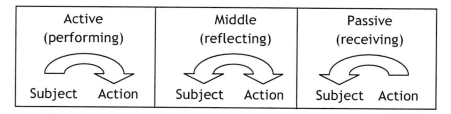

Active (performing)	Middle (reflecting)	Passive (receiving)
Subject Action	Subject Action	Subject Action

The three subject-to-verb relationships of voice are:
1. *active voice:* the verb's subject as *performing* the verb's action ("I am writing to you," 1 Jn 2:1)
2. *middle voice:* the verb's subject as *reflecting* the verb's action, in two main ways:
   - *direct middle*—the verb's subject as reflecting *directly* the action of the verb onto itself ("he hanged himself," Mt 27:5)

- *indirect middle*—the verb's subject as acting with *self-interest* ("Teacher, I *have kept* [in my own self interest] all these things since my youth," Mk 10:20).
3. *passive voice:* the verb's subject as *receiving* the verb's action ("I am being poured out," Phil 2:17).

Voice is indicated two ways in the Greek verb. One way is by inflection in the primary and secondary endings. The other is by a voice suffix attached to the tense stem in the sixth principal part, the -θη of the aorist passive suffix.

Voice and Εἰμί

Be aware that the verb εἰμί expresses a state of being, not action. Therefore, εἰμί *has no voice component*. Thus, when locating or parsing a form of εἰμί, do not include voice. So, ἐστίν is present indicative third plural, *not* present ~~active~~ indicative.

Voice and Deponency

Table 10.7 Old "Deponent" Terminology

Tense	Voice	Terminology	Example	Translation
Present	M/P	Deponent	βούλομαι (βούλομαι)	I wish
Imperf.	M/P	Deponent	ἐβουλόμην (βούλομαι)	I was wishing
Future	Middle	Deponent Future	γνώσομαι (γινώσκω)	I will know
Aorist	Middle	Middle Deponent	ἐγενόμην (γίνομαι)	I became
Aorist	Passive	Passive Deponent	ἐγενήθην (γίνομαι)	I became

Definition. Deponency is a grammatical feature of Latin verbs. A *deponent* is a Latin verb that had active voice forms originally but lost them over time. Traditionally, Greek verbs used to be analyzed with this Latin grammar. The table above summarizes old "deponent" terminology. Notice that the varying terms were an attempt to distinguish "deponency" in different principal parts.

Table 10.8 "Deponent" Aorists

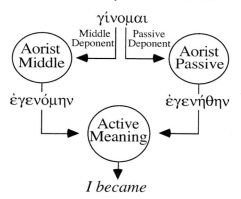

I became

"Deponent" was used for the first principal part found only in middle forms. Then, "deponent future" was the second principal part found only as middle (even though *present* active forms exist). A "middle deponent" was the third principal part found only in middle forms. A "passive deponent" was the sixth principal part found only in passive forms. The student was told to translate all deponent forms "actively." This workaround was problematic, since the advice inevitably left the student with the impression that so-called deponents actually were active voice verbs disguised in middle form, which clearly was not the case. Further, since "middle deponent" and "passive deponent" both were to be translated "actively," the bottom line result came out the same for either form (see the table on "deponent" aorists).

Problems. All this confusion was an artifice of English translation, not Greek grammar. Trying to analyze the Greek verb as "deponent" is now recognized not only as inaccurate, but also misleading and inadequate. Greek verbs are *not* deponent. Why is this Latin category problematic for Greek verbs?

1. *Definition.* First, some of the Greek verbs that show middle forms exclusively in the New Testament were *born*

middle voice. That is, such verbs never existed with active voice endings in the first place. Pretending that such Greek verbs "lost their active voice" (the Latin deponent category) is simply inaccurate.

2. *Classification.* Second, classifying a particular verb as "deponent" is an ambiguous enterprise, since the result depends upon how much Greek one is reading. That is to say, the classification is dependent upon the time span of one's analysis. For example, the dictionary edited by Barclay Newman and published by the United Bible Societies has at least 157 more entries of verbs as -μαι than appear in the Accordance database (not counting here the three textual variants: ἐναντιόομαι, καταβαπτίζομαι, τυρβάζομαι).[2] Why does such a difference exist? Time frame.

The Newman dictionary has a frame of reference of just the New Testament literature, which covers about the first century. In contrast, the popular Accordance software is standardized upon entries as given in the BDAG lexicon,[3] which includes approximately the first three centuries of the Christian church. So, the wider one casts the verb net over time, the *fewer* the number of "deponents" that are caught. Eventually, that is to say, some verbs that show no active forms in the New Testament (i.e., Newman) will be found to exhibit active voice forms somewhere else (i.e., BDAG). So, what really should be classified a "deponent" verb in the first place?

Thus, one should expect lexical confusion, even inconsistency, over this matter of so-called "deponents." A verb such as ψεύδομαι is identified as only middle "in our lit-

---

[2]Barclay M. Newman, Jr., *A Concise Greek-English Dictionary of the New Testament* (New York: United Bible Societies, 1971, 1993). Accordance, Ver. 7.4.1, OakTree Software Specialists, Altamonte Springs, Fla., 2007.

[3]Danker, *A Greek-English Lexicon of the New Testament and Other Early Christian Literature, Third Edition.*

erature" by BDAG, and is listed as -μαι. At the same time, a verb such as ὀνίνημι, also identified as only middle form "in our literature" (BDAG), is *not* entered as a -μαι verb. Why? Just what is the "deponent" classification being applied in these entries, and what is "deponent" supposed to mean at the grammatical level? We seem to throw the word "deponent" around as if the word indicated a true grammatical category, such as "nominative" is for nouns or "perfect" is for verbs, when the word simply is a Latinized confusion of Greek.

3. *Principal Parts.* Third, deponent classification is so convoluted as even to be *tense* dependent. The definition of a "deponent" as not having active voice forms sometimes is not even true across all principal parts for the same verb. For example, the "future deponent" is supposed to be a verb that shows no *future* active forms, yet, the *present* tense of this same verb *does* have active voice forms. As further illustration of this point, note the following examples of contradictions of "deponent" classification in various principle parts of the same verb:

    (1) The verb ἔρχομαι is supposed to be "deponent," but has an active indicative in aorist, perfect, and pluperfect tenses (ἦλθον, ἐλήλυθα, ἐλήλυθει), an active participle in aorist and perfect (ἐλθών, ἐληλυθότα), and an active infinitive in the aorist (ἐλθεῖν).

    (2) The verb γίνομαι is supposed to be "deponent," but has an active indicative in both the perfect and pluperfect tenses (γέγονεν, ἐγεγόνει), an active participle in the perfect (γεγονός), and an active infinitive in the perfect (γεγονέναι).

    (3) The verb κατεφίσταμαι is supposed to be "deponent," but the *only* form of this verb in the New Tes-

tament is an aorist *active* indicative (κατεπέστη-σαν, Acts 18:12)!

These three so-called "deponent" verbs together contribute 452 active voice "hits" in Accordance. Perhaps we might call them "stealth deponents"? In fact, when taken together as a group, all of these so-called "deponent" verbs in the New Testament

Chart 10: "Deponent" Voices

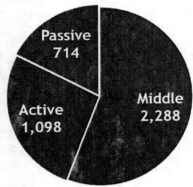

contribute 1,098 active voice hits in Accordance!

Conclusion. In conclusion, all so-called "deponent" verbs in the New Testament are not actually deponent. They occur only as middle simply because: (1) they inherently retain a strong middle voice component in the verb stem itself, and (2) the active voice form is just overwhelmed in common usage, so is either infrequent or non-existent (in some cases even from the beginning).

What is the bottom line? First, we need to quit using the term "deponent" altogether. A Greek verb is active, middle, or passive, period. Some are just lexically middle (lexicon entry is -μαι). For want of a better term, we will call such verbs "lexical middle."

Second, we need to recognize that the Greek middle voice may not come across smoothly in English translation anyway. Remember that the English verb does not have middle voice in the first place. Thus, ἔρχομαι may be glossed as "I come" or "I go," which sounds active voice, but this stylistic difficulty is because trying to bring out the middle voice idea is simply too awkward: "I bring myself along," "I take myself along." The middle voice of ἔρχομαι, or any other -μαι verb in a lexicon, is present grammatically. The middle voice always is not easily or smoothly translated.

While discussion on deponency and Greek verbs may continue, the tide seems to have turned. For an in-depth discussion, one may consult profitably the papers and posts of Carl W. Conrad.[4] For now, we summarize:

+ *Greek verbs are not deponent.*

+ *Greek middle voice is difficult to translate.*

Person and Number

Person is a classification of the verb's subject. *First person* is the person speaking ("I," "we"). *Second person* is the person spoken to ("you," "you"). *Third person* is the person spoken about ("he," "she," "it," "they"). *Number* is whether person is singular or plural. *Pronominal suffixes* are the endings on Greek verbs that indicate person and number. These endings are in two sets, primary and secondary, and two paradigms, one for active, and the other for middle and passive. The same endings are used for both thematic and non-thematic conjugations and all moods except the imperative, which has its own distinctive endings.

The basic rule for person and number is:

+ *A verb agrees with its subject in person and number.*

Greek has at least two exceptions to this basic rule:
1. *Neuter Plural.* A Greek neuter plural can take a singular verb. The idea of a *collective* plural is present (a noun considered as a class or as a collective identity). Observe:

---

[4]The student can follow posts on the biblicalgreek.org/forum by searching the word "deponent." Also, cf. Carl W. Conrad, "New Observations on Voice in the Ancient Greek Verb, November 19, 2002." [cited 10 May 2008]. Online: http://www.ioa.com/~cwconrad/Docs/NewObsAncGrkVc.pdf.

τὰ τέκνα ὑμῶν ἀκάθαρτά ἐστιν, "your *children are unclean*" (1 Cor 7:14). Here, τέκνα is nominative *plural*, but ἐστιν is third person *singular*. The idea "children" is understood in this case as a collective plural.

2. *Compound Subject*. The element of the compound subject closest to the verb can determine the number of the Greek verb. Observe: ἐξῆλθεν ὁ Ἰησοῦς καὶ οἱ μαθηταὶ αὐτοῦ = "*Jesus* and his disciples *went out*" (Mk 8:27). Here, the subject is compound, but note that the verb ἐξῆλθεν is singular. The singular noun Ἰησοῦς, the compound subject element closest to the verb, controls the verb's number.

Six Principal Parts

Principal parts are the essential building blocks needed to produce all tenses and voices for a given verb. English has only three principal parts—present, past, past participle—so must rely on a cumbersome system of auxiliary verbs. Greek has six principal parts, which is more sophisticated, so needs no auxiliary verbs. Before a discussion of these six principal parts, the concept of word formation first must be explored.

Word Formation

Word Roots and Stems

In the hierarchy of word form-ation, including verbs, the first level is the *root*. This is the base for all related word forms. The second level is the *stem*, in which the root forms a trunk for creating related nouns, adjectives, and verbs through noun stems, ad-

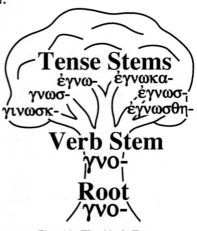

Fig. 11. The Verb Tree

jective stems, and verb stems. *Cognates* are word forms related to the same root, whether noun, adjective, verb. For example, the word root γνο- provides the noun cognate γνῶσις ("knowledge"), as well as the adjective cognate γνωστός ("known"), and the verb cognate γινώσκω ("I know"). Thus, a *cognate accusative* is a direct object noun whose root is the same as the verb; note, for example, φυλάσσοντες φυλακὰς in Lk 2:8, and ἐφοβήθησαν φόβον in Lk 2:9.

Verb and Tense Stems

A *verb stem* is that particular form in which a word root manifests itself as a verb. Verb stems communicate the fundamental "action" of the verb ("know," "teach," "have," "receive," "send," etc.).

Verbs have the additional formation element of a tense stem. A *tense stem* is a formation from the verb stem that creates distinct verb tenses through prefixes, suffixes, and infixes.

Present Tense Formation

A vocabulary word gives the present tense of a verb. Yet, the present tense is one of the most irregular forming tenses in the entire Greek verb system! For example, the verb stem of βαπτίζω is βαπτιδ-, *not* βαπτιζ-. The verb stem of κηρύσσω is κηρυκ-, *not* κηρυσσ-. The verb stem of γινώσκω is γνο-, *not* γινωσκ-. Why is the present tense so different than the verb stem? Verbs have different formation patterns for the present tense because they belong to different stem classes. Some examples of present tense stem classes are:

1. *Identical:* The present stem is identical to the verb stem. This form basically is a regular verb such as λύω.
2. *A -ττ present stem:* Here, a -π stem adds -τ for a -πτ present stem. An example is κρυπ- becoming κρύπτω.

3. *Semivowel iota:* A stem adds "semivowel iota" (iota as a consonant sound), creating various reactions. For example, βαπτιδ- + ι gives the zeta result of βαπτίζω.

4. *Liquid ν:* A stem adds the liquid ν in some form, which generates various reactions. An example is βα- adding ν, to create βαν-, but then lengthening the stem vowel to create the final result of βαίνω.

5. *A -σκ present stem:* A stem adds -σκ or -ισκ. Thus, γνω- reduplicates with iota on the front (γιγνω-), but drops the second gamma (γινω-), then adds the -σκ, creating the present tense stem γινώσκω.

6. *Irregular:* One verb borrows a form from an entirely different verb. One example is λέγω, whose aorist form comes from an entirely different verb root, εἶπον.

These major stem classes can be subdivided, but the list above provides the basic framework for understanding present tense formation from basic verb stems.[5]

Present tense stem formation is presented not because the intermediate student has to master these formations. They are presented to illustrate why the present tense form of the verb that is memorized as a part of vocabulary work often does not help at all in recognizing that same verb in other tenses. The present tense stem is just one of six tense stem patterns. These six tense stem patterns, or principal parts, are the key to the Greek verb.

Principal Parts

Notice in both the omega verb and -μι verb conjugations that present and aorist tenses dominate in frequency. These are the workhorse tenses of the Greek language. Still, the question remains, how does one conquer all these Greek tenses?

---

[5]The advanced student may consult James A. Brooks and Carlton L. Winbery, *Morphology of New Testament Greek: A Review and Reference Grammar* (Lanham, Md.: University Press of America, 1994).

Chart 11: Omega and MI Verb Tense Frequency

Omega Verbs:

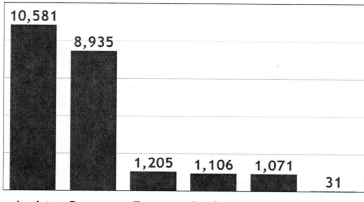

Aorist Present Future Perfect Imperf. Pluperf.

MI Verbs:

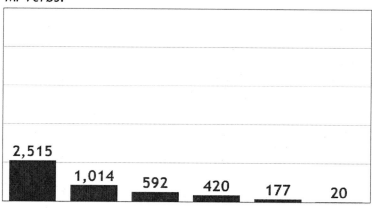

Present Aorist Imperf. Future Perfect Pluperf.

One conquers Greek tenses through principal parts. A *principal part* is a tense stem formation pattern that provides a given tense and voice for a verb. The table below shows one cannot "know" a Greek verb just by memorizing a vocabulary word, which is just the first principal part. One has to know five other principal parts to recognize any form of that verb in the New Testament!

Table 10.9 Principal Parts: Tenses and Voices

Principal Parts	Tenses	Voices		
First	Present	active	middle	passive
	Imperfect	active	middle	passive
Second	Future	active	middle	
Third	First Aorist	active	middle	
	Second Aorist	active	middle	
Fourth	Pluperfect	active		
	Perfect	active		
	Future Perfect	active		
Fifth	Pluperfect		middle	passive
	Perfect		middle	passive
	Future Perfect		middle	passive
Sixth	Aorist			passive
	Future			passive

Principal parts are voice specific. That is, for example, one needs the *second* principal part for future active and middle, but one needs the *sixth* principal part for future passive. Thus:

♦ *Principal parts are voice specific.*

Indicative Verb System

The indicative Greek verb has six morphology slots arranged according to their formation order. Five slots are stem formatives (prefixes, infixes, suffixes), and the sixth is the inflectional ending. Not all slots are used in every formation pattern. No slot is included for a compound preposition, because prepositions are not considered part of the verb stem. The endings are the active, middle, and passive voice forms of the primary and secondary sets.

Table 10.10 Indicative Verb: Morphology Slots

1	2	3	4	5	6
augment	*reduplic.*	*stem*	*suffix*	*vowel*	*ending*

The morphology of these formatives and endings can be organized globally according to patterns, that is, the six principal parts. The table below summarizes the Greek indicative verb system for the omega verb in terms of principal part patterns and morphology.

Table 10.11 Omega Verb: Indicative System

Omega Verb: Indicative System									
		Morphology							
Patterns		Formatives					Endings		
Part	Ten	Aug	Redu	Stem	Suff	Vow	Act	Mid	Pass
1	Pres			Pres		ο/ε	ω	μαι	μαι
	Impf	ἐ		Pres		ο/ε	ν	μην	μην
2	Fut			Fut	σ	ο/ε	ω	μαι	
3	1Aor	ἐ		1Aor	σα		ν	μην	
	2Aor	ἐ		2Aor		ο/ε	ν	μην	
4	Plup	ἐ	λε	Perf	κει		ν		
	Per		λε	Perf	κα		ν		
	FutP		λε	Perf	σ	ο/ε	ω		
5	Plup	ἐ	λε	Perf				μην	μην
	Per		λε	Perf				μαι	μαι
	FutP		λε	Perf	σ			μαι	μαι
6	1Aor	ἐ		1Aor	θη				ν
	Fut			1Aor	θησ	ο/ε			μαι

▱▱▱▱▱▱▱▱▱ EXERCISE 10 ▱▱▱▱▱▱▱▱▱

1. Answer the following on Greek conjugations based on the Mk 15:6-15 passage provided.

15:6 Κατὰ δὲ ἑορτὴν ἀπέλυεν αὐτοῖς ἕνα δέσμιον ὃν παρῃτοῦντο. 15:7 ἦν δὲ ὁ λεγόμενος Βαραββᾶς μετὰ τῶν στασιαστῶν δεδεμένος οἵτινες ἐν τῇ στάσει φόνον πεποιήκεισαν. 15:8 καὶ ἀναβὰς ὁ ὄχλος ἤρξατο αἰτεῖσθαι καθὼς ἐποίει αὐτοῖς. 15:9 ὁ δὲ Πιλᾶτος ἀπεκρίθη αὐτοῖς λέγων· θέλετε ἀπολύσω ὑμῖν τὸν βασιλέα τῶν Ἰουδαίων; 15:10 ἐγίνωσκεν γὰρ ὅτι διὰ φθόνον παραδεδώκεισαν αὐτὸν οἱ ἀρχιερεῖς. 15:11 οἱ δὲ ἀρχιερεῖς ἀνέσεισαν τὸν ὄχλον ἵνα μᾶλλον τὸν Βαραββᾶν ἀπολύσῃ αὐτοῖς. 15:12 ὁ δὲ Πιλᾶτος πάλιν ἀποκριθεὶς ἔλεγεν αὐτοῖς· τί οὖν [θέλετε] ποιήσω [ὃν λέγετε] τὸν βασιλέα τῶν Ἰουδαίων; 15:13 οἱ δὲ πάλιν ἔκραξαν· σταύρωσον αὐτόν. 15:14 ὁ δὲ Πιλᾶτος ἔλεγεν αὐτοῖς· τί γὰρ ἐποίησεν κακόν; οἱ δὲ περισσῶς ἔκραξαν· σταύρωσον αὐτόν. 15:15 Ὁ δὲ Πιλᾶτος βουλόμενος τῷ ὄχλῳ τὸ ἱκανὸν ποιῆσαι ἀπέλυσεν αὐτοῖς τὸν Βαραββᾶν, καὶ παρέδωκεν τὸν Ἰησοῦν φραγελλώσας ἵνα σταυρωθῇ.

1.1 _____ Mk 15:6-15 has how many occurrences of thematic (i.e., -ω) verbs? (Make your own count; then, check with the answer key.)

1.2 ____ Mk 15:6-15 has how many occurrences of non-thematic (-μι) verbs? Identify them (see answer key):

1.3 ____ Mk 15:6-15 has how many occurrences of lexical middle (-μαι) verbs? Identify them (see answer key):

2. Answer the following on Greek tense (kind of action) based on the Mk 15:6-15 passage provided.

2.1 In Mk 15:7, the verb δεδεμένος is a perfect, passive, participle describing Barabbas as "having been imprisoned" with the rebels. What is the significance of this perfect tense?

2.2 In Mk 15:7, the verb πεποιήκεισαν is a pluperfect, active, indicative, 3rd pers. pl. of ποιέω. How would one translate this verb? What is the significance of this pluperfect tense?

2.3 In Mk 15:8, the verb ἐποίει is an imperfect, active, indicative, 3rd pers. sg. of ποιέω. How would one translate this verb? What is the significance of this imperfect tense?

2.4 In Mk 15:9, the verb θέλετε is a present, active, indicative, 2nd pers. pl. of θέλω. How would one translate this verb? What is the significance of this present tense?

2.5 In Mk 15:10, the verb ἐγίνωσκεν is imperfect, active, indicative, 3rd pers. sg. of γινώσκω. How would one translate this verb? What is the significance of this imperfect tense?

2.6 In Mk 15:13, the verb ἔκραξαν is an aorist, active, indicative, 3rd pers. pl. of κράζω. How would one translate this verb? What is the significance of this aorist tense? If the verb had been the imperfect form, ἔκραζον, how would the translation change? What would be the significance of the use of the imperfect tense instead of the aorist?

3. Answer the following on Greek mood.

    3.1 _____ Time is a factor for the Greek verb in what mood only?

    3.2 _____ In this mood related to 3.1 above, primary tenses take what type of endings?

    3.3 _____ In this mood related to 3.1 above, secondary tenses take what type of endings?

    3.4 Provide the four sets of endings for the Greek verb for the active and the middle/passive voices.

	Primary		**Secondary**	
	Active	*Mid. / Pass.*	*Active*	*Mid. / Pass.*
	_____	_____	_____	_____
	_____	_____	_____	_____
	_____	_____	_____	_____
	_____	_____	_____	_____
	_____	_____	_____	_____
	_____	_____	_____	_____

    3.5 _____ In terms of contingency, the subjunctive is the mood of what? Identify some auxiliary verbs that might be used in translation:

    _____

Research four examples of Greek conjunctions that signal the use of the subjunctive mood:

_____

What is the bottom line result of translating a present subjunctive compared to an aorist subjuctive? Why?

_____

What context in Mk 15:6–15 makes these verbs subjunctive?

v. 9—ἀπολύσω: _____

v. 11—ἀπολύσῃ: _____

v. 12—ποιήσω: _____

v. 15—σταυρωθῇ: _____

3.6 _____ In terms of contingency, the optative is the mood of what? Identify the four main optative uses:

_____

3.7 _____ In terms of contingency, the imperative is the mood of what?

The verb σταύρωσον that occurs once each in Mk 15:13 and 15:14 in the passage given above is aorist, active, imperative, 2nd per. sg., from σταυρόω, "I crucify." How is the use of this mood appropriate to the context?

_____

4. Answer the following on Greek voice.

4.1 Voice of a verb indicates the relationship of the verb's _____ to the verb's _____. Describe the three forms of this relationship:

Active: _____

Middle: _____

Passive: _____

4.2 Summarize various problems with labeling Greek verbs as "deponent."

4.3 On the Internet, access the article by Carl Conrad, "New Observations on Voice in the Ancient Greek Verb, November 19, 2002." Be ready to discuss his observations about the Greek passive voice.

5. Answer the following on Greek person and number.

    5.1 State the basic rule on the verb and the verb's subject regarding person and number:

    _____

    5.2 Translate the following and explain the grammar of person and number:

    a. Τῶν δὲ δώδεκα ἀποστόλων τὰ ὀνόματά ἐστιν ταῦτα·

    _____

    b. Καὶ ἔρχεται ἡ μήτηρ αὐτοῦ καὶ οἱ ἀδελφοὶ αὐτοῦ

    _____

6. Answer the following on Greek principal parts.

    6.1 What is the difference between a verb stem and a tense stem?

    _____

    6.2 What is the problem with memorizing the vocabulary form of a verb in the present tense?

    _____

6.3 Define "principal part":

_____

6.4 _____ Each principal part is specific to what component of the verb besides tense?

꙰꙰꙰꙰꙰꙰ MANUSCRIPTS 8 ꙰꙰꙰꙰꙰꙰

Codex Bezae ("D") contains the Gospels, some of 3 John, and Acts. The date is about fifth century. French Reformer Théodore de Bèze (1519-1605) got the text from the monastery of St. Irenaeus at Lyon. Cambridge University Library received the uncial in 1581. The codex has many misspellings, errors, and additions. Below is Lk 6:3b (Οὐδὲ τοῦτο ἀνέγνωτε) to 6:9a (εἶπεν δὲ ὁ Ἰησοῦς πρὸς αὐτούς, Ἐπερωτῶ).[6] Remarkable here is a saying of Jesus found in no other manuscript after 6:4: "On that same day, as he saw a certain man working on the Sabbath, he said to him, 'Man, if you realize what you are doing, you are fortunate, but if you do not know, you are accursed and a transgressor of the law'" (middle line 7 through line 11). This unique saying displaces Lk 6:5 after 6:10.

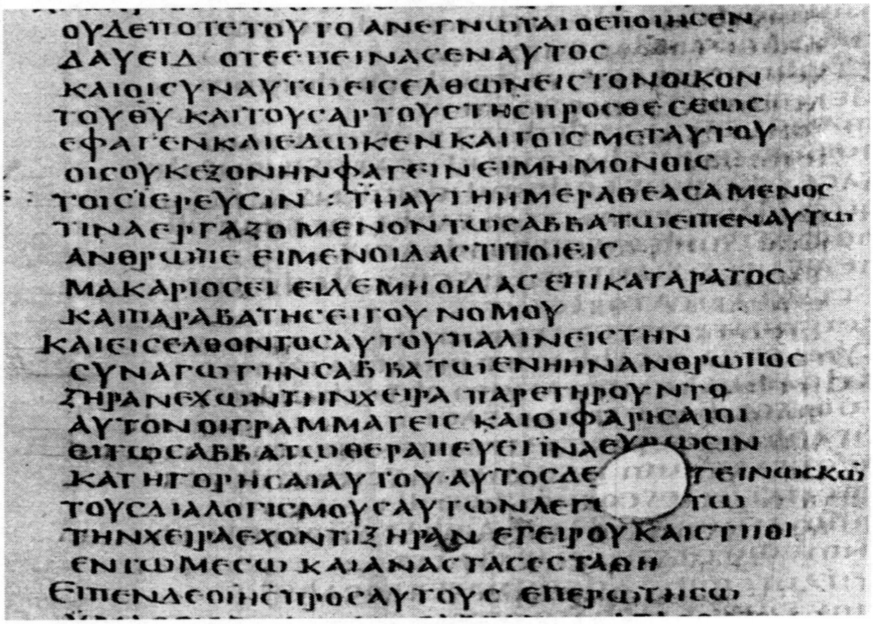

Fig. 12. Codex Bezae at Lk 6:3b-9a.

---

[6]Note πότε inserted between οὐδέ and ἀνέγνωτε, misspelling τότε (line 1). Note misspelling the verb ἐπερωτῶ as ἐπερωτήσω (last word, last line).

CHAPTER 11
PRESENT AND IMPERFECT TENSES

We have organized our review of thematic verb morphology by mood and kind of action. In the next several chapters, we will review the indicative verb. Then, we will cover the other moods. The indicative verb is presented according to kind of action: durative (present, imperfect), perfective (perfect, pluperfect), and undefined (future, aorist).

Durative Tenses

The imperfect tense is built on the present tense stem. Hence, these two tenses comprise the first principal part. Both are durative action, since the present stem that both tenses rely on is durative. One will note that the first

Table 11.1 Principal Parts

Principal Parts	Tenses	Voices		
First	Present	active	middle	passive
	Imperfect	active	middle	passive
Second	Future	active	middle	
Third	First Aorist	active	middle	
	Second Aorist	active	middle	
Fourth	Pluperfect	active		
	Perfect	active		
	Future Perfect	active		
Fifth	Pluperfect		middle	passive
	Perfect		middle	passive
	Future Perfect		middle	passive
Sixth	Aorist			passive
	Future			passive

principal part is the only principal part that comprises all three voices. All other tenses require multiple principal parts to establish all three voices.

Present Morphology

The present tense is a primary tense, so requires no augment. As a primary tense the present tense takes primary endings.

Table 11.2 Present Tense Morphology

1	2	3	4	5	6
augment	reduplic.	stem	suffix	vowel	ending
		Present		o/ε	Primary

$$\lambda\upsilon\text{-}o\text{-}\mu\epsilon\nu$$

Active Voice

Table 11.3 Present Active Indicative

λύω	*I loose, am loosing*
λύεις	*you loose, are loosing (sg)*
λύει	*he (she, it) looses, is loosing*
λύομεν	*we loose, are loosing*
λύετε	*you loose, are loosing (pl)*
λύουσι(ν)	*they loose, are loosing*

Active Paradigm. The thematic vowel pattern for person and number (o, ε, ε, o, ε, o) is hidden by interactions in all except first and second plural. For simplicity, present active indicative forms are learned with *resultant* endings (-ω, -εις, -ει, etc.). Note that moveable -ν regularly shows up in third plural.

Active Translation. Translation is straightforward. The subject does the action. The style of a "to be" auxiliary verb followed by the verb as a participle emphasizes the durative nature of the action in English.

Middle Voice

Middle Paradigm. The second singular form volatilizes due to an intervocalic sigma that elides (-εσαι→-εαι→-η). The third singular and plural forms show a pattern: notice that the plural is formed simply by adding a ν to the singular form: -ται, -νται. This "nu pattern" will be true for secondary middle endings as well.

Table 11.4 Present Middle/Passive Indicative

λύομαι	*I loose, am loosed*
λύῃ	*you loose, are loosed (sg)*
λύεται	*he (she, it) looses, is loosed*
λυόμεθα	*we loose, are loosed*
λύεσθε	*you loose, are loosed (pl)*
λύονται	*they loose, are loosed*

Middle Translation. Use of a reflexive pronoun ("I loose for myself") is an awkward workaround to convey the grammatical thought. This style is only for a direct middle anyway, which is uncommon in the New Testament. More common is the indirect (intensive) middle, in which emphasis is upon the subject's self-interest in the action. In this case, voice often is left untranslated. The reciprocal middle would be the equivalent of the English reciprocal pronoun. Be aware that middle voice often is dropped completely in English translations, so the grammatical significance often relies on exposition, not translation. Examples are:

1. *direct (reflexive) middle:* ἐὰν μὴ βαπτίσωνται οὐκ ἐσθίουσιν, "unless they wash *themselves*, they will not eat" (Mk 7:4);[1] or again, note μετασχηματίζεται, "he transforms *himself*" in 2 Cor 11:14, referring to Satan

2. *indirect (intensive) middle:* ἡμέρας παρατηρεῖσθε καὶ μῆνας, "you *observe* [for yourselves] days and months" (Gal 4:10); or again, note κακῶς αἰτεῖσθε, "you ask wrongly [for yourselves]" in Jas 4:3. Translating middle voice is difficult; note Rom 15:7, προσλαμβάνεσθε

---

[1]The NRSV seems off track on multiple levels in its translation of this verb: "unless they wash *it*." (i.e, the food purchased in the market). First, the verb unnecessarily is converted from *middle* to *active* voice; second, because of the voice change, a fictive direct object has to be shoehorned in that is not present in the text ("it"); and third, the resulting translation suggests a misunderstanding of the entire issue: the ritual act was *not* the washing of *food*, but the *ritual cleansing of the person*, hence the reason for the choice of middle voice by the author.

αλλήλους, "*receive* one another," with the sense in this
context, "as this surely is in your own self-interest!"

3. *reciprocal middle:* συνεβουλεύσαντο, "they took counsel
    with one another" (Mt 26:4)

Middle Meaning. A few verbs show a different meaning in middle versus active voice. These infrequent verbs should be noted as
they are encountered in vocabulary. The table below, not exhaustive, includes some -μι verbs for later reference.

Table 11.5 Lexical Distinction by Voice

Active	Meaning	Middle	Meaning
αἴρω	I take	αἰρέομαι	I choose
ἀποδίδωμι	I give back	ἀποδίδομαι	I sell
ἀπόλλυμι	I destroy	ἀπόλλυμαι	I perish
ἅπτω	I fasten	ἅπτομαι	I touch
ἄρχω	I rule	ἄρχομαι	I begin
γράφω	I write	γράφομαι	I enroll
δανείζω	I lend	δανείζομαι	I borrow
ἵστημι	I place	ἵσταμαι	I stand
λανθάνω	I escape notice	λανθάνομαι	I forget
παύω	I make stop	παύομαι	I cease
πείθω	I persuade	πείθομαι	I obey
φαίνω	I shine	φαίνομαι	I appear
φοβέω	I frighten	φοβέομαι	I fear

Lexical Middle. A *lexical middle* is a verb entered into the
dictionary as -μαι, such as ἔρχομαι. This entry signals that the
verb occurs only as middle voice in the New Testament. Such verbs
are not "deponent." The middle voice simply may or may not be
difficult to bring out in translation. Thus, ἔρχομαι is glossed as "I

come" or "I go," because the middle voice idea ("I bring myself along") is awkward to try to render smoothly in English.

Passive Voice

Passive Translation. Passive forms are identical to the middle voice. Passive voice developed later in the history of the language, borrowing middle forms, relying on context for meaning. Passive voice would translate on the pattern of "I am loosed, am being loosed." One generally can assume that a given form is passive, because, statistically, the passive form outnumbers the middle by three to one (excluding lexical middle verbs). Hence:

♦ *First assume a non-lexical middle/passive is passive.*

Ambiguity still may exist whether a given form is middle or passive. Take Paul's question in Rom 3:9. Is his verb προεχόμεθα middle or passive? If middle, the idea is "do we have an advantage?" If passive, the meaning would be "are we put in a worse position?"

Passive Agency. Passive voice assigns agency of the verb's action to something other than the subject. The subject is acted upon. Sometimes agency is not emphasized. Rather, the focus is just on the action itself. Examples are Πλανᾶσθε = "you are deceived" (Mt 22:29); γαμίζονται = "they are given in marriage" (Mk 12:25); κρίνομαι = "I am being judged" (Acts 23:6).

Sometimes, however, agency is emphasized. The grammar used can indicate the nature of the agency. Personal agency is signaled by ὑπό, intermediate agency by διά, and impersonal agency by ἐν. Examples are:

1. *Personal:* παρακαλούμεθα αὐτοὶ <u>ὑπὸ τοῦ θεοῦ</u> = "we ourselves are being comforted *by God*" (2 Cor 1:4)
2. *Intermediate:* here, agency is personal but intermediate: ἐλπίζω γὰρ ὅτι <u>διὰ τῶν προσευχῶν ὑμῶν</u> χαρισθήσομαι ὑμῖν = "For I hope that *through your prayers* I will be given graciously to you" (Phlm 22); another example is:

σωθησόμεθα <u>δι᾽ αὐτοῦ</u> ἀπὸ τῆς ὀργῆς = "we shall be saved *through him* [Christ] from the wrath" (Rom 5:9)

3. *Impersonal:* <u>ἐν πυρὶ</u> ἀποκαλύπτεται = "will be revealed *by fire*" (1 Cor 3:13)

Table 11.6 Agency and Passive Voice

Agency	Preposition	Case (func.)	Translation
personal	ὑπό	Gen. (abl.)	"by"
intermediate	διά	Gen. (abl.)	"by," "through"
impersonal	ἐν	Dat. (instr.)	"by," "with"

Divine Passive. The so-called "divine passive" is not actually a grammatical category, but just an observation of a habit of mind. One often may assume that a New Testament writer is thinking of God as the passive agent. Predictable verbs in these contexts are "saved" and "raised." Thus, σῴζεσθε, "you are being saved" (1 Cor 15:2); νεκροὶ ἐγείρονται, "the dead are raised" (Lk 7:22); παρακληθήσονται, "they will be comforted" (Mt 5:5).

Imperfect Morphology

The key distinctions from the present are two, both based on the past time factor. One is the augment on the front to indicate past time. The other on the back is secondary endings of past time.

Table 11.7 Imperfect Tense Morphology

1	2	3	4	5	6
augment	reduplic.	stem	suffix	vowel	ending
ἐ		Present		ο/ε	Secondary

$$ἐ\text{-}λυ\text{-}ο\text{-}ν$$

Augmentation

Augmentation for past time has two forms. One is the syllabic augment. The other is the temporal augment. The forms may appear to be complex. However, one can boil the matter down:

♦ *Visible augmentation usually results in an ε, η, ει, or ω.*

Syllabic Augment. Syllabic augment adds the vowel ε to an opening consonant, which adds a syllable to the word. A deviation is a verb beginning with ρ doubling the ρ, yielding the form ἐρρ-. The New Testament does not show rho doubling in the imperfect, but does in the aorist and perfect. Verbs affected are: ῥαβδίζω, ῥαντίζω, ῥέω, ῥιζόω, ῥίπτω, ῥύομαι, and ῥώννυμι.

On rare occasion one may see the diphthong ει instead of ε. The reason is that certain primitive consonant stems with syllabic augment for various reasons dropped some of their consonants, leaving two vowels to volatilize (ε + ε→ει, or ε + ι→ει). Thus, the present tense verb ἔχω actually has a consonant stem σεχ-. The intervocalic sigma elided in the imperfect form (ἐσεχ→ἐεχ→εἶχ).

Temporal Augment. A temporal augment lengthens an opening vowel from short to long on a contract vowel pattern (ε→η, α→η, ο→ω). Verbs that begin with long vowels do not change. Verbs that begin with the variable vowels ι or υ, when short, do actually lengthen to their long forms, but the result can be heard only, not seen in print without a long vowel overstrike (ῑ and ῡ).

Augmentation with diphthongs is unpredictable and simply has to be observed. The diphthongs αι and οι transform into improper long diphthongs on a contract lengthening pattern (αι→ῃ, οι→ῳ). On rare occasions, αι and οι may remain unchanged. The iota diphthong ει also remains unchanged. The upsilon diphthong αυ shows a contract lengthening pattern (αυ→ηυ). The upsilon diphthong ευ, usually representing the adverb εὖ ("well") compounded onto verb stems, is inconsistent. With a consonant, ευ might lengthen (ευ→ηυ). Often, however, ευ simply remains unchanged.

The remaining diphthong forms (ου, υι, ηυ, ωυ) are not involved in verbs in the New Testament.

Table 11.8 Example Augments

Augment	Present	Imperfect
Consonants		
λ→ελ	λύω	ἔλυον
ῥ→ερρ	ῥίπτω	ἔρριπτον
σεχ→ειχ	ἔχω (stem: σεχ-)	εἶχον (ε + ε = εἰ)
Vowels		
α→η	ἀκούω	ἤκουον
ε→η	ἐσθίω	ἤσθιον
ο→ω	ὁμολογέω	ὡμολόγουν
η→η	ἤχω	ἦχον
ω→ω	ὠφελέω	ὠφέλουν
ι→ῑ	ἰσχύω	ἴσχυον
υ→ῡ	ὑμνέω	ὕμνουν
αι→η	αἰτέω	ἤτεον
οι→ῳ	οἰκοδομέω	ᾠκοδόμουν
ει→ει	εἰρηνεύω	εἰρηνεύον
αυ→ηυ	αὐξάνω	ηὔξανον
ευ→ηυ	εὑρίσκω	ηὕρισκον
ευ→ευ	εὐλογέω	εὐλόγουν
ευα→ευη	εὐαγγελίζω	εὐηγγελίζον
Compounds		
(consonant)	ἐνδύω	ἐνέδυνον
(vowel)	συνάγω	συνῆγον
(cons. elision)	ἀναβαίνω	ἀνέβαινον
(vow. elision)	ἀπάγω	ἀπῆγον

Compound Verbs. Remember that the compounded preposition is not considered part of the tense stem in forming principal parts. So, an augment attached to the *tense stem* must go *between* the preposition and the tense stem.

Table 11.9 Compounds

ἐκβάλλω→ἐξέβαλλον

συνάγω→συνῆγον

ἀπάγω→ἀπῆγον

Further, recall that prepositions ending in a vowel affixed to tense stems that themselves begin with a vowel suffer elision (ἀπό + ἄγω = ἀπάγω). Here, the augment occurs *after* the elided vowel, that is, still *between* the preposition and the original stem. Rare exceptions do occur, as in ἀνοίγω → ἤνοιγον. In any compound form, *the verb's accent never precedes the augment.* For example, observe συνῆγον and ἀπῆγον.

Active Voice

Table 11.10 Imperfect Active Indicative

ἔλυον	*I was loosing*
ἔλυες	*you were loosing (sg)*
ἔλυε(ν)	*he (she, it) was loosing*
ἐλύομεν	*we were loosing*
ἐλύετε	*you were loosing (pl)*
ἔλυον	*they were loosing*

The third singular, ἔλυεν, has *no* ending, which exposes the thematic vowel and adds a moveable -ν. The third plural, ἔλυον, represents the -ν option, much more frequent than -σαν. (For imperfect -ω verbs, the -σαν ending occurs only in the two verbs ἔχω and δολιόω.) Otherwise, when the third plural ending is -ν:

♦ *Only context distinguishes first singular and third plural.*

Middle Voice

Table 11.11 Imperfect Middle/Passive Indicative

ἐλυόμην	*I was loosing, was being loosed*
ἐλύου	*you were loosing, were being loosed (sg)*
ἐλύετο	*he (she, it) was loosing, was being loosed*
ἐλυόμεθα	*we were loosing, were being loosed*
ἐλύεσθε	*you were loosing, were being loosed (pl)*
ἐλύοντο	*they were loosing, were being loosed*

Second singular (intervocalic) sigma elides (-εσο→-εο→-ου). Third singular and plural is patterned, simply adding ν (-το, -ντο). Passive forms replicate the middle. Action happens to the subject, is durative, and past time. Translation would be "I was loosed, was being loosed." The grammar of passive agency would apply.

Contract Verbs

Table 11.12 Special Stems

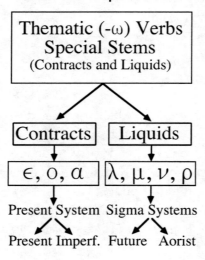

Thematic verbs have two special stems that affect morphology. These stems are contracts and liquids. The contract verb is a verb whose stem ends in one of three vowels: ε, ο, or α. These stem vowels interact with the thematic vowel. This reaction is restricted to the first principal part only. Formation in other principal parts involves a consonant in a suffix or ending. This consonant separates the vowels in question, so the tense stem vowel and thematic vowel have no chance to interact. The contraction of vowels does not take place. Instead, in all other principal parts, contract vowels lengthen.

Contraction Table

The combination of the stem vowel and the thematic vowel (or pronominal suffix, as, for example, in the -ω of the first person singular) produces a resultant long vowel or diphthong. What the student wants to be able to do is know whether the original verb is an epsilon, omicron, or alpha contract to be able to find the verb more quickly in the dictionary, whose lexical form is given as the *uncontracted* verb—that is, an abstract form one never encounters in the New Testament. First, we will overview the contraction possibilities for the first principal part. Then, we provide some "quick tips" for location.

Contraction Chart

The table below summarizes contraction possibilities for the first principal part. The top row represents each particular vowel to be found in the pertinent pronominal suffixes of the first principal part. On the side column are the contract vowels. The intersections of rows and columns give the resultant combinations.

Table 11.13 Contraction Chart: First Principal Part

Contract Vowels	Pronominal Suffix Vowels						
	ε	ει	η	ῃ	ο	ου	ω
ε	ει	ει	η	ῃ	ου	ου	ω
ο	ου	οι	ω	οι	ου	ου	ω
α	α	ᾳ	α	ᾳ	ω	ω	ω

We can summarize the table with two general remarks. First, observe how forms involving ι always survive as ι or iota subscript.

Second, with diphthongs notice that: (1) vowels assimilate, or coalesce, into the same vowel of a diphthong (εει = ει, οου = ου), and (2) different vowels contract with diphthongs, the υ close vowel dropping and the ι close vowel subscripting (αου = ω, αει = ᾳ, εαι = ῃ; but οει = οι is one exception).

Quick Tips

What are some "quick tips" that eliminate the need to memorize this contraction table? The following observations help determine the original contract vowel for present and imperfect verbs, which have the resultant forms η, ῃ, α, ᾳ, ω, and the diphthongs ει, οι, ου. Compare the paradigms to observe that:

1. Any α form is alpha contract only.
2. Any "e" vowel (short ε or long η) is epsilon contract only.
3. Internal ω is alpha contract only (ἀγαπῶμεν).
4. Any ι diphthong is the other vowel (ει→ε; οι→ο).
5. An ου is either an epsilon (ποιοῦμεν) or an omicron (πληροῦμεν) contract.
6. Final ω could be any contract (ποιῶ, πληρῶ, ἀγαπῶ).

These six observations are summarized in the table below.

Table 11.14 Contraction Results

any	ε/ο	ε only		ο only	α only	
ῶ	οῦ	ῇ	εῖ	οῖ	ᾶ	ᾷ

The only ambiguity of result is in final ῶ or the οῦ diphthong. The uncontracted dictionary entry (ποιέω, πληρόω, ἀγαπάω) is an abstraction; the form always is contracted in the New Testament. Contraction involves recognition only. Contraction has no affect on meaning or translation.

Finally, one general observation about accent is helpful:

♦ *Contraction often results in a circumflex accent.*

Sometimes an acute accent is the result. For example, note the pres. mid. ind., sec. pers. sing., λύῃ (λύεσαι → λύεαι → λύῃ).

Contraction Paradigms

Table 11.15 Present Active Contract Verbs

ποιέω	πληρόω	ἀγαπάω
ποιῶ	πληρῶ	ἀγαπῶ
ποιεῖς	πληροῖς	ἀγαπᾷς
ποιεῖ	πληροῖ	ἀγαπᾷ
ποιοῦμεν	πληροῦμεν	ἀγαπῶμεν
ποιεῖτε	πληροῦτε	ἀγαπᾶτε
ποιοῦσι(ν)	πληροῦσι(ν)	ἀγαπῶσι(ν)

Table 11.16 Present Middle/Passive Contract Verbs

ποιέω	πληρόω	ἀγαπάω
ποιοῦμαι	πληροῦμαι	ἀγαπῶμαι
ποιῇ	πληροῖ	ἀγαπᾷ
ποιεῖται	πληροῦται	ἀγαπᾶται
ποιούμεθα	πληρούμεθα	ἀγαπώμεθα
ποιεῖσθε	πληροῦσθε	ἀγαπᾶσθε
ποιοῦνται	πληροῦνται	ἀγαπῶνται

Table 11.17 Imperfect Active Contract Verbs

ποιέω	πληρόω	ἀγαπάω
ἐποίουν	ἐπλήρουν	ἠγάπων
ἐποίεις	ἐπλήρους	ἠγάπας
ἐποίει	ἐπλήρου	ἠγάπα
ἐποιοῦμεν	ἐπληροῦμεν	ἠγαπῶμεν
ἐποιεῖτε	ἐπληροῦτε	ἠγαπᾶτε
ἐποίουν	ἐπλήρουν	ἠγάπων

Table 11.18 Imperfect Middle/Passive Contract Verbs

ποιέω	πληρόω	ἀγαπάω
ἐποιούμην	ἐπληρούμην	ἠγαπώμην
ἐποιοῦ	ἐπληροῦ	ἠγαπῶ
ἐποιεῖτο	ἐπληροῦτο	ἠγαπᾶτο
ἐποιούμεθα	ἐπληρούμεθα	ἠγαπώμεθα
ἐποιεῖσθε	ἐπληροῦσθε	ἠγαπᾶσθε
ἐποιοῦντο	ἐπληροῦντο	ἠγαπῶντο

Some endings such as -οῖ, -ᾷ, and -α are new as verb endings. In addition, the nature of contractions can leave voice, person, and number unclear (cf. πληροῖ), or result in only subtle variations (ἀγαπᾷ vs. ἠγάπα). Note particularly the present active ἀγαπῶ vs. imperfect middle ἠγαπῶ (σ drops: -ασο→-αο→-ῶ).

The Verb Εἰμί

Table 11.19 Present, Imperfect Indicative of Εἰμί

εἰμί	ἤμην	I am, was
εἶ	ἦς (ἦσθα)	you are, were (sg.)
ἐστί(ν)	ἦν	he (she, it) is, was
ἐσμέν	ἦμεν (ἤμεθα)	we are, were
ἐστέ	ἦτε	you are, were (pl.)
εἰσί(ν)	ἦσαν	they are, were

Formation

Εἰμί is part of the -μι verb conjugation. Its high frequency in the New Testament justifies a review in the current chapter, even though its kind of action frequently is more aoristic than durative. Imperfect third plural takes the -σαν ending, rather than -ν. Alternate forms of the imperfect in parentheses are rare. The form ἦσθα occurs in Mt 26:69 and Mk 16:47, and ἤμεθα occurs in Mt 23:30; Acts 27:37; Gal 4:3; and Eph 2:3. Most present tense forms are enclitic, but imperfect forms are not. The verb does not have voice, so one would locate simply as "present indicative."

Grammar

The verb εἰμί is a copulative. This intransitive verb can take substantives in its predicate, but not as direct object. Rather, these forms are predicative and nominative case. Predicate nouns rename the subject. Predicate adjectives describe the subject. Related to the use of copulatives, review the following material on adjectives in Chapter 6:
- the grammar of copulatives
- "verbless predicative" function
- Colwell's Rule: subject vs. predicate nominative (levels of precedence)

Other Copulatives

Two other copulative verbs in Greek are γίνομαι and ὑπάρχω. The verb γίνομαι is a lexical middle. The most common form is the second aorist, middle, third person, singular, ἐγένετο = "it happened," "it took place," or "it came about." The construction καὶ ἐγένετο = "and it came about that" or "now it happened that," is a form often found in narrative material (cf. Mt 7:28; Mk 1:9; Lk 1:23).

The verb ὑπάρχω often is used in terms referring to one's possessions in the sense of "that which exists with [= belongs to] me." The form usually is as a participle, such as the form ὑπάρχων = "being." Use of the verb ὑπάρχω generally is a more literary form of Hellenistic Greek. Two-thirds of the sixty New Testament occurrences of the verb ὑπάρχω are in Luke-Acts alone; Matthew has only three; Mark and John none. Study the following:

1. μεῖζον τῶν λαχάνων ἐστὶν καὶ γίνεται δένδρον = "[the mustard seed] is greater than garden plants and *becomes* a tree" (Mt 13:32); note that δένδρον is nominative

2. Εγίνετο δὲ πάσῃ ψυχῇ φόβος, πολλά τε τέρατα καὶ σημεῖα διὰ τῶν ἀποστόλων ἐγίνετο. = "So great fear *was* upon every person, and many signs and wonders *were taking place* through the apostles." (Acts 2:43)[2]

3. εὐχάριστοι γίνεσθε = "*Be* thankful" (Col 3:15)

4. ἀλλὰ τύπος γίνου = "rather, *be* an example" (1 Tim 4:12); note that τύπος is nominative

5. Μὴ πολλοὶ διδάσκαλοι γίνεσθε = "Let not many *become* teachers" (Jas 3:1); note here that διδάσκαλοι is nominative

6. Αργύριον καὶ χρυσίον οὐχ ὑπάρχει μοι = "'Silver and gold I *do not have* [*does not exist with me*]'" (Acts 3:6)

7. καὶ πάντες ζηλωταὶ τοῦ νόμου ὑπάρχουσιν = "and all *are* zealous for the law" (Acts 21:20); note that ζηλωταί is nominative

8. ὃς ἐν μορφῇ θεοῦ ὑπάρχων = "who, although *being* in the form of God," (Phil 2:6; concessive participle)

Durative Nuances

Translations provided with the paradigms are simply glosses for the general idea. They represent only one nuance among several for these tenses when considered in New Testament passages. In context, present and imperfect tenses can take on various other nuances of meaning. Some of these nuances are reviewed briefly so that the intermediate student can gain greater sophistication in handling these tenses in the New Testament. Remember that translating middle voice retains all the issues raised previously.

---

[2]Notice the *neuter plural* subjects in τέρατα καὶ σημεῖα, but the third *singular* verb form; neuter plural subjects can take singular verbs.

Present Tense Nuances

Descriptive Present

The descriptive present is action that is happening now (the translation used in the paradigms). Neither the beginning nor the end of the action is in mind: Ἴδε νῦν ἐν παρρησίᾳ <u>λαλεῖς</u> = "Behold, now you *are speaking* plainly" (Jn 16:29).

Durative Present

The durative (or "progressive") present denotes action over two points in time, a beginning point continuing even now. Translation often uses English present perfect: τοσαῦτα ἔτη <u>δουλεύω</u> σοι = "all these years *I have served* you" (Lk 15:29).

Historical Present

The historical present is used for dramatic effect, to draw the reader into the story. The narrative is past time (aorist), but suddenly a present tense appears. English shows a similar tense shift in a good story told orally: "We went to the store, and we *hear* this explosion, and *he comes out shouting . . .*" Mostly found in John and Mark in the New Testament, this effect seems to be a feature of Koine style. To retain the ambience of storytelling, maintain the present tense. Thus: καὶ <u>λέγει</u>, Οὐκ εἰμί. = "and he *says*, 'I am not.'" (Jn 1:21). Mark's Gospel particularly shows use of the historical present, providing a characteristic "vividness." For example, observe ἐκβάλλει in Mk 1:12 or λέγει in Mk 2:5.

Aoristic Present

This use is when the present tense kind of action is not durative, but punctiliar or undefined (see Table 10.2). The aoristic present is rare. A few cases show, *by context alone*, that a punctiliar sense is meant. An example is Acts 9:34, <u>ἰᾶταί</u> σε Ἰησοῦς Χριστός = "Jesus Christ *heals* you." For another, note Acts 16:18,

Παραγγέλλω σοι ἐν ὀνόματι Ἰησοῦ Χριστοῦ = "*I command* you in the name of Jesus Christ." Commentaries often will point out this rare use of the present tense. One verb that *is* commonly an aoristic present is εἰμί.

Other Categories

Other uses for the present tense include *iterative* (happens repeatedly), *tendential* or *conative* (action contemplated), and *futuristic* (confident assertion). For these forms, research good resources that describe Greek syntax.

Imperfect Tense Nuances

Descriptive Imperfect

Action is conceived as ongoing with no reference to beginning or end, as with the present, but in past time (the translation used in the paradigms). For example, καὶ οἱ ἄγγελοι διηκόνουν αὐτῷ = "and the angels *were ministering* to him" (Mk 1:13).

Durative Imperfect

This use is parallel to the present tense, only in past time, so the progressive present (or past) perfect is used. For example, ἐντολὴν παλαιὰν ἣν εἴχετε ἀπ' ἀρχῆς = "an old commandment which you *have had* from the beginning" (1 Jn 2:7). This use also is called the "progressive imperfect."

Inceptive Imperfect

Emphasis is upon the beginning of the action in the past. For example, καὶ ἀνοίξας τὸ στόμα αὐτοῦ ἐδίδασκεν αὐτοὺς = "and opening his mouth, he *began to teach* them" (Mt 5:2). Explicitly in the context, the expression "opening his mouth" (ἀνοίξας τὸ στόμα αὐτοῦ) shows that this is the beginning of Jesus' message (what we call the Sermon on the Mount). Implicitly, verse one's context helps establish that Jesus is about to teach the crowds that have gathered around him.

Conative Imperfect

Attempted action is unsuccessful. Time frame is past. Translation can use "was trying to." For example, Gal 1:13: ἐδίωκον τὴν ἐκκλησίαν τοῦ θεοῦ καὶ <u>ἐπόρθουν</u> αὐτήν = "I was persecuting the church of God and *was trying to destroy* it." Paul did not succeed. Simply translating ἐπόρθουν as "I was destroying" could mislead the reader or introduce an idea actually foreign to Paul's thought, as if Paul would be suggesting that, had he continued, he would have succeeded in eradicating the church.

Customary Imperfect

Similar to the iterative present, so sometimes called "iterative imperfect," this use focuses on habit or custom in a past time frame. For example, Καὶ <u>ἐπορεύοντο</u> οἱ γονεῖς αὐτοῦ κατ᾽ ἔτος εἰς Ἰερουσαλὴμ τῇ ἑορτῇ τοῦ πάσχα = "And his parents *used to go* each year to Jerusalem at the feast of Passover" (Lk 2:41). The κατ᾽ ἔτος ("each year") makes the customary action explicit. Luke's theme in this unit is that those surrounding the infancy of Jesus were pious, law-abiding Jews. Here, the imperfect tense of ἐπορεύοντο carefully is chosen to contribute to this picture regarding Jesus' parents. The observant translator should not fail to note the observant parents, an important Lukan nativity theme.

Lexical Middle Voice

A verb lexical middle in the present also is lexical middle in the imperfect, since the imperfect is built on that present tense stem. Note ἔρχομαι, a lexical middle both as present and imperfect: ἐξῆλθον ἐκ τῆς πόλεως καὶ <u>ἤρχοντο</u> πρὸς αὐτόν = "they went out from the city and *were coming* to him" (Jn 4:30). Middle voice is present in ἤρχοντο, but not obvious in translation.

EXERCISE 11

1. Answer the following on present and imperfect verbs based on the Mk 15:6-12 passage provided.

15:6 Κατὰ δὲ ἑορτὴν ἀπέλυεν αὐτοῖς ἕνα δέσμιον ὃν παρῃτοῦντο. 15:7 ἦν δὲ ὁ λεγόμενος Βαραββᾶς μετὰ τῶν στασιαστῶν δεδεμένος οἵτινες ἐν τῇ στάσει φόνον πεποιήκεισαν. 15:8 καὶ ἀναβὰς ὁ ὄχλος ἤρξατο αἰτεῖσθαι καθὼς ἐποίει αὐτοῖς. 15:9 ὁ δὲ Πιλᾶτος ἀπεκρίθη αὐτοῖς λέγων· θέλετε ἀπολύσω ὑμῖν τὸν βασιλέα τῶν Ἰουδαίων; 15:10 ἐγίνωσκεν γὰρ ὅτι διὰ φθόνον παραδεδώκεισαν αὐτὸν οἱ ἀρχιερεῖς. 15:11 οἱ δὲ ἀρχιερεῖς ἀνέσεισαν τὸν ὄχλον ἵνα μᾶλλον τὸν Βαραββᾶν ἀπολύσῃ αὐτοῖς. 15:12 ὁ δὲ Πιλᾶτος πάλιν ἀποκριθεὶς ἔλεγεν αὐτοῖς· τί οὖν [θέλετε] ποιήσω [ὃν λέγετε] τὸν βασιλέα τῶν Ἰουδαίων;

1.1 ἀπέλυεν (15:6)—Locate (parse):

Be able to explain formation elements:
   a. the ἀπ- on the front
   b. the first ε
   c. the εν ending

1.2 παρῃτοῦντο (15:6)—Locate (parse):

Be able to explain formation elements:

   a. the παρ- on the front

   b. the ῃ

   c. the οῦ and its accent

1.3 ἦν (15:7)—Locate (parse):

1.4 ἐποίει (15:8)—Locate (parse):

Be able to explain formation elements:

   a. the ἐ- on the front

   b. the ει ending

1.5 θέλετε (15:9)—Locate (parse):

Be able to explain formation elements:

   a. the θελ- on the front

   b. the second ε

   c. the τε on the end

1.6 ἐγίνωσκεν (15:10)—Locate (parse):

1.7 ἔλεγεν (15:12)—Locate (parse):

---

2. Explain the present and imperfect tense nuances in the following sentences:

   2.1 Κατὰ δὲ ἑορτὴν ἀπέλυεν αὐτοῖς ἕνα δέσμιον ὃν παρῃτοῦντο. (Mk 15:6)

   a. ἀπέλυεν: _____

   b. παρῃτοῦντο: _____

   2.2 καὶ ἀναβὰς ὁ ὄχλος ἤρξατο αἰτεῖσθαι καθὼς ἐποίει αὐτοῖς. (Mk 15:8)

   ἐποίει: _____

   2.3 ἐγίνωσκεν γὰρ ὅτι διὰ φθόνον παραδεδώκεισαν αὐτὸν οἱ ἀρχιερεῖς. (Mk 15:10)

   ἐγίνωσκεν: _____

   2.4 ὁ δὲ Πιλᾶτος πάλιν ἀποκριθεὶς ἔλεγεν αὐτοῖς· (Mk 15:12)

   ἔλεγεν: _____

   2.5 καὶ εἶπαν αὐτῷ· ἀκούεις τί οὗτοι λέγουσιν; ὁ δὲ Ἰησοῦς λέγει αὐτοῖς· ναί. (Mt 21:16)

   a. ἀκούεις: _____

   b. λέγουσιν: _____

   c. λέγει: _____

   2.6 πάντα δὲ τὰ ἔργα αὐτῶν ποιοῦσιν πρὸς τὸ θεαθῆναι τοῖς ἀνθρώποις· (Mt 23:5)

   ποιοῦσιν: _____

2.7 Γρηγορεῖτε οὖν, ὅτι οὐκ οἴδατε ποίᾳ ἡμέρᾳ ὁ κύριος ὑμῶν ἔρχεται. (Mt 24:42)

ἔρχεται: _____

2.8 καὶ ἰδόντες οἱ Φαρισαῖοι ἔλεγον τοῖς μαθηταῖς αὐτοῦ· (Mt 9:11)

ἔλεγον: _____

2.9 Εἶπεν δέ· ἄνθρωπός τις εἶχεν δύο υἱούς. (Lk 15:11)

εἶχεν: _____

2.10 Οἱ δὲ ἀρχιερεῖς καὶ τὸ συνέδριον ὅλον ἐζήτουν ψευδομαρτυρίαν κατὰ τοῦ Ἰησοῦ (Mt 26:59)

ἐζήτουν: _____

3. Translate the following and be ready to explain the grammar of copulatives:

3.1 αὐτὸς υἱὸς Ἀβραάμ ἐστιν

_____

3.2 ὁ μισθὸς ὑμῶν πολὺς ἐν τοῖς οὐρανοῖς·

_____

3.3 ὁ μὲν θερισμὸς πολύς, οἱ δὲ ἐργάται ὀλίγοι·

_____

3.4 ἦσαν δὲ δίκαιοι ἀμφότεροι ἐναντίον τοῦ θεοῦ

_____

3.5 καὶ ἔλεγεν αὐτοῖς· κύριός ἐστιν τοῦ σαββάτου ὁ υἱὸς τοῦ ἀνθρώπου.

_____

_____

3.6 Διὰ δὲ τῶν χειρῶν τῶν ἀποστόλων ἐγίνετο σημεῖα καὶ τέρατα πολλὰ ἐν τῷ λαῷ.

_____

_____

CHAPTER 12
PERFECT AND PLUPERFECT TENSES

The perfect tense system is both easily recognized and exegetically significant. Thus, the student of New Testament Greek is richly rewarded in mastering this system. Two principal parts, fourth and fifth, are involved in formulating the active versus the middle/passive voices.

Perfective Tenses

The pluperfect is built on the perfect stem. Hence, these two tenses comprise the fourth and fifth principal parts. Both tenses are perfective kind of action, since the perfect stem that both rely on is perfective.

Table 12.1 Principal Parts

Principal Parts	Tenses	Voices		
First	Present	active	middle	passive
	Imperfect	active	middle	passive
Second	Future	active	middle	
Third	First Aorist	active	middle	
	Second Aorist	active	middle	
Fourth	Pluperfect	active		
	Perfect	active		
	Future Perfect	active		
Fifth	Pluperfect		middle	passive
	Perfect		middle	passive
	Future Perfect		middle	passive
Sixth	Aorist			passive
	Future			passive

Perfect Active Morphology

The perfect active is the fourth principal part. The perfect tense is a primary tense, so requires no augment. The perfect stem is altered with both a prefix and a suffix. The prefix is called reduplication. The suffix is a -κα pattern parallel to the first aorist -σα pattern. The perfect, while a primary tense, takes *secondary* endings, in the pattern of the first aorist.

Table 12.2 Perfect Active Morphology

1	2	3	4	5	6
augment	reduplic.	stem	suffix	vowel	ending
	λε	Perfect	κα		Secondary

$$\lambda\epsilon\text{-}\lambda\upsilon\text{-}\kappa\alpha\text{-}\mu\epsilon\nu$$

Table 12.3 Perfect Active Indicative

λέλυκα	I have loosed
λέλυκας	you have loosed
λέλυκεν	he (she, it) has loosed
λελύκαμεν	we have loosed
λελύκατε	you have loosed
λελύκασιν (-καν)	they have loosed

The third plural -κασιν (with a moveable -ν) is more frequent than the more typical secondary ending, which, with the suffix, would be -καν. The only verbs showing the -καν option in the New Testament are ὁράω, τηρέω, γινώσκω, ἀποστέλλω, γίνομαι, πίνω, and the second aorist εἶπον associated with λέγω.

Reduplication

The signature of the perfect system is reduplication. The process breaks down into what letter or combination begins the tense stem. Reduplication takes two forms, consonant or augment.

Consonant Reduplication. The basic consonant pattern is repetition. An ε vowel acts to join the reduplicated consonant to the tense stem. The types are:

1. *single consonant:* A single consonant is repeated, inserting an ε (except stems beginning with ρ). Thus, λύω, which begins with the single consonant λ, repeats this λ and inserts an ε, which creates the perfect form λελυ-.

2. *stop with λ/ρ:* The single consonant process also applies to a stop followed by λ or ρ. Notice γράφω, which reduplicates as the perfect stem γεγραφ-, or the verb βλέπω, which reduplicates as βεβλεπ-. Exceptions are χ stems followed by ρ, such as χρίω. These χ stems show smooth patterns, as κέχρικα (see rough to smooth stop).

3. *rough to smooth stop:* Outside the special case of stops followed by λ or ρ above, stop consonants change from rough to smooth. If the single consonant is a rough stop (φ, χ, θ), the repeated consonant takes the form of the corresponding smooth stop (φ→π = πεφ-, χ→κ = κεχ-, θ→τ = τεθ-). So we have φιλέω with the perfect stem πεφιλε-.

Augment Reduplication. The other process uses a vowel as an augment. The vowel usually is ε, η, or ω, similar to the past time augment. A few verbs show exceptions by reduplicating with a consonant (e.g., θνήσκω, μιμνήσκω, πίπτω, and περιτέμνω). Some common types of augment reduplication are detailed below and summarized in the table:

1. *Vowels:* A vowel that opens a stem *lengthens* to create the augment on the pattern of augmentation for past time. Thus, ἀγαπάω reduplicates with the α lengthening to η as ἠγαπα-; or, ὁμολογέω reduplicates as ὠμολογε-.

2. *Complex sibilants:* A stem that opens with a complex sibilant (ζ, ξ, ψ) reduplicates with a vowel. So, ξηραίνω ("I dry up") has the perfect stem ἐξηραν-. For point of reference, no example with the complex sibilant ψ occurs in the New Testament.

3. *Multiple consonants:* A consonant group (e.g., στ-, σφρ-) reduplicates with an ε augment. So, σταυρόω reduplicates as the perfect stem ἐσταυρο-, and σφραγίζω ("I seal") reduplicates into ἐσφραγιδ-. Exceptions are those stops followed by λ or ρ (outlined above).

4. *Rho stems:* Stems beginning with ρ *usually* are augmented and doubled to ἐρρ-. However, to know what a particular rho stem does, consult a lexicon.

Table 12.4 Perfect Reduplication Types

Type	Letters	Example	Perfect
Consonant	Single	λύω	λελυ-
	Stop + λ	βλέπω	βεβλεπ-
	Stop + ρ	γράφω	γεγραφ-
	Aspirated	φιλέω	πεφιλε-
	Stops	χαλάω	κεχαλα-
	(φ, χ, θ)	θύω	τεθυ-
Augment	Vowels	ἀγαπάω	ἠγαπα-
	Iota insert	λαμβάνω	εἴληφ-
	Preserved	ὁράω	ἑορα-
	Vowel	ὁράω	ἑωρα-
	Sibilant	ξηραίνω	ἐξηραν-
	Pairs	σταυρόω	ἐσταυρο-
	Triplets	σφραγίζω	ἐσφραγιδ-
	Rho	ῥέω	ἐρρυη-
	Attic	ἀκούω	ἀκηκο-
	None	οἶδα	οἶδα
Compound	Stem	ἀναβαίνω	ἀναβεβη-

5. *Variations:* One can find minor variations. These variations are generated through elements of root history:
    *   "Iota insert" relates to some ε verbs "inserting" an iota. Examples include εἶπον to εἴρηκα, ἐργάζομαι to the perfect passive εἴργασμαι, and λαμβάνω to the perfect (second active) form εἴληφα.

- <u>Preserved stem vowel</u> relates to the verb ὁράω having two perfect forms, both forms augmenting with ε, but either preserving or lengthening the stem vowel too, as ἑόρακα or ἑώρακα.
- <u>"Attic reduplication"</u> is a feature of the Attic dialect. One has syllable doubling with an additional lengthening of the internal vowel. So, ἀκούω becomes the perfect (second active) ἀκήκοα; ἐγείρω becomes the passive ἐγήγερμαι; ἔρχομαι becomes the perfect (second active) ἐλήλυθα. These Attic forms you just memorize.
- <u>No reduplication</u> is the old perfect (second active) form οἶδα, which has no reduplication. The verb also has lost its perfective force, meaning simply "I know."

Compound Verbs

Compound prepositions are not considered integral to a verb's tense stem. As with past time augments, therefore, reduplication involves the verb's tense stem, *not* the opening compound preposition. Thus, for example, a verb such as ἀναβαίνω, when reduplicated, becomes ἀναβέβηκα.

Tense/Voice Suffix

The perfect active tense/voice suffix is -κα. Since this suffix includes a vowel, no thematic vowel is necessary. The -κα suffix, however, can cause minor stem reactions. Several of these are:

1. *Vowels insert:* Some verbs will insert an η or ω before the tense suffix (μένω→μεμένηκα; πίπτω→πέπτωκα).
2. *Dentals drop:* Dentals will drop before the κ of the -κα suffix. So, ἐλπίζω, stem ἐλπιδ-, drops the δ to give the form ἤλπικα.
3. *Nasal ν drops:* A nasal ν will drop before the κ of the -κα suffix. So, κρίνω, with its nasal stem κριν-, drops the ν to give the form κέκρικα.

Pronominal Suffix

Secondary active endings are used—an exception to the rule that primary tenses take primary endings.

♦ *Perfect active, a primary tense, takes secondary endings.*

First singular has no ending, as in the aorist. Third plural can be -ν, but more often is -σι(ν), a primary ending with moveable -ν. The resultant pattern, when the -κα tense suffix is included, is similar to first aorist: -κα, -κας, -κεν, -καμεν, -κατε, -κασιν (or -καν). The third singular (-κεν) results from no ending, reappearance of the thematic vowel, and movable -ν.

Second Active

The perfect active system has a second variation, a *second active* form (sometimes called "second perfect"). The κ of the -κα suffix falls out. The vowel α is all that remains of the perfect active tense suffix (i.e., -α, -ας, -εν, -αμεν, -ατε, -ασιν). This second active pattern does not affect translation, only the form.

Table 12.5 Perfect Second Active Indicative

γέγραφα	*I have written*
γέγραφας	*you have written*
γέγραφεν	*he (she, it) has written*
γεγράφαμεν	*we have written*
γεγράφατε	*you have written*
γεγράφασιν	*they have written*

The second active examples in the table are not intended as an exhaustive list but as illustrative of the second active form losing the κ of the tense suffix. The paradigm word for the perfect second active is γράφω. (In this case, the stem's ending φ causes this reaction of dropping the κ of the suffix consonant.) Note that a similar process of the dropping of a suffix consonant occurs also in the aorist passive system (dropping the θ of the -θη suffix).

Table 12.6 Perfect Second Active Examples

Verb	Second Active
ἀκούω	ἀκήκοα
γίνομαι	γέγονα
γράφω	γέγραφα
ἔρχομαι	ἐλήλυθα
λαμβάνω	εἴληφα
--------	οἶδα
πάσχω	πέπονθα
πείθω	πέποιθα
πέμπω	πέπομφα
φεύγω	πέφευγα

Contract Verbs

♦ *Contract verbs contract in the first principal part.*

♦ *Contract verbs lengthen in all other principal parts.*

Outside the first principal part, contract verbs lengthen (ε→η, ο→ω, α→η), a grammatical process in broader terms known as *ablaut*, which refers to any vowel change pattern, such as "drink," "drank," "drunk." Contract vowels that end a tense stem contract with thematic vowels used to join the pronominal suffix in the first principal part. In all other principal parts, one has a suffix consonant, such as the κ in the -κα perfect suffix, that separates the contract vowel from other vowels. In the face of this suffix consonant, the contract vowel simply lengthens.

Table 12.7 Perfect Active Indicative: Contracts

ποιέω	πληρόω	ἀγαπάω
πεποίηκα	πεπλήρωκα	ἠγάπηκα
πεποίηκας	πεπλήρωκας	ἠγάπηκας
πεποίηκεν	πεπλήρωκεν	ἠγάπηκεν
πεποιήκαμεν	πεπληρώκαμεν	ἠγαπήκαμεν
πεποιήκατε	πεπληρώκατε	ἠγαπήκατε
πεποιήκασιν	πεπληρώκασιν	ἠγαπήκασιν

Active Translation

Perfect tense in English requires the use of the "have," "has" auxiliary verb. This convention sometimes can be confused with the aorist tense, which also at times has been rendered using the same auxiliary verb. The English sense is completed action. The Greek sense goes further by including on-going results of the completed action.

Perfect Middle Morphology

The perfect middle/passive is the fifth principal part. This part is distinctive because no thematic vowel is used. Primary endings are a return to the expected pattern.

♦ *Perfect middle/passive has no thematic vowel.*

Table 12.8 Perfect Middle/Passive Morphology

1	2	3	4	5	6
augment	reduplic.	stem	suffix	vowel	ending
	λε	Perfect			Primary

$$\lambda\epsilon\text{-}\lambda\upsilon\text{-}\mu\epsilon\theta\alpha$$

Table 12.9 Perfect Middle/Passive Indicative

λέλυμαι	I have loosed, have been loosed
λέλυσαι	you have loosed, have been loosed
λέλυται	he (she, it) has loosed, has been loosed
λελύμεθα	we have loosed, have been loosed
λέλυσθε	you have loosed, have been loosed
λέλυνται	they have loosed, have been loosed

The sigma in the second singular ending (-σαι) is not regarded as intervocalic with the stem vowel, so does not volatilize in contraction, as in the first principal part. Thus, one can contrast λύῃ.

Perfect Middle Volatilization

Table 12.10 Perfect Middle/Passive Volatilization

Tense Stem Ending						
Stops			*Liquid/Nasals*			
Labial	*Palatal*	*Dental*	*Liquid*		*Nasal*	*Suffix*
π, β, φ	κ, γ, χ	τ, δ, θ	λ	ρ	ν	*Letter*
μμ	γμ	σμ	-----	-----	μμ	μ
ψ	ξ	σ	-----	-----	-----	σ
πτ	κτ	στ	-----	-----	-----	τ
φθ	χθ	σθ	λθ	ρθ	νθ	σθ

Consonant Change. The fifth principal part has no thematic vowel. This feature has no affect on vowel stems (-η, -ι, -υ, -ω, and diphthongs). Tense stems, however, that end in a consonant will be face-to-face with consonants of pronominal suffixes. When consonants collide, phonetic changes can take place. To analyze these changes, we can break down the tense stem consonants into stops and liquids. The beginning consonants of the pronominal suffixes involved are μ, σ, τ, σθ.[1] A dash in the table means no reaction; the stem consonant and pronominal suffix consonants remain the same.

A few comments are in order. First, the nasal ν shows several variations. Often verbs ending with -ν drop the ν in their perfect and aorist passive indicative forms (e.g., κέκρικα, κέκριμαι, ἐκρίθην). In contrast, others show -σμαι in the perfect middle, dropping the ν and inserting σ on the letter insert pattern (see below; μιαίνω, μεμίασμαι). On the other hand, notice how the nasal ν can produce a -μμ result. This result is seen in: (1) some perfect middles, as μαραίνω, μεμάραμμαι, (2) compound formation, as ἐνμένω = ἐμμένω, and (3) in some middle/passive participles (having the suffix -μεν), as μεμιαμμένοις (from μιαίνω).

Second, *for consonant stems only*, the *third plural* form of the perfect middle in the New Testament is not the expected -νται ending. Instead, the third plural always is formed periphrastically, that is, with a specific participle construction. The indicative third plural of εἰμί (εἰσί) is combined with the middle participle of the verb. Thus, for example, the perfect middle, third plural of the verb γράφω, which is a consonant stem, would not appear in the New Testament as γεγράφνται. Instead, the third plural would use εἰσί in conjunction with the perfect middle participle of γράφω, creating the hybrid form εἰσὶ γεγραμμένοι = "they have written (for themselves)."

Letter Insert. Besides consonant changes, other verbs simply will insert a letter before the pronominal suffix of the perfect middle. This letter is either an η or σ, which provides euphony in the resultant sound to the Greek ear. An example verb inserting η is βάλλω, which becomes the perfect middle βέβληται (the stem vowel α is lost by vowel gradation). An example of a verb inserting σ is γινώσκω, which becomes the perfect middle form ἔγνωσμαι. Note that, in the case of a σ insert, the second singular and plural

---

[1]The third plural form (-νται) is not represented because this form does not occur; instead, a periphrastic participial construction is used for third plural.

pronominal suffixes (-σαι, -σθε) already have a sigma, so the σ insert is not needed in these two forms.

Table 12.11 Perfect Middle/Passive Indicative: Stops

γράφω	ἄρχω	πείθω
γέγραμμαι	ἦργμαι	πέπεισμαι
γέγραψαι	ἦρξαι	πέπεισαι
γέγραπται	ἦρκται	πέπεισται
γεγράμμεθα	ἤργμεθα	πεπείσμεθα
γέγραφθε	ἦρχθε	πέπεισθε
(εἰσὶ γεγραμμένοι)	(εἰσὶ ἠργμένοι)	(εἰσὶ πεπεισμένοι)

Table 12.12 Perfect Middle/Passive Indicative: Liquids, Insert

ἀγγέλλω	αἴρω	γινώσκω
ἤγγελμαι	ἦρμαι	ἔγνωσμαι
ἤγγελσαι	ἦρσαι	ἔγνωσαι
ἤγγελται	ἦρται	ἔγνωσται
ἠγγέλμεθα	ἤρμεθα	ἐγνώσμεθα
ἤγγελθε	ἦρθε	ἔγνωσθε
(εἰσὶ ἠγγελμένοι)	(εἰσὶ ἠρμένοι)	(εἰσὶ ἐγνωσμένοι)

Perfect Middle Contracts

In the first principal part contract vowels contract. In all other parts, they lengthen. Thus, contract vowels lengthen before the perfect middle pronominal suffix (e.g., πεποίημαι, πεπλήρωμαι, ἠγάπημαι). One contract exception is δέω. Note: δέδεμαι, δέδεσαι, δέδεται, δεδέμεθα, δέδεσθε, δέδενται.

Perfect Middle Translation

Review issues with middle voice. Its use is fading out in New Testament times. Generally, first assume a non-lexical middle is passive. Since in passive voice the subject receives the action, agency of the action often is a focus with passive voice.

1. Μὴ καὶ ὑμεῖς πεπλάνησθε; = "You *have* not also *been deceived*, have you?" (Jn 7:47)

2. ὃ ἐπήγγελται δυνατός ἐστιν καὶ ποιῆσαι = "that which He *had promised* He also was able to do" (Rom 4:21; lexical middle, ἀπαγγέλλομαι)

3. ὅτι δέδεκται ἡ Σαμάρεια τὸν λόγον τοῦ θεοῦ = "that Samaria *had received* the word of God" (Acts 8:14; lexical middle, δέχομαι)

4. δέδεσαι γυναικί; μὴ ζήτει λύσιν· λέλυσαι ἀπὸ γυναικός; μὴ ζήτει γυναῖκα. = "*Are you bound* to a wife? Do not seek to be loosed. *Have you been loosed* from a wife? Do not seek a wife." (1 Cor 7:27)

5. ὅτι ἐτάφη, καὶ ὅτι ἐγήγερται τῇ ἡμέρᾳ τῇ τρίτῃ = "that he was buried, and that he *was raised* the third day" (1 Cor 15:4)

6. θεῷ δὲ πεφανερώμεθα = "but we *have been manifested* unto God" (2 Cor 5:11)

7. καὶ ἐκλέλησθε τῆς παρακλήσεως = "but you *have forgotten* the exhortation" (Heb 12:5)

8. οὗ γάρ εἰσιν δύο ἢ τρεῖς συνηγμένοι εἰς τὸ ἐμὸν ὄνομα = "For where two or three *are gathered together* in my name" (Mt 18:20; consonant stem, periphrastic)

Pluperfect Active Morphology

Table 12.13 Pluperfect Active Morphology

1	2	3	4	5	6
augment	reduplic.	stem	suffix	vowel	ending
ἐ	λε	Perfect	κει		Secondary

$$ἐ\text{-}λε\text{-}λυ\text{-}κει\text{-}μεν$$

Table 12.14 Pluperfect Active Indicative

ἐλελύκειν	*I had loosed*
ἐλελύκεις	*you had loosed*
ἐλέλυκει	*he (she, it) had loosed*
ἐλελύκειμεν	*we had loosed*
ἐλελύκειτε	*you had loosed*
ἐλελύκεισαν	*they had loosed*

The pluperfect is built on the perfect stem. The fourth and fifth principal parts, then, provide the formation patterns. As a secondary tense, the pluperfect takes an augment and secondary endings. The pluperfect's -κει active voice suffix is distinctive.

Augment

Theoretically, the pluperfect is augmented to show past time. Often, however, in actual New Testament forms one finds this pluperfect augment dropped. Pragmatically, the dropping of the augment does not make locating this secondary tense ambiguous. Either the distinctive -κει active voice suffix or the *secondary* middle/passive pronominal suffixes suffice for catching pluperfect forms.

Reduplication

Reduplication is the same as for perfect tense, distinguished by consonant and vowels. One note needs attention. Reduplication of the pluperfect stem and augmentation for past time in *vowel stems* generates the same result (a lengthened vowel). Since the opening vowel already is lengthened in the normal process of *reduplication*, any *further* augmentation to show past time in the pluperfect tense is unnecessary. So, ἀγαπάω, when reduplicated as a perfect stem, would reduplicate by lengthening the vowel, i.e., as ἠγαπη-. Further augmentation to represent the past time of the pluperfect would be redundant. Thus, one still would just have ἠγαπήκειν.

Tense/Voice Suffix

The pluperfect active tense suffix is -κει. This suffix is quite distinctive. That is, this suffix alone is enough to locate a verb as pluperfect. The suffix pattern is like the perfect active -κα.

Consonant Volatilization

Consonant stems ending in stops before the -κει pluperfect suffix would act as in the perfect active, but few actually occur. Liquids and nasals would do similarly. Inserting a letter before the -κει tense suffix shows up in a few forms: λέγω (εἶπον) as the pluperfect active εἰρήκειν; ἐκβάλλω as ἐκβεβλήκειν; and μένω as μεμενήκειν.

Pronominal Suffix

The pluperfect is a secondary tense. Secondary tenses take secondary endings. Endings, then, are like those of other past time verbs, such as the imperfect. However, note that the third plural takes the -σαν option. So, with the -κει tense suffix, the forms are: -κειν, -κεις, -κει, -κειμεν, -κειτε, -κεισαν.

Second Active

Table 12.15 Pluperfect Second Active Indicative

ἐληλύθειν	I had come
ἐληλύθεις	you had come
ἐληλύθει	he (she, it) had come
ἐληλύθειμεν	we had come
ἐληλύθειτε	you had come
ἐληλύθεισαν	they had come

The distinction between first and second active forms in the fourth principal part applies to the pluperfect. In other words, dropping the κ in the -κει pluperfect active suffix makes a second active, on the precise pattern as dropping the κ in the -κα perfect active suffix. In fact, if a verb exists as a perfect second active, that verb by default exists as a pluperfect second active as well (that is, if the pluperfect form even occurs in the New Testament). Our paradigm verb for the pluperfect second active is ἔρχομαι.

Pluperfect Middle Morphology

The pluperfect middle/passive, like the perfect, is based on the fifth principal part. This part is distinctive because no thematic vowel is used. Secondary middle/passive endings are used.

Table 12.16 Pluperfect Middle/Passive Morphology

1	2	3	4	5	6
augment	reduplic.	stem	suffix	vowel	ending
ἐ	λε	Perfect			Secondary

$$ \overset{'}{\epsilon}\text{-}\lambda\epsilon\text{-}\lambda\upsilon\text{-}\mu\epsilon\theta\alpha $$

Table 12.17 Pluperfect Middle/Passive Indicative

ἐλελύμην	I had loosed, had been loosed
ἐλέλυσο	you had loosed, had been loosed
ἐλέλυτο	he (she, it) had loosed, had been loosed
ἐλελύμεθα	we had loosed, had been loosed
ἐλέλυσθε	you had loosed, had been loosed
ἐλέλυντο	they had loosed, had been loosed

The sigma in the second singular ending (-σο) is not regarded as intervocalic with the stem vowel, so does not volatilize, as in the first principal part. Thus, one can contrast ἐλύου.

Volatilization

Consonant. Consonant volatilization would conform to the same volatilization chart of the perfect middle. In reality, the only New Testament verb involved is ἐπιγράφω ("I write on"), which takes the pluperfect middle/passive form ἐπεγεγράμμην.

Third Plural. The *third plural* of this consonant stem would be formed periphrastically, that is, with a participle, as in the perfect middle. One difference from the perfect, though, is that the pluperfect is a *secondary* tense. Correspondingly, the form of εἰμί used would be the imperfect ἦσαν. The construction, then, would be ἦσαν ἐπεγεγραμμένοι. This periphrastic form translates the same as if the verb were a simple pluperfect indicative.

Letter insert. Another volatilization would be the letter insert variety, using either η or σ. One verb that inserts the letter η before the middle ending is βάλλω, which has the pluperfect middle/passive form ἐβεβλήμην.[2]

Pluperfect Contracts

Contracts lengthen before the tense suffix of the pluperfect active and the pronominal suffix of the pluperfect middle. Actual pluperfect contracts, however, are few in number, whether active or middle voice. Of these one can include ποιέω, οἰκοδομέω, and θεμελιόω (and a few -μι verbs). In active voice, examples would be ἐπεποιήκειν and ἐτεθεμελιώκειν. In middle voice, these verbs yield forms such as ἐπεποιήμην and ἐτεθεμελιώμην. Exceptions in which the contract vowel does not lengthen as expected are the pluperfect active of ὁράω, in the form ἑωράκειν, and pluperfect middle/passive of περιδέω ("I wrap"), in the form περιεδεδέμην.

---

[2]Note that this -λλ present tense form of the verb actually is a hidden stem, hiding a single lambda verb stem. In addition, the α vowel in the verb stem is lost by vowel gradation in creating the other principal parts.

"Defective" Perfect, Pluperfect

Overuse of the old perfect second active verb οἶδα washed out its perfective force, becoming almost synonymous with γινώσκω. For this reason, οἶδα sometimes is called a "defective" perfect (i.e., perfect form, but not perfect meaning). Likewise, the ᾔδειν pluperfect form of οἶδα, even though formally a pluperfect, is also "defective." So, ᾔδειν translates simply as an imperfect, "I knew" (with the durative sense, "was knowing").

Table 12.18 The "Defective" Verb Οἶδα, ῌδειν

οἶδα	ᾔδειν	*I know, knew*
οἶδας	ᾔδεις	*you know, knew*
οἶδεν	ᾔδει	*he (she, it) knows, knew*
οἴδαμεν	ᾔδειμεν	*we know, knew*
οἴδατε	ᾔδειτε	*you know, knew*
οἴδασιν	ᾔδεισαν	*they know, knew*

Future Perfect Tense

Table 12.19 Future Perfect Morphology

1	2	3	4	5	6
augment	*reduplic.*	*stem*	*suffix*	*vowel*	*ending*
	λε	Perfect	σ	ο/ε	Primary

$$\lambda\epsilon\text{-}\lambda\upsilon\text{-}\sigma\text{-}o\text{-}\mu\epsilon\nu$$

Active Voice

The future perfect tense is a primary tense. A future perfect uses reduplication, perfect active stem, tense suffix -σ, thematic vowel, and primary active endings. The paradigm λύω given below is only for completeness, since the New Testament has only seven occurrences of the future perfect active, but six are formed using periphrastic participles. The only actual future perfect active in the New Testament is the old perfect οἶδα in Heb 8:11, which inserts η before the future suffix as εἰδήσουσιν: ὅτι πάντες εἰδήσουσίν με ἀπὸ μικροῦ ἕως μεγάλου αὐτῶν = "because all *will know* me, from the least to the greatest of them." However, in this case, notice the simple *future* translation. Remember that the verb οἶδα is defective. Its perfective force washed out. As a future perfect, the perfective aspect reduces down to the basic future tense "I will know." Otherwise, a true future perfect would be translated "they will have known."

Table 12.20 Future Perfect Active Indicative

λελύσω	*I will have loosed*
λελύσεις	*you will have loosed*
λελύσει	*he (she, it) will have loosed*
λελύσομεν	*we will have loosed*
λελύσετε	*you will have loosed*
λελύσουσιν	*they will have loosed*

Middle/Passive Voice

The future perfect middle/passive is rare, occurring in the New Testament only in six periphrastic formations. These six forms are: ἔσομαι πεποιθώς (Heb 2:13); ἔσται δεδεμένον (Mt 16:19); ἔσται λελυμένον (Mt 16:19); ἔσται δεδεμένα (Mt 18:18); ἔσται λελυμένα (Mt 18:18); and ἔσονται διαμεμερισμένοι (Lk 12:52). The translation for such passive voice forms would be "will have been ____ed."

Perfective Nuances

Greek perfective aspect is completed action, like English, but with particular emphasis on on-going consequences. Completed action is communicated by auxiliary verbs in English: "have," "has" (perfect) and "had" (pluperfect). English translation, however, is at something of a loss to bring out the other part of the Greek perfective equation, that is, focus on the on-going consequences of the completed action. Usually this part of the grammar of the perfect tense must be explained in exposition, because this element is difficult to expose in translation.

Table 12.21 Perfective: Completed Action, Continuing Effects

Tense	Action	Effects
Pluperfect	past completed	past continuing
Perfect	past completed	present continuing
Future Perfect	future completed	future continuing

Perfect Tense Nuances

The following discussion presumes the perfective focus on on-going consequences of the completed action. With this perfective aspect in mind, we briefly outline nuances of the use of perfect and pluperfect tenses in the New Testament.

Table 12.22 Perfective Nuance: Completed, Intensive

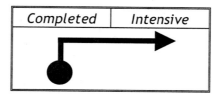

Completed (Consummative)

Here, focus is on the completed action that generated the continuing effects. Translation defaults to the basic "have," "has" auxiliary verbs. For example, we have ἀπεκρίθη ὁ Πιλᾶτος, Ὃ γέγραφα, γέγραφα. = "Pilate answered, 'What I *have written*, I *have written.'"* (Jn 19:22). Simple past tense, encroaching on aorist meaning, also might be used. For example, take Jn 6:32, οὐ Μωϋσῆς <u>δέδωκεν</u> ὑμῖν τὸν ἄρτον ἐκ τοῦ οὐρανοῦ = "it is not Moses who *gave* you the heavenly bread." Context is important in this regard. Notice the explicit aorist form in the previous verse, Jn 6:31, Ἄρτον ἐκ τοῦ οὐρανοῦ <u>ἔδωκεν</u> αὐτοῖς φαγεῖν = "He *gave* them bread from heaven to eat."

Intensive

Here, the continuing effects are emphasized. The existing completed state is the point, so translation often is present tense as a result. Paul described the present state of believers in Christ using this intensive perfect: δι᾽ οὗ καὶ τὴν προσαγωγὴν <u>ἐσχήκαμεν</u> [τῇ πίστει] εἰς τὴν χάριν ταύτην ἐν ᾗ <u>ἐστήκαμεν</u> = "through whom also we *have* access [by faith] into this grace in which we *stand*" (Rom 5:2).

Iterative

Action is completed, basically, but inherent to the context is an idea of repetition over an interval of time. The past is the point. Use of "have, has" is usual. Sometimes the translator may wish to draw out the implication of repetition by inserting "repeatedly" or some similar phrase into the verbal idea. For example: ταῦτα <u>λελάληκα</u> ὑμῖν ἵνα ἐν ἐμοὶ εἰρήνην ἔχητε· = "These things I *have spoken* [i.e., repeatedly] to you in order that in me you might have peace." (Jn 16:33).

Dramatic

Vivid narration or dramatic declaration to involve the reader or listener is the technique. The historical present and dramatic aorist do similarly. The existing state is the point, as with the intensive. Jesus' proclamation in Mt 3:2 seems to have more force and meaning translated this way: Μετανοεῖτε, <u>ἤγγικεν</u> γὰρ ἡ βασιλεία τῶν οὐρανῶν. = "Repent, for the kingdom of heaven *draws near!"*

Pluperfect Tense Nuances

Completed

Again, as with the perfect, the completed action generating the continuing effects is emphasized. Use of the helping verb "had" is normal. For example, καὶ ἤγαγον αὐτὸν ἕως ὀφρύος τοῦ ὄρους ἐφ᾽ οὗ ἡ πόλις <u>ᾠκοδόμητο</u> αὐτῶν = "and they brought him to the leading edge of the hill upon which their city *had been built*" (Lk 4:29).

Intensive

The pluperfect can emphasize the continuing effects, but these effects have come to a conclusion. Therefore, English past tense is used. Translation could use "was/were ____ing" to pull out the ongoing emphasis. Observe: καὶ σκοτία ἤδη <u>ἐγεγόνει</u> καὶ οὔπω ἐληλύθει πρὸς αὐτοὺς ὁ Ἰησοῦς = "and it already *was becoming* dark, but Jesus not yet had come to them" (Jn 6:17; the following ἐληλύθει has a completed nuance).

ⅇⅇⅇⅇⅇⅇⅇⅇ EXERCISE 12 ⅇⅇⅇⅇⅇⅇⅇⅇ

1. Locate the following verb forms. Be ready to answer any questions related to morphology.

   1.1 ἀναβέβηκα: _____

   1.2 ἐλήλυθας: _____

   1.3 ἑώρακεν: _____

   1.4 ἠγαπήκαμεν: _____

   1.5 πεφιλήκατε: _____

   1.6 μεμενήκεισαν: _____

   1.7 οἴδαμεν: _____

   1.8 ᾔδεισαν: _____

   1.9 ἐσταύρωται: _____

   1.10 ἐπεγέγραπτο: _____

   1.11 ἀκηκόασιν: _____

   1.12 ἐκβεβλήκει: _____

   1.13 γεγέννημαι: _____

   1.14 ἀπολέλυσαι: _____

   1.15 κέκριται: _____

1.16 ἡτοίμασται: _____

1.17 τεθεμελίωτο: _____

2. Explain the perfect and pluperfect tense nuances in the following sentences:

   2.1 λέγει αὐτῇ Ἰησοῦς· μή μου ἅπτου, οὔπω γὰρ ἀναβέβηκα πρὸς τὸν πατέρα· (Jn 20:17)

     ἀναβέβηκα: _____

   2.2 αὐτὸς γὰρ ὁ πατὴρ φιλεῖ ὑμᾶς, ὅτι ὑμεῖς ἐμὲ πεφιλήκατε καὶ πεπιστεύκατε ὅτι ἐγὼ παρὰ [τοῦ] θεοῦ ἐξῆλθον. (Jn 16:27)

     a. πεφιλήκατε: _____

     b. πεπιστεύκατε: _____

   2.3 Ἐμοὶ δὲ μὴ γένοιτο καυχᾶσθαι εἰ μὴ ἐν τῷ σταυρῷ τοῦ κυρίου ἡμῶν Ἰησοῦ Χριστοῦ, δι' οὗ ἐμοὶ κόσμος ἐσταύρωται κἀγὼ κόσμῳ. (Gal 6:14)

     ἐσταύρωται: _____

   2.4 Ὃ ἦν ἀπ' ἀρχῆς, ὃ ἀκηκόαμεν, ὃ ἑωράκαμεν τοῖς ὀφθαλμοῖς ἡμῶν, (1 Jn 1:1)

     a. ἀκηκόαμεν: _____

     b. ἑωράκαμεν: _____

   2.5 δὲ εὗρον καθὼς εἰρήκει αὐτοῖς (Lk 22:13)

     εἰρήκει: _____

   2.6 κεκρίκει γὰρ ὁ Παῦλος παραπλεῦσαι τὴν Ἔφεσον (Acts 20:16)

     κεκρίκει: _____

2.7 εἰ γὰρ ἐξ ἡμῶν ἦσαν, μεμενήκεισαν ἂν μεθ᾽ ἡμῶν· (1 Jn 2:19)

μεμενήκεισαν: _____

3. Translate the following. Be ready to locate perfect and pluperfect forms, as well as analyze the perfective nuances.

Κατὰ δὲ ἑορτὴν ἀπέλυεν αὐτοῖς ἕνα δέσμιον ὃν

_____

παρῃτοῦντο. ἦν δὲ ὁ λεγόμενος Βαραββᾶς μετὰ τῶν

_____

στασιαστῶν δεδεμένος οἵτινες ἐν τῇ στάσει φόνον

_____

πεποιήκεισαν. καὶ ἀναβὰς ὁ ὄχλος ἤρξατο αἰτεῖσθαι

_____

καθὼς ἐποίει αὐτοῖς. ὁ δὲ Πιλᾶτος ἀπεκρίθη αὐτοῖς

_____

λέγων· θέλετε ἀπολύσω ὑμῖν τὸν βασιλέα τῶν Ἰουδαίων;

_____

ἐγίνωσκεν γὰρ ὅτι διὰ φθόνον παραδεδώκεισαν αὐτὸν

_____

οἱ ἀρχιερεῖς. οἱ δὲ ἀρχιερεῖς ἀνέσεισαν τὸν ὄχλον ἵνα

_____

μᾶλλον τὸν Βαραββᾶν ἀπολύσῃ αὐτοῖς. ὁ δὲ Πιλᾶτος

_____

πάλιν ἀποκριθεὶς ἔλεγεν αὐτοῖς· τί οὖν [θέλετε]

_____

ποιήσω [ὃν λέγετε] τὸν βασιλέα τῶν Ἰουδαίων; οἱ δὲ

_____

πάλιν ἔκραξαν· σταύρωσον αὐτόν. ὁ δὲ Πιλᾶτος ἔλεγεν

αὐτοῖς· τί γὰρ ἐποίησεν κακόν; οἱ δὲ περισσῶς

ἔκραξαν· σταύρωσον αὐτόν. Ὁ δὲ Πιλᾶτος βουλόμενος

τῷ ὄχλῳ τὸ ἱκανὸν ποιῆσαι ἀπέλυσεν αὐτοῖς τὸν

Βαραββᾶν, καὶ παρέδωκεν τὸν Ἰησοῦν φραγελλώσας ἵνα

σταυρωθῇ.

🝆🝆🝆🝆🝆🝆🝆 MANUSCRIPTS 9 🝆🝆🝆🝆🝆🝆🝆

Papyrus 𝔓⁵² is our oldest New Testament copy, a fragment of John's Gospel, dated around A.D. 100–150. Thus, 𝔓⁵² is only fifty to one hundred years removed from the original of the Gospel. John Rylands Library in Manchester preserves the text. Normally, "recto" is the right-hand book page, or front side of a leaf; "verso" is the left-hand book page, or reverse side of a leaf. Papyri designations are different.[3] The recto of 𝔓⁵² is the image on the left, and the verso is the image on the right. The recto of 𝔓⁵² is Jn 18:31–33. The verso is Jn 18:37–38. Marks are not common on these early papyri. However, note diaeresis over the iota in line two recto (reading as: ΟΥΔΕΝΑΪΝΑΟΛ = ουδενα ἱνα ο λ[ογος]).

Fig. 13. Papyrus 𝔓⁵² at Jn 18:31–33 (left) and Jn 18:37–38 (right).

---

[3]Papyri are made of strips of reed, one layer laid horizontally, the other vertically. The horizontal layer is the "recto," whether front or back of a page; likewise, the vertical layer is the "verso." By folding these double-layer leaves, if the *front* of the first page is horizontal, the *back* of the last page is horizontal (like a bulletin). Thus, with papyri, "recto" or "verso" does not designate front or back pages, but the horizontal or vertical orientation of the reed strips in the layer.

CHAPTER 13
FUTURE AND AORIST TENSES

Both future and aorist tenses are undefined action, distinguished only in time frame. (On rare occasions the future might have durative aspect.) A sigma in the tense suffix pattern for both tenses renders their morphology similar, since they each suffer the same stop consonant volatilization.

Undefined Tenses

The future active and middle is the second principal part. Similarly, the aorist active and middle is the third principal part. The passive voice for both tenses is a new principal part altogether, that is, the sixth. Because

Table 13.1 Principal Parts

Principal Parts	Tenses	Voices		
First	Present	active	middle	passive
	Imperfect	active	middle	passive
Second	Future	active	middle	
Third	First Aorist	active	middle	
	Second Aorist	active	middle	
Fourth	Pluperfect	active		
	Perfect	active		
	Future Perfect	active		
Fifth	Pluperfect		middle	passive
	Perfect		middle	passive
	Future Perfect		middle	passive
Sixth	Aorist			passive
	Future			passive

both stems have undefined aspect, the future passive can be built on the aorist passive stem, which is a key feature of the sixth principal part.

No reason exists as to why the aorist passive principal part is numbered out of logical sequence. One would have expected the aorist passive principal part to be numbered as fourth, that is, immediately after the third principal part of aorist active and middle. The numbering of principal parts is irrevocable from the distant past of Paleolithic Greek.

Future Active and Middle

The future tense is a primary tense, so requires no augment. The future stem is altered with a tense suffix. The suffix is a -σ that will generate consonant reactions. The future as a primary tense takes primary endings, joined by the thematic vowel.

Table 13.2 Future Active and Middle Morphology

1	2	3	4	5	6
augment	*reduplic.*	*stem*	*suffix*	*vowel*	*ending*
		Future	σ	ο/ ε	Primary

$$\lambda\upsilon\text{-}\sigma\text{-}o\text{-}\mu\epsilon\nu$$

$$\lambda\upsilon\text{-}\sigma\text{-}o\text{-}\mu\epsilon\theta\alpha$$

Table 13.3 Future Active Indicative

λύσω	*I will loose*
λύσεις	*you will loose*
λύσει	*he (she, it) will loose*
λύσομεν	*we will loose*
λύσετε	*you will loose*
λύσουσιν	*they will loose*

Table 13.4 Future Middle Indicative

λύσομαι	*I will loose*
λύσῃ	*you will loose*
λύσεται	*he (she, it) will loose*
λυσόμεθα	*we will loose*
λύσεσθε	*you will loose*
λύσονται	*they will loose*

Since primary endings are worked into the thematic vowel in the primary active endings, the future tense appearance is close to the present tense except for the -σ tense suffix. As is typical, the middle second singular volatilizes due to an intervocalic sigma that elides (-εσαι→-εαι→-η). The English future auxiliary verb is "will." Middle voice translation would involve direct, indirect, and reciprocal nuances. Issues of translating middle voice always apply.

Tense Suffix

The signature of the future is the tense suffix. This suffix reacts with stop consonants on the same pattern of sigma volatilization for third declension nouns. We reproduce that sigma volatilization chart presented with third declension nouns for convenience.

Table 13.5 Sigma Volatilization: Stops

Formation	Volatilization Pattern		
	stop consonant	simple sibilant	resultant sibilant
labials	π, β, φ	+ σ	= ψ
palatals	κ, γ, χ	+ σ	= ξ
dentals	τ, δ, θ	+ σ	= σ

Stop Stems. Future tense stems ending in a stop consonant will volatilize with the -σ of the future tense suffix. The result is the same as in third declension nouns: labials yield ψ; palatals yield ξ; and dentals drop, leaving just the tense suffix σ. Thus, one has πέμπω as πέμψω, ἄγω as ἄξω, and πείθω as πείσω.

Hidden Stems. The wording is simply descriptive, not an actual grammatical category. The verb stem from which the future tense stem is formulated is other than what appears in the vocabulary form, which is the present tense stem. Thus, the actual consonant of the future stem reacting to the -σ tense suffix is hidden from the student. The usual hidden consonant is a stop consonant. The following are illustrative categories of present tense stem classes that are "hiding" the actual verb stem consonant:

1. *Double Sigma:* These -σσ present stems in reality end in a palatal (κ, γ, χ). The palatal volatilizes with the sigma suffix. A semivowel iota added to create the present stem results in a characteristic double sigma present stem. A few examples are κηρύσσω (κηρυκ-, κηρύξω), ταράσσω (ταραχ-, ταράξω), and πράσσω (πραγ-, πράξω).

2. *Double Lambda:* These -λλ present stems in reality end in a *single* lambda. Addition of a semivowel iota going to the present stem generates the double lambda present. This single lambda stem reacts as a true liquid future (adds the suffix -εσ; see below), with a typical circumflex accent. A few examples include ἀγγέλλω (ἀγγελ-, ἀγγελῶ), βάλλω (βαλ-, βαλῶ), and ἀποστέλλω (ἀποστελ-, ἀποστελῶ). An exception is μέλλω (μελλήσω).

3. *Zeta Stem:* The -ζ on the present tense stem is not original to the verb stem. Again, a semivowel iota is added to a -δ or -γ verb stem. If the "hidden" -ζ stem actually ends in the dental -δ, the future suffix added to this -δ stem will volatilize as a dental (drops out, leaving only σ). Examples include βαπτίζω (βαπτιδ-, βαπτίσω), δοξάζω (δοξαδ-, δοξάσω), and σῴζω (σωδ-, σώσω).

    A -ζ present stem actually ending in -γ volatilizes with the -σ as a palatal, becoming ξ. Observe κράζω (κραγ-, κράξω) and στηρίζω (στηριγ-, στηρίξω). A few verbs show *both* -δ and -γ forms. Note ἁρπάζω, as both ἁρπάσω *and* ἁρπάξω.

    An interesting -ζ present stem variation is called the "Attic future," because the form derives from the Attic dialect. Some -ζ present stems that hide -δ future stems add the Attic suffix -σε, not -σ, to the -δ future stem. The dental -δ falls out, rendering the σ in the -σε suffix as an intervocalic sigma. Therefore, the suffix σ elides. Finally, the leftover suffix -ε contracts with the thematic vowel. The final result is a "liquid" future look (see below) and characteristic circumflex accent. Two examples of this "Attic future" would be ἐγγίζω (ἐγγιδσε-, ἐγγιῶ) and ἐλπίζω (ἐλπιδσε-, ἐλπιῶ).

4. *Sigma Kappa:* These -σκ or -ισκ present stems in reality often end in either -κ or -χ, which before the -σ future suffix volatilizes predictably to -ξ. An example is διδάσκω (διδακ-, διδάξω). Other -σκ present stems derive from variations, such as -θαν, a liquid. For example, the -σκ compound ἀποθνήσκω really hides a -θαν future stem, which becomes the future liquid middle ἀποθανοῦμαι. The verb γινώσκω endures many changes going into the present tense: (1) the stem is reduplicated (γι-), and the original gamma dropped for euphony; (2) the -σκ suffix is added to the stem γνο-, and the stem vowel lengthened. The future is built on the future stem, γνω-, always found in middle voice (γνώσομαι). Finally, εὑρίσκω actually hides the liquid stem εὑρ-, to which an added ε lengthens to the vowel η on the way to the future as εὑρήσω.

Table 13.6 Hidden Stem Examples

Lexical	Verb Stem	Future
βαπτίζω	βαπτιδ-	βαπτισ-
κράζω	κραγ-	κραξ-
κηρύσσω	κηρυκ-	κηρυξ-
πράσσω	πραγ-	πραξ-
ταράσσω	ταραχ-	ταραξ-
ἀγγέλλω	ἀγγελ-	ἀγγελ-(ˆ)
γινώσκω	γνο-	γνωσ-

Table 13.7 Future Active Indicative: Stops

πέμψω	I will send
πέμψεις	you will send
πέμψει	he (she, it) will send
πέμψομεν	we will send
πέμψετε	you will send
πέμψουσιν	they will send

Contract Verbs. In the first principal part, contract verbs will contract with the thematic vowel. In all other principal parts, they lengthen before tense suffixes, such as a -σ (ε→η, ο→ω, α→η).

Table 13.8 Future Active Indicative: Contracts

ποιέω	πληρόω	ἀγαπάω
ποιήσω	πληρώσω	ἀγαπήσω
ποιήσεις	πληρώσεις	ἀγαπήσεις
ποιήσει	πληρώσει	ἀγαπήσει
ποιήσομεν	πληρώσομεν	ἀγαπήσομεν
ποιήσετε	πληρώσετε	ἀγαπήσετε
ποιήσουσιν	πληρώσουσιν	ἀγαπήσουσιν

Irregular Stems. "Irregular" verbs have stems that appear to be unpredictable from one principal part to the next. In fact, their history shows these verbs are borrowing entirely different stems to form various principal parts. In practical terms, such "irregular" forms of the principal parts must be memorized as if individual vocabulary words in their own right—yet always connected to other verb forms. This irregular verb problem is the same for someone trying to learn English: how does one get from "go" to "went"? (In fact, "went" is past tense of the Old English "wend.") The following table illustrates some examples of irregular future tense verbs. The bottom line is being able to recognize the lexical connections for these irregular forms in the New Testament.

Table 13.9 Irregular Future Examples

Present	Irreg. Future
ἔρχομαι	ἐλεύσομαι
λέγω	ἐρῶ
ὁράω	ὄψομαι
πίνω	πίομαι
πίπτω	πεσοῦμαι
φέρω	οἴσω

Future Lexical Middle

As one would expect, verbs that occur only in middle voice in the present tense (that is, as lexical middle), also occur only in middle voice in the future. Unexpectedly, though, some verbs that do have active voice forms in the present tense *show only middle voice in the future.* Thus, whereas a *present middle* γινώσκομαι *does* have an *active* voice counterpart γινώσκω, the *future middle* γνώσομαι does not. Such unexpected future middle verbs without active voice forms are called *future lexical middle* verbs. Their translation would have the same issues of all lexical middle verbs.

Table 13.10 Future Lexical Middle

Present	Future
ἀνέχω	ἀνέξομαι
γινώσκω	γνώσομαι
λαμβάνω	λήμψομαι
ὁράω	ὄψομαι
τίκτω	τέξομαι
φεύγω	φεύξομαι

Future of Εἰμί

The future tense of εἰμί appears with primary middle endings. Remember, however, that εἰμί does not express voice. The second singular has an intervocalic sigma that volatilizes.

Table 13.11 Future Indicative of Εἰμί

ἔσομαι	*I will be*
ἔσῃ	*you will be (sg.)*
ἔσται	*he (she, it) will be*
ἐσόμεθα	*we will be*
ἔσεσθε	*you will be (pl.)*
ἔσονται	*they will be*

Liquid Future

Table 13.12 Special Stems

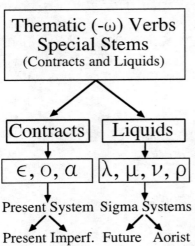

Formation. The thematic verb system has two special stems that affect morphology. These stems are contracts and liquids. The liquid verb is a verb whose stem ends in one of four consonants: λ, μ, ν, or ρ. These liquid verbs use a different future tense suffix. Instead of -σ, a liquid future uses an -εσ suffix. This suffix creates an intervocalic sigma with the thematic vowel. The future sigma is expelled (εσο→εο, εσε→εε), and remaining vowels contract as expected (εο→οῦ, εε→εῖ).

Confusion. The resulting appearance of the liquid future is just like a present tense contract verb, except for the circumflex accent that often results from the contraction. Since a Greek verb normally has an acute accent (you may have noticed by now), then the only distinction between a present tense and a liquid future is the accent alone.

♦ *A liquid future looks exactly like an -ε contract verb.*

Table 13.13 Present Tense Versus Liquid Future

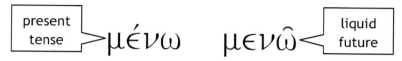

Table 13.14 Liquid Future of Μένω

μενῶ	*I will remain*
μενεῖς	*you will remain*
μενεῖ	*he (she, it) will remain*
μενοῦμεν	*we will remain*
μενεῖτε	*you will remain*
μενοῦσιν	*they will remain*

Variations. Some -λ or -ρ liquid stems form the future in -ησω. These liquid stems do *not* use the -εσ liquid future suffix. Instead, they use the -σ suffix and insert η. Note: θέλω (θελήσω), μέλλω (μελλήσω), βούλομαι (βουλήσομαι), γίνομαι (γενήσομαι), καταβαίνω (καταβήσομαι), and χαίρω (χαρήσομαι). An exception to this -ησω pattern is the "irregular" future of λέγω: ἐρῶ, ἐρεῖς, ἐρεῖ, ἐροῦμεν, ἐρεῖτε, ἐροῦσιν (a liquid future).

The -λλ "hidden" present stem actually is a single lambda future stem, which, as expected, acts as a liquid future (-εσ suffix). Thus, βάλλω is the liquid future βαλῶ, and ἀποστέλλω is ἀποστελῶ. One -λλ exception is the -ησω verb μέλλω, above.

A few verbs simply drop the nasal ν before the future σ (similar to dropping the nasal ν before the κα perfect suffix). An example is ἀποτίνω (ἀποτίσω).

First Aorist Active and Middle

As a secondary tense the aorist requires an augment and takes secondary endings. The -σα tense suffix generates exactly the same consonant reactions as in the future. Since the tense suffix contains a vowel already, the thematic vowel is not necessary.

Table 13.15 First Aorist Active and Middle Morphology

1	2	3	4	5	6
augment	*reduplic.*	*stem*	*suffix*	*vowel*	*ending*
ε		Aorist	σα		Secondary

$$\epsilon\text{-}\lambda\upsilon\text{-}\sigma\alpha\text{-}\mu\epsilon\nu$$

$$\epsilon\text{-}\lambda\upsilon\text{-}\sigma\alpha\text{-}\mu\epsilon\theta\alpha$$

Table 13.16 First Aorist Active Indicative

ἔλυσα	*I loosed*
ἔλυσας	*you loosed (sg.)*
ἔλυσεν	*he (she, it) loosed*
ἐλύσαμεν	*we loosed*
ἐλύσατε	*you loosed (pl.)*
ἔλυσαν	*they loosed*

Table 13.17 First Aorist Middle Indicative

ἐλυσάμην	*I loosed*
ἐλύσω	*you loosed (sg.)*
ἐλύσατο	*he (she, it) loosed*
ἐλυσάμεθα	*we loosed*
ἐλύσασθε	*you loosed (pl.)*
ἐλύσαντο	*they loosed*

Basic Morphology

Aorist formation is a review of the secondary tense morphology that applies to the imperfect. Review augments. Review secondary endings. The active voice ending pattern is similar to the perfect: the first singular drops the -ν ending, leaving only the tense suffix (ἔλυσα). The third singular has no ending, so reverts back to the thematic vowel with moveable -ν (ἔλυσεν). Middle voice second singular is -σο. With the tense suffix, this becomes -σασο. The second (intervocalic) sigma drops, and vowels contract (σαο→σω).

Volatilization

Sigma. The -σα suffix causes the same sigma volatilization as in the future tense. Stop and hidden stems create complex sibilants; thus one has πέμπω: ἔπεμψα, ἐπεμψάμην; κηρύσσω: ἐκήρυξα, ἐκηρυξάμην. Contracts lengthen (ποιέω: ἐποίησα).

Table 13.18 First Aorist Active/Middle Indicative: Stops

ἔπεμψα	ἐπεμψάμην	*I sent*
ἔπεμψας	ἐπέμψω	*you sent (sg.)*
ἔπεμψεν	ἐπέμψατο	*he (she, it) sent*
ἐπέμψαμεν	ἐπεμψάμεθα	*we sent*
ἐπέμψατε	ἐπέμψασθε	*you sent (pl.)*
ἔπεμψαν	ἐπέμψαντο	*they sent*

Liquid Aorist. The liquid aorist reaction is to drop the sigma of the -σα suffix, which leaves only the alpha, sometimes called an *asigmatic aorist* as a result. The lost sigma means the "aorist look" is lost and makes location difficult. A secondary reaction to the loss of the sigma in some verbs is the lengthening of the stem vowel, often to a diphthong, called *compensatory lengthening*. Due to liquid aorist morphology, then, only compensatory lengthening is left to distinguish imperfect and liquid aorist forms of some third singular verbs (ἔμενεν, ἔμεινεν).

Table 13.19 Liquid Aorist

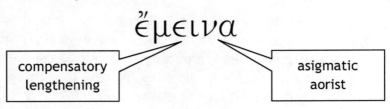

Table 13.20 First Aorist Active Indicative: Liquids

ἔμεινα	*I remained*
ἔμεινας	*you remained (sg.)*
ἔμεινεν	*he (she, it) remained*
ἐμείναμεν	*we remained*
ἐμείνατε	*you remained (pl.)*
ἔμειναν	*they remained*

Liquid Variations. Similar to the future, some liquid stems form the aorist in -ησα. These include θέλω (ἠθέλησα) and χαίρω (ἐχαίρησα). The verbs βούλομαι and μέλλω have no aorist forms in the New Testament. Other liquid verbs show only second aorist forms in the New Testament; for example, γίνομαι (ἐγενόμην), καταβαίνω (κατέβην), βάλλω (ἔβαλον), λαμβάνω (ἔλαβον).

Contracts. Contract verbs contract in the first principal part. In all other parts they lengthen. The -σα aorist tense suffix generates contract lengthening: ποιέω (ἐποί**η**σα), πληρόω (ἐπλήρ**ω**σα), ἀγαπάω (ἠγάπ**η**σα). Two aorist contract exceptions are καλέω and τελέω. Instead of lengthening, the contract vowel remains: ἐκάλεσα, ἐκάλεσας, ἐκάλεσεν, etc. and ἐτέλεσα, etc.

Aorist Lexical Middle

A present lexical middle will be an aorist lexical middle. Thus, λογίζομαι is only aorist middle, ἐλογισάμην. One exception is the second aorist form of ἔρχομαι (ἦλθον) and its compounds. As always, issues of translating these lexical middle verbs apply.

Second Aorist Active and Middle

Grammar

Regular verbs take regular suffixes and endings. Irregular verbs reject these suffixes and form their tenses in other ways. Thus, the regular verb "I work" adds a regular "-ed" suffix for past tense: "I worked." The past tense of "I leave," in contrast, rejects this style of "-ed" suffix, and forms the past tense with a changed stem, "I left." Or, "I go" borrows an entirely different stem, "I went."

Greek is similar. Verbs that accept a -σα suffix to create their past tense are regular and are called first aorist (sometimes "weak aorist"). In contrast, other verbs reject this -σα suffix. Instead, they form the aorist with either (1) a *changed stem* or (2) a *different stem*. Such verbs are called second aorist (sometimes "strong aorist"). Such formation patterns do not affect translation.

The bottom line of the second aorist is like English. That is, just as a person simply has to memorize that "I left" is the past tense of "I leave," or that "I went" is the past tense of "I go," one has to memorize that ἔλιπον is the second aorist of λείπω, or that εἶπον is the second aorist of λέγω. Lexical consultation is essential in determining whether a verb is a first or second aorist.

Morphology

Second aorist morphology is simple:

♦ *Second aorist clones the imperfect, except for stem.*

Thus, one has an augment for past time, a second aorist stem, the thematic vowel, and secondary endings. Mastering second aorists is simply mastering vocabulary—one has to *memorize second aorist stems like vocabulary words*.

Note that the imperfect is built on the *present stem* (first principal part), whereas the second aorist either has a *changed stem* (even if the change is only one letter) or *different stem* altogether. Whereas sometimes differences between imperfect and second aorist stems are dramatic (λέγω, ἔλεγον, εἶπον), sometimes they are more subtle (λείπω, ἔλειπον, ἔλιπον).

Table 13.21 Second Aorist Active and Middle Morphology

1	2	3	4	5	6
augment	*reduplic.*	*stem*	*suffix*	*vowel*	*ending*
ε		2nd Aorist		ε/ο	Secondary

$$\epsilon\text{-}\lambda\iota\pi\text{-}o\text{-}\mu\epsilon\nu$$

$$\epsilon\text{-}\lambda\iota\pi\text{-}o\text{-}\mu\epsilon\theta\alpha$$

Table 13.22 Second Aorist Active Indicative

ἔλιπον	*I left*
ἔλιπες	*you left (sg.)*
ἔλιπεν	*he (she, it) left*
ἐλίπομεν	*we left*
ἐλίπετε	*you left (pl.)*
ἔλιπον	*they left*

Table 13.23 Second Aorist Middle Indicative

ἐλιπόμην	*I left*
ἐλίπου	*you left (sg.)*
ἐλίπετο	*he (she, it) left*
ἐλιπόμεθα	*we left*
ἐλίπεσθε	*you left (pl.)*
ἐλίποντο	*they left*

Formation

The middle second singular (intervocalic) sigma drops, and the remaining vowels contract (εσο→εο→ου). Middle voice once again raises issues of translation already discussed. An important second aorist *lexical middle* is ἐγενόμην, from γίνομαι. Be sure to distinguish carefully this -γεν (*single nu second aorist*) stem from the γενν- (*double nu present*) stem of γεννάω.

First Aorist Imitation

Some second aorist verbs can mimic the first aorist -σα tense suffix rather than using the thematic vowel, but without the sigma (i.e., -α, -ας, -ε, -αμεν, -ατε, -αν). Two common forms in the New Testament that exhibit this behavior are εἶπον for λέγω, and εἶδον for ὁράω. These verbs can be found as εἶπα, εἶπας, εἶπε, etc. and εἶδα, εἶδας, εἶδε, etc. Meaning is not affected.

Table 13.24 Second Aorist: First Aorist Imitation

εἶπα	*I said*
εἶπας	*you said (sg.)*
εἶπεν	*he (she, it) said*
εἴπαμεν	*we said*
εἴπατε	*you said (pl.)*
εἶπαν	*they said*

One verb requires particular attention, because this verb often is incorrectly presented as a "kappa first aorist" (on the pattern of the kappa aorists of the -μι verb system). This verb is φέρω, which has a second aorist, ἤνεγκον, can also show another aorist form, ἤνεγκα. This ἤνεγκα is *not* a "kappa aorist"; rather this verb is a *second aorist* whose stem ends in the -κ but sometimes imitates first aorist endings. The stem ἐνεκ- is reduplicated to ἐνενεκ-, then augmented with vowel gradation to ἠνενκ-; finally, the ν before the palatal assimilates to a nasal, yielding the form ἤνεγκ-.

First and Second Aorist Mixed

A few verbs exhibit *both* a first and a second aorist form. For example, ἁμαρτάνω has both the first aorist form ἡμάρτησα and the second aorist form ἥμαρτον. Meaning is not affected. These verbs show strong second aorist verbs in transition to accepting the weak first aorist suffix.

Table 13.25 First and Second Aorist Mixed

ἡμάρτησα	ἥμαρτον	*I sinned*
ἡμάρτησας	ἥμαρτες	*you sinned (sg.)*
ἡμάρτησεν	ἥμαρτεν	*he (she, it) sinned*
ἡμαρτήσαμεν	ἡμάρτομεν	*we sinned*
ἡμαρτήσατε	ἡμάρτετε	*you sinned (pl.)*
ἡμάρτησαν	ἥμαρτον	*they sinned*

Non-thematic Second Aorist

"Non-thematic second aorist" is a small class of verbs that *do not use a thematic vowel for the aorist active indicative* (ἵστημι, ἀναβαίνω, and γινώσκω). For βαίνω, the original verb stem βα- was lengthened to βη- and augmented for past time, but with no thematic vowel, as ἐ-βη-ν = ἔβην (as a compound, ἀνέβην). For γινώσκω, the original stem γνο- was lengthened to γνω- and then augmented for past time, but with no thematic vowel, as ἔ-γνω-ν = ἔγνων. These two omega verbs are given in the table in their "non-thematic" second aorist active indicative forms.

Table 13.26 Non-thematic Second Aorists

ἀνέβην	ἔγνων	*I went up, I knew*
ἀνέβης	ἔγνως	*you went up, you knew (sg.)*
ἀνέβη	ἔγνω	*he (she, it) went up, he knew*
ἀνέβημεν	ἔγνωμεν	*we went up, we knew*
ἀνέβητε	ἔγνωτε	*you went up, you knew (pl.)*
ἀνέβησαν	ἔγνωσαν	*they went up, they knew*

The Passive System

Passive voice in present and perfect tenses of the first and fifth principal parts simply borrows the middle form of that principal part. Passive voice for future and aorist tenses does not borrow the middle voice form. For these tenses, the passive voice actually has its own distinctive voice suffix added to the tense stem. This distinctive passive voice suffix creates the passive system of the sixth principal part involving aorist and future tenses. Similar to the perfect and pluperfect with their first and second active forms that drop a letter out of the suffix, the passive system has a first and second passive form that drops a letter out of the suffix.

Aorist Passive

Aorist passive is a secondary tense, so takes an augment for past time and uses secondary endings. Because the aorist passive voice suffix includes a vowel, no thematic vowel is necessary, in a pattern similar to the aorist active suffix. Dropping the theta out of the aorist passive suffix creates an aorist second passive.

Endings are secondary, but secondary *active*. Using these active endings on a passive voice does not actually confuse the location, simply because the aorist passive voice suffix is so distinctive. In fact, location is a cinch. All one has to remember is the mantra:

♦ *θη is aorist passive.*

With this nifty little dictum, you are the fastest gun in the west for locating aorist passive forms. The only "gotch ya" are a few -ε contract verbs, such as ἀκολυθέω, *with a θ already in the stem that also lengthens the contract vowel* in other principal parts. The resulting θη configuration is *not* aorist passive, such as the future form ἀκολυθήσω. (Another exception would be the -μι verb τίθημι, whose short stem minus reduplication is the θε.)

Table 13.27 Aorist First and Second Passive Morphology

1	2	3	4	5	6
augment	reduplic.	stem	suffix	vowel	ending
ε		Aorist	θη		Secondary

$$\epsilon\text{-}\lambda\upsilon\text{-}\theta\eta\text{-}\mu\epsilon\nu$$

$$\epsilon\text{-}\gamma\rho\alpha\phi\text{-}\eta\text{-}\mu\epsilon\nu$$

Table 13.28 Aorist First Passive Indicative

ἐλύθην	I was loosed
ἐλύθης	you were loosed (sg.)
ἐλύθη	he (she, it) was loosed
ἐλύθημεν	we were loosed
ἐλύθητε	you were loosed (pl.)
ἐλύθησαν	they were loosed

Table 13.29 Aorist Second Passive Indicative

ἐγράφην	I was written
ἐγράφης	you were written (sg.)
ἐγράφη	he (she, it) was written
ἐγράφημεν	we were written
ἐγράφητε	you were written (pl.)
ἐγράφησαν	they were written

Formation

Secondary active third singular (ἐλύθη) as expected has no ending. Unlike other secondary active patterns, this aorist passive third singular does *not* use a moveable -ν. Note the alternate -σαν ending rather than the simple -ν in third plural. Admittedly, this ending has the same look as a first aorist active third plural ending (ἔλυσαν). In that case, however, the σα is the aorist *tense suffix*.

Theta Volatilization

The θη suffix creates volatilization in the face of the theta consonant. These theta volatilization patterns do not have to be memorized, but they do have to be recognized. You will want to be able to recognize a tense stem that has changed spelling, either with a different consonant immediately in front of the θη suffix or with an inserted vowel. Study the stop and liquid volatilizations.

Table 13.30 Theta Volatilization: Stops

Formation	Stops	Suffix		Result
labials	π, β, [φ]	+ θ	=	φθ [θ drops]
palatals	κ, γ, χ	+ θ	=	χθ
dentals	τ, δ, θ	+ θ	=	σθ

Table 13.31 Theta Volatilization: Liquids

Liquid	Suffix	Result
λ	+ θ	= λθ or ληθ
ρ	+ θ	= ρθ or ρεθ
μ	+ θ	= μηθ
ν	+ θ	= θ or νθ or νηθ

Stops. Stops show *aspiration* in labials and palatals. (They all change to the letter in the third stop column.) The one exception is the labial φ plus θ, which actually causes the θ to drop out, creating a second passive. The palatal χ plus θ simply remains the same, χθ. Dentals drop and insert sigma. Thus, we have πέμπω (ἐπέμφθην), συνάγω (συνήγθην), and πείθω (ἐπείσθην).

Table 13.32 Aorist First Passive Indicative: Stops

ἐπέμφθην	I was sent
ἐπέμφθης	you were sent (sg.)
ἐπέμφθη	he (she, it) was sent
ἐπέμφθημεν	we were sent
ἐπέμφθητε	you were sent (pl.)
ἐπέμφθησαν	they were sent

Liquids. The nasals μ and ν usually react, whereas the liquids λ and ρ usually do not. Any might insert a vowel (either ε or η), as in -ληθ, -μηθ, -νηθ, -ρεθ. The ν drops on occasion. In sum: in theta reactions, three of the liquids—λ, ρ, and μ—*always are retained in some form.* All lambda stem liquids are *second* passives, dropping theta, except βάλλω. A nasal -μ aorist passive does not exist in the New Testament (no aorist passive for νέμω). Thus, we have βάλλω (ἐβλ**ή**θην), λέγω (ἐρρ**έ**θην), and γίνομαι (ἐγεν**ή**θην).

Table 13.33 Aorist First Passive Indicative: Liquids

ἐβλήθην	I was thrown
ἐβλήθης	you were thrown (sg.)
ἐβλήθη	he (she, it) was thrown
ἐβλήθημεν	we were thrown
ἐβλήθητε	you were thrown (pl.)
ἐβλήθησαν	they were thrown

Contracts

Contract verbs contract in the first principal part. In all other parts they lengthen. Contract vowels lengthen before the θη aorist passive suffix: ποιέω (ἐποι**ή**θην), πληρόω (ἐπληρ**ώ**θην), and ἀγαπάω (ἠγαπ**ή**θην). One exception is τελέω, which does not lengthen the ε, but, instead, inserts a sigma. The forms, then, will be ἐτελέσθην, ἐτελέσθης, ἐτελέσθη, etc.

Future Passive

The future first passive borrows the aorist passive stem, adding a sigma to the aorist passive suffix (-θησ), which requires using the thematic vowel. The future passive is a *primary* tense, so has *no augment,* and uses *primary* endings. Second passive drops theta.

Table 13.34 Future First and Second Passive Morphology

1	2	3	4	5	6
augment	reduplic.	stem	suffix	vowel	ending
		Aorist	θησ	ο/ε	Primary

$$\lambda\upsilon\text{-}\theta\eta\sigma\text{-}o\text{-}\mu\epsilon\theta\alpha$$

$$\gamma\rho\alpha\phi\text{-}\eta\sigma\text{-}o\text{-}\mu\epsilon\theta\alpha$$

Table 13.35 Future First Passive Indicative

λυθήσομαι	*I will be loosed*
λυθήσῃ	*you will be loosed (sg.)*
λυθήσεται	*he (she, it) will be loosed*
λυθησόμεθα	*we will be loosed*
λυθήσεσθε	*you will be loosed (pl.)*
λυθήσονται	*they will be loosed*

Table 13.36 Future Second Passive Indicative

γραφήσομαι	*I will be written*
γραφήσῃ	*you will be written (sg.)*
γραφήσεται	*he (she, it) will be written*
γραφησόμεθα	*we will be written*
γραφήσεσθε	*you will be written (pl.)*
γραφήσονται	*they will be written*

Formations

The second singular drops the (intervocalic) σ, then contracts (θησεσαι→θησεαι→θηση). Theta volatilization also applies to future first passive verbs (πεμφθήσομαι). Liquids often will insert a letter (βληθήσομαι). Contracts will lengthen the contract vowel (ποιηθήσομαι). Future second passives (γραφήσομαι) actually look like future middle contract verbs (ποιήσομαι). The only way to distinguish these two principal parts (contract aorist middle, aorist second passive) is to know verb vocabulary, that is, what actually is a contract verb in the first place.

Confusing Terminology

Use of "first" and "second" can be confusing between the third and sixth principal parts. In the third principal part (aorist active and middle), "first" and "second," as in "first aorist" and "second aorist," refer to the *tense stems*. Not so in the sixth principal part. In the sixth principal part (aorist and future passive), "first" and "second," as in "first passive" and "second passive," refer to the *voice suffixes*. A "second aorist" (third part) can be completely unconnected to an aorist "second passive" (sixth part).

Take γράφω, for example. This verb is a *first aorist* in the third principal part (ἔγραψαν), because the nomenclature is based on the *aorist stem accepting a -σα suffix*. The second aorist *simply rejects this -σα suffix* (whether by changing the stem or borrowing from an entirely different verb). However, this first aorist γράφω is an aorist *second passive* in the sixth principal part (ἐγράφην), because the nomenclature here simply is based on *voice suffix form*. In other words, *all aorists as passive take a -θη (-η) voice suffix*.

On the other hand, a second passive aorist always will be a second passive future, because, by definition, the future passive is built on that aorist passive stem. Thus, we have both ἐγράφην and γραφήσομαι. Second passive forms are infrequent in the Greek New Testament, but a few common verbs do have second passives (e.g., ἀποστέλλω, γράφω, and χαίρω).

Lexical Passive

As stated earlier, a present tense lexical middle verb, such as γίνομαι, also is an aorist lexical middle (ἐγενόμην). Correspondingly, this verb also will be an aorist lexical passive (ἐγενήθην). The translation defaults to active voice for either incarnation as aorist middle (third principal part) or aorist passive (sixth principal part). That is, both forms wind up as "I became." Since the future passive is built on the aorist passive stem, then an aorist lexical passive is a future lexical passive. Only six thematic verbs show this feature in the New Testament: ἐπαισχύνομαι, ἰάομαι, λογίζομαι, μεταμέλομαι, μιμνήσκομαι, and χαρίζομαι.

Translation Nuances

Future Nuances

"Undefined" action simply is a way of saying neither of the other two (i.e., not durative, not perfective). Undefined action, therefore, is well suited to anticipating future action without any immediate need to specify the exact nature of that action.

Futuristic (Predictive)

The predictive future is the simple statement that action will take place in future time. Notice the string of predictive futures in the following announcement by Jesus about the Holy Spirit in Jn 16:13: ὁδηγήσει ὑμᾶς ἐν τῇ ἀληθείᾳ πάσῃ· οὐ γὰρ λαλήσει ἀφ᾽ ἑαυτοῦ, ἀλλ᾽ ὅσα ἀκούσει λαλήσει, καὶ τὰ ἐρχόμενα ἀναγγελεῖ ὑμῖν = "He *will lead* you into all truth; for He *will not speak* from Himself, but whatsoever He *will hear*, He *will speak*, and the coming things He *will announce* to you." Notice the various verb stems and their reaction patterns: ὁδηγέω and λαλέω show contract lengthening; ακούω is regular; ἀγγέλλω is a double lambda present, single lambda liquid future.

Imperative

A future can suggest a command, as if in the imperative mood. The form regularly occurs in second person, naturally. Thus, Οὐ φονεύσεις = *"Do not murder"* (literally, "you will not murder," Mt 5:21). Again, note Ἀγαπήσεις τὸν πλησίον σου = *"Love* your neighbor" (Mt 5:43). The context may imply polite request or instruction, as in Lk 1:31, καὶ καλέσεις τὸ ὄνομα αὐτοῦ Ἰησοῦν = "and you *will call* his name Jesus."

Deliberative (Rhetorical)

This nuance occurs in two forms. One variety relates to asking a question: What course of action is now appropriate? One typical example given here is Peter's question to Jesus: Κύριε, πρὸς τίνα ἀπελευσόμεθα; = "Lord, to whom *shall we go?"* (Jn 6:68; observe that this verb is an irregular future, from ἀπέρχομαι).

Another form of this nuance is its use in rhetorical questions. For example, we have Paul's question: ἢ οὐκ οἴδατε ὅτι ἄδικοι θεοῦ βασιλείαν οὐ κληρονομήσουσιν; = "or do you not know that the unrighteous *will not inherit* the kingdom of God?" (1 Cor 6:9). Again, Paul asked the Corinthians, τί γὰρ οἶδας, γύναι, εἰ τὸν ἄνδρα σώσεις; = "For what do you know, O wife, whether *you will save* your husband?" (1 Cor 7:16).

Aorist Nuances

The aorist is the workhorse tense in Greek. Narrative material, such as the Gospels and Acts, has almost twice as many aorist forms as the letters. The student will encounter this tense often.

"Undefined" action simply is a way of saying neither of the other two (i.e., not durative, not perfective). Undefined action, therefore, is well suited to summarizing in a generalizing way any past tense report. In other words, an author would use aorist as a generic description of past activity, not defining anything particular about the action or its process. For example, if asked, "Did you study the lesson?" you might answer, "Yes, I studied the lesson." In point of fact, your study activity perhaps took place over a broad stretch of time, with breaks and other activities interrupting. In reporting your studying, however, you do not bother with these activity details. You just report the action, conceived as a whole. Your aoristic action, "studied," summarizes the action as an overview of the entire process.

Such past tense reporting with undefined overview of the action is the dominant sense of the Greek aorist tense. However, the aorist can have several translation nuances. Listed below are some nuances for the aorist tense, *context always the key*. The graphic in the table below is an attempt to summarize these concepts visually.

Table 13.37 Aorist Tense Nuances: Ingressive, Etc.

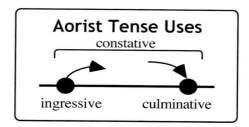

Constative (Summary Report)

Terminology is not fixed. One also will encounter "historical," "holistic," "unitary," etc. "Summary report" views the action from the speaker's perspective and simply announces past action with no comment on aspect, as in "I studied the lesson." For example: καθὼς ἐλάλησεν πρὸς τοὺς πατέρας ἡμῶν, τῷ Ἀβραὰμ καὶ τῷ σπέρματι αὐτοῦ εἰς τὸν αἰῶνα = "even as *he spoke* to our fathers, to Abraham and to his descendants forever" (Lk 1:55).

Note that "spoke" sums up a whole series of events over time, made explicit in the context ("and to his descendents").

Ingressive (Inceptive)

A punctiliar sense surfaces here, but the emphasis is upon the beginning of the action. Typical auxiliary verbs to use for this nuance would include "came," "became," or "began." Sometimes, however, this aorist is translated without an auxiliary verb. One example is Paul's exhortation: Χριστὸς ἀπέθανεν καὶ ἔζησεν = "Christ died and *lived* [i.e., lived again]" (Rom 14:9).

Culminative

Again, the sense is punctiliar, but here emphasis is upon the conclusion of the action. This nuance infringes upon the perfect tense. The aorist, however, infers nothing about on-going consequences, as does the perfect. For example, ἐγὼ ἐβάπτισα ὑμᾶς ὕδατι = "I *have baptized* you with water" (Mk 1:8).

The auxiliary verb "have, has," which is perfective in English, *is not perfective when used with the aorist.* Using "have" or "has," therefore, in a translation may not be wrong (and regularly accompanies English versions in their translations of the aorist), but at the least, the result often might be confused by the general English reader with a perfect tense, since this Greek nuance for the aorist verb is not recognized in the English grammar of "have" as an auxiliary verb. Simply put, as an auxiliary verb, "have" is never undefined action in English, but, rather, always perfective. For the culminative aorist, interests of Greek syntax are in tension with the idioms of English auxiliary verbs, and translation is bewitched.

Epistolary

This use is a feature of letter writing. English idiom is to refer to the writing of a letter from the perspective of the author at the time of writing: "I am writing." Note the present tense idiom.

Greek idiom is different. Greek idiom is to refer to the writing of the letter from the perspective of the reader at the time of reading the letter: "I wrote to you." Note the past tense idiom. This idiom of tense shifting on behalf of the reader's perspective is called the "epistolary aorist." This idiomatic Greek aorist should be translated with an English present for proper English idiom. For example, ἔγραψα ὑμῖν, παιδία = "*I am writing* to you, children" (1 Jn 2:14). This literary convention of tense shifting on behalf of the reader's perspective includes other action as well, such as the sending of an emissary ("I have sent" in Greek = "I am sending" in English, as in Col 4:7-8).

Dramatic

The nuance achieves a dramatic effect. Often in the context something significant has just taken place. Observe the conclusion to the prodigal son parable: ὅτι ὁ ἀδελφός σου οὗτος νεκρὸς ἦν καὶ ἔζησεν = "because this brother of yours was dead and *is alive!*" (Lk 15:32). The aorist here also probably carries something of an inceptive idea, "is alive (again)." Thus, given context, a present tense could be just perfect to translate an aorist tense in the Greek text.[1]

Prophetic

In prophetic speech, a future event is spoken of *as if already accomplished fact* in the surety of fulfillment. This is a cousin to the dramatic aorist. However, this nuance is restricted to contexts of proclamation. Depending on context, translation could use the perfect or future tense. With a perfective nuance, note: Ἔπεσεν ἔπεσεν Βαβυλὼν ἡ μεγάλη = "*Fallen! Fallen!* is Babylon the Great!" (Rev 18:2). Or, with a future nuance, note: τῆς χάριτος ἐξεπέσατε = "you *will fall* from grace" (Gal 5:4).

---

[1]Hmmm: something a little fishy here (present→perfect→aorist), don't you think?

EXERCISE 13

1. Locate the following verbs. Be ready to explain morphology.

1.1 ἔσται: _____

1.2 μισήσεις: _____

1.3 ὑψώσει: _____

1.4 ἀγαπήσεις: _____

1.5 βαλοῦσιν: _____

1.6 ἀποτίσω: _____

1.7 φείσεται: _____

1.8 ἐφείσατο: _____

1.9 Ἠκούσατε: _____

1.10 ἐπετίμησεν: _____

1.11 ἐσταύρωσεν: _____

1.12 ἐκηρύξαμεν: _____

1.13 ἐμείναμεν: _____

1.14 ἐδέξασθε: _____

1.15 ἥξει: _____

1.16 ἐλάβετε: _____

1.17 ἐξῆλθεν: _____

1.18 ἐθεραπεύθη: _____

1.19 ἐρρέθη: _____

1.20 ταπεινωθήσεται: _____

1.21 κηρυχθήσεται: _____

2. Translate the following. Be ready to explain nuances.

   2.1 ἐμείναμεν ἡμέραν μίαν παρ᾽ αὐτοῖς.

   _____

   2.2 ἐγὼ Παῦλος ἔγραψα τῇ ἐμῇ χειρί, ἐγὼ ἀποτίσω·

   _____

   2.3 καὶ βαλοῦσιν τοὺς στεφάνους αὐτῶν ἐνώπιον τοῦ θρόνου.

   _____

   2.4 ἔσται γὰρ τότε θλῖψις μεγάλη οἵα οὐ γέγονεν ἀπ᾽ ἀρχῆς κόσμου ἕως τοῦ νῦν.

   _____

   _____

   2.5 εἰ γὰρ ὁ θεὸς τῶν κατὰ φύσιν κλάδων οὐκ ἐφείσατο, [μή πως] οὐδὲ σοῦ φείσεται.

   _____

   _____

2.6 Ἠκούσατε ὅτι ἐρρέθη· ἀγαπήσεις τὸν πλησίον σου καὶ μισήσεις τὸν ἐχθρόν σου.

_____

_____

2.7 ὅστις δὲ ὑψώσει ἑαυτὸν ταπεινωθήσεται καὶ ὅστις ταπεινώσει ἑαυτὸν ὑψωθήσεται.

_____

_____

2.8 καὶ ἐπετίμησεν αὐτῷ ὁ Ἰησοῦς καὶ ἐξῆλθεν ἀπ᾽ αὐτοῦ τὸ δαιμόνιον καὶ ἐθεραπεύθη ὁ παῖς ἀπὸ τῆς ὥρας ἐκείνης.

_____

_____

2.9 καὶ κηρυχθήσεται τοῦτο τὸ εὐαγγέλιον τῆς βασιλείας ἐν ὅλῃ τῇ οἰκουμένῃ εἰς μαρτύριον πᾶσιν τοῖς ἔθνεσιν, καὶ τότε ἥξει τὸ τέλος.

_____

_____

_____

2.10 εἰ μὲν γὰρ ὁ ἐρχόμενος ἄλλον Ἰησοῦν κηρύσσει ὃν οὐκ ἐκηρύξαμεν, ἢ πνεῦμα ἕτερον λαμβάνετε ὃ οὐκ ἐλάβετε, ἢ εὐαγγέλιον ἕτερον ὃ οὐκ ἐδέξασθε, καλῶς ἀνέχεσθε.

_____

_____

_____

3. Translate the following passage from 1 John. Be ready to locate verb forms, as well as analyze the nuances.

1.1 Ὃ ἦν ἀπ᾽ ἀρχῆς, ὃ ἀκηκόαμεν, ὃ ἑωράκαμεν τοῖς

ὀφθαλμοῖς ἡμῶν, ὃ ἐθεασάμεθα καὶ αἱ χεῖρες ἡμῶν

ἐψηλάφησαν περὶ τοῦ λόγου τῆς ζωῆς— **2** καὶ ἡ ζωὴ

ἐφανερώθη, καὶ ἑωράκαμεν καὶ μαρτυροῦμεν καὶ

ἀπαγγέλλομεν ὑμῖν τὴν ζωὴν τὴν αἰώνιον ἥτις ἦν πρὸς

τὸν πατέρα καὶ ἐφανερώθη ἡμῖν— **3** ὃ ἑωράκαμεν καὶ

ἀκηκόαμεν, ἀπαγγέλλομεν καὶ ὑμῖν, ἵνα καὶ ὑμεῖς

κοινωνίαν ἔχητε μεθ᾽ ἡμῶν. καὶ ἡ κοινωνία δὲ ἡ

ἡμετέρα μετὰ τοῦ πατρὸς καὶ μετὰ τοῦ υἱοῦ αὐτοῦ

Ἰησοῦ Χριστοῦ. **4** καὶ ταῦτα γράφομεν ἡμεῖς, ἵνα ἡ

χαρὰ ἡμῶν ᾖ πεπληρωμένη.

𝕫𝕫𝕫𝕫𝕫𝕫 **MANUSCRIPTS 10** 𝕫𝕫𝕫𝕫𝕫𝕫

Our oldest copy of the Pauline correspondence, papyrus 𝔓⁴⁶, is dated about A.D. 200, but missing the Pastoral Epistles. Eighty-six surviving leaves are kept in two places: the Chester Beatty Library at Dublin and the University of Michigan Library at Ann Arbor. The Eastern Church regarded Paul the author of Hebrews since Hebrews follows Romans in 𝔓⁴⁶. The discovery of 𝔓⁴⁶ (published 1930s) played into the question of the ending of Romans. Below one sees how 𝔓⁴⁶ has Rom 15:33 followed by the doxology of Rom 16:25-27, then Rom 16:1.[2]

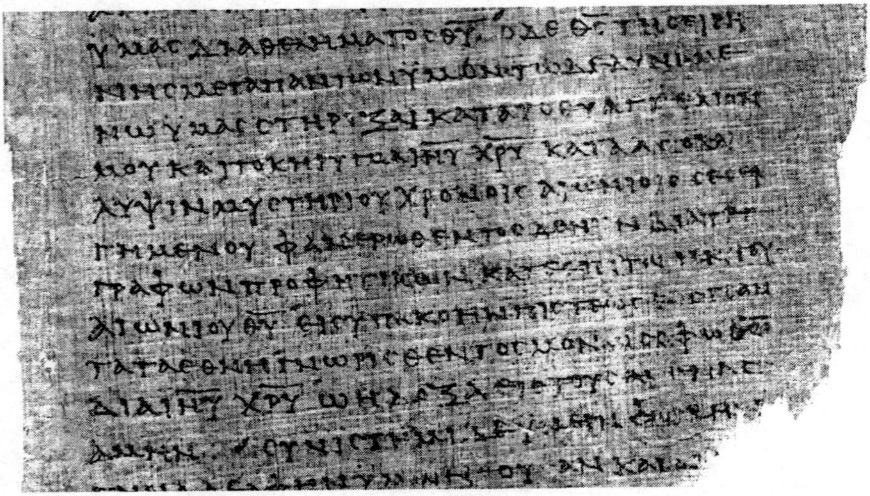

Fig. 14. Papyrus 𝔓⁴⁶ Showing Rom 15:33, 16:25-27, 16:1.

[2]The "doxology" (Rom 16:25-27) occurs in different places in our manuscripts: (1) in the old uncials after chapter 16, (2) in minuscules after chapter 14, and (3) in 𝔓⁴⁶ after chapter 15—the only witness to this placement. Positions of the doxology suggest that Romans could have circulated in at least three different editions. In an article in 1962, T. W. Manson advanced an older theory that Rom 16 was not part of the original letter. He conjectured Paul later added chapter 16 to a copy of Romans sent to Ephesus. Papyrus 𝔓⁴⁶ seemed to support his theory, since a doxology in 𝔓⁴⁶ after chapter 15 suggested the existence of an ancestor having only Rom 1-15. Recent study, however, has rejected Manson's theory and demonstrated conclusively that the original Romans included chapter 16.

CHAPTER 14
MOODS OF CONTINGENCY

Moods of contingency are the three non-indicative moods: subjunctive, optative, and imperative. These moods show increasing contingency in the verbal action. The Greek moods correspond to English moods except for the optative, which is a weaker form of the subjunctive.

Moods of Contingency

Subjunctive Mood

Grammar

Table 14.1 Mood and Contingency

	Indicative (reality)	
Decreasing Reality	Subjunctive (probability)	Increasing Contingency
	Optative (possibility)	
	Imperative (command)	

Indicative infers reality with no contingency, that is, presented as either affirmed or asserted. The subjunctive infers *probable* reality, but some element of contingency bears upon the statement made. The two major uses of the subjunctive mood are for probable reality statements and third class conditional sentences. The most common tense in the subjunctive is the aorist.

No time element is communicated in the subjunctive mood, regardless of tense. Tense communicates verbal aspect only. Thus, present subjunctive is durative, perfect subjunctive perfective, and aorist subjunctive undefined. However, verbal aspect does not always come across into English. Since (1) time is not a factor and (2) aspect is not always translatable, then aorist subjunctive and present subjunctive translations can wind up exactly the same.

Formation

Table 14.2 Subjunctive: Key Formation Elements

1. Mood of contingency
2. All tenses take primary endings (time is not a factor)
3. No aorist augment (time is not a factor)
4. Mood sign is lengthened thematic vowel (η/ω)
5. Tense is aspect only (translations indistinguishable)

Table 14.3 Subjunctive Endings

Active	*Middle/Passive*
-ω	-ωμαι
-ῃς	-ῃ
-ῃ	-ηται
-ωμεν	-ωμεθα
-ητε	-ησθε
-ωσιν	-ωνται

Present. Present subjunctive is straightforward. The subjunctive endings are added directly to the tense stem. As always in the first principal part, contract vowels contract.

First Aorist. First aorist subjunctive has no augment. Lack of an augment presents a problem in conjunction with the suffix. *The aorist -σα suffix looses the alpha in contraction.* So, an aorist subjunctive almost looks like a future tense—but always remember:

◆ *There is no future subjunctive!*

Other aorist formation patterns hold: contracts lengthen, stops volatilize, liquids drop the sigma. Aorist passive has the suffix -θε. (The indicative mood -θη actually is a lengthened -θε.) The ε of the -θε suffix is swallowed up by contraction; only a lengthened thematic vowel and circumflex accent remain.[1] Second passives drop the θ. Second aorist, on the other hand, copies the present tense except for stem.

Perfect. The perfect subjunctive is rare (about twenty times). Half of these are the verb οἶδα as first or second person (εἰδῶ, εἰδῶμεν and εἰδῆς, εἰδῆτε). The other half is periphrastic. In active voice, the subjunctive mood comes from εἰμί as present subjunctive, the perfect active from the perfect active participle. The only two occurrences are ἵνα μὴ πεποιθότες ὦμεν ἐφ᾽ ἑαυτοῖς = "in order that *we should not trust* in ourselves" (2 Cor 1:9) and κἂν ἁμαρτίας ᾖ πεποιηκώς = "and if *he has committed* sins" (Jas 5:15). Middle and passive perfect subjunctives are a similar formulation, but the participles are middle or passive voice; e.g., ὦμεν λελυμένοι.[2]

Table 14.4 Subjunctive Active

Present	2nd Aorist	1st Aorist
λύω	λίπω	λύσω
λύῃς	λίπῃς	λύσῃς
λύῃ	λίπῃ	λύσῃ
λύωμεν	λίπωμεν	λύσωμεν
λύητε	λίπητε	λύσητε
λύωσιν	λίπωσιν	λύσωσιν

---

[1] The LXX does have one future passive subjunctive in Zeph 3:11.
[2] Lk 14:8; Jn 3:27; 6:65; 16:24; 17:19, 23; 1 Cor 1:10; 2 Cor 9:3; Phil 1:10-11.

Table 14.5 Subjunctive Middle

Present	2nd Aorist	1st Aorist
λύωμαι	λίπωμαι	λύσωμαι
λύῃ	λίπῃ	λύσῃ
λύηται	λίπηται	λύσηται
λυώμεθα	λιπώμεθα	λυσώμεθα
λύησθε	λίπησθε	λύσησθε
λύωνται	λίπωνται	λύσωνται

Table 14.6 Subjunctive Passive

Present	2nd Passive	1st Passive
λύωμαι	γραφῶ	λυθῶ
λύῃ	γραφῇς	λυθῇς
λύηται	γραφῇ	λυθῇ
λυώμεθα	γραφῶμεν	λυθῶμεν
λύησθε	γραφῆτε	λυθῆτε
λύωνται	γραφῶσιν	λυθῶσιν

Morphological clones result from various contraction patterns. For example, λύω can be present active *indicative* or present active *subjunctive*. Again, λύῃ can be: (1) present middle/passive indicative, 2ps, (2) present active subjunctive, 3ps, or (3) present middle/passive subjunctive, 2ps. Also, compare aorist forms with themselves or with the future tense (λύσω, λύσῃ). In these cases, one has to rely on context to determine location.

Contracts. With present tense contracts one has an increasing problem distinguishing between indicative and subjunctive moods as one moves from epsilon to omicron to alpha contracts. Only context can resolve the confusion. A brief summary follows:

1. *Epsilon contracts:* only two forms are the same, the active first person singular (ποιῶ) and the middle second person singular (ποιῇ).

2. Omicron contracts: in active voice, all the singulars are the same (πληρῶ, πληροῖς, πληροῖ), but in middle voice, only second person singular (πληροῖ) is the same.

3. *Alpha contracts*: all active and middle forms are the same.

Negative. The negative for the indicative mood is οὐ. The negative for all other moods is μή. Thus, for the subjunctive mood, the negative μή is used. The double negative οὐ μή is emphatic, meaning "never." In *indicative* rhetorical questions, οὐ expects a "yes" answer, but μή expects a "no." So, James asks: μὴ δύναται ἡ πίστις σῶσαι αὐτόν; = "That faith *is not able* to save him, is it?" (Jas 2:14; expected answer: "No, of course not!").

Εἰμί. The verb εἰμί can be subjunctive, but forms sometimes are just one letter. With such brief forms, pay attention to the details. Confusion can occur with relative pronouns (cf. ᾧ, ᾗ, and ᾗς), imperfect indicative (cf. ἦς, ἦτε), conjunctions (ἤ), particles (ἤ), and interjections (ὦ).

Table 14.7 Present Subjunctive of Εἰμί

ὦ	*I might be*
ᾖς	*you might be (sg.)*
ᾖ	*he (she, it) might be*
ὦμεν	*we might be*
ἦτε	*you might be (pl.)*
ὦσιν	*they might be*

Optative Mood

Grammar

The optative infers *possible* reality, but a greater element of contingency bears upon the statement made than with the subjunctive. The English word *optative* derives from the Latin verb *opto*, meaning "I wish." The contingency behind the idea of "wish" helps the English student see that the optative mood is a weaker form of the subjunctive. Conventional use at the time of the New Testament included prayers and benedictions. For this reason, the optative shows up in these formal settings on a regular basis in the New Testament. However, the optative mood occurs just sixty-eight times in the Greek text, so optative forms, in reality, are not encountered that often in translating the New Testament.

No time element is communicated in the optative mood, regardless of tense. Tense communicates verbal aspect only: present optative is durative and aorist optative undefined. (No perfect optative occurs in the New Testament.) However, verbal aspect does not always come across into English. Since (1) time is not a factor and (2) aspect is not always translatable, then both aorist optative and present optative translations can wind up the same.

Formation

Table 14.8 Optative: Key Formation Elements

1. Mood of contingency
2. Takes secondary endings (except -μι; time not a factor)
3. No aorist augment (time not a factor)
4. Thematic vowel always is o
5. Mood sign is ι (sometimes ιε/ιη)
6. Tense is aspect only (translations indistinguishable)

Table 14.9 Optative Endings (with Iota)

Active	*Middle/Passive*
-ιμι	-ιμην
-ις	-ιο
-ι	-ιτο
-ιμεν	-ιμεθα
-ιτε	-ισθε
-ιεν	-ιντο

The endings are secondary except for -μι. The middle second singular forms always react. This reaction is due to the ending -σο setting up an intervocalic sigma (-οισο→-οιο, or -σαισο→-σαιο). Also, the final diphthongs αι and οι, normally considered short for accenting, are considered *long* in the optative (an *exception* to the standard accent rules). The tense stem for each principal part is used to establish the forms. The negative for the optative is μή.

Present. The thematic vowel is ο for the present tense. This creates the resultant endings -οιμι, -οις, -οι, etc. However, only eight thematic verb examples appear in the New Testament, seven in active voice, and one in the middle/passive. No contracted forms of the thematic verb appear at all.

Aorist. The aorist active and middle optative is more frequent in the New Testament than the present optative. The aorist does not have an augment (time is not a factor). The first aorist -σα tense suffix is used, eliminating the need for the ο thematic vowel, and creating the endings -σαιμι, -σαις, -σαι, etc. (The third plural can occur as -σειαν instead of -σαιεν.) The middle forms are -σαίμην, -σαιο, -σαιτο, etc. Contracts lengthen, stops volatilize, and liquids drop the sigma. The *second aorist* active and middle optative copies present tense forms, except for tense stem.

The aorist first passive uses the suffix -θε, an *alternate* mood sign -ιη, and *active* secondary endings. First person takes the -ν ending, and third person takes the -σαν. The resultant endings are -θείην, -θείης, -θείη, etc. Before this passive suffix, contracts lengthen and stops volatilize, as usual. No second passive optative form occurs in the New Testament.

Εἰμί. Optative is rare enough that only one form of εἰμί is represented in the New Testament. The mood indicator -ιη and secondary endings show in the forms: εἴην, εἴης, εἴη, εἴημεν, εἴητε, εἴησαν. However, only the form, εἴη ("may he be," "it might be," etc.), actually appears, and that just twelve times.[3]

---

[3]Except for Jn 13:24, all in Luke-Acts: Lk 1:29; 3:15; 8:9; 9:46; 15:26; 18:36; 22:23; Acts 8:20; 10:17; 20:16; 21:33.

Table 14.10 Optative Active

Present	2nd Aorist	1st Aorist
λύοιμι	λίποιμι	λύσαιμι
λύοις	λίποις	λύσαις
λύοι	λίποι	λύσαι
λύοιμεν	λίποιμεν	λύσαιμεν
λύοιτε	λίποιτε	λύσαιτε
λύοιεν	λίποιεν	λύσαιεν (-ειαν)

Table 14.11 Optative Middle

Present	2nd Aorist	1st Aorist
λυοίμην	λιποίμην	λυσαίμην
λύοιο	λίποιο	λύσαιο
λύοιτο	λίποιτο	λύσαιτο
λυοίμεθα	λιποίμεθα	λυσαίμεθα
λύοισθε	λίποισθε	λύσαισθε
λύοιντο	λίποιντο	λύσαιντο

Table 14.12 Optative Passive

Present	2nd Passive	1st Passive
λυοίμην	--------	λυθείην
λύοιο	--------	λυθείης
λύοιτο	--------	λυθείη
λυοίμεθα	--------	λυθείημεν
λύοισθε	--------	λυθείητε
λύοινται	--------	λυθείησαν

Future Optative. The future optative, extremely rare, does exist, but not in the New Testament. The LXX has five occurrences; the context often is after verbs of saying or thinking within indirect discourse. An example is Job 15:30: ἄνεμος ἐκπέσοι δὲ αὐτοῦ τὸ ἄνθος = "the wind *will sweep away* its flower."[4]

Note on γένοιτο. Seventeen of sixty-eight optatives in the New Testament are in the form γένοιτο, usually as μὴ γένοιτο. All but three of these are in Paul's letters, so quite clearly, this was a characteristic style of Pauline rhetoric.[5] In the negative, the expression might be translated something like "May it never be!"

Frequency. Just five forms cover over half of the optatives in the New Testament. These forms provide 38 of 68 occurrences:

- γένοιτο (γίνομαι, 17x)
- εἴη (εἰμί, 12x)
- δῴη (δίδωμι, 4x)
- θέλοι (θέλω, 3x)
- ἔχοι (ἔχω, 2x)

Imperative Mood

Grammar

The imperative is the contingency of *command*. Commands are highly contingent, except for certain settings, such as the military. (Any parent dealing with children knows this reality.) Thus, the imperative communicates the most contingency of the four Greek moods.

No time element is communicated in the imperative mood, regardless of tense. Tense communicates verbal aspect only: present imperative is durative, perfect imperative perfective, and aorist imperative undefined. However, verbal aspect does not always come across into English. Since (1) time is not a factor and (2) aspect is not always translatable, then aorist imperative and present imperative translations can wind up the same in English.

---

[4]Cf. 1 Kgs 8:57; Job 15:33; 4 Macc 4:23; Sir 38:15.

[5]Lk 1:38; 20:16; Acts 5:24; Rom 3:4, 6, 31; 6:2, 15; 7:7, 13; 9:4; 11:1, 11; 1 Cor 6:15; Gal 2:17; 3:21; 6:14.

Formation

Table 14.13 Imperative: Key Formation Elements

1. Mood of contingency
2. Imperative endings (time not a factor)
3. No aorist augment (time not a factor)
4. Thematic vowel always is ε
5. Tense is aspect only (translations indistinguishable)

Table 14.14 Imperative Endings

Active	*Middle/Passive*
-------	-------
---, ς, θι	-σο
-το	-σθω
-------	-------
-τε	-σθε
-τωσαν	-σθωσαν

Imperative mood has its own set of endings, unique for third person. No first person imperative exists in Greek. (The speaker does not command himself or herself.) The active second singular has three options. In second person, the singular shows some distinctiveness with the no ending or -θι options. Other second person forms are similar to various indicative endings:

1. The -ς (active, 2ps) = -ς of secondary active
2. The -τε (active, 2pp) = -τε of primary active
3. The -σο (middle, 2ps) = -σο of secondary middle
4. The -σθε (middle, 2pp) = -σθε of primary middle

The appropriate stem for each principal part is used. Some of the resultant imperative forms clone their indicative counterparts, especially the second person forms. Context alone decides.

Present. The present active uses the present stem, thematic vowel ε, and the active imperative endings. The second singular opts for no ending, leaving the ε exposed. Second plural looks exactly as the indicative counterpart. All active contracts behave as expected; second plurals look exactly like their indicative counterparts.

The present middle/passive forms are similar to the active, but with middle/passive imperative endings. Second singular volatilizes (intervocalic sigma drops: εσο→εο→ου). Second plural looks like its indicative counterpart. Middle contracts behave as expected. Second singulars drop an intervocalic sigma for double contraction results:

1. The ε contract: εεσο→εεο→εου→οῦ
2. The ο contract: οεσο→οεο→οου→οῦ
3. The α contract: αεσο→αεο→αου→ῶ

Middle contract second plurals look exactly like their indicative counterparts.

Aorist. The first aorist active imperative has no augment and uses the tense suffix -σα. With this suffix, contract verbs lengthen, stops volatilize, and liquids drop the sigma, as usual. Active voice uses active imperative endings, but the -σον ending (2ps) simply is unexplained. Middle voice uses the middle imperative endings, but, once again, the -σαι ending (2ps) is unexplained. The aorist first passive suffix -θη is so distinctive that the use of *active* endings is usually not confusing. Notice that the second singular form, -θηθι, undergoes "deaspiration" of the second theta for purposes of pronunciation, becoming -θητι. Again, for the middle forms, contracts lengthen, stops volatilize, and liquids drop the sigma.

Second aorist copies the present tense except for stem (and the accent, middle second singular). The second passive drops the θ, so the second singular does not need to deaspirate, as in the first passive, and remains -ητι.

Perfect. Perfect imperatives are rare (less than five times, depending on the location). An active form might be ἴστε, from οἶδα (Eph 5:5; Heb 12:17; Jas 1:19). Perfect middle includes πεφίμωσο, from φιμόω (Mk 4:39) and ἔρρωσθε, from ῥώννυμι (Acts 15:29).

One New Testament form possibly is the periphrastic construction: ἔστωσαν . . . περιζωσμέναι (Lk 12:35).

Table 14.15 Imperative Active

Present	2nd Aorist	1st Aorist
------	------	------
λῦε	λίπε	λῦσον
λυέτω	λιπέτω	λυσάτω
------	------	------
λύετε	λίπετε	λύσατε
λυέτωσαν	λιπέτωσαν	λυσάτωσαν

Table 14.16 Imperative Middle

Present	2nd Aorist	1st Aorist
------	------	------
λύου	λιποῦ	λῦσαι
λυέσθω	λίπέσθω	λυσάσθω
------	------	------
λύεσθε	λίπεσθε	λύσασθε
λυέσθωσαν	λιπέσθωσαν	λυσάσθωσαν

Table 14.17 Imperative Passive

Present	2nd Passive	1st Passive
------	------	------
λύου	γράφηθι	λύθητι
λυέσθω	γραφήτω	λυθήτω
------	------	------
λύεσθε	γράφητε	λύθητε
λυέσθωσαν	γραφήτωσαν	λυθήτωσαν

Notice these similarities: (1) λύετε, present active *indicative*, second person plural, *or* present active *imperative*, second plural;

(2) λύεσθε, present middle/passive *indicative*, second person plural, *or* a present middle/passive *imperative*, second plural. Other forms also are similar. The first aorist middle imperative λῦσαι also could be an aorist infinitive or an aorist optative. Thus, the pattern in imperative forms shows one distinct second person form (λῦε), but problems of recognition in others, especially the second person plural forms (λύετε, λύεσθε). Finally, *hear* the difference between active and middle voice: the sharp dental, τ, in the active voice, and the corresponding aspirated form, σθ, in the middle.

Negative. The negative for the indicative mood is οὐ. The negative for all other moods is μή. Thus, for the imperative mood, the negative μή is used. Again, the double negative οὐ μή is emphatic, meaning "never."

Εἰμί. The verb εἰμί can be imperative. The second plural looks just like the indicative, but notice that the imperative form is *not* enclitic (contrast indicative ἐστέ, which in composition is ἐστε).

Table 14.18 Present Imperative of Εἰμί

ἴσθι	*you be (sg.)*
ἔστω (ἤτω)	*he (she, it) must*

ἔστε	*you be (pl.)*
ἔστωσαν	*they must*

Translation Nuances

Subjunctive Nuances

Modal verbs are auxiliary verbs that indicate mood. Since the fundamental idea of subjunctive mood is *contingency*, modal auxiliary verbs implying contingency, such as "might," "should," or "would," can be used. Auxiliary verbs, however, are not necessary. Contingency could be inherent in context, as in some conjunctions.

Inherently, the subjunctive is related to the future. Probability exists only as a future possibility. However, future is used for what *will* take place, subjunctive for what *may* take place. Observe the subjunctive following a string of futures: Τίς ἐξ ὑμῶν <u>ἕξει</u> φίλον καὶ <u>πορεύσεται</u> πρὸς αὐτὸν μεσονυκτίου καὶ **εἴπῃ** αὐτῷ = "Who among you *will have* a friend and *will go* to him in the middle of the night and ***will say*** to him" (Lk 11:5).

Subjunctives traditionally are subdivided by their use in independent or dependent clauses. The following table summarizes typical subjunctive uses. A discussion of these uses follows.

Table 14.19 Subjunctive Uses

Indepen. Clause	Key	Translation
Hortatory	1st per. plu.	*Let us*
Prohibition	aorist with μή	*Do not*
Deliberative	interrogation	*Shall we?*
Emphatic Negation	οὐ μή	*Never!*
Dependent Clause	**Key**	**Translation**
Purpose	ἵνα or ὅπως	*so that*
Result	ἵνα	*as a result*
Relative Pronoun	ὅς, etc.	*whoever, etc.*
Comparison	ὡς	*as*
Temporal	ὅταν, ἕως, ἄχρι, μέχρι	*when, until*
Concession	ἐάν	*even if, although*
Substantive	[grammar]	[subj., obj., etc.]

Independent Clauses

Hortatory ("Let us"). First person plural is the key. Subjunctive mood occurs in an independent clause. The speaker is exhorting others to join in some action. "Let us" in the translation conveys the sense. Thus, Ἀγαπητοί, ἀγαπῶμεν ἀλλήλους = "Beloved, *let us love* one another" (1 Jn 4:7).

Prohibition ("Do not"). Aorist tense with μή is the key. Do not *initiate* an action may be the idea resulting from the aorist aspect. Recent studies, however, have indicated that the idea of "not initiating an action" is overworked. The mood is subjunctive, the negative μή, and usually second person is used in an independent clause. One could use "do not ever." Notice this string of aorist subjunctives: τὰς ἐντολὰς οἶδας· Μὴ φονεύσῃς, Μὴ μοιχεύσῃς, Μὴ κλέψῃς, Μὴ ψευδομαρτυρήσῃς, Μὴ ἀποστερήσῃς = "You know the commandments: 'Do not murder,' 'Do not commit adultery,' 'Do not steal,' 'Do not bear false witness,' 'Do not defraud'" (Mk 10:19).

Deliberative ("Shall we?"). A context of deliberation is the key. Interrogative adverbs or pronouns occur, such as "where?" (πόθεν) "when?" (πότε) or "what?" (τί). A question mark will finish off the expression in an independent clause. Tense and person varies. The speaker questions what is desirable or possible, uncertain of the proper course of action or what might take place. Or, the question simply might be rhetorical, which may involve a sense of simple futurity. Observe:

1. With interrogative pronoun: εἶπεν τῇ μητρὶ αὐτῆς, Τί αἰτήσωμαι; = "she said to her mother, 'What *shall I ask?*'" (Mk 6:24)

2. With interrogative adverb: Πόθεν ἀγοράσωμεν ἄρτους = "Where *shall we buy* bread?" (Jn 6:5)

3. What might take place in the future: ὅτι εἰ ἐν τῷ ὑγρῷ ξύλῳ ταῦτα ποιοῦσιν, ἐν τῷ ξηρῷ τί γένηται; = "If in the green wood they do these things, what *will it be* in the dry?" (Lk 23:31; notice use of the future tense)

Emphatic Negation ("Never!"). Use of οὐ μή is the key. This double negative with the subjunctive is used for emphatic denial in an independent clause. "Never," "surely not," etc. can be used in translation. Thus, καὶ **οὐ μὴ** γνῷς ποίαν ὥραν ἥξω ἐπὶ σέ = "and *you will* **never** *know* what hour I will come upon you" (Rev 3:3). Notice the close tie of subjunctive mood (γνῷς = aor. act. subj., in context given as "will know") and future tense (ἥξω = fut. act. ind. of ἥκω).

Dependent Clauses

Purpose and result examples below are the main use of the subjunctive in dependent clauses. Other uses of the subjunctive fall into various categories of dependent clauses, but not every one catalogued here. Those that are provided are intended to illustrate the flexible use of the subjunctive. The common denominator in all uses is an element of contingency.

Purpose ("So that"). Use of ἵνα or ὅπως[6] is the key. Here, a dependent purpose clause is introduced by ἵνα, ὅπως, or a relative pronoun. As negative, either ἵνα μή, ὅπως μή, μήποτε, μή πως, or μή is used, meaning "lest." Note the following examples:

1. τὸ θυγάτριόν μου ἐσχάτως ἔχει, **ἵνα** ἐλθὼν ἐπιθῇς τὰς χεῖρας αὐτῇ **ἵνα** σωθῇ καὶ ζήσῃ = "My little girl is near death; come, **so that** you *might lay* hands on her **that** *she be made well* and *live!*" (Mk 5:23)
2. **ὅπως** ᾖ σου ἡ ἐλεημοσύνη ἐν τῷ κρυπτῷ = "**that** your alms *might be* in secret" (Mt 6:4)
3. ποιήσωμεν τὰ κακά, **ἵνα** ἔλθῃ τὰ ἀγαθά = "Let us do evil **so that** good *might come*" (Rom 3:8, with a hortatory subjunctive also)

---

[6]The word ὅπως varies in use from an indefinite relative ("that," "in order that") to an indirect interrogative ("how"). This term occasionally is used with the future indicative, but mostly ὅπως is used with the subjunctive. The majority of occurrences are in Matthew and Luke-Acts.

4. ὅπως μὴ <u>καυχήσηται</u> πᾶσα σὰρξ ἐνώπιον τοῦ θεοῦ = "**lest** any flesh *should boast* before God" (1 Cor 1:29)

Result ("As a result"). Use of ἵνα is the key. A dependent result clause is introduced by ἵνα or by ἵνα μή in the negative. (Purpose or result distinctions can be ambiguous.) Thus:

1. ὁ θερίζων μισθὸν λαμβάνει καὶ συνάγει καρπὸν εἰς ζωὴν αἰώνιον, **ἵνα** ὁ σπείρων ὁμοῦ <u>χαίρῃ</u> καὶ ὁ θερίζων = "The reaper is receiving a reward and gathering together fruit unto eternal life, **as a result** the one sowing and the one reaping *rejoice* together." (Jn 4:36)

2. οὐδένα ὑμῶν ἐβάπτισα εἰ μὴ Κρίσπον καὶ Γάιον, **ἵνα μή** τις <u>εἴπῃ</u> ὅτι εἰς τὸ ἐμὸν ὄνομα ἐβαπτίσθητε = "I baptized not one of you, except Crispus and Gaius, **so as a result** no one *could say* that you were baptized in my name!" (1 Cor 1:14-15)

Relative Pronoun ("who"). The relative pronoun with the subjunctive can be used in a third class conditional sentence or to express practical result. Thus, **ὃς δ' ἂν** <u>βλασφημήσῃ</u> εἰς τὸ πνεῦμα τὸ ἅγιον = "but **whoever** *blasphemes* against the Holy Spirit" (Mk 3:29).

Comparison ("as"). In stating comparisons, an element of contingency could be present. The subjunctive could be used in these situations. So:

1. ἵνα ἡ ἡμέρα ὑμᾶς **ὡς** κλέπτης <u>καταλάβῃ</u> = "that the day *might overtake* you **as** a thief" (1 Thess 5:4)

2. <u>ἦτε</u> γὰρ **ὡς** πρόβατα πλανώμενοι = "for *you were* **as** sheep being led astray" (1 Pet 2:25)

Temporal ("when," "until"). Clauses introduced by ὅταν, ἕως, ἄχρι, and μέχρι(ς) have a time element involving contingency. Again, subjunctive mood is used. Note:

1. Καὶ **ὅταν** <u>προσεύχησθε</u> = "And **whenever** *you pray*" (Mt 6:5)

2. Compare: (1) οἱ λοιποὶ τῶν νεκρῶν οὐκ ἔζησαν **ἄχρι** <u>τελεσθῇ</u> τὰ χίλια ἔτη = "The rest of the dead did not

come to life **until** the thousand years *were completed*"
(Rev 20:5); (2) Καὶ **ὅταν** <u>τελεσθῇ</u> τὰ χίλια ἔτη = "And
when the thousand years *is completed*" (Rev 20:7)

3. ἀμὴν γὰρ λέγω ὑμῖν, **ἕως** ἂν <u>παρέλθῃ</u> ὁ οὐρανὸς καὶ ἡ
   γῆ = "for truly I tell you, **until** heaven and earth *pass
   away*" (Mt 5:18)

Concession ("even if," "although"). Concession often is given in
subjunctive mood. Contingency is inherent in such expressions. Observe:

1. **κὰν** ἐμοὶ μὴ <u>πιστεύητε</u> = "**even though** *you do not believe* me" (Jn 10:38)

2. ἀλλὰ καὶ **ἐὰν** ἡμεῖς ἢ ἄγγελος ἐξ οὐρανοῦ <u>εὐαγγελί-
   ζηται</u> [ὑμῖν] παρ᾽ ὃ εὐηγγελισάμεθα ὑμῖν = "but **even
   if** we ourselves or an angel from heaven *should preach* [to
   you] a gospel contradicting the gospel we preached to you"
   (Gal 1:8)

3. ἡμεῖς δὲ **ὡς** ἀδόκιμοι <u>ὦμεν</u> = "**although** we ourselves
   might be disapproved" (2 Cor 13:7)

Substantive. A dependent clause can be substantival, similar to
a purpose clause. Example one shows direct object function, and
example two, apposition:

1. παρεκάλεσαν **ὅπως** <u>μεταβῇ</u> ἀπὸ τῶν ὁρίων αὐτῶν =
   "they pleaded **that** *he might depart* from their region" (Mt
   8:34)

2. ἐμοὶ δὲ εἰς ἐλάχιστόν ἐστιν **ἵνα** ὑφ᾽ ὑμῶν <u>ἀνακριθῶ</u> =
   "but to me it is the smallest thing, **that** *I should be ex-
   amined* by you" (1 Cor 4:3)

Optative Nuances

Subjunctive treats the potential as objectively possible. The
optative, in contrast, treats the potential as only subjectively possible. The optative, then, could be seen as a diluted subjunctive, a
move from assertion to wish.

Thematic Verb

Optatives are infrequent. Use in New Testament times was fading out. The eight present tense optatives of the thematic verb in the New Testament are:

1. καθ᾽ ἡμέραν ἀνακρίνοντες τὰς γραφὰς εἰ ἔχοι ταῦτα οὕτως = "daily investigating the scriptures (to see) if these things *might be* so" (Acts 17:11; cf. Acts 25:16)

2. οὓς ἔδει ἐπὶ σοῦ παρεῖναι καὶ κατηγορεῖν εἴ τι ἔχοιεν πρὸς ἐμέ = "who ought to have been present before you and to make accusation, if *they might have* anything against me" (Lk 24:19)

3. ἐνένευον δὲ τῷ πατρὶ αὐτοῦ τὸ τί ἂν θέλοι καλεῖσθαι αὐτό = "and they signaled to his father as to what *he wished* to name him" (Lk 1:62; cf. Acts 17:18; 1 Pet 3:17)

4. ἀλλ᾽ εἰ καὶ πάσχοιτε διὰ δικαιοσύνην, μακάριοι. = "But even if *you should suffer* for the sake of righteousness, you are blessed!" (1 Pet 3:14)

5. ἔλεγον εἰ βούλοιτο πορεύεσθαι εἰς Ἱεροσόλυμα κἀκεῖ κρίνεσθαι περὶ τούτων = "I was asking if *he was willing* to go to Jerusalem to be judged there concerning these matters" (Acts 25:20)

Basic Types

Voluntative. This use is fundamental. Common contexts are in wishes, prayers, and benedictions. Thus, Αὐτὸς δὲ ὁ θεὸς τῆς εἰρήνης ἁγιάσαι ὑμᾶς ὁλοτελεῖς = "Now *may* the God of peace himself *sanctify* you completely" (1 Thess 5:23).

Futuristic. The particle ἄν occurs with the idea of what might happen in the future if a condition were fulfilled, as in number 3 above (Lk 1:62). Compare: τί ἂν γένοιτο τοῦτο = "what *might happen* because of this" (Acts 5:24).

Deliberative. This use is a report using an indirect question. A direct question asked or reflected on now is being reported indirectly using the contingency of the optative. Thus, ἡ δὲ ἐπὶ τῷ λόγῳ διεταράχθη καὶ διελογίζετο ποταπὸς <u>εἴη</u> ὁ ἀσπασμὸς οὗτος = "But she was disturbed by this word and kept on wondering what sort of greeting this *might be*" (Lk 1:29).

Imperative Nuances

Problem of Person

Imperative translation is straightforward. However, the Greek *third* person command has no exact equivalent in English. Typically one uses the auxiliary verb, "let" ("let him," "let them," etc.). Grammatically, this is a work around, because the subject is transformed into a direct object. Note that, even though formally neither English nor Greek has a first person imperative, a hortatory subjunctive can function similar to a first person command.

Basic Types

Command. This is the default use. Note the following:
1. ἀλλὰ μᾶλλον <u>δουλευέτωσαν</u> = "but *they must serve* all the more" (1 Tim 6:2)
2. πάντοτε <u>χαίρετε</u> = "*rejoice* always" (1 Thess 5:16)
3. καὶ λέγω τούτῳ, <u>Πορεύθητι</u>, καὶ πορεύεται, καὶ ἄλλῳ, <u>Ἔρχου</u>, καὶ ἔρχεται, καὶ τῷ δούλῳ μου, <u>Ποίησον</u> τοῦτο, καὶ ποιεῖ = "and I say to this one, '*Go!*' and he goes, and to another, '*Come!*' and he comes, and to my servant, '*Do* this!' and he does it" (Mt 8:9)

Prohibition. To forbid an ongoing activity, a durative tense can be used to generate the imperative force of command, hence, the *present imperative* with μή. If the action is only anticipated, an undefined tense can be used to forbid beginning the action, which is the *aorist subjunctive* with μή. A good example from 1 John is: Ἀγαπητοί, μὴ παντὶ πνεύματι <u>πιστεύετε</u>, ἀλλὰ <u>δοκιμάζετε</u> τὰ πνεύματα εἰ ἐκ τοῦ θεοῦ ἐστιν = "Beloved, *stop believing* every spirit; rather, *examine* the spirits, (to see) if they are from God" (1 Jn 4:1; by the way, how does one know that these forms of πιστεύετε and δοκιμάζετε, which actually are identical to their indicative counterparts, are definitely imperative in this context?) This traditional understanding (present imperative as stopping action in progress and aorist subjunctive as do not start an action) has been challenged, and rightly so. Do not apply this grammar like a robot oblivious to context. A present imperative may be just a generalized maxim.

Entreaty. The force of a command is diluted to that of request. Socially, inferior rank is implied on the part of the supplicant. Use of "please" might be appropriate. Note:

1. Κύριε, σῶσον, ἀπολλύμεθα = "Lord, *please save* us—we are perishing!" (Mt 8:25)
2. ἐλθέτω ἡ βασιλεία σου = "*Let* your kingdom *come!*" (Mt 6:10)

Permission. One can express consent to someone's request, or to an implied request. Context determines whether this use is politeness or satire. Two examples are:

1. ἀσθενεῖ τις ἐν ὑμῖν; προσκαλεσάσθω τοὺς πρεσβυτέρους τῆς ἐκκλησίας, καὶ προσευξάσθωσαν ἐπ᾽ αὐτὸν = "Is any among you sick? He *may call upon* the elders of the church, and *they may pray* over him" (Jas 5:14)
2. ἀλλὰ ἐλθόντες αὐτοὶ ἡμᾶς ἐξαγαγέτωσαν = "but they may come and themselves *lead* us out!" (Acts 16:37, Paul's indignant irony, illegally jailed, to civic authorities that have abused their powers)

Ἰδού and Ἴδε. Two common aorist imperative forms, ἰδού and ἴδε, are dramatic devices to heighten interest. A particle calling attention, ἰδού (εἰδόμην) means "Lo!" or "Behold!" An interjection, ἴδε (εἶδον) also means "Lo!" or "Behold!" Examples are:

1. ἰδοὺ ἄγγελος κυρίου κατ᾽ ὄναρ ἐφάνη αὐτῷ = "*lo*, an angel of the Lord appeared to him in a dream" (Mt 1:20)
2. ἰδοὺ μάγοι ἀπὸ ἀνατολῶν παρεγένοντο = "*behold,* magi from the east arrived" (Mt 2:1)

3.   Ἴδε ὁ ἀμνὸς τοῦ θεοῦ. = "*Behold*, the Lamb of God!" (Jn 1:36)

4.   ἴδε οὖν χρηστότητα καὶ ἀποτομίαν θεοῦ = "Therefore, *behold* the kindness and severity of God" (Rom 11:22)

𝔷𝔷𝔷𝔷𝔷𝔷𝔷𝔷𝔷 EXERCISE 14 𝔷𝔷𝔷𝔷𝔷𝔷𝔷𝔷𝔷

1.   Answer true or false:

_____ a. The optative mood takes primary endings.

_____ b. The sign of the optative mood is a lengthened thematic vowel.

_____ c. The subjunctive uses the ε thematic vowel.

_____ d. The imperative uses no thematic vowel.

_____ e. In contrast to the subjunctive, the optative does use an augment for the aorist.

_____ f. Differences between tenses in translation often are indistinguishable in the non-indicative moods.

_____ g. The future subjunctive is quite common in the New Testament.

_____ h. With present tense contracts one can have difficulty distinguishing indicative and subjunctive forms.

_____ i. The negative used with all non-indicative moods is μή.

_____ j. Forms of εἰμί as subjunctive exist, but no examples are found in the New Testament.

_____ k. Formally, neither English nor Greek has a first person imperative.

2. Answer the following on the Greek moods.

2.1 _____ What is the Greek mood that expresses probability?

2.2 _____ What is the Greek mood that has the greatest contingency?

2.3 _____ What mood was disappearing in use in New Testament times?

2.4 _____ What tense has its subjunctive/optative forms similar to the present in active/middle voices?

2.5 _____ What is the mood whose third person forms are unique in the New Testament?

2.6 _____ What is the aorist optative form that occurs often in Paul's letters as a part of his rhetoric?

2.7 _____ What is the most frequent form of the present optative of εἰμί?

2.8 _____ What mood has second person plural forms that are indistinguishable from the indicative?

2.9 _____ Inherently the subjunctive logically is related to what tense?

2.10 _____ The negative μή is used with what tense in the subjunctive for prohibition?

2.11 _____ The negative μή is used with what tense in the imperative for prohibition?

2.12 _____ What conjunction is used for a purpose or result subjunctive?

2.13 _____ How does one translate the double negative οὐ μή when used with the subjunctive?

3. Translate the following. Be ready to answer questions of any translation nuances:

3.1 Μὴ κρίνετε, ἵνα μὴ κριθῆτε.

_____

3.2 ἄλλους ἔσωσεν, σωσάτω ἑαυτόν.

_____

3.3 ταῦτα γράφω ὑμῖν ἵνα μὴ ἁμάρτητε.

_____

3.4 καὶ ὅταν ἀκούσωσιν εὐθὺς ἔρχεται ὁ Σατανᾶς.

_____

3.5 λέγει τοῖς μαθηταῖς, Ἄγωμεν εἰς τὴν Ἰουδαίαν πάλιν.

_____

3.6 καὶ διελάλουν πρὸς ἀλλήλους τί ἂν ποιήσαιεν τῷ Ἰησοῦ.

_____

3.7 μὴ γένοιτο· γινέσθω δὲ ὁ θεὸς ἀληθής, πᾶς δὲ ἄνθρωπος ψεύστης.

_____

_____

4. Translate the following passage from 1 John. Be ready to locate verb forms, as well as analyze the nuances.

1.5 Καὶ ἔστιν αὕτη ἡ ἀγγελία ἣν ἀκηκόαμεν ἀπ᾽ αὐτοῦ

_____

καὶ ἀναγγέλλομεν ὑμῖν, ὅτι ὁ θεὸς φῶς ἐστιν καὶ σκοτία

_____

ἐν αὐτῷ οὐκ ἔστιν οὐδεμία. **6** Ἐὰν εἴπωμεν ὅτι

_____

κοινωνίαν ἔχομεν μετ᾽ αὐτοῦ καὶ ἐν τῷ σκότει

_____

περιπατῶμεν, ψευδόμεθα καὶ οὐ ποιοῦμεν τὴν

_____

ἀλήθειαν· **7** ἐὰν δὲ ἐν τῷ φωτὶ περιπατῶμεν ὡς αὐτός

_____

ἐστιν ἐν τῷ φωτί, κοινωνίαν ἔχομεν μετ᾽ ἀλλήλων καὶ τὸ

_____

αἷμα Ἰησοῦ τοῦ υἱοῦ αὐτοῦ καθαρίζει ἡμᾶς ἀπὸ πάσης

_____

ἁμαρτίας. **8** ἐὰν εἴπωμεν ὅτι ἁμαρτίαν οὐκ ἔχομεν,

_____

ἑαυτοὺς πλανῶμεν καὶ ἡ ἀλήθεια οὐκ ἔστιν ἐν ἡμῖν.

_____

9 ἐὰν ὁμολογῶμεν τὰς ἁμαρτίας ἡμῶν, πιστός ἐστιν καὶ

δίκαιος, ἵνα ἀφῇ ἡμῖν τὰς ἁμαρτίας καὶ καθαρίσῃ ἡμᾶς

ἀπὸ πάσης ἀδικίας. **10** ἐὰν εἴπωμεν ὅτι οὐχ

ἡμαρτήκαμεν, ψεύστην ποιοῦμεν αὐτὸν καὶ ὁ λόγος

αὐτοῦ οὐκ ἔστιν ἐν ἡμῖν.

2.1 Τεκνία μου, ταῦτα γράφω ὑμῖν ἵνα μὴ ἁμάρτητε.

καὶ ἐάν τις ἁμάρτῃ, παράκλητον ἔχομεν πρὸς τὸν

πατέρα Ἰησοῦν Χριστὸν δίκαιον· **2** καὶ αὐτὸς ἱλασμός

ἐστιν περὶ τῶν ἁμαρτιῶν ἡμῶν, οὐ περὶ τῶν ἡμετέρων δὲ

μόνον ἀλλὰ καὶ περὶ ὅλου τοῦ κόσμου.

CHAPTER 15
CONDITIONAL SENTENCES

The syntax of conditions in the New Testament should be distinguished carefully from Classical Greek. Older grammars may be faulted for forcing Koine patterns into Classical categories.

Introduction

A conditional sentence is an independent clause modified by an adverbial dependent clause that puts a condition on fulfillment of the independent clause. Normally, the dependent clause is given first, both in English and Greek. The pattern is "if . . . then." Formally, the dependent "if" clause is called the *protasis* (from πρότασις = "putting forward"). The independent "then" clause is called the *apodosis* (from ἀπόδοσις = "giving back"). These two clauses then set forth the full conditional sentence.

Table 15.1 Conditional Clauses

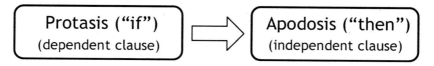

| Protasis ("if") (dependent clause) | ⟹ | Apodosis ("then") (independent clause) |

This two-clause structure in Greek would be: (1) a conditional conjunction signaling the beginning of the conditional sentence, followed by its dependent protasis clause, then (2) the statement of the independent apodosis clause, often signaled with the (untranslatable) particle of contingency, ἄν, occurring somewhere in the apodosis.

Table 15.2 Conditional Sentences: Clauses

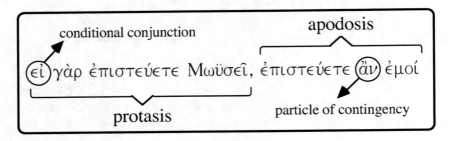

This structure is simple and similar to English. Here, however, is an important Greek conditional sentence dictum:

♦ *The key to any Greek conditional sentence is protasis mood.*

Thus, analysis of any conditional sentence boils down to grammar: the protasis mood. Protasis grammar reveals logic, logic reveals assumptions, and assumptions reveal class conditional sentence. The flowchart below summarizes these observations.

Table 15.3 Conditional Sentences: Flowchart

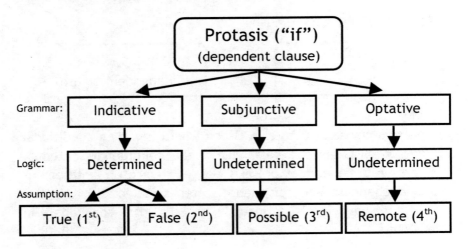

Analysis

Protasis: Grammar

The mood of the protasis verb is the key to understanding any conditional sentence, because verb mood reveals conditional logic. The logic of the condition reveals the two ways the speaker frames the condition. The condition can be framed as either determined or undetermined. Three moods become the basis of this logic.

1. *Indicative (determined):* Use of the indicative mood for the protasis (the "if" verb) reveals a *determined* logic, that is, the condition is determined in the speaker's mind, and assumed either as true or false. Since indicative is the mood of presented reality, this mood is fitting for this use.

2. *Subjunctive (undetermined, possible):* Use of the subjunctive mood for the protasis reveals an *undetermined* logic, that is, the condition is left undetermined in the speaker's mind, but assumed possible. Since subjunctive is a mood of some contingency, this mood is fitting for this use.

3. *Optative (undetermined, remote):* Use of the rare optative mood for the protasis also reveals an *undetermined* logic, that is, the condition is left undetermined in the speaker's mind, but assumed only remote. Since optative is the mood of greater contingency, this mood is fitting for this use.

Protasis: Logic and Assumptions

Determined (True, False)

The speaker already has determined whether the condition is fulfilled or not fulfilled. The condition determined fulfilled would be a *true* condition. The condition determined unfulfilled would be a *false* condition.

True (First Class). The "if" verb is indicative. Here, the speaker assumes the "if" condition true. Determined true is a *first class* conditional sentence. The protasis uses the conjunction εἰ and any indicative mood verb. (On rare occasion ἐάν can be used, which is crasis for εἰ ἄν; cf. Lk 19:40; 1 Thess 3:8.) The apodosis likewise uses any indicative mood. The εἰ on occasion can be translated as "since" when the context makes clear the speaker is setting forth the reality of the "if" clause.

False (Second Class). The "if" verb is indicative. The speaker assumes the "if" condition false. Determined false is a *second class* conditional sentence. This conditional sentence further subdivides into conditions assumed false that the speaker is applying to the present time, or conditions assumed false that the speaker is applying to past time. The grammar of these two time frames is:

1. *False Present*: Conditions assumed false in present time set up the protasis using the conjunction εἰ and any past tense indicative, but usually the imperfect. If stated in the negative, μή is used (with two exceptions in Mk 14:21 and the parallel in Mt 26:24). The apodosis normally is set up using the particle of contingency ἄν (non-translatable) and any past tense indicative. The ἄν can occur anywhere in the apodosis, i.e., not always first. Sometimes this particle is dropped altogether.

2. *False Past*: Conditions assumed false in *past* time use aorist and pluperfect tenses (with two exceptions, the imperfects in Heb 11:15 and Mt 23:30, both contexts past time). The apodosis normally has the particle of contingency ἄν (non-translatable) and any past tense indicative. The ἄν can occur anywhere in the apodosis, that is, not always first, but sometimes is dropped altogether.

Undetermined (Possible, Remote)

Possible (Third Class). The "if" verb is subjunctive. The speaker assumes the "if" condition undetermined, but possible. Undetermined but possible logic is a *third class* conditional sentence. The speaker has not determined whether the hypothetical condition is fulfilled or not fulfilled, but leaves open the possibility.

Quite frequently, the third class conjunction used is ἐάν, and the tense of the apodosis verb is future. However, one should not key in on this particular conjunction as if ἐάν by itself was some guarantee that the third class construction is used. For example, on occasion, one will find the conjunction εἰ in a third class conditional sentence, as in Lk 9:13. Further, while we can generalize by saying the apodosis tense often is future, in fact, any tense in the indicative mood can be found in the apodosis. Even so, future anticipation still is inherent in the context of these third class conditional sentences.

Remote (Fourth Class). The "if" verb is optative. The speaker assumes the "if" condition undetermined, but remote. Undetermined but remote logic is a *fourth class* conditional sentence. The speaker has not determined whether the hypothetical condition is fulfilled or not fulfilled, but the possibility is only remote.

The conjunction used in this fourth class sentence is εἰ. In the fourth class apodosis a particle of contingency occurs, ἄν, which is not translated. Actually, in fact, we do not have a *complete* fourth class conditional sentence in the New Testament. We either find just the protasis or just the apodosis of a fourth class conditional sentence actually expressed, but never both together. Ellipsis of half of the structure leaves the form grammatically incomplete but logically still clear. Often the part that is missing is the apodosis, which would be another verb also in the optative mood.

Structure Summary

The structure of Greek conditional sentences discussed in the previous pages is summarized in the table below. The table gives the class conditional sentence, the protasis logic, the type of conjunction used, and then the tense and mood of the protasis and apodosis clauses.

Table 15.4 Conditional Sentences: Structure

Class	Logic	Conj.	Protasis	Apodosis
1st TRUE	Determined (οὐ in negative)	εἰ (ἐάν)	indicative	any indicative, imperative, subjunctive
2nd FALSE	Determined (μή in negative) a. present time	εἰ	imperfect, or any past tense indicative	past indicative (ἄν optional)
	b. past time	εἰ	aorist indicative	past indicative (ἄν optional)
		εἰ	pluperfect indicative	past indicative (ἄν optional)
3rd POSSIBLE	Undetermined	ἐάν (εἰ)	subjunctive	future, or any indic. (ἄν opt.)
4th REMOTE	Undetermined	εἰ	optative	optative (ἄν optional)

Translation Nuances

First Class (True)

The protasis mood is indicative. The "if" is determined true. Examples below include both conditions *assumed* true and those *asserted* true only for the sake of rhetorical argument. Present tense constructions are common; imperfects are not. Aorist and perfect tenses are more common than imperfect. Since the structure is the same, the examples are focused on present and imperfect tenses.

1. First class, condition assumed true (context essential for this evaluation)
   A. protasis = present indicative
      (1) εἰ ἐκβάλλεις ἡμας = "if you are casting us out" (Mt 8:31; perhaps "*since* you are casting us out")[1]
      (2) εἰ δὲ ἐν πνεύματι θεοῦ ἐγὼ ἐκβάλλω τὰ δαιμόνια = "But if by the Spirit of God I am casting out the demons" (Mt 12:28; perhaps: "*since* by the Spirit of God . . . ")
      (3) εἰ γὰρ πιστεύομεν ὅτι Ἰησοῦς ἀπέθανεν καὶ ἀνέστη = "For if we believe that Jesus died and rose again" (1 Thess 4:14; also: "For *since* we believe . . .")
   B. protasis = imperfect indicative (uncommon)
      (1) εἰ καὶ μετεμελόμην, βλέπω = "Even if I did regret, I see" (2 Cor 7:8; Paul in reference to sending an earlier letter to the Corinthians)
      (2) (other imperfect tense conditions are perhaps examples of mixed classes)
2. First class, condition asserted true only for argument:
   A. protasis = present indicative
      (1) εἰ ὁ σατανᾶς τὸν σατανᾶν ἐκβάλλει = "if Satan casts out Satan" (Mt 12:26)
      (2) καὶ εἰ ἐγὼ ἐν Βεελζεβοὺλ ἐκβάλλω τὰ δαιμόνια = "and if I through Beelzebul am casting out the demons" (Mt 12:27)
      (3) εἰ περιτομὴν ἔτι κηρύσσω, τί ἔτι διώκομαι; = "If I still preach circumcision, why am I still being persecuted?" (Gal 5:11)
   B. protasis = imperfect indicative (most of the examples suggested for this category seem to be ambiguous or of dubious syntax)

---

[1]Wallace's arguments against using "since" in these instances simply are not persuasive; cf. Wallace, *Greek Grammar Beyond the Basics*, pp. 692-94.

Second Class (False)

The protasis mood is indicative. The "if" is determined false. Examples below include both conditions *assumed* false and those *asserted* false only for the sake of rhetorical argument. Any past tense indicative is possible, but the imperfect is common. Notice: (1) the durative aspect of the imperfect verb in the protasis is dropped in English, which defaults to simple preterit, and (2) the English convention using an auxiliary verb "would" in the apodosis.

1. Second class, condition assumed false:
    A. False in present time (imperfect)
        (1) εἰ γὰρ ἐπιστεύετε Μωϋσεῖ, ἐπιστεύετε ἂν ἐμοί = "For if you believed Moses, you would believe me" (Jn 5:46, Jesus to his opponents)
        (2) εἰ δὲ ἑαυτοὺς διεκρίνομεν, οὐκ ἂν ἐκρινόμεθα = "but if we judged ourselves rightly, we would not be judged" (1 Cor 11:31, Paul to Corinthians about the Lord's Supper)
        (3) Εἰ γὰρ ἡ πρώτη ἐκείνη ἦν ἄμεμπτος, οὐκ ἂν δευτέρας ἐζητεῖτο τόπος = "For if that first [covenant] were faultless, no occasion would have been sought for a second" (Heb 8:7, exhorting a Christian audience on the supremacy of Christ)
    B. False in past time (aorist, pluperfect)
        (1) εἰ γὰρ ἔγνωσαν, οὐκ ἂν τὸν κύριον τῆς δόξης ἐσταύρωσαν = "for if they had known, they would not have crucified the Lord of glory" (1 Cor 2:8)
        (2) εἰ δὲ ἐγνώκειτε τί ἐστιν, Ἔλεος θέλω καὶ οὐ θυσίαν, οὐκ ἂν κατεδικάσατε τοὺς ἀναιτίους. = "But if you had known what this means—'I desire mercy and not sacrifice'—you would not have condemned the innocent." (Mt 12:7)
2. Second class, condition asserted false only for argument:
    A. False in present time (imperfect)

(1) εἰ μὴ ἦν οὗτος παρὰ θεοῦ, οὐκ ἠδύνατο ποιεῖν οὐδέν = "if this man were not from God, he would not be able to do anything" (Jn 9:33, the healed blind man responding to his questioners)

(2) Εἰ μὴ ἦν οὗτος κακὸν ποιῶν, οὐκ ἄν σοι παρε-δώκαμεν αὐτόν = "If this man were not an evil-doer, we would not have brought him to you" (Jn 18:30, the Jews to Pilate)

B. False in past time (aorist, pluperfect)

(1) εἰ μὴ ἦλθον καὶ ἐλάλησα αὐτοῖς, ἁμαρτίαν οὐκ εἴχοσαν = "If I had not come and spoken to them, they would not have sin." (Jn 15:22)

(2) Ἀπολελύσθαι ἐδύνατο ὁ ἄνθρωπος οὗτος εἰ μὴ ἐπεκέκλητο Καίσαρα. = "This man could have been released, if he had not appealed to the Emperor." (Acts 26:32)

Third Class (Possible)

The third class conditional sentence uses subjunctive mood to indicate contingency in the "if" clause. The "if" is undetermined, but the speaker entertains the idea that fulfillment of the "if" condition is actually possible. The practical effect is something like "if we say" could infer "which some of you might be saying." Notice the subjunctive mood of the protasis verb in the following:

1. πῶς ἐὰν <u>εἴπω</u> ὑμῖν τὰ ἐπουράνια πιστεύσετε; = "if *I tell* you heavenly things, how will you believe?" (Jn 3:12)

2. ἐὰν ἄλλος <u>ἔλθῃ</u> ἐν τῷ ὀνόματι τῷ ἰδίῳ, ἐκεῖνον λήμ-ψεσθε = "if another person *should come* in his own name, you will receive that one" (Jn 5:43)

3. ὅτι ἐὰν <u>ὁμολογήσῃς</u> ἐν τῷ στόματί σου κύριον Ἰη-σοῦν, καὶ <u>πιστεύσῃς</u> ἐν τῇ καρδίᾳ σου ὅτι ὁ θεὸς αὐ-τὸν ἤγειρεν ἐκ νεκρῶν, σωθήσῃ = "that if *you confess* with your mouth the Lord Jesus, and *believe* in your heart

that God has raised him from the dead, you will be saved" (Rom 10:9)

4. Ἐὰν εἴπωμεν ὅτι κοινωνίαν ἔχομεν μετ᾽ αὐτοῦ καὶ ἐν τῷ σκότει περιπατῶμεν, ψευδόμεθα = "If *we say* that we have fellowship with Him and *are walking* in darkness, we deceive ourselves" (1 Jn 1:6)

5. ἐὰν ὁμολογῶμεν τὰς ἁμαρτίας ἡμῶν, πιστός ἐστιν καὶ δίκαιος ἵνα ἀφῇ ἡμῖν τὰς ἁμαρτίας = "If *we confess* our sins, He is faithful and just in order to forgive us our sins" (1 Jn 1:9)

6. εἰ μήτι πορευθέντες ἡμεῖς ἀγοράσωμεν εἰς πάντα τὸν λαὸν τοῦτον βρώματα = "unless we ourselves go and *buy* food for all these people" (Lk 9:13)

Fourth Class (Remote)

The optative mood indicates significant contingency in the "if" clause. The speaker hardly entertains the idea of fulfillment of the "if" condition. Both protasis and apodosis would be optative. An English illustration would be: "If he *could swim* well, he *might reach* shore." In fact, in the New Testament no complete fourth class conditional sentence occurs; often, the apodosis is missing: ἀλλ᾽ εἰ καὶ πάσχοιτε διὰ δικαιοσύνην, μακάριοι = "But even if *you should suffer* for the sake of righteousness, you are blessed" (1 Pet 3:14, no corresponding optative apodosis).

Use of the optative shows more literary flair. The bulk of New Testament occurrences are in Luke and Acts. This author has a facility with Greek that is a cut above some other New Testament authors. He also uses this mood as an alternate style for indirect discourse used to replace an indicative in secondary sequence, in good Classical Greek style: ἔσπευδεν γὰρ εἰ δυνατὸν εἴη αὐτῷ τὴν ἡμέραν τῆς πεντηκοστῆς γενέσθαι εἰς Ἱεροσόλυμα = "for he was making haste, if *it might be* possible for him to be in Jerusalem on the day of Pentecost" (Acts 20:16).

ᘒᘒᘒᘒᘒᘒᘒᘒ EXERCISE 15 ᘒᘒᘒᘒᘒᘒᘒᘒᘒ

1.3 Matching

_____ 1. protasis

_____ 2. apodosis

_____ 3. εἰ

_____ 4. ἐάν

_____ 5. ἄν

_____ 6. true

_____ 7. false

_____ 8. optative

_____ 9. indicative

_____ 10. subjunctive

_____ 11. imperfect

a. the assumption for 2nd class conditionals

b. grammar indicating determined logic

c. name of independent "then" clause

d. the protasis tense for false in present time

e. grammar for undetermined, but possible

f. name of dependent "if" clause

g. the "if" conjunction used most of the time

h. grammar for undetermined, but remote

i. the assumption for 1st class conditionals

j. the "if" conjunction used in 3rd class mostly

k. non-translated particle in the apodosis

2.   Fill in the following conditional sentences flowchart:

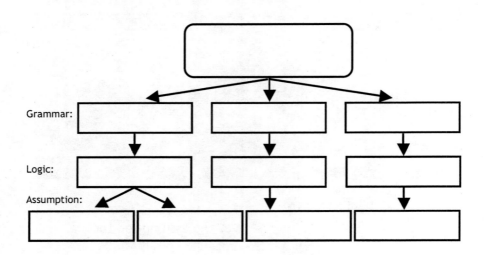

Grammar:

Logic:

Assumption:

3. Translate the following. Be ready to answer conditional sentence questions:

   3.1 εἰ δὲ θέλεις εἰς τὴν ζωὴν εἰσελθεῖν, τήρησον τὰς ἐντολάς.

   _____

   3.2 εἰ υἱὸς εἶ τοῦ θεοῦ, εἰπὲ ἵνα οἱ λίθοι οὗτοι ἄρτοι γένωνται.

   _____

   3.3 εἰ ἠγαπᾶτέ με ἐχάρητε ἂν ὅτι πορεύομαι πρὸς τὸν πατέρα.

   _____

   3.4 καλὸν ἦν αὐτῷ εἰ οὐκ ἐγεννήθη ὁ ἄνθρωπος ἐκεῖνος.

   _____

3.5 Τότε ἐάν τις ὑμῖν εἴπῃ· ἰδοὺ ὧδε ὁ χριστός, ἤ· ὧδε, μὴ πιστεύσητε·

_____

_____

3.6 ζητεῖν τὸν θεόν, εἰ ἄρα γε ψηλαφήσειαν αὐτὸν καὶ εὕροιεν

_____

_____

4. Analyze the conditional sentences in 1 Jn 1:5-10 in exercise #4 of the previous chapter.

5. Translate the following passage from 1 John. Be ready to locate verb forms, as well as analyze conditional sentences.

2.3 Καὶ ἐν τούτῳ γινώσκομεν ὅτι ἐγνώκαμεν αὐτόν, ἐὰν

τὰς ἐντολὰς αὐτοῦ τηρῶμεν. **4** ὁ λέγων ὅτι ἔγνωκα αὐτόν καὶ

τὰς ἐντολὰς αὐτοῦ μὴ τηρῶν, ψεύστης ἐστὶν καὶ ἐν τούτῳ ἡ

ἀλήθεια οὐκ ἔστιν· **5** ὃς δ' ἂν τηρῇ αὐτοῦ τὸν λόγον, ἀληθῶς

ἐν τούτῳ ἡ ἀγάπη τοῦ θεοῦ τετελείωται, ἐν τούτῳ

γινώσκομεν ὅτι ἐν αὐτῷ ἐσμεν. **6** ὁ λέγων ἐν αὐτῷ μένειν

ὀφείλει καθὼς ἐκεῖνος περιεπάτησεν καὶ αὐτὸς [οὕτως]

περιπατεῖν.

2.7 Ἀγαπητοί, οὐκ ἐντολὴν καινὴν γράφω ὑμῖν ἀλλ᾽

ἐντολὴν παλαιὰν ἣν εἴχετε ἀπ᾽ ἀρχῆς· ἡ ἐντολὴ ἡ παλαιά

ἐστιν ὁ λόγος ὃν ἠκούσατε. **8** πάλιν ἐντολὴν καινὴν γράφω

ὑμῖν, ὅ ἐστιν ἀληθὲς ἐν αὐτῷ καὶ ἐν ὑμῖν, ὅτι ἡ σκοτία

παράγεται καὶ τὸ φῶς τὸ ἀληθινὸν ἤδη φαίνει. **9** Ὁ λέγων ἐν

τῷ φωτὶ εἶναι καὶ τὸν ἀδελφὸν αὐτοῦ μισῶν ἐν τῇ σκοτίᾳ

ἐστὶν ἕως ἄρτι. **10** ὁ ἀγαπῶν τὸν ἀδελφὸν αὐτοῦ ἐν τῷ φωτὶ

μένει καὶ σκάνδαλον ἐν αὐτῷ οὐκ ἔστιν· **11** ὁ δὲ μισῶν τὸν

ἀδελφὸν αὐτοῦ ἐν τῇ σκοτίᾳ ἐστὶν καὶ ἐν τῇ σκοτίᾳ

περιπατεῖ καὶ οὐκ οἶδεν ποῦ ὑπάγει, ὅτι ἡ σκοτία ἐτύφλωσεν

τοὺς ὀφθαλμοὺς αὐτοῦ.

2.12 Γράφω ὑμῖν, τεκνία, ὅτι ἀφέωνται ὑμῖν αἱ ἁμαρτίαι

διὰ τὸ ὄνομα αὐτοῦ.

13 γράφω ὑμῖν, πατέρες, ὅτι ἐγνώκατε τὸν ἀπ᾽ ἀρχῆς.

γράφω ὑμῖν, νεανίσκοι, ὅτι νενικήκατε τὸν πονηρόν.

14 ἔγραψα ὑμῖν, παιδία, ὅτι ἐγνώκατε τὸν πατέρα.

ἔγραψα ὑμῖν, πατέρες, ὅτι ἐγνώκατε τὸν ἀπ᾽ ἀρχῆς.

ἔγραψα ὑμῖν, νεανίσκοι, ὅτι ἰσχυροί ἐστε καὶ ὁ λόγος

τοῦ θεοῦ ἐν ὑμῖν μένει καὶ νενικήκατε τὸν πονηρόν.

2.15 Μὴ ἀγαπᾶτε τὸν κόσμον μηδὲ τὰ ἐν τῷ κόσμῳ. ἐάν

τις ἀγαπᾷ τὸν κόσμον, οὐκ ἔστιν ἡ ἀγάπη τοῦ πατρὸς ἐν

αὐτῷ· 16 ὅτι πᾶν τὸ ἐν τῷ κόσμῳ, ἡ ἐπιθυμία τῆς σαρκὸς καὶ

ἡ ἐπιθυμία τῶν ὀφθαλμῶν καὶ ἡ ἀλαζονεία τοῦ βίου, οὐκ

ἔστιν ἐκ τοῦ πατρὸς ἀλλ᾽ ἐκ τοῦ κόσμου ἐστίν. 17 καὶ ὁ

κόσμος παράγεται καὶ ἡ ἐπιθυμία αὐτοῦ, ὁ δὲ ποιῶν τὸ

θέλημα τοῦ θεοῦ μένει εἰς τὸν αἰῶνα.

CHAPTER 16

INFINITIVES

Infinitives and participles are verbals. Verbals are gerbils with their DNA reengineered—that is, verbs remanufactured into nouns, adjectives, and adverbs. Whereas the infinitive is a verbal noun, the participle is a verbal adjective. Both infinitives and participles have similar functions in a sentence.

Introduction

Heritage

Infinitive heritage is a combination of verb and noun. From the verb they carry tense and voice. From the noun they carry case and substantival relationship. Verbals (infinitives and participles) are infinite. *Infinite* means without a subject. As a result, verbals have no first, second, or third person. The absence of a subject also means verbals do not need to express mood. Thus, verbals have no indicative, subjunctive, optative, or imperative.

Table 16.1 Infinitives: Verb and Noun Heritage

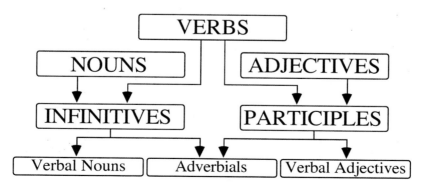

Morphology

Infinitives have their own set of endings that are not to be confused with either noun or verb endings. Infinitive accent is not "irregular," since rules for finite verbs do not apply. The accent is learned by observation for each form. Infinitive endings have four resultant endings, -ειν, -ναι, -σαι, -σθαι, that have volatilized from primitive forms (-εν, -ναι, -αι, -σθαι). Observe that -ειν and -σαι are always active, -σθαι is always middle or passive, and -ναι varies as perfect active or aorist passive.

Table 16.2 Infinitive Endings

Always Active	Always Mid/Pass	Act. or Pass.
-ειν, -σαι	-σθαι	-ναι

Table 16.3 Infinitive Paradigms

	Present	2nd Aor	1st Aor	Perfect
act:	λύειν	λιπεῖν	λῦσαι	λελυκέναι
mid:	λύεσθαι	λιπέσθαι	λύσασθαι	λελύσθαι
pass:	λύεσθαι	γραφῆναι	λυθῆναι	λελύσθαι

Both consonant and vowel reactions already learned help to explain various infinitive forms in the New Testament. Such formulations do not need to be memorized, only recognized. They are described briefly in the following material.

Present Tense

Uncontracted active voice accent is penult acute. Uncontracted middle voice accent is antepenult acute.

Active Voice. The ending is -εν. The theme vowel is ε.
1. Present active: ε + εν = -ειν = λύειν, creating a spurious diphthong (result of contraction)

2. *Contracts:*
   - ε + ειν = -εῖν = ποιεῖν
   - ο + ειν = -οῦν = πληροῦν
   - α + ειν = -ᾶν = ἀγαπᾶν (no iota subscript because ει is a spurious diphthong)

Middle/Passive Voice. The ending is -σθαι. The theme vowel is ε.

1. *Present middle/passive:* ε + σθαι = -εσθαι = λύεσθαι
2. *Contracts:*
   - ε + εσθαι = -εῖσθαι = ποιεῖσθαι
   - ο + εσθαι = -οῦσθαι = πληροῦσθαι
   - α + εσθαι = -ᾶσθαι = ἀγαπᾶσθαι

Perfect Tense

Perfect infinitives are infrequent (under fifty times in the New Testament). The tense stem shows reduplication. The active voice tense suffix is -κε. The ending is -ναι. So, the perfect active form is λελυκέναι. Other patterns are recognizable (e.g., in contract lengthening, as in πεπληρωκέναι, from πληρόω). A perfect second active, dropping the κ of the -κε suffix, is rare. Note the form γεγονέναι (γίνομαι). The perfect middle/passive has the ending -σθαι, but has no thematic vowel (fifth principal part). So, the form, then, is ἀπολελύσθαι (ἀπολύω). Contracts lengthen, as in πεφανερῶσθαι (φανερόω). Perfect middle infinitive stems ending in a stop are quite rare in the New Testament.

Future Tense

Rarely encountered, the future infinitive has the future tense suffix -σ, but this suffix coalesces with another sigma in its εἰμί form. The New Testament has only five occurrences of two verbs. One example is the singular occurrence of εἰσελεύσεσθαι from εἰσέρχομαι in Heb 3:18. The one other example is ἔσεσθαι from εἰμί, which has four occurrences, all of them in Acts (Acts 11:28; 23:30; 24:15; 27:10).

First Aorist Tense

Infinitives do not express a time component, as in the equation for a Greek verb in indicative mood. So, aorist infinitives have no augment.

Active Voice. The actual ending is -αι. The active voice tense suffix is -σα.

1. *Aorist active:* σα + αι = -σαι = λῦσαι (the two alphas coalesce; note perfect mid. ind., 2pp has reduplication and different accent, λέλυσαι)

2. *Contracts:*
   • ε + σαι = -ῆσαι = ποιῆσαι
   • ο + σαι = -ῶσαι = πληρῶσαι
   • α + σαι = -ῆσαι = ἀγαπῆσαι

3. *Stops:*
   • labial: π, β, φ + σαι = -ψαι = πέμψαι
   • palatal: κ, γ, χ + σαι = -ξαι = ἀνοῖξαι (ἀνοίγω)
   • dental: τ, δ, θ + σαι = -σαι = σῶσαι

4. *Liquids:*
   • liquids: λ, ρ + σαι = -λαι or -ραι = ἀπαγγεῖλαι (ἀπαγγέλλω)
   • nasals: ν, μ + σαι = -ναι or -μαι = μεῖναι

Middle Voice. The ending is -σθαι. The middle voice tense suffix is -σα.

1. *Aorist middle:* σα + σθαι = -σασθαι = λύσασθαι

2. *Contracts:*
   • ε + σασθαι = -ήσασθαι = ἀρνήσασθαι (ἀρνέομαι)
   • ο + σασθαι = -ώσασθαι = μισθώσασθαι (μισθόω)
   • α + σασθαι = -ήσασθαι = καταχρήσασθαι (καταχράομαι)

3. *Stops:*
   • labial: π, β, φ + σασθαι = -ψασθαι = μεταπέμψασθαι (μεταπέμπω)
   • palatal: κ, γ, χ + σασθαι = -ξασθαι = ἀνατάξασθαι (ἀνατάσσω)

- dental: τ, δ, θ + σασθαι = -σασθαι = ψεύσασθαι (ψεύδομαι)

4. *Liquids:* ρ+σασθαι = -ρασθαι = κείρασθαι (κείρω)

First Passive Voice. The ending is -ναι. The first passive suffix is -θη.

1. *Aorist passive:* θη + ναι = -θῆναι = λυθῆναι
2. *Contracts:*
   - ε + θηναι = -ηθῆναι = διακονηθῆναι (διακονέω)
   - ο + θηναι = -ωθῆναι = σταυρωθῆναι
   - α + θηναι = -ηθῆναι = γεννηθῆναι (γεννάω)
3. *Stops:*
   - labial: π, β, φ + θηναι = -φθῆναι = προπεμφθῆναι (προπέμπω)
   - palatal: κ, γ, χ + θηναι = -χθῆναι = διορυχθῆναι (διορύσσω)
   - dental: τ, δ, θ + θηναι = -σθῆναι = βαπτισθῆναι
4. *Liquids:* nasal ν + θηναι = -θῆναι or -νθῆναι
   - κριθῆναι (κρίνω)
   - πληθυνθῆναι (πληθύνω)

Second Passive Voice. The second passive voice ending is -ναι, with -η suffix (dropping θ). So, one has η + ναι = -ῆναι = χαρῆναι (χαίρω).

Second Aorist Tense

Second aorist infinitives have no augment and use distinctive second aorist stems. Active and middle voice forms are like the present tense, save for stem and accent. Thus, for second aorist infinitives one has to know vocabulary (i.e., principal parts) and watch accent. The resultant active voice ending is -ειν, as in

Chart 12: Infinitive Tenses

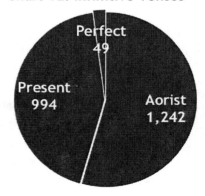

Perfect 49

Present 994

Aorist 1,242

the present. Accent is ultima circumflex. So, the form is βαλεῖν (cf. βάλλειν). The middle voice ending is -εσθαι (with thematic vowel). Accent is penult acute. So, the form is γενέσθαι (cf. γίνεσθαι). Infinitive tense frequency is given in the table above. Excluded is the future infinitive, which occurs only five times.

Grammar

Verbal Characteristics

Tense Aspect

From the verb the infinitive brings tense and voice. This tense, however, is not time. Tense is aspect only. Thus, the present infinitive is durative, the perfect infinitive is perfective, and the aorist infinitive is undefined. Yet, the typical English infinitive form "to _____" can be used for an infinitive translation in any tense. So λύειν, λυεῖν, or λελυκέναι could be "to loose." Notice that the tense aspect does not come across with such a translation. In such situations, one would have to explain the aspect of a Greek infinitive rather than trying to communicate this in a translation. The following examples illustrate the problem of infinitive aspect:

1. *Durative:* Ἀπὸ τότε ἤρξατο ὁ Ἰησοῦς <u>κηρύσσειν</u> καὶ <u>λέγειν</u> = "From that time on, Jesus began *to preach* and *to say*" (Mt 4:17). Notice emphasis on Jesus' *activity*.

2. *Perfective:* κρεῖττον γὰρ ἦν αὐτοῖς μὴ <u>ἐπεγνωκέναι</u> τὴν ὁδὸν τῆς δικαιοσύνης ἢ ἐπιγνοῦσιν <u>ὑποστρέψαι</u> ἐκ τῆς παραδοθείσης αὐτοῖς ἁγίας ἐντολῆς. = "For it would be far better for them not *to have known* the way of righteousness than knowing, *to turn aside* from the holy commandment which has been delivered to them" (2 Pet 2:21). Here, perfective aspect does come across.

3. *Undefined:* οὐ γάρ ἐστιν καλὸν <u>λαβεῖν</u> τὸν ἄρτον τῶν τέκνων καὶ τοῖς κυναρίοις <u>βαλεῖν</u> = "for it is not good

to take bread from the children and *throw* it to the dogs (Mk 7:27). Contextually, these have punctiliar force.

"Subject" Relationship

An infinitive has no subject. On the other hand, this infinitive *can* have a substantive that can be related to its action generally. To understand this infinitive grammar, take this sentence:

Coach wanted *him.*

The student has no confusion that the personal pronoun "him" is direct object of the verb. Hence, as direct object, the pronoun has *objective* inflection, not nominative (not "Coach wanted he").

Now, expand the verb's predicate with an infinitive:

Coach wanted *him* to play shortstop.

Notice that the pronoun *still* functions as direct object of the finite verb, so remains in the *objective* case, not nominative. In addition, though, the pronoun now also is related generally to the action of an infinitive phrase that is extending the finite verb's predicate.

In Greek, this substantive that is related to the infinitive action is called an *accusative of general reference.* This accusative might be called a "surrogate subject." The accusative communicates that this substantive is making only a general reference to the infinitive action in an adverbial manner, and is not actually the grammatical "subject" like a finite verb has. Rom 6:6 illustrates:

τοῦ μηκέτι δουλεύειν ἡμᾶς τῇ ἁμαρτίᾳ
"that *we* might no longer be slaves to sin"

Notice that ἡμᾶς is accusative, not nominative, and functions as an accusative of general reference, translated as "we." The literal idea would be "to serve with reference to us." English sense is more smooth, though, treating ἡμᾶς as a "surrogate subject."

Table 16.4 Accusative of General Reference

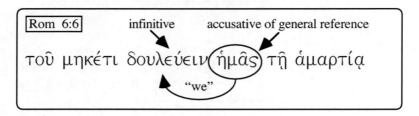

Infinitive Phrase

The infinitive can be part of an entire infinitive phrase. In such a phrase, as a verbal, the infinitive can take:

1. *Direct objects:* ἑαυτὸν οὐ δύναται σῶσαι = "he is not able to save *himself*" (Mk 15:31)
2. *Indirect objects:* Ἔτι πολλὰ ἔχω ὑμῖν λέγειν = "I still have many things to say *to you*" (Jn 16:12)
3. *Adverb modifiers:* Παρακαλοῦμεν δὲ ὑμᾶς, ἀδελφοί, περισσεύειν μᾶλλον = "but we encourage you, brothers, to abound (even) *more*" (1 Thess 4:10)
4. *Prepositional phrases:* εὐκοπώτερόν ἐστιν κάμηλον διὰ τρυπήματος ῥαφίδος διελθεῖν = "to go *through the eye of a needle* is easier for a camel" (Mt 19:24)

Negative Μή

The negative for the indicative mood is οὐ. The infinitive, however, does not have mood. An infinitive, therefore, takes the negative μή.

Noun Characteristics

An infinitive's noun heritage comes out in case relationships. Also, the noun heritage is observed as the infinitive is modified by adjectives or itself modifies other words.

Case Relationships

The infinitive has case function, but without showing case inflection (similar to English substantives). Infinitives appear as indeclinable neuter nouns and take constructions with articles and prepositions. The article always is neuter singular (τό, τοῦ, τῷ):

$$\text{τοῦ λέγειν}$$

Remember that an article does not *have* to be adjacent to its word of concord: <u>τὸ</u> πῶς δεῖ ὑμᾶς <u>περιπατεῖν</u> "how you must *walk*" (1 Thess 4:1; cf. Lk 1:62; 22:24). The infinitive also can be constructed with prepositions and conjunctions:

$$\text{εἰς τὸ λέγειν}$$

These constructions with articles, prepositions, and conjunctions are specialized idioms to be discussed below.

Modifying Relationships

An infinitive can be modified by adjectives, as in Jn 8:26:

<u>πολλὰ</u> ἔχω περὶ ὑμῶν λαλεῖν καὶ κρίνειν
"I have *much* to say and to condemn concerning you"

Similarly, an infinitive itself can modify other words adjectivally, sometimes called "epexegetical," as in Jn 19:10:

<u>ἐξουσίαν</u> ἔχω <u>σταυρῶσαί</u> σε
"I have <u>authority</u> *to crucify* you"

One can compare Rom 15:23, <u>ἐπιποθίαν</u> δὲ ἔχων <u>τοῦ ἐλθεῖν</u> πρὸς ὑμᾶς = "having the <u>desire</u> *to come* to you."

The Verb Εἰμί

The verb εἰμί occurs in only two principal parts, first and second, consisting of the three tenses present, imperfect, and future. The imperfect tense does not have an infinitive form. So, εἰμί occurs as an infinitive only in the present, εἶναι, and in the future, ἔσεσθαι. In fact, the one form ἔσεσθαι covers four of the five future infinitives in the New Testament. Further, εἰμί does not have voice, so εἶναι, for example, is located simply as a "present infinitive" (not "present active infinitive"). An example is Lk 4:41:

ὅτι ᾔδεισαν τὸν χριστὸν αὐτὸν <u>εἶναι</u>
"because they knew that he *was* the Christ"

Translation Nuances

Noun Uses

Subject

Copulative Subject. The infinitive phrase can be subject of the third person singular copulative ἐστίν. The English penchant in this type construction is to use "it" for the subject. Since "it" is an ambiguous word that by default is poor writing, and since "it" only redundantly substitutes for the subject, a better translation and more direct expression is simply to put the actual infinitive phrase in the subject slot of the copulative verb rather than to displace the copulative's subject unnecessarily with "it." An example is Acts 20:35:

Μακάριόν ἐστιν μᾶλλον <u>διδόναι</u> ἢ λαμβάνειν.
"*To give* is more blessed than to receive."

Impersonal Verbs. So-called "impersonal verbs" always are used in the non-personal form of the third person singular (the "it" of the "he," "she," "it"). The impersonal subject of these verbs often is an infinitive. Thus, one can treat such verbs in a manner similar to copulative subjects. That is, one can reject the tendency to begin the translation of an impersonal verb with "it" and instead substitute the infinitive phrase as subject.

Two Greek verbs fit this description. One verb is δεῖ ("it is necessary") and the other is ἔξεστιν ("it is lawful"). Both forms always are used in the impersonal third person singular ("it"). Take the δεῖ in Acts 15:5:

<u>δεῖ περιτέμνειν</u> αὐτοὺς
"<u>to circumcise</u> them <u>is necessary</u>"

Notice avoiding the "it is necessary" style and simply putting the infinitive in the subject slot. An example with ἔξεστιν is Mt 12:12:

ὥστε <u>ἔξεστιν</u> τοῖς σάββασιν καλῶς <u>ποιεῖν</u>
"so that *to do* good on the Sabbath <u>is lawful</u>"

On a number of occasions, the import of δεῖ in English is simply the idea "must." In this type usage, the Greek infinitive actually is converted in translation into a complementary verb that completes the "must" English verb. (Complementary infinitives are discussed below.) Note the following examples:

1. δεῖξαι τοῖς δούλοις αὐτοῦ ἃ <u>δεῖ γενέσθαι</u> = "to show to his servants things which *must take place*" (Rev 1:1)
2. <u>Δεῖ</u> ὑμᾶς <u>γεννηθῆναι</u> ἄνωθεν = "you *must be born* from above" (or "again"; John's typical double meaning; Jn 3:7)
3. <u>Δεῖ</u> τὸν υἱὸν τοῦ ἀνθρώπου πολλὰ <u>παθεῖν</u> = "the Son of man *must suffer* many things" (Lk 9:22)

The δεῖ verb as "must" also can be imperfect. The imperfect form, ἔδει, means "it was necessary," or, in the pattern of a "must" expression, "had (to)": Ἔδει δὲ αὐτὸν διέρχεσθαι διὰ τῆς Σαμαρείας = "But *he had to* go through Samaria" (Jn 4:4).

Direct Object

The infinitive can be a direct object. This function has three main types: direct object, indirect discourse, and complementary.

Direct Object. The infinitive can be a simple direct object. As a direct object, the infinitive will have accusative and genitive case function (but not inflection). An example is Jn 19:12:

ὁ Πιλᾶτος <u>ἐζήτει ἀπολῦσαι</u> αὐτόν
"Pilate <u>was seeking</u> *to release* him"

Indirect Discourse. This category is a subdivision of the direct object use. An infinitive acting as direct object of the main verb represents the entire indirect discourse statement. This use is idiomatic to Greek and difficult to perceive in English, since English does not use this type of grammar for discourse. Distinguish this way of introducing indirect discourse from the use of the conjunction ὅτι with the indicative mood (p. 137). An example is 1 Jn 2:6:

ὁ λέγων ἐν αὐτῷ <u>μένειν</u>

"the one who says *he abides* in him"

This could have been expressed using a ὅτι clause and the reported speech verb having indicative mood: ὁ λέγων <u>ὅτι</u> ἐν αὐτῷ <u>μένει</u> = "the one who says <u>that</u> *he abides* in him." Other examples are Mt 22:23, Lk 24:23, and Rom 2:22.

Complementary. Some verbs require another verb to complete the verbal idea; hence, this second verb is called a *complement*. This complement functionally is a direct object. A *complementary infinitive* is a direct object infinitive required to complete another verb's action. Example verbs that often take a complementary infinitive are ἄρχομαι (as middle, "I begin"), βούλομαι, δέομαι, δύναμαι, θέλω, μέλλω, ὀφείλω, and πειράζω. The -μι verb δύναμαι is common enough in the New Testament that the paradigm is given in this chapter with infinitives. This lexical middle verb's second singular does not volatilize, as is typical, but does have an alternate form (δύνῃ) that imitates this volatilized ending.

Table 16.5 Present Indicative of Δύναμαι

δύναμαι	*I am able*
δύνασαι (δύνῃ)	*you are able (sg.)*
δύναται	*he (she, it) is able*
δυνάμεθα	*we are able*
δύνασθε	*you are able (pl.)*
δύνανται	*they are able*

Study the following complementary infinitive examples:

1. ἄρχομαι: ἤρξαντο λυπεῖσθαι καὶ λέγειν = "they began to be grieved and to say" (Mk 14:19)

2. βούλομαι: με ἐβούλοντο ἀπολῦσαι = "they were willing to release me" (Acts 28:18)

3. δέομαι: διὸ δέομαι μακροθύμως ἀκοῦσαί μου = "so therefore I beg you to hear me patiently" (Acts 26:3)

4. δύναμαι: ἑαυτὸν οὐ δύναται σῶσαι = "he is not able to save himself" (Mk 15:31)

5. θέλω: τί πάλιν θέλετε ἀκούειν; μὴ καὶ ὑμεῖς θέλετε αὐτοῦ μαθηταὶ γενέσθαι; = "Why do you want to hear again? You do not want to become his disciples, do you?" (Jn 9:27)

6. μέλλω: μέλλει γὰρ Ἡρῴδης ζητεῖν τὸ παιδίον τοῦ ἀπολέσαι αὐτό = "for Herod is going to seek the child to destroy him" (Mt 2:13)

7. ὀφείλω: ὃ ὠφείλομεν ποιῆσαι πεποιήκαμεν = "we have done that which we ought to have done" (Lk 17:10)

8. πειράζω: ἐπείραζεν κολλᾶσθαι τοῖς μαθηταῖς = "he was trying to associate with the disciples" (Acts 9:26)

Direct Object Complement

Complements are essential. That is, cut off a complement and you cripple the grammar. For example, a complementary verb is *essential* to completing the verbal idea. If one has "we ought . . .," but no following verb, then the expression begs the question, "ought what?" So, one has this dictum:

♦ *Any complement grammatically is essential.*

Like verbs, a direct object itself can have its own complement. An *object complement* is a *second* accusative *essential* to the meaning of the direct object idea, also called a "double direct object" or "double accusative." To grasp this concept, think of certain verbs such as "ask" or "teach." Not only do you ask *someone*, you also ask *something*. Not only do you teach *someone*, you also teach *something*. In such cases, the *someone* is the first object of the verb, and the *something* is the second, or, the complementary object. Take, for example: "I taught <u>him</u> <u>the lesson</u>." Here, "him" is the *someone*, or first object, and "lesson" is the *something*, or second (i.e., complementary) object. Example Greek verbs that take object complements are ἄγω, αἰτέω, ἀπολύω, ἀποστέλλω, γινώσκω, δέχομαι, δοκέω, ἐγείρω, ἐκβάλλω, εὑρίσκω, ἔχω, θέλω, θεωρέω, καλέω, κηρύσσω, κρίνω, λαμβάνω, λέγω, οἶδα, ὁράω, πιστεύω, and ποιέω.

An infinitive can function as this object complement. Note the following in Acts 13:28:

ἠτήσαντο <u>Πιλᾶτον</u> <u>ἀναιρεθῆναι</u> αὐτόν
"they asked <u>Pilate</u> that he *be killed*"

Here, Πιλᾶτον is the first direct object (the *someone* in the analogy above). The infinitive ἀναιρεθῆναι is a second direct object, or, object complement (the *something* in the analogy).

Apposition

Apposition renames a substantive without using a verb. Often, a word in apposition is set off with commas, but not always: "Bob, our president, is going." An often-cited example of an appositional infinitive is 1 Thess 4:3:

Τοῦτο γάρ ἐστιν θέλημα τοῦ θεοῦ, . . . , <u>ἀπέχεσθαι</u> ὑμᾶς
"For this is the will of God, . . . , *that you abstain*"

Adjective Uses

An infinitive can be an adjective. Some grammars use the term "epexegetic" for this use. Like any adjective, the adjectival infinitive is nonessential to the grammatical expression.

♦ *An adjectival infinitive grammatically is nonessential.*

One can drop the adjectival infinitive and not loose the essential grammatical thought.

Substantive Modifier

Notice how an infinitive modifies the nominal direct object in Pilate's question to Jesus in Jn 19:10:

οὐκ οἶδας ὅτι <u>ἐξουσίαν</u> ἔχω <u>ἀπολῦσαί</u> σε
"Do you not know that I have <u>authority</u> *to release* you?"

A parallel in Paul is Rom 15:23:

<u>ἐπιποθίαν</u> δὲ ἔχων <u>τοῦ ἐλθεῖν</u> πρὸς ὑμᾶς
"having the <u>desire</u> *to come* to you"

Complement Modifier

The infinitive modifies a substantive, but the substantive is the copulative complement. (The infinitive modifies a predicate noun or predicate adjective that follows εἰμί.) The εἰμί subject has to be personal ("I," "you," "he," "she," "we," "they"); otherwise, one has the impersonal "it" construction of ἐστίν; the infinitive in this case functions as a *subject* infinitive. Common adjectives in these personal predicate constructions are "worthy" (ἄξιος), "able" (δύνατος), "unable" (ἀδύνατος), "prepared" (ἕτοιμος), and so forth. An example of a complement modifier is Acts 23:15:

<u>ἕτοιμοί</u> ἐσμεν <u>τοῦ ἀνελεῖν</u> αὐτόν
"we are <u>prepared</u> *to kill* him"

Adverb Uses

The Greek infinitive can express four adverbial functions in its role of modifying the main verb:

1. *Purpose:* Purpose is the default use of the English infinitive and a basic use of the Greek infinitive as well. Purpose is expressed as "to," "in order to," and "so that."
2. *Result:* Result is a statement of consequences. The infinitive provides the consequences of the verbal action. Consequences are expressed with "as a result," "such that."
3. *Cause:* Cause is a statement of reason. The infinitive gives the reason for the verbal action. Cause is expressed as "because."
4. *Time:* Time infers a chronological sequence. The infinitive sets up a chronological frame of reference for the verbal action. The three frames of reference are antecedent, simultaneous, and subsequent. These three time frames are expressed as "before," "while," and "after."

These adverbial functions for the Greek infinitive go beyond English usage, so must be handled with care. As will become clear in the discussion, adverbial infinitives often require conversion into adverbial clauses in English. Fortunately, most adverbial infinitives have construction that makes clear the adverbial role. In fact, any infinitive in construct with an article, preposition, or conjunction *is* adverbial in some way. Thus, we have the dictum:

♦ *Any infinitive in construct always is adverbial.*

A review of the table of adverbial constructions below reveals another important observation: all infinitive constructions except for three are unique to a particular adverbial use. These three ambiguous constructions can be either purpose or result infinitives. They are the anarthrous λύειν, the articular τοῦ λύειν, and the prepositional εἰς τὸ λύειν. Still, the dominant use of all three is purpose. So, if one guesses purpose first for any of these three, one will be right most of the time. Hence, one can conclude for all practical purposes that the adverbial infinitive almost always has unique construction and clear meaning.

♦ *Infinitive construction almost always has clear meaning.*

In terms of translation strategy, the Greek adverbial infinitive often will require adaptation into English. This adaptation usually is on the order of converting the Greek infinitive structure into an English indicative clause.

♦ *Adverbial infinitives often require English indicative clauses.*

Table 16.6 Infinitives: Adverbial Constructions

Constructions	Adverbial Use	Gloss
λύειν εἰς τὸ λύειν πρὸς τὸ λύειν τοῦ λύειν ὡς λύειν	**purpose**	• *to loose* • *so that he looses* • *in order to loose*
λύειν εἰς τὸ λύειν τοῦ λύειν ὥστε λύειν	**result**	• *as a result, he looses* • *such that he looses*
διὰ τὸ λύειν	**cause**	• *because he looses*
πρὸ τοῦ λύειν πρὶν λύειν πρὶν ἢ λύειν	**time:** antecedent	• *before he looses*
ἐν τῷ λύειν	simultaneous	• *while he looses*
μετὰ τὸ λύειν	subsequent	• *after he looses*
ἕως τοῦ λύειν	future (Acts 8:40)	• *until he looses*

Purpose

The *infinitive of purpose* states the purpose expressed in the action of the main verb. Notice how the infinitive structure in some instances is converted into an indicative clause in English. Six constructions are found:

1. *Anarthrous:* ἤλθομεν προσκυνῆσαι αὐτῷ = "we have come *to worship* him" (Mt 2:2)

2. *Articular (τοῦ λύειν):* μετέβη ἐκεῖθεν τοῦ διδάσκειν καὶ κηρύσσειν ἐν ταῖς πόλεσιν αὐτῶν = "he departed from there *to teach* and *to preach* in their cities" (Mt 11:1)

3. *Preposition (εἰς τὸ λύειν):* ἀλλὰ μεταμορφοῦσθε τῇ ἀνακαινώσει τοῦ νοός, εἰς τὸ δοκιμάζειν ὑμᾶς τί τὸ θέλημα τοῦ θεοῦ = "but be transformed by the renewing of your mind, *so that you might approve* what the will of God is" (Rom 12:2)

4. *Preposition (πρὸς τὸ λύειν):* ἐνδύσασθε τὴν πανοπλίαν τοῦ θεοῦ πρὸς τὸ δύνασθαι ὑμᾶς στῆναι πρὸς τὰς μεθοδείας τοῦ διαβόλου = "put on the full armor of God, *so that you be able to stand* against the tricks of the devil" (Eph 6:11)

5. *Particle (ὡς λύειν):* εἰσῆλθον εἰς κώμην Σαμαριτῶν, ὡς ἑτοιμάσαι αὐτῷ = "they entered a village of the Samaritans *in order to prepare* for him" (Lk 9:52)

6. *Conjunction (ὥστε λύειν):* ἀποθανόντες ἐν ᾧ κατειχόμεθα, ὥστε δουλεύειν ἡμᾶς ἐν καινότητι πνεύματος = "having died to that by which we were held fast, *so that we might serve* in newness of the Spirit" (Rom 7:6)

Result

The *infinitive of result* states the result of the action in the main verb. Distinction from infinitive of purpose can be unclear. Notice how the infinitive structure regularly is converted into an indicative clause in English. Four constructions are found:

1. *Anarthrous (λύειν):* διὰ τί ἐπλήρωσεν ὁ σατανᾶς τὴν καρδίαν σου, <u>ψεύσασθαί</u> σε τὸ πνεῦμα τὸ ἅγιον; = "why has Satan filled your heart *such that you lied* to the Holy Spirit?" (Acts 5:3)

2. *Articular (τοῦ λύειν):* ἐκάκωσεν τοὺς πατέρας [ἡμῶν] <u>τοῦ ποιεῖν</u> τὰ βρέφη ἔκθετα αὐτῶν = "he abused [our] fathers, *as a result, they exposed* their infants" (Acts 7:19)

3. *Preposition (εἰς τὸ λύειν):* <u>εἰς τὸ εἶναι</u> αὐτοὺς ἀναπολογήτους = "*so that they are* without excuse" (Rom 1:20); again, τὴν ἀγάπην τῆς ἀληθείας οὐκ ἐδέξαντο <u>εἰς τὸ σωθῆναι</u> αὐτούς = "they received not the love of the truth *with the result that they be saved*" (2 Thess 2:10)

4. *Conjunction (ὥστε λύειν):* ἐθεράπευσεν αὐτόν, <u>ὥστε</u> τὸν κωφὸν <u>λαλεῖν</u> καὶ <u>βλέπειν</u> = "he healed him, *such that* the dumb man *spoke* and *saw*" (Mt 12:22); again, ὁ δὲ Ἰησοῦς οὐκέτι οὐδὲν ἀπεκρίθη, <u>ὥστε θαυμάζειν</u> τὸν Πιλᾶτον = "Jesus no longer answered anything, *so that* Pilate *marveled*." (Mk 15:5)

Cause

The *infinitive of cause* answers the question "why?" The translation uses "because." Always the construction is διὰ τὸ λύειν. Notice how the infinitive structure has to be converted into an indicative clause in English. Study these examples:

1. <u>διὰ τὸ εἶναι</u> αὐτὸν ἐξ οἴκου καὶ πατριᾶς Δαυίδ = "*because he was* of the house and lineage of David" (Lk 2:4)

2. ἦν γὰρ ἐξ ἱκανῶν χρόνων θέλων ἰδεῖν αὐτὸν <u>διὰ τὸ ἀκούειν</u> περὶ αὐτοῦ = "for he had desired to see him for a long time, *because he had heard* about him" (Lk 23:8)

Time

The *infinitive of time* gives a chronological frame of reference related to the main verb action. The action can be (1) antecedent, (2) simultaneous, (3) subsequent, or (4) future to this main verb.

1. Antecedent ("before"):
   - *Preposition (πρὸ τοῦ λύειν):* οἶδεν γὰρ ὁ πατὴρ ὑμῶν ὧν χρείαν ἔχετε πρὸ τοῦ ὑμᾶς αἰτῆσαι αὐτόν = "for your Father knows the need which you have *before you ask* Him" (Mt 6:8)
   - *Conjunction (πρὶν λύειν):* πρὶν ἐλθεῖν ἡμέραν κυρίου τὴν μεγάλην καὶ ἐπιφανῆ = "*before* the great and glorious Day of the Lord *comes*" (Acts 2:20)
   - *Conjunction (πρὶν ἢ λύειν):* πρὶν ἢ συνελθεῖν αὐτοὺς εὑρέθη ἐν γαστρὶ ἔχουσα ἐκ πνεύματος ἁγίου = "*before they came together* she was found with child by the Holy Spirit" (Mt 1:18)
2. Simultaneous ("while")
   - *Preposition (ἐν τῷ λύειν):* καὶ ἐγένετο ἐν τῷ προσεύχεσθαι αὐτὸν = "and it happened that, *while he was praying*" (Lk 9:29)
3. Subsequent ("after"):
   - *Preposition (μετὰ τὸ λύειν):* εἰπὼν ὅτι Μετὰ τὸ γενέσθαι με ἐκεῖ δεῖ με καὶ Ῥώμην ἰδεῖν = "saying, '*After I have been there*, I must see Rome also.'" (Acts 19:21)
4. Future ("until"):
   - *Adverbial Preposition (ἕως τοῦ λύειν):* εὐηγγελίζετο τὰς πόλεις πάσας ἕως τοῦ ἐλθεῖν αὐτὸν εἰς Καισάρειαν = "he continued preaching the good news to all the cities *until he came* to Caesarea" (Acts 8:40; the only New Testament example of this construction)

Infinite Voice

We conclude our discussion on the infinitive with two points about infinite voice. First, infinite voice is relative. Voice connects the verb's action to the verb's subject. However, both infinitives and participles are infinite, that is, not limited by a subject. Thus, to speak of infinite voice is to speak in a relative manner. For an infinitive, voice is related to the substantive with which the infinitive's action is construed (accusative of general reference), which we have styled the "surrogate subject." Similarly, participles can have a "surrogate subject" with which the action of the participle can be construed. Thus, active, middle, and passive voice for both infinitives and participles is speaking in only a relative manner.

Second, verbs that are lexical middle in the indicative also are lexical middle in infinite forms (infinitives and participles). Problems of translating middle voice also apply to infinite verbs.

EXERCISE 16

1. Fill in the following infinitive heritage chart:

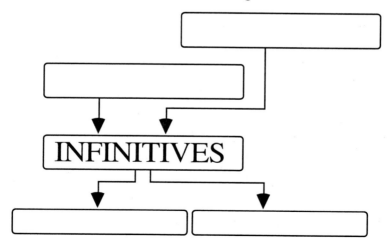

INFINITIVES

2. Answer the following on Greek infinitives:

   2.1 _____ What infinitive endings always are active?

   2.2 _____ What infinitive ending always is middle?

   2.3 _____ What infinitive ending can be either active or passive?

   2.4 _____ Do aorist infinitives show an augment for past time?

   2.5 _____ Do perfect infinitives show reduplication?

   2.6 _____ What is the present active infinitive of ποιέω?

   2.7 _____ What is the aorist active infinitive of βάλλω?

   2.8 _____ What case is the "surrogate subject" that is related generally to the action of the infinitive?

   2.9 _____ What is the negative used with the infinitive?

   2.10 _____ Does the infinitive have case?

   2.11 _____ What is the present infinitive of εἰμί?

   2.12 _____ What is the future infinitive of εἰμί?

   2.13 _____ What type of verb construction sets up an infinitive used as subject?

   2.14 What is an "impersonal verb"? Give two examples.

   _____

   2.15 What is a complementary infinitive?

   _____

2.16 _____ What other direct object function can an infinitive have besides direct object and complementary?

2.17 Match the following adverbial glosses:

____ 1.	ἐν τῷ λύειν	a. _in order to loose_
____ 2.	διὰ τὸ λύειν	b. _such that he looses_
____ 3.	μετὰ τὸ λύειν	c. _because he looses_
____ 4.	ὥστε λύειν	d. _before he looses_
____ 5.	πρὸς τὸ λύειν	e. _while he looses_
____ 6.	πρὸ τοῦ λύειν	f. _after he looses_

3. Translate the following. Be ready to answer questions on infinitive use:

3.1 ἐζήτουν αὐτὸν κρατῆσαι.

_____

3.2 καλόν ἐστιν ἡμᾶς ὧδε εἶναι.

_____

3.3 οὐκ ἔχομεν ἐξουσίαν μὴ ἐργάζεσθαι;

_____

3.4 Οὐδεὶς δύναται δυσὶ κυρίοις δουλεύειν

_____

3.5 πολλὰ ἔχω περὶ ὑμῶν λαλεῖν καὶ κρίνειν

_____

3.6 λέγετε ἐν Βεελζεβοὺλ ἐκβάλλειν με τὰ δαιμόνια

_____

3.7 ἀλλὰ μετὰ τὸ ἐγερθῆναί με προάξω ὑμᾶς εἰς τὴν Γαλιλαίαν.

3.8 πάντα δὲ τὰ ἔργα αὐτῶν ποιοῦσιν πρὸς τὸ θεαθῆναι τοῖς ἀνθρώποις

3.9 πρὸ τοῦ γὰρ ἐλθεῖν τινας ἀπὸ Ἰακώβου μετὰ τῶν ἐθνῶν συνήσθιεν

3.10 Ἐγένετο δὲ ἐν τῷ εἶναι αὐτοὺς ἐκεῖ ἐπλήσθησαν αἱ ἡμέραι τοῦ τεκεῖν αὐτήν

---

4. Analyze the infinitive use in 1 Jn 2:9 in exercise #5 of the previous chapter.

5. Translate the following passage from 1 John. Be ready to locate verb forms, as well as analyze conditional sentences.

   2.18 Παιδία, ἐσχάτη ὥρα ἐστίν, καὶ καθὼς ἠκούσατε ὅτι

ἀντίχριστος ἔρχεται, καὶ νῦν ἀντίχριστοι πολλοὶ γεγόνασιν,

ὅθεν γινώσκομεν ὅτι ἐσχάτη ὥρα ἐστίν. **19** ἐξ ἡμῶν ἐξῆλθαν

ἀλλ᾽ οὐκ ἦσαν ἐξ ἡμῶν· εἰ γὰρ ἐξ ἡμῶν ἦσαν, μεμενήκεισαν

ἂν μεθ᾽ ἡμῶν· ἀλλ᾽ ἵνα φανερωθῶσιν ὅτι οὐκ εἰσὶν πάντες ἐξ

ἡμῶν. **20** καὶ ὑμεῖς χρῖσμα ἔχετε ἀπὸ τοῦ ἁγίου καὶ οἴδατε

πάντες. **21** οὐκ ἔγραψα ὑμῖν ὅτι οὐκ οἴδατε τὴν ἀλήθειαν

ἀλλ᾽ ὅτι οἴδατε αὐτὴν καὶ ὅτι πᾶν ψεῦδος ἐκ τῆς ἀληθείας

οὐκ ἔστιν.

2.22 Τίς ἐστιν ὁ ψεύστης εἰ μὴ ὁ ἀρνούμενος ὅτι Ἰησοῦς

οὐκ ἔστιν ὁ χριστός; οὗτός ἐστιν ὁ ἀντίχριστος, ὁ

ἀρνούμενος τὸν πατέρα καὶ τὸν υἱόν. **23** πᾶς ὁ ἀρνούμενος

τὸν υἱὸν οὐδὲ τὸν πατέρα ἔχει, ὁ ὁμολογῶν τὸν υἱὸν καὶ τὸν

πατέρα ἔχει. **24** ὑμεῖς ὃ ἠκούσατε ἀπ᾽ ἀρχῆς, ἐν ὑμῖν

μενέτω. ἐὰν ἐν ὑμῖν μείνῃ ὃ ἀπ᾽ ἀρχῆς ἠκούσατε, καὶ ὑμεῖς

ἐν τῷ υἱῷ καὶ ἐν τῷ πατρὶ μενεῖτε. **25** καὶ αὕτη ἐστὶν ἡ

ἐπαγγελία ἣν αὐτὸς ἐπηγγείλατο ἡμῖν, τὴν ζωὴν τὴν αἰώνιον.

2.26 Ταῦτα ἔγραψα ὑμῖν περὶ τῶν πλανώντων ὑμᾶς.

27 καὶ ὑμεῖς τὸ χρῖσμα ὃ ἐλάβετε ἀπ᾽ αὐτοῦ, μένει ἐν ὑμῖν

καὶ οὐ χρείαν ἔχετε ἵνα τις διδάσκῃ ὑμᾶς, ἀλλ᾽ ὡς τὸ αὐτοῦ

χρῖσμα διδάσκει ὑμᾶς περὶ πάντων καὶ ἀληθές ἐστιν καὶ οὐκ

ἔστιν ψεῦδος, καὶ καθὼς ἐδίδαξεν ὑμᾶς, μένετε ἐν αὐτῷ.

2.28 Καὶ νῦν, τεκνία, μένετε ἐν αὐτῷ, ἵνα ἐὰν φανερωθῇ

σχῶμεν παρρησίαν καὶ μὴ αἰσχυνθῶμεν ἀπ᾽ αὐτοῦ ἐν τῇ

παρουσίᾳ αὐτοῦ. **29** ἐὰν εἰδῆτε ὅτι δίκαιός ἐστιν, γινώσκετε

ὅτι καὶ πᾶς ὁ ποιῶν τὴν δικαιοσύνην ἐξ αὐτοῦ γεγέννηται.

CHAPTER **17**

PARTICIPLE MORPHOLOGY

Infinitives and participles are verbals. Whereas the infinitive is a verbal noun, the participle is a verbal adjective. Before investigating participle translation, the student will benefit from an overview of participle formation.

Introduction

Heritage

Participle heritage is a combination of verb and adjective. From the verb they carry tense and voice. From the adjective they carry case, concord, and substantival relationships. Verbals (i.e., infinitives and participles) are infinite. Infinite means without a subject. Thus, verbals have no first, second, or third person. The absence of a subject also means verbals do not need to express mood. Thus, verbals have no indicative, subjunctive, optative, or imperative.

Table 17.1 Participles: Verb and Adjective Heritage

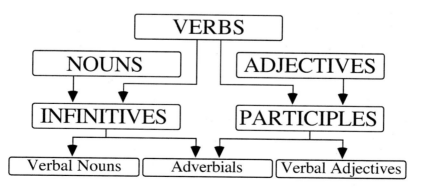

Morphology

Heritage and Morphology

Table 17.2 Heritage/Morphology

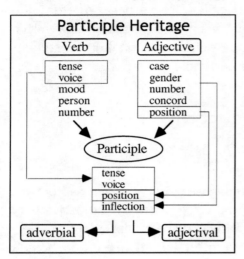

Participle forms reflect their heritage. From verbs they show principal part components in making tense and voice. Yet, participles are timeless, so they do not have an augment. From the adjective participles show case, gender, and number through first, second, and third declension inflections. The adjective background also raises issues of construction with the article, that is, position. As one can see, studying participles is a good way to review the entire Greek verb and noun system (and adjectives as well).

Morphology Hints

Before surveying participle forms, some morphology hints might be helpful for mastering these constructions:
- focus on suffix patterns
- know that -μεν- always is middle (passive)
- become familiar with predictable volatilization patterns
- memorize *nominative singular* forms like vocabulary words
- know mas./neu. *active* is *third* declension, *middle* is *second*

The table below provides a convenient summary of paticiple suffix patterns.

Table 17.3 Participle Suffix Patterns

Tense	Active Ms./Nu.	Active Fem.	Middle	Passive Ms./Nu.	Passive Fem.
Present	-οντ-	-ουσ-	-ομεν-	-ομεν-	-ομεν-
2nd Aorist	-οντ-	-ουσ-	-ομεν-	-εντ-	-εισ-
1st Aorist	-σαντ-	-σασ-	-σαμεν-	-θεντ-	-θεισ-
Perfect	-κοτ-	-κυι-	-μεν-	-μεν-	-μεν-

Of the predictable volatilization patterns for participles, note these two patterns in particular that happen regularly across all principal parts governed by third declension inflection:

1. *Nominative Singular and Dative Plural:* In third declension masculine and neuter forms, the nominative singular and dative plural can hide the participle suffix, just as noun stems are hidden in these slots. Thus, one still has to recognize certain nominative and dative participle endings without the typical suffix visible:
   - present: λύων, λύουσιν
   - aorist: λύσας, λύσασιν
   - perfect: λελυκώς, λελυκόσιν
   - aorist passive: λυθείς, λυθεῖσιν

   Nominative forms are frequent in participles, so be sure to memorize these forms in particular like vocabulary words.

2. *Neuter Forms:* In third declension, neuter nominative and accusative singular also react and hide the suffix pattern. Thus, one still has to recognize the following as neuter participle endings without the typical suffix appearance: λῦον, λῦσαν, λελυκός, and λυθέν.

Active Voice

Present Active

Table 17.4 Present Active Morphology

$$\lambda\upsilon\text{-}o\nu\tau\text{-}\epsilon\varsigma$$

Formation. Formation uses the first principal part. The active participle suffix is -ντ. Phonetic changes obscure this suffix in some forms. The thematic vowel o is added to the -ντ suffix. Inflection by gender is added. Masculine and neuter use third declension endings, following ἄρχων, in which the nominative singular form becomes -ων, and the dative plural form becomes -ουσιν, because -οντ→-ον→-ων and -οντσι→-οσι→-ουσι. Feminine uses first declension endings, following δόξα, but feminine forms react with the participle stem, based on primitive feminine endings making an -ουσ, involving the semivowel iota as -οντι→-ονσ→-οσ→-ουσ. Recall that neuter third declension has no nominative/accusative singular ending. In the participle, no ending leaves exposed the suffix -οντ as the ending. A Greek word cannot end with τ, so the τ drops. The remaining thematic vowel, o, however, does not take compensatory lengthening.

Participle accent is not "irregular," since rules for finite verbs do not apply. Accent follows that of nouns and adjectives. Once the accent of the nominative masculine singular in a tense and voice is known, one can observe that: (1) general rules of accent are followed, (2) accent is persistent, (3) the genitive feminine plural of active voice (and aorist passive) has the typical circumflex on the ultima, as in first declension nouns.

Table 17.5 Present Active Participle (-οντ-, -ουσ-)

Masculine		Neuter	
Singular	*Plural*	*Singular*	*Plural*
λύων	λύοντες	λῦον	λύοντα
λύοντος	λυόντων	λύοντος	λυόντων
λύοντι	λύουσιν	λύοντι	λύουσιν
λύοντα	λύοντας	λῦον	λύοντα

Feminine	
Singular	*Plural*
λύουσα	λύουσαι
λυούσης	λυουσῶν
λυούσῃ	λυούσαις
λύουσαν	λυούσας

Volatilization. Contract verbs show contraction with these resultant endings in typical patterns. For ε contracts: ε+ω = ω, ε+ο = ου, ε+ου = ου, so ποιῶν, ποιοῦντος, etc. For ο contracts: ο+ω = ω, ο+ο = ου, ο+ου = ου, so πληρῶν, πληροῦντος, etc. For α contracts: α+ω = ω, α+ο = ω, α+ου = ω, so ἀγαπῶν, ἀγαπῶντος, etc.

Perfect Active

Table 17.6 Perfect First Active Morphology

λϵ-λυ-κοτ-ϵϛ

First Active. Formation uses the fourth principal part. Some of the perfect active participle formation is explainable. The perfect active stem is reduplicated. The tense suffix is -κ. However, a different participle suffix indicator is used, generating reactions—

some inexplicable, including inexplicable endings involving the archaic letter digamma, which dropped before vowels:

1. Masculine suffix becomes -κοτ and masculine nominative singular -κως, because -κοτς→-κος→-κως (τ dropping before σ, and compensatory lengthening).
2. Neuter nominative singular ending becomes -κος, because -κοτς→-κος (τ dropping before σ, but *no* compensatory lengthening; this neuter sigma ending is inexplicable).
3. Dative plural becomes -κοσιν, because -κοτσι→-κοσι (again, τ drops before the σ; however, the short vowel in this pattern does *not* lengthen).

Accent is ultima acute. Feminine follows καρδία, but primitive feminine forms react with the tense stem, inexplicably winding up as -κυι. The reactions perhaps involve the old digamma letter, a semivowel (or consonantal) iota, and simply dropping the -οτ.

Table 17.7 Perfect First Active Participle (-κοτ-, -κυι-)

Masculine		Neuter	
Singular	*Plural*	*Singular*	*Plural*
λελυκώς	λελυκότες	λελυκός	λελυκότα
λελυκότος	λελυκότων	λελυκότος	λελυκότων
λελυκότι	λελυκόσιν	λελυκότι	λελυκόσιν
λελυκότα	λελυκότας	λελυκός	λελυκότα

Feminine	
Singular	*Plural*
λελυκυῖα	λελυκυῖαι
λελυκυίας	λελυκυιῶν
λελυκυίᾳ	λελυκυίαις
λελυκυῖαν	λελυκυίας

Volatilization. Contracts lengthen: πεποιηκώς, πεπληρωκώς, ἠγαπηκώς; a few exceptions occur, such as δέω (δεδεκώς) and ὁράω (ἑωρακώς). No perfect participle stems with stops are encountered, except a few dentals, such as ἐλπίζω, which has the form ἠλπικώς. Examples of the letter insert variety include: ἔχω (ἐσχηκώς); μένω compounded, as in ὑπομένω (ὑπομεμενηκώς); βάλλω (βεβληκώς); and εἶπον, for λέγω, whose perfect form is εἰρηκώς.

Second Active. This system is similar to the perfect first active, but the -κ of the suffix is dropped, as expected. The perfect tense sign is lost as a result. The most common verb is the old second perfect, οἶδα, "I know," but this verb has lost perfective force and translates with simple present tense.

Table 17.8 Perfect Second Active Participle (-οτ-, -υι-)

	Masculine		Neuter
Singular	*Plural*	*Singular*	*Plural*
εἰδώς	εἰδότες	εἰδός	εἰδότα
εἰδότος	εἰδότων	εἰδότος	εἰδότων
εἰδότι	εἰδόσιν	εἰδότι	εἰδόσιν
εἰδότα	εἰδότας	εἰδός	εἰδότα

	Feminine
Singular	*Plural*
εἰδυῖα	εἰδυῖαι
εἰδυίας	εἰδυιῶν
εἰδυῖᾳ	εἰδυίαις
εἰδυῖαν	εἰδυίας

Future Perfect Active

Extremely rare, the future perfect participle as active voice in the New Testament is found only once. That form, however, actually is periphrastic (incorporating a construction with εἰμί). The future tense derives from εἰμί, and the perfect tense derives from the participle: ἔσομαι πεποιθώς ("I will trust," Heb 2:13).

Future Active

Table 17.9 Future Active Morphology

$$λυ\text{-}σοντ\text{-}ες$$

Formation uses the second principal part. The future active is similar to first aorist, but with a -σοντ- thematic vowel pattern, rather than the -σαντ- pattern (λύσοντες rather than λύσαντες). Contracts lengthen (ποιήσων); stops change (ἄξων); liquids drop sigma (κρινῶν). In fact, the future active participle occurs only ten times in the New Testament: σώσων, Mt 27:49; παραδώσων, Jn 6:64; προσκυνήσων, Acts 8:27; συναντήσοντά, Acts 20:22; ἄξων, Acts 22:5; προσκυνήσων, Acts 24:11; ποιήσων, Acts 24:17; κατακρινῶν, Rom 8:34; ἀποδώσοντες, Heb 13:17; and κακώσων, 1 Pet 3:13.

First Aorist Active

Table 17.10 First Aorist Active Morphology

$$λυ\text{-}σαντ\text{-}ες$$

Formation. Formation uses the third principal part. Augment for past time is not used. First aorist active tense suffix is -σα. The -ντ participle suffix is added. Reactions occur in some forms:

1. Nominative singular becomes -σας, because -σαντς→-σας (ντ dropping before σ, then compensatory lengthening, but lengthening invisible).
2. Neuter singular becomes -σαν, because -σαντ→-σαν (τ cannot stand at the end of a word).
3. Dative plural becomes -σασιν, because -σαντσι→-σασι (again, ντ drops before the σ).

Accent is penult acute. Masculine and neuter is third declension. Feminine follows first declension δόξα, but primitive forms show stem reactions, yielding -σασ, involving the semivowel iota, as in -σαντι→-σανσ→-σασ (τι going to σ).

Volatilization. Contracts lengthen; thus, ποιήσας, πληρώσας, ἀγαπήσας (with a few exceptions, as in καλέω, καλέσας). Stems with stops are as expected; thus, the labial πέμπω is πέμψας; palatal κηρύσσω (κηρυκ-) is κηρύξας; dental πείθω is πείσας. Liquid ἐγείρω becomes ἐγείρας, and κρίνω becomes κρίνας.

Table 17.11 Aorist Active Participle (-σαντ-, -σασ-)

Masculine		Neuter	
Singular	*Plural*	*Singular*	*Plural*
λύσας	λύσαντες	λῦσαν	λύσαντα
λύσαντος	λυσάντων	λύσαντος	λυσάντων
λύσαντι	λύσασιν	λύσαντι	λύσασιν
λύσαντα	λύσαντας	λῦσαν	λύσαντα

Feminine	
Singular	*Plural*
λύσασα	λύσασαι
λυσάσης	λυσασῶν
λυσάσῃ	λυσάσαις
λύσασαν	λυσάσας

Second Aorist Active

Table 17.12 Second Aorist Active Morphology

$$\lambda \iota \pi \text{-} \text{ο} \nu \tau \text{-} \epsilon \varsigma$$

Like infinitives, the second aorist active participle duplicates the present active, except for stem and accent (ultima acute).

Table 17.13 Second Aorist Active Participle (-οντ-, -ουσ-)

Masculine		Neuter	
Singular	*Plural*	*Singular*	*Plural*
λιπών	λιπόντες	λιπόν	λιπόντα
λιπόντος	λιπόντων	λιπόντος	λιπόντων
λιπόντι	λιποῦσιν	λιπόντι	λιποῦσιν
λιπόντα	λιπόντας	λιπόν	λιπόντα

Feminine	
Singular	*Plural*
λιποῦσα	λιποῦσαι
λιπούσης	λιπουσῶν
λιπούσῃ	λιπούσαις
λιποῦσαν	λιπούσας

Middle/Passive Voice

Present Middle/Passive

Table 17.14 Present Middle/Passive Morphology

$$\lambda\upsilon\text{-}o\mu\epsilon\nu\text{-}o\iota$$

Formation. Memorize "-μεν- is middle" and one has any middle participle for any tense.

♦ *The suffix -μεν- always is a middle (passive) participle.*

The thematic vowel, o, and participial suffix, -μεν, are added to the present stem. Present middle/passive participles follow the adjective ἀγαθός exactly except for the oxytone accent. Participle accent is not "irregular," since rules for finite verbs do not apply. Nominative masculine singular accent is antepenult acute. Then observe that: (1) general rules of accent are followed, (2) accent is persistent, (3) the genitive feminine plural does *not* have the typical circumflex on the ultima, as in first declension nouns.

Table 17.15 Present Middle/Passive Participle (-ομεν-)

Masculine		Neuter	
Singular	*Plural*	*Singular*	*Plural*
λυόμενος	λυόμενοι	λυόμενον	λυόμενα
λυομένου	λυομένων	λυομένου	λυομένων
λυομένῳ	λυομένοις	λυομένῳ	λυομένοις
λυόμενον	λυομένους	λυόμενον	λυόμενα

Feminine	
Singular	*Plural*
λυομένη	λυόμεναι
λυομένης	λυομένων
λυομένῃ	λυομέναις
λυομένην	λυομένας

Volatilization. For ε contracts: ε+ο = ου, so ποιούμενος etc. For ο contracts: ο+ο = ου, so πληρούμενος, etc. For α contracts: α+ο = ω, so ἀγαπώμενος, etc.

Lexical Middle. Lexical middle in the indicative also is a lexical middle participle. Thus, the lexical middle verb πορεύομαι has present middle participle forms of πορευόμενος, πορευομένη, and πορευόμενον. The middle voice is difficult of translation; the typical strategy is to translate these participle forms actively.

Perfect Middle/Passive

Table 17.16 Perfect Middle/Passive Morphology

$$\lambda\epsilon\text{-}\lambda\upsilon\text{-}\mu\epsilon\nu\text{-}οι$$

Formation. Formation uses the fifth principal part. This part has reduplication and a voice suffix but no thematic vowel. The reduplicated stem is λελυ-. The voice indicator is -μεν. Endings are like ἀγαθός, without oxytone accent. Accent is penult acute.

Table 17.17 Perfect Middle/Passive Participle (-μεν-)

Masculine		Neuter	
Singular	*Plural*	*Singular*	*Plural*
λελυμένος	λελυμένοι	λελυμένον	λελυμένα
λελυμένου	λελυμένων	λελυμένου	λελυμένων
λελυμένῳ	λελυμένοις	λελυμένῳ	λελυμένοις
λελυμένον	λελυμένους	λελυμένον	λελυμένα

Feminine	
Singular	*Plural*
λελυμένη	λελυμέναι
λελυμένης	λελυμένων
λελυμένη	λελυμέναις
λελυμένην	λελυμένας

Volatilization. Contracts lengthen, as expected: πεποιημένος, πεπληρωμένος, and ἠγαπημένος (with a few exceptions, as δέω, δεδεμένος). Stops also react as expected: the labial καταλείπω becomes καταλελειμμένος, and γράφω is γεγραμμένος; the palatal διώκω is δεδιωγμένος, and συνάγω is συνηγμένος; the dental ἑτοιμάζω is ἡτοιμασμένος. Liquid examples are κρίνω, κεκριμένος; ἀποστέλλω, ἀπεσταλμένος; σπείρω, ἐσπαρμένος. A letter insert would be περιβάλλω, as περιβεβλημένος.

Future Middle

Formation uses the second principal part. The future middle is similar to first aorist, but with a -σομεν- thematic vowel pattern, rather than the -σαμεν- (λυσόμενοι rather than λυσάμενοι). In fact, the only future middle participle in the New Testament is the form γενησόμενον, in 1 Cor 15:37.

Table 17.18 Future Middle Morphology

$$\lambda\upsilon\text{-}\sigma o\mu\epsilon\nu\text{-}o\iota$$

First Aorist Middle

Table 17.19 First Aorist Middle Morphology

$$\lambda\upsilon\text{-}\sigma\alpha\mu\epsilon\nu\text{-}o\iota$$

Formation. Forms are as expected. The aorist stem with suffix is λυσα-. The voice indicator is -μεν. Endings are like ἀγαθός, but without the oxytone accent. The accent is antepenult acute.

Table 17.20 First Aorist Middle Participle (-σαμεν-)

Masculine		Neuter	
Singular	*Plural*	*Singular*	*Plural*
λυσάμενος	λυσάμενοι	λυσάμενον	λυσάμενα
λυσαμένου	λυσαμένων	λυσαμένου	λυσαμένων
λυσαμένῳ	λυσαμένοις	λυσαμένῳ	λυσαμένοις
λυσάμενον	λυσαμένους	λυσάμενον	λυσάμενα

Feminine	
Singular	*Plural*
λυσαμένη	λυσάμεναι
λυσαμένης	λυσαμένων
λυσαμένῃ	λυσαμέναις
λυσαμένην	λυσαμένας

Volatilization. Reaction patterns are like the active voice, since the aorist suffix continues to be used. For example, the contract ποιέω is ποιησάμενος. The labial stop περιβλέπω is περιβλεψάμενος. The liquid κείρω is κειράμενος, and so forth.

Second Aorist Middle

Table 17.21 Second Aorist Middle Morphology

λιπ-ομεν-οι

The second aorist middle participle is a carbon copy of the present middle, except stem. Even the accent is antepenult acute.

Table 17.22 Second Aorist Middle Participle (-ομεν-)

Masculine		Neuter	
Singular	*Plural*	*Singular*	*Plural*
λιπόμενος	λιπόμενοι	λιπόμενον	λιπόμενα
λιπομένου	λιπομένων	λιπομένου	λιπομένων
λιπομένῳ	λιπομένοις	λιπομένῳ	λιπομένοις
λιπόμενον	λιπομένους	λιπόμενον	λιπόμενα

Feminine	
Singular	*Plural*
λιπομένη	λιπόμεναι
λιπομένης	λιπομένων
λιπομένη	λιπομέναις
λιπομένην	λιπομένας

Aorist Passive

First Passive. Formation uses the sixth principal part. The passive suffix, however, is an original -θε, not the lengthened -θη of the indicative. Otherwise, formation is like aorist active. Accent is ultima acute. Nominative singular and dative plural of the masculine and neuter react (for the usual reasons):

1. Nominative singular becomes -θείς, because the process is -θεντς→-θες→-θεις (ντ dropping before σ, then compensatory lengthening).
2. Neuter singular becomes -θέν, because the process shows -θεντ→-θεν (τ cannot stand at the end of a word).
3. Dative plural becomes -θεῖσιν, because the process shows -θεντσι→-θεσι→-θεισι (ντ drops before σ; stem undergoes compensatory lengthening).

Again, the feminine forms react too, winding up as -θεῖσα, for the usual reasons involving a semivowel iota that has produced the -θεντι→-θενσ→-θεσ→-θεισ reaction (τι going to σ, then ν dropping before the σ, and compensatory lengthening).

Table 17.23 Aorist Passive Morphology

$$\lambda\upsilon\text{-}\theta\epsilon\nu\tau\text{-}\epsilon\varsigma$$

Table 17.24 Aorist First Passive Participle (-θεντ-, -θεισ-)

Masculine		Neuter	
Singular	*Plural*	*Singular*	*Plural*
λυθείς	λυθέντες	λυθέν	λυθέντα
λυθέντος	λυθέντων	λυθέντος	λυθέντων
λυθέντι	λυθεῖσιν	λυθέντι	λυθεῖσιν
λυθέντα	λυθέντας	λυθέν	λυθέντα

Feminine	
Singular	*Plural*
λυθεῖσα	λυθεῖσαι
λυθείσης	λυθεισῶν
λυθείσῃ	λυθείσαις
λυθεῖσαν	λυθείσας

Volatilization. Various reactions take on familiar patterns. Contracts lengthen: ποιηθείς, πληρωθείς, ἀγαπηθείς. Stems with stops are as expected. Thus, the labial πέμπω is πεμφθείς, and a palatal κηρύσσω (κηρυκ-) is κηρυχθείς. Liquid ἐγείρω becomes ἐγερθείς. Often in the gospels ἀποκρίνομαι is the aorist passive, ἀποκριθείς, which drops the ν before the θ. A letter insert example would be εὑρίσκω, as εὑρεθείς, inserting the ε.

Second Passive. The second passive system, as expected, drops the θ of the -θε passive participle suffix. Then, resultant endings show up as -είς, -εῖσα, -έν. The participial suffix is -ντ.

Table 17.25 Aorist Second Passive Participle (-εντ-, -εισ-)

Masculine		Neuter	
Singular	*Plural*	*Singular*	*Plural*
γραφείς	γραφέντες	γραφέν	γραφέντα
γραφέντος	γραφέντων	γραφέντος	γραφέντων
γραφέντι	γραφεῖσιν	γραφέντι	γραφεῖσιν
γραφέντα	γραφέντας	γραφέν	γραφέντα

Feminine	
Singular	*Plural*
γραφεῖσα	γραφεῖσαι
γραφείσης	γραφεισῶν
γραφείσῃ	γραφείσαις
γραφεῖσαν	γραφείσας

The New Testament has only thirty-five examples of the second passive participle. These examples involve just nine verbs and their compounds: ἀποστέλλω; ἁρπάζω; διατάσσω and ὑποτάσσω; ἐμπλέκω; καταλλάσσω; σπείρω and διασπείρω; συνθάπτω; στρέφω and ἐπιστρέφω; and φύω and συμφύω.

Future Passive

Table 17.26 Future Passive Morphology

$$\lambda\upsilon\text{-}\theta\eta\sigma\text{-}o\mu\epsilon\nu\text{-}o\iota$$

The aorist passive stem is used, but with the suffix -θη instead of -θε. The -σ future suffix is added, and the thematic vowel and middle/passive voice indicator, -ομεν, finished off with standard adjectival endings. Future passive, in fact, has only one example in the New Testament, the contract λαλέω, as λαληθησομένων (Heb 3:5). The LXX has only fourteen examples. One is Eccl 1:9:

τί τὸ πεποιημένον αὐτὸ τὸ ποιηθησόμενον
"what has been done is what will be done"

Εἰμί as Participle

Present Tense

Table 17.27 Εἰμί as Present Participle

Masculine		Neuter	
Singular	*Plural*	*Singular*	*Plural*
ὤν	ὄντες	ὄν	ὄντα
ὄντος	ὄντων	ὄντος	ὄντων
ὄντι	οὖσιν	ὄντι	οὖσιν
ὄντα	ὄντας	ὄν	ὄντα

Feminine	
Singular	*Plural*
οὖσα	οὖσαι
οὔσης	οὐσῶν
οὔσῃ	οὔσαις
οὖσαν	οὔσας

As a participle, εἰμί occurs only in present and future tenses. The verb εἰμί as a present participle is just the present active inflectional endings with accent. Genitive feminine plural accent follows the noun rule. Since εἰμί does not express voice, location is simply "present participle," *not* "present *active* participle."

Future Tense

Luke 22:49 has the one instance of εἰμί as a future participle:

ἰδόντες δὲ οἱ περὶ αὐτὸν τὸ ἐσόμενον εἶπαν . . .
"when those who were around him saw *what was going to happen*, they said . . ."

This participle is direct object of the aorist participle ἰδόντες.

Participle Frequency

Participle frequency by tense and by case is given in the chart below. (Future participle has only thirteen occurrences in the New Testament.) Nominative function is predominant. Participles most often in some way relate to the subject of a verb or have copulative construction.

Chart 13: Participle Tenses and Cases

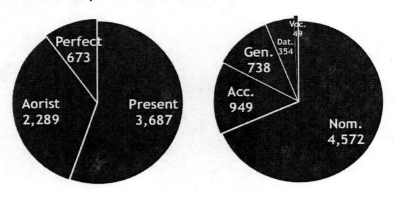

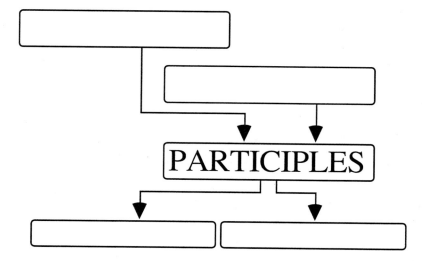

EXERCISE 17

1. Fill in the following participle suffix table:

Tense	Active Ms./Nu.	Active Fem.	Middle	Passive Ms./Nu.	Passive Fem.
Present					
2nd Aorist					
1st Aorist					
Perfect					

2. Fill in the following participle heritage chart:

PARTICIPLES

3. Fill in the following participle heritage/morphology chart:

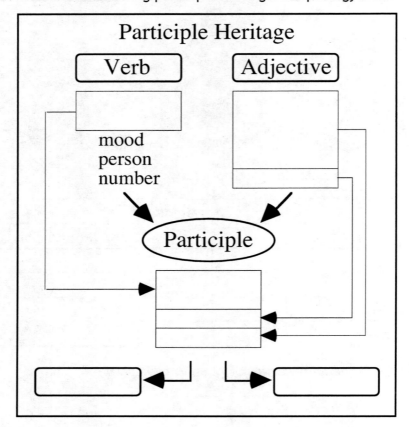

4. Key points on mastering participle morphology are:

   4.1 focus on _____ patterns

   4.2 know that _____ always is middle (passive)

   4.3 become familiar with predictable _____ patterns

   4.4 memorize _____ forms like vocabulary words

   4.5 know that mas./neu. _active_ is _____, _middle_ is _____

5. Locate the following participle forms:

5.1 λυσαμένους: _____

5.2 λυθεῖσαι: _____

5.3 ἀγαπῶντος: _____

5.4 λελυμένου: _____

5.5 πεμφθείς: _____

5.6 λυθησομένῳ: _____

5.7 λυούσαις: _____

5.8 λιπόν: _____

5.9 λύσαντες: _____

5.10 λελυκώς: _____

5.11 λυθέντων: _____

6. Be ready to locate participles in translations of 1 Jn 1:1-2:29 as a part of exercises since chapter 13.

7. Translate the following passage from 1 John. Be ready to locate participle forms.

3.1 ἴδετε ποταπὴν ἀγάπην δέδωκεν ἡμῖν ὁ πατήρ, ἵνα

_____

τέκνα θεοῦ κληθῶμεν, καὶ ἐσμέν. διὰ τοῦτο ὁ κόσμος οὐ

_____

γινώσκει ἡμᾶς, ὅτι οὐκ ἔγνω αὐτόν. **2** ἀγαπητοί, νῦν τέκνα

_____

θεοῦ ἐσμεν, καὶ οὔπω ἐφανερώθη τί ἐσόμεθα. οἴδαμεν ὅτι

_____

ἐὰν φανερωθῇ, ὅμοιοι αὐτῷ ἐσόμεθα, ὅτι ὀψόμεθα αὐτὸν

καθώς ἐστιν. **3** καὶ πᾶς ὁ ἔχων τὴν ἐλπίδα ταύτην ἐπ᾽ αὐτῷ

ἁγνίζει ἑαυτόν, καθὼς ἐκεῖνος ἁγνός ἐστιν.

4 Πᾶς ὁ ποιῶν τὴν ἁμαρτίαν καὶ τὴν ἀνομίαν ποιεῖ, καὶ

ἡ ἁμαρτία ἐστὶν ἡ ἀνομία. **5** καὶ οἴδατε ὅτι ἐκεῖνος

ἐφανερώθη, ἵνα τὰς ἁμαρτίας ἄρῃ, καὶ ἁμαρτία ἐν αὐτῷ οὐκ

ἔστιν. **6** πᾶς ὁ ἐν αὐτῷ μένων οὐχ ἁμαρτάνει· πᾶς ὁ

ἁμαρτάνων οὐχ ἑώρακεν αὐτὸν οὐδὲ ἔγνωκεν αὐτόν.

7 Τεκνία, μηδεὶς πλανάτω ὑμᾶς· ὁ ποιῶν τὴν

δικαιοσύνην δίκαιός ἐστιν, καθὼς ἐκεῖνος δίκαιός ἐστιν·

8 ὁ ποιῶν τὴν ἁμαρτίαν ἐκ τοῦ διαβόλου ἐστίν, ὅτι ἀπ᾽ ἀρχῆς

ὁ διάβολος ἁμαρτάνει. εἰς τοῦτο ἐφανερώθη ὁ υἱὸς τοῦ θεοῦ,

ἵνα λύσῃ τὰ ἔργα τοῦ διαβόλου. **9** Πᾶς ὁ γεγεννημένος ἐκ

τοῦ θεοῦ ἁμαρτίαν οὐ ποιεῖ, ὅτι σπέρμα αὐτοῦ ἐν αὐτῷ

μένει, καὶ οὐ δύναται ἁμαρτάνειν, ὅτι ἐκ τοῦ θεοῦ

γεγέννηται. **10** ἐν τούτῳ φανερά ἐστιν τὰ τέκνα τοῦ θεοῦ καὶ

τὰ τέκνα τοῦ διαβόλου· πᾶς ὁ μὴ ποιῶν δικαιοσύνην οὐκ

ἔστιν ἐκ τοῦ θεοῦ, καὶ ὁ μὴ ἀγαπῶν τὸν ἀδελφὸν αὐτοῦ.

11 Ὅτι αὕτη ἐστὶν ἡ ἀγγελία ἣν ἠκούσατε ἀπ᾽ ἀρχῆς,

ἵνα ἀγαπῶμεν ἀλλήλους, **12** οὐ καθὼς Κάϊν ἐκ τοῦ πονηροῦ

ἦν καὶ ἔσφαξεν τὸν ἀδελφὸν αὐτοῦ· καὶ χάριν τίνος ἔσφαξεν

αὐτόν; ὅτι τὰ ἔργα αὐτοῦ πονηρὰ ἦν τὰ δὲ τοῦ ἀδελφοῦ αὐτοῦ

δίκαια.

13 [Καὶ] μὴ θαυμάζετε, ἀδελφοί, εἰ μισεῖ ὑμᾶς ὁ

κόσμος. **14** ἡμεῖς οἴδαμεν ὅτι μεταβεβήκαμεν ἐκ τοῦ

θανάτου εἰς τὴν ζωήν, ὅτι ἀγαπῶμεν τοὺς ἀδελφούς· ὁ μὴ

ἀγαπῶν μένει ἐν τῷ θανάτῳ. **15** πᾶς ὁ μισῶν τὸν ἀδελφὸν

αὐτοῦ ἀνθρωποκτόνος ἐστίν, καὶ οἴδατε ὅτι πᾶς

ἀνθρωποκτόνος οὐκ ἔχει ζωὴν αἰώνιον ἐν αὐτῷ μένουσαν.

16 ἐν τούτῳ ἐγνώκαμεν τὴν ἀγάπην, ὅτι ἐκεῖνος ὑπὲρ ἡμῶν

τὴν ψυχὴν αὐτοῦ ἔθηκεν· καὶ ἡμεῖς ὀφείλομεν ὑπὲρ τῶν

ἀδελφῶν τὰς ψυχὰς θεῖναι. **17** ὃς δ᾽ ἂν ἔχῃ τὸν βίον τοῦ

κόσμου καὶ θεωρῇ τὸν ἀδελφὸν αὐτοῦ χρείαν ἔχοντα καὶ

κλείσῃ τὰ σπλάγχνα αὐτοῦ ἀπ᾽ αὐτοῦ, πῶς ἡ ἀγάπη τοῦ θεοῦ

μένει ἐν αὐτῷ; **18** Τεκνία, μὴ ἀγαπῶμεν λόγῳ μηδὲ τῇ

γλώσσῃ ἀλλὰ ἐν ἔργῳ καὶ ἀληθείᾳ.

19 [Καὶ] ἐν τούτῳ γνωσόμεθα ὅτι ἐκ τῆς ἀληθείας

ἐσμέν, καὶ ἔμπροσθεν αὐτοῦ πείσομεν τὴν καρδίαν ἡμῶν,

20 ὅτι ἐὰν καταγινώσκῃ ἡμῶν ἡ καρδία, ὅτι μείζων ἐστὶν ὁ θεὸς τῆς καρδίας ἡμῶν καὶ γινώσκει πάντα. **21** Ἀγαπητοί,

ἐὰν ἡ καρδία [ἡμῶν] μὴ καταγινώσκῃ, παρρησίαν ἔχομεν

πρὸς τὸν θεὸν **22** καὶ ὃ ἐὰν αἰτῶμεν λαμβάνομεν ἀπ᾽ αὐτοῦ,

ὅτι τὰς ἐντολὰς αὐτοῦ τηροῦμεν καὶ τὰ ἀρεστὰ ἐνώπιον

αὐτοῦ ποιοῦμεν.

23 Καὶ αὕτη ἐστὶν ἡ ἐντολὴ αὐτοῦ, ἵνα πιστεύσωμεν τῷ

ὀνόματι τοῦ υἱοῦ αὐτοῦ Ἰησοῦ Χριστοῦ καὶ ἀγαπῶμεν

ἀλλήλους, καθὼς ἔδωκεν ἐντολὴν ἡμῖν. **24** καὶ ὁ τηρῶν τὰς

ἐντολὰς αὐτοῦ ἐν αὐτῷ μένει καὶ αὐτὸς ἐν αὐτῷ· καὶ ἐν

τούτῳ γινώσκομεν ὅτι μένει ἐν ἡμῖν, ἐκ τοῦ πνεύματος οὗ

ἡμῖν ἔδωκεν.

Ancient inscriptions included abbreviations and local dialects affecting spelling and grammar. The inscription below, from the Ephesus Museum in Selçuk, Turkey, is an honorific recording the benefaction of Gaius Laecanius Bassus, proconsul of Asia, A.D. 80-81 (cf. *I. Eph.* III.695.17). He was from a well-known family of Roman senators, the Laecanii, and served as one of the two consuls of Rome in A.D. 64 during Nero's political meltdown and the fire of Rome, the probable context for the martyrdoms of Peter and Paul. The inscription memorializes the proconsul's benefactions. One benefaction is the Fountain of Laecanius Bassus that stands southwest of the Agora in Ephesus. These lines read, "Gaius Laecanius Bassus, who was proconsul and benefactor on behalf of all the cities, also took care for . . ."

Fig. 15. Inscription, Proconsul Gaius Laecanius Bassus

CHAPTER 18
PARTICIPLE TRANSLATION

The participle is a verbal adjective. This dual nature of verb and adjective sets the course of participle translation. The participle can be used as an adjective. A review of adjective grammar, therefore, would be profitable. As another incarnation of the verb, the participle also can function adverbially.

Introduction

Characteristics

Verb Characteristics

Components. The participle expresses tense and voice only, that is, does not carry components related to the subject (mood, person, number). Tense, however, is aspect only. Aspect might be easier to convey in translation with participles than with infinitives due to limitations of the English infinitive. Voice is relative to how the participle's action is construed in conjunction with the main verb, not to the participle having a subject.

Modifiers. A participle can have its own modifiers. As such, the participle can:

- take its own direct object: "and after taking *food*," Acts 9:19
- take an indirect object: "while he was saying these things *to them*," Mt 9:18
- be modified by an adverb: "proclaiming the kingdom of God and teaching about the Lord Jesus Christ with all boldness and *without hindrance*," Acts 28:31
- be modified by a prepositional phrase: "while he was teaching *in the synagogue at Capernaum*," Jn 6:59)

Negative. The participle does not express mood. A participle, therefore, takes the negative μή. On rare occasion one does see the negative οὐ (17 times). For example, notice οὐ βλέπων = "not seeing," Lk 6:42 (cf. 2 Cor 12:1; Gal 4:27; Col 2:19; Heb 11:1).

Adjective Characteristics

Case. The participle has case function *and* case inflection (unlike the infinitive, which has case function but not inflection). Case indicates the participle's function in the sentence. Concord declares how the participle relates to other elements in a sentence. Thus, careful observation of concord is crucial to any participle's translation.

Function. Adjectival participles function like adjectives, that is, they can have attributive, substantival, or predicative roles in a sentence (indicated in part by case inflection). For example:

- *attributive*, modifying a substantive: "the time of the *appearing* star," Mt 2:7
- *substantival*, standing in for a substantive, such as the subject or the direct object: "if you love *those who love* you," Mt 5:46
- *predicate*, the predicate adjective of an εἰμί construction: "you will be *silent* and *unable* to speak," Lk 1:20

Procedure

Translating participles boils down to answering three questions:
1. What is the construction?
2. What is the concord?
3. What is the aspect?

These three questions can build the logical process of understanding participles and their use. Construction is the easiest dividing line between adjectival and adverbial uses. Concord is crucial to establishing the function of an adjectival participle or construing the adverbial participle's action in relationship to the main verb. Aspect communicates the burden of the Greek tense stem. Notice how the participle translation flowchart provided below is constructed around these three questions.

Table 18.1 Participle Translation Flowchart

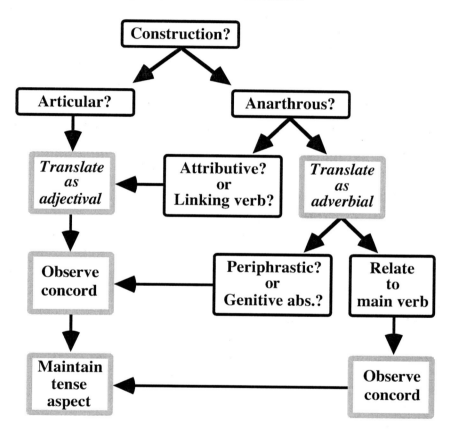

The flowchart guides this discussion of translating participles. First, translating articular participles as adjectives will be covered. Then, translating anarthrous participles will be covered. Our problem with the anarthrous construction, as will be seen, is that this type of construction, like its adjective counterpart, fundamentally is ambiguous. Often, though, anarthrous participles are adverbial.

Articular Participles

The premier question in translating participles is, what is the construction? Construction means whether the participle is articular or anarthrous. Articular construction is clear because:

♦ *Articular participles always are adjectives.*

> *Translation Tip #1:*
> Often, a *relative pronoun clause* will do the trick in translating articular participles, along the lines of "the one *who* . . . ," "*that which* . . . ," etc.

The articular participle provides a fastball straight down the middle that can be knocked out of the park—this participle is an adjective, no question. One only needs to be familiar with the three uses of the adjective. Thus, a quick review of adjective use would be helpful.

The second question is, what is the concord? With articular participles, concord will express the adjectival function. Attributive participles will be in concord with the substantive modified. Substantival participles will be in concord with their substantive function as subject, direct object, or object of a preposition. Predicate participles will be nominative.

The third question is, what is the aspect? If present tense, try to pull out durative kind of action. If perfect tense, try to pull out perfective action (perhaps with the "have, has" auxiliary verb). If aorist or future tense, leave the action undefined.

Attributive Use

The following examples show articular participles being used as adjectives attributively. Observe concord carefully:

1. καὶ ἐπληρώθη ἡ γραφὴ <u>ἡ λέγουσα</u> = "and the scripture was fulfilled *which says*" (Jas 2:23)

2. ἐργάζεσθε μὴ τὴν βρῶσιν <u>τὴν ἀπολλυμένην</u> ἀλλὰ τὴν βρῶσιν <u>τὴν μένουσαν</u> εἰς ζωὴν αἰώνιον = "Do not work for the food *which perishes* but for the food *which abides* unto eternal life" (Jn 6:27)
3. Ὃς δ᾽ ἂν σκανδαλίσῃ ἕνα τῶν μικρῶν τούτων <u>τῶν πιστευόντων</u> εἰς ἐμέ = "But whoever causes to stumble one of the least of these *who believe* in me" (Mt 18:6)
4. ἐλαλοῦμεν <u>ταῖς συνελθούσαις</u> γυναιξίν = "we began speaking to the women *who had gathered together*" (Acts 16:13)
5. οὐ τὸ σῶμα <u>τὸ γενησόμενον</u> σπείρεις = "you do not sow the body *that will be*" (1 Cor 15:37)
6. οὐδεὶς τῶν ἀνδρῶν ἐκείνων <u>τῶν κεκλημένων</u> = "none of those men *who were invited*" (Lk 14:24)

Remember: the article may not be *adjacent* to the participle. For example, a prepositional phrase can intervene:
1. <u>τοῖς</u> ἀπὸ τῶν ἐθνῶν <u>ἐπιστρέφουσιν</u> ἐπὶ τὸν θεόν = "*those* from among the Gentiles *who are turning* to God" (Acts 15:19)
2. οὗτός ἐστιν ὁ ἄρτος <u>ὁ</u> ἐκ τοῦ οὐρανοῦ <u>καταβαίνων</u> = "this is the bread *coming down* from heaven" (Jn 6:50)

Substantival Use

In this use, the articular participle becomes the grammatical equivalent of a noun. The participle is the subject or an object (direct object, indirect object, or object of a preposition). This use can be distinguished from the attributive use, because:

♦ *Substantival participles stand alone.*

That is, no noun of concord is nearby to modify. The following examples show articular participles being used as adjectives substantively. Observe concord carefully:

1. *Subject:*
   - τεθνήκασιν γὰρ <u>οἱ ζητοῦντες</u> τὴν ψυχὴν τοῦ παι-δίου = "for *those who were seeking* the child's life have died" (Mt 2:20)
   - <u>ὁ εὑρὼν</u> τὴν ψυχὴν αὐτοῦ ἀπολέσει αὐτήν = "*the one who finds* his life will lose it" (Mt 10:39); observe time frame: the main verb is future, so the aorist participle is construed as present
   - ἐξῆλθεν <u>ὁ τεθνηκὼς</u> = "*the one who had died* came out" (Jn 11:44); observe time frame: the main verb is past, so the perfect participle is construed as pluperfect
2. *Direct Object:*
   - ἵνα <u>τὰ λείποντα</u> ἐπιδιορθώσῃ = "in order that you might set straight *the things that are remaining*" (Tit 1:5)
   - κύριος . . . τὸ δεύτερον <u>τοὺς μὴ πιστεύσαντας</u> ἀπώλεσεν = "the Lord . . . a second time destroyed *those who disbelieved*" (Jude 5)
   - ἐξῆλθον δὲ ἰδεῖν τὸ γεγονὸς = "they came out to see *what had happened*" (Lk 8:35)
3. *Indirect Object:*
   - ὁ πατὴρ ὑμῶν ὁ ἐν τοῖς οὐρανοῖς δώσει ἀγαθὰ <u>τοῖς αἰτοῦσιν</u> αὐτόν = "your Father in heaven will give good gifts *to those who ask* him" (Mt 7:11)
   - μὴ ἐρεῖ τὸ πλάσμα <u>τῷ πλάσαντι</u> = "the molded object will not say *to the one who molded* (Rom 9:20)
   - Εἴπατε <u>τοῖς κεκλημένοις</u> = "say *to those who have been invited*" (Mt 22:4)
4. *Prepositional Object: (with or without preposition)*
   - προσεύχεσθε ὑπὲρ <u>τῶν διωκόντων</u> ὑμᾶς = "pray for *those who persecute* you" (Mt 5:44)
   - ἀλλ᾽ ἐν τούτοις πᾶσιν ὑπερνικῶμεν διὰ <u>τοῦ ἀγα-πήσαντος</u> ἡμᾶς = "but in all these things we are more

than conquerors through *the one who loved* us" (Rom 8:37)

- εἰς μαρτύριον <u>τῶν λαληθησομένων</u> = "as a witness of *that which would be spoken* (later)" (Heb 3:5)
- περὶ δὲ <u>τῶν πεπιστευκότων</u> ἐθνῶν ἡμεῖς ἐπεστεί-λαμεν = "now concerning Gentiles *who have believed* we sent a letter" (Acts 21:25)

5. *Predicate Noun.* Predicate *noun* use *must* have the article:

- θεὸς γάρ ἐστιν <u>ὁ ἐνεργῶν</u> ἐν ὑμῖν = "for God is *the one who works* in you" (Phil 2:13)
- οὗτοί εἰσιν <u>οἱ ἀκούσαντες</u> = "these are *the ones who hear*" (Lk 8:14); observe time frame: main verb is present, so aorist participle is construed as present
- Καὶ τίς <u>ὁ κακώσων</u> ὑμᾶς; = "who is *the one who will harm* you?" (Lk 8:14); εἰμί is assumed in the question
- ὑμεῖς δέ ἐστε <u>οἱ διαμεμενηκότες</u> μετ᾽ ἐμοῦ = "but you are *the ones who have remained* with me" (Lk 22:28)

Anarthrous Participles

The three main questions of construction, concord, and aspect still apply. However, the answer to the first is not an immediate homerun, as with the articular participle, which clearly is an adjective and can be translated straightaway without much fuss.

The premier question in translating participles is, what is the construction? Anarthrous construction is the dark side of the force:

♦ *Anarthrous participles are ambiguous.*

The anarthrous participle, so to speak, has a built in cloaking device. Grammatically, you do not know what you have without some contextual reconnaisance. That is, the anarthrous participle can be *adjective* or *adverb*, which is a huge swath of ground to cover. If

used as an adjective, the anarthrous participle most probably is either attributive or predicative. If used as an adverb, the anarthrous
participle will modify the main verb.

The second question is, what is the concord? With anarthrous
participles used as adjectives, concord will signal the adjectival
function. Anarthrous *attributive* participles will be in concord with
the substantive modified. The uncommon anarthrous *substantival*
adjective is an object complement, hence accusative. *Predicative*
participles will be nominative. With anarthrous participles used as
adverbs, concord will express the participle's "surrogate subject."

The third question is, what is the aspect? If present tense, try
to pull out durative kind of action. If perfect tense, try to pull out
perfective action (perhaps with the "have, has" auxiliary verb). If
aorist or future tense, leave the action undefined. Further, if used
as an adverb and the adverbial function is temporal, then the
present participle's action will be simultaneous to the main verb,
and the aorist participle's action will be antecedent to the main
verb.

Adjectival Use

Anarthrous participles can be either adjectival or adverbial.
Notice the left-right branching function on the participle flowchart
under the anarthrous question. The left branch is adjectival use.
The right branch is adverbial use. Notice in the left branch that the
anarthrous participle, if adjectival, generally will have two of the
three adjective functions, that is, either attributive or predicative.
Rarely, a few anarthrous participles *might* be construed as object
complements, sometimes called the "double accusative" (second
direct object)—but such use with participles is debatable.

Attributive

The anarthrous participle as attributive adjective is not too
hard to spot. First, one has to have a noun in the neighborhood.

Second, the participle must be in concord with the nearby noun. This concord should suggest a modifying function for the participle to an observant student. The following are examples:

1. προσῆλθεν αὐτῷ γυνὴ <u>ἔχουσα</u> ἀλάβαστρον μύρου βαρυτίμου = "a woman *who had* a jar of expensive ointment came to him" (Mt 26:7)
2. σὺ ἂν ᾔτησας αὐτὸν καὶ ἔδωκεν ἄν σοι ὕδωρ <u>ζῶν</u> = "you would have asked him and he would have given you *living* water" (Jn 4:10)
3. καὶ ὧδε μὲν δεκάτας <u>ἀποθνήσκοντες</u> ἄνθρωποι λαμβάνουσιν = "and here *mortal* men receive the tithe" (Heb 7:8)
4. ὁ κατὰ τὸ πολὺ αὐτοῦ ἔλεος ἀναγεννήσας ἡμᾶς εἰς ἐλπίδα <u>ζῶσαν</u> = "who according to his great mercy begat us unto a *living* hope" (1 Pet 1:3)
5. ὅμοιός ἐστιν ἀνθρώπῳ <u>οἰκοδομήσαντι</u> οἰκίαν = "he is like a man *who built* a house" (Lk 6:49)
6. παραλυτικὸν ἐπὶ κλίνης <u>βεβλημένον</u> = "a paralytic *who was lying* on a bed" (Mt 9:2)

Predicative

The second use of the anarthrous adjectival participle is predicative. The anarthrous participle as predicate adjective is not too hard to spot. First, one has to have a linking verb in the neighborhood. Second, the participle must be in nominative case. Third, predicate *adjective* use must be *anarthrous*. Predicative construction apparently is not found with aorist participles. Note:

1. καὶ ἐγενόμην νεκρὸς καὶ ἰδοὺ <u>ζῶν</u> εἰμι = "and I was dead, and, behold, I am *alive*" (Rev 1:18)
2. ἦν ἡμέρας τρεῖς <u>μὴ βλέπων</u>, "he was *sightless* for three days" (Acts 9:9)
3. Ἦν δὲ <u>θυμομαχῶν</u> Τυρίοις καὶ Σιδωνίοις = "now he was *angry* with Tyre and Sidon" (Acts 12:20)

4. οὗ ἡ οἰκία ἦν συνομοροῦσα τῇ συναγωγῇ = "whose house was *adjacent* to the synagogue" (Acts 18:7)

5. καὶ τὰ ἱμάτια αὐτοῦ ἐγένετο στίλβοντα λευκὰ λίαν = "and his garments became *brilliant*, exceedingly white" (Mk 9:3)

6. καὶ ἦν ὑποτασσόμενος αὐτοῖς = "and he was *obedient* to them" (Lk 2:51)

7. καὶ ἰδοὺ ἔσῃ σιωπῶν καὶ μὴ δυνάμενος λαλῆσαι = "and behold, you will be *silent* and *unable* to speak" (Lk 1:20)

8. οὐδὲν γάρ ἐστιν κεκαλυμμένον ὃ οὐκ ἀποκαλυφθή-σεται = "for nothing is *hidden* that will not be revealed" (Mt 10:26)

Note that a linking verb does not *have* to be explicit. One could have the "verbless" predicative structure, which, by definition, is the articular nominative noun and anarthrous nominative adjective (in this case, anarthrous participle). Take Heb 4:12 for example:

Ζῶν γὰρ ὁ λόγος τοῦ θεοῦ
"For the word of God is *living*"

Notice how ὁ λόγος functions as the articular nominative noun; Ζῶν functions as the anarthrous nominative adjective.

Object Complement?

Some anarthrous adjectival participles have been analyzed as object complements. However, these better might be described as direct object clauses. Examples are rare. Study the following:

1. παρέστησεν αὐτὴν ζῶσαν = "he presented her *alive*" (Acts 9:41)

2. εἶδον ἤδη αὐτὸν τεθνηκότα = "when he saw him already *dead*"(Jn 19:33)

3. καὶ ἐλθὸν εὑρίσκει σεσαρωμένον καὶ κεκοσμημένον = "and when he comes he finds it *having been swept clean* and *put in order*" (Lk 11:25)

4. πᾶν πνεῦμα ὃ ὁμολογεῖ Ἰησοῦν Χριστὸν ἐν σαρκὶ ἐληλυθότα = "every spirit that confesses Jesus Christ *has come* in the flesh" (1 Jn 4:2)

5. ὁ Φίλιππος ἤκουσεν αὐτοῦ ἀναγινώσκοντος = "Philip heard him reading" (Acts 8:30)

Adverbial Use

> *Translation Tip #2:*
> An adverbial participle often requires conversion into an indicative verb in a dependent clause that modifies the main verb of the independent clause.

The main use of anarthrous participles is adverbial. If used as an adverb, the anarthrous participle will modify the main verb, that is, the verb of the independent clause. Thus, one must find the main verb, know the main verb's own grammar and context, and construe the participle in relationship to this main verb. In fact, this adverbial use is the dominant function of anarthrous participles. As a timesaving shortcut, therefore, know that:

♦ *Anarthrous participles most often are adverbial.*

If one first assumes that the anarthrous participle is adverbial, that assumption will be correct a majority of the time.

Adverbial use has at least nine categories. Realize that the *translator* must make the decision by context which of the nine adverbial categories is most likely for a given participle. At times multiple categories seem to fit. One has to make a subjective decision which option best seems to communicate the author's intent. These categories will be described briefly and examples provided. Notice how the participles often are converted into indicative verbs that function in dependent adverbial clauses related to the main verb.

Temporal

Assumption. Temporal participles add a temporal clause that modifies the main verb. This temporal use is a good place to start with adverbial participles, because:

♦ *Many adverbial participles are temporal.*

Thus, when one first hits an anarthrous participle, make two quick assumptions on the law of probabilities for translation purposes:
    1.   Assume the anarthrous participle is adverbial.
    2.   Assume the adverbial participle is temporal.
These two assumptions generally will save time. Context will clue one in quickly when the situation with the anarthrous participle is otherwise.

Further, with temporal participles, two important observations need to be kept in mind. One is about time frame. The other is about relative time.

Time Frame. First, *the time frame of the sentence comes from the main verb in the independent clause.* If the main verb is past tense, the time frame of the entire sentence is past time. If the main verb is present tense, the time frame of the entire sentence is present time. Thus, adverbial participles derive their time frame from the main verb, not their own tense, which communicates aspect only. Remember that the participle is timeless.

> **Translation Tip #3:**
> With temporal participles and their relative time:
> (1) for aorist tense set up "when" or "after" clause
> (2) for present tense set up "while" or "as" clause

Relative Time. Second, *the action of the temporal participle is expressed as time relative to the main verb.* This "relative time" is either antecedent to the main verb or simultaneous with the main verb. The distinction is easy to make. If an adverbial participle is temporal:

♦ *Aorist participles are antecedent to the main verb.*

♦ *Present participles are simultaneous to the main verb.*

In practical terms, these two dictums mean: (1) translate the aorist temporal participle using "when" or "after" conjunctions to set up the dependent clause; (2) translate the present temporal participle using "while" or "as" conjunctions to set up the dependent clause.

Perfect temporal participles can be handled by the sense of the context. One could use the straight "-ing" form ("having loosed"). Or, one could try an antecedent or simultaneous relative time.

Surrogate Subject. Neither infinitive nor participle takes a subject. Grammatically, both are infinite. The infinitive, however, can have a "surrogate subject." This surrogate subject technically is called the accusative of general reference, because the word that is "subject" of the infinitive is placed in the accusative case.

Like the infinitive, the participle also can have a "surrogate subject." However, unlike the infinitive, the participle's surrogate subject can be any case, not just accusative, depending on which grammatical element is serving as "subject." The participle, then, will declare its "subject" by inflecting itself to be in concord with the grammatical element serving as the surrogate subject.

Table 18.2 Participle Concord and Surrogate Subject

1. ἐρχόμεθα αὐτῷ βλέποντες ταῦτα

2. ἐρχόμεθα αὐτῷ βλέποντι ταῦτα

Sentence one above translates, "we are coming to him while *we* are seeing these things." Sentence two translates, "we are coming to him while *he* is seeing these things." Notice how concord declares the participle's "subject." The *nominative* (plural) inflection of the participle βλέποντες in sentence one declares that the "subject" of the participle is the subject of the main verb, thus the translation, "while *we* are seeing." The *dative* (singular) inflection of the participle βλέποντι in sentence two declares that the "subject" of the participle is some dative element nearby, which is the pronoun αὐτῷ, thus, the alternate translation, "while *he* is seeing."

Examples. Study these examples of anarthrous participles taken as temporal. Observe the "when" or "after" style for aorist participles and the "while" or "as" style for present participles. Perfect participles are handled variously by sense of context:

1. ἀκούσας δὲ ὁ βασιλεὺς Ἡρῴδης ἐταράχθη = "but *when* King Herod *heard*, he was troubled" (Mt 2:3); notice the participle ἀκούσας is *nominative*, so the subject of the main verb, Ἡρῴδης, is subject of the participle

2. καὶ ἀναστὰς ἦλθεν πρὸς τὸν πατέρα ἑαυτοῦ = "and *after* he *arose*, he went to his father" (Lk 15:20)

3. εἰστήκεισαν δὲ οἱ δοῦλοι καὶ οἱ ὑπηρέται ἀνθρακιὰν πεποιηκότες = "and the servants and the officers were standing, *having made* a charcoal fire" (Jn 18:18)

4. ἐληλακότες οὖν ὡς σταδίους εἴκοσι πέντε ἢ τριάκοντα θεωροῦσιν τὸν Ἰησοῦν = "therefore, *after having rowed* about twenty five or thirty stadia, they saw Jesus" (Jn 6:19)

5. Ἀκούοντα δὲ τὰ ἔθνη ἔχαιρον καὶ ἐδόξαζον τὸν λόγον τοῦ κυρίου = "and *as* they *were listening*, the Gentiles began to rejoice and to glorify the word of the Lord" (Acts 13:48); notice the *time frame* of the sentence is *past* time, since the main verbs, ἔχαιρον and ἐδόξαζον, are past time; thus, the *present* participle, Ἀκούοντα, which is dependent on the independent clause for its time frame, is rendered *past* time, "were listening"

6. Καὶ διεπορεύετο κατὰ πόλεις καὶ κώμας διδάσκων καὶ πορείαν ποιούμενος εἰς Ἱεροσόλυμα = "and he was traveling along city and village *as he was teaching* and *making* his journey to Jerusalem" (Lk 13:22)

7. <u>Συνηγμένων</u> δὲ τῶν Φαρισαίων ἐπηρώτησεν αὐτοὺς ὁ Ἰησοῦς = "Now *while* the Pharisees *were gathered toge-ther*, Jesus questioned them" (Mt 22:41); also an example of the genitive absolute (see below)

Purpose

Purpose uses the participle to express the motive or reason for the main verb's action. Translation can convert the participle into a dependent clause beginning with "so that," "in order to," "for the purpose of." Since the infinitive in English by default is a pur-pose statement, the purpose participle also can be converted into a simple infinitive. The plain "-ing" form of the participle also can be used.

1. ἕτεροι δὲ <u>πειράζοντες</u> σημεῖον ἐξ οὐρανοῦ ἐζήτουν παρ᾽ αὐτοῦ = "but others *in order to test* were seeking a sign out of heaven from him" (Lk 11:16)
2. ἦλθεν <u>ζητῶν</u> καρπὸν ἐν αὐτῇ = "he came *seeking* fruit on it" (Lk 13:6)
3. ἐλεημοσύνας <u>ποιήσων</u> εἰς τὸ ἔθνος μου παρεγενόμην = "I came *to present* offerings to my nation" (Acts 24:7)

Cause

Cause uses the participle to express the cause of the main verb's action. The participle can be converted into an indicative verb in a dependent clause that is begun with the conjunctions "because," "since," or "for."

1. Εὐχαριστῶ τῷ θεῷ μου . . . <u>ἀκούων</u> σου τὴν ἀγάπην καὶ τὴν πίστιν = "I give thanks to my God . . . *because I hear* of your love and your faith" (Phlm 4, 5)
2. πολλοὶ ἐπίστευσαν εἰς αὐτὸν τῶν Σαμαριτῶν διὰ τὸν λόγον τῆς γυναικὸς <u>μαρτυρούσης</u> ὅτι Εἶπέν μοι πάντα ἃ ἐποίησα = "Many of the Samaritans believed in him because of the word of the woman, *because she testified*, 'He told me all the things that I have done'" (Jn 4:39)

3. κρίναντας τοῦτο, ὅτι εἷς ὑπὲρ πάντων ἀπέθανεν = "*because we determined* this, that one died for all" (2 Cor 5:15)

4. ὁ οὖν Ἰησοῦς κεκοπιακὼς ἐκ τῆς ὁδοιπορίας ἐκαθέζετο = "therefore, *because Jesus was weary* from the journey, he was sitting" (Jn 4:6)

Condition

Condition uses the participle to express a condition that limits the main verb's action. The participle can be converted into an indicative verb in a dependent clause that is begun with the conjunction "if." The conjunction εἰ is not required.

1. ταῦτα γὰρ ποιοῦντες οὐ μὴ πταίσητέ ποτε = "for *if you do* these things you will never stumble" (2 Pet 1:10)

2. ἐξ ὧν διατηροῦντες ἑαυτοὺς εὖ πράξετε = "from which, *if you keep* yourselves, you will do well" (Acts 15:29)

3. πῶς ἡμεῖς ἐκφευξόμεθα τηλικαύτης ἀμελήσαντες σωτηρίας; = "how shall we escape *if we neglect* so great a salvation?" (Heb 2:3)

Concession

Concession uses the participle to express a concession against the main verb's action. The participle can be set up as a dependent clause that is begun with the conjunctions "although," "even though," "though," or "whereas."

1. βλέποντες οὐ βλέπουσιν καὶ ἀκούοντες οὐκ ἀκούουσιν οὐδὲ συνίουσιν = *although seeing*, they do not see, and *although hearing*, they do not hear" (Mt 13:13)

2. τυφλὸς ὢν ἄρτι βλέπω = "*whereas I was* blind, now I see" (Jn 9:25)

3. διότι γνόντες τὸν θεὸν οὐχ ὡς θεὸν ἐδόξασαν = "for, *even though they knew* God, they did not glorify as God" (Rom 1:21)

4. ἀνεῳγμένων δὲ τῶν ὀφθαλμῶν αὐτοῦ οὐδὲν ἔβλεπεν = "but *though* his eyes *were open*, he could see nothing" (Acts 9:8)

Means

Means uses the participle to express the means facilitating the main verb's action. The participle phrase can use the conjunctions "by" or "through."

1. τοῦτο γὰρ ποιῶν καὶ σεαυτὸν σώσεις καὶ τοὺς ἀκούοντάς σου = "for *by doing* this you will save both yourself and your hearers" (1 Tim 4:16)
2. σταυρώσαντες δὲ αὐτὸν διεμερίσαντο τὰ ἱμάτια αὐτοῦ βάλλοντες κλῆρον = "and after they crucified him, they divided his garments among themselves *by casting lots*" (Mt 27:35)
3. ὃν καὶ ἀνεῖλαν κρεμάσαντες ἐπὶ ξύλου = "whom they also put to death *by hanging him* on a tree" (Acts 10:39)
4. Ἰδοὺ ὁ βασιλεύς σου ἔρχεταί σοι, πραῢς καὶ ἐπιβεβηκὼς ἐπὶ ὄνον = "Behold, your king comes to you, humble and *mounted* on a donkey" (Mt 21:5)

Manner

Manner uses the participle to express the manner or attitude accompanying the main verb's action. Usually this participle is expressing emotion or other action that intensifies the main verb. The participle often is translated in a simple "-ing" or "-ed" form.

1. καὶ ἐλάλει εὐλογῶν τὸν θεόν = "and he began to speak *blessing* God" (Lk 1:64)
2. καὶ ὑπέστρεψαν οἱ ποιμένες δοξάζοντες καὶ αἰνοῦντες τὸν θεὸν = "and the shepherds returned *glorifying* and *praising* God" (Lk 2:20)
3. ἦλθαν σπεύσαντες = "they went away *with haste*" (Lk 2:16)

4. ὥστε γυμνοὺς καὶ <u>τετραυματισμένους</u> ἐκφυγεῖν ἐκ τοῦ οἴκου ἐκείνου = "such that they fled from that house naked and *wounded*" (Acts 19:16)

Complementary

Complementary (or supplementary) uses the participle to complete the main verb's action. Hence, the complementary participle is essential. This use is a function parallel to that of the complementary infinitive. Common in this use are main verbs related to appearing, beginning, being, ceasing, continuing, and showing. The participle often is translated in its simple "-ing" form.

1. οὐ παύομαι <u>εὐχαριστῶν</u> ὑπὲρ ὑμῶν = "I do not cease *giving thanks* for you" (Eph 1:16)
2. θέλεις εἰς Ἱεροσόλυμα <u>ἀναβὰς</u> = "Do you want *to go up* to Jerusalem?" (Acts 25:9)

Circumstantial

Circumstantial uses the participle to add action that is not essential to the main verb. This use often is invoked to deal with double verbs of saying, such as "he answered and said," which is redundant and derives from a Semitic idiom of the Old Testament. The "and said" part of the phrase is the participle converted into an indicative verb joined to the main verb with "and."

1. ὁ δὲ Πιλᾶτος ἀπεκρίθη αὐτοῖς <u>λέγων</u> = "but Pilate answered them *and said*" (Mk 15:9)
2. ἠκολούθησαν τῷ Ἰησοῦ ἀπὸ τῆς Γαλιλαίας <u>διακονοῦσαι</u> αὐτῷ = "they followed Jesus from Galilee *and ministered* to him" (Mt 27:55)

Idiomatic Use

Two further uses of the participle one could say are adverbial. These uses could have been included as categories in the section immediately above on adverbial use. Yet, these types of participles also are idiomatic. They have peculiarities to them grammatically. As idioms, they stand out, and so are treated as their own section.

Periphrasis

Periphrasis is a "phrasing around," a roundabout way of saying something. A periphrastic construction uses *two* verbal forms—a form of a linking verb and a participle—when one finite verb would have sufficed. Periphrasis may represent an emphasis on the *durative* aspect of the tense. This type of pleonasm (overfullness) is a peculiarity of Koine style (cf. "Koine Style," p. 4), a Koine habit of mind. That is, even the better New Testament writers can show periphrastic expressions on occasion. Instead of a normal present indicative verb, as one example, one will find εἰμί in the present tense linked to a present participle for the same effect. Thus, the present participle is linked to a form of εἰμί to create present, imperfect, and future periphrastic tenses. Or, a form of εἰμί in the future tense can be linked to the perfect participle to create the equivalent of a future perfect indicative.

Table 18.3 Periphrastic Tenses: Examples

1. *Present periphrastic:*
   εἰσὶν διδάσκοντες = διδάσκουσιν = "they are teaching"
2. *Imperfect periphrastic:*
   ἦν ἐκβάλλων = ἐξέβαλλον = "he was casting out"
3. *Future periphrastic:*
   ἔσονται πίπτοντες = πεσοῦνται = "they will fall"
4. *Perfect periphrastic:*
   ἐστε σεσῳσμένοι = σέσωσθε = "you have been saved"
5. *Future perfect periphrastic:*
   ἔσται λελυμένον = λελύσται = "will have been loosed"

Grammatically, periphrastic construction can be understood as a complementary participle. The participle completes the verbal idea begun in the linking verb. If so, periphrasis would be the most common complementary use in the New Testament. Syntactically, the construction is predicative (because of the linking verb). The adjectival focus as a predicate adjective would be in view. Either way, periphrastic constructions translate in a straightforward manner. Be aware that the linking verb is not always adjacent to the participle, and, on rare occasion, even can be found after the participle. Study the following examples:

1. οἱ ἄνδρες οὓς ἔθεσθε ἐν τῇ φυλακῇ εἰσὶν ἐν τῷ ἱερῷ ἑστῶτες καὶ διδάσκοντες τὸν λαόν = "the men whom you put in prison *are standing* in the temple and *teaching* the people" (Acts 5:25)

2. ἦν ἐκβάλλων δαιμόνιον = "*he was casting out* a demon" (Lk 11:14)

3. μόνον δὲ ἀκούοντες ἦσαν ὅτι ὁ διώκων ἡμᾶς ποτε νῦν εὐαγγελίζεται τὴν πίστιν ἥν ποτε ἐπόρθει = "but they only *were hearing*, "The one who formerly persecuted us is now evangelizing the faith which he once was persecuting" (Gal 1:23); notice the εἰμί form is after the participle

4. καὶ οἱ ἀστέρες ἔσονται ἐκ τοῦ οὐρανοῦ πίπτοντες = "and the stars *will fall* from heaven" (Mk 13:25)

5. Τῇ γὰρ χάριτί ἐστε σεσῳσμένοι διὰ πίστεως = "For by grace *you have been saved* through faith" (Eph 2:8)

6. καὶ ὃ ἐὰν λύσῃς ἐπὶ τῆς γῆς ἔσται λελυμένον ἐν τοῖς οὐρανοῖς = "whatever you loose on earth *will have been loosed* in heaven" (Mt 16:19)

Genitive Absolute

Concept. A *genitive absolute* is a genitive participle clause that is independent of the main verb. This independence is signaled grammatically by an abrupt shift in construction to the genitive case. A tip-off to one very common genitive absolute construction is a change of subject. A participial clause starts off with "they," for example, but the finite verb's subject might be "he." Such a participial clause is independent of the main verb and its subject. While the clause does add more information to the main verb, the clause is nonessential to the action of the main verb. Even though other adverbial participles, such as the circumstantial, are said to be nonessential to the action of the main verb, they are not in the same way grammatically *independent* of the main verb like the genitive absolute.

Construction. As the name suggests, the construction is easy to spot: both the participle and the noun construed with the participle will be genitive. To translate, establish the surrogate subject of the genitive participle and treat the genitive participle as if a temporal adverbial clause. Thus, the two-step process is:

1. *Surrogate subject:* treat the genitive noun or pronoun in the neighborhood as the "subject" of the participle.
2. *Temporal nuance:* give the participle a temporal nuance or other adverbial translation.

Study the following examples:

1. *Present:* Καὶ πορευομένων αὐτῶν ἐν τῇ ὁδῷ εἶπέν τις πρὸς αὐτόν = "And *as they were going along the way* a certain man said to him" (Lk 9:57). Notice carefully: (1) the abrupt subject shift from "they" in the participle to "a certain man" in the main verb; (2) the genitive clause is nonessential, and (3) the clause is grammatically *independent* of the main verb.

2. *Aorist:* Καταβάντος δὲ αὐτοῦ ἀπὸ τοῦ ὄρους ἠκολούθησαν αὐτῷ ὄχλοι πολλοί = "And *after he came down from the mountain,* a large crowd followed him" (Mt 8:1). Notice the genitive construction and the subject shift. The whole clause not only is nonessential but also is independent of the main verb.

3. *Perfect:* Συνηγμένων δὲ τῶν Φαρισαίων ἐπηρώτησεν αὐτοὺς ὁ Ἰησοῦς = "And *while the Pharisees were gathered together,* Jesus asked them" (Mt 22:41). Notice the genitive construction and the subject shift. The whole

clause not only is nonessential but also is independent of the main verb.

4. *Copulative:* Καὶ <u>ὄντος αὐτοῦ</u> ἐν Βηθανίᾳ ἐν τῇ οἰκίᾳ Σίμωνος τοῦ λεπροῦ <u>κατακειμένου αὐτοῦ</u> ἦλθεν γυνὴ = "And *while he was* in Bethany at the home of Simon the leper, *as he was reclining*, a woman came" (Mk 14:3). Notice the genitive construction and the subject shift. This example actually stacks up two genitive absolutes back to back. The direct story line is the main indicative verb, "a woman came." The two genitive participle constructions having a different subject are grammatically independent of the main verb, "she came," even though adding more information to the scene.

Caveat. In identifying the genitive absolute, do not get carried away with tagging every genitive participle encountered as a genitive absolute. Not all genitive participles are genitive absolutes. For example, note Acts 8:30:

ὁ Φίλιππος ἤκουσεν αὐτοῦ <u>ἀναγινώσκοντος</u>
"Philip heard him *reading*"

This participle is *essential* to the main verb. The participle is part of a direct object clause that indicates what Philip heard (some might give this as an object complement). The case is genitive because ἀκούω can take its direct object in the genitive, as in this example. The participle's adverbial function is *not* grammatically independent of the main verb, as is the genitive absolute.

Conclusion

General Question

Other Tenses?

Have you noticed the absence of "imperfect" or "pluperfect" participles? These tenses are unnecessary in participles. Their function is temporal. Imperfect sets durative action in past time. Pluperfect sets perfective action in past time. These time and aspect functions already are covered in relating adverbial participles to a main verb. The main verb sets the time frame of the sentence. If the main verb is *past* tense, then a present adverbial participle's effect is imperfect, and the perfect adverbial participle's effect is pluperfect. Observe the imperfect result of this present (temporal) participle: ὑπέστρεψαν εἰς Ἰερουσαλὴμ <u>ἀναζητοῦντες</u> αὐτόν = "they returned to Jerusalem and *were looking for* him" (Lk 2:45; "to look for" if taken as purpose). Observe the pluperfect result of this perfect (causal) participle: ἐδέξαντο αὐτὸν οἱ Γαλιλαῖοι πάντα <u>ἑωρακότες</u> ὅσα ἐποίησεν = "the Galileans welcomed him *because they had seen* all the things that he had done" (Jn 2:9).

Periphrastic Results

Periphrastic constructions also illustrate how the question of other tenses is answered. With εἰμί as imperfect, notice the resultant *imperfect* force with the present participle:

1. Καὶ <u>ἦσαν</u> οἱ μαθηταὶ Ἰωάννου καὶ οἱ Φαρισαῖοι <u>νηστεύοντες</u> = "And the disciples of John and the Pharisees *were fasting*" (Mk 2:18)

2. καὶ ὡς <u>ἀτενίζοντες</u> <u>ἦσαν</u> εἰς τὸν οὐρανὸν = "and as *they were gazing* into heaven" (Acts 1:10)

Notice the resultant *pluperfect* force with the perfect participle:

1. ὃ <u>ἦν</u> <u>λελατομημένον</u> ἐκ πέτρας = "which *had been hewn* out of rock" (Mk 15:46)

2. καὶ <u>ἦν</u> αὐτῷ <u>κεχρηματισμένον</u> = "and *it had been revealed* to him" (Lk 2:26)

3. Καὶ ἦλθεν εἰς Ναζαρά, οὗ <u>ἦν</u> <u>τεθραμμένος</u> = "and he came to Nazareth where *he had been brought up*" (Lk 4:16)

4. <u>ἦσαν</u> γὰρ <u>προεωρακότες</u> Τρόφιμον τὸν Ἐφέσιον ἐν τῇ πόλει σὺν αὐτῷ = "for *they earlier had seen* Trophimus the Ephesian in the city with him" (Acts 21:29)

Adverbial Summary

A general summary of translation strategy for adverbial participles might be helpful to summarize the above discussion in a useful format. The following table provides a synopsis of both regular and idiomatic adverbial uses. The suggested translations do not cover every circumstance in which one might encounter an adverbial participle in the New Testament, of course. As always, context always is the deciding factor for translating an adverbial participle, along with attempting to meet the expectations of smooth English idiom.

Table 18.4 Adverbial Participle: Translation Summary

Regular	Translation Strategy
Temporal	after, when, while, as, -ing
Purpose	to, -ing, so that, in order to, etc.
Cause	because, since, for
Condition	if, whether
Concession	whereas, although, even though, though
Means	by, through
Manner	-ing (or, with ____)
Complementary	-ing, to
Circumstantial	[indicative] and [indicative]
Idiomatic	**Translation Strategy**
Periphrastic	-ing or -ed (cf. complementary)
Gen. Absolute	after, when, while, as, -ing (cf. temporal)

EXERCISE 18

1. Translate the following, as required. Be ready to answer any questions on participle use:

   1.1 ἰδόντες δὲ τὸν ἀστέρα ἐχάρησαν [first, translate as temporal; then, translate as causal]

   1. _____

   2. _____

   1.2 ἐπορεύετο γὰρ τὴν ὁδὸν αὐτοῦ χαίρων

   _____

   1.3 ἀνήρ τίς ἐστιν καταλελειμμένος ὑπὸ Φήλικος δέσμιος

   _____

   1.4 ἐὰν γὰρ ἀγαπήσητε τοὺς ἀγαπῶντας ὑμᾶς, τίνα μισθὸν ἔχετε;

   _____

   _____

   1.5 διότι γνόντες τὸν θεὸν οὐχ ὡς θεὸν ἐδόξασαν ἢ ηὐχαρίστησαν [translate as concession]

   _____

   _____

1.6 καὶ οὐκ ἐγὼ μόνος ἀλλὰ καὶ πάντες οἱ ἐγνωκότες τὴν ἀλήθειαν

_____

_____

1.7 Καὶ εἰσελθόντος αὐτοῦ εἰς Ἱεροσόλυμα ἐσείσθη πᾶσα ἡ πόλις λέγουσα· τίς ἐστιν οὗτος;

_____

_____

2. Be ready to identify participle use in translations of 1 Jn 1:1-3:24 as a part of exercises since chapter 13.

3. Translate the following passage from 1 John. Be ready to identify participle use.

4.1 Ἀγαπητοί, μὴ παντὶ πνεύματι πιστεύετε ἀλλὰ

_____

δοκιμάζετε τὰ πνεύματα εἰ ἐκ τοῦ θεοῦ ἐστιν, ὅτι πολλοὶ

_____

ψευδοπροφῆται ἐξεληλύθασιν εἰς τὸν κόσμον. **2** ἐν τούτῳ

_____

γινώσκετε τὸ πνεῦμα τοῦ θεοῦ· πᾶν πνεῦμα ὃ ὁμολογεῖ

_____

Ἰησοῦν Χριστὸν ἐν σαρκὶ ἐληλυθότα ἐκ τοῦ θεοῦ ἐστιν,

_____

3 καὶ πᾶν πνεῦμα ὃ μὴ ὁμολογεῖ τὸν Ἰησοῦν ἐκ τοῦ θεοῦ οὐκ

_____

ἔστιν· καὶ τοῦτό ἐστιν τὸ τοῦ ἀντιχρίστου, ὃ ἀκηκόατε ὅτι

_____

ἔρχεται, καὶ νῦν ἐν τῷ κόσμῳ ἐστὶν ἤδη.

4 ὑμεῖς ἐκ τοῦ θεοῦ ἐστε, τεκνία, καὶ νενικήκατε

αὐτούς, ὅτι μείζων ἐστὶν ὁ ἐν ὑμῖν ἢ ὁ ἐν τῷ κόσμῳ. **5** αὐτοὶ

ἐκ τοῦ κόσμου εἰσίν, διὰ τοῦτο ἐκ τοῦ κόσμου λαλοῦσιν καὶ

ὁ κόσμος αὐτῶν ἀκούει. **6** ἡμεῖς ἐκ τοῦ θεοῦ ἐσμεν, ὁ

γινώσκων τὸν θεὸν ἀκούει ἡμῶν, ὃς οὐκ ἔστιν ἐκ τοῦ θεοῦ

οὐκ ἀκούει ἡμῶν. ἐκ τούτου γινώσκομεν τὸ πνεῦμα τῆς

ἀληθείας καὶ τὸ πνεῦμα τῆς πλάνης.

7 Ἀγαπητοί, ἀγαπῶμεν ἀλλήλους,

ὅτι ἡ ἀγάπη ἐκ τοῦ θεοῦ ἐστιν,

καὶ πᾶς ὁ ἀγαπῶν ἐκ τοῦ θεοῦ γεγέννηται

καὶ γινώσκει τὸν θεόν.

8 ὁ μὴ ἀγαπῶν οὐκ ἔγνω τὸν θεόν,

ὅτι ὁ θεὸς ἀγάπη ἐστίν.

9   ἐν τούτῳ ἐφανερώθη ἡ ἀγάπη τοῦ θεοῦ ἐν ἡμῖν,

ὅτι τὸν υἱὸν αὐτοῦ τὸν μονογενῆ ἀπέσταλκεν ὁ θεὸς

εἰς τὸν κόσμον ἵνα ζήσωμεν δι᾽ αὐτοῦ.

10   ἐν τούτῳ ἐστὶν ἡ ἀγάπη,

οὐχ ὅτι ἡμεῖς ἠγαπήκαμεν τὸν θεὸν

ἀλλ᾽ ὅτι αὐτὸς ἠγάπησεν ἡμᾶς

καὶ ἀπέστειλεν τὸν υἱὸν αὐτοῦ

ἱλασμὸν περὶ τῶν ἁμαρτιῶν ἡμῶν.

11 Ἀγαπητοί, εἰ οὕτως ὁ θεὸς ἠγάπησεν ἡμᾶς, καὶ ἡμεῖς

ὀφείλομεν ἀλλήλους ἀγαπᾶν. 12 θεὸν οὐδεὶς πώποτε

τεθέαται. ἐὰν ἀγαπῶμεν ἀλλήλους, ὁ θεὸς ἐν ἡμῖν μένει καὶ

ἡ ἀγάπη αὐτοῦ ἐν ἡμῖν τετελειωμένη ἐστίν. 13 Ἐν τούτῳ

γινώσκομεν ὅτι ἐν αὐτῷ μένομεν καὶ αὐτὸς ἐν ἡμῖν, ὅτι ἐκ

τοῦ πνεύματος αὐτοῦ δέδωκεν ἡμῖν. **14** καὶ ἡμεῖς τεθεάμεθα

καὶ μαρτυροῦμεν ὅτι ὁ πατὴρ ἀπέσταλκεν τὸν υἱὸν σωτῆρα

τοῦ κόσμου. **15** Ὃς ἐὰν ὁμολογήσῃ ὅτι Ἰησοῦς ἐστιν ὁ υἱὸς

τοῦ θεοῦ, ὁ θεὸς ἐν αὐτῷ μένει καὶ αὐτὸς ἐν τῷ θεῷ. **16** καὶ

ἡμεῖς ἐγνώκαμεν καὶ πεπιστεύκαμεν τὴν ἀγάπην ἣν ἔχει ὁ

θεὸς ἐν ἡμῖν.

Ὁ θεὸς ἀγάπη ἐστίν, καὶ ὁ μένων ἐν τῇ ἀγάπῃ ἐν τῷ θεῷ

μένει καὶ ὁ θεὸς ἐν αὐτῷ μένει. **17** Ἐν τούτῳ τετελείωται ἡ

ἀγάπη μεθ᾽ ἡμῶν, ἵνα παρρησίαν ἔχωμεν ἐν τῇ ἡμέρᾳ τῆς

κρίσεως, ὅτι καθὼς ἐκεῖνός ἐστιν καὶ ἡμεῖς ἐσμεν ἐν τῷ

κόσμῳ τούτῳ. **18** φόβος οὐκ ἔστιν ἐν τῇ ἀγάπῃ ἀλλ᾽ ἡ τελεία ἀγάπη ἔξω βάλλει τὸν φόβον, ὅτι ὁ φόβος κόλασιν ἔχει, ὁ δὲ

φοβούμενος οὐ τετελείωται ἐν τῇ ἀγάπῃ. **19** ἡμεῖς ἀγαπῶμεν,

ὅτι αὐτὸς πρῶτος ἠγάπησεν ἡμᾶς. **20** ἐάν τις εἴπῃ ὅτι ἀγαπῶ

τὸν θεὸν καὶ τὸν ἀδελφὸν αὐτοῦ μισῇ, ψεύστης ἐστίν· ὁ γὰρ

μὴ ἀγαπῶν τὸν ἀδελφὸν αὐτοῦ ὃν ἑώρακεν, τὸν θεὸν ὃν οὐχ

ἑώρακεν οὐ δύναται ἀγαπᾶν. **21** καὶ ταύτην τὴν ἐντολὴν

ἔχομεν ἀπ᾽ αὐτοῦ, ἵνα ὁ ἀγαπῶν τὸν θεὸν ἀγαπᾷ καὶ τὸν

ἀδελφὸν αὐτοῦ.

CHAPTER 19
MI VERBS: FIRST PRINCIPAL PART

Greek verbs divide into two major conjugations: -ω verbs and -μι verbs. The -μι verb does not always show a theme vowel in its formation. Otherwise, these verbs in general follow -ω verb formation, except in the first principal part.

Introduction

MI verbs are older than -ω verbs. One encounters them often in translating Homer's *Iliad* or *Odyssey*, for example. Some endings are the more primitive verb endings as a result. The first person singular, -μι, from which the conjugation derives its name, is an example. The -μι verb eventually began losing out to the growing dominance of -ω verbs. By New Testament times, they are on their way out. Depending on who is counting, about 30 different -μι verbs appear in the New Testament. Compounds increase their number to about 116-119. A few -μι verbs actually are quite frequent. The verb εἰμί, even though a -μι verb, was introduced with -ω verbs because of its tremendous frequency (2,462 times!) and its importance for adjective and participle grammar. Δίδωμι occurs 613 times, including compounds. The lexical middle δύναμαι, introduced with infinitives, occurs 210 times.

The -μι verb conjugation mostly follows the -ω verb formation patterns, if a lengthened stem vowel is recognized. The main difference is in the first principal part of the present and imperfect tenses. Not even the second aorist -μι verb is entirely distinctive, since we do have some -ω verbs that have a non-thematic second aorist as well (i.e., γινώσκω and compounds of βαίνω; cf. Table 13.26). This chapter focuses on this distinctive first principal part of -μι verbs.

Present Tense

Indicative Mood

Morphology

Table 19.1 MI Verb: Present Tense Morphology

1	2	3	4	5	6
augment	reduplic.	stem	suffix	vowel	ending
	δι	Present			Primary

$$δι\text{-}δω\text{-}μεν$$

Table 19.2 MI Verb: Present Indicative

δίδωμι	δίδομαι	I give, am given
δίδως	δίδοσαι	you give, are given (sg.)
δίδωσιν	δίδοται	he (she, it) gives, are given
δίδομεν	διδόμεθα	we give, are given
δίδοτε	δίδοσθε	you give, are given (pl.)
διδόασιν	δίδονται	they give, are given

Active Voice

The -μι verb active indicative has four key formation components:

1. lengthening
2. reduplication
3. non-thematic
4. primary -μι endings

These fomation components are typical of many -μι verbs. Each component will be described briefly.

Lengthening. The present active indicative -μι verb lengthens the short stem vowel in *singular* forms. Since the lexical form is the first singular, all vocabulary forms of -μι verbs include this lengthened stem vowel. Thus, the original tense stem of a -μι verb is the *corresponding short vowel of the vocabulary form*. So the tense stem of δίδωμι, minus the reduplication, is δο-. For τίθημι the stem is θε-. The stem of ἵστημι is στα-. The verb ἀφίημι is compounded with ἀπό, which elides to ἀφ- before rough breathing. The stem of ἀφίημι, really just ἵημι, is only one letter, ἑ- (seriously).

Reduplication. Secondly, about half of -μι verbs reduplicate in the present system. Recall reduplication in the fourth and fifth principal parts of the -ω verb (perfect system). There, the reduplication pattern used the vowel ε, as in λελυ-. The pattern for -μι verbs is similar, only the vowel is ι. Almost half of -μι verbs are *not* reduplicated (cf. ἀπόλλυμι, δείκνυμι, and φημί). If one has noticed already, some -ω verbs *also* reduplicate the present stem, as in, for example, the verbs: γίνωσκω = γιγνώσκω (but γ before ν drops); μιμνήσκομαι; πίπτω; and τίκτω (which swaps letters, τκ→κτ, a process called "metathesis").

Phonetic processes have to be kept in mind in reduplication. With τίθημι, the reduplicated stem θιθη- deaspirates to the form τιθη- for pronunciation. For ἵστημι, the reduplicated stem σιστη- drops the initial σ before the vowel, picks up rough breathing as a result, and becomes ἵστη. The verb ἀφίημι, stem ἑ-, reduplicates with the reduplication vowel ι, and rough breathing as ἱη-.

Non-thematic. Thirdly, -μι verbs do not use a theme vowel. This feature is similar to the fifth principal part in the -ω verb of the perfect middle. While typically no theme vowel is used, a few exceptions do occur. These exceptions are:

1. *Future tense*: which does incorporate a thematic vowel in the *resultant* primary endings
2. *Subjunctive mood*: which includes a long thematic vowel in *resultant* subjunctive endings
3. *Imperative mood*: in the single form of the present active imperative, second singular

Otherwise, absent the theme vowel, pronominal endings are joined directly to the lengthened, reduplicated stem.

Table 19.3 MI Verb: Primary Active Endings

-μι	I
-ς	you (sg)
-σι	he, she, it
-μεν	we
-τε	you (pl)
-ασι	they

Primary Endings. Fourthly, the suffix endings for the primary active -μι verb are added. These -μι verb endings are regular, but they are learned in their resultant forms. The primary pattern learned for the -ω verb (-ω, -εις, -ει, etc.) is a *resultant* pattern. In a similar way, the -μι verb pattern also is learned as a resultant pattern. For point of reference, the original primitive endings were -μι, -σι, -τι, -μεν, -τε, -ντι. These endings then become the resultant endings of -μι, -ς, -σι, -μεν, -τε, -ασι. Because the ending -μι becomes familiar quickly due to vocabulary work, the only notably different forms that require attention are the two third person forms of -σι and -ασι.

Middle Voice

The present indicative middle and passive formation is similar to the active, with two distinctions:
1. *No lengthening:* the short stem vowel does *not* lengthen in the singular forms as in the active voice
2. *Middle endings:* primary middle endings are used

Also, note that the second singular does *not* react, as so often in the -ω verb due to an intervocalic sigma. The reason is that this sigma is not considered intervocalic with the -μι verb *stem* vowel.

Contingency Moods

Table 19.4 MI Verb: Subjunctive and Imperative

Subjunctive		_Imperative_	
διδῶ	διδῶμαι	-------	-------
διδῷς	διδῷ	δίδου	δίδοσο
διδῷ	διδῶται	διδότω	διδόσθω
διδῶμεν	διδώμεθα	-------	-------
διδῶτε	διδῶσθε	δίδοτε	δίδοσθε
διδῶσιν	διδῶνται	διδότωσαν	διδόσθωσαν

Subjunctive

The subjunctive, *by definition*, requires a lengthened thematic vowel as the mood sign. Thus, all subjunctives, whether -ω verb or -μι verb, take lengthened thematic vowel endings. The -μι verb has a short vowel in its stem. Hence, with subjunctive -μι verbs, one has a recipe for contraction. The lengthened thematic vowels of the subjunctive mood contract with the short vowels of -μι verb stems. Whatever the exact nature of the contraction, the result is a long syllable with a circumflex accent, except for the antepenult acute in the middle first plural. These contracted verb stems, with reduplication, are the basic look of the present subjunctive. Be aware that second and third singular (διδῷς, διδῷ) can have the alternate forms of διδοῖς and διδοῖ, respectively.

Imperative

The imperative, *by definition*, has a distinct set of imperative endings that signal the imperative mood. Thus, all imperatives, whether -ω verb or -μι verb, take these imperative endings. Short vowel stems contract in one form, the active second singular, which opts for no ending, leaving the thematic vowel ε exposed to contract with the stem vowel (e.g., ο + ε = ου or ε + ε = ει; note that only this form appropriates the thematic vowel; the others are non-thematic). These imperative endings, with reduplication, are the basic look of the present imperative.

Optative

Only two -μι verbs actually have present optatives in the New Testament, and in only three forms. The verb εἰμί has the form εἴη, and δύναμαι has the two forms δυναίμην and δύναιντο.

Imperfect Tense

Morphology

Table 19.5 MI Verb: Imperfect Tense Morphology

1	2	3	4	5	6
augment	*reduplic.*	*stem*	*suffix*	*vowel*	*ending*
ἐ	δι	Present			Secondary

$$\overset{\text{᾿}}{ε}\text{-}δι\text{-}δο\text{-}μεν$$

Table 19.6 MI Verb: Imperfect Indicative

ἐδίδουν	ἐδιδόμην	*I was giving, was given*
ἐδίδους	ἐδίδοσο	*you were giving, were given (sg.)*
ἐδίδου	ἐδίδοτο	*he (she, it) was giving, was given*
ἐδίδομεν	ἐδιδόμεθα	*we were giving, were given*
ἐδίδοτε	ἐδίδοσθε	*you were giving, were given (pl.)*
ἐδίδοσαν	ἐδίδοντο	*they were giving, were given*

The imperfect tense occurs only in the indicative mood. Thus, the imperfect of -μι verbs involves only two paradigms, the active and middle/passive voices of the indicative.

Active Indicative

Pattern

The pattern is first principal part. That is, the imperfect -μι verb is built on the present tense stem. Formation components are almost the same as a result, only with allowance for a past time tense in augment and endings. The imperfect active, then, has five key components:
1. lengthening
2. reduplication
3. augment
4. non-thematic
5. secondary endings

These formation components are typical of many -μι verbs. Each component will be described briefly.

Components

Lengthening. Imperfect active indicative of -μι verbs lengthens short stem vowels in *singular* forms (as in present tense); yet, the pattern varies. For δίδωμι, lengthening is -ου. For τίθημι, however, note this variation in singular forms: τιθη-, τιθει-, τιθει-. Such patterns should not need to be memorized, only recognized as some type of lengthening in singular forms.

Reduplication. The imperfect is built on the first principal part, so uses the present tense stem. The reduplication pattern is the same as present tense, using the vowel ι (for about half of all -μι verbs).

Augment. Any secondary tense is augmented. Typical patterns of syllabic and temporal augment of the -ω verb apply to -μι verbs also.

Non-thematic. Regularly, -μι verbs do not use a theme vowel ("athematic"). As in the present tense, pronominal endings are joined directly to the reduplicated stem.

Secondary Endings. The -μι verb secondary endings are regular. Most of the time, the third plural takes the -σαν option. On occasion, the third plural does take the -ν option. If so, the stem vowel is lengthened. This lengthening generates a slightly altered ending pattern (e.g., -ουν or -ην).

Middle Indicative

Indicative middle and passive is similar to the active, with only two distinctions: (1) the short stem vowel is *not* lengthened, and (2) secondary middle endings are used. The second singular does not react.

Dual Conjugations

As pointed out at the beginning of this chapter, the -μι verb was on its way out in New Testament times, giving way to the dominance of -ω verbs. This transitional status of the -μι verb shows up in the New Testament in that a few verbs actually are found in *both* the -μι and -ω conjugations. These dual-conjugation verbs evidence the -ω conjugation in the actual process of taking over a given -μι verb. Observing vocabulary will disclose verbs that can be found in both conjugations. Examples would include ἀπόλλυμι (cf. ἀπολλύω) and δείκνυμι (cf. δεικνύω). For example, μὴ τῷ βρώματί σου ἐκεῖνον ἀπόλλυε ὑπὲρ οὗ Χριστὸς ἀπέθανεν = "*Do not destroy* with your food that one for whom Christ died" (Rom 14:15). This imperative form shows the thematic vowel ending of the -ω verb system. Again, we have, τί σημεῖον δεικνύεις ἡμῖν ὅτι ταῦτα ποιεῖς; = "What sign *are you doing* for us since you are doing these things?" (Jn 2:18). As a -μι verb, the active second singular ending would have been δεικνύς.

EXERCISE 19

1. Describe briefly the four key formation components of the present active indicative -μι verb:

    1.1 _____

    1.2 _____

    1.3 _____

    1.4 _____

2. Describe briefly the five key formation components of the imperfect active indicative -μι verb:

    2.1 _____

    2.2 _____

    2.3 _____

    2.4 _____

    2.5 _____

3. Identify the three exceptions to the non-thematic nature of the -μι verb:

    3.1 _____

3.2 _____

3.3 _____

4. Answer true or false:

____ a. The imperfect active -μι verb lengthens the verb stem vowel in singular forms.

____ b. All -μι verbs reduplicate in the present system.

____ c. The endings -σι and -ασι represent the primary active third person of the -μι verb.

____ d. The middle second singular -μι verb ending reacts due to an intervocalic sigma.

____ e. The present subjunctive -μι verb almost always has circumflex accent on the verb-stem vowel.

____ f. The vowel of reduplication is the same ε vowel of the perfect reduplication process.

____ g. The only -μι verbs with present optatives in the New Testament are εἰμί and δύναμαι.

____ h. The secondary active endings of the -μι verb are the same endings as for the -ω verb.

____ i. Some verbs can be found in both the -μι verb and the -ω verb conjugations.

5. Locate the following forms of the -μι verb τίθημι:

5.1 τιθέασιν: _____

5.2 τίθενται: _____

5.3 τιθῶμεν: _____

5.4 τιθέτω: _____

5.5 ἐτίθεσθε: _____

6. Translate the following:

6.1 παντὶ αἰτοῦντί σε δίδου

_____

6.2 ὅταν παραδιδῷ τὴν βασιλείαν τῷ θεῷ

_____

6.3 καὶ δείκνυσιν αὐτῷ πάσας τὰς βασιλείας τοῦ κόσμου

_____

6.4 καὶ τὴν δύναμιν καὶ ἐξουσίαν αὐτῶν τῷ θηρίῳ διδόασιν

_____

6.5 ὁ υἱὸς τοῦ ἀνθρώπου παραδίδοται εἰς χεῖρας ἁμαρτωλῶν

_____

6.6 καὶ ἐτίθουν παρὰ τοὺς πόδας τῶν ἀποστόλων, διεδίδετο δὲ ἑκάστῳ καθότι ἄν τις χρείαν εἶχεν.

_____

_____

7. Answer the following questions related to the manuscript lines of 𝔓⁶⁶ and 𝔓⁷⁵ at the end of this chapter (p. 454):

7.1 _____ Which manuscript has the negative οὐ twice in the same line, once as οὐχ and once as οὐκ?

7.2 _____ Does either manuscript show any iota subscripts? When did iota subscript begin to be used?

7.3 _____ Which scribe spelled ἀλήθεια as ἀλήθια? This type of vowel substitution, such as ι for ει, represents a spelling variation known as *itacism*, that is, the confusion of like-sounding vowels or diphthongs.

7.4 _____ Which scribe changed the word order by pulling the second ἀλήθεια before the negative (not shown) after the word ὅτι?

7.5 _____ What punctuation mark is clearly visible in 𝔓⁶⁶?

8. Translate the following passage from 1 John. Be ready to identify -μι verbs.

5.1 Πᾶς ὁ πιστεύων ὅτι Ἰησοῦς ἐστιν ὁ Χριστὸς, ἐκ τοῦ

_____

θεοῦ γεγέννηται, καὶ πᾶς ὁ ἀγαπῶν τὸν γεννήσαντα ἀγαπᾷ

_____

[καὶ] τὸν γεγεννημένον ἐξ αὐτοῦ. **2** ἐν τούτῳ γινώσκομεν ὅτι

_____

ἀγαπῶμεν τὰ τέκνα τοῦ θεοῦ, ὅταν τὸν θεὸν ἀγαπῶμεν καὶ

_____

τὰς ἐντολὰς αὐτοῦ ποιῶμεν. **3** αὕτη γάρ ἐστιν ἡ ἀγάπη τοῦ

_____

θεοῦ, ἵνα τὰς ἐντολὰς αὐτοῦ τηρῶμεν, καὶ αἱ ἐντολαὶ αὐτοῦ

_____

βαρεῖαι οὐκ εἰσίν. **4** ὅτι πᾶν τὸ γεγεννημένον ἐκ τοῦ θεοῦ

_____

νικᾷ τὸν κόσμον· καὶ αὕτη ἐστὶν ἡ νίκη ἡ νικήσασα τὸν

_____

κόσμον, ἡ πίστις ἡμῶν.

_____

5.5 Τίς [δέ] ἐστιν ὁ νικῶν τὸν κόσμον εἰ μὴ ὁ πιστεύων

ὅτι Ἰησοῦς ἐστιν ὁ υἱὸς τοῦ θεοῦ; **6** οὗτός ἐστιν ὁ ἐλθὼν δι᾽

ὕδατος καὶ αἵματος, Ἰησοῦς Χριστός, οὐκ ἐν τῷ ὕδατι μόνον

ἀλλ᾽ ἐν τῷ ὕδατι καὶ ἐν τῷ αἵματι· καὶ τὸ πνεῦμά ἐστιν τὸ

μαρτυροῦν, ὅτι τὸ πνεῦμά ἐστιν ἡ ἀλήθεια. **7** ὅτι τρεῖς εἰσιν

οἱ μαρτυροῦντες, **8** τὸ πνεῦμα καὶ τὸ ὕδωρ καὶ τὸ αἷμα, καὶ

οἱ τρεῖς εἰς τὸ ἕν εἰσιν. **9** εἰ τὴν μαρτυρίαν τῶν ἀνθρώπων

λαμβάνομεν, ἡ μαρτυρία τοῦ θεοῦ μείζων ἐστίν· ὅτι αὕτη

ἐστὶν ἡ μαρτυρία τοῦ θεοῦ ὅτι μεμαρτύρηκεν περὶ τοῦ υἱοῦ

αὐτοῦ. **10** ὁ πιστεύων εἰς τὸν υἱὸν τοῦ θεοῦ ἔχει τὴν

μαρτυρίαν ἐν ἑαυτῷ, ὁ μὴ πιστεύων τῷ θεῷ ψεύστην

πεποίηκεν αὐτόν, ὅτι οὐ πεπίστευκεν εἰς τὴν μαρτυρίαν ἣν

μεμαρτύρηκεν ὁ θεὸς περὶ τοῦ υἱοῦ αὐτοῦ. **11** Καὶ αὕτη

ἐστὶν ἡ μαρτυρία, ὅτι ζωὴν αἰώνιον ἔδωκεν ἡμῖν ὁ θεός, καὶ

αὕτη ἡ ζωὴ ἐν τῷ υἱῷ αὐτοῦ ἐστιν. **12** ὁ ἔχων τὸν υἱὸν ἔχει

τὴν ζωήν· ὁ μὴ ἔχων τὸν υἱὸν τοῦ θεοῦ τὴν ζωὴν οὐκ ἔχει.

5.13 Ταῦτα ἔγραψα ὑμῖν ἵνα εἰδῆτε ὅτι ζωὴν ἔχετε

αἰώνιον, τοῖς πιστεύουσιν εἰς τὸ ὄνομα τοῦ υἱοῦ τοῦ θεοῦ.

14 Καὶ αὕτη ἐστὶν ἡ παρρησία ἣν ἔχομεν πρὸς αὐτὸν ὅτι ἐάν

τι αἰτώμεθα κατὰ τὸ θέλημα αὐτοῦ ἀκούει ἡμῶν. **15** καὶ ἐὰν

οἴδαμεν ὅτι ἀκούει ἡμῶν ὃ ἐὰν αἰτώμεθα, οἴδαμεν ὅτι

ἔχομεν τὰ αἰτήματα ἃ ᾐτήκαμεν ἀπ᾽ αὐτοῦ.

5.16 Ἐάν τις ἴδῃ τὸν ἀδελφὸν αὐτοῦ ἁμαρτάνοντα

ἁμαρτίαν μὴ πρὸς θάνατον, αἰτήσει καὶ δώσει αὐτῷ ζωήν,

τοῖς ἁμαρτάνουσιν μὴ πρὸς θάνατον. ἔστιν ἁμαρτία πρὸς

θάνατον· οὐ περὶ ἐκείνης λέγω ἵνα ἐρωτήσῃ. **17** πᾶσα ἀδικία ἁμαρτία ἐστίν, καὶ ἔστιν ἁμαρτία οὐ πρὸς θάνατον.

5.18 Οἴδαμεν ὅτι πᾶς ὁ γεγεννημένος ἐκ τοῦ θεοῦ οὐχ

ἁμαρτάνει, ἀλλ᾽ ὁ γεννηθεὶς ἐκ τοῦ θεοῦ τηρεῖ αὐτὸν καὶ ὁ

πονηρὸς οὐχ ἅπτεται αὐτοῦ. **19** οἴδαμεν ὅτι ἐκ τοῦ θεοῦ

ἐσμεν καὶ ὁ κόσμος ὅλος ἐν τῷ πονηρῷ κεῖται. **20** οἴδαμεν

δὲ ὅτι ὁ υἱὸς τοῦ θεοῦ ἥκει καὶ δέδωκεν ἡμῖν διάνοιαν ἵνα

γινώσκωμεν τὸν ἀληθινόν, καὶ ἐσμὲν ἐν τῷ ἀληθινῷ, ἐν τῷ

υἱῷ αὐτοῦ Ἰησοῦ Χριστῷ. οὗτός ἐστιν ὁ ἀληθινὸς θεὸς καὶ

ζωὴ αἰώνιος.

5.21 Τεκνία, φυλάξατε ἑαυτὰ ἀπὸ τῶν εἰδώλων.

▓▓▓▓▓▓▓ MANUSCRIPTS 11 ▓▓▓▓▓▓▓

John 8:44 has spelling variations for the -μι verb ἵστημι in two manuscripts, 𝔓⁶⁶ and 𝔓⁷⁵ (late second to early third century papyrus manuscripts, Bodmer collection), that yield different tenses. The only way to know the difference in tenses is whether the verb is spelled with rough or smooth breathing. Yet, neither 𝔓⁶⁶ nor 𝔓⁷⁵ has breathing marks. So, how do we know two different tenses are meant by the scribes? A neat trick!

The negative οὐ has alternate spellings: οὐκ before smooth breathing (e.g., οὐκ εἰμί) and οὐχ before rough breathing (e.g., οὐχ ἡ γραφή). The verb ἵστημι is spelled the same in two tenses—an odd development of Koine Greek. The perfect tense is normal: ἕστηκεν. Observe the rough breathing. The imperfect tense form, ἔστηκεν, inexplicably mimics the perfect form. Note the *smooth* breathing. At Jn 8:44, scribes had trouble with the εστηκεν form of ἵστημι. Some thought the form was imperfect (smooth breathing). Others thought the form was perfect (rough breathing). We know this because the negative precedes the verb. The perfect form with rough breathing requires the negative to be spelled οὐχ. The imperfect form with smooth breathing requires the negative to be spelled οὐκ. Note carefully: spelling demonstrates that 𝔓⁶⁶ has the imperfect tense in mind but 𝔓⁷⁵ the perfect tense. (The sigma in uncial script is C, which looks like our capital "C.")

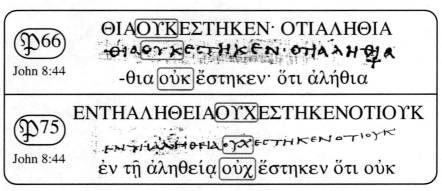

Fig. 16. Papyrus Manuscripts 𝔓⁶⁶ and 𝔓⁷⁵ at Jn 8:44.

CHAPTER 20
MI VERBS: OTHER PARTS

Greek verbs divide into two major conjugations: -ω verbs and -μι verbs. The -μι verb morphology divides into two groups. The first group is the first principal part producing the present and imperfect tenses. The second group is all other principal parts.

Analysis

The reason why -μι verb morphology easily divides into two groups is that, outside the first principal part, -μι verbs are formed just like their -ω verb counterparts. Thus, after presenting the first principal part, which establishes the present and imperfect tenses, presenting the rest of the -μι verb system is simply a review of the other principal part patterns of the -ω verb system. As a result, the basic principal part patterns must be fixed firmly in memory.

Forms in the tables are given to illustrate the tense, though some forms do not occur in the New Testament. Because the first principal part of the -μι verb has a characteristic reduplication, then the following three generalizations can reduce the need for memorizing -μι verb paradigms:

♦ *Any ι vowel -μι verb reduplication can be only present or imperfect tense.*

♦ *Any ε vowel -μι verb reduplication can be only perfect or pluperfect tense.*

♦ *Non-reduplicated -μι verb stems are either aorist or future tense.*

That is, the one feature of reduplication alone covers four of the six tenses in a -μι verb! Recognize reduplication in any form and one has nailed location of a given -μι verb.

Perfective Tenses

Indicative Mood

Table 20.1 MI Verb: Perfect Active Morphology

1	2	3	4	5	6
augment	reduplic.	stem	suffix	vowel	ending
	δε	Perfect	κα		Secondary

$$\delta\epsilon\text{-}\delta\omega\text{-}\kappa\alpha\text{-}\mu\epsilon\nu$$

Table 20.2 MI Verb: Perfect Middle/Passive Morphology

1	2	3	4	5	6
augment	reduplic.	stem	suffix	vowel	ending
	δε	Perfect			Secondary

$$\delta\epsilon\text{-}\delta o\text{-}\mu\epsilon\theta\alpha$$

Table 20.3 MI Verb: Pluperfect Active Morphology

1	2	3	4	5	6
augment	reduplic.	stem	suffix	vowel	ending
ἐ	δε	Perfect	κει		Secondary

$$\dot{\epsilon}\text{-}\delta\epsilon\text{-}\delta\omega\text{-}\kappa\epsilon\iota\text{-}\mu\epsilon\nu$$

Table 20.4 MI Verb: Pluperfect Middle/Passive Morphology

1	2	3	4	5	6
augment	reduplic.	stem	suffix	vowel	ending
ἐ	δε	Perfect			Secondary

$$ \overset{\text{᾿}}{ἐ}\text{-}δε\text{-}δω\text{-}μεθα $$

Table 20.5 MI Verb: Perfect and Pluperfect Indicative

Perfect		Pluperfect	
Active	*Middle*	*Active*	*Middle*
δέδωκα	δέδομαι	ἐδεδώκειν	ἐδεδόμην
δέδωκας	δέδοσαι	ἐδεδώκεις	ἐδέδοσο
δέδωκεν	δέδοται	ἐδεδώκει	ἐδέδοτο
δεδώκαμεν	δεδόμεθα	ἐδεδώκειμεν	ἐδεδόμεθα
δεδώκατε	δέδοσθε	ἐδεδώκειτε	ἐδέδοσθε
δέδωκαν	δέδονται	ἐδεδώκεισαν	ἐδέδοντο

The perfect active is regular, but observe the long stem vowel. The perfect middle is regular, but with a short stem vowel, and no intervocalic sigma in the second singular. Pluperfect is regular, but normally drops the augment, as in the -ω verb. The middle also has no intervocalic sigma in the second singular.

Contingency Moods

Perfect subjunctive and imperative are not included, because these forms are quite rare. An example of a subjunctive form is the middle/passive periphrastic construction ᾖ δεδομένον in Jn 3:27 (cf. 6:65). An example of the imperative would be Ἔρρωσθε (ῥώννυμι) in Acts 15:29.

Undefined Tenses

Future Indicative

Table 20.6 MI Verb: Future Active Morphology

1	2	3	4	5	6
augment	*reduplic.*	*stem*	*suffix*	*vowel*	*ending*
		Future	σ	ο/ε	Primary

$$δω\text{-}σ\text{-}ο\text{-}μεν$$

Table 20.7 MI Verb: Future Middle Morphology

1	2	3	4	5	6
augment	*reduplic.*	*stem*	*suffix*	*vowel*	*ending*
		Future	σ	ο/ε	Primary

$$δω\text{-}σ\text{-}ο\text{-}μεθα$$

Table 20.8 MI Verb: Future Passive Morphology

1	2	3	4	5	6
augment	*reduplic.*	*stem*	*suffix*	*vowel*	*ending*
		Aorist	θησ	ο/ε	Primary

$$δο\text{-}θησ\text{-}ο\text{-}μεθα$$

Table 20.9 MI Verb: Future Indicative

Active	Middle	Passive
δώσω	δώσομαι	δοθήσομαι
δώσεις	δώσῃ	δοθήσῃ
δώσει	δώσεται	δοθήσεται
δώσομεν	δωσόμεθα	δοθησόμεθα
δώσετε	δώσεσθε	δοθήσεσθε
δώσουσιν	δώσονται	δοθήσονται

Indicative forms are regular. The future passive is built on the aorist passive stem (sixth principal part), so shows the *short* stem vowel. The second singular of both middle and passive reacts with an intervocalic sigma. Remember that the future tense is not used in contingency moods. This is true for both -ω verbs and -μι verbs.

First Aorist Indicative

Table 20.10 MI Verb: First Aorist Active Morphology

1	2	3	4	5	6
augment	reduplic.	stem	suffix	vowel	ending
ἐ		Aorist	σα/κα		Secondary

$$\overset{,}{\epsilon}\text{-}ζω\text{-}σα\text{-}μεν, \; \overset{,}{\epsilon}\text{-}δω\text{-}κα\text{-}μεν$$

Table 20.11 MI Verb: First Aorist Middle Morphology

1	2	3	4	5	6
augment	reduplic.	stem	suffix	vowel	ending
ἐ		Aorist	σα		Secondary

$$\overset{,}{\epsilon}\text{-}ζω\text{-}σα\text{-}μεθα$$

Table 20.12 MI Verb: First Aorist Passive Morphology

1	2	3	4	5	6
augment	reduplic.	stem	suffix	vowel	ending
ἐ		Aorist	θη		Secondary

$$\overset{\text{ʾ}}{ἐ}\text{-}ζω\text{-}σθη\text{-}μεν$$

Table 20.13 MI Verb: First Aorist Indicative

	Active		
Regular	*"Kappa Aor."*	*Middle*	*Passive*
ἔζωσα	ἔδωκα	ἐζωσάμην	ἐζώσθην
ἔζωσας	ἔδωκας	ἐζώσω	ἐζώσθης
ἔζωσεν	ἔδωκεν	ἐζώσατο	ἐζώσθη
ἐζώσαμεν	ἐδώκαμεν	ἐζωσάμεθα	ἐζώσθημεν
ἐζώσατε	ἐδώκατε	ἐζώσασθε	ἐζώσθητε
ἔζωσαν	ἔδωκαν	ἐζώσαντο	ἐζώσθησαν

Active Indicative

Our δίδωμι paradigm is not helpful in the aorist. Patterns can show *both* first *and* second aorist forms in the *same* voice and mood (cf. active subjunctive). Further, its active indicative has an odd "kappa aorist." Thus, in the aorist, our -μι verb paradigms switch to the more regular ζώννυμι (ζω-) and δείκνυμι (δεικ-).

Regular. Note that two different paradigms are necessary for the first aorist active -μι verb. One is for a "kappa aorist." This kappa aorist is a variant formation pattern found in only three -μι verbs, but these three verbs and their compounds are frequent in the New Testament. So, the variation has to be remembered well. The regular first aorist active -μι verb can be represented by the paradigm word ζώννυμι, which mainly occurs in compounds in both the LXX and the New Testament. Other -μι verbs in this regular category are: ἀπόλλυμι (which inserts an ε as ἀπώλεσα), ἵστημι and its compounds (ἀνίστημι, ἀφίστημι, ἐξίστημι, καθίστημι, μεθίστημι, παρίστημι, and συνίστημι), ἐμπίπλημι, ἐπίμπρημι, κεράννυμι, συνκεράννυμι, ἐκπετάννυμι, σβέννυμι, and a whole series of palatal stops: δείκνυμι and compounds (ἀναδείκνυμι, ἀποδείκνυμι, ὑποδείκνυμι), ῥήγνυμι and its compounds (διαρήγνυμι, προσρήγνυμι = προσρήσσω), μίγνυμι, πήγνυμι, κατάγνυμι, and συζεύγνυμι.

Kappa Aorist. In contrast to this regular aorist formation pattern, three -μι verbs, δίδωμι, τίθημι, and ἵημι compounds, are called "kappa aorists." *Kappa aorist* describes the typical -σα first aorist suffix pattern being replaced by a -κα, yielding an alternate pattern -κα, -κας, -κεν, -καμεν, -κατε, -καν. To be sure, this "kappa aorist" suffix pattern easily could be confused with the perfect tense. However, to keep straight aorist and perfect forms, note carefully these two formation features of the kappa aorist: (1) past time augment, and (2) no reduplication (i.e., recognize the difference between ἔδωκα vs. δέδωκα).

Middle Indicative

The first aorist middle -μι verb in the New Testament is rare, because most -μι verbs are *second aorist* in their *middle* voice formation. The paradigm is ζώννυμι. In the paradigm, as in the -ω verb, the intervocalic second singular sigma reacts as expected with the typical contraction result. Only two verbs actually are involved in the New Testament. The compound form διαζώννυμι occurs as διεζώσατο in Jn 21:7. The other verb is ἐνδείκνυμι, showing two forms: ἐνεδείξατο in 2 Tim 4:14, and ἐνεδείξασθε in Heb 6:10.

Passive Indicative

The -θη suffix is key (sixth principal part). First passive can show a short-vowel stem (ἐδόθην) or insert σ (ἐζώσθην). Second passive -μι verbs are rare, but any -γνυμι stem is a candidate.

First Aorist Contingency Moods

Table 20.14 MI Verb: First Aorist Subjunctive and Imperative

Subjunctive		Imperative	
δείξω	δείξωμαι	-------	-------
δείξῃς	δείξῃ	δεῖξον	δείξαι
δείξῃ	δείξηται	δειξάτω	δειξάσθω
δείξωμεν	δειξώμεθα	-------	-------
δείξητε	δείξησθε	δείξατε	δείξασθε
δείξωσιν	δείξωνται	δειξάτωσαν	δειξάσθωσαν

Subjunctive

Aorist subjunctive has no augment and takes primary endings with lengthened thematic vowel as the mood sign. Thus, the aorist subjunctive -μι verb *does* have a thematic vowel. However, first aorist subjunctive -μι verbs are uncommon in the New Testament.

The first aorist active subjunctive is encountered in ἀπόλλυμι, which inserts an ε before the -σα tense suffix, yielding the forms ἀπολέσω, ἀπολέσῃς, ἀπολέσῃ, etc. Also, δείκνυμι, whose stem is δεικ-, shows palatal volatilization with the -σ of the aorist tense suffix; the one example is δείξω (Acts 7:3).

The first aorist middle subjunctive -μι verb is rare. Two forms of ἐνδείκνυμι show up three times: once as ἐνδείξωμαι (Rom 9:17) and twice as ἐνδείξηται (Eph 2:7; 1 Tim 1:16).

Imperative

Aorist imperative has no augment, aorist tense suffix, and takes imperative endings. Aorist imperative forms of the -μι verb tend to show more second aorist forms than first aorist.

The first aorist active imperative shows forms of δείκνυμι and two of its compounds, ἐπιδείκνυμι and ἀναδείκνυμι. One also encounters an example from παρίστημι, which normally is second aorist in the imperative, but first aorist as παραστήσατε (Rom 6:13, 19). Two other first aorist active imperatives are κεράσατε from κεράννυμι (Rev 18:6), and χρῆσον from κίχρημι (Lk 11:5).

The first aorist middle imperative -μι verb has only one occurrence. This form is ζῶσαι (ζώννυμι) in Acts 12:8.

Second Aorist Indicative

Table 20.15 MI Verb: Second Aorist Active Morphology

1	2	3	4	5	6
augment	reduplic.	stem	suffix	vowel	ending
ἐ		Aorist			Secondary

$$\overset{\text{'}}{\epsilon}\text{-}\sigma\tau\eta\text{-}\mu\epsilon\nu$$

Table 20.16 MI Verb: Second Aorist Middle Morphology

1	2	3	4	5	6
augment	reduplic.	stem	suffix	vowel	ending
ἐ		Aorist			Secondary

$$\overset{\text{'}}{\epsilon}\text{-}\delta o\text{-}\mu\epsilon\theta\alpha$$

Table 20.17 MI Verb: Sec. Aorist Indicative (Ἵστημι, Δίδωμι)

Active	Middle
ἔστην	ἐδόμην
ἔστης	ἔδου
ἔστη	ἔδοτο
ἔστημεν	ἐδόμεθα
ἔστητε	ἔδοσθε
ἔστησαν	ἔδοντο

Active Indicative

Remember that the second aorist -ω verb has no aorist tense suffix in active voice and takes a thematic vowel, producing a resultant look like the imperfect. However, also remember that some -ω verb second aorists are "non-thematic," that is, they do not take the theme vowel. The two -ω verb examples of non-thematic second aorists are ἀνέβην (ἀναβαίνω) and ἔγνων (γινώσκω).

The second aorist in the -μι verb also is non-thematic. The -μι verb's own stem vowel suffices for accepting the pronominal suffix. One exception would be "kappa aorists," second aorist verbs that are first aorist in active voice (δίδωμι, τίθημι, and ἵημι; but, παρέδοσαν, Lk 1:2). The stem vowel is altered with a tense suffix.

Classification of -μι verbs as second aorist is not always neat and tidy. For example, forms of ἵστημι defy being pigeon-holed. This verb and its compounds usually are first aorist, but not always. The only first person forms are second aorist (ἐξέστημεν, 2 Cor 5:13; ἀντέστην, Gal 2:11), as is one of the three forms in second person (ἀντικατέστητε, Heb 12:4). Further, over one third (39%) of the third person forms are second aorist (33 of 84)! Thus, classifying -μι verbs as either first or second aorist is a challenge.

Middle Indicative

Only three second aorist -μι verbs have a middle indicative in the New Testament: ἀπόλλυμι, δίδωμι, and τίθημι. Unexpectedly, their second singulars react, the sigma in each apparently taken as intervocalic, even though a verb stem vowel is involved (either as οσο→οο→ου or as εσο→εο→ου). Two unusual formations in these second aorist middle verbs are encountered. First, δίδωμι forms in the New Testament present unexpected variations that seem influenced by the -ω conjugation, specifically ἀπέδετο (Heb 12:16) and ἐξέδετο (Mt 21:33; Mk 12:1; Lk 20:9). Second, the aorist middle forms of ἀπόλλυμι strangely exhibit a thematic vowel in the third person forms of ἀπώλετο and ἀπώλοντο. So, once again, saying -μι verbs are non-thematic is not carved in stone.

Second Aorist Contingency Moods

Table 20.18 MI Verb: Second Aorist Subjunctive and Imperative

Subjunctive			Imperative		
δῶ	δῶμαι	δοθῶ	-------	-------	-------
δῷς	δῷ	δοθωῇς	δός	δοῦ	δόθητι
δῷ	δῷται	δοθωῇ	δότω	δόσθω	δοθήτω
δῶμεν	δώμεθα	δοθῶμεν	-------	-------	-------
δῶτε	δῶσθε	δοθῆτε	δότε	δόσθε	δόθητε
δῶσιν	δῶνται	δοθῶσι	δότωσαν	δόσθωσαν	δοθήτωσαν

Subjunctive

The -μι verb shows mostly *second* aorist forms in the contingency moods. Sometimes, however, one might find a -σ suffix on the stem, as in the subjunctive of δίδωμι. If so, that verb in that particular form is showing a first aorist configuration: note δώσῃ (Jn 17:2) and δώσωμεν (Rev 19:7). In the active voice, second aorist subjunctives involve δίδωμι, τίθημι, ἵημι, and ἵστημι. In the middle voice, just two verbs are involved: third person forms of ἀπόλλυμι (ἀπόληται, ἀπόλωνται), as well as just one form of ἀποτίθημι (ἀποθώμεθα, Rom 13:12). The passive subjunctive has a *first passive* suffix (as does imperative): δοθῶ.

Imperative

Second aorist active imperatives involve δίδωμι, τίθημι, ἵημι, and ἵστημι. Second aorist middle involves only three forms of τίθημι: θέσθε (Lk 9:44), ἀπόθεσθε (Col 3:8), and παράθου (2 Tim 2:2). Passive imperative has a *first passive* suffix: δόθητι.

Optative

The second aorist optative -μι verb is rare. The two New Testament verbs involved show four occurrences of δῴη (δίδωμι; Rom

15:5; 2 Thess 3:16; 2 Tim 1:16, 18), along with the one occurrence of ὀναίμην (ὀνίνημι; Phlm 20).

Infinitives

Present

The active voice infinitive ending for the present tense -μι verb is -ναι, and middle/passive is -σθαι. Thus, διδόναι and δίδοσθαι are the present active and middle/passive infinitives, respectively. The verb εἰμί has the infinitive form εἶναι.

Perfect

The perfect -μι verb infinitive is rare. The compound ἐξίστημι has the perfect active infinitive ἐξεστακέναι (Acts 8:11). The perfect second active form ἑστάναι is from ἵστημι (cf. Lk 13:25; Acts 12:14; 1 Cor 10:12).

Future and Aorist

The future -μι verb infinitive is rare in the New Testament. The verb εἰμί has all four examples in the form ἔσεσθαι (Acts 11:28; 23:30; 24:15; 27:10).

The active voice infinitive ending for the aorist tense -μι verb is -σαι for first aorist and -ναι for second aorist. The middle voice is -σθαι, and the passive is -ναι. An example of the first aorist active infinitive is παραστῆσαι (παρίστημι). The verb δείκνυμι, stem δείκ-, has the volatilized form δεῖξαι. The verb ἀπόλλυμι, which inserts an ε, has the form ἀπολέσαι. Second aorist forms are evidenced in δοῦναι (δίδωμι), θεῖναι (τίθημι), and στῆναι (ἵστημι).

The aorist middle infinitive shows up six times: in compounds of τίθημι, ἀποθέσθαι (Eph 4:22) and καταθέσθαι (Acts 24:27;

25:9); as ἀπολέσθαι (ἀπόλλυμι, Lk 13:33; 2 Pet 3:9); and as ἐνδείξασθαι (ἐνδείκνυμι, Rom 9:22). The more common aorist passive infinitive, which has an *active* ending, has examples in the forms δοθῆναι, τεθῆναι, and σταθῆναι.

Participles

Participle formation in the -μι verb follows -μι verb principal parts. Volatilization is as expected, if the stem is recognized. Thus, the verb δείκνυμι, stem δεικ-, is δειχθείς in the aorist passive. A problem in volatilization, though, will be -μι verb stems, such as the θε- of τίθημι. Some stems can be confused with tense/voice prefixes and suffixes. In some forms, τίθημι ends up like naked endings, such as in the aorist active participle: θείς, θεῖσα, θέν. Note particularly, however, τίθημι as *aorist passive*: τεθείς, τεθεῖσα, τεθέν. This form looks like perfect reduplication. Here, however, the opening τε- *is* the original verb stem, not reduplication. The original stem θε- had to deaspirate (from rough stop to corresponding smooth) for pronunciation in order to blend with the following θ of the ending (θεθείς → τεθείς).

Almost all aorist -μι verb participles are second aorist. For first aorist forms, simply recognize nominative masculine forms, such as ἀπολέσας (ἀπόλλυμι, Mt 10:39; Lk 9:25; 15:4) or κρεμάσαντες (κρεμάννυμι, Acts 5:30; 10:39). Also, be aware of the normal stop volatilization, as in διαρρήξας, διαρρήξαντες, (διαρήγνυμι, Mk 14:63; Acts 14:14).

Almost all perfect active participle forms relate to ἵστημι and compounds, as in ἑστηκώς, παρεστηκώς. The second perfect is seen in ἑστώς, ἑστῶσα, ἑστός, all of which have contracted and taken on other reactions (also note compounds; e.g., παρεστώς). A compounded form of δίδωμι, παραδίδωμι, is found in the form παραδεδωκώς. The verb τίθημι has the perfect participle form τεθεικώς.

Table 20.19 MI Verb: Present Active Participle

Masculine (ἄρχων)		Neuter (3rd Decl.)		Feminine (δόξα)	
διδούς	διδόντες	διδόν	διδόντα	διδοῦσα	διδοῦσαι
διδόντος	διδόντων	διδόντος	διδόντων	διδούσης	διδουσῶν
διδόντι	διδοῦσιν	διδόντι	διδοῦσιν	διδούσῃ	διδούσαις
διδόντα	διδόντας	διδόν	διδόντα	διδοῦσαν	διδούσας

Table 20.20 MI Verb: Present Middle/Passive Participle

Masculine (ἀγαθός)		Neuter (ἀγαθός)		Feminine (ἀγαθός)	
διδόμενος	διδόμενοι	διδόμενον	διδόμενα	διδομένη	διδόμεναι
διδομένου	διδομένων	διδομένου	διδομένων	διδομένης	διδομένων
διδομένῳ	διδομένοις	διδομένῳ	διδομένοις	διδομένη	διδομέναις
διδόμενον	διδομένους	διδόμενον	διδόμενα	διδομένην	διδομένας

Table 20.21 MI Verb: Second Aorist Active Participle

Masculine (ἄρχων)		Neuter (3rd Decl.)		Feminine (δόξα)	
δούς	δόντες	δόν	δόντα	δοῦσα	δοῦσαι
δόντος	δόντων	δόντος	δόντων	δούσης	δουσῶν
δόντι	δοῦσιν	δόντι	δοῦσιν	δούσῃ	δούσαις
δόντα	δόντας	δόν	δόντα	δοῦσαν	δούσας

Table 20.22 MI Verb: Second Aorist Middle Participle

Masculine (ἀγαθός)		Neuter (ἀγαθός)		Feminine (ἀγαθός)	
δόμενος	δόμενοι	δόμενον	δόμενα	δομένη	δόμεναι
δομένου	δομένων	δομένου	δομένων	δομένης	δομένων
δομένῳ	δομένοις	δομένῳ	δομένοις	δομένη	δομέναις
δόμενον	δομένους	δόμενον	δόμενα	δομένην	δομένας

Table 20.23 MI Verb: Aorist First Passive Participle

Masculine (3rd Decl.)		Neuter (3rd Decl.)		Feminine (δόξα)	
δοθείς	δοθέντες	δοθέν	δοθέντα	δοθεῖσα	δοθεῖσαι
δοθέντος	δοθέντων	δοθέντος	δοθέντων	δοθείσης	δοθεισῶν
δοθέντι	δοθεῖσιν	δοθέντι	δοθεῖσιν	δοθείσῃ	δοθείσαις
δοθέντα	δοθέντας	δοθέν	δοθέντα	δοθεῖσαν	δοθείσας

Table 20.24 MI Verb: Perfect First Active Participle

Masculine (3rd Decl.)		Neuter (3rd Decl.)		Feminine (καρδία)	
δεδωκώς	δεδωκότες	δεδωκός	δεδωκότα	δεδωκυῖα	δεδωκυῖαι
δεδωκότος	δεδωκότων	δεδωκότος	δεδωκότων	δεδωκυίας	δεδωκυιῶν
δεδωκότι	δεδωκόσιν	δεδωκότι	δεδωκόσιν	δεδωκυίᾳ	δεδωκυίαις
δεδωκότα	δεδωκότας	δεδωκός	δεδωκότα	δεδωκυῖαν	δεδωκυίας

Table 20.25 MI Verb: Perfect Middle/Passive Participle

Masculine (ἀγαθός)		Neuter (ἀγαθός)		Feminine (ἀγαθός)	
δεδομένος	δεδομένοι	δεδομένον	δεδομένα	δεδομένη	δεδομέναι
δεδομένου	δεδομένων	δεδομένου	δεδομένων	δεδομένης	δεδομένων
δεδομένῳ	δεδομένοις	δεδομένῳ	δεδομένοις	δεδομένῃ	δεδομέναις
δεδομένον	δεδομένους	δεδομένον	δεδομένα	δεδομένην	δεδομένας

Other Paradigms

The three most common New Testament -μι verbs are δίδωμι, τίθημι, and ἵστημι. The standard paradigm is δίδωμι. Because of their use, especially in compound forms, the two verbs τίθημι and ἵστημι are outlined here in addition to δίδωμι in the two common appearances as present or aorist tense to aid the student. Their participles boil down to recognizing *reduplicated* present or *non-reduplicated* aorist stems (i.e., τιθείς vs. θείς; ἱστάς vs. στάς).

Table 20.26 MI Verb: Present of Τίθημι

Indicative		Subjunctive		Imperative	
τίθημι	τίθεμαι	τιθῶ	τιθῶμαι	-------	-------
τίθης	τίθεσαι	τιθῇς	τιθῇ	τίθει	τίθεσο
τίθησιν	τίθεται	τιθῇ	τιθῆται	τιθέτω	τιθέσθω
τίθεμεν	τιθέμεθα	τιθῶμεν	τιθώμεθα	-------	-------
τίθετε	τίθεσθε	τιθῆτε	τιθῆσθε	τίθετε	τίθεσθε
τιθέασιν	τίθενται	τιθῶσιν	τιθῶνται	τιθέτωσαν	τιθέσθωσαν

Table 20.27 MI Verb: Aorist of Τίθημι

Indicative		Subjunctive		Imperative	
ἔθηκα	ἐθέμην	θῶ	θῶμαι	-------	-------
ἔθηκας	ἔθου	θῇς	θῇ	θές	θοῦ
ἔθηκεν	ἔθετο	θῇ	θῆται	θέτω	θέσθω
ἐθήκαμεν	ἐθέμεθα	θῶμεν	θώμεθα	-------	-------
ἐθήκατε	ἔθεσθε	θῆτε	θῆσθε	θέτε	θέσθε
ἔθηκαν	ἔθεντο	θῶσιν	θῶνται	θέτωσαν	θέσθωσαν

Table 20.28 MI Verb: Imperfect, Aorist Passive of Τίθημι

Imperfect		AorP: Indicative	Subjunc.	Imperative
ἐτίθην	ἐτιθέμην	ἐτέθην	τεθῶ	-------
ἐτίθεις	ἐτίθεσο	ἐτέθης	τεθῇς	τέθητι
ἐτίθει	ἐτίθετο	ἐτέθη	τεθῇ	τεθήτω
ἐτίθεμεν	ἐτιθέμεθα	ἐτέθημεν	τεθῶμεν	-------
ἐτίθετε	ἐτίθεσθε	ἐτέθητε	τεθῆτε	τέθητε
ἐτίθεσαν	ἐτίθεντο	ἐτέθησαν	τεθῶσι	τεθήτωσαν

Table 20.29 MI Verb: Present of Ἵστημι

Indicative		Subjunctive		Imperative	
ἵστημι	ἵσταμαι	ἱστῶ	ἱστῶμαι	-------	-------
ἵστης	ἵστασαι	ἱστῇς	ἱστῇ	ἵστη	ἵστασο
ἵστησιν	ἵσταται	ἱστῇ	ἱστῆται	ἱστάτω	ἱστάσθω
ἵσταμεν	ἱστάμεθα	ἱστῶμεν	ἱστώμεθα	-------	-------
ἵστατε	ἵστασθε	ἱστῆτε	ἱστῆσθε	ἱστάτε	ἵστασθε
ἱστᾶσιν	ἵστανται	ἱστῶσιν	ἱστῶνται	ἱστάτωσαν	ἱστάσθωσαν

Table 20.30 MI Verb: Aorist of Ἵστημι

Indicative		Subjunctive		Imperative	
ἔστην	ἐστάμην	στῶ	στῶμαι	-------	-------
ἔστης	ἔστασο	στῇς	στῇ	στῆθι	στάσο
ἔστη[1]	ἔστατο	στῇ	στῆται	στήτω	στάσθω
ἔστημεν	ἐστάμεθα	στῶμεν	στώμεθα	-------	-------
ἔστητε	ἔστασθε	στῆτε	στῆσθε	στῆτε	στάσθε
ἔστησαν	ἔσταντο	στῶσιν	στῶνται	στήτωσαν	στάσθωσαν

Table 20.31 MI Verb: Imperfect, Aorist Passive of Ἵστημι

Imperfect		AorP: Indicative	Subjunc.	Imperative
ἵστην	ἱστάμην	ἐστάθην	σταθῶ	-------
ἵστης	ἵστασο	ἐστάθης	σταθῇς	στάθητι
ἵστη	ἵστατο	ἐστάθη	σταθῇ	σταθήτω
ἵσταμεν	ἱστάμεθα	ἐστάθημεν	σταθῶμεν	-------
ἵστατε	ἵστασθε	ἐστάθητε	σταθῆτε	στάθητε
ἵστασαν	ἵσταντο	ἐστάθησαν	σταθῶσι	σταθήτωσαν

---

[1]Can show a first aorist form of ἔστησεν. Cf. Mt 4:5; 18:2; Mk 9:36; Lk 4:9; 9:47; Acts 17:31; 22:30.

EXERCISE 20

1. The key to -μι verb location is reduplication, for those verbs that reduplicate (and the most frequent ones do):

   1.1 _____ and _____ What -μι verb tenses are represented by ι vowel reduplication?

   1.2 _____ and _____ What -μι verb tenses are represented by ε vowel reduplication?

   1.3 _____ and _____ What -μι verb tenses are represented by non-reduplication?

2. Answer the following:

   2.1 Define "kappa aorist."

   _____

   2.2 _____ The term "kappa aorist" applies to what voice only?

   2.3 _____ What are two alternate forms of the -μι verb stem δω- that one will see in conjugated forms?

   2.4 _____ What are two alternate forms of the -μι verb stem θη- that one will see in conjugated forms?

2.5 _____ What is the alternate form of the -μι verb stem στη- that one will see in conjugated forms?

3. Locate the following forms of the -μι verb δίδωμι:

    3.1 ἔδωκας: _____

    3.2 δέδωκας: _____

    3.3 δέδοσθε: _____

    3.4 ἔδοσθε: _____

    3.5 ἐδόθημεν: _____

    3.6 δῷς: _____

    3.7 δόσθωσαν: _____

    3.8 διδόντες: _____

    3.9 δομένην: _____

    3.10 δοθέντας: _____

4. Translate the following:

    4.1 ἐπέθηκαν αὐτῷ τὸν σταυρόν.

    _____

    4.2 καὶ ἀναστὰς ἠκολούθησεν αὐτῷ.

    _____

    4.3 Γνωρίζομεν δὲ ὑμῖν, ἀδελφοί, τὴν χάριν τοῦ θεοῦ τὴν δεδομένην ἐν ταῖς ἐκκλησίαις τῆς Μακεδονίας

    _____

    _____

5. Translate the following passage from Luke. Be ready to identify -μι verbs. Then, compare this edited text with the uncial
   lines of Sinaiticus (p. xxvi) and Vaticanus (p. 520).

   2.1 Ἐγένετο δὲ ἐν ταῖς ἡμέραις ἐκείναις ἐξῆλθεν δόγμα

παρὰ Καίσαρος Αὐγούστου ἀπογράφεσθαι πᾶσαν τὴν

οἰκουμένην. **2** αὕτη ἀπογραφὴ πρώτη ἐγένετο ἡγεμονεύοντος

τῆς Συρίας Κυρηνίου. **3** καὶ ἐπορεύοντο πάντες

ἀπογράφεσθαι, ἕκαστος εἰς τὴν ἑαυτοῦ πόλιν. **4** Ἀνέβη δὲ

καὶ Ἰωσὴφ ἀπὸ τῆς Γαλιλαίας ἐκ πόλεως Ναζαρὲθ εἰς τὴν

Ἰουδαίαν εἰς πόλιν Δαυὶδ ἥτις καλεῖται Βηθλέεμ, διὰ τὸ

εἶναι αὐτὸν ἐξ οἴκου καὶ πατριᾶς Δαυίδ, **5** ἀπογράψασθαι

σὺν Μαριὰμ τῇ ἐμνηστευμένῃ αὐτῷ, οὔσῃ ἐγκύῳ. **6** Ἐγένετο

δὲ ἐν τῷ εἶναι αὐτοὺς ἐκεῖ ἐπλήσθησαν αἱ ἡμέραι τοῦ τεκεῖν

αὐτήν, **7** καὶ ἔτεκεν τὸν υἱὸν αὐτῆς τὸν πρωτότοκον, καὶ

ἐσπαργάνωσεν αὐτὸν καὶ ἀνέκλινεν αὐτὸν ἐν φάτνῃ, διότι

οὐκ ἦν αὐτοῖς τόπος ἐν τῷ καταλύματι.

2.8 Καὶ ποιμένες ἦσαν ἐν τῇ χώρᾳ τῇ αὐτῇ

ἀγραυλοῦντες καὶ φυλάσσοντες φυλακὰς τῆς νυκτὸς ἐπὶ τὴν

ποίμνην αὐτῶν. **9** καὶ ἄγγελος κυρίου ἐπέστη αὐτοῖς καὶ

δόξα κυρίου περιέλαμψεν αὐτούς, καὶ ἐφοβήθησαν φόβον

μέγαν. **10** καὶ εἶπεν αὐτοῖς ὁ ἄγγελος· μὴ φοβεῖσθε, ἰδοὺ

γὰρ εὐαγγελίζομαι ὑμῖν χαρὰν μεγάλην ἥτις ἔσται παντὶ τῷ

λαῷ, **11** ὅτι ἐτέχθη ὑμῖν σήμερον σωτὴρ ὅς ἐστιν χριστὸς

κύριος ἐν πόλει Δαυίδ. **12** καὶ τοῦτο ὑμῖν τὸ σημεῖον,

εὑρήσετε βρέφος ἐσπαργανωμένον καὶ κείμενον ἐν φάτνῃ.

13 καὶ ἐξαίφνης ἐγένετο σὺν τῷ ἀγγέλῳ πλῆθος στρατιᾶς

οὐρανίου αἰνούντων τὸν θεὸν καὶ λεγόντων·

14 δόξα ἐν ὑψίστοις θεῷ

καὶ ἐπὶ γῆς εἰρήνη

ἐν ἀνθρώποις εὐδοκίας.

2.15   Καὶ ἐγένετο ὡς ἀπῆλθον ἀπ᾽ αὐτῶν εἰς τὸν

οὐρανὸν οἱ ἄγγελοι, οἱ ποιμένες ἐλάλουν πρὸς ἀλλήλους·

διέλθωμεν δὴ ἕως Βηθλέεμ καὶ ἴδωμεν τὸ ῥῆμα τοῦτο τὸ

γεγονὸς ὃ ὁ κύριος ἐγνώρισεν ἡμῖν. **16** καὶ ἦλθαν

σπεύσαντες καὶ ἀνεῦραν τήν τε Μαριὰμ καὶ τὸν Ἰωσὴφ καὶ

τὸ βρέφος **17** ἰδόντες δὲ ἐγνώρισαν περὶ τοῦ ῥήματος τοῦ

λαληθέντος αὐτοῖς περὶ τοῦ παιδίου τούτου. **18** καὶ πάντες

οἱ ἀκούσαντες ἐθαύμασαν περὶ τῶν λαληθέντων ὑπὸ τῶν

ποιμένων πρὸς αὐτούς·

APPENDIX 1
GLOSSARY

This glossary provides brief definitions and explanations of key grammatical terms used in this grammar or related to topics covered in the discussions.

Ablaut—any pattern of vowel changes representing grammatical processes.

Accidence—study focusing on word inflections, sometimes used synonymously with morphology.

Accusative of General Reference—a substantive in accusative case grammatically related to an infinitive; specifies that which produces the infinitive action, and, so, functions like a "subject."

Active Voice—the subject of the verb performs the verbal action. ("I hit.")

Adverbial Prepositions—old adverbs with dual nature; still acting as adverbs, they also had prepositional function, i. e., were used mainly with noun structures; can be found by themselves (modifying a verb). Cf. *Proper Preposition*.

Adverbials—with numbers, those numbering terms used as adverbs, such as "once," "twice," and diagrammed under the verb.

Adverbial Use—with infinitives and participles, that use in which the verbal heritage is dominant and the grammatical function is to modify or make an additional assertion related to the main verb.

Adversative—coordinating conjunctions showing contrast, antithesis, or opposition.

Alpha Privative—the letter alpha prefixed to a word to negate the meaning, similar to the Latin prefix "un-," as in "unlike" (νόμος = "law"; ἄνομος = "lawless").

Alpha Pure ("α pure")—first declension stem with α throughout the singular.

Anarthrous—construction without the definite article.

Antecedent—the word, phrase, or clause to which a pronoun refers.

Antepenult—the third syllable from the end of a Greek word.

Aorist—one of three aspects of the Greek verb; verbal action as undefined, or in a given context, punctiliar (cf. *Punctiliar*).

Aoristic Perfect—a dubious category for the perfect tense in which perfective aspect supposedly has washed out, so that translation becomes aoristic by default.

Aoristic Present—rare use of present tense in which the context reveals a focus on a punctiliar aspect.

Apodosis—the "then" clause of a conditional sentence that specifies the results of the condition; functions and diagrams as an independent clause.

Apposition—placement side by side or in close proximity of two grammatical elements with equal syntactical relation to other parts of the sentence; acts as explanatory material. Cf. *Epexegetic.*

Articular—composition with the Greek article, also called *arthrous.*

Ascriptive Attributive—an articular adjective in simple attributive position, i.e., normally situated before the anarthrous noun modified.

Asigmatic—liquid aorist formation that looses the sigma of the aorist tense suffix.

Aspect—alternate term for kind of action in the equation of meaning of Greek verbs.

Aspiration—the degree of air allowed to flow around the tongue when using the mouth cavity for pronunciation, creating a rough sound; with stops, the consonants φ, χ, and θ are aspirated.

Assimilation—See *Coalescence.*

Athematic—alternate term describing the -μι verb conjugation, which does not use a theme vowel before the pronominal suffixes.

Attic Future—a dental delta tense stem that forms the future with the suffix -σε, forcing the dental consonant to drop; the sigma becomes intervocalic and drops; the remaining vowels contract.

Attic Reduplication—a perfect reduplication pattern that doubles the opening syllable and simultaneously lengthens the internal vowel (ἀκούω to the second perfect form ἀκήκοα).

Attributive Position—the adjective attributes a quality to the noun, which limits the noun's meaning.

Augmentation—adding a vowel prefix to tense stems beginning with a consonant or lengthening the opening vowel of a tense stem to indicate past time.

Byzantine—Constantinople, capital of the Eastern Roman Empire—later renamed Byzantium—fell to the Turks in A.D. 1453. Greek manuscripts produced in the scriptoriums there, today called Byzantine, went with Christians fleeing West, affecting the transmission of the New Testament.

Cardinal Numerals—the counting numbers ("one," "two," "three").

Closed Vowels—the mouth is relatively closed as they are pronounced. Cf. *Open Vowels.*

Coalescence—two of the same letters merge into one in word formation (e. g., σ + σ = σ).

Cognates—all words related to the same root, whether noun, adjective, or verb.

Codex—book form with folded leaves sewn together, as opposed to the scroll.

Colwell's Rule—clarifies which of two nominatives is subject and which is predicate.

Compensatory Lengthening—compensating for the loss of letters by lengthening a remaining vowel.

Complementary—any grammatical element that is essential to completing the meaning, such as a complementary infinitive.

Completed Perfect—use of perfect tense in which the context reveals an emphasis upon the completed action that generated the continuing effects.

Complex Sentence—an independent clause with at least one dependent clause; subordinating conjunctions indicate complex sentences.

Complex Sibilant—the "s" sounding consonants ψ, ξ, and ζ.

Compound Predicate—two verbal structures joined by a conjunction.

Compound Sentence—two or more independent clauses joined by conjunctions.

Compound Subject—two subjects joined by a conjunction.

Compound Verb—verb modified by adding a prepositional prefix.

Conative Imperfect—use of imperfect tense in which the context reveals a focus on attempted, but unsuccessful, action, translated, "tried to . . . ."

Concord—grammatical agreement, such as in case, gender, and number for nouns.

Conjugation—variously used to refer to: (1) an entire group of verbs with similar inflected forms, or (2) a presentation of all the inflected forms of a verb, or (3) the individual pattern of inflection for a given tense stem in a given tense, voice, and mood.

Conjunctions—function words that join words, phrases, clauses, and sentences.

Consonant Declension—the third declension, as all stems end either in consonants or ι and υ acting as semivowels (*consonantal iota* with "y" sound, *consonantal upsilon* with "w" sound).

Consonantal Iota—See *Semivowels*.

Consonantal Upsilon—See *Semivowels*.

Constative Aorist—use of aorist tense as a summary report of past action.

Contract Verbs—verbs whose stems end in one of the three vowels ε, ο, or α, which contract with pronominal suffix vowels in the first principal part, or lengthen in other principal parts.

Contraction—the reaction of certain vowels in word formation resulting in a long vowel or diphthong; contract verbs are a special category in verb formation.

Coordinate Clause—a clause with parallel grammatical status to a related clause, joined by a coordinate conjunction.

Coordinate Conjunction—connects two identically constructed grammatical elements.

Copulative—expresses equality or similarity of words or clauses; one function of εἰμί; cf. *Equative*.

Coronis—mark like an apostrophe used to indicate a dropped letter.

Crasis—merging of two words into one for pronunciation, often dropping a letter, such as κἀγώ for καὶ ἐγώ.

Culminative Aorist—use of aorist tense in which the context reveals an emphasis upon the conclusion of the action.

Customary Imperfect—use of imperfect tense in which the context reveals a focus on habit or custom, translated, "used to . . . ."

Deaspiration—altering a rough stop (φ, χ, θ) to its corresponding smooth stop (π, κ, τ) for pronunciation purposes (e. g., the imperative ending -θηθι to -θητι).

Declension—a word group involving nouns, pronouns and adjectives with a similar inflection pattern; Greek has three basic patterns: first, second, and third declensions.

Degrees—relates to making comparisons in three modes: positive, comparative, and superlative ("new," "newer," "newest").

Deliberative Future—use of future tense for rhetorical questions or in questions about an appropriate course of action to take; also called "rhetorical future."

Denotation—the explicit dictionary meaning of a word or grammatical element.

Dependent Clause—a clause that cannot stand by itself as a sentence, and grammatically acts as a noun, adjective, or adverb. Also called a subordinate clause.

Deponent—a category of Latin verbs that loose their active voice forms over time. In the past, this Latin deponent category has been applied mistakenly to lexical middle Greek verbs.

Descriptive Imperfect—similar to the descriptive present, action as ongoing with no reference to beginning or end, only past time.

Descriptive Present—action simply presented as ongoing with no reference to the beginning or the end of the action, or its result.

Diaeresis—a double dot over the second vowel of two vowels together to separate pronunciation into two vowels rather than as a diphthong.

Digamma—an archaic letter of the Greek alphabet, written as Ϝ, pronounced similarly to the English "w." Irregularities of word formation seem to be traceable to the sounding of this letter.

Direct Discourse—direct quotation.

Direct Middle—the verb's subject directly reflects the verbal action back onto itself.

Disyllabic—a word having just two syllables.

Divine Passive—the reader is to presume the agent of the passive voice is God.

Double Accusative—a verb having two accusative direct objects; also called "object complement."

Dramatic Aorist—use of aorist tense for dramatic effect in which the context reveals something significant has just taken place.

Dramatic Perfect—use of perfect tense in which the context reveals an emphasis upon a dramatic declaration or vivid narration. Cf. *Historical Present, Dramatic Aorist*.

Durative—one of three aspects of the Greek verb; verbal action as ongoing, in process.

Durative Imperfect—similar to the durative present, only past time.

Durative Present—action over two points in time, a beginning point that continues even now; translation often uses English present perfect.

Edited Text—used to refer to the printed *Greek New Testament*. We have no original manuscripts, and no two copies agree exactly. What to print as the Greek text must be decided at every point of significant variation by a team of editors using the scientific principles of textual criticism.

Elision—dropping of a letter, such as dropping a vowel at the end of one word before a vowel or diphthong that begins the next word.

Ellipsis—omission of words obviously understood, but grammatically necessary.

Emphasis—see *Position*.

Emphatic Pronoun—Koine tendency to include personal pronouns (more obvious in first, second person) with the verb to emphasize the subject already in the verb.

Enclitic—a word that loses its accent, leaning on the previous word for accent.

Epexegetic—additional explanatory material.

Epistolary Aorist—idiomatic use of aorist tense in letter writing that adopts the later perspective of the reader when referring to the writing of the letter; translated with the English idiom of present tense.

Equative—possessing equal status or function, as εἰμί can act as an equative verb; cf. *Copulative*.

Erasmus—Renaissance scholar credited with standardizing the pronunciation of Koine Greek using Latin; also produced the first published Greek New Testament, coming off the new Gutenberg printing press in 1516. Erasmus's text was the basis for other published Greek New Testaments, including the Beza text used by the King James translators for the 1611 Authorized Version.

Eta Pure ("η pure")—first declension stem with η throughout the singular.

First Active—that perfect and pluperfect active form that retains the kappa of the perfect active tense suffix.

First Class—conditional sentence category; condition is assumed true; the mood used is indicative.

First Passive—that future and aorist passive form that retains the theta of the passive suffix of the sixth principal part.

Fourth Class—conditional sentence category; condition is assumed undetermined, but remote; the mood used is optative.

Future Perfect—rare use of the perfect tense with a focus on the future continuing effects of the completed action; only Heb 8:11 in the New Testament.

Futuristic Future—use of future tense in which the context reveals a simple focus on action to happen in the future; also called "predictive future."

Gamma Nasal—a consonant combination in which the initial gamma takes on a nasal pronounciation.

Genitive Absolute—a participle in the genitive case with no syntactical relationship to the rest of the sentence; an abrupt change of subject from participle to main verb is typical; the participle adds information, but is independent of the main verb and its subject; a genitive noun is treated as "subject" of the participle.

Gradation—changes which vowels undergo in the process of word formation.

Hidden Stem—descriptive term for tense stems whose actual form is hidden in the present tense stem formulation of a verb memorized as vocabulary.

Historical Present—in a narrative context of past tense, use of a present tense as a dramatic aspect for vividness, but translated as past tense with the past context.

Idiom—meaning which transcends denotation of individual grammatical elements, the linguistic expressions of a given language that lie closest to the heart of a particular culture and time.

Imperative Future—use of future tense in which the context reveals a focus on command.

Impersonal Verb—a verb always used in neuter third person singular, such as δεῖ and ἔξεστι.

Improper Diphthongs—vowels containing iota subscript; the iota might seem to create a diphthong sound, but does not, because the iota actually is not pronounced.

Inceptive Imperfect—use of imperfect tense in which the context reveals a focus on the beginning of the action, translated, "began to . . . ."

Independent Clause—a verb and its related subject.

Indirect Discourse—indirect quotation; grammatically functions as direct object of the main verb.

Indirect Middle—the verb's subject acts with self-interest in the action.

Infinite—verbal forms not limited by a subject, such as infinitives and participles.

Inflection—patterns of changes in word endings that indicate word relationships.

Ingressive Aorist—use of an aorist tense in which the context reveals an emphasis upon the beginning of the action; also called "inceptive aorist."

Intensive Perfect—use of perfect tense in which the context reveals an emphasis upon the continuing effects of the completed action.

Intensive Pronoun—specialized use of the third personal pronoun either for the equivalent of the English adjective "the same" or for a reflexive idea (i.e., "-self").

Interior Cases—descriptive term for the genitive and dative rows of a paradigm.

Interjection—part of speech such as exclamatory words that stand alone in sentence.

Intervocalic Sigma—a sigma between two vowels; the construction can volatilize, the sigma dropping, the remaining two vowels contracting.

Intransitive Verb—does not require a direct object for completion. ("He ran.")

Itacism—spelling variations in our Greek manuscripts resulting from confusion of like-sounding vowels or diphthongs, such as interchanging ι and ει.

Iterative Perfect—use of perfect tense in which the context reveals an emphasis upon repetition over an interval of time; the past is the point.

Kappa Aorist—are three -μι verbs in particular that substitute a -κα pattern for the -σα first aorist suffix (δίδωμι, τίθημι, ἵημι).

Lectionary—Christian worship developed a system of readings (called "lections") from the Gospels and Epistles, apparently following the pattern of synagogue worship, which used readings from the Law and the Prophets each Sabbath. The Christian readings were coordinated with Sundays and the Christian calendar. A book containing these Scripture lections is called a lectionary. Lectionary study contributes to a knowledge of the history of the New Testament text.

Lengthening—changing a short vowel to a corresponding long vowel or diphthong.

Lexical Form—the form of the initial entry of a word in a Greek dictionary; for verbs, the present active indicative, first person singular form; for nouns, the nominative singular form.

Lexical Middle—verbs in the dictionary ending in -μαι. In an earlier generation of grammars, these verbs had been analyzed as "deponent," a Latin category that does not accurately describe or reflect the true nature of the middle voice in Greek verbs.

Liquid—a continuant consonant (i.e., a consonant that sounds as long as air is allowed to flow) pronounced with a breathing pattern through the mouth cavity, but no interruption of airflow, as with stops; generates a class of reactions in word formation; typically includes nasals.

Liquid Aorist—a liquid verb that forms the aorist active indicative by dropping the sigma of the -σα aorist suffix before the liquid consonant that ends the tense stem; only the alpha of the suffix remains; a further reaction can be the occasional compensatory lengthening of a stem vowel.

Liquid Future—a liquid verb that forms the future active indicative with the suffix -εσ, creating an intervocalic sigma that drops, resulting in contraction of the remaining vowels.

Liquid Verb—a verb whose tense stem ends in a liquid consonant.

Location—specifying an individual word's component grammatical parts.

Main Verb—a finite verb, usually; a descriptive term in connection with adverbial participles, whose relationship usually is to a finite verb nearby.

Majuscule—close in meaning to the term uncial (a handwriting style using large letters, similar to our capital letters, all run together) but really refers just to capital letters themselves.

Metathesis—process in word formation of swapping letters, such as τκ to κτ.

Middle Voice—the subject reflects the verbal action upon itself. ("I hit myself.")

Minuscule—a reform in handwriting beginning about the ninth century using small case letters in a cursive (connected together) style.

Modal Verb—an auxiliary verb that indicates mood, particularly contingency, such as "might," "could," "should."

Monosyllabic—a word having just one syllable.

Morphology—study of phonology (pronunciation, phonetic change, and accent) and word formation (inflection, derivation, and compounds). Cf. *Accidence*.

Moveable ν—addition of the letter ν to a pronominal suffix to smooth pronunciation for the following word beginning with a vowel, or when the verb comes at the end of a clause or sentence.

Nasal—a continuant consonant (i.e., a consonant that sounds as long as air is allowed to flow) produced with a breathing pattern through the nose, but creating no friction (noise), in contrast to liquids, sibilants, and stops; generates a class of reactions in word formation.

Nomina Sacra—sacred names abbreviated in manuscripts of the New Testament as standard scribal procedure, indicated with a line above the letters.

Nominative Absolute—a nominative with no inherent grammatical relationship to the sentence.

Non-thematic—joining the pronominal suffix directly to the tense stem without a thematic vowel.

Non-thematic Second Aorists—a small class of verbs that includes the -ω verbs ἀναβαινω and γινώσκω and the -μι verb ἵστημι that do not use a thematic vowel in the second aorist active indicative.

Oblique—all other cases besides the nominative; sometimes called "objective" cases, as they function as objects of prepositions or direct/indirect objects of verbs, whereas the nominative does not.

Open Vowels—the mouth is relatively open as the vowels are pronounced. The degree of openness often is illustrated in the "vowel pyramid," but any graphic is an attempt to schematize the relative position of tongue and jaw.

Positions of the tongue up and down are described as high, medium, and low. Positions of the tongue front to back are known as front, central, and back. The

high	ι		υ
medium	η		ω
low	ε	α	o
	front	center	back

seven vowel pronunciations combine these two tongue positions: three vowels are low (front = ε, central = α, and back = o), two vowels are medium (front = η and back = ω), and two vowels are high (front = ι and back = υ). Of these, alpha is the most open, iota and upsilon the least open (cf. *Closed Vowels*).

Ordinal Numerals—ordering numbers indicating sequence ("first," "second"); used as adjectives.

Ὅτι Recitative—used to refer to the occurrence of ὅτι understood to be introducing a direct quote; the ὅτι is left untranslated.

Oxytone—any noun having an acute accent in the ultima of the lexical form.

Paradigm—a pattern used to illustrate all other words in that class or category.

Passive Voice—the subject of the verb receives the verbal action. ("I was hit.")

Penult—the second syllable from the end of a Greek word.

Perfect—a Greek tense that expresses completed action with ongoing *present* consequences, similar to the English present perfect.

Periphrasis—a construction using two verbal forms, a participle and a linking verb, when one finite verb would have sufficed; "phrasing around," a roundabout way of saying something; represents a typical Koine tendency toward overemphasis.

Persistent Accent—in noun declensions, the tendency of the accent to remain in the syllable of the lexical form, in as much as rules allow.

Pluperfect—in English, the tense expressing past action completed prior to a specified time, formed with a past participle and auxiliary verbs: "had written"; in Greek, ongoing *past* consequences.

Polysyllabic—a word having three or more syllables.

Position—used in several ways; with **adjectives**, the article is constructed with the adjective (called "articular" construction) indicating attributive function; cf. *Attributive, Articular*; with **word order**, the position first in a clause, i.e, the "primary" or "positive" position, or any position later in the clause, the

Primary Position

primary position = emphatic repetition
of pronominal suffix

Σὺ πιστεύεις εἰς τὸν υἱὸν τοῦ ἀνθρώπου;
[Do you (yourself) believe in the Son of Man? (Jn 9:35)]

Postpositive Position

postpositive position

Οὕτως γὰρ ἠγάπησεν ὁ θεὸς τὸν κόσμον,
[For God loved the world in this manner (Jn 3:16)]

"postpositive" position. Word order is not as crucial in Greek as in English, but position can indicate *some* meaning. The head of the sentence or the clause is called the "primary position," or also "positive position." A Greek word can be placed in primary position for *emphasis*. A common example occurs with personal pronouns. The Greek verb already has a pronominal suffix. A personal pronoun beginning the clause intensifies the meaning from "you," for example, to "you *yourself*." Some words never occur first in a clause, so are called *postpositives*. Examples would be γάρ and δέ. Postpositives are positioned as the second or later word in the Greek clause. Their regular position in English translation is first.

Postpositives—words that never occur first in a clause.

Potentiality—the potential reality of a statement, with degrees of contingency.

Predicate Adjective—an adjective in predicate position (that is, in an anarthrous construction).

Predicate Nominative—a nominative noun in predicate position (anarthrous).

Predicative Position—an anarthrous adjective used to make an assertion about a related noun, which requires a form of "to be," whether implicit or explicit.

Preposition—a word "pre-positioned" before a substantive to clarify the grammatical connection between that substantive and other elements in the sentence, such as verbs or other substantives. Cf. *Adverbial Preposition, Proper Preposition*.

Preterit—the simple past tense in English: "wrote."

Primary Position—the head of a sentence or clause; also called "positive position."

Proclitics—a word having no accent of its own that leans to the following word.

Progressive Imperfect—alternate name for the durative imperfect.

Progressive Present—alternate name for the durative present.

Pronominal Suffixes—endings attached to tense stems that give person and number of the subject.

Proper Prepositions—former adverbs now composed exclusively with nouns; never used by themselves; that is, they always are part of a prepositional phrase. Cf. *Adverbial Preposition*.

Prophetic Aorist—use of aorist tense in prophetic contexts that reveal an emphasis upon the action as if already accomplished fact, the surety of fulfillment.

Protasis—the "if" clause of a conditional sentence that puts forth the condition; functions and diagrams as a dependent clause.

Punctiliar—aoristic verbal aspect taken as a point in time in a particular context.

Recessive Accent—in verb conjugations, the tendency of the accent to move as far away from the ultima as rules allow.

Reciprocal Middle—action as middle voice in which the subject participates in the action as part of a group cooperating together.

Recto—in manuscripts, normally the right-hand book page; however, with papyri, the horizontal layer of reed strips, whether front or back page.

Reduplication—creation of a tense stem prefix by repeating an opening consonant and inserting a vowel, or by augmenting an opening vowel.

Relative Clause—a dependent (subordinate) clause introduced by a relative pronoun.

Restrictive Attributive—an articular adjective positioned after an articular noun to add emphatic force (ὁ ποιμὴν ὁ καλός = "the *good* shepherd," Jn 10:11). Cf. *Ascriptive Attributive.*

Scripto Continua—style of writing in ancient manuscripts of the New Testament; all letters were formed as uncials, with no word divisions and no punctuation.

Second Active—an alternate perfect and pluperfect active form that drops the kappa of the perfect first active tense suffix; also called "strong" perfect and "strong" pluperfect.

Second Aorist—an alternate form of the aorist tense stem that does not affect meaning; also called "strong" aorist (The form probably is older than first aorist, having survived the developmental tendency to alter aorist stems with a tense suffix, which generated a "weak" or "first" aorist.)

Second Class—conditional sentence category; condition is assumed false; mood used is indicative.

Second Passive—an alternate future and aorist passive form that drops the theta of the passive suffix of the sixth principal part.

Semivowels—the two vowels ι and υ whose history includes an older vocalization as a consonant, as in "y" and "w." Affects pronunciation and word formation. Also known as consonantal iota and consonantal upsilon.

Sharp's Rule—actually six rules, together clarifying the significance of personal nouns joined by καί, grammatical observations—under specific parameters—that reveal whether these nouns are thought of as distinct entities or as the same person or aspect. As formulated by Granville Sharp in 1798, the nouns must be: (1) of personal description and (2) of the same case. I have taken liberty to condense Sharp's rules into the following format ("A" = article, "N" = noun, "Same" = applying to the same person or aspect, "Distinct" = applying to distinct persons or aspects):

SAME: 1. $[A_1N_1]$ καί N_2
2. $[A_1N_1]$ $[A_2N_2]$ (exception: a string of dependent genitives)
3. $[A_1N_1]$ N_2
DISTINCT: 4. When the nouns do not relate to personal description
5. N_1 καί N_2 (exception: constructions with numeral εἷς)
6. $[A_1N_1]$ καί $[A_2N_2]$

Once studied, these six rules can be reduced even further: (1) any construction with καί absent relates to the same person or aspect (#2-3); (2) any *symmetrical* construction with καί—all nouns articular or *all* nouns anarthrous—relates to the distinct persons or aspects (#5-6); and (3) only one construction with καί relates to the same person, and this construction is asymmetrical; only the first noun has the article (#1). Rule #1 traditionally is the preeminent one for exegesis.

Sigma Volatilization—a pattern of interaction between the sibilant σ and the stop consonants.

Simple Sentence—an independent clause by itself.

Spurious Diphthong—when ει results from combinations other than ε + ι, and ου results from combinations other than ο + υ, or compensatory lengthening has taken place.

Stop—a consonant pronounced with a breathing pattern through the mouth cavity, creating air friction, hence a noise, as with liquids, but further complicated by the use of the tongue to stop the airflow momentarily, both at various points and with varying degrees of release.

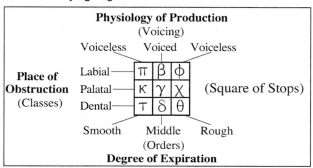

The two important questions about stop sounds are *where* and *how*. First, answering the question *where* provides two sets of terms: (1) those related to **physiology of production**, i.e., the use of the vocal chords ("voiced," "voiceless"), and (2) those related to the **place of obstruction**, controlling the airflow ("stops"). The stop consonants created with the vocal chords ("voiced") are β, γ, δ. The stop consonants created without the vocal chords ("voiceless") involve the two sets of π, κ, τ and φ, χ, θ. Further, these stop consonants subdivide into three stop *classes* of where the airflow is obstructed: (1) at the throat ("palatal/guttural"), (2) behind the teeth ("dental/lingual"), or (3) with the lips ("labial").

Second, answering the question regarding *how* provides a third set of terms related to stop consonant sounds. The direction and degree of the airflow can be controlled, determining how noisy the sound is. Noise is created by the friction of moving air. The air can be moved through two main passage ways, the nose or the mouth. Air forced through the nasal cavity escapes without friction (*nasals* μ and ν). Air forced through the mouth cavity escapes with only slight friction, hence a little noise (*liquids* λ and ρ, and σ). However, air moved through the mouth cavity also can add further sophistication to sound production through the manipulation of tongue or lips. Airflow can be manipulated both through specific placement (labial, palatal, dental) and through degree of air allowed to flow in that placement. How the obstruction of the air is removed creates **degrees of expiration** of the air—the three stop *orders*. The flow may be released: (1) completely, with less noise, by smoothly and sharply releasing the blocked air ("sharp," "smooth")—π, κ, τ, (2) somewhat, with a little more noise, by more openly releasing the blocked air ("flat," "middle")—β, γ, δ, or (3) barely, with even greater noise, by fully aspirating the sound with an open release ("aspirate," "rough")—φ, χ, θ. The crux of the matter relates to the voiceless stops—the smooth (sharp) π, κ, τ, and the rough (aspirate) φ, χ, θ—on either side of the voiced. Note how these often interrelate in Greek.

Finally, a ***continuant*** is a consonant whose sound quality does not change as long as air is allowed to flow (voiced = μ, ν, λ; voiceless = σ, φ, χ, θ). A *fricative* is a consonant forced through a constricted passage. Technically, the aspirates φ, χ, θ are not stops, but fricative continuants. The rough breathing is a fricative continuant, which explains some volatilizations.

Subordinate Clause—See *Dependent Clause*.

Subordinate Conjunction—conjunction that introduces a dependent clause; quite common is ὅτι.

Substantive—any word functioning as a noun or noun equivalent.

Surrogate Subject—descriptive term for the grammatical element associated with the action of the infinite forms of infinitives and participles.

Syllabic Augment—augmentation of a tense stem that begins with a consonant by adding a vowel, thereby adding another syllable to the word.

Syncopation—suppressing a short vowel between two single consonants for pronunciation; "weak syncopation" means the suppression occurs in only three forms (the genitive and dative singular, dative plural); "strong syncopation" means that the suppression occurs in *all* forms except for the nominative singular.

Syntax—word arrangements that carry meaning across through particular use in a sentence—in contrast to morphology (or, accidence), which studies word formation and inflection, as well as rudimentary elements of grammar.

Temporal Augment—augmentation of a tense stem beginning with a vowel by lengthening that vowel, theoretically thereby adding time to the pronunciation.

Textual Criticism—the study of differing copies of manuscripts to determine the most likely original reading, but also, in New Testament textual criticism, to write a history of those manuscripts.

Third Class—conditional sentence category; condition is assumed undetermined, but possible; mood used is subjunctive.

Transitive Verb—verbal action that takes a direct object. ("She wrote a book.")

Two Termination—adjectives with just two inflections for the three genders.

Ultima—the last syllable on the end of a Greek word.

Uncial—a handwriting style using all large letters, similar to our capital letters.

Verso—in manuscripts, normally the left-hand book page; however, with papyri, the vertical layer of reed strips, whether front or back page.

Volatilization—a descriptive term applied to the patterned reactions in word formation surrounding particular letter combinations; the most common are those involving sigma, stops, theta, elision, and contraction.

APPENDIX 2
PARADIGMS

These paradigms are a summary of material presented in the grammar. The paradigms are not exhaustive. Certain forms are not covered in these paradigms, such as certain third declension patterns, for example. Movable -ν is included in most forms, since this pattern is so common in the New Testament.

Declensions

Second Declension			
Mas/Fem		Neuter	
Sg	Pl	Sg	Pl
-ος	-οι	-ον	-α
-ου	-ων	-ου	-ων
-ῳ	-οις	-ῳ	-οις
-ον	-ους	-ον	-α

First Declension						Third Declension					
Singular					Pl	Mas/Fem		Neuter			
Fem			Mas		All	All		Sg	Pl	Sg	Pl
-α	-η	-α	-ης	-ας	-αι	-ς, --	-ες	--	-α	-ος	-η
-ας	-ης	-ης	-ου	-ου	-ων	-ος	-ων	-ος	-ων	-ους	-ων
-ᾳ	-η	-η	-η	-ᾳ	-αις	-ι	-σιν	-ι	-σιν	-ει	-σιν
-αν	-ην	-αν	-ην	-αν	-ας	-α, -ν	-ας	--	-α	-ος	-η

Greek Article

Masculine		Neuter		Feminine	
ὁ	οἱ	τό	τά	ἡ	αἱ
τοῦ	τῶν	τοῦ	τῶν	τῆς	τῶν
τῷ	τοῖς	τῷ	τοῖς	τῇ	ταῖς
τόν	τούς	τό	τά	τήν	τάς

Nouns

2D Masculine		2D Neuter		2D Mas. Oxytone	
λόγος	λόγοι	δῶρον	δῶρα	υἱός	υἱοί
λόγου	λόγων	δώρου	δώρων	υἱοῦ	υἱῶν
λόγῳ	λόγοις	δώρῳ	δώροις	υἱῷ	υἱοῖς
λόγον	λόγους	δῶρον	δῶρα	υἱόν	υἱούς
2D Neu. Oxytone		**2D Feminine**		**1D "α pure"**	
ἱερόν	ὁδός	ὁδός	ὁδοί	καρδία	καρδίαι
ἱεροῦ	ὁδοῦ	ὁδοῦ	ὁδῶν	καρδίας	καρδιῶν
ἱερῷ	ὁδῷ	ὁδῷ	ὁδοῖς	καρδίᾳ	καρδίαις
ἱερόν	ὁδόν	ὁδόν	ὁδούς	καρδίαν	καρδίας
1D Antepenult		**1D "α pure" Oxytone**		**1D "η pure"**	
ἀλήθεια	ἀλήθειαι	χαρά	χαραί	ἀγάπη	ἀγάπη
ἀληθείας	ἀληθειῶν	χαρᾶς	χαρῶν	ἀγάπης	ἀγάπης
ἀληθείᾳ	ἀληθείαις	χαρᾷ	χαραῖς	ἀγάπη	ἀγάπη
ἀλήθειαν	ἀληθείας	χαράν	χαράς	ἀγάπην	ἀγάπην
1D "η pure" Oxytone		**1D Sibilant**		**1D Mas. -ης Nom.**	
γραφή	γραφαί	δόξα	δόξαι	μαθητής	μαθηταί
γραφῆς	γραφῶν	δόξης	δοξῶν	μαθητοῦ	μαθητων
γραφῇ	γραφαῖς	δόξῃ	δόξαις	μαθητῇ	μαθηταῖς
γραφήν	γραφάς	δόξαν	δόξας	μαθητήν	μαθητάς
1D Mas. -ας Nom.		**1D "α pure" contract**		**1D "α pure" contract**	
μεσσίας	μεσσίαι	γῆ	-------	συκῆ	-------
μεσσίου	μεσσιῶν	γῆς	-------	συκῆς	-------
μεσσίᾳ	μεσσίαις	γῇ	-------	συκῇ	-------
μεσσίαν	μεσσίας	γῆν	-------	συκῆν	-------

1D "α pure" contract		1D Proper Name		Irreg. Proper Name	
μνᾶ	-------	Ἰωάννης	-------	Ἰησοῦς	-------
μνᾶς	-------	Ἰωάννου	-------	Ἰησοῦ	-------
μνᾷ	-------	Ἰωάννῃ	-------	Ἰησοῦ	-------
μνᾶν	-------	Ἰωάννην	-------	Ἰησοῦν	-------
3D Labial		**3D Palatal**		**3D Dental -ν acc.**	
λίψ	λίβες	σάρξ	σάρκες	χάρις	χάριτες
λιβός	λίβων	σαρκός	σαρκῶν	χάριτος	χαρίτων
λιβί	λίψι(ν)	σαρκί	σαρξί(ν)	χάριτι	χάρισι(ν)
λίβα	λίβας	σάρκα	σάρκας	χάριν	χάριτας
3D Dental -α acc.		**3D Den. -ητος stem**		**3D Den. -ματ stem**	
ἐλπίς	ἐλπίδες	πραΰτης	πραΰτητες	σῶμα	σώματα
ἐλπίδος	ἐλπίδων	πραΰτητος	πραυτήτων	σώματος	σωμάτων
ἐλπίδι	ἐλπίσι(ν)	πραΰτητι	πραΰτησιν	σώματι	σώμασιν
ἐλπίδα	ἐλπίδας	πραΰτητα	πραΰτητας	σῶμα	σώματα
3D Den. -ντ stem		**3D Den. -ντ stem**		**3D Den. -κτ stem**	
ἄρχων	ἄρχοντες	ὀδούς	ὀδόντες	νύξ	νύκτες
ἄρχοντος	ἀρχόντων	ὀδόντος	ὀδόντων	νυκτός	νυκτῶν
ἄρχοντι	ἄρχουσιν	ὀδόντι	ὀδοῦσιν	νυκτί	νύξι(ν)
ἄρχοντα	ἄρχοντας	ὀδόντα	ὀδόντας	νύκτα	νύκτας
3D Sibilant -ος nom.		**3D Liquid long η**		**3D Liquid long ω**	
ἔθνος	ἔθνη	σωτήρ	σωτῆρες	αἰών	αἰῶνες
ἔθνους	ἐθνῶν	σωτῆρος	σωτήρων	αἰῶνος	αἰώνων
ἔθνει	ἔθνεσιν	σωτῆρι	σωτῆρσιν	αἰῶνι	αἰῶσιν
ἔθνος	ἔθνη	σωτῆρα	σωτῆρας	αἰῶνα	αἰῶνας
3D Liquid η→ε		**3D Liquid ω→ο**		**3D Weak Syncopation**	
ἀστήρ	ἀστέρες	εἰκών	εἰκόνες	πατήρ	πατέρες
ἀστέρος	ἀστέρων	εἰκόνος	εἰκόνων	πατρός	πατέρων
ἀστέρι	ἀστέρσιν	εἰκόνι	εἰκόσιν	πατρί	πατράσιν
ἀστέρα	ἀστέρας	εἰκόνα	εἰκόνας	πατέρα	πατέρας
3D Strong Syncopation		**3D Vowel -ι stem**		**3D Vowel -υ stem**	
ἀνήρ	ἄνδρες	πίστις	πίστεις	ἰχθύς	ἰχθύες
ἀνδρός	ἀνδρῶν	πίστεως	πίστεων	ἰχθύος	ἰχθύων
ἀνδρί	ἀνδράσιν	πίστει	πίστεσιν	ἰχθύι	ἰχθύσιν
ἄνδρα	ἄνδρας	πίστιν	πίστεις	ἰχθύν	ἰχθύας

3D Diphthong -ευ stem		3D Diphthong -ου stem		
ἱερεύς	ἱερεῖς	νοῦς	νόες	
ἱερέως	ἱερέων	νοός	νοῶν	
ἱερεῖ	ἱερεῦσιν	νοΐ	νουσίν	
ἱερέα	ἱερεῖς	νοῦν	νόας	

Adjectives

2D Masculine Oxytone		2D Neuter Oxytone		1D η pure Oxytone	
ἀγαθός	ἀγαθοί	ἀγαθόν	ἀγαθά	ἀγαθή	ἀγαθαί
ἀγαθοῦ	ἀγαθῶν	ἀγαθοῦ	ἀγαθῶν	ἀγαθῆς	ἀγαθῶν
ἀγαθῷ	ἀγαθοῖς	ἀγαθῷ	ἀγαθοῖς	ἀγαθῇ	ἀγαθαῖς
ἀγαθόν	ἀγαθούς	ἀγαθόν	ἀγαθά	ἀγαθήν	ἀγαθάς
2D Antepenult Acute		**2D Antepenult Acute**		**1D α pure**	
δίκαιος	δίκαιοι	δίκαιον	δίκαια	δικαία	δίκαιαι
δικαίου	δικαίων	δικαίου	δικαίων	δικαίας	δικαίων
δικαίῳ	δικαίοις	δικαίῳ	δικαίοις	δικαίᾳ	δικαίαις
δίκαιον	δικαίους	δίκαιον	δίκαια	δικαίαν	δικαίας
2D Contraction, Mas.		**Neuter**		**Feminine**	
χρυσοῦς	χρυσοῖ	χρυσοῦν	χρυσᾶ	χρυσῆ	χρυσαῖ
χρυσοῦ	χρυσῶν	χρυσοῦς	χρυσῶν	χρυσῆς	χρυσῶν
χρυσῷ	χρυσοῖς	χρυσῷ	χρυσοῖς	χρυσῇ	χρυσαῖς
χρυσοῦν	χρυσοῦς	χρυσοῦν	χρυσᾶ	χρυσήν	χρυσᾶς
2D 2 Termination M/F		**Neuter**			
ἔρημος	ἔρημοι	ἔρημον	ἔρημα		
ἐρήμου	ἐρήμων	ἐρήμου	ἐρήμων		
ἐρήμῳ	ἐρήμοις	ἐρήμῳ	ἐρήμοις		
ἔρημον	ἐρήμους	ἔρημον	ἔρημα		
3D 2 Termination M/F		**Neuter**			
ἀληθής	ἀληθεῖς	ἀληθές	ἀληθῆ		
ἀληθοῦς	ἀληθῶν	ἀληθοῦς	ἀληθῶν		
ἀληθεῖ	ἀληθέσιν	ἀληθεῖ	ἀληθέσιν		
ἀληθῆ	ἀληθεῖς	ἀληθές	ἀληθῆ		

3D Liquid 2 Term. M/F		Neuter			
ἄφρων	ἄφρονες	ἄφρον	ἄφρονα		
ἄφρονος	ἀφρόνων	ἄφρονος	ἀφρόνων		
αφρονι	ἄφροσιν	αφρονι	ἄφροσιν		
ἄφρονα	ἄφρονας	ἄφρον	ἄφρονα		
Mixed 1: 3-3-1 Mas.		Neuter		Feminine	
ταχύς	ταχεῖς	ταχύ	ταχέα	ταχεῖα	ταχεῖαι
ταχέως	ταχέων	ταχέως	ταχέων	ταχείας	ταχειῶν
ταχεῖ	ταχέσιν	ταχεῖ	ταχέσιν	ταχείᾳ	ταχείαις
ταχύν	ταχεῖς	ταχύ	ταχέα	ταχεῖαν	ταχείας
Mixed 2: 3-3-1 Mas.		Neuter		Feminine	
πᾶς	πάντες	πᾶν	πάντα	πᾶσα	πᾶσαι
παντός	πάντων	παντός	πάντων	πάσης	πασῶν
παντί	πᾶσιν	παντί	πᾶσιν	πάσῃ	πάσαις
πάντα	πάντας	πᾶν	πάντα	πᾶσαν	πάσας
Mixed 3: 3-3-1 Mas.		Neuter		Feminine	
μέλας	μέλανες	μέλαν	μέλανα	μέλαινα	μέλαιναι
μέλανος	μελάνων	μέλανος	μελάνων	μελαίνης	μελαινῶν
μέλανι	μέλασιν	μέλανι	μέλασιν	μελαίνῃ	μελαίναις
μέλανα	μέλανας	μέλαν	μέλανα	μέλαιναν	μελαίνας
Mixed 4: 3-2-1 Mas.		Neuter		Feminine	
μέγας	μεγάλοι	μέγα	μεγάλα	μεγάλη	μεγάλαι
μεγάλου	μεγάλων	μεγάλου	μεγάλων	μεγάλης	μεγάλων
μεγάλῳ	μεγάλοις	μεγάλῳ	μεγάλοις	μεγάλῃ	μεγάλαις
μέγαν	μεγάλους	μέγα	μεγάλα	μεγάλην	μεγάλας
Mixed 5: 3-2-1 Mas.		Neuter		Feminine	
πολύς	πολλοί	πολύ	πολλά	πολλή	πολλαί
πολλοῦ	πολλῶν	πολλοῦ	πολλῶν	πολλῆς	πολλῶν
πολλῷ	πολλοῖς	πολλῷ	πολλοῖς	πολλῇ	πολλαῖς
πολύν	πολλούς	πολύ	πολλά	πολλήν	πολλάς

Comparisons

Comparative, Mas.		Neuter		Feminine	
-τερος	-τεροι	-τερον	-τερα	-τερα	-τεραι
-τερου	-τερων	-τερου	-τερων	-τερας	-τερων
-τερῳ	-τεροις	-τερῳ	-τεροις	-τερᾳ	-τεραις
-τερον	-τερους	-τερον	-τερα	-τεραν	-τερας
Superlative, Mas.		Neuter		Feminine	
-τατος	-τατοι	-τατον	-τατα	-τατα	-ταται
-τατου	-τατων	-τατου	-τατων	-τατας	-τατων
-τατῳ	-τατοις	-τατῳ	-τατοις	-τατᾳ	-ταταις
-τατον	-τατους	-τατον	-τατα	-ταταν	-τατας
Comparative, M/F		Neuter			
-ιων	-ιονες	-ιον	-ιονα		
-ιονος	-ιονων	-ιονος	-ιονων		
-ιονι	-ιοσι	-ιονι	-ιοσι		
-ιονα	-ιονας	-ιον	-ιονα		
Superlative, Mas.		Neuter		Feminine	
-ιστος	-ιστοι	-ιστον	-ιστα	-ιστη	-ισται
-ιστου	-ιστων	-ιστου	-ιστων	-ιστης	-ιστων
-ιστῳ	-ιστοις	-ιστῳ	-ιστοις	-ιστη	-ισταις
-ιστον	-ιστους	-ιστον	-ιστα	-ιστην	-ιστας

Numerals: Cardinal

"One," Masculine		Neuter		Feminine	
εἷς	-------	ἕν	-------	μία	-------
ἑνός	-------	ἑνός	-------	μιᾶς	-------
ἑνί	-------	ἑνί	-------	μιᾷ	-------
ἕνα	-------	ἕν	-------	μίαν	-------
"Two," Mas/Fem/Neu					
-------	δύο				
-------	δύο				
-------	δυσί				
-------	δύο				

"Three," Mas/Fem	Neuter	
------- τρεῖς	------- τρία	
------- τριῶν	------- τριῶν	
------- τρισί	------- τρισί	
------- τρεῖς	------- τρία	
"Four," Mas/Fem	**Neuter**	
------- τέσσαρες	------- τέσσαρα	
------- τεσσάρων	------- τεσσάρων	
------- τέσσαρσι	------- τέσσαρσι	
------- τέσσαρας	------- τέσσαρα	
"Two hundred," Mas	**Neuter**	**Feminine**
------- διακόσιοι	------- διακόσια	------- διακόσιαι
------- διακοσίων	------- διακοσίων	------- διακοσίων
------- διακοσίοις	------- διακοσίοις	------- διακοσίαις
------- διακοσίους	------- διακόσια	------- διακοσίας

Numerals: Ordinal

"First," Masculine		Neuter		Feminine	
πρῶτος	πρῶτοι	πρῶτον	πρῶτα	πρώτη	πρῶται
πρώτου	πρώτων	πρώτου	πρώτων	πρώτης	πρώτων
πρώτῳ	πρώτοις	πρώτῳ	πρώτοις	πρώτῃ	πρώταις
πρῶτον	πρώτους	πρῶτον	πρῶτα	πρώτην	πρώτας

Pronouns

Personal, 1st (I, we)			
ἐγώ	ἡμεῖς		
ἐμοῦ	ἡμῶν		
ἐμοί	ἡμῖν		
ἐμέ	ἡμᾶς		
Personal, 2nd (you)			
σύ	ὑμεῖς		
σοῦ	ὑμῶν		
σοί	ὑμῖν		
σέ	ὑμᾶς		

Pers., 3ʳᵈ (he, they)		Neuter (it, they)		Feminine (she, they)	
αὐτός	αὐτοί	αὐτό	αὐτά	αὐτή	αὐταί
αὐτοῦ	αὐτῶν	αὐτοῦ	αὐτῶν	αὐτῆς	αὐτῶν
αὐτῷ	αὐτοῖς	αὐτῷ	αὐτοῖς	αὐτῇ	αὐταῖς
αὐτόν	αὐτούς	αὐτό	αὐτά	αὐτήν	αὐτάς
Possessive, 1ˢᵗ Sg. (my)		Neuter (Sg.)		Feminine (Sg.)	
ἐμός	ἐμοί	ἐμόν	ἐμά	ἐμή	ἐμαί
ἐμοῦ	ἐμῶν	ἐμοῦ	ἐμῶν	ἐμῆς	ἐμῶν
ἐμῷ	ἐμοῖς	ἐμῷ	ἐμοῖς	ἐμῇ	ἐμαῖς
ἐμόν	ἐμούς	ἐμόν	ἐμά	ἐμήν	ἐμάς
Possessive, 1ˢᵗ Pl. (our)		Neuter (Pl.)		Feminine (Pl.)	
ἡμέτερος	ἡμέτεροι	ἡμέτερον	ἡμέτερα	ἡμετέρα	ἡμέτεραι
ἡμετέρου	ἡμετέρων	ἡμετέρου	ἡμετέρων	ἡμετέρας	ἡμετέρων
ἡμετέρῳ	ἡμετέροις	ἡμετέρῳ	ἡμετέροις	ἡμετέρα	ἡμετέραις
ἡμέτερον	ἡμετέρους	ἡμέτερον	ἡμέτερα	ἡμετέραν	ἡμετέρας
Possessive, 2ⁿᵈ (your)		Neuter (Sg.)		Feminine (Sg.)	
σός	σοί	σόν	σά	σή	σαί
σοῦ	σῶν	σοῦ	σῶν	σῆς	σῶν
σῷ	σοῖς	σῷ	σοῖς	σῇ	σαῖς
σόν	σούς	σόν	σά	σήν	σάς
Possessive, 2ⁿᵈ (your)		Neuter (Pl.)		Feminine (Pl.)	
ὑμέτερος	ὑμέτεροι	ὑμέτερον	ὑμέτερα	ὑμετέρα	ὑμέτεραι
ὑμετέρου	ὑμετέρων	ὑμετέρου	ὑμετέρων	ὑμετέρας	ὑμετέρων
ὑμετέρῳ	ὑμετέροις	ὑμετέρῳ	ὑμετέροις	ὑμετέρα	ὑμετέραις
ὑμέτερον	ὑμετέρους	ὑμέτερον	ὑμέτερα	ὑμετέραν	ὑμετέρας
Poss., 3ʳᵈ (his, their)		Neuter (its, their)		Feminine (her, their)	
ἴδιος	ἴδιοι	ἴδιον	ἴδια	ἰδία	ἴδιαι
ἰδίου	ἰδίων	ἰδίου	ἰδίων	ἰδίας	ἰδίων
ἰδίῳ	ἰδίοις	ἰδίῳ	ἰδίοις	ἰδίᾳ	ἰδίαις
ἴδιον	ἰδίους	ἴδιον	ἴδια	ἰδίαν	ἰδίας
Reflexive, 1ˢᵗ (myself)		Neuter		F (myself, ourselves)	
---------	---------	---------	---------	---------	---------
ἐμαυτοῦ	ἑαυτῶν	---------	---------	ἐμαυτῆς	ἑαυτῶν
ἐμαυτῷ	ἑαυτοῖς	---------	---------	ἐμαυτῇ	ἑαυταῖς
ἐμαυτόν	ἑαυτούς	---------	---------	ἐμαυτήν	ἑαυτάς

Reflex., 2nd (yourself)		Neuter		F (yourself, yourselves)	
---------	---------	---------	---------	---------	---------
σεαυτοῦ	ἑαυτῶν	---------	---------	σεαυτῆς	ἑαυτῶν
σεαυτῷ	ἑαυτοῖς	---------	---------	σεαυτῇ	ἑαυταῖς
σεαυτόν	ἑαυτούς	---------	---------	σεαυτήν	ἑαυτάς

Reflex., 3rd (himself)		N (itself, themselves)		F (herself, themselves)	
---------	---------	---------	---------	---------	---------
ἑαυτοῦ	ἑαυτῶν	ἑαυτοῦ	ἑαυτῶν	ἑαυτῆς	ἑαυτῶν
ἑαυτῷ	ἑαυτοῖς	ἑαυτῷ	ἑαυτοῖς	ἑαυτῇ	ἑαυταῖς
ἑαυτόν	ἑαυτούς	ἑαυτό	ἑαυτά	ἑαυτήν	ἑαυτάς

Recip. (one another)					
---------	---------				
---------	ἀλλήλων				
---------	ἀλλήλοις				
---------	ἀλλήλους				

Demon. (this, these)		Neuter (this, these)		Feminine (this, these)	
οὗτος	οὗτοι	τοῦτο	ταῦτα	αὕτη	αὗται
τούτου	τούτων	τούτου	τούτων	ταύτης	τούτων
τούτῳ	τούτοις	τούτῳ	τούτοις	ταύτῃ	ταύταις
τοῦτον	τούτους	τοῦτο	ταῦτα	ταύτην	ταύτας

Demon. (that, those)		Neuter (that, those)		Feminine (that, those)	
ἐκεῖνος	ἐκεῖνοι	ἐκεῖνο	ἐκεῖνα	ἐκείνη	ἐκεῖναι
ἐκείνου	ἐκείνων	ἐκείνου	ἐκείνων	ἐκείνης	ἐκείνων
ἐκείνῳ	ἐκείνοις	ἐκείνῳ	ἐκείνοις	ἐκείνῃ	ἐκείναις
ἐκεῖνον	ἐκείνους	ἐκεῖνο	ἐκεῖνα	ἐκείνην	ἐκείνας

Correlative (such)		Neuter (such)		Feminine (such)	
τοιοῦτος	τοιοῦτοι	τοιοῦτο	τοιοαῦτα	τοιαύτη	τοιαῦται
τοιούτου	τοιούτων	τοιούτου	τοιούτων	τοιαύτης	τοιαύτων
τοιούτῳ	τοιούτοις	τοιούτῳ	τοιούτοις	τοιαύτῃ	τοιαύταις
τοιοῦτον	τοιούτους	τοιοῦτο	τοιαῦτα	τοιαύτην	τοιαύτας

Relative (who, whom)		Neuter (which, what)		Feminine (who, whom)	
ὅς	οἵ	ὅ	ἅ	ἥ	αἵ
οὗ	ὧν	οὗ	ὧν	ἧς	ὧν
ᾧ	οἷς	ᾧ	οἷς	ᾗ	αἷς
ὅν	οὕς	ὅ	ἅ	ἥν	ἅς

Interrog. M/F (who?)		Neuter (which? what?)		
τίς	τίνες	τί	τίνα	
τίνος	τίνων	τίνος	τίνων	
τίνι	τίσι(ν)	τίνι	τίσι(ν)	
τίνα	τίνας	τί	τίνα	
Indefinite M/F (certain)		**Neuter** (something)		
τις	τινες	τι	τινα	
τινος	τινων	τινος	τινων	
τινι	τισι(ν)	τινι	τισι(ν)	
τινα	τινας	τι	τινα	
Indef. Rel. (whoever)		Neuter (which ones)		Feminine (whoever)
ὅστις	οἵτινες	ὅτι	ἅτινα	ἥτις αἵτινες
-------	-------	-------	-------	------- -------
-------	-------	-------	-------	------- -------
-------	-------	-------	-------	------- -------
Negative (no one)		Neuter (anything)		Feminine (no one)
οὐδείς	-------	οὐδέν	-------	οὐδεμία -------
οὐδενός	-------	οὐδενός	-------	οὐδεμιᾶς -------
οὐδενί	-------	οὐδενί	-------	οὐδεμιᾷ -------
οὐδένα	-------	οὐδέν	-------	οὐδεμίαν -------

Verb Endings

Omega Verb		MI Verb	
Active	*Mid. / Pass.*	*Active*	*Mid. / Pass.*
Ind—Primary		**Ind—Primary**	
-ω	-μαι	-μι (-ω)	-μαι
-εις	-σαι (η)	-ς (-εις)	-σαι (-η)
-ει	-ται	-σι (-ει)	-ται
-ομεν	-μεθα	-μεν (-ομεν)	-μεθα
-ετε	-σθε	-τε (-ετε)	-σθε
-ουσι	-νται	-ασι (-ουσι)	-νται
Ind—Secondary		**Ind—Secondary**	
-ν	-μην	-ν	-μην
-ς	-σο (-ου, -ω)	-ς	-σο (-ου)
-- (-εν)	-το	--	-το
-μεν	-μεθα	-μεν	-μεθα
-τε	-σθε	-τε	-σθε
-ν, -σαν	-ντο	-ν, -σαν	-ντο
Subjunctive		**Subjunctive**	
-ω	-μαι	-ῶ	-ῶμαι
-ῃς	-ῃ	-ῷς (-ῇς)	-ῷ (-ῇ)
-ῃ	-ται	-ῷ (-ῇ)	-ῷται (-ῇται)
-ωμεν	-μεθα	-ῶμεν	-ώμεθα
-ητε	-σθε	-ῶτε (-ῆτε)	-ῶσθε (-ῆσθε)
-ωσι	-νται	-ῶσι	-ῶνται
Imperative		**Imperative**	
----	----	----	----
--, -ς, -θι	-σο (-ου)	--, -ς, -θι	-σο (-ου)
-τω	-σθω	-τω	-σθω
----	----	----	----
-τε	-σθε	-τε	-σθε
-τωσαν	-σθωσαν	-τωσαν	-σθωσαν
Optative		**Optative**	
-ιμι	-ιμην	-ιμι	-ιμην
-ις	-ιο	-ις	-ιο
-ι	-ιτο	-ι	-ιτο
-ιμεν	-ιμεθα	-ιμεν	-ιμεθα
-ιτε	-ισθε	-ιτε	-ισθε
-ιεν	-ιντο	-ιεν	-ιντο

Omega Verb: Present, Imperfect

PRESENT		IMPERFECT	
Active	*M/P*	*Active*	*M/P*
Indicative		**Indicative**	
λύω	λύομαι	ἔλυον	ἐλυόμην
λύεις	λύῃ	ἔλυες	ἐλύου
λύει	λύεται	ἔλυε	ἐλύετο
λύομεν	λυόμεθα	ἐλύομεν	ἐλυόμεθα
λύετε	λύεσθε	ἐλύετε	ἐλύεσθε
λύουσι	λύονται	ἔλυον	ἐλύοντο
Subjunctive			
λύω	λύωμαι		
λύῃς	λύῃ		
λύῃ	λύηται		
λύωμεν	λυώμεθα		
λύητε	λύησθε		
λύωσι	λύωνται		
Imperative			
-------	-------		
λῦε	λύου		
λυέτω	λυέσθω		
-------	-------		
λύετε	λύεσθε		
λυέτωσαν	-έσθωσαν		
Optative			
λύοιμι	λυοίμην		
λύοις	λύοιο		
λύοι	λύοιτο		
λύοιμεν	λυοίμεθα		
λύοιτε	λύοισθε		
λύοιεν	λύοιντο		
Infinitive			
λύειν	λύεσθαι		
Participle			
λύων	λυόμενος		
λύουσα	λυομένη		
λῦον	λυόμενον		

Omega Verb Contraction: Present Tense

PRESENT ACTIVE			PRESENT MIDDLE/PASSIVE		
ε	ο	α	ε	ο	α
Indicative			**Indicative**		
-ῶ	-ῶ	-ῶ	-οῦμαι	-οῦμαι	-ῶμαι
-εῖς	-οῖς	-ᾷς	-ῇ	-οῖ	-ᾷ
-εῖ	-οῖ	-ᾷ	-εῖται	-οῦται	-ᾶται
-οῦμεν	-οῦμεν	-ῶμεν	-ούμεθα	-ούμεθα	-ώμεθα
-εῖτε	-οῦτε	-ᾶτε	-εῖσθε	-οῦσθε	-ᾶσθε
-οῦσι	-οῦσι	-ῶσι	-οῦνται	-οῦνται	-ῶνται
Subjunctive			**Subjunctive**		
-ῶ	-ῶ	-ῶ	-ῶμαι	-ῶμαι	-ῶμαι
-ῇς	-οῖς	-ᾷς	-ῇ	-οῖ	-ᾷ
-ῇ	-οῖ	-ᾷ	-ῆται	-ῶται	-ᾶται
-ῶμεν	-ῶμεν	-ῶμεν	-ώμεθα	-ώμεθα	-ώμεθα
-ῆτε	-ῶτε	-ᾶτε	-ῆσθε	-ῶσθε	-ᾶσθε
-ῶσι	-ῶσι	-ῶσι	-ῶνται	-ῶνται	-ῶνται
Imperative			**Imperative**		
-------	-------	-------	-------	-------	-------
-ει	-ου	-α	-οῦ	-οῦ	-ῶ
-είτω	-ούτω	-άτω	-είσθω	-ούσθω	-άσθω
-------	-------	-------	-------	-------	-------
-εῖτε	-οῦτε	-ᾶτε	-εῖσθε	-οῦσθε	-ᾶσθε
-είτωσαν	-ούτωσαν	-άτωσαν	-είσθωσαν	-ούσθωσαν	-άσθωσαν
Infinitive			**Infinitive**		
-εῖν	-οῦν	-ᾶν	-εῖσθαι	-οῦσθαι	-ᾶσθαι
Participle			**Participle**		
-οῦντ-	-οῦντ-	-ῶντ-	-ουμεν-	-ουμεν-	-ωμεν-
-οῦσ-	-οῦσ-	-ῶσ-	-ουμεν-	-ουμεν-	-ωμεν-
-οῦντ-	-οῦντ-	-ῶντ-	-ουμεν-	-ουμεν-	-ωμεν-

Omega Verb Contraction: Imperfect Tense

IMPERFECT ACTIVE			IMPERFECT MIDDLE/PASSIVE		
ε	ο	α	ε	ο	α
Indicative			**Indicative**		
-ουν	-ουν	-ων	-ούμην	-ούμην	-ώμην
-εις	-ους	-ας	-οῦ	-οῦ	-ῶ
-ει	-ου	-α	-εῖτο	-οῦτο	-ᾶτο
-οῦμεν	-οῦμεν	-ῶμεν	-ούμεθα	-ούμεθα	-ώμεθα
-εῖτε	-οῦτε	-ᾶτε	-εῖσθε	-οῦσθε	-ᾶσθε
-ουν	-ουν	-ων	-οῦντο	-οῦντο	-ῶντο

Omega Verb: Future

FUTURE			
Active	*Middle*	*1ˢᵗ Passive*	*2ⁿᵈ Passive*
Indicative			
λύσω	λύσομαι	λυθήσομαι	γραφήσομαι
λύσεις	λύσῃ	λυθήσῃ	γραφήσῃ
λύσει	λύσεται	λυθήσεται	γραφήσεται
λύσομεν	λυσόμεθα	λυθησόμεθα	γραφησόμεθα
λύσετε	λύσεσθε	λυθήσεσθε	γραφήσεσθε
λύσουσι	λύσονται	λυθήσονται	γραφήσονται
Subjunctive			
Imperative			
Optative			
Infinitive			
λύσειν	λύσεσθαι	λυθήσεσθαι	γραφήσεσθαι
Participle			
λύσων	λυσόμενος	λυθησόμενος	γραφησόμενος
λύσουσα	λυσομένη	λυθησομένη	γραφησομένη
λύσον	λυσόμενον	λυθησόμενον	γραφησόμενον

Omega Verb: Liquid Future

LIQUID FUTURE[1]			
Active	*Middle*	*1st Passive*	*2nd Passive*
Indicative			
μενῶ	μενοῦμαι	βληθήσομαι	φανήσομαι
μενεῖς	μενῇ	βληθήσῃ	φανήσῃ
μενεῖ	μενεῖται	βληθήσεται	φανήσεται
μενοῦμεν	μενούμεθα	βληθησόμεθα	φανησόμεθα
μενεῖτε	μενεῖσθε	βληθήσεσθε	φανήσεσθε
μενοῦσι	μενοῦνται	βληθήσονται	φανήσονται
Infinitive			
μενεῖν	μενεῖσθαι	βληθήσεσθαι	φανήσεσθαι
Participle			
μενῶν	μενούμενος	βληθησόμενος	φανησόμενος
μενοῦσα	μενουμένη	βληθησομένη	φανησομένη
μενοῦν	μενούμενον	βληθησόμενον	φανησόμενον

---

[1]Liquid verbs involve *active and middle* voices only (second, third principal parts of future and aorist). Their passive voice is regular (sixth principal part).

Omega Verb: First Aorist

FIRST AORIST			
Active	*Middle*	*1ˢᵗ Pass.*	*2ⁿᵈ Pass.*
Indicative			
ἔλυσα	ἐλυσάμην	ἐλύθην	ἐγράφην
ἔλυσας	ἐλύσω	ἐλύθης	ἐγράφης
ἔλυσε	ἐλύσατο	ἐλύθη	ἐγράφη
ἐλύσαμεν	ἐλυσάμεθα	ἐλύθημεν	ἐγράφημεν
ἐλύσατε	ἐλύσασθε	ἐλύθητε	ἐγράφητε
ἔλυσαν	ἐλύσαντο	ἐλύθησαν	ἐγράφησαν
Subjunctive			
λύσω	λύσωμαι	λυθῶ	γραφῶ
λύσῃς	λύσῃ	λυθῇς	γραφῇς
λύσῃ	λύσηται	λυθῇ	γραφῇ
λύσωμεν	λυσώμεθα	λυθῶμεν	γραφῶμεν
λύσητε	λύσησθε	λυθῆτε	γραφῆτε
λύσωσι	λύσωνται	λυθῶσι	γραφῶσι
Imperative			
-------	-------	-------	-------
λῦσον	λῦσαι	λύθητι	γράφηθι
λυσάτω	λυσάσθω	λυθήτω	γραφήτω
-------	-------	-------	-------
λύσατε	λύσασθε	λύθητε	γράφητε
-------	-------	-------	γραφήτωσαν
Optative			
λύσαιμι	λυσαίμην	λυθείην	
λύσαις	λύσαιο	λυθείης	
λύσαι	λύσαιτο	λυθείη	
λύσαιμεν	λυσαίμεθα	λυθείημεν	
λύσαιτε	λύσαισθε	λυθείητε	
λύσαιεν	λύσαιντο	λυθείησαν	
Infinitive			
λῦσαι	λύσασθαι	λυθῆναι	γραφῆναι
Participle			
λύσας	λυσάμενος	λυθείς	γραφείς
λύσασα	λυσαμένη	λυθεῖσα	γραφεῖσα
λύσαν	λυσάμενον	λυθέν	γραφέν

Omega Verb: Liquid Aorist

LIQUID AORIST[2]			
Active	*Middle*	*1st Passive*	*2nd Passive*
Indicative			
ἔμεινα	ἐμεινάμην	ἐβλήθην	ἐστάλην
ἔμεινας	ἐμείνω	ἐβλήθης	ἐστάλης
ἔμεινε	ἐμείνατο	ἐβλήθη	ἐστάλη
ἐμείναμεν	ἐμεινάμεθα	ἐβλήθημεν	ἐστάλημεν
ἐμείνατε	ἐμείνασθε	ἐβλήθητε	ἐστάλητε
ἔμειναν	ἐμείναντο	ἐβλήθησαν	ἐστάλησαν
Subjunctive			
μείνω	μείνωμαι	βληθῶ	σταλῶ
μείνῃς	μείνῃ	βληθῇς	σταλῇς
μείνῃ	μείνηται	βληθῇ	σταλῇ
μείνωμεν	μεινώμεθα	βληθῶμεν	σταλῶμεν
μείνητε	μείνησθε	βληθῆτε	σταλῆτε
μείνωσι	μείνωνται	βληθῶσι	σταλῶσι
Imperative			
-------	-------	-------	-------
μεῖνον	μεῖναι	βλήθητι	στάλητι
μεινάτω	μεινάσθω	βληθήτω	σταλήτω
-------	-------	-------	-------
μείνατε	μείνασθε	βλήθητε	στάλητε
μεινάντων	μεινάσθων	βληθέντων	σταλέντων
Optative			
μείναιμι	μειναίμην	βληθείην	σταλείην
μείναις	μείναιο	βληθείης	σταλείης
μείναι	μείναιτο	βληθείη	σταλείη
μείναιμεν	μειναίμεθα	βληθείημεν	σταλείημεν
μείναιτε	μείναισθε	βληθείητε	σταλείητε
μείναιεν	μείναιντο	βληθείησαν	σταλείησαν
Infinitive			
μεῖναι	μείνασθαι	βληθῆναι	σταλῆναι
Participle			
μείνας	μεινάμενος	βληθείς	σταλείς
μείνασα	μειναμένη	βληθεῖσα	σταλεῖσα
μεῖναν	μεινάμενον	βληθέν	σταλέν

[2]Liquid verbs involve *active and middle* voices only (second, third principal parts of future and aorist). Their passive voice is regular (sixth principal part).

Omega Verb: Second Aorist

	SECOND AORIST		
Active	*Middle*	*1ˢᵗ Pass.*	*2ⁿᵈ Pass.*
Indicative			
ἔλιπον	ἐλιπόμην	ἐβλήθην	ἀνηγγέλην
ἔλιπες	ἐλίπου	ἐβλήθης	ἀνηγγέλης
ἔλιπε	ἐλίπετο	ἐβλήθη	ἀνηγγέλη
ἐλίπομεν	ἐλιπόμεθα	ἐβλήθημεν	ἀνηγγέλημεν
ἐλίπετε	ἐλίπεσθε	ἐβλήθητε	ἀνηγγέλητε
ἔλιπον	ἐλίποντο	ἐβλήθησαν	ἀνηγγέλησαν
Subjunctive			
λίπω	λίπωμαι	βληθῶ	ἀναγγελῶ
λίπῃς	λίπῃ	βληθῇς	ἀναγγελῇς
λίπῃ	λίπηται	βληθῇ	ἀναγγελῇ
λίπωμεν	λιπώμεθα	βληθῶμεν	ἀναγγελῶμεν
λίπητε	λίπησθε	βληθῆτε	ἀναγγελῆτε
λίπωσι	λίπωνται	βληθῶσι	ἀναγγελῶσι
Imperative			
-------	-------	-------	
λίπε	λιποῦ	βλήθητι	ἀναγγέληθι
λιπέτω	λιπέσθω	βληθήτω	ἀναγγελήτω
-------	-------	-------	
λίπετε	λίπεσθε	βλήθητε	ἀναγγέλητε
λιπέτωσαν	λιπέσθωσαν	βληθήτωσαν	ἀναγγελήτωσαν
Optative			
λίποιμι	λιποίμην	βληθείην	ἀναγγέλειεν
λίποις	λίποιο	βληθείης	ἀναγγέλειες
λίποι	λίποιτο	βληθείη	ἀναγγέλειε
λίποιμεν	λιποίμεθα	βληθείημεν	ἀναγγέλειεμεν
λίποιτε	λίποισθε	βληθείητε	ἀναγγέλειετε
λίποιεν	λίποιντο	βληθείησαν	ἀναγγέλειεσαν
Infinitive			
λιπεῖν	λιπέσθαι	βληθῆναι	ἀναγγελῆναι
Participle			
λιπών	λιπόμενος	βληθείς	ἀναγγελείς
λιποῦσα	λιπομένη	βληθεῖσα	ἀναγγελεῖσα
λιπόν	λιπόμενον	βληθέν	ἀναγγελέν

Omega Verb: Perfect

	PERFECT	
1st Active	*2nd Active*	*M/P*
Indicative		
λέλυκα	γέγραφα	λέλυμαι
λέλυκας	γέγραφας	λέλυσαι
λέλυκε	γέγραφε	λέλυται
λελύκαμεν	γεγράφαμεν	λελύμεθα
λελύκατε	γεγράφατε	λέλυσθε
λελύκασι	γεγράφασι	λέλυνται
Subjunctive		
ὦ λελυκώς		ὦ λελυμένος
ᾖς λελυκώς		ᾖς λελυμένος
ᾖ λελυκώς		ᾖ λελυμένος
ὦμεν λελυκότες		ὦμεν λελυμένοι
ἦτε λελυκότες		ἦτε λελυμένοι
ὦσι λελυκοτες		ὦσι λελυμένοι
Imperative		
-------		-------
λέλυκε		λέλυσο
λελυκέτω		λελύσθω
-------		-------
λελύκετε		λέλυσθε
λελυκέτωσαν		λελύσθωσαν
Optative		
Infinitive		
λελυκέναι	γεγονέναι	λελύσθαι
Participle		
λελυκώς	εἰδώς	λελύμενος
λελυκυῖα	εἰδυῖα	λελυμένη
λελυκός	εἰδός	λελυμένον

Omega Verb: Pluperfect

	PLUPERFECT	
1st Active	*2nd Active*	*M/P*
Indicative		
ἐλελύκειν	ἐληλύθειν	ἐλελύμην
ἐλελύκεις	ἐληλύθεις	ἐλέλυσο
ἐλέλυκει	ἐληλύθει	ἐλέλυτο
ἐλελύκειμεν	ἐληλύθειμεν	ἐλελύμεθα
ἐλελύκειτε	ἐληλύθειτε	ἐλέλυσθε
ἐλελύκεισαν	ἐληλύθεισαν	ἐλέλυντο
Subjunctive		
Imperative		
Optative		
Infinitive		
Participle		

MI Verb: Δίδωμι—Present, Imperfect, Second Aorist

PRESENT		IMPERFECT		SECOND AORIST	
Active	*M/P*	*Active*	*M/P*	*Active*	*Middle*
Indicative		**Indicative**		**Indicative**	
δίδωμι	δίδομαι	ἐδίδουν	ἐδιδόμην	ἔδωκα[3]	ἐδόμην
δίδως	δίδοσαι	ἐδίδους	ἐδίδοσο	ἔδωκας	ἔδου
δίδωσι	δίδοται	ἐδίδου	ἐδίδοτο	ἔδωκε	ἔδοτο
δίδομεν	διδόμεθα	ἐδίδομεν	ἐδιδόμεθα	ἐδώκαμεν	ἐδόμεθα
δίδοτε	δίδοσθε	ἐδίδοτε	ἐδίδοσθε	ἐδώκατε	ἔδοσθε
διδόασι	δίδονται	ἐδίδοσαν	ἐδίδοντο	ἔδωκαν	ἔδοντο
Subjunctive		(or ἐδίδουν)		**Subjunctive**	
διδῶ				δῶ	δῶμαι
διδῷς				δῷς	δῷ
διδῷ				δῷ	δῶται
διδῶμεν				δῶμεν	δώμεθα
διδῶτε				δῶτε	δῶσθε
διδῶσι				δῶσι	δῶνται
Imperative				**Imperative**	
-------				-------	-------
δίδου				δός	δοῦ
διδότω				δότω	δόσθω
-------				-------	-------
δίδοτε				δότε	δόσθε
διδότωσαν				δότωσαν	δόσθωσαν
Optative				**Optative**	
				δῴην	
				δῴης	
				δῴη	
				δῴημεν	
				δῴητε	
				δῴησαν	
Infinitive				**Infinitive**	
διδόναι	δίδοσθαι			δοῦναι	
Participle				**Participle**	
διδούς	διδόμενος			δούς	
-------	-------			-------	
διδόν	διδόμενον			-------	

---

[3]"Kappa" (first) aorist in active indicative only. Also, the subjunctive mood can show first aorist forms: δώσω, δώσῃς, δώσῃ, δωσώμεν, δώσητε, δωσώσι.

MI Verb: Ζώννυμι, Δείκνυμι—Regular First Aorist and Δίδωμι—Future

REGULAR FIRST AORIST			FUTURE		
Active	*Middle*	*Passive*	*Active*	*Middle*	*Passive*
Indicative			**Indicative**		
ἔζωσα	ἐζωσάμην	ἐζώσθην	δώσω	δώσομαι	δοθήσομαι
ἔζωσας	ἐζώσω	ἐζώσθης	δώσεις	δώσῃ	δοθήσῃ
ἔζωσεν	ἐζώσατο	ἐζώσθη	δώσει	δώσεται	δοθήσεται
ἐζώσαμεν	ἐζωσάμεθα	ἐζώσθημεν	δώσομεν	δωσόμεθα	δοθησόμεθα
ἐζώσατε	ἐζώσασθε	ἐζώσθητε	δώσετε	δώσεσθε	δοθήσεσθε
ἔζωσαν	ἐζώσαντο	ἐζώσθησαν	δώσουσι	δώσονται	δοθήσονται
Subjunctive					
δείξω	δείξωμαι	δειχθῶ			
δείξῃς	δείξῃ	δειχθῇς			
δείξῃ	δείξηται	δειχθῇ			
δείξωμεν	δειξώμεθα	δειχθῶμεν			
δείξητε	δείξησθε	δειχθῆτε			
δείξωσι	δείξωνται	δειχθῶσι			
Imperative					
--------	--------	--------			
δεῖξον	δείξαι	δείχθητι			
δειξάτω	δειξάσθω	δειχθήτω			
--------	--------	--------			
δείξατε	δείξασθε	δείχθητε			
δειξάτωσαν	δειξάσθωσαν	δειχθήτωσαν			
Infinitive					
δείξαι		δειχθῆναι			
Participle			**Participle**		
δείξας		δειχθείς	δώσων		
		δειχθεῖσα	-------		
		δειχθέν	-------		

MI Verb: Δίδωμι—Perfect, Pluperfect

PERFECT		PLUPERFECT
Active	*M/P*	*Active*
Indicative	**Indicative**	**Indicative**
δέδωκα	δέδομαι	ἐδεδώκειν
δέδωκας	δέδοσαι	ἐδεδώκεις
δέδωκε	δέδοται	ἐδεδώκει
δεδώκαμεν	δεδόμεθα	ἐδεδώκειμεν
δεδώκατε	δέδοσθε	ἐδεδώκειτε
δέδωκαν	δέδονται	ἐδεδώκεισαν
Subjunctive		
	ὦ δεδομένος	
	ᾖς δεδομένος	
	ᾖ δεδομένος	
	ὦμεν δεδομένοι	
	ἦτε δεδομένοι	
	ὦσι δεδομένοι	
Participle		
δεδωκώς	δεδομένος	
-------	δεδομένη	
-------	δεδομένον	

MI Verb: Τίθημι—Present, Imperfect, Second Aorist

PRESENT		IMPERFECT		SECOND AORIST	
Active	*M/P*	*Active*	*M/P*	*Active*	*Middle*
Indicative		**Indicative**		**Indicative**	
τίθημι	τίθεμαι	ἐτίθην	ἐτιθέμην		ἐθέμην
τίθης	τίθεσαι	ἐτίθεις	ἐτίθεσο		ἔθου
τίθησι	τίθεται	ἐτίθει	ἐτίθετο		ἔθετο
τίθεμεν	τιθέμεθα	ἐτίθεμεν	ἐτιθέμεθα		ἐθέμεθα
τίθετε	τίθεσθε	ἐτίθετε	ἐτίθεσθε		ἔθεσθε
τιθέασι	τίθενται	ἐτίθεσαν	ἐτίθεμην		ἔθεντο
Subjunctive		(or ἐτίθουν)		**Subjunctive**	
τιθῶ				θῶ	θῶμαι
τιθῇς				θῇς	θῇ
τιθῇ				θῇ	θῆται
τιθῶμεν				θῶμεν	θώμεθα
τιθῆτε				θῆτε	θῆσθε
τιθῶσι				θῶσι	θῶνται
Imperative				**Imperative**	
-------	-------			-------	-------
τίθει	τίθεσο			θές	θέσο
τιθέτω	τιθέσθο			θέτω	θέσθω
-------	-------			-------	-------
τίθετε	τίθεσθε			θέτε	θέσθε
τιθέτωσαν	τιθέσθωσαν			θέτωσαν	θέσθωσαν
Infinitive				**Infinitive**	
τιθέναι	τίθεσθαι			θεῖναι	θέσθαι
Participle				**Participle**	
τιθείς	τιθέμενος			θείς	θέμενος
-------	τιθεμένη			-------	-------
-------	τιθέμενον			-------	-------

MI Verb: Τίθημι—First Aorist, Future, Perfect, Pluperfect

FIRST AORIST			FUTURE		
Active	*Middle*	*Passive*	*Active*	*Middle*	*1st Passive*
Indicative			**Indicative**		
ἔθηκα		ἐτέθην	θήσω	θήσομαι	τεθήσομαι
ἔθηκας		ἐτέθης	θήσεις	θήσῃ	τεθήσῃ
ἔθηκε		ἐτέθη	θήσει	θήσοται	τεθήσεται
ἐθήκαμεν		ἐτέθημεν	θήσομεν	θησόμεθα	τεθησόμεθα
ἐθήκατε		ἐτέθητε	θήσετε	θήσεσθε	τεθήσεσθε
ἔθηκαν		ἐτέθησαν	θήσουσι	θήσονται	τεθήσονται
Subjunctive					
		τεθῶ			
		τεθῇς			
		τεθῇ			
		τεθῶμεν			
		τεθῆτε			
		τεθῶσι			
Infinitive					
		τεθῆναι			
Participle					
		τεθείς			

PERFECT		PLUPERFECT	
Active	*M/P*	*Active*	*M/P*
Indicative	**Indicative**	**Indicative**	
τέθεικα	τέθειμαι		ἐτεθείμην
τέθεικας	τέθεισαι		ἐτεθείσο
τέθεικε	τέθειται		ἐτεθείτο
τεθείκαμεν	τεθείμεθα		ἐτεθείμεθα
τεθείκατε	τέθεισθε		ἐτεθείσθε
τέθεικαν	τέθεινται		ἐτεθείντο
Participle			
τεθεικώς	τεθειμένος		
-------	-------		
-------	-------		

MI Verb: Ἵστημι—Present, Imperfect, Second Aorist

PRESENT		IMPERFECT		SECOND AORIST	
Active	*M/P*	*Active*	*M/P*	*Active*	*Middle*
Indicative		**Indicative**		**Indicative**	
ἵστημι	ἵσταμαι	ἵστην	ἱστάμην	ἔστην	
ἵστης	ἵστασαι	ἵστης	ἵστασο	ἔστης	
ἵστησι	ἵσταται	ἵστη	ἵστατο	ἔστη	
ἵσταμεν	ἱστάμεθα	ἵσταμεν	ἱστάμεθα	ἔστημεν	
ἵστατε	ἵστασθε	ἵστατε	ἵστασθε	ἔστητε	
ἱστᾶσι	ἵστανται	ἵστασαν	ἵσταντο	ἔστησαν	
				Subjunctive	
				στῶ	
				στῇς	
				στῇ	
				στῶμεν	
				στῆτε	
				στῶσι	
Imperative				**Imperative**	
-------	-------			-------	
ἵσταθι	ἵστασο			στῆθι (στά)	
ἱστάτω	ἱστάσθω			στήτω	
-------	-------			-------	
ἵστατε	ἵστασθε			στῆτε	
ἱστάτωσαν	ἱστάσθωσαν			στήτωσαν	
Infinitive				**Infinitive**	
ἱστάναι	ἵστασθαι			στῆναι	στάσθαι
Participle				**Participle**	
ἱστάς	ἱστάμενος			στάς	στάμενος
-------	-------			στᾶσα	σταμένη
-------	-------			στάν	στάμενον

MI Verb: Ἵστημι—First Aorist, Future, Perfect, Pluperfect

FIRST AORIST			FUTURE		
Active	*Middle*	*Passive*	*Active*	*Middle*	*Passive*
Indicative			**Indicative**		
ἔστησα		ἐστάθην	στήσω	στήσομαι	σταθήσομαι
ἔστησας		ἐστάθης	στήσεις	στήσῃ	σταθήσῃ
ἔστησε		ἐστάθη	στήσει	στήσεται	σταθήσεται
ἐστήσαμεν		ἐστάθημεν	στήσομεν	στησόμεθα	σταθησόμεθα
ἐστήσατε		ἐστάθητε	στήσετε	στήσεσθε	σταθήσεσθε
ἔστησαν		ἐστάθησαν	στήσουσι	στήσονται	σταθήσονται
Subjunctive					
στήσω		σταθῶ	**PERFECT**		**PLUPERFECT**
στήσῃς		σταθῇς	*Active*	*M/P*	*Active*
στήσῃ		σταθῇ	**Indicative**		**Indicative**
στήσωμεν		σταθῶμεν	ἔστηκα		εἱστήκειν
στήσητε		σταθῆτε	ἔστηκας		εἱστήκεις
στήσουσι		σταθῶσι	ἔστηκε		εἱστήκει
Imperative			ἑστήκαμεν		εἱστήκειμεν
-------			ἑστήκατε		εἱστήκειτε
στῆσον			ἔστηκαν		εἱστήκεισαν
στησάτω			**Infinitive**		
-------			ἑστακέναι		
στήσατε			**Participle**		
στησάτωσαν			ἑστηκώς		
Infinitive			ἑστηκυῖα		
στῆσαι		σταθῆναι	ἑστηκός		
Participle					
στήσας		σταθείς			

MI Verb: Ἵημι—Present, Imperfect, Second Aorist

PRESENT		IMPERFECT		SECOND AORIST	
Active	*M/P*	*Active*	*M/P*	*Active*	*Middle*
Indicative		**Indicative**			
ἵημι	ἵεμαι	ἵην			
ἵης	ἵεσαι	ἵης			
ἵησι	ἵεται	ἵη			
ἵεμεν	ἱέμεθα	ἵεμεν			
ἵετε	ἵεσθε	ἵετε			
ἱεῖσι	ἵενται	ἵεσαν			
Subjunctive				**Subjunctive**	
ἱῶ				ὧ	
ἱῆς				ἧς	
ἱῇ				ἧ	
ἱῶμεν				ὧμεν	
ἱῆτε				ἧτε	
ἱῶσι				ὧσι	
Imperative				**Imperative**	

ἵεθι				ἕς	
ἱέτω				ἕτω	

ἵετε				ἕτε	
ἱέωσαν				ἕτωσαν	
Infinitive				**Infinitive**	
ἱέναι				εἷναι	
Participle				**Participle**	
ἱείς	-------			εἵς	
-------	ἱεμένη				-------
-------	ἱέμενον				-------

MI Verb: Ἵημι—First Aorist, Future, Perfect

FIRST AORIST		FUTURE		PERFECT	
Active	*Passive*	*Active*	*Passive*	*Active*	*M/P*
Indicative		**Indicative**		**Indicative**	
ἧκα	ἕθην	ἥσω	ἐθήσομαι		εἷμαι
ἧκας	ἕθης	ἥσεις	ἐθήσῃ		εἷσαι
ἧκε	ἕθη	ἥσει	ἐθήσεται		εἷται
ἥκαμεν	ἐθημεν	ἥσομεν	ἐθησόμεθα		εἵμεθα
ἥκατε	ἐθητε	ἥσετε	ἐθήσεσθε		εἷσθε
ἧκαν	ἐθησαν	ἥσουσι	ἐθήσονται		εἷνται
Subjunctive					
	ἑθῶ				
	ἑθῇς				
	ἑθῇ				
	ἑθῶμεν				
	ἑθῆτε				
	ἑθῶσι				

MI Verb: Εἰμί—Complete Conjugation

PRESENT	IMPERFECT	FUTURE
Indicative	**Indicative**	**Indicative**
εἰμί	ἤμην	ἔσομαι
εἶ	ἦς (ἦσθα)	ἔσῃ
ἐστί	ἦν	ἔσται
ἐσμέν	ἦμεν (ἤμεθα)	ἐσόμεθα
ἐστέ	ἦτε	ἔσεσθε
εἰσί	ἦσαν	ἔσονται
Subjunctive		
ὦ		
ᾖς		
ᾖ		
ὦμεν		
ἦτε		
ὦσι		
Imperative		

ἴσθι		
ἔστω (ἤτω)		

ἔστε		
ἔστωσαν		
Optative		
εἴην		
εἴης		
εἴη		
εἴημεν		
εἴητε		
εἴησαν		
Infinitive		**Infinitive**
εἶναι		ἔσεσθαι
Participle		**Participle**
ὤν		ἐσόμενος
οὖσα		ἐσομένη
ὄν		ἐσόμενον

Miscellaneous:[4] (1) **Φημί**, (2) **Κεῖμαι**, (3) **Γινώσκω**

φημί		κεῖμαι		γινώσκω
Present *Active* **Indicative**	**Imperfect** *Active* **Indicative**	**Present** *Middle* **Indicative**	**Imperfect** *Middle* **Indicative**	**2nd Aorist** *Active* **Indicative**
φημί	ἔφην	κεῖμαι	ἐκείμην	ἔγνων
φής	ἔφης	κεῖσαι	ἔκεισο	ἔγνως
φησί	ἔφη	κεῖται	ἔκειτο	ἔγνω
φαμέν	ἔφαμεν	κείμεθα	ἐκείμεθα	ἔγνωμεν
φατέ	ἔφατε	κεῖσθε	ἔκεισθε	ἔγνωτε
φασί	ἔφασαν	κεῖνται	ἔκειντο	ἔγνωσαν
				Subjunc.
				γνῶ
				γνῷς
				γνῷ (γνοῖ)
				γνῶμεν
				γνῶτε
				γνῶσι
				Imperative

				γνῶθι
				γνώτω

				γνῶτε
				γνώτωσαν
				Infinitive
				γνῶναι
		Participle		**Participle**
		κείμενος		γνούς
		κειμένη		γνοῦσα
		κείμενον		γνόν

[4]The verb φημί occurs in only four forms: φημί, φησί, φασί, and ἔφη. The verb κεῖμαι is a common lexical middle -μι verb. The -ω verb γινώσκω has an athematic second aorist like ἵστημι. Also, the verb δείκνυμι and compounds is quite regular except for what appear to be atypical participial forms: δεικνύς, δεικνῦσα, δεικνύν. Rare -μι verb forms include: (1) ἵσημι, in two perfect forms ἴσασι (act. ind.) and ἴστε (act. imp.), perhaps connected to εἴδω; (2) ἐπίσταμαι, conjugated like ἵστημι; (3) εἶμι, "I go," easily confused with εἰμί, "I am"; present = εἶμι, εἶς, εἶ, etc.; imperfect = ᾔειν, ᾔεις, ᾔει, etc.; participial = ἰών, ἰοῦσα, ἰόν; and compounded forms = ἄπειμι, εἴσειμι, ἔξειμι, ἔπειμι, σύνειμι.

▤▤▤▤▤▤ MANUSCRIPTS 12 ▤▤▤▤▤▤

Luke is the only writer to date the nativity story, which he closely ties to the reign of Caesar Augustus, and for a reason. Augustus ended centuries of Roman civil wars and molded the Roman Republic into what became the Roman Empire, the longest lasting empire in history. Augustus was celebrated by the Roman poet Virgil: "Now a generation descends from heaven on high . . . smile on the birth of the child . . . and a golden race spring up throughout the world! Thine own Apollo now is king! . . . He shall have the gift of divine life, . . . and shall sway a world to which his father's virtues have brought peace" (Virgil, *Eclogue* 4.4-52). Note carefully Luke's subtle counterstatement: "born for you a Savior, who is Christ the Lord. . . . and on earth peace . . ." (Lk 2:11, 14).

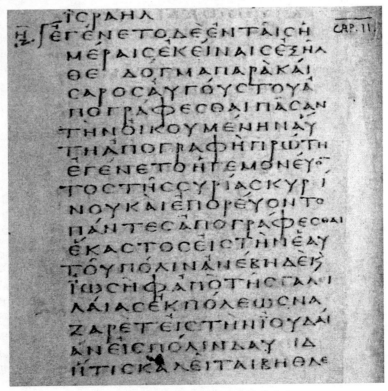

Fig. 17. Codex Vaticanus at Lk 2:1-4.

APPENDIX 3
PRINCIPAL PARTS

This principal parts list is given for indicative first person singular in the traditional order. Dashes indicate a part that does not occur in the New Testament. Multiple lines indicate alternate forms. Bold indicates fifty or more times in the New Testament. Italics indicates liquid verbs. Asterisk indicates a second aorist. Generally, non-compounded forms are given, except for very common verbs, but the compounded forms easily can be derived from them.

First	Second	Third	Fourth	Fifth	Sixth
ἀγαλλιάω	----------	ἠγαλλίασα	----------	----------	ἠγαλλιάθην
ἀγανακτέω	----------	ἠγανάκτησα	----------	----------	----------
ἀγαπάω	ἀγαπήσω	ἠγάπησα	ἠγάπηκα	ἠγάπημαι	ἠγαπήθην
ἀγγαρεύω	ἀγγαρεύσω	ἠγγάρευσα	----------	----------	----------
ἀγγέλλω	*ἀγγελῶ*	ἤγγειλα	ἤγγελκα	ἤγγελμαι	*ἠγγέλην*
ἁγιάζω	----------	ἡγίασα	----------	ἡγίασμαι	ἡγιάσθην
ἁγνίζω	----------	ἥγνισα	ἥγνικα	ἥγνισμαι	ἡγνίσθην
ἀγνοέω	----------	ἠγνόησα	ἠγνόηκα	ἠγνόημαι	ἠγνοήθην
ἀγοράζω	----------	ἠγόρασα	ἠγόρακα	ἠγόρασμαι	ἠγοράσθην
ἀγρεύω	----------	ἤρευσα	----------	----------	----------
ἄγω	ἄξω	ἤγαγον*	ἦχα	ἦγμαι	ἤχθην
ἀδικέω	ἀδικήσω	ἠδίκησα	ἠδίκηκα	ἠδίκημαι	ἠδικήθην
ἀθετέω	ἀθετήσω	ἠθέτησα	----------	----------	----------
αἰνέω	----------	ἤνεσα	ἤνεκα	ἤνημαι	ᾐνέσθην
αἱρέω	αἱρήσομαι	εἷλα			
εἷλον*	ᾕρηκα	ᾕρημαι	ᾑρέθην		
αἴρω	*ἀρῶ*	ἦρα	ἦρκα	ἦρμαι	ἤρθην
αἰσθάνομαι	αἰσθήσομαι	ᾐσθόμην	----------	ᾔσθημαι	----------
αἰσχύνω	αἰσχυνθήσομαι	-------	----------	----------	ᾐσχύνθην
αἰτέω	αἰτήσω	ᾔτησα	ᾔτηκα	ᾔτημαι	ᾐτήθην
ἀκολουθέω	ἀκολουθήσω	ἠκολούθησα	ἠκολούθηκα	ἠκολούθημαι	ἠκολουθήθην
ἀκούω	ἀκούσω	ἤκουσα	ἀκήκοα	ἤκουσμαι	ἠκούσθην
ἀλείφω	----------	ἤλειψα	ἀλήλιφα	ἀλήλιμμαι	ἠλείφθην

ἀλλάσσω	ἀλλάξω	ἤλλαξα	ἤλλαχα	ἤλλαγμαι	ἠλλάγην
ἁμαρτάνω	ἁμαρτήσω	ἡμάρτησα ἥμαρτον*	ἡμάρτηκα	ἡμάρτημαι	ἡμαρτήθην
ἀμελέω	----------	ἡμέλησα	----------	----------	----------
ἀμφιέννυμι	----------	ἡμφίεσα	----------	ἡμφίεσμαι	----------
ἀναβαίνω	ἀναβήσομαι	ἀνέβην*	ἀναβέβηκα	----------	----------
ἀναγκάζω	----------	ἠνάγκασα	----------	----------	ἠναγκάσθην
ἀναθεματίζω	---------	ἀνεθεμάτισα	--------	----------	----------
ἀναλίσκω	----------	ἀνήλωσα	ἀνήλωκα	ἀνήλωμαι	ἀνηλώθην
ἀνατέλλω	ἀνατελῶ	ἀνέτειλα	ἀνατέταλκα	ἀνατέταλμαι	----------
ἀνατρέπω	----------	ἀνέτρεψα	----------	----------	----------
ἀνίστημι	ἀναστήσω	ἀνέστησα	ἀνέστηκα	ἀνέστημαι	ἀνεστάθην
ἀνοίγω	ἀνοίξω	ἀνέῳξα ἠνέῳξα ἤνοιξα	ἀνέῳγα	ἀνέῳγμαι ἠνέῳγμαι	ἀνεῴχθην ἠνεῴχθην ἠνοίχθην ἠνοίγην
ἀντλέω	----------	ἤντλησα	ἤντληκα	----------	----------
ἀξιόω	----------	ἠξίωσα	ἠξίωκα	ἠξίωμαι	ἠξιώθην
ἀπαγγέλλω	ἀπαγγελῶ	ἀπήγγειλα	----------	ἀπήγγελμαι	ἀπηγγέλην
ἀπαντάω	ἀπαντήσω	ἀπήντησα	ἀπήντηκα	ἀπήντημαι	ἀπηντήθην
ἀπατάω	----------	ἠπάτησα	ἠπάτηκα	ἠπάτημαι	ἠπατήθην
ἀπειθέω	----------	ἠπείθησα	----------	----------	----------
ἀπειλέω	----------	ἠπείλησα ἠπειλησάμην	----------	----------	----------
ἀπέρχομαι	ἀπελεύσομαι	ἀπῆλθον*	ἀπελήλυθα	----------	----------
ἀπιστέω	----------	ἠπίστησα	----------	----------	----------
ἀποθνῄσκω	ἀποθανοῦμαι	ἀπέθανον*	----------	----------	----------
ἀποκεφαλίζω	---------	ἀπεκεφάλισα	--------	----------	----------
ἀποκρίνομαι	---------	ἀπεκρινάμην	--------	----------	ἀπεκρίθην
ἀποκτείνω	ἀποκτενῶ	ἀπέκτεινα	----------	----------	ἀπεκτάνθην
ἀπόλλυμι	ἀπολέσω ἀπολῶ	ἀπώλεσα	ἀπώλεκα ἀπόλωλα	ἀπολώλεσμαι	ἀπωλέσθην
ἀπολογέομαι	--------	ἀπελογησάμην	------	----------	ἀπελογήθην
ἀπολύω	ἀπολύσω	ἀπέλυσα	----------	ἀπολέλυμαι	ἀπελύθην
ἀπορέω	----------	ἠπόρησα	ἠπόρηκα	ἠπόρημαι	ἠπορήθην
ἀποστεγάζω	---------	ἀπεστέγασα	----------	----------	----------
ἀποστέλλω	ἀποστελῶ	ἀπέστειλα	ἀπέσταλκα	ἀπέσταλμαι	ἀπεστάλην
ἀποστερέω	----------	ἀπεστέρησα	ἀπεστέρηκα	ἀπεστέρημαι	ἀπεστερήθην
ἀποτινάσσω	----------	ἀπετίναξα	----------	----------	----------
ἅπτω	----------	ἧψα ηψάμην	----------	----------	----------
ἀπωθέω	----------	ἀπῶσα	----------	----------	----------
ἀρέσκω	----------	ἤρεσα	----------	----------	ἠρέσθην

ἀριθμέω	----------	ἠρίθμησα	ἠρίθμηκα	ἠρίθμημαι	----------
ἀριστάω	----------	ἠρίστησα	----------	----------	----------
ἀρκέω	----------	ἤκεσα	----------	----------	ἠρκέσθην
ἁρμόζω	----------	ἥρμοσα	----------	----------	----------
ἀρνέομαι	ἀρνήσομαι	ἠρνησάμην	----------	ἤρνημαι	----------
ἁρπάζω	ἁρπάσω	ἥρπασα	ἥρπακα	ἥρπασμαι	ἡρπάσθην
ἄρχω	ἄρξω	ἦρξα	----------	----------	----------
ἀσεβέω	----------	ἠσέβησα	----------	----------	----------
ἀσθενέω	----------	ἠσθένησα	ἠσθένηκα	----------	----------
ἀσπάζομαι	----------	ἠσπασάμην	----------	----------	----------
ἀστοχέω	----------	ἠστόχησα	----------	----------	----------
ἀστράπτω	----------	----------	----------	----------	----------
ἀσφαλίζω	----------	ἠσφάλισα	----------	----------	ἠσφαλίσθην
ἀτακτέω	----------	ἠτάκτησα	----------	----------	----------
ἀτενίζω	----------	ἠτένισα	----------	----------	----------
ἀτιμάζω	----------	ἠτίμασα	----------	----------	ἠτιμάσθην
αὐγάζω	----------	ηὔγασα	----------	----------	----------
αὐλέω	----------	ηυλήσα	----------	----------	----------
αὐλίζομαι	----------	----------	----------	----------	ηὐλίσθην
αὐξάνω	αὐξήσω	ηὔξησα	----------	----------	ηὐξήθην
ἀφίημι	ἀφήσω	ἀφῆκα	----------	ἀφέωμαι	ἀφέθην
(ἀφίω, ἀφέω)					
ἀφικνέομαι	----------	ἀφικόμην	----------	----------	----------
ἀφορίζω	ἀφορίσω	ἀφώρισα	----------	ἀφώρισμαι	ἀφωρίσθην
βάλλω	βαλῶ	ἔβαλον*	βέβληκα	βέβλημαι	ἐβλήθην
βαπτίζω	βαπτίσω	ἐβάπτισα	----------	βεβάπτισμαι	ἐβαπτίσθην
βάπτω	βάψω	ἔβαψα	----------	βέβαμμαι	----------
βαρέω	βαρήσω	----------	----------	βεβάρημαι	ἐβαρήθην
βασανίζω	----------	ἐβασάνισα	----------	----------	ἐβασανίσθην
βασιλεύω	βασιλεύσω	ἐβασίλευσα	----------	----------	----------
βασκαίνω	----------	ἐβάσκανα	----------	----------	----------
βαστάζω	βαστάσω	ἐβάστασα	----------	----------	----------
βδελύσσομαι	--------	----------	----------	ἐβδέλυγμαι	----------
βεβαιόω	βεβαιώσω	ἐβεβαίωσα	----------	----------	ἐβεβαιώθην
βιάζω	----------	----------	----------	----------	----------
βιόω	----------	ἐβίωσα	----------	----------	----------
βλάπτω	----------	ἔβλαψα	----------	----------	----------
βλαστάνω	----------	ἐβλάστησα	----------	----------	----------
βλέπω	βλέψω	ἔβλεψα	----------	----------	----------
βοάω	----------	ἐβόησα	----------	----------	----------
βοηθέω	----------	ἐβοήθησα	----------	----------	----------
βολίζω	----------	ἐβόλισα	----------	----------	----------
βόσκω	----------	----------	----------	----------	----------

βουλεύω	βουλεύσω	ἐβούλευσα	----------	----------	----------
βούλομαι	----------	----------	----------	----------	ἐβουλήθην
βραδύνω	----------	----------	----------	----------	----------
βρέχω	----------	ἔβρεξα	----------	----------	----------
γαμέω	----------	ἔγημα ἐγάμησα	γεγάμηκα	----------	ἐγαμήθην
γελάω	γελάσω	----------	----------	----------	----------
γεμίζω	----------	ἐγέμισα	----------	----------	ἐγεμίσθην
γεννάω	γεννήσω	ἐγέννησα	γεγέννηκα	γεγέννημαι	ἐγεννήθην
γεύομαι	γεύσομαι	ἐγευσάμην	----------	----------	----------
γίνομαι	γενήσομαι	ἐγενόμην*	γέγονα	γεγένημαι	ἐγενήθην
γινώσκω	γνώσομαι	ἔγνων*	ἔγνωκα	ἔγνωσμαι	ἐγνώσθην
γνωρίζω	γνωρίσω	ἐγνώρισα	----------	----------	ἐγνωρίσθην
γογγύζω	----------	ἐγόγγυσα	----------	----------	----------
γράφω	γράψω	ἔγραψα	γέγραφα	γέγραμμαι	ἐγράφην
γρηγορέω	----------	ἐγρηγόρησα	----------	----------	----------
δάκνω	----------	----------	----------	----------	----------
δακρύω	----------	ἐδάκρυσα	----------	----------	----------
δανίζω	----------	ἐδάνισα	----------	----------	----------
δαπανάω	δαπανήσω	ἐδαπάνησα	----------		

δεῖ [impersonal, third singular form; imperfect, ἔδει]

δειγματίζω	----------	ἐδειγμάτισα	----------	----------	----------
δείκνυμι (δεικνύω)	δείξω	ἔδειξα	----------	δέδειγμαι	ἐδείχθην
δειπνέω	δειπνήσω	ἐδείπνησα	----------	----------	----------
δεκατόω	----------	----------	δεδεκάτωκα	δεδεκάτωμαι	----------
δέομαι	----------	----------	----------	δεδέημαι	ἐδεήθην
δέρω	----------	ἔδειρα	----------	----------	ἐδάρθην
δέχομαι	δέξομαι	ἐδεξάμην	----------	δέδεγμαι	ἐδέχθην
δέω	----------	ἔδησα	δέδεκα	δέδεμαι	ἐδέθην
δηλόω	δηλώσω	ἐδήλωσα	----------	----------	ἐδηλώθην
διακονέω	διακονήσω	διηκόνησα	----------	----------	διηκονήθην
διανοίγω	----------	διήνοιξα	----------	διήνοιγμαι	διηνοίχθην
διαφημίζω	----------	διεφήμισα	----------	----------	διεφημίσθην
διδάσκω	διδάξω	ἐδίδαξα	----------	----------	ἐδιδάχθην
δίδωμι	δώσω	ἔδωκα	δέδωκα	δέδομαι	ἐδόθην
δικαιόω	δικαιώσω	ἐδικαίωσα	----------	δεδικαίωμαι	ἐδικαιώθην
διψάω	διψήσω	ἐδίψησα	----------	----------	----------
διώκω	διώξω	ἐδίωξα	----------	δεδίωγμαι	ἐδιώχθην
δοκέω	----------	ἔδοξα	----------	----------	----------
δοκιμάζω	δοκιμάσω	ἐδοκίμασα	----------	δεδοκίμασμαι	--------
δοξάζω	δοξάσω	ἐδόξασα	----------	δεδόξασμαι	ἐδοξάσθην
δουλεύω	δουλεύσω	ἐδούλευσα	δεδούλευκα	----------	----------

δουλόω	δουλώσω	ἐδούλωσα	----------	δεδούλωμαι	ἐδουλώθην
δύναμαι	δυνήσομαι	----------	----------	----------	ἠδυνήθην
δυναμόω	----------	----------	----------	----------	ἐδυναμώθην
δωρέομαι	----------	ἐδωρησάμην	----------	δεδώρημαι	----------
ἐάω	ἐάσω	εἴασα	----------	----------	----------
ἐγγίζω	ἐγγιῶ	ἤγγισα	ἤγγικα	----------	----------
ἐγείρω	ἐγερῶ	ἤγειρα	----------	ἐγήγερμαι	ἠγέρθην
ἐθίζω	----------	----------	----------	εἴθισμαι	----------
εἴκω	----------	εἶξα	----------	----------	----------
εἰμί	ἔσομαι	----------	----------	----------	----------
(impf. ἤμην)					
εἰσέρχομαι	εἰσελεύσομαι	εἰσῆλθον*	εἰσελήλυθα	----------	----------
ἐκβάλλω	ἐκβαλῶ	ἐξέβαλον*	----------	----------	ἐξεβλήθην
ἐκδικέω	ἐκδικήσω	ἐξεδίκησα	----------	----------	----------
ἐκκεντέω	ἐκκεντήσω	ἐξεκέντησα	----------	----------	----------
ἐκχέω	ἐκχεῶ	ἐξέχεα	ἐκκέχυκα	----------	----------
ἐλαττόω	----------	ἠλάττωσα	----------	ἠλάττωμαι	----------
ἐλαύνω	----------	----------	ἐλήλακα	----------	----------
ἐλέγχω	ἐλέγξω	ἤλεγξα	----------	----------	ἠλέγχθην
ἐλεέω	ἐλεήσω	ἠλέησα	----------	ἠλέημαι	ἠλεήθην
ἐλευθερόω	ἐλευθερώσω	ἠλευθέρωσα	----------	----------	ἠλευθερώθην
ἐλίσσω	ἐλίξω	----------	----------	----------	----------
ἕλκω	ἑλκύσω	εἵλκυσα	----------	----------	----------
(ἑλκύω)					
ἐλπίζω	ἐλπιῶ	ἤλπισα	ἤλπικα	----------	----------
ἐμβριμάομαι	--------	ἐνεβριμησάμην	-----	----------	ἐνεβριμήθην
ἐμφανίζω	ἐμφανίσω	ἐνεφάνισα	----------	----------	ἐνεφανίσθην
ἐνθυμέομαι	----------	----------	----------	----------	ἐνεθυμήθην
ἐντέλλομαι	ἐντελοῦμαι	ἐνετειλάμην	----------	ἐντέταλμαι	----------
ἐνυπνιάζομαι	--------	----------	----------	----------	ἐνυπνιάσθην
ἐξαρτίζω	----------	ἐξήρτισα	----------	ἐξήρτισμαι	----------
ἐξέρχομαι	ἐξελεύσομαι	ἐξῆλθον*	ἐξελήλυθα	----------	----------

ἔξεστιν ̈ τηιρτψ-ονε τιμεσ ̈ τηρεε τιμεσ ασ τηε παρτιχιπλε φορμ ἐξόν̈

ἐξετάζω	----------	ἐξήτασα	----------	----------	----------
ἐξουδενέω	----------	----------	----------	----------	ἐξουδενήθην
ἐξουθενέω	----------	ἐξουθένησα	----------	ἐξουθένημαι	ἐξουθενήθην
ἐπερωτάω	ἐπερωτήσω	ἐπηρώτησα	----------	----------	----------
ἐπιθυμέω	ἐπιθυμήσω	ἐπεθύμησα	----------	----------	----------
ἐπιμελέομαι	ἐπιμελήσομαι	-------	----------	----------	ἐπεμελήθην
ἐπιορκέω	ἐπιορκήσω	----------	----------	----------	----------
ἐπιποθέω	----------	ἐπεπόθησα	----------	----------	----------
ἐπισκέπτομαι	ἐπισκέψομαι	ἐπεσκεψάμην	----	----------	----------
ἐπισκιάζω	ἐπισκιάσω	ἐπεσκίασα	----------	----------	----------

ἐπίσταμαι	----------	----------	----------	----------	----------
ἐπιχειρέω	----------	ἐπεχείρησα	----------	----------	----------
ἐραυνάω	----------	ἠραύνησα	----------	----------	----------
ἐργάζομαι	----------	εἰργασάμην ἠργασάμην	----------	εἴργασμαι	----------
ἐρημόω	----------	----------	----------	ἠρήμωμαι	ἠρημώθην
ἑρμηνεύω	----------	----------	----------	----------	----------
ἔρχομαι	ἐλεύσομαι	ἦλθον*	ἐλήλυθα	----------	----------
ἐρωτάω	ἐρωτήσω	ἠρώτησα	----------	----------	----------
ἐσθίω	φάγομαι	ἔφαγον*	----------	----------	----------
ἑτοιμάζω	----------	ἡτοίμασα	ἡτοίμακα	ἡτοίμασμαι	ἡτοιμάσθην
εὐαγγελίζω	--------	εὐηγγέλισα	----------	εὐηγγέλισμαι	εὐηγγελίσθην
εὐαρεστέω	----------	εὐηρέστησα	εὐηρέστηκα	----------	----------
εὐδοκέω	----------	εὐδόκησα ηὐδόκησα	----------	----------	----------
εὐκαιρέω	----------	εὐκαίρησα	----------	----------	----------
εὐλαβέομαι	----------	----------	----------	----------	εὐλαβήθην
εὐλογέω	εὐλογήσω	εὐλόγησα	εὐλόγηκα	εὐλόγημαι	----------
εὑρίσκω	εὑρήσω	εὗρησα εὗρον*	εὗρηκα	----------	εὑρέθην
εὐφραίνω	----------	----------	----------	----------	ηὐφράνθην εὐφράνθην
εὐχαριστέω	--------	ηὐχαρίστησα	--------	----------	ηὐχαριστήθην
ἔχω (impf. εἶχον)	ἕξω	ἔσχον*	ἔσχηκα	----------	----------
ζάω	ζήσω	ἔζησα	----------	----------	----------
ζέω	----------	----------	----------	----------	----------
ζηλόω	----------	ἐζήλωσα	----------	----------	----------
ζημιόω	----------	----------	----------	----------	ἐζημιώθην
ζητέω	ζητήσω	ἐζήτησα	----------	----------	ἐζητήθην
ζυμόω	----------	----------	----------	----------	ἐζυμώθην
ζώννυμι	ζώσω	ἔζωσα	----------	----------	----------
ἡγέομαι	----------	ἡγησάμην	----------	ἥγημαι	----------
ἥκω	ἥξω	ἧξα	----------	----------	----------
ἡσυχάζω	----------	ἡσύχασα	----------	----------	----------
θαμβέω	----------	----------	----------	----------	ἐθαμβήθην
θανατόω	θανατώσω	ἐθανάτωσα	----------	----------	ἐθανατώθην
θάπτω	----------	ἔθαψα	----------	----------	ἐτάφην
θαυμάζω	----------	ἐθαύμασα	----------	----------	ἐθαυμάσθην
θεάομαι	----------	ἐθεασάμην	----------	τεθέαμαι	ἐθεάθην
θέλω (impf. ἤθελον)	----------	ἠθέλησα	----------	----------	----------
θεμελιόω	θεμελιώσω	ἐθεμελίωσα	----------	τεθεμελίωμαι	----------

θεραπεύω	θεραπεύσω	ἐθεράπευσα	----------	τεθεράπευμαι	ἐθεραπεύθην
θεωρέω	θεωρήσω	ἐθεώρησα	----------	----------	----------
θησαυρίζω	----------	ἐθησαύρισα	----------	τεθησαύριμαι	--------
θιγγάνω	----------	ἔθιγον*	----------	----------	----------
θλίβω	----------	----------	----------	τέθλιμμαι	----------
θνήσκω	----------	----------	τέθνηκα	----------	----------
θραύω	----------	----------	----------	τέθραυσμαι	----------
θυμόω	----------	----------	----------	----------	ἐθυμώθην
θύω	----------	ἔθυσα	----------	τέθυμαι	ἐτύθην
ἰάομαι	ἰάσομαι	ἰασάμην	----------	ἴαμαι	ἰάθην
ἵστημι	στήσω	ἔστησα	ἕστηκα	----------	ἐστάθην
(ἔστην)					
ἰσχύω	ἰσχύσω	ἴσχυσα	----------	----------	----------
καθαρίζω	καθαριῶ	ἐκαθάρισα	----------	κεκαθάρισμαι	ἐκαθαρίσθην
καθεύδω	----------	----------	----------	----------	----------
κάθημαι	καθήσομαι	----------	----------	----------	----------
καίω	----------	----------	----------	κέκαυμαι	----------
κακόω	κακώσω	ἐκάκωσα	----------	----------	----------
καλέω	καλέσω	ἐκάλεσα	κέκληκα	κέκλημαι	ἐκλήθην
καλύπτω	καλύψω	ἐκάλυψα	----------	κεκάλυμμαι	ἐκαλύφθην
κάμπτω	κάμψω	ἔκαμψα	----------	----------	----------
καταβαίνω	καταβήσομαι	κατέβην*	καταβέβηκα	----------	----------
καταράομαι	----------	κατηρασάμην	--------	κατήραμαι	----------
καταργέω	καταργήσω	κατήργησα	κατήργηκα	κατήργημαι	κατηργήθην
καταρτίζω	καταρτίσω	κατήρτισα	----------	κατήρτισμαι	----------
κατηγορέω	κατηγορήσω	κατηγόρησα	----------	----------	----------
καυματίζω	----------	ἐκαυμάτισα	----------	----------	ἐκαυματίσθην
καυκάομαι	καυχήσομαι	ἐκαυχησάμην	--------	κεκαύχημαι	----------
κεῖμαι	----------	---------	----------	----------	----------
κελεύω	----------	ἐκέλευσα	----------	----------	----------
κενόω	κενώσω	ἐκένωσα	----------	κεκένωμαι	ἐκενώθην
κεράννυμι	----------	ἐκέρασα	----------	κεκέρασμαι	----------
κερδαίνω	*κερδανῶ*	*ἐκέρδησα*	----------	----------	*ἐκερδήθην*
	κερδήσω				
κηρύσσω	----------	ἐκήρυξα	----------	----------	ἐκηρύχθην
κινέω	κινήσω	ἐκίνησα	----------	----------	ἐκινήθην
κίχρημι	----------	ἔχρησα	----------	----------	----------
κλαίω	κλαύσω	ἔκλαυσα	----------	----------	----------
κλάω	----------	ἔκλασα	----------	----------	----------
κλείω	κλείσω	ἔκλεισα	----------	κέκλεισμαι	ἐκλείσθην
κλέπτω	κλέψω	ἔκλεψα	----------	----------	----------
κληρονομέω	κληρονομήσω	ἐκληρονόμησα	κεκληρονόμηκα	----	----------
κλίνω	----------	ἔκλινα	κέκλικα	----------	----------

κοιμάω	----------	----------	----------	κεκοίμημαι	ἐκοιμήθην
κοινόω	----------	ἐκοίνωσα	κεκκοίνωκα	κεκοίνωμαι	----------
κοινωνέω	----------	ἐκοινώνησα	κεκοινώνηκα	--------	----------
κολάζω	----------	ἐκόλασα	----------	----------	----------
κομίζω	κομίσομαι	ἐκόμισα	----------	----------	----------
κοπιάω	----------	ἐκοπίασα	κεκοπίακα	----------	----------
κόπτω	κόψομαι	ἔκοψα	----------	----------	----------
κοσμέω	----------	ἐκόσμησα	----------	κεκόσμημαι	----------
κράζω	κράξω	ἔκραξα	κέκραγα	----------	----------
κρατέω	κρατήσω	ἐκράτησα	κεκράτηκα	κεκράτημαι	----------
κρίνω	κρινῶ	ἔκρινα	κέκρικα	κέκριμαι	ἐκρίθην
κρύπτω	----------	ἔκρυψα	----------	κέκρυμμαι	ἐκρύβην
κτάομαι	----------	ἐκτησάμην	----------	----------	----------
κτίζω	----------	ἔκτισα	----------	ἔκτισμαι	ἐκτίσθην
κυρόω	----------	ἐκύρωσα	----------	κεκύρωμαι	----------
κωλύω	----------	ἐκώλυσα	----------	----------	ἐκωλύθην
λαγχάνω	----------	ἔλαχον	----------	----------	----------
λαλέω	λαλήσω	ἐλάλησα	λελάληκα	λελάλημαι	ἐλαλήθην
λαμβάνω	λήμψομαι	ἔλαβον*	εἴληφα	----------	----------
λάμπω	λάμψω	ἔλαμψα	----------	----------	----------
λανθάνω	----------	ἔλαθον*	----------	----------	----------
λατρεύω	λατρεύσω	ἐλάτρευσα	----------	----------	----------
λέγω	ἐρῶ	εἶπον*	εἴρηκα	εἴρημαι	ἐρρέθην
λείπω	----------	----------	----------	----------	----------
λιθάζω	----------	ἐλίθασα	----------	----------	ἐλιθάσθην
λογίζομαι	----------	ἐλογισάμην	----------	----------	ἐλογίσθην
λοιδορέω	----------	ἐλοιδόρησα	----------	----------	----------
λούω	----------	ἔλουσα	----------	λέλουμαι	----------
λυπέω	----------	ἐλύπησα	λελύπηκα	----------	ἐλυπήθην
λυτρόω	----------	ἐλύτρωσα	----------	----------	ἐλυτρώθην
λύω	λύσω	ἔλυσα	λέλυκα	λέλυμαι	ἐλύθην
μαθητεύω	----------	ἐμαθήτευσα	----------	----------	ἐμαθητεύθην
μαίνομαι	----------	----------	----------	----------	----------
μανθάνω	----------	ἔμαθον*	μεμάθηκα	----------	----------
μαραίνω	----------	----------	----------	----------	ἐμαράνθην
μαρτυρέω	μαρτυρήσω	ἐμαρτύρησα	μεμαρτύρηκα	μεμαρτύρημαι	ἐμαρτυρήθην
μαστιγόω	μαστιγώσω	ἐμαστίγωσα	----------	----------	----------
μάχομαι	----------	----------	----------	----------	----------
μεγαλύνω	----------	----------	----------	----------	ἐμεγαλύνθην
μεθύσκω	----------	----------	----------	----------	ἐμεθύσθην
μελετάω	----------	ἐμελέτησα	----------	----------	----------
μέλλω	μελλήσω	----------	----------	----------	----------

μέλω (impers. 3rd sg., μέλει imperfect, ἔμελεν; pres. imperative, μελέτω)

μέμφομαι	----------	----------	----------	----------	----------
μένω	*μενῶ*	ἔμεινα	*μεμένηκα*	----------	----------
μερίζω	μεριῶ	ἐμέρισα	----------	μεμέρισμαι	ἐμερίσθην
μεριμνάω	μεριμνήσω	ἐμερίμνησα	----------	----------	----------
μεταμέλομαι	μεταμελήσομαι	------	----------	----------	μετεμελήθην
μετρέω	----------	ἐμέτρησα	----------	----------	-ἐμετρήθην
μηνύω	----------	ἐμήνυσα	----------	----------	ἐμηνύθην
μιαίνω	----------	----------	----------	*μεμίαμμαι*	*ἐμιάνθην*
μείγνυμι	----------	ἔμιξα	----------	μέμιγμαι	----------
(μειγνύω)					
μιμνήσκομαι	μνήσω	----------	----------	μέμνημαι	ἐμνήσθην
μισέω	μισήσω	ἐμίσησα	μεμίσηκα	μεμίσημαι	----------
μισθόω	----------	ἐμίσθωσα	----------	----------	----------
μνημονεύω	----------	ἐμνημόνευσα	--------	----------	----------
μοιχεύω	μοιχεύσω	ἐμοίχευσα	----------	----------	ἐμοιχεύθην
μολύνω	----------	*ἐμόλυνα*	----------	----------	*ἐμολύνθην*
μορφόω	----------	----------	----------	----------	ἐμορφώθην
μυέω	----------	----------	----------	μεμύημαι	----------
μυρίζω	----------	ἐμύρισα	----------	----------	----------
μωμάομαι	----------	ἐμωμησάμην	----------	----------	ἐμωμήθην
μωραίνω	----------	*ἐμώρανα*	----------	----------	*ἐμωράνθην*
νεκρόω	----------	ἐνέκρωσα	----------	νενέκρωμαι	----------
νέμω	----------	----------	----------	----------	*ἐνεμήθην*
νεύω	----------	ἔνευσα	----------	----------	----------
νηστεύω	νηστεύσω	ἐνήστευσα	----------	----------	----------
νήφω	----------	ἔνηψα	----------	----------	----------
νικάω	νικήσω	ἐνίκησα	νενίκηκα	----------	----------
νίπτω	----------	ἔνιψα	----------	----------	----------
νοέω	----------	ἐνόησα	----------	----------	----------
νομίζω	----------	ἐνόμισα	----------	----------	----------
νομοθετέω	----------	----------	----------	νενομοθέτημαι	------
νυστάζω	----------	ἐνύσταξα	----------	----------	----------
ξενίζω	----------	ἐξένισα	----------	----------	ἐξενίσθην
ξηραίνω	----------	ἐξήρανα	----------	ἐξήραμμαι	ἐξηράνθην
ὁδεύω	----------	----------	----------	----------	----------
ὀδυνάω	----------	----------	----------	----------	----------
ὄζω	----------	ὤζησα	----------	----------	----------
οἶδα	εἰδήσω	----------	οἶδα (εἰδῆτε, εἰδῆς = subjunctive forms)		
οἰκέω	οἰκήσω	ᾤκησα	----------	----------	----------
οἰκοδομέω	οἰκοδομήσω	ᾠκοδόμησα	----------	οἰκοδόμημαι	οἰκοδομήθην
οἴομαι	----------	----------	----------	----------	----------
(οἶμαι)					
ὀκνέω	----------	ὤκνησα	----------	----------	----------

ὁμιλέω	----------	ὡμίλησα	----------	----------	----------
ὀμνύω	----------	ὤμοσα	----------	----------	----------
(ὄμνυμι)					
ὁμοιόω	ὁμοιώσω	ὡμοίωσα	----------	----------	ὡμοιώθην
ὁμολογέω	ὁμολογήσω	ὡμολόγησα	----------	----------	----------
ὀνειδίζω	----------	ὠνείδισα	----------	----------	----------
ὀνίνημι	----------	ὠνάμην	----------	----------	----------
ὀνομάζω	----------	ὠνόμασα	----------	----------	ὠνομάσθην
ὁπλίζω	----------	ὥπλισα	----------	ὥπλισμαι	----------
ὁράω	ὄψομαι	εἶδον*	ἑώρακα	----------	ὤφθην
			ἑόρακα		
ὀργίζω	ὀργιῶ	----------	----------	----------	ὠργίσθην
ὀρέγω	----------	----------	----------	----------	----------
ὁρίζω	----------	ὥρισα	----------	ὥρισμαι	ὡρίσθην
ὁρμάω	----------	ὥρμησα	----------	----------	----------
ὀρύσσω	----------	ὤρυξα	----------	----------	----------
ὀρχέομαι	----------	ὠρχησάμην	----------	----------	----------
ὀφείλω	----------	----------	----------	----------	----------
παγιδεύω	----------	ἐπαγίδευσα	----------	----------	----------
παιδεύω	----------	ἐπαίδευσα	----------	πεπαίδευμαι	ἐπαιδεύθην
παίζω	παίξω	ἔπαιξα	----------	----------	ἐπαίχθην
παίω	----------	ἔπαισα	----------	----------	----------
παλαιόω	----------	ἐπαλαίωσα	πεπαλαίωκα	----------	ἐπαλαιώθην
παραδίδωμι	παραδώσω	παρέδωκα	παραδέδωκα	παραδέδομαι	παρεδόθην
παρακαλέω	--------	παρεκάλεσα	--------	παρακέκλημαι	παρεκλήθην
παραμυθέομαι	παραμυθήσομαι	παρεμυθησάμην	----- -------		----------
παροξύνω	----------	----------	----------	----------	----------
παρρησιάζομαι	--------	ἐπαρρησιασάμην	----	----------	----------
πάσχω	----------	ἔπαθον*	πέπονθα	----------	----------
πατάσσω	πατάξω	ἐπάτησα	----------	----------	----------
παύω	παύσω	ἔπαυσα	----------	πέπαυμαι	----------
πειθαρχέω	----------	ἐπειθάρκησα	--------	----------	----------
πείθω	πείσω	ἔπεισα	πέποιθα	πέπεισμαι	ἐπείσθην
πεινάω	πεινάσω	ἐπείνασα	----------	----------	----------
πειράζω	----------	ἐπείρασα	----------	πεπείραμαι	ἐπειράθην
πέμπω	πέμψω	ἔπεμψα	----------	----------	ἐπέμφθην
πενθέω	πενθήσω	ἐπένθησα	----------	----------	----------
περιπατέω	περιπατήσω	περιεπάτησα	--------	----------	----------
περισσεύω	----------	ἐπερίσσευσα	--------	----------	ἐπερισσεύθην
περιτέμνω	----------	περιέτεμον*	----------	περιτέτμημαι	περιετμήθην
πετάομαι	----------	----------	----------	----------	----------
(πέτομαι)					
πήγνυμι	----------	ἔπηξα	----------	----------	----------

πηδάω	----------	ἐπήδησα	----------	----------	----------
πιάζω	----------	ἐπίασα	----------	----------	ἐπιάσθην
πικραίνω	πικρανῶ	----------	----------	----------	ἐπικράνθην
πίμπλημι	----------	ἔπλησα	----------	----------	ἐπλήσθην
πίνω	πίομαι	ἔπιον*	πέπωκα	----------	----------
πιπράσκω	----------	----------	πέπρακα	πέπραμαι	ἐπράθην
πίπτω	πεσοῦμαι	ἔπεσον* ἔπεσα	πέπτωκα	----------	----------
πιστεύω	πιστεύσω	ἐπίστευσα	πεπίστευκα	πεπίστευμαι	ἐπιστεύθην
πλανάω	πλανήσω	ἐπλάνησα	----------	πεπλάνημαι	ἐπλανήθην
πλάσσω	----------	ἔπλασα	----------	----------	ἐπλάσθην
πλεονάζω	----------	ἐπλεόνασα	----------	----------	----------
πλεονεκτέω	----------	ἐπλεονέκτησα	-------	----------	ἐπλεονεκτήθην
πλέω	----------	----------	----------	----------	----------
πληθύνω	πληθυνῶ	----------	----------	----------	ἐπληθύνθην
πληρόω	πληρώσω	ἐπλήρωσα	----------	πεπλήρωμαι	ἐπληρώθην
πλήσσω	----------	----------	----------	----------	ἐπλήγην
πλουτέω	----------	ἐπλούτησα	πεπλούτηκα	----------	----------
πνέω	----------	ἔπνευσα	----------	----------	----------
πνίγω	----------	ἔπνιξα	----------	----------	----------
ποιέω	ποιήσω	ἐποίησα	πεποίηκα	πεποίημαι	----------
ποιμαίνω	ποιμανῶ	ἐποίμανα	----------	----------	----------
πολεμέω	πολεμήσω	ἐπολέμησα	----------	----------	----------
πορεύομαι	πορεύσομαι	----------	----------	πεπόρευμαι	ἐπορεύθην
πορνεύω	----------	ἐπόρνευσα	----------	----------	----------
ποτίζω	----------	ἐπότισα	πεπότικα	----------	ἐποτίσθην
πραγματεύομαι	-----	ἐπραγματευσάμην	---	----------	----------
πράσσω	πράξω	ἔπραξα	πέπραχα	πέπραγμαι	----------
προσέρχομαι	-------	προσῆλθον*	προσελήλυθα	-------	----------
προσεύχομαι	προσεύξομαι	προσηυξάμην	------	----------	----------
προσκυνέω	προσκυνήσω	προσεκύνησα	-------	----------	----------
προφητεύω	προφητεύσω	ἐπροφήτευσα	----------	----------	----------
πταίω	----------	ἔπταισα	----------	----------	----------
πτοέω	----------	----------	----------	----------	ἐπτοήθην
πτύσσω	----------	ἔπτυξα	----------	----------	----------
πτύω	----------	ἔπτυσα	----------	----------	----------
πυνθάνομαι	----------	ἐπυθόμην	----------	----------	----------
πωλέω	----------	ἐπώλησα	----------	----------	----------
πωρόω	----------	ἐπώρωσα	----------	πεπώρωμαι	ἐπωρώθην
ῥαβδίζω	----------	----------	----------	----------	ἐραβδίσθην
ῥαντίζω	----------	ἐράντισα	----------	ῥερράντισμαι	----------
ῥαπίζω	----------	ἐράπισα	----------	----------	----------

ῥέω	ῥεύσω	----------	----------	----------	----------
	ῥεύσομαι				
ῥήγνυμι	ῥήξω	ἔρρηξα	----------	----------	----------
(ῥήσσω)					
ῥιζόω	----------	----------	----------	ἐρρίζωμαι	----------
ῥίπτω	----------	ἔρριψα	----------	ἔρριμμαι	----------
		ἔριψα			
ῥύομαι	ῥύσομαι	ἐρρυσάμην	----------	----------	ἐρρύσθην
		ἐρυσάμην			ἐρύσθην
ῥώννυμι	----------	----------	----------	ἔρρωμαι	----------
σαλεύω	----------	ἐσάλευσα	----------	σεσάλευμαι	ἐσαλεύθην
σαλπίζω	σαλπίσω	ἐσάλπισα	----------	----------	----------
σβέννυμι	σβέσω	ἔσβεσα	----------	----------	----------
σέβομαι	----------	----------	----------	----------	----------
σείω	σείσω	----------	----------	----------	ἐσείσθην
σημαίνω	----------	ἐσήμανα	----------	----------	----------
σήπω	----------	----------	σέσηπα	----------	----------
σθενόω	σθενώσω	----------	----------	----------	----------
σιγάω	----------	ἐσίγησα	----------	σεσίγημαι	----------
σιωπάω	σιωπήσω	ἐσιώπησα	----------	----------	----------
σκανδαλίζω	----------	ἐσκανδάλισα	-------	----------	ἐσκανδαλίσθην
σκάπτω	σκάψω	ἔσκαψα	----------	----------	----------
σκευάζω	σκευάσω	ἐσκεύασα	----------	ἐσκεύασμαι	ἐσκευάσθην
σκηνόω	σκηνώσω	ἐσκήνωσα	----------	----------	----------
σκιρτάω	----------	ἐσκίρτησα	----------	----------	----------
σκληρύνω	----------	ἐσκλήρυνα	----------	----------	ἐσκληρύνθην
σκοπέω	----------	----------	----------	----------	----------
σκορπίζω	----------	ἐσκόρπισα	----------	----------	ἐσκορπίσθην
σκοτίζω	----------	----------	----------	----------	ἐσκοτίσθην
σκοτόω	----------	----------	----------	ἐσκότωμαι	ἐσκοτώθην
σκύλλω	----------	----------	----------	ἔσκυλμαι	----------
σοφίζω	----------	ἐσόφισα	----------	----------	----------
σπαράσσω	----------	ἐσπάραξα	----------	----------	----------
σπαργανόω	----------	ἐσπαργάνωσα	-------	ἐσπαργάνωμαι	-------
σπάω	----------	ἔσπασα	----------	----------	----------
σπείρω	----------	ἔσπειρα	----------	ἔσπαρμαι	ἐσπάρην
σπένδω	----------	----------	----------	----------	----------
σπεύδω	----------	ἔσπευσα	----------	----------	----------
σπιλόω	----------	----------	----------	ἐσπίλωμαι	----------
σπλαγχνίζομαι	--------	----------	----------	----------	ἐσπλαγχνίσθην
σπουδάζω	σπουδάσω	ἐσπούδασα	----------	----------	----------
σταυρόω	σταυρώσω	ἐσταύρωσα	----------	ἐσταύρωμαι	ἐσταυρώθην
στέλλω	στελῶ	ἔστειλα	ἔσταλκα	ἔσταλμαι	ἐστάλην

στενάζω	----------	ἐστέναξα	----------	----------	----------
στερεόω	----------	ἐστερέωσα	----------	----------	ἐστερεώθην
στεφανόω	----------	ἐστεφάνωσα	----------	ἐστεφάνωμαι	----------
στηρίζω	στηρίξω	ἐστήριξα	----------	ἐστήριγμαι	ἐστηρίχθην
	στηρίσω	ἐστήρισα			
στοιχέω	στοιχήσω	----------	----------	----------	----------
στρατεύω	----------	----------	----------	----------	----------
στρέφω	στρέψω	ἔστρεψα	----------	ἔστραμμαι	ἐστράφην
στρώννυμι	----------	ἔστρωσα	----------	ἔστρωμαι	ἐστρώθην
(στρωννύω)					
συγχέω	----------	----------	----------	συγκέχυμαι	συνεχύθην
(συγχύνω)					
συλάω	----------	ἐσύλησα	----------	----------	----------
συμπαθέω	----------	ἐσυμπάθησα	----------	----------	----------
συνάγω	συνάξω	συνήγαγον*	----------	συνῆγμαι	συνήχθην
σύρω	----------	----------	----------	----------	----------
σφάζω	σφάξω	ἔσφαξα	----------	ἔσφαγμαι	ἐσφάγην
σφραγίζω	----------	ἐσφράγισα	----------	ἐσφράγισμαι	ἐσφραγίσθην
σχίζω	σχίσω	ἔσχισα	----------	----------	ἐσχίσθην
σχολάζω	----------	ἐσχόλασα	----------	----------	----------
σῴζω	σώσω	ἔσωσα	σέσωκα	σέσωμαι	ἐσώθην
(σῴζω, variation has no iota subscript)					
σωφρονέω	----------	ἐσωφρόνησα	----------	----------	----------
ταλαιπωρέω	----------	ἐταλαιπώρησα	-------	----------	----------
ταπεινόω	ταπεινώσω	ἐταπείνωσα	----------	----------	ἐταπεινώθην
ταράσσω	----------	ἐτάραξα	----------	τετάραγμαι	ἐταράχθην
τάσσω	τάξω	ἔταξα	τέταχα	τέταγμαι	ἐτάχθην
τείνω	*τενῶ*	ἔτεινα	----------	----------	----------
τελειόω	----------	ἐτελείωσα	τετελείωκα	τετελείωμαι	ἐτελειώθην
τελευτάω	----------	ἐτελεύτησα	τετελεύτηκα	----------	----------
τελέω	τελέσω	ἐτέλεσα	τετέλεκα	τετέλεσμαι	ἐτελέσθην
τήκω	----------	----------	----------	----------	----------
τηρέω	τηρήσω	ἐτήρησα	τετήρηκα	τετήρημαι	ἐτηρήθην
τίθημι	θήσω	ἔθηκα	τέθεικα	τέθειμαι	ἐτέθην
τίκτω	τέξω	ἔτεκον*	----------	----------	ἐτέχθην
	τέξομαι				
τίλλω	----------	----------	----------	----------	----------
τιμάω	τιμήσω	ἐτίμησα	----------	τετίμημαι	----------
τιμωρέω	----------	----------	----------	----------	ἐτιμωρήθην
τίνω	*τίσω*	----------	----------	----------	----------
τολμάω	τολμήσω	ἐτόλμησα	----------	----------	----------
τραυματίζω	----------	ἐτραυμάτισα	-------	τετραυμάτισμαι	------

τρέπω	τρέψω	ἔτρεψα	----------	----------	ἐτρέφθην
					ἐτράπην
τρέφω	----------	ἔθρεψα	----------	τέθραμμαι	ἐθρέφθην
					ἐτράφην
τρέχω	----------	ἔδραμον*	----------	----------	----------
τρίβω	τρίψω	ἔτριψα	----------	τέτριμμαι	----------
τυγχάνω	----------	ἐτύχησα	τετύχηκα	----------	----------
		ἔτυχον*	τέτευχα		
			τέτυχα		
τύπτω	----------	----------	----------	----------	----------
τυφλόω	----------	ἐτύφλωσα	τετύφλωκα	----------	----------
τυφόω	----------	----------	----------	τετυφωμαι	ἐτυφώθην
ὑβρίζω	----------	ὕβρισα	----------	----------	ὑβρίσθην
ὑγιαίνω	----------	----------	----------	----------	----------
ὑμνέω	ὑμνήσω	ὕμνησα	----------	----------	----------
ὑπάγω	----------	----------	----------	----------	----------
ὑπάρχω	----------	----------	----------	----------	----------
ὑστερέω	----------	ὑστέρησα	ὑστέρηκα	----------	ὑστερήθην
ὑψόω	ὑψώσω	ὕψωσα	----------	----------	ὑψώθην
φαίνω	φανῶ	ἔφηνα	----------	----------	ἐφάνθην
		ἔφανα			ἐφάνην
φανερόω	φανερώσω	ἐφανέρωσα	----------	πεφανέρωμαι	ἐφανερώθην
φείδομαι	φείσομαι	ἐφεισάμην	----------	----------	----------
φέρω	οἴσω	ἤνεγκα*	ἐνήνοχα	----------	ἠνέχθην
φεύγω	φεύξομαι	ἔφυγον*	πέφευγα	----------	----------
φημί [three other NT forms: ἔφη (impf., act.), φησί (pre., act.), φασί (pre., act.)]					
φθάνω	----------	ἔφθασα	----------	----------	----------
		ἔφθην			
φθέγγομαι	----------	ἐφθεγξάμην	----------	----------	----------
φθείρω	*φθερῶ*	ἔφθειρα	----------	ἔφθαρμαι	----------
φιλέω	----------	ἐφίλησα	πεφίληκα	----------	----------
φιλοτιμέομαι	----------	----------	----------	----------	----------
φιμόω	φιμώσω	ἐφίμωσα	----------	πεφίμωμαι	ἐφιμώθην
φοβέω	----------	----------	----------	----------	ἐφοβήθην
φονεύω	φονεύσω	ἐφόνευσα	----------	----------	----------
φορέω	φορέσω	ἐφόρεσα	----------	πεφόρημαι	ἐφορήθην
φορτίζω	----------	----------	----------	πεφόρτισμαι	----------
φραγελλόω	----------	ἐφραγέλλωσα	----------	----------	----------
φράζω	----------	ἔφρασα	----------	----------	----------
φρίσσω	----------	----------	----------	----------	----------
φρονέω	φρονήσω	ἐφρόνισα	----------	----------	----------
φρουρέω	φρουρήσω	----------	----------	----------	----------
φυλάσσω	φυλάξω	ἐφύλαξα	----------	----------	----------

φυτεύω	----------	ἐφύτευσα	----------	πεφύτευμαι	ἐφυτεύθην
φύω	----------	ἔφυσα	----------	----------	ἐφύην
		ἔφυν			
φωνέω	φωνήσω	ἐφώνησα	----------	----------	ἐφωνήθην
φωτίζω	φωτίσω	ἐφώτισα	----------	πεφώτισμαι	ἐφωτίσθην
χαίρω	*χαρήσομαι*	----------	----------	----------	*ἐχάρην*
χαλάω	χαλάσω	ἐχάλασα	----------	----------	ἐχαλάσθην
χαρίζομαι	χαρίσομαι	ἐχαρισάμην	----------	κεχάρισμαι	ἐχαρίσθην
χαριτόω	----------	ἐχαρίτωσα	----------	κεχαρίτωμαι	----------
χέω	χεῶ	ἔχεα	----------	κέχυμαι	ἐχύθην
χορηγέω	χορηγήσω	ἐχορήγησα	----------	----------	----------
χορτάζω	----------	ἐχόρτασα	----------	----------	ἐχορτάσθην
χράομαι	----------	ἐχρησάμην	----------	κέχρημαι	----------
χρηματίζω	χρηματίσω	ἐχρημάτισα	----------	κεχρημάτισμαι	ἐχρηματίσθην
χρίω	----------	ἔχρισα	----------	----------	----------
χρονίζω	χρονίσω	----------	----------	----------	----------
	χρονιῶ				
χρυσόω	----------	----------	----------	κεχρύσωμαι	----------
χωρέω	----------	ἐχώρησα	----------	----------	----------
χωρίζω	χωρίσω	ἐχώρισα	----------	κεχώρισμαι	ἐχωρίσθην
ψάλλω	*ψαλῶ*	----------	----------	----------	----------
ψεύδομαι	----------	ἐψευσάμην	----------	----------	----------
ψηλαφάω	----------	ἐψηλάφησα	----------	----------	----------
ψηφίζω	----------	ἐψήφισα	----------	----------	----------
ὠδίνω	----------	----------	----------	----------	----------
ὠφελέω	ὠφελήσω	ὠφέλησα	----------	----------	ὠφελήθην

L uke mentions city officials of Thessalonica related to the disturbance about Paul, and identifies these local magistrates as "politarchs" (πολιτάρχης, Acts 17:6, 8). We had no reference to such a title in any of ancient literature, whether Greek or Latin. Therefore, some concluded Luke made a mistake or just invented the term. Then, only recently in modern times as a result of ongoing archeological research, inscriptions began turning up in Macedonia and elsewhere with this precise term, verifying Luke's accuracy in using this correct designation in this local reference in the province of Macedonia. The image below is from the outside yard of the Archeological Museum of Berea in Macedonia. This inscription is on the base of a pedestal. Only the right half of the lines are shown below. The end of the third line has Luke's term, ΠΟΛΕΙΤΑΡΧΟΥΝΤΩ(Ν), πολειτάρχουντω(ν). The last letter of the line has flaked off or worn off, but the exact same ending is used in the last word of the line above, so one can tell that a N is missing at the end of line three. Note the spelling variation of the ι as the diphthong ει (called an "itacism").

Fig. 18. Inscription, Politarchs, Berea Museum, Macedonia.

APPENDIX 4
LEXICAL MIDDLE

The following list combines New Testament verbs entered as -μαι in concording programs based on BDAG plus additional -μαι entries in the Newman dictionary. The additional Newman verbs are marked with an asterisk. This list illustrates the problem with identifying the lexical middle verb.

A, α

ἀγωνίζομαι, *I struggle*
αἱρέομαι, *I choose**
αἰσθάνομαι, *I understand*
αἰσχύνομαι, *I am ashamed**
ἀκαιρέομαι, *I am without opportunity*
ἅλλομαι, *I leap*
ἀμύνομαι, *I come to help*
ἀναβάλλομαι, *I postpone**
ἀναγνωρίζομαι, *I make known again**
ἀναδέχομαι, *I welcome*
ἀνάκειμαι, *I am seated at table*
ἀναλογίζομαι, *I consider closely*
ἀνατάσσομαι, *I compile*
ἀνατίθεμαι, *I lay before**
ἀνδρίζομαι, *I act like a man*
ἀνεμίζομαι, *I am driven by the wind**
ἀνέρχομαι, *I go up, come up*
ἀνέχομαι, *I endure*
ἀνθομολογέομαι, *I give thanks*
ἀνταγωνίζομαι, *I struggle*
ἀνταποκρίνομαι, *I reply*
ἀντέχομαι, *I hold firmly to*
ἀντιδιατίθεμαι, *I oppose**
ἀντίκειμαι, *I welcome*
ἀντιλαμβάνομαι, *I help*

ἀντιπαρέρχομαι, *I pass by on the other side of the road*
ἀντιστρατεύομαι, *I war against*
ἀντιτάσσομαι, *I resist**
ἀπάγχομαι, *I hang myself**
ἀπαλλοτριόομαι, *I am a stranger to**
ἀπαρνέομαι, *I disown*
ἀπασπάζομαι, *I say good-bye*
ἀπεκδέχομαι, *I await expectantly*
ἀπεκδύομαι, *I disarm*
ἀπέρχομαι, *I go away*
ἀπογίνομαι, *I die*
ἀποδέχομαι, *I welcome*
ἀπόκειμαι, *I welcome*
ἀποκρίνομαι, *I answer*
ἀπολογέομαι, *I defend myself*
ἀπολούομαι, *I cleanse myself**
ἀπομάσσομαι, *I wipe off**
ἀποτάσσομαι, *I say good-bye**
ἀποτρέπομαι, *I avoid**
ἀποφθέγγομαι, *I speak*
ἀποφορτίζομαι, *I unload*
ἀποχωρίζομαι, *I separate**
ἀπωθέομαι, *I push aside**
ἁρμόζομαι, *I promise in marriage**
ἀρνέομαι, *I deny*
ἀσπάζομαι, *I greet*

αὐλίζομαι, I spend the night
ἀφικνέομαι, I reach
ἀφίσταμαι, I leave, incite to revolt*
ἀχρειόομαι, I am worthless*

B, β

βδελύσσομαι, I detest
βουλεύομαι, I plan, decide*
βούλομαι, I want

Γ, γ

γεύομαι, I taste
γίνομαι, I am, become

Δ, δ

δαιμονίζομαι, I am demon possessed
δέομαι, I ask
δέχομαι, I receive
διαβεβαιόομαι, I speak confidently
διαγίνομαι, I pass time
διαδέχομαι, I receive possession of
διακατελέγχομαι, I refute
διαλέγομαι, I discuss, debate
διαλλάσσομαι, I am reconciled to
διαλογίζομαι, I discuss, argue
διαμαρτύρομαι, I declare solemnly
διαμάχομαι, I protest violently
διαπονέομαι, I am greatly annoyed
διαπορεύομαι, I travel through
διαπραγματεύομαι, I make a profit
διαπρίομαι, I am furious*
διαστέλλομαι, I order, command*
διαταράσσομαι, I am deeply troubled*
διατίθεμαι, I make a will*
διαχειρίζομαι, I kill*
διαχωρίζομαι, I go away*
διενθυμέομαι, I think over
διέρχομαι, I go through
διηγέομαι, I tell
διϊκνέομαι, I go all the way through, penetrate
διϊσχυρίζομαι, I insist
δογματίζομαι, I obey rules*
δράσσομαι, I am able
δύναμαι, I am able
δωρέομαι, I give

E, ε

ἐγκαυχάομαι, I boast
ἐγκομβόομαι, I put on
ἐγκρατεύομαι, I exercise self-control
εἰσδέχομαι, I welcome
εἰσέρχομαι, I go (come) into
εἰσκαλέομαι, I invite in
εἰσπορεύομαι, I go in, come in
εκδαπανάομαι, I spend myself fully*
ἐκδέχομαι, I wait for
ἐκδίδομαι, I lease*
ἐκδιηγέομαι, I tell
ἐκθαμβέομαι, I am greatly surprised*
ἐκκαίομαι, I am inflamed*
ἐκκρέμαμαι, I hang upon*
ἐκλανθάνομαι, I forget completely
ἐκλέγομαι, I choose, select
ἐκλύομαι, I give up, faint
ἐκπλήσσομαι, I am amazed*
ἐκπορεύομαι, I go out, come out
ἐκστρέφομαι, I am perverted*
ἐκτίθεμαι, I explain*
ἐκτρέπομαι, I wander, go astray*
ἑλκόομαι, I am covered with sores*
ἐμβριμάομαι, I speak harshly to
ἐμμαίνομαι, I am enraged
ἐμπλέκομαι, I am mixed up in*
ἐμπορεύομαι, I am in business
ἐναγκαλίζομαι, I take into my arms
ἐναντιόυμαι, I oppose, deny (Acts 13:45, variant)*
ἐνάρχομαι, I begin
ἐνδείκνυμαι, I show*
ἐνδέχομαι, it is possible
ἐνδοξάζομαι, I receive glory
ἐνθυμέομαι, I think about
ἐντέλλομαι, I command
ἐντρέφομαι, I live on, feed on*
ἐνυπνιάζομαι, I dream
ἐνωτίζομαι, I pay close attention to
ἐξαιτέομαι, I ask permission*
ἐξάλλομαι, I jump up
ἐξαπορέομαι, I despair*

ἐξέρχομαι, *I come out, go out*
ἐξηγέομαι, *I tell, relate*
ἐξηχέομαι, *I ring out, sound forth**
ἐπαγγέλλομαι, *I promise*
ἐπαγωνίζομαι, *I struggle in behalf of*
ἐπαθροίζομαι, *I increase, crowd around**
ἐπαισχύνομαι, *I am ashamed*
ἐπακροάομαι, *I listen to*
ἐπαναπαύομαι, *I rest on*
ἐπανέρχομαι, *I return*
ἐπανίσταμαι, *I turn against**
ἐπεισέρχομαι, *I come upon*
ἐπεκτείνομαι, *I stretch toward*
ἐπενδύομαι, *I put on*
ἐπέρχομαι, *I come upon*
ἐπιγίνομαι, *I spring up*
ἐπιδέχομαι, *I receive*
ἐπιδιατάσσομαι, *I add to* (a will)
ἐπίκειμαι, *I lie on*
ἐπιλαμβάνομαι, *I take hold of*
ἐπιλανθάνομαι, *I forget*
ἐπιμελέομαι, *I take care of*
ἐπιπορεύομαι, *I come to*
ἐπισκέπτομαι, *I visit, care for*
ἐπισκευάζομαι, *I make ready*
ἐπισπάομαι, *I remove the marks of circumcision*
ἐπίσταμαι, *I know, understand*
ἐπονομάζομαι, *I call myself**
ἐργάζομαι, *I work*
ἐρεύγομαι, *I declare, tell*
ἐρημόομαι, *I am made waste, desolate**
ἔρχομαι, *I come*
ἑσσόομαι, *I am worse off*
εὐλαβέομαι, *I act in reverence*
εὐοδόομαι, *I have things go well, earn**
εὐπορέομαι, *I have financial means**
εὔχομαι, *I pray*
ἐφάλλομαι, *I jump on*
ἐφικνέομαι, *I reach*

Z, ζ

H, η
ἡγέομαι, *I consider*
ἡττάομαι, *I am defeated*

Θ, θ
θαμβέομαι, *I am amazed**
θεάομαι, *I see*
θερμαίνομαι, *I warm myself**
θροέομαι, *I am alarmed**
θυμόομαι, *I am furious**

I, ι
ἰάομαι, *I heal, cure*
ἱλάσκομαι, *I bring about forgiveness for*

K, κ
καθέζομαι, *I sit down*
κάθημαι, *I sit, live, stay*
κακουχέομαι, *I am ill-treated**
καταβαπτίζομαι, *I wash myself (variant?)**
καταβαρύνομαι, *I am very heavy**
καταγωνίζομαι, *I conquer*
κατακαλύπτομαι, *I cover my head**
κατακαυχάομαι, *I boast against*
κατάκειμαι, *I lie (in bed), am sick, recline at table*
κατανύσσομαι, *I am stabbed*
καταποντίζομαι, *I sink, drown**
καταράομαι, *I curse*
κατασοφίζομαι, *I deceive by trickery*
καταχράομαι, *I make full use of*
κατεργάζομαι, *I accomplish*
κατέρχομαι, *I come down, go down*
κατεφίσταμαι, *I attack* (Acts 18:12)
[κατεφίστημι, *I attack*]*
κατιόομαι, *I rust**
κατοπτρίζομαι, *I behold, reflect**
καυσόομαι, *I am burned up**
καυχάομαι, *I boast*
κεῖμαι, *I lie, exist*
κλυδωνίζομαι, *I am tossed by the sea*
κνήθομαι, *I feel an itching**

κοιμάομαι, *I sleep, die**
κολλάομαι, *I unite myself with**
κραταιόομαι, *I become strong**
κτάομαι, *I acquire*
κυλίομαι, *I roll about**

Λ, λ

λογίζομαι, *I reckon*
λυμαίνομαι, *I harass, destroy*
λυτρόομαι, *I redeem**

Μ, μ

μαίνομαι, *I am insane*
μαντεύομαι, *I tell fortunes*
μαραίνομαι, *I wither away**
μαρτύρομαι, *I testify*
μασάομαι, *I gnaw, bite*
ματαιόομαι, *I am given to worthless or futile speculation**
μάχομαι, *I quarrel, fight*
μεθύσκομαι, *I get drunk**
μέμφομαι, *I find fault with*
μεταβάλλομαι, *I change my mind**
μετακαλέομαι, *I send for, summon**
μεταμέλομαι, *I regret*
μεταμορφόομαι, *I am transformed**
μεταπέμπομαι, *I send for**
μετεωρίζομαι, *I worry*
μηκύνομαι, *I grow**
μιμέομαι, *I imitate*
μιμνήσκομαι, *I remember*
μισθόομαι, *I hire**
μνηστεύομαι, *I am engaged**
μοιχάομαι, *I commit adultery**
μονόομαι, *I am left alone**
μυέομαι, *I learn the secret of**
μυκάομαι, *I roar*
μωμάομαι, *I find fault with*

Ν, ν

νομοθετέομαι, *I am given the law**
νοσφίζομαι, *I keep back for myself, embezzle**

Ξ, ξ

ξυράομαι, *I shave**

Ο, ο

ὀδυνάομαι, *I am in great pain**
οἴομαι, *I suppose*
ὁμείρομαι, *I yearn for*
ὀνίναμαι, *I benefit, profit**
ὁπλίζομαι, *I arm myself**
ὀπτάνομαι, *I appear*
ὀργίζομαι, *I am angry**
ὀρέγομαι, *I am eager for**
ὀρχέομαι, *I dance*
ὀχλέομαι, *I trouble, harras**

Π, π

παραβιάζομαι, *I urge*
παραβολεύομαι, *I risk*
παραγίνομαι, *I come, arrive*
παραδέχομαι, *I accept, receive*
παραιτέομαι, *I ask for*
παρακαθέζομαι, *I sit*
παράκειμαι, *I am present*
παραλέγομαι, *I sail along*
παραλογίζομαι, *I deceive*
παραλύομαι, *I am paralyzed**
παραμυθέομαι, *I console*
παραπορεύομαι, *I pass by*
παρεισέρχομαι, *I slip in, come in*
παρέρχομαι, *I pass by*
παροίχομαι, *I go by*
παροξύνομαι, *I am upset**
παρρησιάζομαι, *I speak boldly*
παχύνομαι, *I grow dull, insensitive**
πειράομαι, *I try*
περιβλέπομαι, *I look around**
περιεργάζομαι, *I am a busybody*
περιέρχομαι, *I travel about*
περίκειμαι, *I am placed around, bound, surrounded*
περιλείπομαι, *I remain*
περιποιέομαι, *I obtain, win**
περισπάομαι, *I am distracted**
περπερεύομαι, *I am conceited*
πέτομαι, *I fly*
πίμπραμαι, *I swell up, burn with fever**
πιστόομαι, *I firmly believe**

πολιτεύομαι, *I live, conduct my life*
πορεύομαι, *I go, proceed*
πραγματεύομαι, *I trade, do business*
προαιρέομαι, *I decide**
προαιτιάομαι, *I accuse beforehand*
προβλέπομαι, *I have in store**
προγίνομαι, *I happen previously*
προενάρχομαι, *I begin beforehand*
προεπαγγέλλομαι, *I promise from the beginning*
προέρχομαι, *I go ahead*
προευαγγελίζομαι, *I proclaim the good news beforehand*
προέχομαι, *I am better off**
προηγέομαι, *I outdo*
προκαλέομαι, *I irritate*
πρόκειμαι, *I am set before*
προμαρτύρομαι, *I predict*
προπορεύομαι, *I go before*
προσανατίθεμαι, *I go for advice, add to**
προσαπειλέομαι, *I threaten further**
προσδέομαι, *I need*
προσδέχομαι, *I wait for*
προσεργάζομαι, *I make more* (profit)
προσέρχομαι, *I come to, go to*
προσεύχομαι, *I pray*
προσκαλέομαι, *I call to myself**
προσκληρόομαι, *I join**
προσκλίνομαι, *I join**
προσκολλάομαι, *I am united (in marriage)**
προσλαμβάνομαι, *I welcome**
προσορμίζομαι, *I moor, tie up**
προσποιέομαι, *I act as if**
προσπορεύομαι, *I come to*
προτίθεμαι, *I plan, purpose**
προτρέπομαι, *I am encouraged**
προχειρίζομαι, *I choose*
πτοέομαι, *I am terrified**
πτύρομαι, *I am frightened**
πυνθάνομαι, *I inquire, ask*
πυρόομαι, *I burn**

Ρ, ρ

ῥιζόομαι, *I am firmly rooted**
ῥιπίζομαι, *I am tossed about**
ῥύομαι, *I save, rescue*
ῥώννυμι, *I am healthy**

Σ, σ

σαίνομαι, *I am disturbed**
σεβάζομαι, *I worship*
σέβομαι, *I worship*
σεληνιάζομαι, *I am an epileptic*
σημειόομαι, *I take note of**
σκοτίζομαι, *I am darkened**
σκοτόομαι, *I am darkened**
σπάομαι, *I draw**
σπένδομαι, *I am poured out as a drink offering**
σπλαγχνίζομαι, *I am moved with compassion*
στέλλομαι, *I guard against, avoid**
στενοχωρέομαι, *I am held in check**
στρατεύομαι, *I serve as a soldier, war**
συγκάθημαι, *I sit with*
συγκακουχέομαι, *I share hardship with*
συγκατατίθεμαι, *I agree with**
συγκαταψηφίζομαι, *I am enrolled with*
συγκεράννυμαι, *I unite**
συγχράομαι, *I associate on friendly terms*
συλλογίζομαι, *I discuss*
συλλυπέομαι, *I am deeply grieved**
συμμερίζομαι, *I share with**
συμμορφίζομαι, *I take on the same form as**
συμπαραγίνομαι, *I assemble*
συμπαρακαλέομαι, *I am encouraged together**
συμπορεύομαι, *I go along with*
συμφύομαι, *I grow up with**
συναγωνίζομαι, *I help*
συναλίζομαι, *I eat with, assemble**
συνανάκειμαι, *I sit at table with*

συναναπαύομαι, *I have a time of rest with*

συναντιλαμβάνομαι, *I help*

συναπάγομαι, *I am carried away, led astray**

συναπόλλυμι, *I perish with**

συναρμολογέομαι, *I am joined together**

συναυξάνομαι, *I grow together**

συνδέομαι, *I am in prison with**

συνδοξάζομαι, *I share in another's glory**

συνεισέρχομαι, *I go in with*

συνέπομαι, *I accompany*

συνέρχομαι, *I come together*

συνευωχέομαι, *I eat together*

συνήδομαι, *I delight in*

συνθάπτομαι, *I am burried together with**

συνθλάομαι, *I am broken to pieces**

συντίθεμαι, *I agree, arrange**

συνυποκρίνομαι, *I join in acting with insincerity*

συσταυρόομαι, *I am crucified with**

συσχηματίζομαι, *I am conformed to**

Τ, τ

τήκομαι, *I dissolve, am melted**

τραχηλίζομαι, *I am laid bare**

τυρβάζομαι, *I am troubled* (Luke 10:41, variant)*

τύφομαι, *I smolder**

τυφόομαι, *I am swollen with pride**

Υ, υ

ὑπεραίρομαι, *I am puffed up with pride**

ὑπερεκχύννομαι, *I run over**

ὑποδέομαι, *I put on**

ὑποδέχομαι, *I receive*

ὑποκρίνομαι, *I pretend*

Φ, φ

φαντάζομαι, *I appear**

φείδομαι, *I spare, refrain from*

φθέγγομαι, *I speak*

φιλοτιμέομαι, *I make it my ambition*

φοβέομαι, *I fear**

Χ, χ

χαρίζομαι, *I grant, give*

χειμάζομαι, *I am storm-tossed**

χράομαι, *I make use of*

χρηστεύομαι, *I am kind*

Ψ, ψ

ψεύδομαι, *I lie, speak untruth*

ψύχομαι, *I grow cold, die out (of love)**

Ω, ω

ὠνέομαι, *I buy*

ὠρύομαι, *I roar* (of lions)

APPENDIX 5
ANSWER KEY

This answer key provides answers to even-numbered exercises, as well as other select questions. The key is intended to guide the student and affirm the learning process, but not to be a crutch.

Exercise 1
1.2 Line 2: ιθεονυμ-σασικαε
1.4 literary and non-literary
1.6 Alexander the Great
1.7b "Holy Ghost Greek"
1.8 (1) *overemphasis*: historical present, vivid perfect, direct for indirect discourse;
(2) *overfullness*: compound verb followed by preposition, periphrasis;
(3) *other*: absence of conjunctions (overuse of καί)
2.2 voiceless
2.4 voiceless
2.5 Line 2: ημεραιςεκιναι(ς, very small C at margin)
2.5 Line 4: παραΚαισαροσΑ
2.5 Line 6: φεσθεπασαντην
2.5 Line 8: τηναπογραφην
2.5 Line 10: ηγεμονευοντ(ος, very small OC at margin)
3.1 Line 2: ἐξ-ε-πλήσ-σον-το ἐ-πὶ τῇ δι-δα-χῇ αὐ-τοῦ· ἦν γὰρ
3.2 b F, d T, f F, h F
3.3b βλέπομεν, βλέπει, βλεπομένη
3.4b λόγοι, λόγοις, λόγῳ

Exercise 2
1. b T, d F
2.2 circumflex
2.4 first

3.2 three: σάββατον (neu.), θεός (mas.), ἄνθρωπος (mas.)
4. Mk 1:21-22

Exercise 3
1.2 accusative; obj. of prep. (prep. phrase is adverbial)
1.4 accusative; direct obj.
1.6 genitive; possession
1.8 dative; obj. of prep. (prep. phrase is association)
1.10 vocative; direct address
1.12 genitive; ablative of separation
1.14 genitive; relationship
1.16 dative; indirect obj.
2.2 *through the revelation of Jesus Christ*; objective

Exercise 4
1. b T, d T
2.2 anarthrous
2.4 not translated; idiom with proper name
2.6 yes, δέ, line 14

Exercise 5
1. b T, d F, f F
2.2 α or ν
2.4 nom. sg., dat. pl.
2.6 ντ
2.8 coalescence

3.2   ποιμήν, ποιμένος, ποιμένι,
       ποιμένα
       ποιμένες, ποιμένων, ποιμέσιν,
       ποιμένας
3.4   βασιλεύς, βασιλέως, βασιλεῖ,
       βασιλέα
       βασιλεῖς, βασιλέων,
       βασιλεῦσιν, βασιλεῖς
4.   γραμματεύς, semivowel stem;
       πνεῦμα, neuter ματ stem

Exercise 6
2.2a   Table 6.1, δίκαιος; b anarthrous;
       c attributive
2.4a   Table 6.6, μέγας; b anarthrous; c
       attributive

Exercise 7
1.2   proper
1.4a   acc.; b abl.; c abl.; d acc.; e
       abl.; f abl.; g ins.
1.6a   vowel elision before following
       vowel; b both vowel elision and
       consonant aspiration due to rough
       breathing
2.2   clause
2.4   combines an independent clause
       with at least one dependent
       clause
2.6   noun, adjective, adverb
2.8   22 times; illustrates Koine style
       (see p. 5)

Exercise 8
1.2   third
2.2   substantive
3.2   *once, twice*
4.2   -ιων, -ιον
5.2   -τατα, -ιστα
6.2   often the compared element
       drops the full clause, leaving only
       the subject of the clause
6.4   ablative, accusative

Exercise 9
1.2   b F, d F
1.4   Inflected: ἀκούομεν

we hear
       Emphatic: ἡμεῖς ἀκούομεν
       we hear
       Intensive: αὐτοὶ ἀκούομεν
       we ourselves hear
       Doubled: αὐτοὶ ἡμεῖς ἀκούομεν
       we ourselves hear
1.6   adjective
1.8   indefinite
2.2   first
2.4b   *who,* subject
2.6   indefinite
2.8   1c, 2b, 3d, 4a

Exercise 10
1.1   *33 thematic verbs:* 24 finite; 2 in-
       finitives (15:8, αἰτεῖσθαι; 15:15,
       ποιῆσαι); 7 participles (15:7,
       λεγόμενος, δεδεμένος; 15:8,
       ἀναβάς; 15:9, λέγων; 15:12,
       ἀποκριθείς; 15:15, βουλόμενος,
       φραγελλώσας)
1.2   *2 non-thematic verbs:* 15:10,
       παραδεδώκεισαν (παραδίδωμι);
       15:10, παρέδωκεν (παραδίδωμι)
1.3   *4 lexical verbs:* 15:6, παρῃτοῦντο
       (παραιτέομαι); 15:9, 12, ἀπεκρί-
       θη, ἀποκριθείς (ἀποκρίνομαι);
       15:15, βουλόμενος (βούλομαι)
2.2   *had committed* [murder],
       completed action, completed
       effects
2.4   *are you desiring,* continuous
       action, thus, decided attitude
2.6   *they cried out,* undefined action,
       thus, summary report
       they were crying out, continuous
       action, emphasis on actual action
3.2   primary endings
3.6   possible reality; fourth class
       conditional sentences, wishes,
       benedictions, and prayers
5.2b   *and his mother and brothers
       come;* plural subject but singular
       verb; element of the compound
       subject closest to the verb
       affects the number of the verb,

hence, *mother*, which is singular, affects the verb's number

6.2 the present tense stem often is the most altered tense stem

6.4 voice

Exercise 11

1.2 παρῃτοῦντο, impf., mid. (dep.), ind., 3pp, παραιτέομαι, *I ask*
a. παρ- is the compound preposition παρά with elided vowel
b. η- is the past time augment of the diphthong αι-
c. οῦ- is the contraction of ε and ο yielding circumflex accent

1.4 ἐποίει, impf., act., ind., 3ps, ποιέω, *I do*
a. ἐ- is the augment for past time
c. ει is the contraction of ε and ε

1.6 ἐγίνωσκεν, impf., act., ind., 3ps, γινώσκω, *I know*

2.2 ἐποίει, customary impf., for habitual or repeated action

2.4 ἔλεγεν, descriptive impf., no emphasis on beginning or end

2.6 ποιοῦσιν, descriptive pres., no emphasis on beginning or end

2.8 ἔλεγον, inceptive impf., emphasis on beginning, *began to say*

2.10 ἐζήτουν, conative impf., action attempted, *were trying to seek*

3.2 *your reward is great in heaven*, verbless predicative

3.4 *both were righteous before God*, pronoun precedence; *both* is an adjective here used as pronoun

Exercise 12

1.2 ἐλήλυθας, perf., act., ind., 2ps, ἔρχομαι, *I come, go*

1.4 ἠγαπήκαμεν, perf., act., ind., 1pp, ἀγαπάω, *I love*

1.6 μεμενήκεισαν, pluperf., act., ind., 3pp, μένω, *I remain*

1.8 ᾔδεισαν, pluperf. (defective), act., ind., 3pp, οἶδα, *I know*

1.10 ἐπεγέγραπτο, pluperf., pass., ind., 3ps, ἐπιγράφω, *I write upon*

1.12 ἐκβεβλήκει, pluperf., act., ind., 3ps, ἐκβάλλω, *I cast out*

1.14 ἀπολέλυσαι perf., pass., ind., 2ps, ἀπολύω, *I release, divorce*

1.16 ἡτοίμασται, perf., pass., ind., 3ps, ἐτοιμάζω *I prepare*

2.2 a. πεφιλήκατε, intensive perf., on-going consequences
b. πεπιτεύκατε, completed perf., completed action

2.4 a. ἀκηκόαμεν, iterative perf., repeated instances
b. ἑωράκαμεν, iterative perf., repeated instances

2.6 κεκρίκει, completed perf., emphasis on completed action

Exercise 13

1.2 μισήσεις, fut., act., ind., 2ps, μισέω, *I hate*

1.4 ἀγαπήσεις, fut., act., ind., 2ps, ἀγαπάω, *I love*

1.6 ἀποτίσω, fut., act., ind., 1ps, ἀποτίνω, *I repay*

1.8 ἐφείσατο, aor., mid. (dep.), ind., 3ps, φείδομαι, *I spare*

1.10 ἐπετίμησεν, fut., act., ind., 3ps, ἐπιτιμάω, *I rebuke*

1.12 ἐκηρύξαμεν, aor., act., ind., 1pp, κηρύσσω, *I proclaim*

1.14 ἐδέξασθε, aor., mid. (dep.), ind., 2pp, δέξομαι, *I receive*

1.16 ἐλάβετε, aor., act., ind., 2pp, λαμβάνω, *I take, receive*

1.18 ἐθεραπεύθη, aor., pass., ind., 3ps, θεραπεύω, *I heal*

1.20 ταπεινωθήσεται, fut., pass., ind., 3ps, ταπεινόω, *I humble*

2.2 *I, Paul, am writing in my own hand, I will repay* (epistolary aorist)

2.4 *There will be great tribulation such as has not happened form the beginning of the world until now.* (predictive future)

2.6 *You have heard that it has been said: Love your neighbor and hate your enemy.* (culminative aorist; imperative future)

2.8 *And Jesus rebuked him and cast out the demon from him, and the child was healed from that hour.* (constative aorist; but *healed* seems to be an ingressive aorist)

2.10 *For if the one who comes is preaching another Jesus whom we did not preach, or you are receiving a different spirit which you did not receive, or a different gospel which you did not accept, you bear well.* (constative or culminative aorist)

Exercise 14

1   b F, d F, f T, h T, j F
2.2 imperative
2.4 second aorist
2.6 γένοιτο
2.8 imperative
2.10 aorist
2.12 ἵνα

3.2 *He saved others. Let him save himself.* (command imperative)

3.4 *And when they hear, immediately Satan comes.* (temporal subjunc.)

3.6 *And they were discussing with one another what they might do with Jesus.* (deliberative subj.)

Exercise 15

3.2 *If you are the Son of God, tell these stones to become bread.* (indicative, determined, asserted true, 1st)

3.4 *It would be better for him if that man had not been born.* (indicative, determined, asserted false, 2nd)

3.6 *so that (they should) seek God, if somehow indeed they might touch him and might find him.*

(optative, undetermined, remote, 4th)

Exercise 16

2.2 -σθαι
2.4 no
2.6 ποιεῖν
2.8 accusative
2.10 yes
2.12 ἔσεσθαι
2.14 at times, a verb that refuses to speak to you; at other times, a verb that occurs only in third person neuter: δεῖ and ἔξεστιν
2.16 indirect object

3.2 *To be here is good for us.* (subject)

3.4 *No one is able to serve two masters.* (complementary)

3.6 *You are saying that I cast out the demons by Beelzebul.* (indirect discourse as direct object)

3.8 *But they do all their works in order to be seen by men.* (adverbial of purpose)

3.10 *Now it happened that, while they were there, the days for her to give birth were fulfilled.* (*while they were there* = adverbial of time; *for her to give birth* = adverbial of purpose)

Exercise 17

4.2 -μεν- always is middle
4.4 nominative forms
5.2 λυθεῖσαι: aor., pass., part., nom., fem., pl.
5.4 λελυμένου: perf., mid./pass., part., gen., mas./neu., sg.
5.6 λυθησομένῳ: fut., pass., part., dat., mas./neu., sg.
5.8 λιπόν: aor., act., part., nom./acc., neu., sg.
5.10 λελυκώς: perf., act., part., nom., mas., sg.

Exercise 18

1.2 *For he was going along his way rejoicing.* (*rejoicing* = adverbial of manner)

1.4 *For if you love those who love you, what reward do you have?* (*those who love you* = substantival, dir. obj.)

1.6 *And not I only, but also all those who have known the truth* (*those who have known* = substantival, subject)

Exercise 19

3.1 future tense
3.2 subjunctive mood
3.3 imperative mood
4. b F, d F, f F, h T
5.2 τίθενται: pres., mid./pass., ind., 3pp
5.4 τιθέτω: imperative, act., ind., 3ps

6.2 *When he delivers over the kingdom to God*

6.4 *And their power and authority they give to the beast*

6.6 *And they were placing at the feet of the apostles, and they were distributing to each person just as anyone was having need*

Exercise 20

1.2 perfect and pluperfect
2.2 active voice
2.4 -θε- and -θου-
3.2 δέδωκας: perf., act., ind., 2ps
3.4 ἔδοσθε: aor., mid., ind., 2pp
3.6 δῷς: aor., act., subj., 2ps
3.8 διδόντες: pres., act., part., nom., mas., pl.
3.10 δοθέντας: aor., pass., part., acc., mas., sg.
4.2 *And after he arose, he followed him.*

P aul appeared before Lucius Junius Gallio, the proconsul of Achaia (Greece), while Paul was in Corinth (Acts 18:12). A letter sent by the Emperor Claudius that happens to mention this Gallio as proconsul was preserved in a Greek inscription that was discovered in Delphi, Greece. Due to this inscription, we can date Gallio's proconsulship (A.D. 51-52), and, as a result, can estimate fairly closely Paul's time in Corinth. The inscription is held in the Archeological Museum of Delphi. Below is that part of the inscription that includes Gallio's name (ΓΑΛΛΙΩΝ).

Fig. 19. Inscription, Proconsul Lucius Junius Gallio.

VOCABULARY 1
FREQUENCY: 136+

Our goal is words that occur 15 or more times in the New Testament, including second aorists, a total of 841 words. Seven vocabulary lists give decreasing frequency. This list has 130 words.

ἀγαπάω, I love
ἄγγελος, -ου, ὁ, messenger, angel
ἅγιος, -α, -ον, holy; pl. noun, saints
ἀδελφός, -οῦ, ὁ, brother
ἀκούω, I hear
ἀλλά, but, except
ἁμαρτία, -ας, ἡ, sin
ἄν, part. of contingency
ἀνήρ, ἀνδρός, ἡ, man, husband
ἄνθρωπος, -ου, ὁ, man
ἀπό, gen., from
ἀποκρίνομαι, I answer
αὐτός, -ή, -ό, himself, herself, itself, same; he, she, it
ἀφίημι, I let go, permit, forgive
βασιλεία, -ας, ἡ, kingdom
γάρ, for
γῆ, γῆς, ἡ, earth, land
γίνομαι, I become, am

γινώσκω, I know, understand
γράφω, I write
δέ, but, and
διά, gen., through; acc., on account of
δίδωμι, I give
δόξα, -ης, ἡ, glory
δύναμαι, I can, am able
ἐάν, if
ἑαυτοῦ, of himself
ἔβην (βαίνω), I went
ἐγείρω, I raise up
ἐγενόμην (γίνομαι), I became
ἐγώ, I
ἔδωκα (δίδωμι), I gave
ἔθνος, -ους, τό, a nation; pl., Gentiles
εἰ, if
εἶδον (ὁράω), I saw
εἰμί, I am
εἶπον (λέγω), I said
εἰς, acc., into
εἷς, μία, ἕν, one

εἰσέρχομαι, I go, come in/into, enter
ἐκ, ἐξ, gen., out of, from
ἐκεῖνος, -η, -ο, that
ἔλαβον (λαμβάνω), I took, received
ἐν, dat., in
ἐξέρχομαι, I go out
ἐπί, gen., over, on, at the time of; dat., on the basis of, at; acc., on, to, against
ἔργον, -ου, τό, work
ἔρχομαι, I come, go
ἐσθίω, I eat
εὑρίσκω, I find
ἔχω, I have, hold
ἕως, until; gen., as far as
ζάω, I live
ἤ, or
ἦλθον (ἔρχομαι), I went
ἡμέρα, -ας, ἡ, day
θέλω, I will, wish, want
θεός, -οῦ, ὁ, god, God

ἰδού, *see!, behold!*
Ἰησοῦς, -οῦ, ὁ, *Jesus*
ἵνα, *in order that, that*
Ἰουδαῖος, -ου, ὁ, *Jew*
ἵστημι, *I cause to stand, I stand*
καθώς, *as, even as*
καί, *and, even, also*
καλέω, *I call, name, invite*
καρδία, -ας, ἡ, *heart*
κατά, gen., *down from, against;* acc., *according to, throughout, during*
κόσμος, ου, ὁ, *world*
κύριος, -ου, ὁ, *lord, master, sir*
λαλέω, *I speak*
λαμβάνω, *I take, receive*
λαός, -οῦ, ὁ, *people*
λέγω, *I say, speak*
λόγος, -ου, ὁ, *word*
μαθητής, -οῦ, ὁ, *disciple*
μέγας, μεγάλη, μέγα, *large, great*
μέν, postpositive particle, *on the one hand, indeed* (or untrans.)
μετά, gen., *with;* acc., *after*
μή, *not, lest*
νόμος, -ου, ὁ, *law, the Law*
νῦν, *now*
ὁ, ἡ, τό, *the*
οἶδα, *I know*

ὄνομα, *name*
ὁράω, *I see*
ὅς, ἥ, ὅ, *who, which*
ὅστις, ἥτις, ὅτι, *whoever, whichever, whatever*
ὅτι, *that, because*
οὐ, οὐκ, οὐχ, *not*
οὐδέ, *and not, not even, neither, nor*
οὐδείς, οὐδεμία, οὐδέν, *no one, nothing*
οὖν, *therefore*
οὐρανός, *heaven, sky*
οὗτος, αὕτη, τοῦτο, *this; he, her, it*
οὕτως, *thus*
ὄχλος, -ου, ὁ, *crowd, multitude*
πάλιν, *again*
παρά, gen. *from;* dat., *beside, in the presence of;* acc., *alongside of*
πᾶς, πᾶσα, πᾶν, *every, all*
πατήρ, πατρός, ὁ, *father*
Παῦλος, -ου, ὁ, *Paul*
περί, gen., *concerning, about;* acc., *around*
Πέτρος, -ου, ὁ, *Peter*
πιστεύω, *I have faith (in), believe*
πίστις, -εως, ἡ, *faith, belief, trust*
πνεῦμα, -ατος, τό, *spirit, the Spirit*

ποιέω, *I do, make*
πόλις, -εως, ἡ, *city*
πολύς, πολλή, πολύ, *much;* pl., *many*
πορεύομαι, *I go, proceed*
πρός, acc., *to, towards, with*
προφήτης, -ου, ὁ, *prophet*
πρῶτος, -η, -ον, *first*
σάρξ, σαρκός, ἡ, *flesh*
σύ, *you*
σῶμα, -ατος, τό, *body*
τέ, *and*
τις, τι, *someone/thing, a certain one/thing, anyone/thing*
τίς, τί, *who? what? which? why?*
τότε, *then, at that time*
υἱός, -οῦ, ὁ, *son*
ὑπέρ, gen., *in behalf of;* acc., *above*
ὑπό, gen., *by;* acc., *under*
φωνή, -ῆς, ἡ, *sound, voice*
χάρις, -ιτος, ἡ, *grace*
χείρ, χειρός, ἡ, *hand*
Χριστός, *Christ, messiah*
ὡς, *as, that, how, about*

VOCABULARY 2
FREQUENCY: 135-67

Our goal is words that occur 15 or more times in the New Testament, including second aorists, a total of 841 words. Seven vocabulary lists give decreasing frequency. This list has 131 words.

᾽Αβραάμ, *Abraham*
ἀγαθός, -ή, -ον, *good*
ἀγάπη, -ης, ἡ, *love*
ἄγω, *I lead*
αἷμα, -ατος, τό, *blood*
αἴρω, *I take up/away*
αἰτέω, *I ask*
αἰών, -ῶνος, ὁ, *age*
ἀκολουθέω, *I follow*
ἀλήθεια, -ας, ἡ, *truth*
ἀλλήλων, *of one another*
ἄλλος, -η, -ο, *other, another*
ἀμήν, *verily, truly, amen*
ἀναβαίνω, *I go up*
ἀνίστημι, *I cause to rise; I arise*
ἀνοίγω, *I open*
ἀπέθανον (ἀποθνήσκω), *I died*
ἀπέρχομαι, *I depart*
ἀποθνήσκω, *I die*
ἀποκτείνω, *I kill*

ἀπόλλυμι, *I destroy; middle, I perish*
ἀποστέλλω, *I send*
ἀπόστολος, -ου, ὁ, *apostle*
ἄρτος, -ου, ὁ, *bread, loaf*
ἀρχιερεύς, -έως, ὁ, *chief/high priest*
ἄρχω, *I rule; often middle, I begin*
βάλλω, *I throw, put*
βαπτίζω, *I baptize*
βασιλεύς, -έως, ὁ, *king*
βλέπω, *I see*
γεννάω, *I beget*
δεῖ, *it is necessary*
διδάσκω, *I teach*
δίκαιος, -α, -ον, *right, just, righteous*
δικαιοσύνη, -ης, ἡ, *righteousness*
δοῦλος, -ου, ὁ, *slave*
δύναμις, -εως, ἡ, *power*
δύο, *two*

δώδεκα, *twelve*
ἔβαλον (βάλλω), *I threw*
ἔγνων (γινώσκω), *I knew*
εἰρήνη, -ης, ἡ, *peace*
ἕκαστος, -η, -ον, *each*
ἐκβάλλω, *I cast out*
ἐκεῖ, *there*
ἐκκλησία, -ας, ἡ, *assembly, congregation, church*
ἐμός, ἐμή, ἐμόν, *my, mine*
ἐντολή, -ῆς, ἡ, *commandment*
ἐνώπιον, gen., *before*
ἐξουσία, -ας, ἡ, *authority*
ἔπεσον (πίπτω), *I fell*
ἑπτά, *seven*
ἕτερος, -α, -ό, *other, another, different*
ἔτι, *still, yet, even*

εὐαγγέλιον, -ου, τό, good news, the Gospel

εὗρον (εὑρίσκω), I found

ἔφαγον (ἐσθίω), I ate

ζητέω, I seek

ζωή, -ῆς, ἡ, life

ἤγαγον (ἄγω), I led

θάλασσα, -ης, ἡ, sea

θάνατος, -ου, ὁ, death

ἴδιος, -α, -ον, one's own

ἱερόν, -οῦ, τό, temple

Ἰερουσαλήμ, ἡ, Jerusalem

Ἰσραήλ, ὁ, Israel

Ἰωάννης, -ου, ὁ, John

κἀγώ, and I

κάθημαι, I sit

καιρός, -οῦ, ὁ, time, appointed time, season

καλός, -ή, -όν, good, beautiful

καρπός, -οῦ, ὁ, fruit

καταβαίνω, I go down

κεφαλή, -ῆς, ἡ, head

κρίνω, I judge, decide

μᾶλλον, more, rather

μαρτυρέω, I bear witness, testify

μέλλω, I am about to

μένω, I remain

μηδείς, μηδεμία, μηδέν, no one

μήτηρ, μητρός, ἡ, mother

μόνος, -η, -ον, alone, only

Μωϋσῆς, -έως, ὁ, Moses

νεκρός, -ά, -όν, dead; noun, dead body, corpse

ὁδός, -ου, ἡ, way, road, journey

οἰκία, -ας, ἡ, house

οἶκος, -ου, ὁ, house

ὅλος, -η, -ον, whole

ὅπου, where, whither

ὅσος, -η, -ον, as great as, as many as

ὅταν, whenever

ὅτε, when

οὔτε, neither, nor

ὀφθαλμός, -οῦ, ὁ, eye

παραδίδωμι, I hand over, betray

παρακαλέω, I exhort beseech, , console

πέμπω, I send

περιπατέω, I walk; I live

πίνω, I drink

πίπτω, I fall

πιστός, -ή, -όν, faithful, believing

πληρόω, I fill, fulfill

πλοῖον, -ου, τό, boat

πονηρός, -ά, -όν, evil

πούς, ποδός, ὁ, foot

προσέρχομαι, I come to

προσεύχομαι, I pray

πρόσωπον, -ου, τό, face

πῦρ, πυρός, τό, fire

πῶς, how?

ῥῆμα, -ατος, τό, word

σάββατον, -ου, τό, the Sabbath

σημεῖον, -ου, τό, sign

Σίμων, -ος, ὁ, Simon

στόμα, -ατος, τό, mouth

σύν, dat., with

σῴζω, I save

τέκνον, -ου, τό, child

τηρέω, I keep

τίθημι, I place

τόπος, -ου, ὁ, place

τρεῖς, τρία, three

ὕδωρ, ὕδατος, τό, water

ὑπάγω, I depart

Φαρισαῖος, -ου, ὁ, Pharisee

φοβέω, I fear

φῶς, φωτός, τό, light

χαίρω, I rejoice

ψυχή, -ῆς, ἡ, soul, life, self

ὥρα, -ας, ἡ, hour

ὥστε, so that

VOCABULARY 3
FREQUENCY: 66-41

Our goal is words that occur 15 or more times in the New Testament, including second aorists, a total of 841 words. Seven vocabulary lists give decreasing frequency. This list has 127 words.

ἀγαπητός, -ή, -όν, *beloved, dear*

αἰώνιος, -ον, *eternal*

ἁμαρτάνω, *I sin*

ἁμαρτωλός, -όν, *sinful*; noun, *sinner*

ἀνάστασις, -εως, ἡ, *resurrection*

ἄξιος, -α, -ον, *worthy*

ἀπαγγέλλω, *I report, announce*

ἀποδίδωμι, *I give back, pay*; mid., *I sell*

ἀπολύω, *I release*

ἄρα, *then, therefore*

ἀρχή, -ῆς, ἡ, *beginning*

ἀσπάζομαι, *I greet, salute*

ἄχρι, ἄχρις, gen., *as far as, up to*; conj., *until*

Γαλιλαία, -ας, ἡ, *Galilee*

γλῶσσα, -ης, ἡ, *tongue, language*

γενεά, -ᾶς, ἡ, *generation*

γραμματεύς, -έως, ὁ, *scribe*

γραφή, -ῆς, ἡ, *writing, Scripture*

δαιμόνιον, -ου, τό, *demon*

Δαυίδ, ὁ, *David*

δεξιός, -ά, -όν, *right* (opp. left)

δεύτερος, -α, -ον, *second*

δέχομαι, *I receive*

δέω, *I bind*

διδάσκαλος, -ου, ὁ, *teacher*

διέρχομαι, *I pass through*

διό, *wherefore*

διώκω, *I pursue, persecute*

δοκέω, *I think; seem*

δοξάζω, *I glorify*

ἐγγίζω, *I come near*

εἶλον (αἱρέω), *took up*

εἴτε, *if, whether*

ἐλπίς, -ίδος, ἡ, *hope*

ἔμπροσθεν, gen., *in front of, before*

ἔξω, *without*; gen., *outside*

ἐπαγγελία, -ας, ἡ, *promise*

ἐπερωτάω, *I ask, question, demand of*

ἐπιγινώσκω, *I come to know, recognize*

ἐργάζομαι, *I work*

ἔρημος, -ον, *solitary, deserted*; noun, *the desert, wilderness*

ἐρῶ, *I shall say*

ἐρωτάω, *I ask, entreat*

ἔσχατος, -η, -ον, *last*

ἔτος, -ους, τό, *year*

εὐαγγελίζω, *I bring good news, preach good tidings*

εὐθύς, *straight-way, immediately*

εὐλογέω, *I bless*

ἤδη, *now, already*

ἤνεγκα (φέρω), *I brought*

Ἡρῴδης, -ου, ὁ,
Herod
θαυμάζω, I marvel,
wonder at
θέλημα, -ατος, τό,
will
θεραπεύω, I heal
θεωρέω, I look at,
behold
θηρίον, -ου, τό, beast
θλῖψις, -εως, ἡ, tri-
bulation, affliction
θρόνος, -ου, ὁ, throne
Ἰάκωβος, -ου, ὁ,
Jacob. James
Ἱεροσόλυμα, τά or ἡ,
Jerusalem
ἱμάτιον, -ου, τό,
garment
Ἰουδαία, -ας, ἡ,
Judea
Ἰούδας, -α, ὁ, Judah,
Judas
καθίζω, I seat, sit
καινός, -ή, -όν, new
κακός, -ή, -όν, bad,
evil
κατοικέω, I inhabit,
dwell
κηρύσσω, I proclaim,
preach
κράζω, I cry out
κρατέω, I grasp
κρίσις, -εως, ἡ,
judgment
λίθος, -ου, ὁ, stone
λοιπός, -ή, -όν, re-
maining; n.: the rest;
adv.: for the rest

λύω, I loose
μακάριος, -α, -ον,
blessed, happy
μέρος, -ους, τό, part
μέσος, -η, -ον,
middle, in the midst
μηδέ, but not, nor,
not even
μικρός, -ά, -όν,
small, little
ναός, -οῦ, ὁ, temple
νύξ, νυκτός, ἡ, night
ὅμοιος, -α, -ον, like
ὅπως, so that, that
ὄρος, ὄρους, τό,
mountain
οὐαί, woe! alas!
οὐκέτι, no longer
οὐχί, not
παιδίον, -ου, τό,
infant, child
πάντοτε, always
παραβολή, -ῆς, ἡ,
parable
παραλαμβάνω, I
receive
παρίστημι, I am
present, stand by
πάσχω, I suffer
πείθω, I persuade
Πιλᾶτος, -ου, ὁ,
Pilate
πλεῖον, -ονος, (cf.
πολύς) larger, more
ποῦ, where?
πρεσβύτερος, -α, -ον,
elder
πρό, gen., before
προσκυνέω, I worship

προσφέρω, I bring to,
offer
σεαυτοῦ, of yourself
σήμερον, today
σοφία, -ας, ἡ, wisdom
σπείρω, I sow
σπέρμα, -ατος, τό,
seed
σταυρόω, I crucify
συνάγω, I gather
together
συναγωγή, -ῆς, ἡ,
synagogue
σωτηρία, -ας, ἡ,
salvation
τέσσαρες, -ων, four
τιμή, -ῆς, ἡ, honor,
price
τοιοῦτος, -αύτη,
-οῦτο, such
τρίτος, -η, -ον, third
τυφλός, -ή, -όν, blind
ὑπάρχω, I am, exist;
τὰ ὑπάρχοντα,
one's possessions
φανερόω, I manifest
φέρω, I carry, bear
φημί, I say
φόβος, -ου, ὁ, fear
φυλακή, -ῆς, ἡ,
guard, prison, watch
φωνέω, I call
χαρά, -ᾶς, ἡ, joy,
delight
χρεία, -ας, ἡ, need
χρόνος, -ου, ὁ, time
χωρίς, gen., without
ὧδε, here

VOCABULARY 4
FREQUENCY: 40-28

Our goal is words that occur 15 or more times in the New Testament, including second aorists, a total of 841 words. Seven vocabulary lists give decreasing frequency. This list has 127 words.

ἁγιάζω, I sanctify

ἀγοράζω, I buy

ἀγρός, -οῦ, ὁ, field

ἀδικέω, I wrong, do wrong

ἀκάθαρτος, -ον, unclean

ἀληθινός, -ή, -όν, true

ἀναγινώσκω, I read

ἄνεμος, -ου, ὁ, wind

ἅπας, -ασα, -αν, all

ἅπτω, I touch

ἀρνέομαι, I deny

ἀρνίον, -ου, τό, lamb

ἄρτι, now, just now

ἄρχων, -οντος, ὁ, ruler

ἀσθενέω, I am weak

Βαρναβᾶς, -ᾶ, ὁ, Barnabas

βιβλίον, -ου, τό, book

βλασφημέω, I revile, blaspheme

βούλομαι, I wish, determine

γαμέω, I marry

γνῶσις, -εως, ἡ, wisdom

δείκνύω and δείκνυμι, I show

διάβολος, -ον, slanderous, accusing falsely; noun, the Accuser, the Devil

διαθήκη, -ης, ἡ, covenant

διακονέω, I wait upon, serve, minister

διακονία, -ας, ἡ, waiting at table, service, ministry

διάκονος, -ου, ὁ and ἡ, servant, administrator, deacon

διδαχή, -ῆς, ἡ, teaching

δικαιόω, I justify, declare righteous

δυνατός, -ή, -όν, powerful, possible

ἐγγύς, near

ἐκεῖθεν, from there

ἐκπορεύομαι, I go out

ἐλεέω, I have mercy

ἐλπίζω, I hope

ἐμαυτοῦ, of myself

ἔξεστι, it is lawful

ἐπιθυμία, -ας, ἡ, eager desire, passion

ἐπικαλέω, I call, name; mid., I invoke, appeal to

ἔπιον (πίνω), I drank

ἐπιστρέφω, I turn to, return

ἐπιτίθημι, I lay upon

ἐπιτιμάω, I rebuke, warn

ἑτοιμάζω, I prepare

εὐθέως, immediately

εὐχαριστέω, I give thanks

ἐχθρός, -ά, -όν, hating; noun, an enemy

ἡγέομαι, I am chief; I think, regard

Ἠλίας, -ου, ὁ, Elijah

ἥλιος, -ου, ὁ, the sun

θυγάτηρ, -τρός, ἡ, daughter

θύρα, -ας, ἡ, door

θυσία, -ας, ἡ, *sacrifice*
ἴδε, *see! behold*
ἱερεύς, -έως, ὁ, *priest*
ἱκανός, -ή, -όν,
 sufficient, able,
 considerable
ἰσχυρός, -ά, -όν,
 strong
ἰσχύω, *I am strong*
Ἰωσήφ, ὁ, *Joseph*
καθαρίζω, *I cleanse*
Καίσαρ, -ος, ὁ, *Caesar*
καλῶς, *well*
καυχάομαι, *I boast*
κλαίω, *I weep*
λογίζομαι, *I account,*
 reckon
μαρτυρία, -ας, ἡ,
 testimony, evidence
μάρτυς, -υρος, ὁ,
 witness
μάχαιρα, -ης, ἡ, *sword*
μέλος, -ους, τό,
 member
μετανοέω, *I repent*
μήτε, *neither, nor*
μισέω, *I hate*
μισθός, -οῦ, ὁ, *wage,*
 reward
μνημεῖον, -ου, τό,
 tomb, monument
μυστήριον, -ου, τό,
 mystery
ναί, *truly, yes*
νικάω, *I conquer*
οἰκοδομέω, *I build,*
 edify
οἶνος, -ου, ὁ, *wine*

ὀλίγος, -η, -ον, *little,*
 few
ὁμοίως, *likewise*
ὀπίσω, gen., *behind,*
 after
ὀργή, -ῆς, ἡ, *anger*
οὖς, ὠτός, τό, *ear*
ὀφείλω, *I owe, ought*
παραγγέλλω, *I*
 command, charge
παραγίνομαι, *I come,*
 arrive
παράκλησις, -εως, ἡ,
 exhortation,
 consolation
παρέρχομαι, *I pass by,*
 pass away; I arrive
παρρησία, -ας, ἡ,
 boldness, confidence
πάσχα, τό (not
 inflected), *passover*
πειράζω, *I test, tempt,*
 attempt
πέντε, *five*
περισσεύω, *I abound,*
 am rich
περιτομή, -ῆς, ἡ,
 circumcision
πλανάω, *I lead astray*
πλῆθος, -ους, τό,
 multitude
πλήν, *however, but,*
 only; gen., except
πλούσιος, -α, -ον, *rich*
πόθεν, *from where*
ποῖος, -α, -ό, *what sort*
 of? what?
ποτέ, *at some time,*
 once, ever

ποτήριον, -ου, τό, *cup*
πράσσω, *I do, perform*
πρόβατον, -ου, τό,
 sheep
προσευχή, -ῆς, ἡ,
 prayer
προσκαλέομαι, *I*
 summon
προφητεύω, *I prophesy*
πτωχός, -ή, -όν, *poor;*
 noun, *poor man*
Σατανᾶς, -ᾶ, ὁ, *Satan,*
 Adversary
σκανδαλίζω, *I cause*
 to stumble
σκότος, -ους, τό,
 darkness
συνείδησις, -εως, ἡ,
 conscience
συνέρχομαι, *I come*
 together
τελέω, *I finish, fulfill*
τέλος, -ους, τό, *end*
ὑπομονή, -ῆς, ἡ,
 steadfast endurance
ὑποστρέφω, *I return*
ὑποτάσσω, *I subject,*
 put in subjection
φαίνω, *I shine, appear*
φεύγω, *I flee*
Φίλιππος, -ου, ὁ,
 Philip
φίλος, -η, -ον, *loving;*
 noun, *friend*
φυλάσσω, *I guard*
φυλή, -ῆς, ἡ, *tribe*
χώρα, -ας, ἡ, *country*
ὥσπερ, *just as, even as*

VOCABULARY 5
FREQUENCY: 27-21

Our goal is words that occur 15 or more times in the New Testament, including second aorists, a total of 841 words. Seven vocabulary lists give decreasing frequency. This list has 124 words.

ἀγνοέω, *I do not know*
ἀδελφή, -ῆς, ἡ, *sister*
ἀδικία, -ας, ἡ, *unrighteousness*
Αἴγυπτος, -ου, ἡ, *Egypt*
ἀκοή, -ῆς, ἡ, *hearing; report*
ἀληθής, -ές, *true*
ἀμπελών, -ῶνος, ὁ, *vineyard*
ἀναβλέπω, *I look up, receive sight*
ἀνάγω, *I lead up; mid., I put to sea, set sail*
ἀναιρέω, *I take up; kill*
ἀντί, gen., *instead of, for*
ἄπιστος, -ον, *unbelieving, faithless*
ἀποκαλύπτω, *I reveal*
ἀσθένεια, -ας, ἡ, *weakness*
ἀσθενής, -ές, *weak*
ἀστήρ, -έρος, ὁ, *star*
αὐξάνω, *I cause to grow; increase*

βασιλεύω, *I reign*
βαστάζω, *I bear, carry*
γέ, *indeed even*
γνωρίζω, *I make known*
γρηγορέω, *I watch*
δέκα, *ten*
δένδρον, -ου, τό, *tree*
δέομαι, *I beseech*
διδασκαλία, -ας, ἡ, *teaching*
διότι, *because*
δοκιμάζω, *I prove, approve*
δουλεύω, *I serve*
εἰκών, -όνος, ἡ, *image*
ἐκλέγομαι, *I pick out, choose*
ἐκλεκτός, -ή, -όν, *chosen, elect*
ἔλεος, -ους, τό, *pity, mercy*
ἐλεύθερος, -α, -ον, *free*
Ἕλλην, -ος, ὁ, *Greek*
ἐνδύω, *I put on, clothe*
ἕνεκα or ἕνεκεν, gen., *on account of*

ἐνεργέω, *I work, produce*
ἑορτή, -ῆς, ἡ, *feast*
ἔπαθον (πάσχω), *I suffered*
ἐπεί, *when, since*
ἐπιστολή, -ῆς, ἡ, *letter*
εὐδοκέω, *I think it good, am well pleased with*
ἐφίστημι, *I stand over, come upon*
ἔφυγον (φεύγω), *I fled*
ζῷον, -ου, τό, *living creature, animal*
ἥκω, *I have come*
Ἠσαΐας, -ου, ὁ, *Isaiah*
θεάομαι, *I behold*
θερίζω, *I reap*
θυσιαστήριον, -ου, τό, *altar*
Ἰακώβ, ὁ, *Jacob*
ἰάομαι, *I heal*
καθαρός, -ά, -όν, *clean*
καθεύδω, *I sleep*

καθίστημι, I set,
    constitute
κἀκεῖνος, -η, -ο, and
    that one
καταλείπω, I leave
καταργέω, I bring to
    naught, abolish
κατεργάζομαι, I work
    out
κατηγορέω, I accuse
κεῖμαι, I lie, am laid
κελεύω, I order
κοιλία, -ας, ἡ, belly;
    womb
κοπιάω, I toil
κρίμα, -ατος, τό,
    judgment
κωλύω, I forbid, hinder
κώμη, -ης, ἡ, village
λατρεύω, I serve,
    worship
λευκός, -ή, -όν, white
λυπέω, I grieve
Μακεδονία, -ας, ἡ,
    Macedonia
μανθάνω, I learn
Μαρία, -ας, ἡ, Mary
Μαριάμ, ἡ, Mary
μετάνοια, -ας, ἡ,
    repentance
μηκέτι, no longer
μήποτε, lest,
    perchance
μιμνήσκομαι, I
    remember
μνημονεύω, I
    remember

νέος, -α, -ον, new,
    young
νεφέλη, -ης, ἡ, cloud
νοῦς, νοός, ὁ, mind
ὀμνύω or ὄμνυμι, I
    swear, take an oath
ὁμολογέω, I confess,
    profess
οὗ, where
οὔπω, not yet
παῖς, παιδός, ὁ and ἡ,
    boy, girl, child,
    servant
πάρειμι, I am present;
    I have arrived
παρουσία, -ας, ἡ,
    presence, coming
πεινάω, I hunger
πειρασμός, -οῦ, ὁ,
    temptation
πέραν, gen., beyond
περιβάλλω, I put
    around, clothe
πίμπλημι, I fill
πληγή, -ῆς, ἡ, blow,
    wound, plague
πλοῦτος, -ου, ὁ,
    wealth
πνευματικός, -ή, -όν,
    spiritual
πορνεία, -ας, ἡ,
    fornication
πόσος, -η, -ον, how
    great? how much?
προσέχω, I attend to,
    give heed to
πωλέω, I sell

σκεῦος, -ους, τό,
    vessel; pl., goods
σός, σή, σόν, your,
    yours
σταυρός, -οῦ, ὁ, cross
στέφανος, -ου, ὁ,
    crown
στρατιώτης, -ου, ὁ,
    soldier
στρέφω, I turn
συνέδριον, -ου, τό,
    council, Sanhedrin
συνίημι, I understand
σωτήρ, -ῆρος, ὁ,
    Saviour
τελειόω, I fulfill, make
    perfect
τελώνης, -ου, ὁ, tax
    gatherer
τεσσαράκοντα, forty
τιμάω, I honor
Τιμόθεος, -ου, ὁ,
    Timothy
ὑπακούω, I obey
φιλέω, I love
φρονέω, I think
χαρίζομαι, I give
    freely, forgive
χήρα, -ας, ἡ, widow
χιλίαρχος, -ου, ὁ,
    tribune, captain
χιλιάς, -άδος, ἡ,
    thousand
ὡσεί, as, like, about

VOCABULARY 6
FREQUENCY: 20-17

Our goal is words that occur 15 or more times in the New Testament, including second aorists, a total of 841 words. Seven vocabulary lists give decreasing frequency. This list has 110 words.

αἰτία, -ας, ἡ, *cause, accusation*

ἀκροβυστία, -ας, ἡ, *uncircumcision*

ἀληθῶς, *truly*

ἀνάγκη, -ης, ἡ, *necessity*

Ἀντιοχεία, -ας, ἡ, *Antioch*

ἀπέχω, *I have received (payment); I am distant*

ἀποκάλυψις, -εως, ἡ, *revelation*

ἀπώλεια, -ας, ἡ, *destruction*

ἀργύριον, *silver, money*

ἀρέσκω, *I please*

ἀριθμός, -ους, ὁ, *number*

Ἀσία, -ας, ἡ, *Asia*

ἄφεσις, -εως, ἡ, *sending away, remission*

βάπτισμα, -ατος, τό, *baptism*

βλασφημία, -ας, ἡ, *reproach, blasphemy*

βρῶμα, -ατος, τό, *food*

γένος, -ους, τό, *race, kind*

γεωργός, -οῦ, ὁ, *farmer*

γονεύς, -έως, ὁ, *parent*

δέησις, -εως, ἡ, *entreaty*

δεσμός, -οῦ, ὁ, *fetter, bond*

διακρίνω, *I judge, dis-criminate,; mid., I doubt*

δῶρον, -ου, τό, *gift*

ἔδραμον (τρέχω), *I ran*

εἰσπορεύομαι, *I enter*

ἑκατόν, *one hundred*

ἑκατοντάρχης (-αρ-χος), -ου, ὁ, *centurion*

ἐλέγχω, *I convict, reprove*

ἔμαθον (μαν-θάνω), *I learned*

ἐξίστημι, *I amaze, am amazed*

ἐπαίρω, *I lift up*

ἐπάνω, *above; gen., over*

ἐπαύριον, *tomorrow*

ἐπιβάλλω, *I lay upon*

ἐπίγνωσις, -εως, ἡ, *knowledge*

ἐπιλαμβάνομαι, *I take hold of*

ἐπιτρέπω, *I permit*

ἐπουράνιος, -ιον, *heavenly*

ἔσχον (ἔχω), *I had*

ἕτοιμος, -η, -ον, *ready, prepared*

ἔτυχον (τυγχάνω), *I obtained*

ἐχάρην (χαίρω), *I was glad*

ἡγεμών, -όνος, ὁ, *leader (Roman: gov.)*

θησαυρός, -οῦ, ὁ, *storehouse, treasure*

θυμός, -ους, ὁ, *wrath*
ἵππος, -ου, ὁ, *horse*
Ἰσαάκ, ὁ, *Isaac*
ἰχθύς, -ύος, ὁ, *fish*
Καισάρεια, -ας, ἡ,
  Caesarea
κἄν, *and if*
καταγγέλλω, *I*
  proclaim
κατακρίνω, *I condemn*
καταλύω, *I destroy; I*
  lodge
κατέχω, *I hold back,*
  hold fast
κενός, -ή, -όν, *empty,*
  vain
κερδαίνω, *I gain*
κληρονομέω, *I inherit*
κοιμάω, *I sleep, fall*
  asleep
κοινωνία, -ας, ἡ,
  fellowship;
  contribution
κόπος, -ου, ὁ, *labor,*
  trouble
κρείττων or
  κρείσσων, -ονος,
  better
κριτής, -οῦ, ὁ, *judge*
κρυπτός, -ή, -όν,
  hidden
κρύπτω, *I conceal*
κτίσις, -εως, ἡ,
  creation, creature
μαρτύριον, -ου, τό,
  testimony, witness
μεριμνάω, *I am*
  anxious, distracted

μέχρι or μέχρις, *until;*
  gen., *as far as*
μήν, μηνός, ὁ, *month*
μήτι, interrogative;
  expects "no"
νηστεύω, *I fast*
νίπτω, *I wash*
νυνί, *now*
ξύλον, -ου, τό, *weed,*
  tree
οἰκοδομή, -ῆς, ἡ,
  building; edification
παλαιός, -ά, -όν, *old*
παράπτωμα, -ατος, τό,
  trespass
παρατίθημι, *I set*
  before; mid., *I*
  entrust
παραχρῆμα,
  immediately
περισσότερος, -α,
  -ον, *greater, more*
περιτέμνω, *I*
  circumcise
πλήρωμα, -ατος, τό,
  fullness
πλησίον, *near;* noun,
  neighbor
ποιμήν, -ένος, ὁ,
  shepherd
πόλεμος, -ου, ὁ, *war*
πολλάκις, *often*
ποταμός, -οῦ, ὁ, *river*
πότε, *when?*
προάγω, *I lead forth,*
  go before
προστίθημι, *I add, add*
  to

προφητεία, -ας, ἡ,
  prophecy
πυλών, -ῶνος, ὁ,
  vestibule, gateway
ῥίζα, -ης, ἡ, *root*
ῥύομαι, *I rescue,*
  deliver
σκηνή, -ῆς, ἡ, *tent,*
  tabernacle
σοφός, -ή, -όν, *wise*
ταράσσω, *I trouble*
τέλειος, -α, -ον,
  complete, perfect,
  mature
τίκτω, *I give birth to*
τοσοῦτος, -αύτη,
  -οῦτο, *so great, so*
  much; pl., *so many*
τρέχω, *I run*
ὑπηρέτης, -ου, ὁ,
  servant, assistant
ὑποκριτής, -οῦ, ὁ,
  hypocrite
ὑπομένω, *I tarry; I*
  endure
ὑψόω, *I lift up, exalt*
φανερός, -ά, -όν,
  manifest
χάρισμα, -ατος, τό,
  gift
χρυσοῦς, -ῆ, -οῦν,
  χρύσεος, -α, -ον,
  (contract forms)
  golden
ὦ, *O!*
ὡσαύτως, *likewise*

VOCABULARY 7
FREQUENCY: 16-15

Our goal is words that occur 15 or more times in the New Testament, including second aorists, a total of 841 words. Seven vocabulary lists give decreasing frequency. This list has 92 words.

ἀθετέω, I reject
ἀνακρίνω, I examine
ἀνέχομαι, I endure
ἀνομία, -ας, ἡ, lawlessness
ἀπάγω, I lead away
γάμος, -ου, ὁ, marriage, wedding
γεύομαι, I taste
γνωστός, -ή, -όν, known
γυμνός, -ή, -όν, naked
Δαμασκός, -ου, ἡ, Damascus
δεῖπνον, -ου, τό, supper
δέρω, I beat
δέσμιος, -ου, ὁ, prisoner
δηνάριον, -ου, τό, denarius
διαλογίζομαι, I debate
διαμαρτύρομαι, I testify solemnly
διατάσσω, I command
διψάω, I thirst

εἶτα, then, next
ἐκτείνω, I stretch forth
ἐκχέω, I pour out
ἐλαία, -ας, ἡ, olive tree
ἐμβαίνω, I embark
ἐντέλλω, I command
ἐπαγγέλλομαι, I promise
ἔπειτα, then
ἐπιθυμέω, I desire
ἐπιμένω, I continue
ἐργάτης, -ου, ὁ, workman
εὐλογία, -ας, ἡ, blessing
εὐσέβεια, -ας, ἡ, piety, godliness
εὐχαριστία, -ας, ἡ, thanksgiving
Ἔφεσος, -ου, ἡ, Ephesus
ζῆλος, -ου, ὁ, zeal, jealousy
ἥμαρτον (ἁμαρτάνω), I sinned

θεμέλιος, -ου, ὁ, foundation
θρίξ, τριχός, ἡ, hair
Ἰορδάνης, -ου, ὁ, Jordan
κακῶς, badly
καταλαμβάνω, I overtake, apprehend
κατέρχομαι, I come down, go down
Καφαρναούμ, ἡ, Capernaum
κλείω, I shut
κλέπτης, -ου, ὁ, thief
κληρονόμος, -ου, ὁ, heir
κτίζω, I create
Λάζαρος, -ου, ὁ, Lazarus
λῃστής, -οῦ, ὁ, robber
λύπη, -ης, ἡ, pain, grief
μοιχεύω, I commit adultery
νήπιος, -ου, ὁ, infant, child
νομίζω, I suppose

νυμφίος, -ου, ὁ,
  bridegroom
ξηραίνω, I dry up
ὅθεν, from where,
  wherefore
οἰκουμένη, -ης, ἡ,
  (inhabited) world
ὁμοιόω, I make like,
  liken
οὐδέποτε, never
ὀψία, -ας, ἡ, late,
  evening
πάθημα, -ατος, τό,
  suffering
παρέχω, I offer, afford
παρθένος, -ου, ἡ, ὁ,
  virgin
παύω, I cease
περισσός, -ή, -όν,
  excessive, abundant
πέτρα, -ας, ἡ, rock
πλήρης, -ες, full

ποτίζω, I give drink
προλέγω, I say
  beforehand
προσδοκάω, I wait for
πώς, somehow, perhaps
ῥαββί, particle, (my)
  rabbi, master,
  teacher
σαλεύω, I shake
Σαῦλος, -ου, ὁ, Saul
σκάνδαλον, -ου, τό, a
  cause of stumbling
σκοτία, -ας, ἡ,
  darkness
συκῆ, -ῆς, ἡ, fig tree
συλλαμβάνω, I take,
  conceive
συμφέρω, I bring
  together; imper., it is
  profitable
συνίστημι,
  συνιστάνω, trans., I

commend; intrans., I
  stand with, consist
σφραγίζω, I seal
σφραγίς, -ῖδος, ἡ, seal
ταχέως, quickly, soon
τέρας, -ατος, τό,
  wonder
τολμάω, I dare
τράπεζα, -ης, ἡ, table
τροφή, -ῆς, ἡ, food
τύπος, -ου, ὁ, mark,
  example
ὑπακοή, -ῆς, ἡ,
  obedience
ὑστερέω, I lack
χορτάζω, I eat to the
  full, am satisfied, am
  filled
χόρτος, -ου, ὁ, grass,
  hay
ὠφελέω, I profit

VOCABULARY
GREEK–ENGLISH

This index includes the total list of vocabulary words that are assigned in this text. The first number is the vocabulary list; the second number is the New Testament frequency. Second aorist verbs are included (third principal part). Their frequency number includes all inflected second aorist forms and their compounds.

Ἀβραάμ, *Abraham* 2.73
ἀγαθός, *good* 2.102
ἀγαπάω, *I love* 1.143
ἀγάπη, *love* 2.116
ἀγαπητός, *beloved* 3.61
ἄγγελος, *messenger* 1.175
ἁγιάζω, *I sanctify* 4.28
ἅγιος, *holy* 1.233
ἀγνοέω, *I do not know* 5.22
ἀγοράζω, *I buy* 4.30
ἀγρός, *field* 4.36
ἄγω, *I lead* 2.67
ἀδελφή, *sister* 5.26
ἀδελφός, *brother* 1.343
ἀδικέω, *I wrong* 4.28
ἀδικία, *unrighteousness* 5.25
ἀθετέω, *I reject* 7.16
Αἴγυπτος, *Egypt* 5.25
αἷμα, *blood* 2.97
αἴρω, *I take up* 2.101
αἰτέω, *I ask* 2.70

αἰτία, *cause* 6.20
αἰών, *age* 2.122
αἰώνιος, *eternal* 3.71
ἀκάθαρτος, *unclean* 4.32
ἀκοή, -ῆς, ἡ, *hearing* 5.24
ἀκολουθέω, *I follow* 2.90
ἀκούω, *I hear* 1.428
ἀκροβυστία, *uncircumcision* 6.20
ἀλήθεια, *truth* 2.109
ἀληθής, *true* 5.26
ἀληθινός, *true* 4.28
ἀληθῶς, *truly* 6.18
ἀλλά, *but* 1.638
ἀλλήλων, *of one another* 2.100
ἄλλος, *other* 2.155
ἁμαρτάνω, *I sin* 3.43
ἁμαρτία, *sin* 1.173
ἁμαρτωλός, *sinful* 3.47
ἀμήν, *truly* 2.129
ἀμπελών, *vineyard* 5.23

ἄν, *particle* 1.166
ἀναβαίνω, *I go up* 2.82
ἀναβλέπω, *I look up* 5.25
ἀναγινώσκω, *I read* 4.32
ἀνάγκη, *necessity* 6.17
ἀνάγω, *I lead up* 5.23
ἀναιρέω, *I take up* 5.24
ἀνακρίνω, *I examine* 7.16
ἀνάστασις, *resurrection* 3.42
ἄνεμος, *wind* 4.31
ἀνέχομαι, *I endure* 7.15
ἀνήρ, *man* 1.216
ἄνθρωπος, *man* 1.550
ἀνίστημι, *I arise* 2.108
ἀνοίγω, *I open* 2.77
ἀνομία, *lawlessness* 7.15
ἀντί, *instead of* 5.22
Ἀντιοχεία, *Antioch* 6.18

ἄξιος, worthy 3.41
ἀπαγγέλλω, I announce 3.45
ἀπάγω, I lead away 7.15
ἅπας, all 4.34
ἀπέθανον (ἀποθνή- σκω), I died 2.88
ἀπέρχομαι, I depart 2.117
ἀπέχω, I have received 6.19
ἄπιστος, unbelieving 5.23
ἀπό, from 1.646
ἀποδίδωμι, I give back 1.48
ἀποθνήσκω, I die 2.111
ἀποκαλύπτω, I reveal 5.26
ἀποκάλυψις, revelation 6.18
ἀποκρίνομαι, I answer 1.231
ἀποκτείνω, I kill 2.74
ἀπόλλυμι, I destroy 2.90
ἀπολύω, I release 3.66
ἀποστέλλω, I send 2.132
ἀπόστολος, apostle 2.80
ἅπτω, I touch 4.39
ἀπώλεια, destruction 6.18
ἄρα, then 3.53
ἀργύριον, silver 6.20
ἀρέσκω, I please 6.17
ἀριθμός, number 6.18
ἀρνέομαι, I deny 4.33

ἀρνίον, lamb 4.30
ἄρτι, now 4.36
ἄρτος, bread, loaf 2.97
ἀρχή, beginning 3.55
ἀρχιερεύς, chief priest 2.122
ἄρχω, I rule 2.86
ἄρχων, ruler 4.37
ἀσθένεια, weakness 5.24
ἀσθενέω, I am weak 4.33
Ἀσία, Asia 6.18
ἀσθενής, weak 5.26
ἀσπάζομαι, I greet 3.59
ἀστήρ, star 5.24
αὐξάνω, I increase 5.21
αὐτός, he 1.5597
ἄφεσις, sending away 6.17
ἀφίημι, I let go 1.143
ἄχρι, until 3.49
βάλλω, I throw, put 2.122
βαπτίζω, I baptize 2.77
βάπτισμα, baptism 6.19
Βαρναβᾶς, Barnabas 4.28
βασιλεία, kingdom 1.162
βασιλεύς, -έως, ὁ, king 2.115
βασιλεύω, I reign 5.21
βαστάζω, I bear 5.27
βιβλίον, book 4.34
βλασφημέω, I blaspheme 4.34
βλασφημία, blasphemy 6.18

βλέπω, I see 2.133
βούλομαι, I wish 4.37
βρῶμα, food 6.17
Γαλιλαία, Galilee 3.61
γαμέω, I marry 4.28
γάμος, marriage 7.16
γάρ, for 1.1041
γέ, indeed 5.26
γενεά, generation 3.43
γεννάω, I beget 2.97
γένος, race 6.20
γεύομαι, I taste 7.15
γεωργός, farmer 6.19
γῆ, earth 1.250
γίνομαι, I become 1.669
γινώσκω, I know 1.222
γλῶσσα, tongue 3.50
γνωρίζω, I make known 5.25
γνῶσις, wisdom 4.29
γνωστός, known 7.15
γονεύς, parent 6.20
γραμματεύς, -έως, ὁ, scribe 3.63
γραφή, writing 3.50
γράφω, I write 1.191
γρηγορέω, I watch 5.22
γυμνός, naked 7.15
δαιμόνιον, demon 3.63
Δαμασκός, Damascus 7.15
Δαυίδ, David 3.59
δέ, but 1.2792
δέησις, entreaty 6.18
δεῖ, it is necessary 2.101
δείκνυμι, I show 4.30
δεῖπνον, supper 7.16
δέκα, ten 5.25

δένδρον, *tree*   5.25
δεξιός, *right*   3.54
δέομαι, *I beseech*   5.22
δέρω, *I beat*   7.15
δέσμιος, *prisoner*   7.16
δεσμός, *bond*   6.18
δεύτερος, *second*   3.43
δέχομαι, *I receive*   3.56
δέω, *I bind*   3.43
δηνάριον, *denarius*
                       7.16
διά, *through*   1.667
διάβολος, *slanderous*
                       4.37
διαθήκη, *covenant*   4.33
διακονέω, *I serve*   4.37
διακονία, *service*   4.34
διάκονος, *servant*   4.29
διακρίνω, *I*
   discriminate   6.19
διαλογίζομαι, *I*
   debate   7.16
διαμαρτύρομαι, *I*
   testify solemnly 7.15
διατάσσω, *I command*
                       7.16
διδασκαλία, *teaching*
                       5.21
διδάσκαλος, *teacher*
                       3.59
διδάσκω, *I teach*   2.97
διδαχή, *teaching*   4.30
δίδωμι, *I am able*   1.415
διέρχομαι, *I pass*
   through   3.43
δίκαιος, *righteous*   2.79
δικαιοσύνη,
   righteousness   2.92
δικαιόω, *I justify*   4.39
διό, *wherefore*   3.53

διότι, *because*   5.23
διψάω, *I thirst*   7.16
διώκω, *I pursue*   3.45
δοκέω, *I think*   3.62
δοκιμάζω, *I approve*
                       5.22
δόξα, *glory*   1.166
δοξάζω, *I glorify*   3.61
δουλεύω, *I serve*   5.25
δοῦλος, *slave*   2.126
δύναμαι, *I can, am*
   able   1.210
δύναμις, -εως, ἡ,
   power   2.119
δυνατός, *powerful*   4.32
δύο, *two*   2.135
δώδεκα, *twelve*   2.75
δῶρον, *gift*   6.19
ἐάν, *if*   1.350
ἑαυτοῦ, *of himself*
                       1.319
ἔβαλον (βάλλω), *I*
   threw   2.132
ἔβην (βαίνω, com-
   pounds), *I went*   1.140
ἐγγίζω, *I come near*
                       3.42
ἐγγύς, *near*   4.31
ἐγείρω, *I raise up*
                       1.144
ἐγενόμην (γίνομαι),
   I became   1.486
ἔγνων (γινώσκω), *I*
   knew   2.135
ἐγώ, *I*   1.2666
ἔδραμον (τρέχω), *I*
   ran   6.18
ἔδωκα (δίδωμι), *I*
   gave   1.280
ἔθνος, *nation*   1.162

εἰ, *if*   1.502
εἶδον (ὁράω), *I saw*
                       1.350
εἰκών, *image*   5.23
εἷλον (αἱρέω), *I took*
   up   3.41
εἰμί, *I am*   1.2462
εἶπον (λέγω), *I said*
                       1.937
εἰρήνη, *peace*   2.92
εἰς, *into*   1.1767
εἷς, *one*   1.345
εἰσέρχομαι, *I come*
   into   1.194
εἰσπορεύομαι, *I enter*
                       6.18
εἶτα, *then, next*   7.15
εἴτε, *if, whether*   3.65
ἐκ, ἐξ, *out of*   1.914
ἕκαστος, *each*   2.82
ἑκατόν, *one hundred*
                       6.17
ἑκατοντάρχης,
   centurion   6.20
ἐκβάλλω, *I cast out*
                       2.81
ἐκεῖ, *there*   2.105
ἐκεῖθεν, *from there*
                       4.37
ἐκεῖνος, *that*   1.265
ἐκκλησία, *church*   2.114
ἐκλέγομαι, *I choose*
                       5.22
ἐκλεκτός, *elect*   5.22
ἐκπορεύομαι, *I go out*
                       4.33
ἐκτείνω, *I stretch*
   forth   7.16
ἐκχέω, *I pour out*   7.16

ἔλαβον (λαμβάνω), *I took* 1.272

ἐλαία, *olive tree* 7.15

ἐλέγχω, *I convict* 6.17

ἐλεέω, *I have mercy* 4.28

ἔλεος, *mercy* 5.27

ἐλεύθερος, *free* 5.23

Ἕλλην, *Greek* 5.25

ἐλπίζω, *I hope* 4.31

ἐλπίς, *hope* 3.53

ἔμαθον (βάλλω), *I learned* 6.19

ἐμαυτοῦ, *of myself* 4.37

ἐμβαίνω, *I embark* 7.16

ἐμός, *my, mine* 2.76

ἔμπροσθεν, *before* 3.48

ἐν, *in* 1.2752

ἐνδύω, *I put on* 5.27

ἕνεκα, *on account of* 5.24

ἐνεργέω, *I work* 5.22

ἐντέλλω, *I command* 7.15

ἐντολή, *commandment* 2.67

ἐνώπιον, *before* 2.94

ἐξέρχομαι, *I go out* 1.218

ἔξεστι, *it is lawful* 4.31

ἐξίστημι, *I amaze* 6.17

ἐξουσία, *authority* 2.102

ἔξω, *outside* 3.63

ἑορτή, *feast* 5.25

ἐπαγγελία, *promise* 3.52

ἐπαγγέλλομαι, *I promise* 7.15

ἔπαθον (πάσχω), *I suffered* 5.26

ἐπαίρω, *I lift up* 6.19

ἐπάνω, *above* 6.19

ἐπαύριον, *tomorrow* 6.17

ἐπεί, *when* 5.26

ἔπειτα, *then* 7.16

ἐπερωτάω, *I ask* 3.56

ἔπεσον (πίπτω), *I fell* 2.122

ἐπί, *over* 1.890

ἐπιβάλλω, *I lay upon* 6.18

ἐπιγινώσκω, *I know* 3.44

ἐπίγνωσις, *knowledge* 6.20

ἐπιθυμέω, *I desire* 7.16

ἐπιθυμία, *passion* 4.38

ἐπικαλέω, *I call,* 4.30

ἐπιλαμβάνομαι, *I take hold of* 6.19

ἐπιμένω, *I continue* 7.16

ἔπιον (πίνω), *I drank* 4.39

ἐπιστολή, *letter* 5.24

ἐπιστρέφω, *I return* 4.36

ἐπιτίθημι, *I lay upon* 4.39

ἐπιτιμάω, *I rebuke* 4.29

ἐπιτρέπω, *I permit* 6.18

ἐπουράνιος, *heavenly* 6.19

ἑπτά, *seven* 2.88

ἐργάζομαι, *I work* 3.41

ἐργάτης, *workman* 7.16

ἔργον, *work* 1.169

ἔρημος, *deserted* 3.48

ἔρχομαι, *I go* 1.632

ἐρῶ, *I shall say* 3.46

ἐρωτάω, *I ask* 3.63

ἐσθίω, *I eat* 1.158

ἔσχατος, *last* 3.52

ἔσχον (ἔχω), *I had* 6.20

ἕτερος, *another* 2.98

ἔτι, *yet* 2.93

ἑτοιμάζω, *I prepare* 4.40

ἕτοιμος, *ready* 6.17

ἔτος, *year* 3.49

ἔτυχον (τυγχάνω), *I obtained* 6.17

εὐαγγελίζω, *I bring good news* 3.54

εὐαγγέλιον, *good news* 2.76

εὐδοκέω, *I think it good* 5.21

εὐθέως, *immediately* 4.36

εὐθύς, *immediately* 3.59

εὐλογέω, *I bless* 3.41

εὐλογία, *blessing* 7.16

εὑρίσκω, *I find* 1.176

εὗρον (εὑρίσκω), *I found* 2.95

εὐσέβεια, *piety* 7.15

εὐχαριστέω, *I give thanks* 4.38

εὐχαριστία, *thanksgiving* 7.15

ἔφαγον (ἐσθίω), *I ate* 2.99

Ἔφεσος, *Ephesus* 7.16

ἐφίστημι, I stand over 5.21

ἔφυγον (φεύγω), I fled 5.26

ἐχάρην (χαίρω), I was glad 6.20

ἐχθρός, hating 4.32

ἔχω, I have 1.708

ἕως, until 1.146

ζάω, I live 1.140

ζῆλος, zeal 7.16

ζητέω, I seek 2.117

ζωή, life 2.135

ζῷον, living creature 5.23

ἤ, or 1.343

ἤγαγον (ἄγω), I led 2.108

ἡγεμών, leader 6.20

ἡγέομαι, I am chief 4.28

ἤδη, already 3.61

ἥκω, I have come 5.26

ἦλθον (ἔρχομαι), I came 1.982

Ἠλίας, Elijah 4.29

ἥλιος, the sun 4.32

ἥμαρτον (ἁμαρτάνω), I sinned 7.15

ἡμέρα, day 1.389

ἤνεγκα (φέρω), I brought 3.62

Ἡρῴδης, Herod 3.43

Ἠσαΐας, Isaiah 5.22

θάλασσα, sea 2.91

θάνατος, death 2.120

θαυμάζω, I marvel 3.43

θεάομαι, I behold 5.22

θέλημα, will 3.62

θέλω, I will 1.208

θεμέλιος, foundation 7.15

θεός, God 1.1317

θεραπεύω, I heal 3.43

θερίζω, I reap 5.21

θεωρέω, I look at 3.58

θηρίον, beast 3.46

θησαυρός, treasure 6.17

θλῖψις, tribulation 3.45

θρίξ, hair 7.15

θρόνος, throne 3.62

θυγάτηρ, daughter 4.28

θυμός, wrath 6.18

θύρα, door 4.39

θυσία, sacrifice 4.28

θυσιαστήριον, altar 5.23

Ἰακώβ, Jacob 5.27

Ἰάκωβος, Jacob 3.42

ἰάομαι, I heal 5.26

ἴδε, see! 4.29

ἴδιος, one's own 2.114

ἰδού, behold! 1.200

ἱερεύς, priest 4.31

ἱερόν, temple 2.72

Ἱεροσόλυμα, Jerusalem 3.62

Ἱερουσαλήμ, Jerusalem 2.77

Ἰησοῦς, Jesus 1.917

ἱκανός, sufficient 4.39

ἱμάτιον, garment 3.60

ἵνα, in order that 1.663

Ἰορδάνης, Jordan 7.15

Ἰουδαία, Judea 3.44

Ἰουδαῖος, Jew 1.194

Ἰούδας, Judas 3.44

ἵππος, horse 6.17

Ἰσαάκ, Isaac 6.20

Ἰσραήλ, Israel 2.68

ἵστημι, I cause to stand 1.154

ἰσχυρός, strong 4.29

ἰσχύω, strong 4.28

ἰχθύς, fish 6.20

Ἰωάννης, John 2.135

Ἰωσήφ, Joseph 4.35

κἀγώ, and I 2.76

κάθημαι, I sit 2.91

καθαρίζω, I cleanse 4.31

καθαρός, clean 5.27

καθεύδω, I sleep 5.22

καθίζω, I seat 3.46

καθίστημι, I set 5.21

καθώς, even as 1.182

καί, and 1.9161

καινός, new 3.42

καιρός, time 2.85

Καῖσαρ, Caesar 4.29

Καισάρεια, Caesarea 6.17

κἀκεῖνος, and that one 5.22

κακός, bad 3.50

κακῶς, badly 7.16

καλέω, I call 1.148

καλός, good 2.101

καλῶς, well 4.37

κἄν, and if 6.17

καρδία, heart 1.156

καρπός, fruit 2.67

κατά, down from 1.473

καταβαίνω, I go down 2.81

καταγγέλλω, I proclaim 6.18

κατακρίνω, I condemn
        6.18
καταλαμβάνω, I
    overtake   7.15
καταλείπω, I leave 5.24
καταλύω, I destroy 6.17
καταργέω, I abolish
        5.27
κατεργάζομαι, I work
    out   5.22
κατέρχομαι, I go down
        7.16
κατέχω, I hold back
        6.17
κατηγορέω, I accuse
        5.23
κατοικέω, I inhabit
        3.44
καυχάομαι, I boast
        4.37
Καφαρναούμ,
    Capernaum   7.16
κεῖμαι, I lie   5.24
κελεύω, I order   5.25
κενός, empty   6.18
κερδαίνω, I gain   6.17
κεφαλή, head   2.75
κηρύσσω, I preach
        3.61
κλαίω, I weep   4.40
κλείω, I shut   7.16
κλέπτης, thief   7.16
κληρονομέω, I inherit
        6.18
κληρονόμος, heir 7.15
κοιλία, womb   5.22
κοιμάω, I sleep   6.18
κοινωνία, fellowship
        6.19
κοπιάω, I toil   5.23

κόπος, labor   6.18
κόσμος, world   1.186
κράζω, I cry out   3.55
κρατέω, I grasp   3.47
κρείττων, better   6.19
κρίμα, judgment   5.27
κρίνω, I judge   2.114
κρίσις, judgment   3.47
κριτής, judge   6.19
κρυπτός, hidden   6.17
κρύπτω, I conceal   6.18
κτίζω, I create   7.15
κτίσις, creation   6.19
κύριος, lord   1.717
κωλύω, I forbid   5.23
κώμη, village   5.27
Λάζαρος, Lazarus 7.15
λαλέω, I speak   1.296
λαμβάνω, I take   1.258
λαός, people   1.142
λατρεύω, I serve   5.21
λέγω, I say   1.2353
λευκός, white   5.25
λῃστής, robber   7.15
λίθος, stone   3.59
λογίζομαι, I reckon
        4.40
λόγος, word   1.330
λοιπός, remaining 3.55
λυπέω, I grieve   5.26
λύπη, pain   7.16
λύω, I loose   3.42
μαθητής, disciple 1.261
μακάριος, happy   3.50
Μακεδονία,
    Macedonia   5.22
μᾶλλον, more   2.81
μανθάνω, I learn   5.25
Μαρία, Mary   5.27
Μαριάμ, Mary   5.27

μαρτυρέω, I bear
    witness   2.76
μαρτυρία, testimony,
    evidence   4.37
μαρτύριον, witness
        6.19
μάρτυς, witness   4.35
μάχαιρα, sword   4.29
μέγας, great   1.243
μέλλω, I am about to
        2.109
μέλος, member   4.34
μέν, particle   1.179
μένω, I remain   2.118
μεριμνάω, I am
    anxious   6.19
μέρος, part   3.42
μέσος, middle   3.58
μετά, with   1.469
μετανοέω, I repent 4.34
μετάνοια, repentance
        5.22
μέχρι, until   6.17
μή, not   1.1042
μηδέ, but not   3.56
μηδείς, no one   2.90
μηκέτι, no longer 5.22
μήν, month   6.19
μήποτε, lest   5.25
μήτε, neither   4.34
μήτηρ, mother   2.83
μήτι, interrogative 6.18
μικρός, small   3.46
μιμνήσκομαι, I
    remember   5.23
μισέω, I hate   4.40
μισθός, wage   4.29
μνημεῖον, tomb   4.40
μνημονεύω, I
    remember   5.21

μοιχεύω, I commit
   adultery   7.15
μόνος, alone   2.114
μυστήριον, mystery
                    4.28
Μωϋσῆς, Moses   2.80
ναί, yes   4.33
ναός, temple   3.45
νεκρός, dead   2.128
νέος, new   5.24
νεφέλη, cloud   5.25
νήπιος, infant   7.15
νηστεύω, I fast   6.20
νικάω, I conquer   4.28
νίπτω, I wash   6.17
νομίζω, I suppose   7.15
νόμος, law   1.194
νοῦς, mind   5.24
νυμφίος, bridegroom
                    7.16
νῦν, now   1.147
νυνί, now   6.20
νύξ, night   3.61
ξηραίνω, I dry up   7.15
ξύλον, tree   6.20
ὁ, ἡ, τό, the   1.19867
ὁδός, road   2.101
ὅθεν, from where   7.15
οἶδα, I know   1.318
οἰκία, house   2.93
οἰκοδομέω, I build 4.40
οἰκοδομή, building 6.18
οἶκος, house   2.114
οἰκουμένη, world   7.15
οἶνος, wine   4.34
ὀλίγος, little   4.40
ὅλος, whole   2.109
ὀμνύω, I swear   5.26
ὅμοιος, like   3.45
ὁμοιόω, I liken   7.15

ὁμοίως, likewise   4.30
ὁμολογέω, I confess
                    5.26
ὄνομα, name   1.231
ὀπίσω, behind   4.35
ὅπου, where   2.82
ὁράω, I see   1.454
ὀργή, anger   4.36
ὄρος, mountain   3.63
ὅπως, that   3.53
ὅς, ἥ, ὅ, who, which
                    1.1407
ὅσος, as great as   2.110
ὅστις, ἥτις, ὅτι,
   whoever, whichever,
   whatever   1.144
ὅταν, whenever   2.123
ὅτε, when   2.103
ὅτι, that, because
                    1.1296
οὐ, οὐκ, οὐχ, not
                    1.1622
οὗ, where   5.24
οὐαί, woe!   3.46
οὐδέ, and not   1.143
οὐδείς, no one   1.227
οὐκέτι, no longer   3.47
οὖν, therefore   1.499
οὔπω, not yet   5.26
οὐρανός, heaven   1.273
οὖς, ear   4.36
οὔτε, neither   2.86
οὗτος, αὕτη, τοῦτο,
   this   1.1387
οὕτως, thus   1.208
οὐχί, not   3.54
ὀφείλω, I owe   4.35
ὀφθαλμός, eye   2.100
ὄχλος, crowd   1.175
ὀψία, late   7.15

πάθημα, suffering   7.16
παιδίον, child   3.52
παῖς, boy   5.24
παλαιός, old   6.19
πάλιν, again   1.141
πάντοτε, always   3.41
παρά, alongside   1.194
παραβολή, parable   3.50
παραγγέλλω, I
   command   4.32
παραγίνομαι, I arrive
                    4.37
παραδίδωμι, I hand
   over   2.119
παρακαλέω, I beseech
                    2.109
παράκλησις,
   exhortation   4.29
παραλαμβάνω, I
   receive   3.49
παράπτωμα, trespass
                    6.19
παρατίθημι, I set
   before   6.19
παραχρῆμα,
   immediately   6.18
πάρειμι, I am present
                    5.24
παρέρχομαι, I pass by
                    4.29
παρέχω, I offer   7.16
παρθένος, virgin   7.15
παρίστημι, I am
   present   3.41
παρουσία, coming   5.24
παρρησία, boldness
                    4.31
πᾶς, πᾶσα, πᾶν, every,
   all   1.1243
πάσχα, passover   4.29

πάσχω, I suffer   3.42
πατήρ, father   1.413
Παῦλος, Paul   1.158
παύω, I cease   7.15
πείθω, I persuade 3.52
πεινάω, I hunger   5.23
πειράζω, I test   4.38
πειρασμός,
    temptation   5.21
πέμπω, I send   2.79
πέντε, five   4.38
πέραν, beyond   5.23
περί, around   1.333
περιβάλλω, I put
    around   5.23
περιπατέω, I walk 2.95
περισσεύω, I abound
    4.39
περισσός, excessive
    7.15
περισσότερος,
    greater, more   6.19
περιτέμνω, I
    circumcise   6.17
περιτομή, circumcision
    4.36
πέτρα, rock   7.15
Πέτρος, Peter   1.156
Πιλᾶτος, Pilate   3.55
πίμπλημι, I fill   5.24
πίνω, I drink   2.73
πίπτω, I fall   2.90
πιστεύω, I believe
    1.241
πίστις, faith   1.243
πιστός, faithful   2.67
πλανάω, I lead astray
    4.39
πλεῖον, more   3.44
πληγή, wound   5.22

πλῆθος, multitude 4.31
πλήν, however   4.31
πληρόω, I fill   2.86
πλήρωμα, fullness 6.17
πλησίον, near   6.17
πλοῖον, boat   2.67
πλούσιος, rich   4.28
πλοῦτος, wealth   5.22
πνεῦμα, spirit   1.379
πνευματικός, spiritual
    5.26
πόθεν, from where 4.29
ποιέω, I do   1.568
ποιμήν, shepherd 6.18
ποῖος, what sort of?
    4.33
πόλεμος, war   6.18
πλήρης, full   7.16
πόλις, city   1.163
πολλάκις, often   6.18
πολύς, much   1.416
πονηρός, evil   2.78
πορεύομαι, I go 1.153
πορνεία, fornication
    5.25
πόσος, how great? 5.27
ποταμός, river   6.17
πότε, when?   6.19
ποτέ, at some time 4.29
ποτήριον, cup   4.31
ποτίζω, I give drink 7.15
ποῦ, where?   3.52
πούς, foot   2.93
πράσσω, I do   4.39
πρεσβύτερος, elder
    3.66
πρό, before   3.47
προάγω, I go before
    6.20
πρόβατον, sheep   4.39

προλέγω, I say
    beforehand   7.15
πρός, towards   1.700
προσδοκάω, I wait for
    7.16
προσέρχομαι, I come
    to   2.86
προσευχή, prayer 4.36
προσεύχομαι, I pray
    2.85
προσέχω, I attend to
    5.24
προσκαλέω, I summon
    4.29
προσκυνέω, I worship
    3.60
προστίθημι, I add 6.18
προσφέρω, I offer 3.47
πρόσωπον, face   2.76
προφητεία, prophecy
    6.19
προφητεύω, I prophesy
    4.28
προφήτης, prophet
    1.144
πρῶτος, first   1.155
πτωχός, poor   4.34
πυλών, vestibule   6.18
πῦρ, fire   2.71
πωλέω, I sell   5.22
πῶς, how?   2.118
πώς, somehow   7.15
ῥαββί, rabbi   7.15
ῥῆμα, word   2.68
ῥίζα, root   6.17
ῥύομαι, I deliver   6.17
σάββατον, Sabbath 2.68
σαλεύω, I shake   7.15
σάρξ, flesh   1.147
Σατανᾶς, Satan   4.36

Σαῦλος, Saul　7.15
σεαυτοῦ, of yourself　3.43
σημεῖον, sign　2.77
σήμερον, today　3.41
Σίμων, Simon　2.75
σκανδαλίζω, I cause to stumble　4.29
σκάνδαλον, a cause of stumbling　7.15
σκεῦος, vessel　5.23
σκηνή, tent　6.20
σκοτία, darkness　7.16
σκότος, darkness　4.31
σός, your　5.26
σοφία, wisdom　3.51
σοφός, wise　6.20
σπείρω, I sow　3.52
σπέρμα, seed　3.43
σταυρός, cross　5.27
σταυρόω, I crucify 3.46
στέφανος, crown　5.25
στόμα, mouth　2.78
στρατιώτης, soldier　5.26
στρέφω, I turn　5.21
σύ, you　1.2906
συκῆ, fig tree　7.16
συλλαμβάνω, I take　7.16
συμφέρω, I bring together　7.15
σύν, with　2.128
συνάγω, I gather together　3.59
συναγωγή, synagogue　3.56
συνέδριον, council 5.22
συνείδησις, conscience　4.30

συνέρχομαι, I come together　4.30
συνίημι, I understand　5.26
συνίστημι, I commend　7.16
σφραγίζω, I seal　7.15
σφραγίς, seal　7.16
σῴζω, I save　2.106
σῶμα, body　1.142
σωτήρ, Saviour　5.24
σωτηρία, salvation 3.46
ταράσσω, I trouble 6.17
ταχέως, quickly　7.15
τέ, and　1.215
τέκνον, child　2.99
τέλειος, complete　6.19
τελειόω, I fulfill　5.23
τελέω, I finish　4.28
τέλος, end　4.40
τελώνης, tax gatherer　5.21
τέρας, wonder　7.16
τεσσαράκοντα, forty　5.22
τέσσαρες, four　3.41
τηρέω, I keep　2.70
τίθημι, I place　2.100
τίκτω, I give birth to　6.18
τιμάω, I honor　5.21
τιμή, honor　3.41
Τιμόθεος, Timothy 5.24
τις, τι, someone, something　1.525
τίς, τί, who? what?　1.555
τοιοῦτος, such　3.57
τολμάω, I dare　7.16
τόπος, place　2.94

τοσοῦτος, so great 6.20
τότε, then　1.160
τράπεζα, table　7.15
τρεῖς, three　2.69
τρέχω, I run　6.20
τρίτος, third　3.56
τροφή, food　7.16
τύπος, mark　7.15
τυφλός, blind　3.50
ὕδωρ, water　2.76
υἱός, son　1.377
ὑπάγω, I depart　2.79
ὑπακοή, obedience 7.15
ὑπακούω, I obey　5.21
ὑπάρχω, I exist　3.60
ὑπέρ, above　1.150
ὑπηρέτης, assistant　6.20
ὑπό, under　1.220
ὑποκριτής, hypocrite　6.17
ὑπομένω, I tarry　6.17
ὑπομονή, steadfast endurance　4.32
ὑποστρέφω, I return　4.35
ὑποτάσσω, I subject　4.38
ὑστερέω, I lack　7.16
ὑψόω, I lift up　6.20
φαίνω, I shine　4.31
φανερός, manifest 6.18
φανερόω, I make manifest　3.49
Φαρισαῖος, Pharisee　2.98
φέρω, I carry　3.66
φεύγω, I flee　4.29
φημί, I say　3.66
φιλέω, I love　5.25

Φίλιππος, *Philip*	4.36	χαρίζομαι, *I give*		χρυσοῦς, *golden*	6.18
φίλος, *loving*	4.29	freely	5.23	χώρα, *country*	4.28
φοβέω, *I fear*	2.95	χάρις, *grace*	1.155	χωρίς, *apart from*	3.41
φόβος, *fear*	3.47	χάρισμα, *gift*	6.17	ψυχή, *life*	2.103
φρονέω, *I think*	5.26	χείρ, *hand*	1.177	ὦ, *O!*	6.20
φυλακή, *prison*	3.47	χήρα, *widow*	5.26	ὧδε, *here*	3.61
φυλάσσω, *I guard*	4.31	χιλίαρχος, *tribune*	5.21	ὥρα, *hour*	2.106
φυλή, *tribe*	4.31	χιλιάς, *thousand*	5.23	ὡς, *as*	1.503
φωνέω, *I call*	3.43	χορτάζω, *I eat to the*		ὡσαύτως, *likewise*	6.17
φωνή, *sound*	1.139	full	7.16	ὡσεί, *about*	5.21
φῶς, *light*	2.73	χόρτος, *grass*	7.15	ὥσπερ, *just as*	4.36
χαίρω, *I rejoice*	2.74	χρεία, *need*	3.49	ὥστε, *so that*	2.83
χαρά, *joy*	3.59	Χριστός, *Christ*	1.529	ὠφελέω, *I profit*	7.15
		χρόνος, *time*	3.54		

VOCABULARY
ENGLISH DERIVATIVES

English words that etymologically are derived from standard vocabulary words or related cognate groups have been given with a short definition and an etymological connection. The abbreviation "lit." stands for "literally."[1]

ἀγαπάω, *I love*, **agapanthus** (a genus of plants which includes the African lily; lit., "flower lover"); see **Agape**

ἀγαπητός, *beloved*, **agapanthus** (a genus of plants which includes the African lily; lit., "flower lover"); see **Agape**

ἀγαθός, *good*, **Agatha** (lit., "good"), **agathism** (the doctrine that all things tend towards good)

ἀγάπη, *love*, see ἀγαπητός, **Agape** (the fellowship meal of the early church; lit., "love [feast]")

ἀγγέλλω, *I tell, announce*, **angel** (a heavenly messenger), **evangelist** (a messenger of good news, particularly the Christian gospel)

ἄγγελος, *angel*; see ἀγγέλλω

ἁγιάζω, *I sanctify*, **Hagiographa** (third of three Old Testament divisions; lit., "sacred writings"), **hagiography** (biography of saints; lit., "writing of the saints"), **hagiology** (literature dealing with the lives of saints), **hagioscope** (a small opening in an interior wall of a church to view inside; lit., "to see the sacred")

ἅγιος, *holy*, see ἁγιάζω

ἀγοράζω, *I buy*, **agora** (a marketplace in ancient Greece)

ἀγρός, *field*, **agronomy** (the management of land), cf. Latin *ager, agri* (agrarian, agriculture)

ἄγω, *I lead*, **demagogue** (a person who stirs up people to gain power; lit., "a people leader"), **pedagogue** (school

---

[1]Dr. Jeff Cate, my former student, compiled these derivatives. Definitions and etymologies are based on Ernest Klein, *Klein's Comprehensive Etymological Dictionary of the English Language* (New York, Oxford, Amsterdam: Elsevier Scientific Publishing Company, 1971); E. G. Withycombe, *The Oxford Dictionary of English Christian Names*, 2d ed. (Oxford: Clarendon Press, 1950); *The American Heritage Dictionary*, 2d ed. (Boston: Houghton Mifflin Company, 1991); C. T. Onions, ed., *The Oxford Dictionary of English Etymology* (Oxford: Clarendon Press, 1966); *Webster's New World Dictionary*; and Frederic M. Wheelock, *Latin*, 3d ed. (New York: Barnes and Noble Books, 1963).

teacher, educator; lit., "child lead-er"), **stratagem** (military maneuver designed to surprise an enemy; lit., "to lead an army"), **synagogue** (a building for Jewish gatherings; lit., "assembly" or "to lead together"; cf. σύν + ἄγω), cf. Latin *ago* (agenda, agent, agile, agitate)

ἀδελφή, *sister*, cf. ἀδελφός (Philadel-phia)

ἀδελφός, *brother*, **Philadelphia** (lit., "brotherly love")

ἀήρ, *air*, **aerial** (pertaining to the air), **aerobic** (living or occurring only in the presence of oxygen), **aerody-namics** (branch of mechanics study-ing forces of air; lit., "air power"), **aeronautics** (science of aircraft design and operation; lit., "air-sail-ing"), **aeroplane** (British var-iation of airplane), **aerosol** (suspen-sion of colloidal particles in a gas; lit., "an air solution"), **aerospace** (earth's atmosphere), cf. Latin *aer, aeris*

αἷμα, *blood*, **anemia** (or anaemia; a deficiency of oxygen-carrying mate-rial in the blood; lit., "without blood"), **anemic** (or anaemic; list-less, weak, or pallid; lit., "without blood"), **hematology** (science of studying blood), **hemoglobin** (oxy-gen-carrying substance in blood; lit., "blood drop"), **hemophilia** (disorder characterized by excessive bleeding; lit., "blood lover"), **hemorrhage** (profuse discharge of blood; lit., "a blood flow"), **leukemia** (white blood cell cancer; lit., "white blood")

αἴρω, *I take up, take away*, **aorta** (the main artery of the heart that carries blood to the body; lit., "that which raises"), **dieresis** (or diaeresis; a mark [¨] placed over a pair of vowels indicating the two sounds are sep-arate; lit., "to take apart")

αἰών, *age, eternity*, **eon** (an extreme-ly long period of time)

αἰώνιος, *eternal, unending*, **eon** (ex-tremely long period), cf. αἰών

ἀκαθαρτός, *unclean*, **catharsis** (a process of purging)

ἀκοή, *hearing, report*, **acoumeter** (an instrument measuring the power of the sense of hearing), **acoustical** and **acoustics** (pertaining to sound or hearing)

ἀκολουθέω, *I follow*, **acolyte** (an attendant or follower; lit., "follow-er"), **anacoluthon** (an abrupt change within a sentence to a second con-struction inconsistent with the first; lit., "not following")

ἀκούω, *I hear*, see ἀκοή

ἀλλήλων, *of one another*, **parallel** (being equal distant apart; lit., "be-side one another")

ἄλλος, *other*, **allegory** (a symbolic representation; lit., "speaking the other"), **allergy** (adverse reaction to a substance; lit., "other work"), **allotropy** (variation of physical pro-perties without change of substance, e.g., charcoal and diamonds; lit., "other kind")

ἁμαρτάνω, *I sin*, **hamartiology** (theo-logical study of the doctrine of sin)

ἁμαρτία, *sin*, see ἁμαρτάνω

ἁμαρτωλός, *sinful, sinner*, cf. ἁμαρ-τία (hamartiology)

ἀνά, *up*, **anabolic** (something which builds up living tissue; lit., "to throw up"), **analogy** (an affinity between two otherwise unrelated things), **analysis** (examina-tion by studying component parts; lit., "to break up"), **anatomy** (the biological study of the body; lit., "to cut up" or "to dissect"), **anode** (positively charged electrode; lit., "the way up"; cf. ἀνά + ὁδός)

ἀναβαίνω, *I go up*, **Anabasis** (military advance, such as that of Cyrus the Younger into Asia Minor, as narrated by Xenophon; lit., "to go up"), **anabatic** (pertaining to rising wind currents; lit., "to go up"), cf. βαίνω (acrobat, diabetes)

ἀνάστασις, *resurrection*, cf. ἀνά + ἵστημι

ἄνεμος, *wind*, **anemometer** (instrument for measuring wind; lit., "wind measurement"), **sea anemone** (flower-like marine organism; lit., "sea wind")

ἀνήρ, *man, husband*, **Alexander** (lit., "defending men"), **Andrew** (lit., "manly"), **androgen** (male sex hormone), **androgenous** (pertaining to production of male offspring; lit., "male offspring"), **androgynous** (having both male and female characteristics; lit., "male-female"), **android** (possessing human fea-tures), **Neandrathal** (prehistoric man; lit., "new man"), **philander** (to engage in casual love affairs; lit., "a loving man"), **polyandry** (having more than one husband; lit., "many husbands")

ἄνθρωπος, *man*, **anthropocentric** (regarding humankind as the central fact or final aim of the universe), **anthropology** (study of humankind), **anthropogenesis** (scientific study of the origin of humankind; lit., "the beginning of man"), **anthropoid** (resembling humans, such as apes), **anthropomorphic** (ascribing human features to a nonhuman object or being; lit., "the form of man"),

anthropophagus (cannibal or eater of human flesh; lit., "human eater"), **misanthrope** (person who hates or mistrusts people; lit., "human hater"), **philanthropy** (a desire to help humankind; lit., "human lover")

ἀντί, *against*, **anti-** (anything opposed to something else: Antibacterial, antibiotic, Antichrist, anticlimax, antidote, antifreeze, antinomian, anti-Semitism), **antonym** (opposite meaning to another word; lit., "name against"), **antithesis** (direct contrast; lit., "set against")

ἄξιος, *worthy*, **axiology** (study of values and value judgments; lit., "study of worth"), **axiom** (self-evident or universally recognized truth; lit., "worthy statement")

ἅπαξ, *once*, **hapax legomenon** (word which occurs only once in the Greek New Testament; lit., "spoken once")

ἀπό, *away from*, **apostasy** (abandoning belief formerly held; lit., "to stand away from"), **apostle** (one who is sent out; lit., "sent out"), **apostrophe** (sign indicating omission of letter(s); lit., "to turn away")

ἀποδίδωμι, *I give back*, **apodosis** (the clause that states the consequence of a conditional statement; lit., "given back")

ἀποκαλύπτω, *I reveal*, **apocalypse** (a prophetic revelation; lit., "revelation"), **apocalyptic** (pertaining to a prophetic disclosure), **eucalyptus** (an Australian evergreen; lit., "well covered"; cf. εὐ + καλύπτω)

ἀπόλλυμι, *I destroy, perish*, **Apollyon** (name of the bottomless pit angel in Revelation; lit., "the Destroyer")

ἀποστέλλω, *I send, send out*, **apostle** (a missionary of the early church;

lit., "one sent out"), **apostolic** (having to do with the Apostles)

ἀπόστολος, *apostle*, see ἀποστέλλω

ἅπτομαι, *I touch*, **haptometer** (instrument for measuring the sense of touch), **periapt** (charm worn as protection against misfortune; lit., "fastened around"), **synapse** (point of contact where nerve impulses are transmitted between neurons; lit., "to touch together")

ἀρχή, *beginning*, **archangel** (celestial being above angel rank; lit., "chief angel"), **archenemy** (primary opponent; lit., "chief enemy"), **archetype** (first model of later patterns; lit., "chief model"), cf. ἄρχαιος (archaeology, archaic, ar-chaism)

ἀρχιερεύς, *chief priest*, cf. ἀρχή + ἱερεύς

ἄρχομαι, *I begin*, cf. ἀρχαίος (archaeology, archaic, archaism), ἀρχή (archangel, archenemy, archetype)

ἄρχω, *I rule*, **anarchy** (the absence of political authority; lit., "without a ruler"), **Archelaus** (lit., "ruler of the people"), **ethnarch** (the ruler of a province or people; lit., "nation ruler"), **gynarchy** (government by women; lit., "female rule"), **matriarch** (a woman who rules a family or tribe; lit., "mother ruler"), **monarch** (a sole hereditary ruler; lit., "only ruler"), **oligarchy** (government by a few; lit., "few rulers"), **patriarch** (the male leader of a family or tribe; lit., "father ruler"), **tetrarch** (a governor of one of the four divisions of a country, especially in the Roman Empire; lit., "four rulers")

ἄρχων, *ruler*, see ἄρχω

ἀσθένεια, *weakness*, **asthenia** (lack or loss of bodily strength), **asthenic** (slender, lightly muscled human physique), **asthenopia** (eyestrain resulting in dim vision; lit., "weak sight"), **asthenosphere** (less rigid layer of earth's mantle), **neurasthenia** (fatigue once thought to result from exhaustion of the nervous system)

ἀσθενέω, *I am weak*, see ἀσθένεια

ἀσθενής, *sick, weak*, see ἀσθένεια

ἀστήρ, *star*, **aster** (daisy-like flower; lit., "star"), **asterisk** (a star-shaped symbol [*]; lit., "a little star"), **asteroid** (a small celestial body in an orbit), **astrology** (study of the stars for influence on human affairs), **astronaut** (a navigator of a spacecraft; lit., "star sailor"), **astronomy** (scientific study of the universe beyond earth), **disaster** (misfortune causing widespread destruction; originally, the evil influence of a celestial body)

αὐξάνω, *I cause to grow*, **auxin** (plant hormone that causes growth), cf. Latin *augeo* (augment, auxiliary)

αὐτός, *he, him*, **autobiography** (biography of a person written by that same person; lit., "writing one's own life"), **autogenous** (self-generated or self-produced; lit., "self beginning"), **autograph** (a person's own signature or handwriting; lit., "self written"), **automatic** (acting in an independent manner; lit., "self-acting"), **automobile** (a self-propelled vehicle; lit., "self-moving"), **autonomous** (independent or self-governing; lit., "self law"), **autopsy** (examination of a corpse to determine the cause of death; lit., "self seeing")

ἀφίημι, *I permit, forgive*, **aphesis** (loss of a vowel from the beginning of a word; e.g., "squire" for "esquire"; lit., "sent away") ἄφρων, *foolish*, cf. ἀ + φρωνέω (lit., "not thinking")

βάλλω, *I throw*, **ballistics** (the study of projectiles), **diabolical** (devilish or satanic; cf. διάβολος; lit., "to cast against"), **emblem** (an object which functions as a symbol; lit., "to insert" or "to throw in"), **embolism** (the obstruction of a blood vessel by a clot or air bubble; lit., "insertion" or "thrown in"), **hyperbole** (an exaggeration; lit., "over throw"), **parable** (a simple story to illustrate a lesson or moral; lit., "to compare" or "to throw alongside"), **symbol** (something that represents something else; lit., "to throw together"), **metabolism** (physical and chemical processes involved in a living organism; lit., "thrown across")

βαπτίζω, *I baptize*, **baptism** (the Christian sacrament or ordinance involving immersion into or sprinkling of water), **Baptists** (the Protestant denomination which emphasizes the ordinance of baptism)

βασιλεία, *kingdom*, **Basil** (the Greek church father of the fourth century; lit., "kingly"), **basilica** (a type of a Roman building used as a court or place of assembly later used as churches; lit., "kingly")

βασιλεύς, *king*, see βασιλεία

βασιλικός, *royal*, see βασιλεία

βιβλίον, *book*, **Bible** (the sacred book of Christianity), **bibliography** (list of books), **bibliolatry** (excessive adherence to the Bible; lit., "Bible worship"), **bibliomania** (excessive desire for books; lit., "book madness"), **bibliophile** (one who loves and collects books; lit., "book lover"), **bibliotheca** (library or book collection; lit., "book case")

βλασφημέω, *I blaspheme*, **blaspheme** (to speak of something sacred in an irreverent manner), **blasphemous** (impiously irreverent), **blasphemy** (a profane act or utterance against something sacred)

βούλομαι, *I wish, am willing*, **abulia** (loss of ability to decide or act independently; lit., "without a will"), **Aristobulus** (lit., "best counselor"), **boule** (the senate of 400 founded in ancient Athens by Solon; lit., "council"), **bouleuterion** (a Greek senate house), cf. Latin *volo* (involuntary, volition, volitive, voluntary, volunteer, voluptuous)

γαμέω, *I marry*, **bigamy** (married to two persons; lit., "two marriages"), **gamete** (a sex cell which combines with another sex cell to produce a new organism), **misogamy** (hatred of marriage; lit., "marriage-hate"), **monogamy** (being married to only one person; lit., "only marriage"), **polygamy** (being married to more than one person at the same time; lit., "many marriages")

γάμος, *marriage*, see γαμέω

γενεά, *generation*, **genealogy** (the recorded history of one's ancestors)

γένος, *race*, **androgenous** (pertaining to production of male offspring; lit., "male offspring"), **eugenics** (study of hereditary improvement by genetic control; lit., "good offspring"), **genocide** (the systematic killing of a whole race; lit., "to kill a race"), **homogenous** (of the same or similar nature or kind; lit., "same kind"), cf. Latin *genus, generis* (degenerate, gender, general, generic, generous, genitive, genuine, genus)

γῆ, *earth, land,* **apogee** (point in an orbit farthest from the focus; lit., "away from the earth"), **geography** (study of the earth and its features), **geology** (scientific study of earth), **geometry** (the mathematics based on points, lines, angles, surfaces, and solids; lit., "earth measure"), **George** (lit., "earth worker"), **geothermal** (pertaining to the internal heat of the earth; lit., "earth heat"), **perigee** (point in an orbit closest to the focus; lit., "near the earth")

γίνομαι, *I am (become, take place),* **anthropogenesis** (scientific study of the origin of humankind; lit., "the beginning of man"), **autogenous** (self-generated or self-produced; lit., "self beginning"), **Genesis** (first book of the Bible; lit., "the beginning"), **genetic** (pertaining to the origin or development of something), **parthenogenesis** (reproduction by the development of an unfertilized ovum, seed, or spore; lit., "virgin beginning"), **pyrogenous** (produced by or producing heat; lit., "fire producing"), **orogenesis** (formation of a mountain; lit., "mountain beginning")

γινώσκω, *I know,* see γνῶσις

γλῶσσα, *tongue,* **epiglottis** (cartilage that covers the windpipe during swallowing; lit., "upon the tongue"), **glossary** (explanatory list of difficult terms), **glossolalia** (uttering of unintelligible sounds; lit., "tongue speaking"), **polyglot** (a speech or writing in several languages; lit., "many tongues")

γνωρίζω, *I make known,* see γνῶσις

γνῶσις, *wisdom,* **agnostic** (someone who believes that God's existence cannot be known), **diagnosis** (critical analysis of the nature of something; lit., "to know through"), **gnomic** (characterized by brief statements of truth), **Gnosticism** (early Christian belief that centered on spiritual knowledge), **physiognomy** (the face or countenance as an index to character; lit., "physically known"), **prognosis** (prediction or a forecast; lit., "to know beforehand")

γράμμα, *letter,* **cardiogram** (curve traced by a cardiograph to diagnose heart defects), **grammar** (systematic study of a language), **grammatical** (relating to rules of a language; lit., "of letters"), **pentagram** (five pointed star used in magic), **telegram** (a communication by telegraph; lit., "end letter"), **Tetragrammaton** (Hebrew letters often transliterated as YHWH and used as a proper name for God; lit., "four letters")

γραμματεύς, *scribe,* see γράμμα

γραφή, *writing, Scripture,* **agrapha** (sayings of Jesus not recorded in the gospels; lit., "unwritten"), **autograph** (a person's own signature or handwriting; lit., "self written"), **bibliography** (list of books), **biography** (written account of a person's life; lit., "life writing"), **calligraphy** (art of fine handwriting; lit., "beautiful writing"), **chirography** (penmanship; lit., "hand writing"), **chronograph** (instrument that records time intervals; lit., "time writing"), **epigraph** (inscription, as on a statute or building; lit., "written upon"), **geography** (study of earth and its features), **graph** (a drawing that exhibits a numerical relationship), **graphic** (pertaining to written representation), **graphite** (allotrope of carbon used in lead pencils), **Hagiographa** (third of three divisions of the Old Testament; lit., "the sacred writings"), **lithography** (printing process that uses a large flat surface; lit., "stone writing"), **opistograph** (ancient document written on both front and back sides; lit., "writing behind"), **paragraph** (a division in a writing that expresses a complete thought: originally, a mark placed in the margin *beside* the new section), **phonograph** (device reproducing recorded sound; lit., "sound writing"), **photograph** (image or picture recorded a light-sensitive surface; lit., "light writing"), **pornography** (sexually explicit writings or pictures; lit., "immoral writings"), **pseudepigrapha** (spurious writing falsely attributed to important people; lit., "falsely ascribed"), **seismograph** (instrument used to record earthquake measurements; lit., "earthquake writings"), **topography** (graphical representation of physical features of a region; lit., "place writing")

γράφω, *I write*, see γραφή

γρηγορέω, *I watch*, **Gregory** (lit., "watchful")

γυνή, *woman*, **androgynous** (having both male and female characteristics; lit., "male-female"), **gynarchy** (government by women; lit., "female rule"), **gynecocracy** (political ascendancy of women; lit., "female power"), **gynecology** (medical science of female physiology), **gynophore** (stalk of a pistil, seed-bearing

organ of a flower); **misogyny** (hatred of women; lit., "women-hate")

δαιμόνιον, *demon*, **demon** (evil being), **demoniac** (possessed by a demon), **demonic** (pertaining to evil powers), **demonology** (study of demons), **pandemonium** (abode of all demons in John Milton's *Paradise Lost*; lit., "all the demons")

δείκνυμι, *I show*, **apodictic** (clearly proven or shown; lit., "shown away from"), **paradigm** (list of all inflectional forms of a word; lit., "shown alongside")

δέκα, *ten*, **decalogue** (the Ten Commandments; lit., "the ten words"), **decapolis** (the district near Galilee comprised of ten hellenistic cities; lit., "ten cities"), **decade** (a period of ten years), **decathlon** (an athletic contest consisting of ten events), cf. Latin *decem* (December, decemvir, decimal, decimeter)

δένδρον, *tree*, **dendrite** (a mineral crystalizing within another in a tree-branching pattern; branches of nerve cells transmitting impulses), **dendrology** (botanical study of trees), **philodendron** (tropical American vine; lit., "loves trees"), **Rhododendron** (evergreen shrub with pink or purple flowers; lit., "a rose tree")

δεξιός, *right* (direction), cf. Latin *dexter*, *dextra*, *dextrum* (ambidextrous, dexterity, dexterous)

δεύτερος, *second*, **deuteragonist** (in Classical Greek drama, the character of second importance; lit., "second actor"), **deuteranopia** (red-green color-blindness; lit., "without seeing the second"; so called because green is given as the second of the primary colors), **deuterium** (heavy isotope of hydrogen, with atomic weight of 2), **deuterocanonical** (the designation for the Apocrypha by the Council of Trent in 1548; lit., "canonized second"), **Deuteronomy** (Old Testament book that contains the second giving of Mosaic law; lit., "second law")

δέω, *I bind*, **anadem** (wreath or garland for the head; lit., "to bind up"), **asyndeton** (omission of conjunctions in constructions that normally would need them; lit., "without being bound together"), **diadem** (a royal crown or headband; lit., "to bind across")

διά, *through*, **diabetes** (disease affecting urine passage; lit., "going through"), **diagnosis** (process of determining the nature of a problem; lit., "known through"), **diagonal** (lit., line going from angle to angle), **dialogue** (conversation between two persons; lit., "words between"), **diameter** (the width of a circle; lit., "measure through"), **diaphanous** (transparently thin; lit., "appears through"), **Diaspora** (Dispersion of the Jews throughout the world after the Babylonian captivity; lit., "to scatter through[out]")

διάβολος, *Devil* (adj.: slanderous, falsely accusing), **diabolical** (devilish, satanic; lit., "to cast against")

διακονέω, *I serve*, **deacon** (a layman who assists clergy), **diaconal** (pertaining to deacons or the diaconate), **diaconate** (rank or office of deacon)

διακονία, *service, ministry*, see διακονέω

διδάσκαλος, *teacher*, **Didache** (lit., "the Teaching," an early Christian writing among the Apostolic Fathers, "Teaching of the Twelve Apostles"),

didactics (art or science of teaching), **didactic** (intended to instruct)

διδάσκω, *I teach*, see διδάσκαλος

διδαχή, *teaching*, see διδάσκαλος

δίδωμι, *I give, grant, allow*, **antidote** (remedy to counteract a poison; lit., "given against"), **apodosis** (clause that states the consequence of a conditional statement; lit., "given away"), **dose** (amount of medicine taken at one time; lit., "given")

δικαιόω, *I justify*, **syndicate** (combination control of a business; lit., "together equals"), **theodicy** (vindication of divine justice; lit., "justice of the gods")

δικαίως, *justly* (adv.), see δικαιόω

δίκαιος, *righteous*, see δικαιόω

δοκέω, *I think, seem*, **Docetism** (the heresy that Christ only seemed to have a body), **dogma** (system of doctrines), **dogmatic** (stating an opinion positively or arrogantly)

δόξα, *glory*, **doxology** (liturgical formula of praise to God; lit., "to speak glory"), **heterodox** (not in agreement with accepted belief; lit., "other opinion"), **orthodox** (agreement with accepted belief; lit., "correct opinion"), **paradox** (apparent contradiciton that still may be true; lit., "against opinion")

δοξάζω, *I glorify, honor*, see δόξα

δύναμαι, *I am able*, **aerodynamics** (branch of mechanics dealing with the forces exerted by air; lit., "air power"), **dynamic** (pertaining to energy or force), **dynamo** (generator), **dynasty** (family or group that maintains power for several generations; lit., "standing in power"), **dynamite** (a powerful explosive), **thermodynamics** (branch of physics dealing with transformation of heat into mechanical energy; lit., "heat power")

δύναμις, *power*, see δύναμαι

δυνατός, *powerful, able*, see δύναμαι

δύο, *two*, **duet** (musical composition for two people), **duo** (a pair or a couple), **dyad** (two units regarded as a pair), **dyothelitism** (theological doctrine that Christ had two wills, both human and divine; lit., "two wills"), cf. Latin *duo*

δώδεκα, *twelve*, **dodecagon** (polygon with twelve sides; lit., "twelve angles"), **dodecahedron** (polyhedron with twelve faces; lit., "twelve bases"), **dodecaphonic** (relating to twelve-tone music; lit., "twelve sounds")

δῶρον, *gift*, **Dorothy** (or Dorothea; lit., "gift of God"), **Pandora** (Greek mythology, the first mortal woman who opened a box releasing all evil into the world; lit., "all giving"), **Theodore** (lit., "God's gift")

ἔθνος, *nation, gentile*, **ethnarch** (the ruler of a province or people; lit., "nation ruler"), **ethnic** (pertaining to a cultural, racial or national group), **ethnicity** (the condition of belonging to a cultural group), **ethnocentrism** (belief in the superiority of one's own ethnic group), **ethnology** (anthropological study of culture)

ἐγώ, *I*, **ego** (the self), **egocentric** (self-centered or selfish), **egoism** (ethical doctrine that morality has its foundations in self-interest), **egomania** (obsessive preoccupation with the self), **egotism** (excessive reference to oneself in speaking or writing), cf. Latin *ego*

εἶδον (ὁράω), *I saw*, **idea** (a mental image; lit., "something seen")

εἴκοσι, *twenty*, **icosahedron** (polyhedron having twenty faces; lit., "twenty bases")

εἰκών, *likeness, image*, **icon** (an image or representation), **iconoclast** (one who attacks traditional ideas; lit., "an image breaker")

εἰμί, *I am*, **Homoiousion** (fourth-century, Arian teaching that Jesus the Son and God the Father were of similar but different substance; lit., "similar essence"), **ontogeny** (development of an individual organism from origin to death), **ontology** (the branch of philosophy that deals with being), **parousia** (theological term for the second coming of Christ; cf. παρά, + εἰμί), cf. εξουσία

εἰρήνη, *peace*, **eirenicon** (a proposal for peace), **Irenaeus** (lit., "peaceful"), **Irene** (lit., "peace"), **irenic** (conciliatory or promoting peace)

εἰς, *into*, **eisegesis** (reading a meaning into a text; lit., "to lead into")

εἷς, μία, ἕν, *one*, **henotheism** (belief in one god without denying existence of others; lit., "one god"), **hyphen** (a punctuation mark used to connect the parts of a compound word; lit., "under one")

ἐκ, *out of*, **ecstasy** (a state of intense joy; lit., "to drive out of one's senses" or "to stand out"), **exegesis** critical analysis of a text to obtain meaning; lit., "to lead out"), **Exodus** (the journey of the Hebrew people out of Egypt; lit., "the journey out")

ἑκατόν, *one hundred*, **hecatomb** (a sacrifice of a hundred oxen to the gods of ancient Greece and Rome), **hectometer** (a hundred meter unit)

ἐκκλησία, *church*, **ecclesia** (political assembly of citizens of ancient Greek city-state), **ecclesiastical** (pertaining to the church), **ecclesiology** (theological study of church doctrine)

ἐκλεκτός, *chosen*, *elect*, **eclectic** (consisting of components selected from diverse sources)

ἐλεάω (also ἐλεέω), *I have mercy*, **alms** (charitable giving to the poor), **eleemosynary** (dependent upon alms or charity)

ἔλεος, *mercy*, *pity*, see ἐλεάω

Ἕλλην, *Greek*, *gentile*, **hellenism** (spread of Greek culture in the ancient world), **Hellenist** (person who adopted Greek language and culture), **Panhellenic** (pertaining to the unifying of the Greek peoples or to Greek-letter fraternities and sororities; lit., "all the Greeks)

ἐν, *in*, **emblem** (object that functions as a symbol; lit., "to insert" or "to throw in"), **embolism** (obstruction of a blood vessel by a clot or air bubble; lit., "insertion" or "thrown in"), **embryo** (fetus or unborn organism; lit., "that which grows in [the body]"), **empathy** (sympathetic understanding of another person; lit., "feeling within"), **emphasis** (speaking with force in the voice; lit., "speaking on"), **emporium** (a trading place; lit., "on the road"), **encephalitis** (inflammation of the brain; lit., "in the head"), **enclitic** (a word dependent on the preceeding word; lit., "leaning on"), **encyclical** (something which is circular or general; lit., "in a circle"), **endemic** (something prevalent in a particular group; lit., "in or among the people")

ἕνδεκα, *eleven*, **hendecasyllabic** (a verse containing eleven syllables; lit., "eleven syllables")

ἐνδύω, *I put on*, *clothe*, **endue** (to provide)

ἐννέα, *nine*, **ennead** (a group or set of nine)

ἕξ, *six*, **hexagon** (figure with six sides and six angles; lit., "six angles"), **hexameter** (line of verse containing six metrical feet), **Hexapla** (Origen's Old Testament compilation consisting of six Hebrew and Greek texts written side by side), **Hexateuch** (designation for the first six books of the Bible; lit., "six books"), cf. Latin *sex* (sextet, sextant)

ἐξουσία, *authority*, cf. ἐκ + εἰμί

ἔξω, *outside* (adv.), **exotic** (something foreign; lit., "from the outside"), **exoteric** (pertaining to the outside or external)

ἐπί, *on*, *upon*, **epicenter** (location directly above an earthquake's center; litarlly, "on the center"), **epidemic** (disease that strikes a large portion of a population; lit., "on the people"), **epidermis** (outer layer of skin; lit., "on the skin"), **epiglottis** (the cartilage that closes the windpipe during swallowing; lit., "on the tongue"), **epilepsy** (chronic nervous disease characterized by convulsions; lit., "to seize upon"), **epilogue** (conclusion of a writing or drama; lit., "a saying in addition" or "a word upon"), **epiphany** (manifestation of the divine; lit., "to shine upon"), **episcopal** (governed by bishops or overseers; lit., "overseen"), **epitaph** (inscription on a tomb; lit., "on a tomb"), **epithet** (a descriptive name or title; lit., "placed upon"), **epitome** (something that embodies or exemplifies a large whole; lit., "to cut upon") ἐπιστολή, *letter*, **epistle** (a letter)

ἐπιστρέφω, *I turn to, return*, cf. στρέφω (apostrophe, catastrophe, strophe)

ἑπτά, *seven*, **heptagon** (figure with seven sides and seven angles; lit., "seven angles"), **heptameter** (a unit of verse consisting of seven feet), **heptarchy** (rule of seven people), **heptathlon** (an athletic competition consisting of seven events), cf. Latin *septem* (September, septuagenarian, Septuagesima, Septuagint)

ἐργάζομαι, *I work (accomplish)*, **allergy** (an adverse reaction to a substance; lit., "other work"), **energy** (power for work), **erg** (a measurable unit of energy or work), **ergonomics** (the study of workers), **George** (lit., "earth worker"), **metallurgy** (the science of metal working), **synergism** (action of two or more subjects that achieves effects of which each is individually incapable; lit., "work together"), **thaumaturge** (performer of miracles or magic feats; lit., "miracle worker")

ἔργον, *work*, see ἐργάζομαι

ἔρημος, *wilderness*, **eremite** (religious recluse), **hermit** (a person who has withdrawn from society), **hermitage** (a secluded retreat, e.g., Andrew Jackson's home)

ἔσχατος, *last*, **eschatology** (the theological study of the end times)

ἕτερος, *another*, **heterodox** (not in agreement with accepted belief; lit., "other opinion"), **heterosexual** (attraction to the opposite sex)

ἔτος, *year*, **Etesian Winds** (prevailing northerly summer winds of the Mediterranean; lit., "yearly winds")

εὐαγγελίζω, *I bring good news*, **evangelism** (process of gospel proclamation), **evangelist** (gospel proclaimer), **evangelize** (to proclaim the gospel)

εὐαγγέλιον, *gospel, good news*, see εὐαγγελίζω

εὐλογέω, *I bless*, **eulogize** (to praise or commend; lit., "to speak well of"), **eulogy** (spoken or written tribute; lit., "good word")

εὑρίσκω, *I find*, **eureka** (an exclamation of triumph or discovery; lit., "I found it"; Archimedes supposedly exclaimed *eureka* when he discovered how to measure the volume of an irregular solid and thereby determine the purity of a gold object), **heuristic** (pertaining to an educational method in which the student learns by discovery)

εὐχαριστέω, *I give thanks*, **Eucharist** (Christian communion; lit., "thanksgiving" or "good favor")

ἔφαγον (ἐσθίω), *I ate*, **anthropophagus** (cannibal or eater of human flesh; lit., "human eater"), **esophagus** (the tube for the passage of food to the stomach), **sarcophagus** (stone coffin; lit., "to eat flesh" because a limestone coffin accelerates disintegration)

ἔχω, *I have*, **epoch** (particular period of history; lit., "to hold upon")

ζωή, *life*, **Mesozoic** (third era of geologic time; lit., "middle of life"), **protozoa** (one-celled, primitive form of animal life; lit., "first life"), **Zoe** (lit., "life"), **zoo** (park for keeping animals), **zoology** (scientific study of animals)

ζῷον, *living creature*, see ζωή

ἡγεμών, *governor*, *ruler*, **eisegesis** (reading a meaning into a text; lit., "to lead into"), **exegesis** (critical analysis of a text to obtain meaning; lit., "to lead out"), **hegemony** (predominant influence of one state over another; lit., "leadership")

ἡγέομαι, *I am chief, think, regard*, see ἡγεμών

ἥλιος, *sun*, **aphelion** (the orbital point farthest from the sun; lit., "away from the sun"), **heliocentric** (having the sun as the center), **Helios** (Greek sun god who drove his chariot daily across the sky), **heliotrope** (plant that turns toward the sun; lit., "sun turn"), **Helium** (gaseous element discovered from the solar spectrum), **perihelion** (the orbital point nearest the sun; lit., "near the sun")

ἡμέρα, *day*, **ephemeral** (lasting only one day), **ephemerid** (a short-lived mayfly insect), **ephemeris time** (astronomical time based on earth's rotation), **hemerocallis** (a day lily)

θαυμάζω, *I marvel, wonder*, **thaumaturge** (a performer of miracles or magic feats; lit., "miracle worker")

θάλασσα, *sea*, **thalassic** (pertaining to seas or oceans)

θάνατος, *death*, **Athanasius** (Greek patriarch of Alexandria; lit., "deathless"), **euthanasia** (killing or allowing a person to die for merciful reasons; lit., "good death"), **thanatopsis** (meditation upon death; lit., "seeing death"), **Thanatos** (death personified or a philosophical notion)

θεάομαι, *I behold*, **theater** (a place to observe dramatic performances)

θέλω, *I wish, desire*, **dyothelitism** (theological doctrine that Christ had two wills, both human and divine; lit., "two wills"), **monothelitism** (theological doctrine that Christ had only one will but two natures; lit., "only one will")

θεός, *God*, **atheism** (denial of God's existence; lit., "no god"), **henotheism** (belief in one god without denying existence of others; lit., "one god"), **monotheism** (belief in only one God; lit., "only god"), **pantheism** (belief that God is the sum of all things; lit., "all is God"), **pantheon** (a temple for all the gods; lit., "all the gods"), **polytheism** (the belief in many gods; lit., "many gods"), **theocracy** (government of religious leaders who claim to rule by divine authority; lit., "the power of God"), **theodicy** (a vindication of divine justice), **theology** (study of the nature of God and religious truth; lit., "the study of God"), **theophany** (a divine manifestation; lit., "the appearance of a god"), **Theophilus** (lit., "loved of God"), **theotokos** (a theological term for Mary, the mother of Jesus; lit., "God bearer"), cf. Latin *deus, dei* (deify, deity)

θεραπεύω, *I heal*, **chemotherapy** (treatment of disease with chemicals), **therapeutic** (having healing powers), **therapy** (treatment of an illness or disability)

θεωρέω, *I observe*, **theorem** (an idea that is demonstrably true), **theory** (idea based on limited information)

θηρίον, *beast*, **theriomorphic** (having the form of a beast)

θρόνος, *throne*, **throne** (a royal chair for a ruler)

ἰάομαι, *I heal*, **geriatrics** (the medical study of old age; lit., "old age healing"), **pediatrics** (medical treatment of infants and children; lit., "child healing"), **psychiatry** (medical study and treatment of mental illness; lit., "soul healing"); cf. the "ia" in words

ἴδιος, *one's own*, **idiom** (an expression peculiar to one's own language), **idiosyncrasy** (a behavior characteristic to a particular individual; lit., "one's own mixture together"), **idiot** (foolish or stupid person; lit., "a person concerned with his own interests")

ἱερεύς, *priest*, **hierophant** (interpreter of sacred mysteries; lit., "a revealer of sacred things"), **Hierapolis** (ancient city of Asia Minor; lit., "sacred city"), **hierarchy** (a body of persons organized according to rank of authority; lit., "priestly rule"), **hieroglyphics** (pictorial system of writing in ancient Egypt; lit., "sacred carvings"), **Jerome** (or Hieronymos [Ἱερώνυμος]; biblical scholar of the fourth to fifth centuries; lit., "sacred name"), cf. ἱερόν

ἱερόν, *temple*, see ἱερεύς

ἵστημι, *I place, set, cause to stand*, **apostasy** (abandoning former belief; lit., "to stand away from"), **apostate** (a person who abandons a former belief; lit., "one standing away from"), **dynasty** (family or group that maintains power for several generations; lit., "standing in power"), **ecstasy** (a state of intense joy; lit., "to drive out of one's senses" or "to stand out"), **epistemology** (branch of philosophy that investigates the nature and origin of knowledge; lit., "the study of knowledge"; cf. ἐπί, + ἵστημι + λόγος, **hypostasis** (the substance or essence of something; lit., "standing under")

ἰχθύς, *fish*, ΙΧΘΥΣ (a Greek acronym for Ἰησοῦς Χριστός, Θεοῦ Υἱός, Σωτήρ ("Jesus Christ, God's Son, Savior"), which also spelled "fish"), **ichthyology** (the study of fish)

καθαρίζω, *I cleanse*, **catharsis** (a process of purging)

καθαρός, *clean, pure*, see καθαρίζω

καθίζω, *I seat, sit*, cf. καθέδρα ("a bishop's chair"; cathedra, cathedral)

καινός, *new*, **Cenozoic** (the last era of geological time; lit., "new life")

κακός, *bad*, **cacodyl** (a poisonous oil with an obnoxious smell; lit., "bad odor"), **cacography** (bad handwriting or spelling; lit., "bad writing"), **cacophony** (a jarring, disconcordant sound; lit., "bad sound")

κακῶς, *badly* (adv.), see κακός

καλέω, *I call*, **ecclesia** (the political assembly of citizens of an ancient Greek city-state, cf. ἐκ + καλέω), **ecclesiastical** (pertaining to the church), **ecclesiology** (theological study of the doctrine of the church), **Paraclete** (theological term for the Holy Spirit, cf. παρά, + καλέω)

καλός, *good*, **calisthenics** (exercises to develop muscles and well-being; lit., "beautiful strength"), **calligraphy** (the art of fine handwriting; lit., "beautiful writing"), **kaleidoscope** (tubular instrument that makes changing designs for the eyes; lit., "to see beautiful forms")

καλῶς, *well* (adv.), see καλός

καρδία, *heart*, **cardiac** (pertaining to the heart), **cardio-pulmonary** (pertaining to the heart and lungs), **cardiogram** (the curve traced by a cardiograph to diagnose heart defects), **cardiology** (medical study of diseases and functions of the heart) καρπός, *fruit*, **carpology** (area of botany concerned with fruit and seeds), **homocarpous** (having all the fruits of a flowerhead alike), **macrocarpous** (having large fruit), **parthenocarpy** (production of fruit without fertilization; lit., "virgin fruit"), **Polycarp** (lit., "much fruit")

κατά, *down*, **cataclysm** (a great flood; lit., "to wash against"), **catalog** (list of items; lit., "word down"), **catastrophe** (a sudden change towards misfortune; lit., "a turn against"), **catechism** (oral instruction; lit., "to resound" or "to sound down"), **category** (a group of items; lit., "accused" or "judged down"), **catheter** (a medical tube to remove fluids from the body; lit., "to send down"), **cathode** (negatively charge electrode; lit., "the way down")

καταβαίνω, *I go down*, Cf. βαίνω (acrobat, Anabasis, anabatic, diabetes)

κατηγορέω, *I accuse*, cf. κατά + ἀγορά ("against the assembly")

κεφαλή, *head*, **acephalous** (headless or lacking a clearly defined head; lit., "without a head"), **brachycephalic** (having a short, almost round head; lit., "short headed"), **cephalic** (of the head or skull), **encephalitis** (a brain inflammation), **enkephalins** (chemicals in the brain), **macrocephalous** (having a large head)

κηρύσσω, *I preach*, **kerygma** (theological term for the message proclaimed by the early church)

κοινωνία, *fellowship*, cf. κοινή (cenobite, Koine Greek)

κόσμος, *world*, **cosmic** (pertaining to the universe), **cosmogony** (the study of the evolution of the universe; lit., "world creation"), **cosmology** (study of the universe), **cosmonaut** (astronaut, especially one from the former Soviet Union; lit., "world sailor"), **cosmopolitan** (common to the whole world; lit., "world citizen"), **cosmorama** (an exhibition of scenes from all over the world; lit., "world view"), **cosmos** (the universe as an orderly, harmonious whole), **microcosm** (smaller system representing a larger system; lit., "small world")

κρατέω, *I grasp, seize*, **aristocracy** (government by the nobility; lit., "the best in power"), **democracy** (government by the people; lit., "people in power"), **plutocrat** (a person with political influence or control because of wealth; lit., "power in wealth")

κρίνω, *I judge, decide*, **crisis** (decisive situation or turning point), **criterion** (standard on which a judgment is based), **critic** (one who forms and expresses judgments), **critical** (characterized by careful or severe judgment), **critique** (critical review of a work), **diacritical** (marking a distinction; lit., "to distinguish" or "to judge through"), **endocrine** (secreting internally; lit., "to separate inside"), **hypocrite** (person who professes and acts in a contradictory manner; lit., "an actor" or "one under examination")

κρίσις, *judgment*, see κρίνω

λαλέω, *I speak*, **glossolalia** (an uttering of unintelligible sounds; lit., "tongue speaking")

λαμβάνω, *I take, receive*, **analeptic** (restorative or stimulating, especially of a medicine; lit., "to take up"), **epilepsy** (disorder characterized by attacks of seizures; lit., "to take or seize upon"), **syllable** (single unin-terrupted sound of a spoken lan-guage; lit., "to take together")

λαός, *people*, **Archelaus** (lit., "ruler of the people"), **laity** (the common people collectively as distinguished from clergy, professionals), **Nicholas** (lit., "victory of the people")

λέγω, *I say*, **dialect** (a certain form of a spoken language; lit., "to speak across or through"), **hapax lego-menon** (word that only occurs one time in the Greek New Testament; lit., "spoken once"), **lecture** (spoken exposition of a given subject for instructional purposes), **legend** (un-verified popular story handed down from earlier times), **prolegomenon** (a critical introduction; lit., "to say beforehand")

λείπω, *I leave*, **eclipse** (the partial or complete obscuring of a celestial body; lit., "to leave out"), **ellipsis** (the omission of a word necessary for syntax but not necessary for under-standing; lit., "to lack within")

λευκός, *white*, **leukemia** (cancer of the white blood cells; lit., "white blood"), **leukocyte** (white corpuscle in the blood)

λέων, *lion*, cf. Latin *leo, leonis* (Leo, Leonard, leopard, lion)

λίθος, *stone*, **lithification** (formation of sedimentary rock from silt), **lithium** (soft, silvery metallic ele-ment), **lithography** (printing process that uses a flat surface; lit., "stone writing"), **litholysis** (treatment for kidney stones; lit., "to break up stones"), **lithophyte** (a plant that grows on a rocky surface; lit., "stone plant"), **lithosphere** (the outer rigid shell of the earth's crust), **monolith**

(a single large block of stone), **neo-lithic** (last period of the stone age; lit., "new stone age"), **paleolithic** (the earliest stone age period; lit., "old stone age")

λογίζομαι, *I account, reckon*, **logic** (the science of correct reasoning), **logical** (in accordance with reason)

λόγος, *word*, **alogi** (early opponents of the Logos doctrine in the Johannine literature; lit., "without the Logos"), **alogia** (inability to speak; lit., "with-out words"), **analogy** (correspond-ence between subjects otherwise dissimilar), **apologetics** (branch of theology that deals with the defense and proof of Christianity), **biology** (science of living organisms and life processes; lit., "the study of life"), **decalogue** (the Ten Commandments; lit., "the ten words"), **dialogue** (a conversation between two persons; lit., "words between"), **epilogue** (a short addition to the conclusion of a literary or dramatic work), **logic** (the science of correct reasoning), **mono-logue** (long speech given by only one person; lit., "the only word"), **syllo-gism** (form of deductive reasoning consisting of a major premise, minor premise, and a conclusion), **trilogy** (a group of three dramatic or literary works related in subject or theme)

λύω, *I loose*, **analysis** (the separation of a subject into its constituent parts for study), **catalyst** (substance that increases the rate of a chemical reaction without being consumed in the process), **electrolysis** (chemical change produced by an electric current), **Hippolytus** (lit., "letting horses loose"), **litholysis** (treatment for a kidney stone; lit., "to break up stones"), **paralysis** (loss or impairment of the movement of a part of the body)

μαθητής, *disciple*, **mathematics** (the science of numbers and their relationships), **polymath** (person learned in many fields; lit., "much learning")

μακάριος, *blessed*, **macarize** (to pronounce happy or blessed; lit., "to bless")

μανθάνω, *I learn*, see μαθητής

μαρτυρέω, *I witness, testify*, **martyr** (a person whose testimony is sealed by their death), **martyrdom** (death of a martyr)

μαρτυρία, testimony, witness, see μαρτυρέω

μάρτυς, *witness*, see μαρτυρέω

μέγας, *large, great*, **megahertz** (one million cycles per second, especially in radio frequency; lit., "many cycles"), **megalith** (a very large stone; lit., "large stone"), **megalomania** (mental disorder characterized by delusions of grandeur, power, and wealth; lit., "madness of greatness"), **megalopolis** (region made up of several large cities; lit., "large city"), **megaphone** (device used to amplify a voice; lit., "loud sound"), **omega** (the last letter of the Greek alphabet; lit., "the great O")

μέλας, *black*, **melancholy** (sadness, depression; lit., "black bile"), **melanin** (a dark pigment in skin or hair), **melanoma** (a dark-pigmented malignant tumor)

μέρος, *part*, **isomer** (any of two or more chemical compounds whose molecules contain the same atoms but in different arrangements; lit., "equal parts"), **pentamerous** (having five similar parts; lit., "five parts"),

polymer (a substance consisting of giant molecules formed from smaller molecules of the same substance; lit., "many parts")

μέσον, *in the midst of*, **Mesolithic** (the cultural period between the Paleolithic and Neolithic ages; lit., "the middle stone age"), **Mesopotamia** (the region between the Tigris and Euphrates rivers; lit., "between the rivers"), **mesosphere** (the layer of air between the stratosphere and thermosphere; also layer of the earth between the athenosphere and the earth's core; lit., "the middle sphere"), **Mesozoic** (the third era of geologic time; lit., "middle of life")

μέσος, *middle*, see μέσον

μεσσίας, *messiah*, **Messiah** (the anticipated Jewish deliverer), **messianic** (pertaining to the messiah)

μετά, *with*, **metabolism** (physical and chemical processes involved in a living organism; lit., "thrown across"), metamorphosis, **metaphor** (a figure of speech; lit., "to carry across"), **metathesis** (transposition of letters or sounds in a word; lit., "transposed" or "place after"), **method** (means or manner of procedure; lit., "the way across")

μήτηρ, *mother*, **metropolis** (a major city; lit., "mother city"), cf. Latin *mater, matris* (maternal, matriarchy, matrimony, matricide, matriculate, matron)

μικρός, *small*, **microbe** (a minute life form; lit., "small life"), **microbiology** (the study of microorganisms), **microcosm** (small system representing a larger system; lit., "small world"), **microscope** (optical instrument that enlarges images; lit., "to see the small"), **omicron** (fifteenth letter of the Greek alphabet; lit., "the small O")

μιμνῄσκομαι, *I remember,* **amnesia** (partial or total lost of memory; lit., "without memory"), **amnesty** (general pardon by a government for offenders; lit., "not remembered"), **anamnesis** (recollection or complete case history of a patient; lit., "to recall again"), **mnemonic** (an aid to memory)

μισέω, *I hate,* **misanthrope** (a person who hates or mistrusts people; lit., "to hate persons"), **misogamy** (hatred of marriage; lit., "marriage-hate"), **misogyny** (hatred of women; lit., "hates women"), **misology** (hatred of reason or enlightenment), **misoneism** (hatred of change; lit., "hate the new")

μνημεῖον, *tomb, monument,* see μιμνῄσκομαι

μόνος, *only, alone,* **monarch** (the sole hereditary ruler; lit., "only ruler"), **monk** (one who secludes himself to a religious order; lit., "alone"), **monogamy** (being married to only one person; lit., "only marriage"), **monograph** (a book on a single subject; lit., "single writing"), **monolith** (a single large block of stone; lit., "single stone"), **monologue** (a long speech given by only one person; lit., "the only word"), **monorail** (a railway with a single rail serving as track; lit., "single rail"), **monotheism** (belief in only one God; lit., "only god"), **monothelitism** (theological doctrine that Christ had only one will but two natures; lit., "only one will"), **monotone** (speaking words without changing pitch; lit., "only one tone")

μύριοι, *ten thousand,* **myriad** (a very large, indefinite number)

νεκρός, *dead,* **necrology** (list of people who have died), **necromancy** (divination by means of a corpse; lit., "divination of the dead"), **necrophobia** (a morbid fear of death or corpses; lit., "fear of the dead"), **necrophilia** (an obsessive fascination with death or corpses; lit., "to love death"), **necropolis** (a cemetery, especially a large one of an ancient city; lit., "city of the dead"), **necrosis** (the death or decay of tissue in part of a body or plant)

νέος, *new,* **misoneism** (hatred of change; lit., "hate the new"), **Neolithic** (last period of the stone age; lit., "new stone age"), **Neon** (a gaseous element; lit., "new"), **neo-orthodoxy** (a modern theological movement that seeks to revive adherence to certain doctrines), **neophyte** (a new convert; lit., "a new plant"), **Neoplatonism** (modified form of Platonism)

νεφέλη, *cloud,* **nepheline** (a mineral used with ceramics and enamels; lit., "cloudy" because it becomes cloudy when placed in nitric acid), **nephelometer** (device used to measure particles in a liquid; lit., "cloud measurement"), **nephology** (study of clouds), cf. Latin *nebula, nebulae* (nebula, nebulous)

νικάω, *I conquer,* **Berenice** (Macedonian Greek for "victory bringer"), **Eunice** (lit., "good victory"), **Nicodemus** (lit., "victory of the people"), **Nicholas** (lit., "victory of the people"), **Nike** (the Greek goddess of victory; lit., "victory")

νόμος, *law*, **agronomy** (soil and plant management), **antinomian** (emphasis on faith without the law; lit., "against the law"), **autonomous** (self-governing or self-ruling; lit., "self law"), **Deuteronomy** (the Old Testament book which contains the second giving of the Mosaic law; lit., "second law"), **economy** (management of community resources; lit., "household law"), **gastronomy** (the management of good eating; lit., "stomach law"), **taxonomy** (science and principles of classification; lit., "arrangement law")

νοῦς, *mind, thought*, **noetic** (pertaining to or apprehended by intellect), **paranoia** (mental disorder characterized by delusions of persecution; lit., "beyond the mind"), cf. μετάνοια ("repentance"; lit., "mind change")

νύξ, *night*, **nyctalopia** (night blindness; lit., "night blindness"), **nyctatropism** (tendency of leaves of some plants to change their position at night; lit., "turns at night"), cf. Latin *nox, noctis* (equinox, noctiluca, noctuid, nocturnal, nocturne)

ὁδός, *way, road*, **anode** (a positively charged electrode; lit., "the way up"; cf. ἀνά, + ὁδός), **cathode** (a negatively charge electrode; lit., "the way down"; cf. κατά + ὁδός), **electrode** (conductor through which an electric current passes; lit., "an electric path"), **episode** (an incident that is part of a narrative but forms a separate unit; lit., "upon into the way"; cf. ἐπί, + εἰς + ὁδός), **Exodus** (journey of the Hebrews out of Egypt; lit., "the journey out"),

method (a means or manner of procedure; lit., "the way across"; cf. μετά + ὁδός), **odometer** (instrument used to measure travel; lit., "a journey measure"), **period** (interval of time; lit., "the way around"; cf. περί + ὁδός), **synod** (council or assembly of churches; lit., "the way together"; cf. σύν + ὁδός)

ὀδούς, *tooth*, **odontology** (study of teeth), **orthodontist** (a dentist who corrects tooth irregularities; lit., "a tooth straightener"), **periodontal** (occurring around a tooth or affecting gums; lit., "around the tooth")

οἰκία, *house, family, household*, **ecocide** (destruction of an environment; lit., "house killer"), **ecology** (science of relationships between organisms and their environment), **economy** (management of a community's resources; lit., "household law"), **ecosystem** (an ecological community with its environment, considered as a unit), **ecumenical** (universal or worldwide in range)

οἶκος, *house*, see οἰκία

οἶνος, *wine*, **wine** (the fermented juice of grapes), cf. Latin *vinum, vini* (vine, vinegar, viniculture, vintage, vinyl)

ὀκτώ, *eight*, **octagon** (figure with eight sides and eight angles; lit., "eight angles"), **octopus** (a marine creature with eight legs; lit., "eight feet"), cf. Latin *octo* (octave, octavo, octet, October, octogenarian)

ὀλίγος, *little, few*, **oligarchy** (government controlled by a few people; lit., "the rule of a few")

ὅλος, *whole, complete, all, entire*, **catholic** (general or universal in scope; lit., "according to the whole"), **holocaust** (great or total destruction, such as that of the Jews by the Nazis; lit., "to burn the whole"), **holograph** (document written wholly in the handwriting of the person under whose name it appears), **holistic** (emphasis on the whole and of interdependence of individual parts)

ὅμοιος, *like*, **homeostasis** (physiological equilibrium within an organism; lit., "standing constant"), **homoeoteleuton** (an incorrect copy of an original text caused by the similar ending of lines; lit., "similar endings"), **homoiotherm** (a warm-blooded animal; lit., "constant warmth"), **Homoiousion** (fourth-century Arian teaching that Jesus the Son and God the Father were of similar but different substance; lit., "similar essence")

ὄνομα, *name*, **acronym** (word formed from the initial letters of words; lit., "high name"), **antonym** (word with a meaning opposite to that of another word; lit., "name against"), **binomial** (mathematical expression formed by two terms connected with a plus or minus sign; lit., "two names"), **homonym** (one of two or more words that have the same sound but different meanings; lit., "similar name"), **Jerome** (Hieronymos [Ἱερώνυμος]; biblical scholar, fourth to fifth centuries; lit., "sacred name"), **onomasticon** (a vocabulary of proper names), **onomatopoeia** (formation of words by making their sounds; lit., "making a name"), **patronymic** (a name received from a paternal ancestor, e.g. "Stevenson"; lit., "father's name"), **polynomial** (a mathematical expression consisting of two or more terms; lit., "many names"), **pseudonym** (a fictitious name assumed by an author; lit., "false name"), **synonym** (a word having the same meaning as that of another in the same language; lit., "name together"), cf. Latin *nomen, nominis* (cognomen, denomination, ignominy, nomenclature, nominate, nominative, nominal, noun, pronoun, renown)

ὀπίσω, *after, behind*, **opistograph** (an ancient document written on both the front and back sides; lit., "writing behind")

ὁράω, *I see*, **cosmorama** (exhibition of scenes from all over the world; lit., "world view"), **diorama** (a view through a small opening), **panorama** (an open view in all directions; lit. "seeing all")

ὄρος, *mountain*, **ore** (a mined mineral or metal), **orogenesis** (the formation of a mountain; lit., "mountain beginning"), **orogenic belt** (belt of mountain building), **orogeny** (an episode in mountain formation), **orography** (the study of the physical geography of mountains and mountain ranges), **orology** (the study of mountains)

οὐρανός, *heaven*, **Uranium** (a heavy, radioactive element; lit., "heavenly"), **uranography** (scientific study of celestial bodies; lit., "writing the heavens"), **Uranus** (seventh planet rotating around the sun; lit., "heavenly")

οὖς, *ear*, **otology** (scientific study of the ear), **otoscope** (instrument used to view the ear) οὗτος, *this, these,* **tautology** (needless repetition of the same sense in different words; lit., "same saying")

ὀφθαλμός, *eye,* **Antigonus Monophthalmos** (Alexander the Great's general who ruled Asia Minor and was so named after he lost an eye in battle; lit., "the one-eyed"), **ophthalmology** (branch of medicine dealing with structure, functions, and diseases of the eye)

ὄχλος, *crowd,* **ochlocracy** (government by the masses or mob rule; lit., "crowd power"), **ochlophobia** (abnormal fear of crowds; lit., "crowd fear")

παιδίον, *child,* **pedagogue** (a school teacher or educator; lit., "child leader"), **pediatrics** (medical treatment of infants and children; lit., "child healing")

παῖς, παιδός, *boy, girl, child, servant,* **pedagogue** (school teacher, educator; lit., "child leader"), **pediatrics** (medical treatment of in-fants and children; lit., "child healing")

πάλιν, *again* (adv.), **palimpsest** (document that has been erased and rewritten; lit., "to scrape again"), **palindrome** (a word or words reading the same backwards and forwards; e.g., "level" or "a man, a plan, a canal, Panama"; lit., "to run again")

παρά, *beside,* **parable** (a simple story to illustrate a lesson or moral; lit., "to throw alongside" or "to compare"), **paradigm** (list of all inflectional forms of a word; lit., "shown alongside"), **paragraph** (a division in a writing which expresses a complete thought. Originally, a mark was placed in the margin *beside* the new section), **paramedic**, **parallel** (being equidistant apart; lit., "beside one another"), **parenthesis** (punctuation marks used to set off explanatory remarks; lit., "set in alongside")

παραβολή, *parable,* **parable** (a simple story to illustrate a lesson or moral; lit., "to throw alongside" or "to compare")

παρακαλέω, *I comfort,* **Paraclete** (a theological designation for the Holy Spirit)

παράκλησις, *exhortation, consolation,* **Paraclete** (a theological designation for the Holy Spirit)

πάρειμι, *I am present,* **parousia** (the theological term for Christ's second coming)

παρθένος, *virgin,* **parthenocarpy** (the production of fruit without fertilization; lit., "virgin fruit"), **parthenogenesis** (reproduction by the development of an unfertilized ovum, seed, or spore; lit., "virgin beginning"), **Parthenon** (ancient temple of Greek goddess Athena Parthenos, "Athena the Virgin," on the Acropolis in Athens; lit., "the virgin")

παρουσία, *presence,* **parousia** (the theological term for Christ's second coming)

παρρησία, *boldness, confidence,* cf. παρά, + ῥέω (diarrhea, hemorrhage)

πᾶς, *every, all, whole,* **Pan-American** (refers to North, South, and Central America collectively; lit., "all the Americas"), **pandemonium** (abode of all demons in John Milton's *Paradise Lost*; lit., "all the demons"), **Pandora** (Greek mythology's first mortal woman who opened a box releasing all evil into the world; lit., "all giving"), **Panhellenic** (unity of all Greek peoples or pertaining to

Greek-letter fraternities and sororities; lit., "all the Greeks), **panorama** (an open view in all directions; lit. "seeing all"), **pantheism** (belief that God is the sum of all things; lit., "all is God"), **pantheon** (a temple for all the gods; lit., "all the gods")

πάσχα, *Passover*, **paschal lamb** (lamb eaten at the feast of the Passover)

πατήρ, *father*, **patriarch** (male leader of a family or tribe; lit., "father ruler"), **patriot** (a person who loves and supports his country; lit., "of one's fathers"), **patristic** (pertaining to the fathers of the early church), **patronymic** (a name received from a paternal ancestor, e.g. "Stevenson"; lit., "father's name"), cf. Latin *pater, patris* (paternal, paternity, patrician, patrimony, patron)

πέντε, *five*, **pentagon** (figure with five sides and five angles; lit., "five angles"), **pentagram** (a five-pointed star used in magic), **pentamerous** (having five similar parts; lit., "five parts"), **pentameter** (a line of verse containing five metrical feet), **Pentateuch** (the first five books of the Bible; lit., "five books"), **pentathlon** (an athletic competition consisting of five events)

πεντήκοντα, *fifty*, **Pentecost** (Jewish or Christian festival celebrated fifty days after Passover; lit., "the fiftieth")

περί, *around*, **pericope** (small section of a literary work; lit., "to cut around"), **perigee** (the point at which the moon is closest to the earth; lit., "around the earth"), **perihelion** (the point at which the earth is closest to the sun; lit., "around the sun"), **perimeter** (the circumference or outside outline of an object; lit., "measure around"), **periodontal** (occurring around a tooth or affecting the gums; lit., "around the tooth"), **periphery** (the outermost region of a precise boundary; lit., "to carry around"), **periphrastic** (circumlocution or round about way of saying something; lit., "to point around"), **periscope** (device used to aid vision when sight is blocked or limited; lit., "to look around")

περιπατέω, *I walk*, **peripatetic** (pertaining to walking, such as Aristotle's teaching method of philosophizing while walking)

πίνω, *I drink*, **symposium** (a meeting or conference for discussion of some topic; lit., "to drink together"), cf. Latin *poto* (potion)

πίπτω, *I fall*, **peripeteia** (a sudden change of events as in a literary work; lit., "to fall around"), **symptom** (an indication of a condition or event; lit., "to fall together")

πλανάω, *I deceive, lead astray*, **planet** (a nonluminous celestial body in an orbit; lit., "a wanderer")

πλείων, *more than* (also πλέον), **pleonasm** (a redundancy of speech), **pleonastic** (use of excessive amount of words)

πλῆθος, *crowd*, **plethora** (an overabundance or excess; lit., "fullness"), **plethoric** (excessive in quantity)

πλήρης, *full*, **pleroma** (in Valentinian Gnosticism, the *pleroma* was the fullness of the spiritual world as pairs of aeons; lit., "fullness")

πληρόω, *I fulfill*, see πλήρης

πλούσιος, *rich*, **Pluto** (Roman god of the dead and the underworld), **plu-**

tocracy (government by the wealthy; lit., "wealthy power"), **plutocrat** (a person with political influence or control because of wealth; lit., "power in wealth")

πνεῦμα, *spirit, wind,* **pneumatic** (a device powered by compressed air), **pneumatology** (Christian doctrine of the Holy Spirit), **pneumonia** (infection or inflammation of the lungs)

πνευματικός, *spiritual,* see πνεῦμα

ποιέω, I *do, make,* **onomatopoeia** (formation of words by making their sounds; lit., "making a name"), **pharmacopoeia** (official book listing drugs and their formulas; lit., "making drugs"), **poem** (literary composition; lit., "something that is made")

ποιμήν, *shepherd,* **poimenic** (pastoral in nature; lit., "shepherdly"; cf. Latin *pastor, pastoris* ["shepherd"])

πόλις, *town,* **acropolis** (elevated part of an ancient Greek city such as in Athens; lit., "the high city"), **decapolis** (ancient district near Galilee comprised of ten hellenistic cities; lit., "ten cities"), **Hierapolis** (an ancient city of Asia Minor; lit., "sacred city"), **Indianapolis** (lit., "city of Indiana"), **megalopolis** (a vast, populous urban area; lit., "a great city"), **metropolis** (major city; lit., "mother city"), **necropolis** (a cemetery, especially a large one of an ancient city; lit., "the city of the dead"), **Tripoli** (lit., "three cities"); cf. πολιτή (cosmopolitan, politics)

πολύς, *much, many,* **polyandry** (having more than one husband; lit., "many husbands"), **polygamy** (being married to more than one person at the same time; lit., "many marriages"), **polyglot** (a speech or writing in several languages; lit., "many tongues"), **polygon** (a multi-sided figure; lit., "many angles"), **polymath** (a person learned in many fields; lit., "much learning"), **polynomial** (mathematical expression consisting of two or more terms; lit., "many names"), **polytheism** (belief in many gods; lit., "many gods")

πορεύομαι, I *go (proceed, travel),* **pore** (an opening in the skin through which fluids pass)

πορνεία, *fornication,* **pornography** (sexually explicit writings or pictures; lit., "immoral writings")

πούς, *foot,* **octopus** (marine creature having eight legs; lit., "eight feet"), **platypus** (semiaquatic mammal with webbed feet; lit., "flat feet"), **podiatry** (the study and treatment of foot ailments; lit., "foot healing"), **podium** (an elevated platform for a speaker; cf. podion, diminutive form of πούς), **tripod** (a three-legged stand; lit., "three feet")

πράσσω, I *do, practice,* **praxis** (practical application or exercise for learning), cf. Latin *practico* (practical, practice)

πρεσβύτερος, *elder,* **presbyter** (an elder in the church), **Presbyterian** (denomination of churches governed by a group of elders)

πρό, *before,* **problem** (source of perplexity which needs a solution; lit., "thrown before"), **prognosis** (prediction or a forecast; lit., "to know before"), **program** (public notice; lit., "to write before"), **prolegomenon** (an introduction; lit., "spoken before"), **prolepsis** (anticipation; "to take before"), **prologue** (introduction to a literary work; lit., "a word before"), **prophylactic** (preventive precaution; lit., "to guard before"), **protasis** ("if" clause of conditional sentences; lit., "to arrange before")

πρός, *near, toward,* **proselyte** (convert to Judaism; lit., "one who has come to")

πρόσωπον, *face,* **prosopography** (a description of a person's appearance or character; lit., "face writing")

προφητεύω, *I prophesy,* **prophet** (one who speaks by divine inspiration; lit., "to speak before"; cf. πρό + φημί)

προφήτης, *prophet,* see προφητεύω

πρῶτος, *first,* **protagonist** (the main character in a drama or novel; lit., "the first actor"), **protein** (food substance essential for tissue growth; lit., "primary"), **proton** (a positively charged subatomic particle; lit., "first"), **protoplasm** (colloidal substance essential to living matter; lit., "primary form"), **prototype** (the first example of an object; lit., "first model"), **protozoa** (a one-celled, primitive form of animal life; lit., "first life")

πῦρ, *fire,* **pyre** (a pile of wood for burning a corpse in a funeral rite), **pyretic** (characterized or affected by fever), **Pyrex** (heat-resistant glassware for cooking), **pyrogenous** (produced by or producing heat; lit., "fire producing"), **pyromania** (compulsion to start destructive fires; lit., "fire madness"), **pyrotechnic** (pertaining to fireworks; lit., "fire art" or "fire skill")

ῥῆμα, *word,* cf. ῥητορική (rhetoric)

σάββατον, *sabbath,* **Sabbath** (the seventh day of the week), **sabbatical** (a period of rest or study usually after an interval of time)

σάρξ, *flesh,* **sarcasm** (sharp, mocking remark intended to wound another; lit., "to tear flesh"), **sarcoma** (a malignant tumor usually in connective tissue), **sarcophagus** (a stone coffin; lit., "to eat flesh" because limestone coffins accelerated disintegration)

σημεῖον, *sign, miracle,* **semantics** (study of words and nonverbal symbols), **semaphore** (device that uses flags, lights, or arms to signal; lit., "signal carrier"), **semiology** (science dealing with signs or sign language)

σκανδαλίζω, *I cause to stumble,* **scandal** (disgraceful circumstance), **scandalize** (to shock disgracefully)

σκότος, *darkness,* **scotobiotic** (capable of living in darkness; lit., "dark life"), **scotoma** (area of diminished vision within a visual field), **scotopia** (ability to see in dim light; lit., "darkness vision"), **scotoscope** (device used to enhance night vision; lit., "darkness vision")

σοφία, *wisdom,* **philosophy** (pursuit of wisdom by intellectual means; lit., "the love of wisdom"), **Sophia** (lit., "wise"), **sophism** (plausible but fallacious argument), **sophist** (member of a philosophical school in ancient Greece), **sophisticated** (refinement or complexity), **sophomore** (second year student; lit., "a wise fool"), **sophomoric** (immature and overconfident; lit., "foolishly wise")

σοφός, *wise,* see σοφία

σπέρμα, *seed,* **sperm** (male reproductive cells; lit., "seed"), **spermatozoa** (fertilizing gametes of a male animal; lit., "seed animal"), **sperm-**

icide (an agent that kills sperm; lit., "seed killer")

στόμα, *mouth*, **Chrysostom** (gifted fourth-century orator; lit., "golden mouth"), **stoma** (minute opening on the surface of a leaf; lit., "mouth"), **stomach** (principle digestive organ in mammals)

συγγενής, *relative*, cf. σύν + γενός

συκῆ, *fig tree*, **sycamore** (a broad leaf tree; lit., "mulberry fig"), **syconium** (the fleshy fruit of a fig), **sycophant** (person who attempts to win favor or gain advance by flattering influential people; lit., "to show figs")

σύν, *with, together*, **asyndeton** (omission of conjunctions in constructions which normally would need them; lit., "without being bound together"), **symbol** (something that represents something else; lit., "to throw together"), **symphony** (a harmonious combination of musical sounds; lit., "to sound together"), **symposium** (a meeting or conference for discussion of some topic; lit., "to drink together"), **symptom** (indication of a condition or event; lit., "to fall together"), **synagogue** (building for Jewish gatherings; lit., "assembly" or "to lead together"; cf. σύν + ἄγω), **synapse** (the point of contact where nerve impulses are transmitted between neurons; lit., "to touch together"), **syndrome** (characteristics of a situation; lit., "run together"), **synchronize** (to occur at the same time; lit., "timed together"), **synod** (a council or assembly of churches; lit., "the way together"; cf. σύν + ὁδός), **synonym** (a word having the same meaning as that of another in the same language; lit., "name

together"), **synoptic** (arranging similar items side by side; lit., "seen together"), **synthesis** (the combination of separate elements to form a whole; lit., "placed together")

συνάγω, *I gather together*, **synagogue** (building for Jewish gatherings; lit., "assembly" or "to lead together"; cf. σύν + ἄγω)

συναγωγή, *synagogue*, see συνάγω

συνέδριον, *Sanhedrin*, **Sanhedrin** (Jewish legal council)

σῶμα, *body*, **chromosome** (cell part responsible for hereditary characteristics; lit., "body color"), **psychosomatic** (a physical disorder originating in or aggravated by the mind; lit., "mind-body")

σωτήρ, *savior*, **soteriology** (theological study of salvation)

σωτηρία, *salvation*, see σωτήρ

ταχέως (ταχύ), *soon* (adv.), **tachometer** (an instrument that measures rotational speed; lit., "speed measure"), **tachycardia** (excessively rapid heartbeat; lit., "swift heart"), **tachygraphy** (rapid writing or shorthand; lit., "fast writing"), **tachypnea** (excessively rapid respiration; lit., "fast breathing")

ταχύς, *quick*, see ταχέως

τέκνον, *child*, **theotokos** (theological term for Mary, the mother of Jesus; lit., "God bearer")

τελέω, *I complete, fulfill*, **telegram** (a communication by telegraph; lit., "end letter"), **telegraph** (device that transmits messages by wire; lit., "end writing"), **teleology** (philosophical study of design or purpose), **telephone** (a device that transmits sounds from one location to another; lit., "end sound"), **telescope** (device used to see distant objects; lit., "to see the end"), **telic** (directed toward a goal or purpose)

τέλος, *end*, see τελέω

τέσσαρες, *four*, **Diatessaron** (Tatian's harmony of the four gospels; lit., "through four"), **tetragon** (four-sided polygon; lit., "four angles"), **Tetragrammaton** (four Hebrew letters usually transliterated as YHWH used as a proper name for God; lit., "four letters"), **tetrahedron** (a solid figure with four triangular faces; lit., "four bases"), **tetrarch** (a governor of one of the four divisions of a country, especially in the Roman Empire; lit., "four rulers")

τίθημι, *I put, place, lay*, **antithesis** (direct contrast; lit., "set against"), **bibliotheca** (library or book collection; lit., "book case"), **hypothesis** (an assumption or explanation; lit., "placed under"), **metathesis** (the transposition of letters or sounds in a word; lit., "transposed" or "place after"), **parenthesis** (punctuation marks used to set off explanatory remarks; lit., "set in alongside"; cf. παρά, + ἐν + τίθημι), **synthesis** (the combination of separate elements to form a whole; lit., "placed together"), **thesis** (proposition; lit., "something placed")

τιμάω, *I honor*, **Timothy** (cf. Τιμόθεος; lit., "honor of God")

τιμή, *honor, price*, see τιμάω

τόπος, *place*, **isotope** (any of two or more forms of an element having the same atomic number but different atomic weights; lit., "equal place"), **topic** (subject of discussion or conversation; lit., "place"), **topography** (detailed description of an area; lit.,

"place writing"), **utopia** (an ideally perfect place; lit., "not a place")

τρεῖς, *three*, **triad** (a group of three), **triangle** (figure with three sides and three angles; lit., "three angles"), **trigonometry** (mathematical study of triangles; lit., "measurement of triangles"), **trio** (musical composition for three), **tripod** (three-legged stand; lit., "three feet"), cf. Latin *tres, tria* (trident, triumvirate, trivia)

τυφλός, *blind*, **typhlology** (scientific study of blindness)

ὕδωρ, *water*, **dehydrate** (to lose water or moisture), **hydrant** (large discharge pipe for providing water), **hydraulic** (operated by water or fluid), **hydroelectric** (generating electricity by moving water), **hydrogen** (gaseous element producing water when burned; lit., "water producing"), **hydrolysis** (decomposition of a chemical compound by reaction with water; lit., "loosing by water"), **hydrophobia** (the fear of water), **hydroplane** (to skim on the surface of water), **hydrothermal** (pertaining to hot water; lit., "hot water")

ὑγιής, *healthy*, **hygiene** (the science of health and prevention of disease), **hygienic** (tending to promote or preserve health)

υἱός, *son*, Mark Antony made a pun about the well-known brutality of Herod the Great: "It is better to be his pig (ὗς) than his son (υἱός)."

ὑπάγω, *I go away*, cf. ἄγω, **demagogue** (one who stirs up people to gain power; lit., "a people leader"), **pedagogue** (school teacher or educator; lit., "child leader"), **stratagem** (a military maneuver designed to surprise an enemy; lit., "to lead an army"), **synagogue** (building for Jewish gatherings; lit., "assembly" or "to lead together"; cf. σύν + ἄγω), cf. Latin *ago* (agenda, agent, agile, agitate)

ὑπέρ, *over, above*, **hyper-** (something overdone or exaggerated: hyperactive, hypercritical, hypersensitive), **hyperbola** (a geometrical curve; lit., "over thrown"), **hyperbole** (exaggeration; lit., "over throw"), **hyperglycemic** (a diabetic condition of having too much sugar; lit., "over sugar")

ὑπό, *under*, **hypodermic** (medical instrument used to inject substances under the skin; lit., "under the skin"), **hypoglycemic** (diabetic condition of too little blood sugar; lit., "under sugar"), **hypostasis** (the substance or essence of something; lit., "standing under"), **hypotaxis** (subordinate relationship of clauses with connectives), **hypotenuse** (the side of a right triangle opposite the right angle; lit., "stretched under"), **hypothesis** (assumption or explanation; lit., "placed under")

ὑποστρέφω, *I return*, cf. στρέφω (apostrophe, catastrophe, strophe)

ὑποτάσσω, *I put in subjection*, **hypotaxis** (the subordinate relationship of clauses with connectives)

φαίνω, *I shine, appear*, **diaphanous** (transparently thin; lit., "appears through"), **Epiphany** (festival commemorating the manifestation of Christ to the magi; lit., "manifest" or "appears to"), **fantasy** (creative imagination; lit., "an appearance"), **phantasm** (imaginary image that only seems to appear; lit., "an appearance"), **phantom** (something

that apparently is seen but has no physical reality; lit., "an appearance"), **phenomenon** (an occurrence that is perceptible by the senses; lit., "something which appears"), **theophany** (a divine manifestation; lit., "the appearance of a god")

φέρω, *I bring, carry*, **Christopher** (lit., "Christ bearer"), **euphoria** (a feeling of well-being; lit., "to carry good"), **metaphor** (a figure of speech; lit., "to carry across"), **periphery** (the outermost region within a precise boundary; lit., "to carry around"), **phosphorus** (highly reactive element that burns easily; lit., "light carrier"), **semaphore** (device that uses flags, lights, or arms to signal; lit., "signal carrier"), cf. Latin *fero* (fertile, circumference, confer, defer, differ, infer, offer, prefer, proffer, refer, suffer, transfer)

φεύγω, *I flee*, cf. Latin *fugio* (centrifugal, fugitive, refuge, subterfuge, Tempus Fugit)

φημί, *I say*, **aphasia** (a total or partial loss of the power to speak; lit., "without speech"), **blasphemy** (profane act or utterance against the sacred), **emphasis** (speaking with a force of voice; lit., "speaking on"), **euphemism** (using a less direct word or phrase for one considered offensive; lit., "speaking well")

φιλέω, *I love*, **bibliophile** (one who loves and collects books; lit., "book lover"), **hemophilia** (disorder characterized by excessive bleeding; lit., "blood lover"), **Philadelphia** (lit., "brotherly love"), **philander** (to engage in casual love affairs; lit., "a loving man"), **philanthropy** (a desire to help humankind; lit., "human lover"), **philharmonic** (devoted to or appreciating music; lit., "harmony loving"), **philhellene** (one who loves Greece or the Greeks; lit., "Greek lover"), **Philip** (lit., "lover of horses"), **philodendron** (a tropical American vine; lit., "loves trees"), **philosophy** (intellectual pursuit of wisdom; lit., "the love of wisdom"), **Theophilus** (lit., "loved of God")

φίλος, *loving*, see φιλέω

φόβος, *fear*, **acrophobia** (an abnormal fear of being in high places), **claustrophobia** (fear of confined spaces; lit., "fear of closed space"), **hydrophobia** (fear of water), **necrophobia** (a morbid fear of death or corpses; lit., "fear of the dead"), **ochlophobia** (an abnormal fear of crowds; lit., "crowd fear"), **phobia** (a strong fear or dislike)

φρονέω, *I think*, **phrenic** (pertaining to the mind), **phrenology** (system of analyzing character and mental faculties based on head shape), **schizophrenia** (a mental disorder characterized by split personality; lit., "split mind")

φυλακή, *guard, prison, watch*, **phylactery** (a small box that contained portions of the Hebrew Scriptures for Jewish men), **phylaxis** (inhibiting of infection by the body), **prophylactic** (protective or preventative; lit., "guarding beforehand"), **prophylaxis** (protective treatment against disease; lit., "guarding beforehand")

φυλάσσω, *I guard, keep*, **phylactery** (small box that contains portions of the Hebrew Scriptures for Jewish men), **phylaxis** (inhibiting of infection by the body), **prophylactic** (protective or preventative; lit., "guard-ing beforehand"), **prophylaxis** (protective treatment against disease; lit., "guarding beforehand")

φυλή, *tribe*, **phyle** (a large citizen's group based on kinship in an ancient Greek city-state; lit., "tribe"), **phylogeny** (origin and evolution of a group or race of animal or plants; lit., "beginning of a tribe"), **phylum** (a main division of the animal or plant kingdom; lit., "a tribe")

φωνέω, *I call*, **euphony** (pleasant combination of agreeable sounds; lit., "good sound"), **megaphone** (device used to amplify the voice; lit., "loud sound"), **phoneme** (the smallest unit of speech), **phonetics** (linguistical study of sounds), **phonics** (study of sound and speech), **symphony** (a harmonious combination of musical sounds; lit., "to sound together"), **telephone** (a device that transmits sounds from one location to another; lit., "end sound"), **xylophone** (a wooden musical percussion instrument; lit., "wood sound")

φωνή, *voice* (sound), see φωνέω

φῶς, *light*, **aphotic zone** (that part of the ocean in total darkness; lit., "the zone without light"), **disphotic zone** (that part of the ocean with reduced light; lit., "zone with little light"), **phosphorus** (highly reactive element that burns easily; lit., "light carrier"), **phot** (unit of illumination), **photograph** (an image or picture recorded on a light-sensitive surface; lit., "light writing"), **photosynthesis** (process of plant cells converting chemicals and light into energy; lit., "to place light together")

χαρίζομαι, *I give, grant, pardon, forgive*, **charisma** (charm or personal magnetism; lit., "favor" or "a divine gift"), **charismatic** (emphasizing the spiritual or divine gifts; lit., "divine gifts"), **Charissa** (lit., "grace"), **Eucharist** (Christian communion; lit., "thanksgiving" or "good favor")

χάρις, *grace, favor*, see χαρίζομαι

χείρ, *hand*, **chirography** (penmanship; lit., "hand writing"), **chiromancy** (palm-reading; lit., "hand divination"), **chiropractic** (therapy by manipulating the spinal column or joints; lit., "hand done")

χίλιοι, *one thousand*, **chiliasm** (the doctrine that Christ will rule for one thousand years), **kilometer** (distance of a thousand meters; lit., "thousand meters"), **kilogram** (a weight of a thousand grams; lit., "thousand grams"), **kiloliter** (a unit of volume equal to a thousand liters; lit., "thousand liters"), **kilowatt** (a unit of power equal to a thousand watts; lit., "thousand watts")

Χριστός, *Christ*, **Christ** (English transliteration of the Greek word *christos* used for the Hebrew word *Messiah*, meaning "anointed one"), **Christology** (the study of Christ's person and qualities), cf. χρίω ("to anoint"; hence, "christen")

χρόνος, *time*, **anachronism** (a chronological disorder of events; lit., "backward in time"), **chronic** (prolonged or occurring for a long time), **chronicle** (an extended account of historical events), **chronograph** (an instrument that records time intervals; lit., "time writing"), **chronology** (determination of dates and the sequence of events), **synchronize** (to occur at the same time; lit., "timed together")

χρυσοῦς, *golden*, **chrysanthemum** (a gold-color flower; lit., "gold flower"), **chryselephantine** (made of gold and ivory; lit., "gold and ivory"), **chrysolite** (yellow or greenish gem; lit., "gold stone"), **Chrysostom** (the eloquent preacher of the fourth century; lit., "golden-mouthed")

χώρα, *country* (district), **chorography** (the technique of mapping a region or district; lit., "region writing")

ψυχή, *life, soul*, **psyche** (the soul or spirit), **psychiatry** (medical study and treatment of mental illness; lit., "soul healing"), **psychology** (science of mental processes and behavior; lit., "study of the soul"), **psychopath** (one with personality disorder), **psychosis** (severe mental disorder), **psychosomatic** (physical disorder originating in or aggravated by the mind; lit., "mind-body")

ὥρα, *hour*, **horologe** (a timepiece), **horology** (science or art of measuring time or making timepieces), **horoscope** (the aspect of the planets and stars at the time of a person's birth), **hour** (one of the 24 parts of the day)

SUBJECT INDEX

This subject index is provided with an element of redundancy to facilitate locating topics more easily. A level of detail also is provided in order to make the text more useful and to cross-reference topics.